Transforming Neuropsychology and Cognitive Psychology With AI and Machine Learning

Rohit Bansal
Stanford Institute of Management and Technology, Australia

Gunjan Shuklaa
SICA College, Indore, India

Fazla Rabby
Stanford Institute of Management and Technology, Australia

Tariq Maqableh
Charles Sturt University, Australia

Remya Lathabhavan
Indian Institute of Management, Bodh Gaya, India

IGI Global
Scientific Publishing
Publishing Tomorrow's Research Today

Vice President of Editorial Melissa Wagner
Managing Editor of Acquisitions Mikaela Felty
Managing Editor of Book Development Jocelynn Hessler
Production Manager Mike Brehm
Cover Design Phillip Shickler

Published in the United States of America by
IGI Global Scientific Publishing
701 East Chocolate Avenue
Hershey, PA, 17033, USA
Tel: 717-533-8845
Fax: 717-533-8661
Website: https://www.igi-global.com E-mail: cust@igi-global.com

Library of Congress Cataloging-in-Publication Data

Names: Bansal, Rohit, 1982- editor. | Maqableh, Tariq, 1987- editor. | Shuklaa, Gunjan, 1982- editor. | Rabby, Fazla, 1978- editor. | Lathabhavan, Remya, 1984- editor.
Title: Transforming neuropsychology and cognitive psychology with AI and machine learning / edited by Rohit Bansal, Tariq Maqableh, Gunjan Shuklaa, Fazla Rabby, Remya Lathabhavan.
Description: Hershey, PA : IGI Global Scientific Publishing, [2025] | Includes bibliographical references and index. | Summary: "This book serves as a comprehensive resource for the latest advancements in AI algorithms and Machine Learning within neuropsychology and cognitive psychology"-- Provided by publisher.
Identifiers: LCCN 2024054392 (print) | LCCN 2024054393 (ebook) | ISBN 9798369393413 (hardcover) | ISBN 9798369393420 (paperback) | ISBN 9798369393437 (ebook)
Subjects: LCSH: Cognitive psychology. | Neuropsychology. | Machine learning.
Classification: LCC BF201 .T73 2025 (print) | LCC BF201 (ebook) | DDC 153--dc23/eng/20250313
LC record available at https://lccn.loc.gov/2024054392
LC ebook record available at https://lccn.loc.gov/2024054393

British Cataloguing in Publication Data
A Cataloguing in Publication record for this book is available from the British Library.

Table of Contents

Detailed Table of Contents

Advanced technologies enable mental health professionals to refine therapeutic approaches, enhancing responsiveness to patients' unique needs. In this chapter, we explored such approaches that integrate cognitive behavioural therapy (CBT) with machine learning (ML) and artificial intelligence (AI) to enhance mental health services. It begins by defining key concepts of both CBT and ML, focusing on how ML improves the accuracy, accessibility, and personalization of therapeutic interventions. Practical examples illustrate ML uses in therapy, such as chatbots that assist in CBT, virtual reality tools simulating therapeutic settings, and real-time monitoring tools for tracking patient progress. Ethical considerations are also discussed, highlighting the importance of maintaining patient confidentiality and the therapeutic relationship. The chapter concludes by noting how ML and CBT integration could improve mental health access, accuracy in diagnosis, and individualized treatment.

Advancements in artificial intelligence (AI) are revolutionizing neurophysiology, enhancing precision and efficiency in assessing brain and nervous system function. AI-driven neurophysiological assessment integrates machine learning, deep neural networks, and advanced data analytics to process complex data from electroencephalography, and electromyography techniques. This technology enables earlier diagnosis of neurological disorders like epilepsy and Alzheimer's by detecting subtle neural patterns that may be missed by human analysis. AI also facilitates real-time monitoring and predictive analytics, improving outcomes in critical care and neurorehabilitation. Challenges include ensuring data quality, addressing ethical concerns, and overcoming computational limits. The integration of AI into neurophysiology offers a precise, scalable, and accessible approach to treating neurological disorders. This chapter discusses the methodologies, applications, and future directions of AI in neurophysiological assessment, emphasizing its transformative impact in clinical and research fields.

This chapter examines how artificial intelligence (AI) is improving neuropsychological practice and how AI tools can be used to diagnose treat and rehabilitate cognitive disorders. Through a critical analysis of recent research and developing patterns the chapter emphasizes AIs potential for neuropsychology real-time interventions personalized care and early detection. It explores how artificial intelligence (AI) has advanced to create tools like virtual assistants chatbots and machine learning algorithms that have greatly enhanced neuropsychological testing and treatment. AI in neurorehabilitation shows encouraging results improving the precision and effectiveness of treatment regimens particularly for patients with brain injuries or cognitive decline. The chapter also examines the effects of AI on neuropsychological training and education with a focus on preparing the next generation of neuropsychologists for practice settings enhanced by AI.

This chapter examines how Artificial Intelligence (AI) and Machine Learning (ML) are being used in neuropsychology, focusing on how they can significantly improve the study and treatment of cognitive issues like Mild Cognitive Impairment (MCI) and Alzheimer's Disease (AD). Traditional methods in neuropsychology often depend on subjective evaluations, which can reduce the accuracy of diagnoses and delay necessary treatments. AI and ML use large amounts of data to find early signs of cognitive problems and provide better predictive analysis, helping with early detection and more accurate treatment. From a research standpoint, AI offers new tools to examine complex data from brain scans, genetic information, and behaviour tests. Machine learning can identify patterns that suggest how diseases might progress, which could lead to important discoveries in finding markers for

AI in neuropsychological assessment within employee selection and performance evaluation, exploring its potential benefits and challenges. Through a comprehensive review of current research on the latest advancements and evolving trends in AI for HR practices and neuropsychological assessment, this study aims to provide HR professionals with detailed insights into the various tools that can be used for transforming HR processes.

The rapid advancement of Artificial Intelligence (AI) and Machine Learning (ML) has introduced transformative capabilities in the detection and management of cognitive impairments. These impairments represent significant challenges in healthcare, characterized by complex symptoms and progressive deterioration. Traditional diagnostic and management methods often face limitations due to the subtleties in early symptom detection and the need for comprehensive data analysis. AI algorithms offer powerful tools to address these challenges. The integration of these AI algorithms into clinical practice provides several advantages: enhanced diagnostic accuracy through sophisticated data analysis, personalized treatment plans tailored to individual patient profiles, and predictive models that forecast disease progression. This chapter highlights the potential of artificial intelligence to transform the management of mental retardation and shows how these technologies can be used to overcome the limitations of traditional and advances in the field of mental health.

The chapter explores the transformative role of artificial intelligence (AI) and natural language processing (NLP) technologies in enhancing mental health care. This chapter provides a comprehensive overview of the current landscape of AI and NLP applications in mental health, detailing the mechanisms through which chatbots and virtual assistants operate. It discusses the various types of chatbots, their advantages in promoting early intervention and reducing stigma. Furthermore, the chapter addresses the methodologies of fine-tuning and prompt engineering that optimize these digital tools for specific therapeutic contexts. By integrating empirical research findings and theoretical insights, this chapter elucidates how AI and NLP-driven solutions can bridge gaps in traditional mental health services, ultimately contributing to improved outcomes for individuals and communities. The findings underscore the importance of ongoing research and development in this field, advocating for the continued integration of technology in mental health support systems

Music significantly influences our emotions and overall well-being in daily life. This proposed system seeks to revolutionize the music listening experience by harnessing the power of cognitive psychology, AI, and machine learning through advanced facial emotion detection. By integrating a facial recognition API, the system captures and analyzes the user's facial expressions in real time, accurately mapping these emotions to corresponding music genres, playlists, or individual tracks. The implementation follows a logical framework that connects emotion detection directly with music selection, featuring a state-of-the-art music player specifically designed to intuitively interpret human emotions using a web camera interface. The ultimate objective of this system is to enhance the user's mood and emotional well-being by curating music that aligns perfectly with the emotional cues derived from their facial expressions. This approach merges cognitive psychology

neurological illnesses, and the essential function of cognition in detecting cognitive decline. The increasing potential of neurological machine learning likely overcomes the aforementioned deficiencies—consistent monitoring and early identification in mental health—through automation. This research will ultimately address AI-related concerns regarding the longitudinal monitoring of individuals with mental illnesses. Neurocognitive testing may leverage machine learning to significantly advance the evaluation and early management of cognitive health, hence facilitating future research to enhance and broaden the capabilities of neurolearning and cognitive neuropsychology.

Preface

The convergence of Artificial Intelligence (AI) and machine learning represents a significant advancement in understanding and addressing neurological and psychological conditions. Artificial Intelligence (AI) and Machine Learning (ML) are transforming neuropsychology and cognitive psychology by providing new tools and methodologies for research, diagnosis, and treatment. The role of Artificial Intelligence (AI) in neuropsychology is multifaceted, enhancing various aspects of research, diagnosis, treatment, and overall understanding of the brain and its functions. AI can develop and administer neuropsychological tests that are adaptive and can tailor difficulty based on real-time responses, providing more accurate and efficient assessments. Further, AI algorithms can automate the scoring of neuropsychological tests and provide detailed interpretations, reducing human error and increasing consistency. AI can analyze subtle patterns in test performance that might indicate early signs of cognitive decline, potentially identifying conditions like Alzheimer's disease much earlier than traditional methods. Machine learning models can predict the onset and progression of diseases by analyzing historical and real-time patient data, enabling earlier and more accurate diagnoses. Further, Machine learning algorithms can adapt therapeutic interventions in real-time based on patient responses, optimizing cognitive-behavioral therapy (CBT) and other treatment modalities. ML can analyze data from smartphones and wearable devices to assess cognitive and emotional states continuously, providing a more comprehensive picture of a patient's condition outside of clinical settings. Machine learning techniques can analyze functional connectivity in the brain, helping to identify networks involved in various cognitive processes and how they are disrupted in different disorders.

CHAPTER OVERVIEW

Accordingly, the book "Transforming Neuropsychology and Cognitive Psychology With AI and Machine Learning" aimed at highlight the synergies between these fields and explore innovative applications, methodologies, and future prospects. This book will serve as a comprehensive resource for the latest advancements in AI algorithms and Machine Learning within neuropsychology and cognitive psychology.

Chapter one "Cognitive Behavioral Therapy and Machine Learning" explored such approaches that integrate cognitive behavioural therapy with machine learning and artificial intelligence to enhance mental health services.

Chapter two "AI-Enhanced Neurophysiological Assessment" discussed the methodologies, applications, and future directions of AI in neurophysiological assessment, emphasizing its transformative impact in clinical and research fields.

Chapter three "AI-Powered Breakthroughs-Revolutionizing Cognitive Psychology and Neuropsychology with Machine Learning" examined how artificial intelligence is improving neuropsychological practice and how AI tools can be used to diagnose treat and rehabilitate cognitive disorders.

Chapter four "Integration of AI with ML for Neuropsychological Applications" examined how Artificial Intelligence and Machine Learning are being used in neuropsychology, focusing on how they can significantly improve the study and treatment of cognitive issues like Mild Cognitive Impairment and Alzheimer's Disease.

Chapter five "Transforming Minds AI and Machine Learning Applications in Cognitive Neuroscience" analyzed emotional states and behaviours.

Chapter six, "Leveraging Artificial Intelligence in Neuropsychological Assessment- Transforming Employee Selection and Performance Evaluation" analysed the role of AI in neuropsychological assessment within employee selection and performance evaluation, exploring its potential benefits and challenges.

Chaper seven "AI Algorithms For Early Detection Of Cognitive Impairments" highlighted the potential of artificial intelligence to transform the management of mental retardation and shows how these technologies can be used to overcome the limitations of traditional and advances in the field of mental health.

Chapter eight "AI in Neuroimaging and Brain Analysis" highlighted the integration of AI in neuroimaging offers unprecedented opportunities to enhance our understanding of the brain, improve diagnostic accuracy, and personalize treatment strategies for neurological disorders.

Chapter nine "Hey Friend I am a Spiritual Robot! How May I help You!: Integrating Spiritual Robotics in College Counseling" presented a novel perspective on how spiritual robots can enhance the well-being of students at college and help them perform better at educational as well as personal level.

Chapter ten "Development of AI and NLP Driven Chatbots and Virtual Assistants for Mental Health Support" provided a comprehensive overview of the current landscape of AI and NLP applications in mental health, detailing the mechanisms through which chatbots and virtual assistants operate.

Chapter eleven "NeuroSymphony – AI Tailored Music for Cognitive and Emotional States" explored how music significantly influences our emotions and overall well-being in daily life.

Chapter twelve "Predictive Analysis of Medicinal Plants for Central Nervous System Diseases using Machine Learning" proposed a cutting-edge machine learning approach to accurately predict the effectiveness of medicinal plants in treating CNS diseases.

Chapter thirteen "Predictive Analytics in Clinical Psychology - Role of Machine Learning in Future Mental Health Care" highlighted the integration of natural language processing (NLP) for analysing patient interactions, wearable technologies for real-time monitoring, and reinforcement learning for adaptive therapeutic interventions.

Chapter fourteen "Machine Learning for Combating Mental Health Stigma" depicted that machine learning reduces biases, enhances patient interactions, and fosters inclusivity.

Chapter fifteen "Use of virtual reality (VR) and AI in therapeutic settings" explored the transformative impact of virtual reality and artificial intelligence in therapeutic settings.

Chapter sixteen "Enhancing ADHD Support through a Human-AI Collaboration Framework- Integrating AI-Driven Assessments and Post-Therapy Mentorship" proposed a Human-AI Collaboration Model for ADHD Support encompassing Diagnosis, Therapeutic Support, and Post-Therapy Monitoring and Mentoring.

Chapter seventeen "Exploring the Association Between Caregiving Activities and Neuropsychological Disorders Deep Learning Model and Emerging Solutions" compared the frequency and intensity of caregiving activities, assess caregivers' physical and mental health status, and identify significant health behaviors associated with caregiving intensity.

Chapter eighteen "Developments, hardships, and prospective directions in the field of neuroscience and neurological machine learning for behavioral evaluation" examined the current state of neuroscience, emphasizing the use of machine learning to improve behavioral assessment and its therapeutic applications.

We highly appreciate everyone involved in the publication of this book.

Rohit Bansal
Stanford Institute of Management and Technology, Australia

Tariq Maqableh
Charles Sturt University, Australia

Gunjan Shuklaa
SICA College, Indore, India

Fazla Rabby
Stanford Institute of Management and Technology, Australia

Remya Lathabhavan
Indian Institute of Management, Bodh Gaya, India

Chapter 1
Cognitive Behavioral Therapy (CBT) and Machine Learning (ML)

Yashasvi Walia
Manipal University Jaipur, India

Rajnish Kumar Gupta
https://orcid.org/0000-0001-9354-360X
Manipal University Jaipur, India

ABSTRACT

Advanced technologies enable mental health professionals to refine therapeutic approaches, enhancing responsiveness to patients' unique needs. In this chapter, we explored such approaches that integrate cognitive behavioural therapy (CBT) with machine learning (ML) and artificial intelligence (AI) to enhance mental health services. It begins by defining key concepts of both CBT and ML, focusing on how ML improves the accuracy, accessibility, and personalization of therapeutic interventions. Practical examples illustrate ML uses in therapy, such as chatbots that assist in CBT, virtual reality tools simulating therapeutic settings, and real-time monitoring tools for tracking patient progress. Ethical considerations are also discussed, highlighting the importance of maintaining patient confidentiality and the therapeutic relationship. The chapter concludes by noting how ML and CBT integration could improve mental health access, accuracy in diagnosis, and individualized treatment.

DOI: 10.4018/979-8-3693-9341-3.ch001

1. INTRODUCTION

1.1 Overview of Cognitive Behavioral Therapy (CBT)

Cognitive Behavior Therapy (CBT) is a time-sensitive, structured, present-oriented psychotherapy that helps individuals identify the most important goals and overcome obstacles that get in the way. CBT is based on the cognitive model: how individuals perceive a situation is more closely connected to their reaction than the situation itself (Beck, 2020). CBT is considered one of the well-researched and widely used psychotherapy approaches. CBT, developed by Aaron T. Beck, MD—widely regarded as the father of Cognitive Behavioral Therapy and a leading figure in psychopathology research—has become a revolutionary treatment since its inception in the 1960s and 1970s. With proven effectiveness in over 2,000 clinical trials, CBT has been successfully applied to a broad range of mental disorders, psychological issues, and medical conditions with psychological components (Beck & Fleming, 2021). It is a problem-focused therapy that addresses current issues rather than exploring the past. It combines cognitive and behavioral approaches to address and modify thought patterns and behaviors contributing to emotional distress. Thus, helping individuals identify and change distressing thoughts and behaviors to improve coping skills and well-being (Chand et al., 2022).

Cognitive Approach, the term "Cognitive" is derived from the Latin verb "cognoscere," which means "to recognize." It is about forming a clear idea of our thoughts, attitudes, and expectations. The goal is to recognize and change false and distressing beliefs, such as over-generalizing or catastrophizing. These negative thought patterns often lead to self-fulfilling prophecies and emotional distress. Cognitive therapy teaches individuals to replace these harmful thoughts with more realistic, manageable ones, allowing them to gain better control over their emotions and thinking. While, behavioral approach, has its origins in "behaviorism", which assumes that human behavior is learned and can be modified. It identifies problematic behavior patterns that make life more difficult and works on changing them. By using techniques like relaxation exercises or increasing activity, individuals can adopt healthier behaviors, reducing distress and improving their well-being. CBT integrates these two approaches to provide a comprehensive therapeutic intervention, helping individuals not only change distorted thinking but also adopt healthier behaviors, leading to more effective management of mental health challenges. Thus, sessions involve setting goals, using relaxation and problem-solving techniques, tracking thoughts, etc. CBT is commonly used to treat mental health conditions like depression, anxiety, and OCD, as well as physical conditions like chronic pain. Its overall success depends on active participation, honesty, and effort of both therapist and patient. The duration of CBT varies depending on the severity of the problem, with sessions typically lasting one hour and occurring weekly.

1.2 Origin of CBT

CBT was developed by Dr. Aaron T. Beck in the 1960s when he observed that patients with depression exhibited distorted and irrational thinking patterns, or 'cognitive distortions'. His clinical observations led him to conceptualize depression as more of a cognitive disorder than a mood disorder, paving the way for a new approach to psychotherapy. Dr. Beck's cognitive theory of depression was first outlined in his work Cognitive Therapy for Depression (1979), which combined treatment protocols with empirical research—an innovation previously seen in behavior therapy (Beck et al., 2024). The evolution of Cognitive Behavioral Therapy (CBT) is rooted in both psychoanalysis and behaviorism (Jan Scott & Aaron T. Beck, 2008). While cognitive therapy focuses on conscious processes, it incorporates structured interventions influenced by behaviorism (Weishaar, 1993).

Early in the 20th century, psychodynamic models explored unconscious drives, while behaviorists rejected these ideas, favoring empirical observations (Clak & Beck, 1999). Aaron Beck's research marked a shift in the mid-20th century, emphasizing that conscious cognition shapes feelings and behaviors (Beck, 1967). Beck's cognitive model identified distorted cognitive processing and distinct profiles for different disorders (Greenberg & Beck, 1989). Initially subscribing to psychoanalysis, Beck found that negative beliefs and automatic thoughts, rather than unconscious drives, underpinned depressive symptoms. His cognitive therapy method, which departed from traditional psychoanalytic approaches, demonstrated its efficacy in treating depression, showing better results than medication (Rush et al., 1977). As interest grew, Beck and other clinicians expanded this approach to treat anxiety, personality disorders, and substance use. The therapy evolved into Cognitive Behavioral Therapy (CBT) with the integration of behavioral strategies. Various CBT models, including rational emotive therapy, schema-focused therapy, and dialectical behavioral therapy, have emerged. CBT is now one of the most extensively researched and empirically supported psychotherapies, proving effective in treating a wide range of mental health conditions and medical issues such as chronic pain and insomnia (Beck & Fleming, 2021). Its research-based framework has earned recognition from bodies like the National Institute of Clinical Excellence (NICE), solidifying its place in clinical practice (Jan Scott & Aaron T Beck, 2008). Many CBT approaches have emerged over the decades, reaching varied degrees of application and success. CBTs can be organized into three major divisions: *1) coping skills therapies,* which stress the development of a repertoire of skills designed to give the patient the instruments to cope with a variety of problem situations; *2) problem-solving therapies,* which emphasize the development of general strategies to deal with a broad range of personal difficulties; and *3) restructuring therapies,* which emphasize the assumption that emotional problems are a consequence of maladaptive thoughts, being the goal of treatment to reframe distorted thinking and to promote adaptive thoughts (Knapp & Beck, 2008).

1.3 Basics of CBT

A. CBT Triangle

The cognitive triangle, or the triangle of cognitive behavioural therapy (CBT), offers a framework for comprehending the interactions and influences between thoughts, feelings, and behaviors (Figure 1). It is an essential part of cognitive behavioural therapy (CBT), which is frequently used to treat mental health conditions like stress, anxiety, and depression. Every component can affect others, resulting in a vicious cycle that can cause issues like unhelpful thinking that generates needless feelings or avoidance behaviors that keep anxiety levels high. But this interdependence also works to CBT's benefit because addressing one component, like reversing negative thought patterns, can have a positive effect on feelings and actions, which can help with conditions like panic attacks. For example, the process by which a person assesses and interprets a circumstance or event, impacting their emotional and behavioral reaction, is known as cognitive appraisal. This assessment determines whether the situation is perceived as positive, negative, or neutral, and shapes how a person feels and acts based on their interpretation. For example, Sarah developed social anxiety after some uncomfortable social interactions. She appraised these situations as evidence that others were judging her negatively. This negative appraisal heightened her anxiety and caused her to avoid social settings. Through cognitive behavioral therapy (CBT), she learned to reappraise these interactions more realistically, recognizing that occasional awkwardness is normal and not a sign of harsh judgment. This shift in appraisal helped reduce her anxiety and allowed her to engage socially with more confidence.

Important Elements of the CBT Triangle are as follows:

- Thoughts: This part refers to cognitive processes, beliefs, and interpretations in our minds. Our thoughts can be influenced by past experiences, culture, and cognitive distortions (like black-and-white thinking or catastrophizing). These ideas affect how we feel, behave, and see the world, other people, and ourselves.

- Feelings: Emotions or feelings are our responses to our thoughts and the world around us. These can range from fleeting emotions like frustration to deeper, long-lasting emotions like anxiety or sadness. Identifying and understanding emotions is crucial for managing mental health effectively.
- Behaviors: It refers to the actions we take in response to our thoughts and feelings. These behaviors may be external, such as avoiding situations or interacting with others, or internal, like rumination. The relationship between thoughts, feelings, and behaviors is bi-directional: unhealthy behaviors can reinforce negative thoughts and feelings, while positive behaviors can improve emotional well-being.

Figure 1. Cognitive Behavioral Therapy (CBT) Triangle

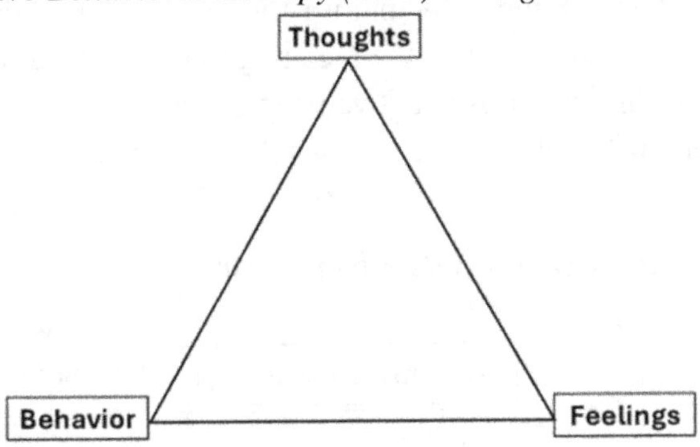

B. CBT is about meanings

Cognitive behavioural therapy (CBT) helps people analyze and challenge the ideas that influence their perceptions by focusing on the meanings they ascribe to their experiences. CBT goes far deeper into the cognitive processes that affect emotions and behaviors, even though it is frequently misunderstood as only treating surface-level problems or fixing flawed thinking. Consider Sarah, for example, who developed social anxiety as a result of a string of awkward social situations. She eventually came to feel that people were continuously criticizing her. Her therapist helped her explore this belief during her cognitive behavioural therapy sessions, assisting her in realizing that being awkward occasionally is a normal human experience and does not always translate into being perceived negatively by others. Through this process, Sarah gradually realized that her perception was distorted by her anxiety, which significantly contributed to her feelings of inadequacy. This change in perspective not only gave her more self-assurance but also inspired her to interact with people more freely. In a similar vein, Tamara's experience with OCD serves as an example of how CBT can change a person. After being initially imprisoned by her obsessive behaviors and the conviction that they were required to avoid harm, Tamara collaborated with her therapist to confront these ideas. She was able to overcome her limiting thoughts and live a more satisfying life by realizing that her fears were irrational and changing the way she thought about safety and control. The experiences of Tamara and Sarah both highlight how cognitive behavioural therapy (CBT) enables people to reframe their perceptions of reality, promoting more adaptive behaviors and healthier emotional reactions.

C. Appraisals matter

The insight of the CBT model is that it is not events that bother us. Instead, it is the way that we interpret events – the meaning that we give to them – that gives rise to our feelings. This explains why two people experiencing the same event can react in completely different ways. Let's consider a few examples:

Figure 2. How we interpret events determines how we feel about them

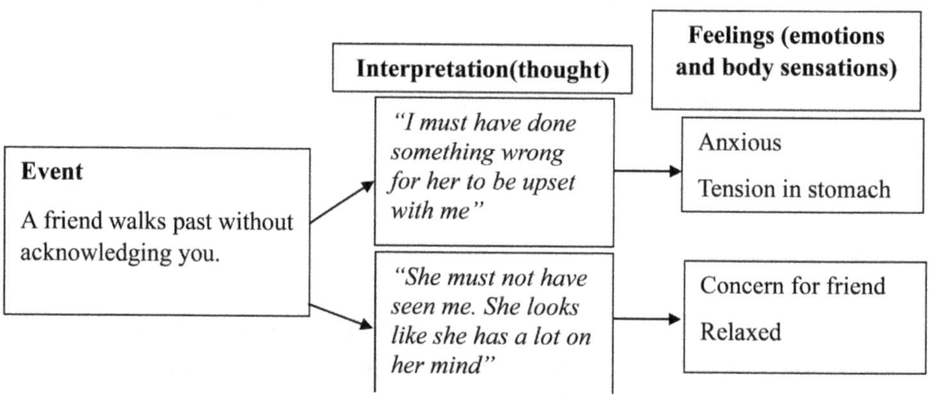

Figure 3. How interpreting events determines how we feel about them

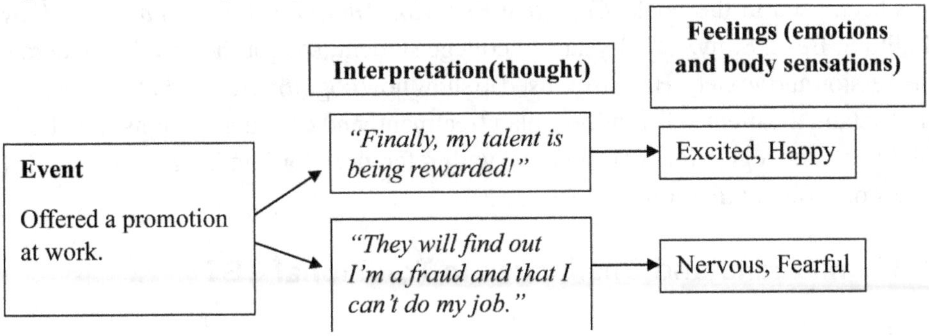

The above examples suggest that our interpretation of events significantly influences how we feel and respond to situations. Personalizing a friend's behavior can lead to anxiety, while a more neutral interpretation results in a different outcome. Similarly, a promotion can be viewed with excitement or anxiety, depending on the interpretation. This concept, echoed by thinkers like Epictetus and Shakespeare, highlights how our thoughts shape our emotional responses. While we cannot always control our circumstances, we can control how we interpret them. As Viktor Frankl emphasized, our greatest freedom lies in choosing our attitude and perspective in any situation.

D. Principles of CBT

Despite personalised CBT treatment for each individual, it follows a few key principles applicable to all patients. These principles are as follows:

- CBT is based on an ever-evolving formulation of patients' problems and an individual conceptualization of each patient in cognitive terms.
- CBT requires a sound therapeutic alliance.
- CBT emphasizes collaboration and active participation.
- CBT is goal-oriented and problem-focused.
- CBT initially emphasizes the present.
- CBT is educative, aims to teach the patient to be her therapist, and emphasizes relapse prevention.
- CBT aims to be time limited.
- CBT sessions are structured.
- CBT teaches patients to identify, evaluate, and respond to their dysfunctional thoughts and beliefs.
- CBT uses a variety of techniques to change thinking, mood, and behavior.

To illustrate CBT principles in depression, a case study of an ideal patient, Sally has been used in the book- *Cognitive Behavior Therapy: Basics and Beyond,* by Judith S. Beck. Sally, an 18-year-old college student, sought therapy for moderate depression and anxiety. Her case is used to show how cognitive theory helps therapists understand a patient's difficulties, plan treatment, and conduct sessions. The book highlights strategies for typical cases, with references for handling more complex cases or different diagnoses (Beck, 2020).

1.4 Limitations and Challenges in Traditional CBT

CBT remains a widely used and empirically supported treatment, applied in diverse settings and adapted for different populations, including children, adults, and the elderly. However, building on CBT's proven effectiveness and improving its quality and accessibility—especially for underserved neighborhoods and diverse populations—remains a challenge for academics and clinicians. This includes adapting treatments to different cultural contexts, expanding digital and online methods of delivery, and integrating CBT into primary care and public health settings (Beck & Fleming, 2021). The integration of Artificial Intelligence (AI) and Machine Learning (ML) into CBT introduces a host of promising applications that could further enhance the effectiveness, accessibility, and personalization of therapy (Jiang et al., 2024). Chatbots, virtual assistants, and real-time monitoring systems are examples of AI-powered technologies that have the potential to increase the scalability and responsiveness of therapy. With the ability to provide remote and on-demand therapeutic support, these developments may be especially helpful to people who face social, economic, or geographic obstacles to traditional in-person therapy. AI has the potential to personalize treatment by analyzing vast datasets and spotting behavioral patterns, which will allow interventions to be tailored to each patient's unique needs. Nevertheless, the dependence on digital tools presents difficulties, including addressing the digital divide, guaranteeing fair access to technology, and avoiding cultural biases in AI models. Dr. Aaron Beck's lifelong goal of using cognitive behavioural therapy (CBT) to lessen human suffering is still a driving force. The integration of AI and ML supports this goal by offering to increase the effectiveness and reach of therapy. Even though these innovations have the potential to be revolutionary, they must be developed and applied with careful consideration of ethical issues, such as protecting patient data privacy, preserving the human connection that is essential to therapy, and making sure that AI enhances rather than replaces the role of the therapist. As the CBT community honors its 70-year legacy, integrating AI and ML into research and practice holds the potential to revolutionize the way CBT is delivered, studied, and disseminated globally, ensuring that more individuals receive high-quality, evidence-based care.

2. OVERVIEW OF ARTIFICIAL INTELLIGENCE (AI) AND MACHINE LEARNING (ML)

The term artificial intelligence (AI) refers to the ability of machines to carry out tasks like reasoning, problem-solving, and natural language comprehension that normally require human-like intelligence. In the 1950s, the idea of artificial intelligence (AI) first surfaced, with an emphasis on theoretical frameworks for machines that could mimic human cognitive processes (Bini, 2018). By the 21st century, AI has become a major focus of computer science research and application after developing dramatically over the decades and gaining traction in a variety of fields. These days, artificial intelligence (AI) is incorporated into many facets of daily life, from big data analysis and driverless cars to tailored suggestions on websites like Netflix and Amazon. AI's adaptability and potential to revolutionize sectors like healthcare, transportation, finance, and more are demonstrated by these applications (Dave et al., 2022).

Machine Learning (ML) is a core or a key subset of AI. It focuses on algorithms allowing computers to learn from data and improve their performance over time without explicit programming. These algorithms are continuously refined by comparing predictions with known outcomes, enhancing their ability to make accurate recommendations or decisions over time (Helm et al., 2020). ML has become a well-known tool because of its capacity to effectively process enormous volumes of data and derive significant insights that human analysts might miss. The development of machine learning has produced several approaches that can be divided into four categories: supervised, unsupervised, semi-supervised, and reinforcement learning. Different approaches are used by each category according to the type of data that is available, enabling customized solutions for a range of applications. In conclusion, machine learning (ML) is particularly concerned with the ability of machines to learn from experience and make defensible decisions based on data, whereas artificial intelligence (AI) embodies the more general goal of developing intelligent systems that can replicate human thought processes. This collaboration between AI and ML is spurring innovation in a variety of fields, radically altering the way we use technology and improving our capacities in problem-solving and decision-making.

2.1 Machine Learning (ML)

The concept of Machine Learning (ML) was first coined by Arthur Samuel in 1959. According to him, ML is defined as the field of study that gives computers the ability to learn without being explicitly programmed (Samuel, 1959). Machine learning (ML) is used to help machines process data more effectively when human interpretation falls short. With the rise of large datasets, ML's demand has grown, allowing industries to extract relevant information from data. The core goal of ML is for machines to learn from data without explicit programming. Researchers and programmers have explored various approaches to enable machines to solve complex problems involving vast datasets. Data scientists like to point out that there is no single one-size-fits-all type of algorithm that is best to solve a problem. The kind of algorithm employed depends on the kind of problem we wish to solve, the number of variables, the kind of model that would suit it best, and so on. ML relies on different algorithms to solve data problems.

2.1.1 Types of Machine Learning

Machine learning algorithms are trained by utilizing labeled, unlabelled, or hybrid datasets. Consequently, the nature of the requisite data for a particular task dictates the archetype of the machine learning model that is formulated. Consequently, four fundamental categories of machine learning have been established and developed: supervised, unsupervised, semi-supervised, and reinforcement learning (Alnuaimi & Albaldawi, 2024).

A. **Supervised Learning (SL):** Supervised Learning (SL) is a type of machine learning where the system learns to make predictions based on labeled data. It works similarly to how a person learns with the help of a teacher—using specific examples to figure out general rules. In SL, the system is trained with data that already has correct answers (labels), and the goal is to use that knowledge to predict outcomes for new, unseen data. There are two main types of supervised learning:
    a. Regression: This method helps in understanding the relationship between a dependent variable (what you want to predict) and one or more independent variables (the factors influencing the prediction). For example, in market trends or weather forecasting, regression is used to predict continuous outcomes like prices or temperatures. The most common type is linear regression, where a straight line is used to model the relationship between variables (Praba et al., 2021).
    b. Classification: This method involves sorting data into categories. It's about placing data into pre-defined classes based on the features of that data (Bansal, 2023). A simple example is classifying emails as "spam" or "not spam." Classification works with both structured (organized) and unstructured (unorganized) data, and the goal is to assign unknown data to a known category or label (Brownlee, 2022).

While both regression and classification can be used to make predictions in machine learning, the key difference is that regression predicts continuous values (like a price or temperature), while classification predicts discrete categories (like "spam" or "not spam"). Both learn from labeled datasets but apply them to different types of problems.

B. **Unsupervised Learning:** Unsupervised learning is a machine learning technique where the system is trained without having any labeled data or predefined outcomes. Unlike supervised learning, where the system learns from examples with known answers, unsupervised learning requires the machine to find hidden patterns and structures in the data on its own. This type of learning is useful when we don't know the exact categories or labels, and the machine has to analyze the data independently (Ali et al., 2021; Sandhya & Charanjeet, 2016). For instance, if we provide a set of images containing cats and dogs (but without labeling them as "cat" or "dog"), the machine will automatically try to separate them based on their features, such as size, shape, or behavior. Over the time, the system learns to distinguish between these groups even though it has not been explicitly told what a "cat" or a "dog" is. If we later input new pictures of cats and dogs, the machine will be able to categorize them based on the previous patterns it identified. There are two main types and the most common of unsupervised learning algorithms, clustering and association analysis.
   a. Clustering: Clustering involves grouping data into clusters based on their inherent similarities. For example, an online store might use clustering algorithms to group customers by their shopping behaviors. Customers who frequently buy similar types of products or shop at specific times could be clustered together. Another example would be grouping visitors to a store based on how often they visit. Clustering helps in organizing data when the categories or groups are unknown beforehand.
   b. Association: Association analysis focuses on discovering relationships between different items in a dataset. This technique is commonly used in recommendation systems. For example, a supermarket might discover that customers who purchase a specific item, like bread, are also likely to buy butter. Based on this information, the system can suggest related items to customers. Association analysis helps identify the probability of one event occurring when another related event happens, such as customers who buy A also tend to buy B.

In summary, unsupervised learning is a powerful approach for analyzing unlabeled data, discovering hidden patterns, and making data-driven predictions without predefined categories. It is widely used in areas like customer segmentation, recommendation systems, and anomaly detection. Through techniques like clustering and association, unsupervised learning plays a crucial role in helping machines understand and categorize complex data sets.

C. **Semi-Supervised Learning:** Semi-supervised learning (SSL) is a powerful technique that combines supervised and unsupervised learning to improve learning accuracy. It addresses the challenge of limited labeled data by leveraging the abundance of unlabelled data (Ali et al., 2021; Sandhya & Charanjeet, 2016). With more common supervised machine learning methods, we can train a machine learning algorithm on a 'labeled' dataset in which each record includes the outcome information. SSL finds applications in diverse fields like speech analysis, web content classification, protein sequence classification, and text document classifiers (Rastogi et al., 2020).
D. **Reinforcement Learning:** Reinforcement Learning (RL) is a machine learning method where a software agent learns to make decisions by interacting with its environment through trial and error. Instead of knowing the correct answers beforehand, the agent tries different actions, receiving feedback as rewards for positive outcomes and punishments for negative ones. Over time, it learns which actions yield the best results, improving its decision-making process (Rastogi et al., 2020). Unlike supervised learning, where the model is trained with labeled data, RL allows the agent to learn from its own experiences. Although sometimes considered a subset of semi-supervised learning, RL is widely recognized as a distinct form of machine learning studied across various disciplines due to its generality (Ram, 2022). These disciplines include game theory, control theory, operations research, information theory, simulation-based optimization, multi-agent systems, swarm intelligence, statistics, and genetic algorithms. A practical example is autonomous driving, where a car learns to navigate by continuously adjusting its actions based on road conditions and feedback (Alnuaimi & Albaldawi, 2024). Some main points in reinforcement learning:
    - Input: The input should be from the initial stage where the model starts.
    - Output: There are multiple outputs to any problem.
    - Training: As the training depends on input, the model will return the state, and the user will decide to reward or discard the model based on its output.

2.1.2 Need for Machine Learning (ML)

Machine learning (ML) has revolutionized the way we approach problems involving large amounts of data, complex decisions, and dynamic environments. By enabling computers to learn from data and improve their performance without being explicitly programmed, ML is becoming an important tool in both scientific and psychological domains. Its application goes beyond traditional programming methods, making it particularly useful in areas requiring adaptability and continuous learning. Here are some specific areas where machine learning is being used:

- Predictive modeling: A key component of ML, allows scientists to forecast outcomes based on patterns in large datasets. This ability is vital in fields like genomics, where predictive models help identify individuals at risk for diseases based on genetic information, thus revolutionizing personalized medicine. In psychology, predictive models assist in mental health research by predicting which individuals may be at risk for disorders like depression or anxiety, based on behavioral data and cognitive patterns.
- Natural language processing (NLP): ML has practical implications in both science and psychology. In the scientific community, NLP tools help analyze vast amounts of textual data, such as scientific papers or patient reports, making it easier to draw insights from them. In psychology, NLP plays a crucial role in understanding human emotions and communication. Chatbots designed using NLP can serve as therapeutic tools, offering mental health support by analyzing users' emotional tone, suggesting coping strategies, or even intervening during a crisis.
- Computer vision: It enables machines to interpret and analyze visual data. In scientific fields like medicine, this helps in areas like medical imaging, where ML systems assist in diagnosing diseases by recognizing patterns in MRI or CT scans. In psychology, computer vision can be applied to analyze human behavior by studying facial expressions, body language, and eye movements, providing insights into emotional states, or detecting mental health issues such as autism.
- Fraud detection: ML models identify anomalies in financial transactions, similar principles can be applied in psychological research to detect abnormal patterns in behavior, potentially signaling distress or deception. This has implications for forensic psychology, where algorithms can be trained to recognize suspicious behavior in criminal investigations or legal proceedings.
- Recommendation systems: This ML tool has immense potential in both consumer industries and psychology. These systems analyze users' past behavior to make personalized suggestions, whether for products, movies, or content. From a psychological perspective, recommendation systems may help tailor therapy sessions or mental health apps by offering coping strategies, therapeutic content, or even self-care routines based on a person's mental state or past activities.

In essence, the increasing integration of machine learning across scientific and psychological domains marks a shift towards more data-driven, adaptive, and personalized solutions. As research evolves, so does the ability to apply ML in ways that benefit not only technology and business but also human understanding and well-being. ML's power to learn, adapt, and improve makes it indispensable for both scientific discovery and psychological practice, offering new ways to analyze human behavior, diagnose mental health issues, and even deliver personalized interventions for improved emotional and cognitive health.

2.1.3 Machine Learning and Psychology

AI and psychology are increasingly interconnected, with machine learning (ML) offering new ways to understand human cognition and behavior. Just as humans learn through feedback, ML algorithms, optimize their actions based on trial-and-error experiences. AI models can simulate complex decision-making and problem-solving, aiding research in areas like mental health diagnosis and behavior prediction (Vieira et al., 2022). From a psychological perspective, machine learning holds the potential to model complex cognitive processes. Algorithms can simulate decision-making, problem-solving, and even social interactions, creating a new frontier for studying the human mind. In turn, psychological theories can inform the design of more efficient and human-like AI systems. When applied to therapies like Cognitive Behavioral Therapy (CBT), AI can enhance treatment by identifying patterns in thought and behavior and offering more personalized interventions for conditions like depression, anxiety, and PTSD, offering the potential for more accurate diagnoses and tailored treatments. This synergy allows therapists to leverage data-driven insights, improving treatment outcomes and creating adaptive, patient-centered approaches. Psychologists are experimenting with AI to predict behaviors, diagnose mental illnesses, and improve treatment outcomes. AI has been used to analyze brain scans for pain, understand personality traits, and predict issues like social media addiction and alcohol abuse (Dave et al., 2022). Thus, the need for machine learning is grounded not only in its technical capabilities but also in its capacity to enhance our understanding of both the physical world and the human experience. This synergy between science, psychology, and machine learning is leading us toward more intelligent, adaptive systems that not only solve complex problems but also contribute to a deeper understanding of human cognition, behavior, and mental health.

2.1.4 Machine Learning Applications for Various Disorders

Artificial intelligence (AI) and machine learning (ML) have become highly effective tools in psychology, especially for diagnosing and predicting mental health disorders. These technologies analyze large volumes of data to find trends that can greatly improve diagnosis and treatment strategies. A variety of mental health conditions, including Post-traumatic stress disorder (PTSD), anxiety, obsessive-compulsive disorder (OCD), depression, and suicidal thoughts, are being treated with machine learning models, such as random forests, support vector machines (SVMs), and neural networks. These models present encouraging opportunities to increase the precision of mental health assessments and predictions by combining demographic, psychological, and medical data.

- PTSD: Post-traumatic stress disorder development following hospitalization is predicted by models such as XGBoost and SVM using psychological and physical predictors (such as pulse rate and PTSD symptoms).
- Anxiety Disorders: Auto-sklearn, naïve Bayes, and logistic regression models are useful for forecasting the course and outcome of anxiety disorders. These models employ biological, psychological, and clinical data; however, the accuracy of the results is only moderate.
- OCD: Using brain imaging data, machine learning models and MRI scans are used to predict the severity of OCD, with a special emphasis on brain regions that affect obsessive-compulsive behavior.
- Depression: Using information from self-reported surveys, electroencephalography (EEG) scans, and facial recognition, machine learning models like random forests and neural networks help diagnose and forecast the severity of depression.
- Suicidal Behaviour and Self-Injury: Models such as random forests forecast the likelihood of self-harm and hospital readmission, while natural language processing and machine learning techniques are utilized to evaluate the risk of suicide using data from therapy sessions. These techniques examine patient information, including past self-harm incidents and medical records.

In conclusion, machine learning provides cutting-edge resources for mental health treatment, enabling psychologists to predict the onset, severity, and course of treatment of a variety of disorders with better accuracy. However, before incorporating these techniques completely into clinical practice, there are still issues that need to be resolved, such as data availability and model performance (Dave et al., 2022).

2.2 Integration of Machine Learning in CBT

CBT, a widely-used psychological intervention, helps individuals develop healthier responses to stress, anxiety, and depression by addressing the connections among thoughts, emotions, and behaviors. Machine learning, with its capacity to analyze patterns within large datasets and make predictive insights, now enhances CBT by improving diagnostic accuracy and enabling more personalized treatments.

The integration of Cognitive Behavioural Therapy (CBT) and Machine Learning (ML) has created new opportunities for behavioral analysis and mental health treatment in recent years. Since the COVID-19 pandemic, mental health issues have increased significantly, with higher rates of depression, anxiety, and suicidal thoughts (Penninx et al., 2022). CBT, a widely-used psychological intervention, helps individuals develop healthier responses to stress, anxiety, and depression by addressing the connections among thoughts, emotions, and behaviors. Machine learning, with its capacity to analyze patterns within large datasets and make predictive insights, now enhances CBT by improving diagnostic accuracy and enabling more personalized treatments. Although CBT is one of the most effective treatments available, traditional in-person therapy faces obstacles such as limited access and the stigma surrounding mental health. To address these challenges, computer-based and internet-based CBT (CCBT and ICBT) have been developed, though they still face limitations, including reduced interactivity and high dropout rates (Webb et al., 2017).

Human behavior is shaped by a complex interplay of actions, cognition, and emotions. Actions are visible behaviors; cognition encompasses thoughts and mental representations, such as skills and knowledge; and emotions, often intense and momentary, strongly influence behavior though not always logically. Understanding these interactions is key to identifying behavioral patterns and abnormalities. Additionally, behavior is influenced by social and personal factors like socioeconomic status, cultural norms, personality traits, and formative experiences (Gifford & Nilsson, 2014). Understanding the principles underlying human behavior helps inform therapeutic approaches, including CBT, which effectively addresses behavioral and emotional challenge (Sarter et al., 2021).

2.2.1 Machine Learning in Cognitive Behavioral Therapy

Cognitive behavioural therapy (CBT) is becoming more and more effective in a variety of applications as machine learning is incorporated into it. In political psychology and philosophy, 'cognition' refers to the deliberate mental processes involved in gaining knowledge and understanding. Cognitive neuroscience, which explores mental functions such as perception, memory, and reasoning, closely aligns with this concept. In contrast, emotion describes a temporary state driven by intense experiences, such as joy or fear, and is often viewed as distinct from cognitive processes. However, recent studies suggest that cognition and emotion are deeply interconnected, influencing one another within the brain. This interdependence means that our thoughts, emotions, and behaviors collectively shape our actions. Cognitive Behavioral Therapy (CBT) leverages these connections by helping individuals understand how their thoughts affect their feelings and behaviors. By addressing unhelpful thought patterns, CBT has proven effective in improving mental health, particularly in treating conditions like anxiety and depression (Dave et al., 2022). A few key applications of Machine Learning in CBT are as follows:

- Stress and Emotion Detection: Since emotions have a direct impact on thoughts and behaviors, they are essential to cognitive behavioural therapy. Real-time monitoring of clients' emotional distress through the analysis of behavioral cues (e.g., body language) and physiological signals (e.g., skin conductance, heart rate) is known as stress and emotion detection. To identify stress and emotional distress, machine learning algorithms can examine behavioral cues like body language and facial expressions as well as physiological signals like skin conductance, heart rate, and EEG. This makes it possible to monitor clients' mental states in real-time, which helps therapists to provide timely support, intervene when stress levels rise, and modify therapy sessions in response to clients' emotional reactions.
- Detection of Abnormal Behaviour: In cognitive behavioural therapy, recognizing maladaptive or abnormal behaviors is essential to creating treatment plans. To identify behaviors that differ from social norms, machine learning models can examine data from wearable technology, public surveillance systems, or recordings of therapy sessions. In situations like severe mental health disorders or substance abuse, where clients may be at risk of hurting themselves or others, this application is extremely helpful. Early detection can stop dangerous situations from getting worse and result in timely interventions.
- Deception and Lie Detection: In addition to mental health, forensic and legal domains can benefit from the detection of lies and deception. By examining both verbal and non-verbal indicators, including tone of voice, facial expressions, and physiological data, machine learning models can distinguish between dishonest and truthful actions. In therapeutic settings, these methods—which are frequently implemented through polygraph examinations or deception detection algorithms—are employed to ascertain the emotional states and stress levels of clients.

2.2.2 Case Studies Showing Successful ML-Driven CBT Interventions

A growing field of study that seeks to improve the efficacy and accessibility of mental health treatments is the combination of machine learning (ML) and cognitive behavioural therapy (CBT). The possible advantages of this integration are demonstrated in several case studies. A study by Karyotaki et al. (2021) assessed the use of machine learning algorithms to forecast treatment outcomes in online cognitive behavioural therapy, and the results showed a mean balanced accuracy of 78.1%. This outcome demonstrated the ability of machine learning to customize interventions based on patient data, enhancing therapeutic efficacy, in addition to surpassing the clinical usefulness benchmark of 67% (Karyotaki et al., 2021). Another important study concentrated on forecasting CBT dropout rates for individuals suffering from panic disorder. The researchers obtained remarkable accuracy rates of 88% and 85%, respectively, by employing a variety of machine learning techniques, such as random forest and light gradient boosting algorithms. To improve retention rates, clinicians can take proactive measures by using machine learning (ML) to identify patients who are at risk of discontinuing therapy (Ogawa, 2024). Moreover, new opportunities for customizing CBT interventions have been made possible by developments in AI technologies, especially deep learning, and large language models. Fitzpatrick et al. (2017), for instance, investigated the use of conversational agents driven by natural language processing to support CBT techniques in real time, showing enhanced patient engagement and treatment protocol adherence. These AI-powered solutions can offer prompt assistance and feedback, overcoming some of the drawbacks of conventional in-person therapy (K. K. Fitzpatrick et al., 2017). Overall, these case studies show that incorporating machine learning into cognitive behavioural therapy (CBT) not only has the potential to improve therapeutic approaches but also increases patient retention and engagement in mental health services. More individualized and efficient treatment options for people dealing with mental health issues may become available as this field develops.

2.2.3 Machine Learning, AI Models, and Tools for Therapeutic Enhancements

Recent advancements in artificial intelligence (AI) using Machine learning (ML) offer new possibilities for improving mental health services. These ML advancements can enhance diagnosis, treatment personalization, and accessibility, offering solutions like AI-driven CBT models and conversational agents. These advancements help tailor CBT interventions to individual needs, making therapy more precise and accessible (Vieira et al., 2022). A schematic representation of integrating AI in various stages of CBT treatment provides a clear systematic process of CBT in machine learning (Figure 4) (Jiang et al., 2024).

Figure 4. Integration of AI in various stages of CBT treatment

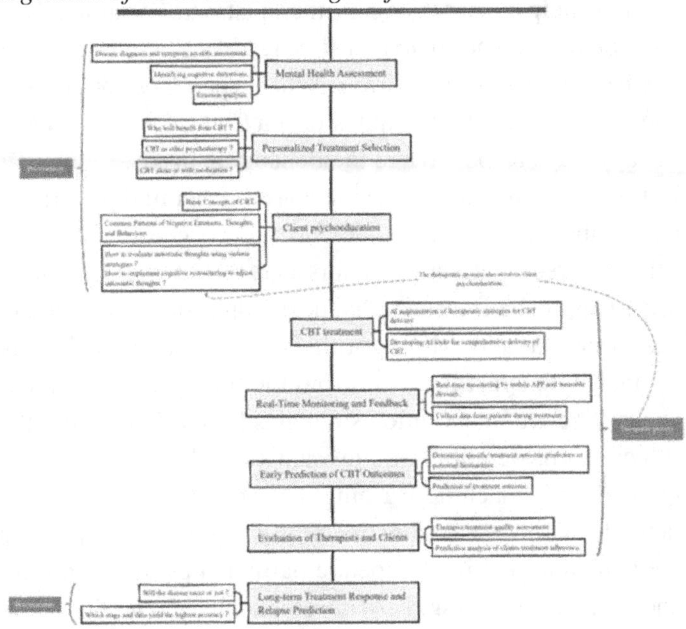

A. ML implementation in CBT:

- Personalization of Treatment: To personalize treatment plans in therapy, ML algorithms can examine vast amounts of data about each patient, including demographic information and past treatment outcomes. This customized approach ensures that interventions closely match the individual psychological profile and requirements of every patient, which may result in better treatment of mental health issues. Therapists can use the most effective therapeutic approaches right away by using algorithms that, for instance, can determine which approaches have produced the best results for comparable patients in the past.
- Accessibility: CBT is much more accessible when machine learning-powered tools like chatbots and virtual therapy platforms are used. People in underserved or remote areas, where traditional therapy options may be scarce, can benefit from these technologies by receiving support and therapeutic interventions. ML tools can help to close the gap in mental health services by providing asynchronous support and

instant resources, increasing access to therapy for people who might otherwise encounter obstacles.

- Real-Time Monitoring: Machine learning makes it easier to continuously track patients' progress using mobile apps and wearable technology. With the help of these gadgets, therapists can dynamically modify treatment plans in response to real-time feedback on physiological indicators like heart rate and stress levels. When a patient's condition changes, this continuous evaluation enables prompt interventions, guaranteeing that therapy stays responsive to their changing needs.
- Data-Driven Insights: Machine learning can find patterns and trends in large datasets that help guide clinical procedures. By finding relationships between patient behaviors and therapeutic outcomes, this data-driven approach improves diagnostic precision and treatment effectiveness. For example, ML algorithms can guide clinical decision-making by analyzing aggregate data from multiple patients to uncover insights about effective intervention strategies for particular conditions.
- Ethical Considerations: Significant ethical concerns are raised by the integration if machine learning into cognitive behavioral therapy, particularly with regard to patients' privacy and potential degradation of the human aspect in therapeutic partnerships. It is vital to strike a balance between utilizing these developments and retaining the fundamental human aspects of empathy and understanding in therapy, as therapists depend more and more on technology for insights and monitoring. Addressing these ethical concerns is necessary to ensure that technology integration enhances patient care rather than detracts from it.

In brief, by personalizing treatment, increasing accessibility, facilitating real-time monitoring, offering data-driven insights, and bringing to light ethical issues that need to be addressed as technology in mental health care continues to advance, the use of machine learning in cognitive behavioural therapy holds great promise for improving therapeutic outcomes.

B. Developing ML tools for comprehensive delivery of CBT

In real-world practice, CBT strategies are usually combined to meet the specific needs of each client, even though they are frequently discussed separately. Advances in ML in recent years have resulted in the creation of digital tools that creatively and novelly apply the concepts and methods of cognitive behavioural therapy. These resources provide a more comprehensive approach to treatment by combining several CBT techniques. A notable development in this field is the emergence of chatbots driven by artificial intelligence, commonly referred to as relational or conversational agents. These chatbots can simulate human therapists by interacting with users through both spoken and non-spoken dialogue. This makes it possible for them to offer individualized, effective, and easily accessible CBT treatment at any time of day or night. According to a review, 10 of the 17 chatbots that provided psychotherapy were based on CBT. These chatbots—Woebot, Wysa, Tess, and Youper, among others—have gained notoriety for their capacity to provide psychological support and assist users in resolving mental health issues. They are useful instruments for delivering mental health care because of their accessibility and application of CBT techniques (Abd-Alrazaq et al., 2019). The increasing need for digital tools for mental health has prompted researchers to create new AI-based systems based on CBT. These tools, which combine ML and CBT to assist patients in better managing their mental health, are state-of-the-art in mental health care. A summarized outline of specific AI tools currently utilized in CBT interventions are presented in Table 1.

Table 1. AI tools used in cognitive behavioral therapy

AI Tools	Description
Woebot (Kathleen Kara Fitzpatrick et al., 2017) https://woebothealth.com/	A chatbot that provides CBT-based treatment for anxiety and depression by interacting with users through interactive CBT tools, emotion tracking, and daily conversations. When it finds language that raises red flags, it directs users to other sources.
Wysa (Inkster et al., 2018) https://www.wysa.com/	A chatbot for therapy that uses positive psychology, cognitive behavioural therapy, and mindfulness to treat stress, anxiety, and depression. It provides safe and compassionate support by using pre-written dialogues created by clinicians.
Youpers (Mehta et al., 2021) https://youpers.com/en/	Offers CBT interventions that are customized based on users' emotional states. It uses mental health evaluations, symptom monitoring, and real-time emotion analysis.
Tess (Fulmer et al., 2018) https://www.x2ai.com/uprisehealth	A psychological AI chatbot that offers quick reminders, psychoeducation, and mental health support; it also adapts its responses according to user input and prioritizes cognitive behavioural therapy.
BetterHelp https://www.betterhelp.com/	An AI-powered online therapy platform that pairs clients with certified therapists and provides a range of therapeutic modalities, including psychodynamic and cognitive behavioural therapy.
Rumi (Oliveira et al., 2021) https://www.rumimentalhealth.com/	A chatbot that explores thoughts, feelings, and behaviors using rumination-focused cognitive behavioural therapy (CBT) to lessen symptoms of depression and anxiety.
Cloud Bot (Rizea, 2022)	CBT is provided by a chatbot that uses natural language processing (NLP), with a special emphasis on cognitive restructuring to help users with mental health concerns.

continued on following page

Table 1. Continued

AI Tools	Description
Saarthi (Rani et al., 2023) https://saarthimentalhealth.wordpress.com/	An AI and natural language processing (NLP) chatbot that provides evidence-based cognitive behavioural therapy (CBT) in real-time and remote health monitoring to reduce anxiety and depression and facilitate long-term mental health tracking.
SchizoBot (Nwoye et al., 2024)	A chatbot that uses artificial neural networks to provide cognitive behavioural therapy (CBT) for managing schizophrenia can help clinicians administer therapy consistently.
XIAO AN (Su et al., 2022)	A Chinese AI psychotherapy robot that treats anxiety disorders effectively uses cognitive behavioural therapy (CBT) to track emotions and deliver therapy.
Emohaa (Sabour et al., 2023)	A Chinese chatbot with two platforms: ES-Bot for unstructured emotional support and CBT-Bot for structured CBT exercises.

AI-powered chatbots help people manage their mental health outside of regular therapy hours by offering efficient, individualized, and convenient Cognitive Behavioural Therapy (CBT) support. Because these AI agents are available around the clock, they are especially helpful for people who are having trouble getting in-person therapy because of things like lengthy wait times or a lack of resources. However, it is important to understand that chatbots cannot completely replace human therapists, even though they can ease the strain on healthcare systems and supplement traditional therapy, particularly in complex cases that call for empathy and nuanced understanding. To uphold clinical standards and advance user well-being, developers and mental health professionals must work together to ensure that these tools provide accurate and moral guidance.

3. CHALLENGES AND LIMITATIONS

3.1 Technical Challenges

- Privacy and Data Security: One of the main obstacles to incorporating machine learning (ML) into cognitive behavioural therapy (CBT) is making sure that patients' private data is protected. Strong security measures must be put in place to protect patients' confidentiality as the healthcare industry faces rising data breach risks. Preventing serious harm to people and preserving the credibility of mental health services depends on the ethical management of personal health data. Complexity is further increased by adhering to legal requirements like the Health Insurance Portability and Accountability Act

(HIPAA), which calls for the use of sophisticated encryption and access control systems to safeguard personal data.

- Understanding Human Emotion: Large datasets are easily processed by ML algorithms, but they frequently fall short of understanding the complexity of human emotions. Machine learning systems may not be as effective in therapeutic settings, particularly when emotional sensitivity is essential, because they lack the depth of knowledge required to capture emotional nuances. This drawback emphasizes how AI must be used as a helpful tool in addition to human therapists, not as a substitute, to maintain the therapeutic process's compassionate elements.

3.2 Clinical Challenges

- Resistance to Tech-Driven Therapy: Some patients' resistance to technology-enhanced cognitive behavioural therapy is a major obstacle to its adoption, frequently stemming from their lack of knowledge about or mistrust of technology-based interventions. Many people who are seeking therapy might favor in-person, conventional interactions over virtual or online ones. The adoption of ML-driven therapeutic approaches may be slowed by this resistance, underscoring the necessity of educational initiatives and a slow rollout of technology in therapeutic settings.
- Maintaining the Therapeutic Alliance: Treatment success depends on the therapeutic alliance or the relationship of cooperation between a patient and a therapist. To guarantee that this connection is maintained, ML must be carefully considered when incorporated into CBT. Higher adherence to therapy and improved treatment outcomes have been repeatedly linked to strong therapeutic relationships. Thus, any new technology should be developed to strengthen and enhance this crucial component of therapy rather than reducing it.

3.3 Ethical and Legal Challenges

- Ethical Considerations: The application of machine learning to mental health treatment raises several ethical questions, such as privacy concerns, the requirement for informed consent, and the possibility of algorithmic bias. Biases in the training data used for machine learning can result in unfair treatment recommendations that disproportionately impact marginalized communities. These ethical conundrums must be resolved to develop just and efficient AI tools for mental health treatment.

- Legal Conditions: Navigating the legal environment around the application of AI in healthcare is both difficult and essential. Healthcare practitioners must ensure that current laws about patient confidentiality and informed consent are followed when integrating ML solutions. Legal frameworks must change as technology advances to protect patient rights and promote innovation in providing mental health services.

4. CONCLUSION AND FUTURE DIRECTIONS

The integration of Artificial Intelligence (AI) and Machine Learning (ML) in cognitive behavioral analysis marks a significant advancement in the field of psychology. This chapter outlined how AI can be used to identify and forecast stressful, emotional, dishonest, and aberrant behavior by utilizing its capacity to examine intricate relationships between variables that are frequently beyond human comprehension. User-centric insights are crucial in several industries, including marketing, healthcare, and security, where these applications have broad implications. Even though AI is still in its infancy, it has the potential to yield revolutionary new applications in these domains. With a focus on unimodal and multimodal sensing mechanisms, feature extraction methods, AI/ML models, datasets, and the associated challenges, this chapter has summarised the salient features of previous researches. A bright future is presented by AI-based cognitive behavioural analysis, but more study is necessary to completely comprehend its potential and constraints. Crucially, this emerging field needs to make sure AI systems are created morally, considering how society will be affected in terms of privacy, justice, and personal welfare. The chapter also showed how AI methods, particularly machine learning and deep learning, are already being used to address significant problems like mental health diagnosis, suicide, self-harm prediction, and behavioral intervention accuracy. Although the results of the reviewed studies are encouraging, they also point out the need for adaptation and further development, laying the groundwork for more sophisticated uses of AI in psychology.

Future Directions

Several crucial issues must be resolved to get past the present obstacles and fully utilize AI's potential in cognitive behavioral analysis:

- Tools and Techniques: Strong, flexible, and user-friendly multimodal devices with sensors like heart rate (HR), heart rate variability (HRV), and galvanic skin response (GSR) are desperately needed. Accurate behavioral analysis requires consistent and dependable data collection, which these devices will make possible. Reducing noise and artifacts can be achieved by combining enhanced methods for EEG or ECG with already-existing modalities, such as physiological signals and video. This method will increase the general comprehension of cognitive behaviors in addition to improving the quality of the data.

- Techniques and Algorithms: Self-reports, behavioral observations, and physiological data should all be incorporated into AI models to give a more thorough and impartial understanding of cognitive-behavioral processes. Models will be more robust, interpretable, and equitable if they can better handle missing data and modalities. Furthermore, bias in behavioral analysis will be decreased by improving generalization across various cultural and linguistic contexts by fine-tuning pre-trained models with larger, more varied datasets. By improving the precision and accuracy of these models, deep learning techniques in particular hold great promise for enhancing the detection of stress, emotion, deception, and abnormal behavior.
- Assessment and Policy Formulation: Given the delicate nature of psychological research, behavioral data protection is crucial. Consistency and reliability across studies will be improved by creating strategies to protect data privacy and security as well as standardizing procedures for data collection, analysis, and reporting. The development of succinct evaluation techniques and diagnostic instruments will enable more efficient evaluations of AI detection systems. Legislators must concentrate on creating moral frameworks that protect the privacy of patients and users while encouraging advancements in AI-powered cognitive behavioral analysis.
- Accessibility and Enhancement of Data: The advancement of AI-based cognitive behavioural analysis depends on the availability of high-quality, diverse data. By creating repositories, crowdsourcing projects, and data-sharing platforms, researchers will be able to exchange and pool data from various fields, enhancing the caliber of AI models. The scarcity of some data types can be addressed by creating synthetic datasets using data augmentation techniques, such as the use of generative models like GANs. AI models will also be more inclusive and applicable to a larger range of populations if data diversity is increased by incorporating samples from various age, demographic, and cultural groups.

An overview of the present and potential applications of AI and ML in cognitive behavioural therapy is provided in this chapter. It establishes the foundation for further study in this emerging field by concentrating on the identification of stress, emotion, dishonesty, and aberrant behavior. AI methods will provide increasingly sophisticated and customized applications for comprehending human behavior as they develop further. AI will revolutionize not only psychological research but also practical applications in security, healthcare, and other fields with the integration of reliable devices, sophisticated algorithms, and safe, standardized data practices. The need for flexible models, ethical AI development, and data privacy issues highlight the significance of continuous research and interdisciplinary cooperation. AI-based cognitive behavioral analysis has the potential to completely transform the knowledge and treatment of mental health conditions with ethical application and ongoing development, providing fresh hope for more precise diagnosis, prompt interventions, and improved patient outcomes.

REFERENCES

Abd-Alrazaq, A. A., Alajlani, M., Alalwan, A. A., Bewick, B. M., Gardner, P., & Househ, M. (2019). An overview of the features of chatbots in mental health: A scoping review. *International Journal of Medical Informatics*, 132, 103978. DOI: 10.1016/j.ijmedinf.2019.103978 PMID: 31622850

Ali, N. H., Abdulmunem, M. E., & Ali, A. E. (2021). Learning evolution: A survey. *Iraqi Journal of Science*, •••, 4978–4987. DOI: 10.24996/ijs.2021.62.12.34

Alnuaimi, A., & Albaldawi, T. (2024). An overview of machine learning classification techniques. *BIO Web of Conferences, 97*, 00133. https://doi.org/DOI: 10.1051/bioconf/20249700133

Bansal, S. (2023). ANALYTIXLABS. *MACHINE LEARNING What is Classification Algorithm in Machine Learning? With Examples, 25 JANUARY 2023.[Online]. Available:https://www. analytixlabs. co. in/blog/classification-in-machine-learning.*

Beck, A. (1967). Depression: clinical, experimental, and theoretical aspects. *Harper & Row google schola, 2*, 103-113.

Beck, A. T., Rush, A. J., Shaw, B. F., Emery, G., DeRubeis, R. J., & Hollon, S. D. (2024). *Cognitive therapy of depression*. Guilford Publications.

Beck, J. S. (2020). *Cognitive behavior therapy: Basics and beyond*. Guilford Publications.

Beck, J. S., & Fleming, S. (2021). A Brief History of Aaron T. Beck, MD, and Cognitive Behavior Therapy. *Clinical Psychology in Europe*, 3(2), e6701. DOI: 10.32872/cpe.6701 PMID: 36397957

Bini, S. A. (2018). Artificial intelligence, machine learning, deep learning, and cognitive computing: What do these terms mean and how will they impact health care? *The Journal of Arthroplasty*, 33(8), 2358–2361. DOI: 10.1016/j.arth.2018.02.067 PMID: 29656964

Brownlee, J. (2022). *Machine learning mastery*. Machine Learning Mastery.

Chand, S., Kuckel, D., & Huecker, M. (2022). [*StatPearls][Internet] [. Treasure Island] [FL][: StatPearls Publishing.*]. *Cognitive Behaviour Therapy*, 2022(May), 29.

Clak, D. A., & Beck, A. T. (1999). *Scientific foundations of cognitive theory and therapy of depression*. John Wiley & Sons.

Dave, R., Sargeant, K., Vanamala, M., & Seliya, N. (2022). Review on psychology research based on artificial intelligence methodologies. *Journal of Computer and Communications*, 10(5), 113–130. DOI: 10.4236/jcc.2022.105008

Fitzpatrick, K. K., Darcy, A., & Vierhile, M. (2017). Delivering Cognitive Behavior Therapy to Young Adults With Symptoms of Depression and Anxiety Using a Fully Automated Conversational Agent (Woebot): A Randomized Controlled Trial. *JMIR Mental Health*, 4(2), e19. DOI: 10.2196/mental.7785 PMID: 28588005

Fitzpatrick, K. K., Darcy, A., & Vierhile, M. (2017). Delivering cognitive behavior therapy to young adults with symptoms of depression and anxiety using a fully automated conversational agent (Woebot): A randomized controlled trial. *JMIR Mental Health*, 4(2), e7785. DOI: 10.2196/mental.7785 PMID: 28588005

Fulmer, R., Joerin, A., Gentile, B., Lakerink, L., & Rauws, M. (2018). Using psychological artificial intelligence (Tess) to relieve symptoms of depression and anxiety: Randomized controlled trial. *JMIR Mental Health*, 5(4), e9782. DOI: 10.2196/mental.9782 PMID: 30545815

Gifford, R., & Nilsson, A. (2014). Personal and social factors that influence pro-environmental concern and behavior: A review. *International Journal of Psychology*, 49(3), 141–157. PMID: 24821503

Greenberg, M. S., & Beck, A. T. (1989). Depression versus anxiety: A test of the content-specificity hypothesis. *Journal of Abnormal Psychology*, 98(1), 9–13. DOI: 10.1037/0021-843X.98.1.9 PMID: 2708648

Helm, J. M., Swiergosz, A. M., Haeberle, H. S., Karnuta, J. M., Schaffer, J. L., Krebs, V. E., Spitzer, A. I., & Ramkumar, P. N. (2020). Machine Learning and Artificial Intelligence: Definitions, Applications, and Future Directions. *Current Reviews in Musculoskeletal Medicine*, 13(1), 69–76. DOI: 10.1007/s12178-020-09600-8 PMID: 31983042

Inkster, B., Sarda, S., & Subramanian, V. (2018). An empathy-driven, conversational artificial intelligence agent (Wysa) for digital mental well-being: Real-world data evaluation mixed-methods study. *JMIR mHealth and uHealth*, 6(11), e12106. DOI: 10.2196/12106 PMID: 30470676

Jiang, M., Zhao, Q., Li, J., Wang, F., He, T., Cheng, X., . . . Fu, G. (2024). A Generic Review of Integrating Artificial Intelligence in Cognitive Behavioral Therapy. *arXiv preprint arXiv:2407.19422.*

Karyotaki, E., Efthimiou, O., Miguel, C., Bermpohl, F. M. G., Furukawa, T. A., Cuijpers, P., & Forsell, Y. (2021). Internet-Based Cognitive Behavioral Therapy for Depression: A Systematic Review and Individual Patient Data Network Meta-analysis. *JAMA Psychiatry*, 78(4), 361–371. DOI: 10.1001/jamapsychiatry.2020.4364 PMID: 33471111

Knapp, P., & Beck, A. T. (2008). Cognitive therapy: Foundations, conceptual models, applications and research. *The British Journal of Psychiatry*, 30, s54–s64. DOI: 10.1590/S1516-44462008000600002 PMID: 19039445

Mehta, A., Niles, A. N., Vargas, J. H., Marafon, T., Couto, D. D., & Gross, J. J. (2021). Acceptability and effectiveness of artificial intelligence therapy for anxiety and depression (Youper): Longitudinal observational study. *Journal of Medical Internet Research*, 23(6), e26771. DOI: 10.2196/26771 PMID: 34155984

Nwoye, E. O., Muslehat, A. A., Umeh, C., Okodeh, S. O., & Woo, W. L. (2024). SchizoBot: Delivering Cognitive Behavioural Therapy for Augmented Management of Schizophrenia. *Digital Technologies Research and Applications*, 3(2), 24–40. DOI: 10.54963/dtra.v3i2.225

Ogawa, S. (2024). Predicting Dropout From Cognitive Behavioral Therapy for Panic Disorder Using Machine Learning Algorithms. *Journal of Clinical Medicine Research*, 16(5), 251–255. DOI: 10.14740/jocmr5167 PMID: 38855785

Oliveira, A. L. S., Matos, L. N., Junior, M. C., & Delabrida, Z. N. C. (2021). An Initial Assessment of a Chatbot for Rumination-Focused Cognitive Behavioral Therapy (RFCBT) in College Students. Computational Science and Its Applications–ICCSA 2021: 21st International Conference, Cagliari, Italy, September 13–16, 2021, Proceedings, Part VI 21, Penninx, B. W., Benros, M. E., Klein, R. S., & Vinkers, C. H. (2022). How COVID-19 shaped mental health: from infection to pandemic effects. *Nature Medicine*, 28(10), 2027–2037.

Praba, R., Darshan, G., Roshanraj, T., & Prakash, B. (2021). Study on machine learning algorithms. *Int. J. Sci. Res. Comput. Sci. Eng. Inf. Technol*, 7, 67–72.

Ram, A. (2022). Short Review on Machine Learning and its Application. *Special Education*, 1(43).

Rani, K., Vishnoi, H., & Mishra, M. (2023). A mental health chatbot delivering cognitive behavior therapy and remote health monitoring using NLP and AI. 2023 International Conference on Disruptive Technologies (ICDT), Rastogi, V., Satija, S., Sharma, D. P. K., & Singh, S. (2020). Machine learning algorithms: Overview. *International Journal of Advanced Research in Engineering and Technology*, 11(9).

Rizea, A. (2022). Deep Learning-based Solution for Mental Health Issues. *DATA-BASE SYSTEMS*, 57.

Rush, A. J., Beck, A. T., Kovacs, M., & Hollon, S. (1977). Comparative efficacy of cognitive therapy and pharmacotherapy in the treatment of depressed outpatients. *Cognitive Therapy and Research*, 1(1), 17–37. DOI: 10.1007/BF01173502

Sabour, S., Zhang, W., Xiao, X., Zhang, Y., Zheng, Y., Wen, J., Zhao, J., & Huang, M. (2023). A chatbot for mental health support: Exploring the impact of Emohaa on reducing mental distress in China. *Frontiers in Digital Health*, 5, 1133987. DOI: 10.3389/fdgth.2023.1133987 PMID: 37214342

Samuel, A. L. (1959). Machine learning. *Technology Review*, 62(1), 42–45.

Sandhya, N., & Charanjeet, K. (2016). A review on machine learning techniques. *International Journal on Recent and Innovation Trends in Computing and Communication*, 4(3), 451–458.

Sarter, L., Heider, J., Kirchner, L., Schenkel, S., Witthöft, M., Rief, W., & Kleinstäuber, M. (2021). Cognitive and emotional variables predicting treatment outcome of cognitive behavior therapies for patients with medically unexplained symptoms: A meta-analysis. *Journal of Psychosomatic Research*, 146, 110486. DOI: 10.1016/j.jpsychores.2021.110486 PMID: 33879330

Scott, J., & Beck, A. T. (2008). Cognitive behavioural therapy. In Murray, R. M., Kendler, K. S., McGuffin, P., Wessely, S., & Castle, D. J. (Eds.), *Essential Psychiatry* (4th ed., pp. 636–651). Cambridge University Press., https://doi.org/DOI, DOI: 10.1017/CBO9780511544125.029

Scott, J., & Beck, A. T. (2008). Cognitive behavioural therapy. *This page intentionally left blank*, 636.

Su, S., Wang, Y., Jiang, W., Zhao, W., Gao, R., Wu, Y., & Li, K. (2022). Efficacy of artificial intelligence-assisted psychotherapy in patients with anxiety disorders: A prospective, national multicenter randomized controlled trial protocol. *Frontiers in Psychiatry*, 12, 799917. DOI: 10.3389/fpsyt.2021.799917 PMID: 35126211

Vieira, S., Liang, X., Guiomar, R., & Mechelli, A. (2022). Can we predict who will benefit from cognitive-behavioural therapy? A systematic review and meta-analysis of machine learning studies. *Clinical Psychology Review*, 97, 102193. https://doi.org/https://doi.org/10.1016/j.cpr.2022.102193. DOI: 10.1016/j.cpr.2022.102193 PMID: 35995023

Webb, C. A., Rosso, I. M., & Rauch, S. L. (2017). Internet-based cognitive-behavioral therapy for depression: Current progress and future directions. *Harvard Review of Psychiatry*, 25(3), 114–122. DOI: 10.1097/HRP.0000000000000139 PMID: 28475503

Chapter 2
AI-Enhanced Neurophysiological Assessment

Deepak Kumar
https://orcid.org/0009-0002-7598-5484
Shri Gopichand College of Pharmacy, India

Punet Kumar
https://orcid.org/0000-0001-6047-6615
Shri Gopichand College of Pharmacy, India

Sushma Pal
https://orcid.org/0009-0000-3036-9982
Shri Gopichand College of Pharmacy, India

Sangam Singh
https://orcid.org/0000-0002-1341-4451
Oxford College of Pharmacy, India

ABSTRACT

Advancements in artificial intelligence (AI) are revolutionizing neurophysiology, enhancing precision and efficiency in assessing brain and nervous system function. AI-driven neurophysiological assessment integrates machine learning, deep neural networks, and advanced data analytics to process complex data from electroencephalography, and electromyography techniques. This technology enables earlier diagnosis of neurological disorders like epilepsy and Alzheimer's by detecting subtle neural patterns that may be missed by human analysis. AI also facilitates real-time monitoring and predictive analytics, improving outcomes in critical care and neurorehabilitation. Challenges include ensuring data quality, addressing

DOI: 10.4018/979-8-3693-9341-3.ch002

ethical concerns, and overcoming computational limits. The integration of AI into neurophysiology offers a precise, scalable, and accessible approach to treating neurological disorders. This chapter discusses the methodologies, applications, and future directions of AI in neurophysiological assessment, emphasizing its transformative impact in clinical and research fields.

INTRODUCTION

Neurophysiological evaluation methods such as electroencephalography, electromyography, and magnetoencephalography play an important role in assessing nervous system function. The EEG captures the brain's electrical wave activity and is crucial in diagnosing conditions like epilepsy and sleep disorders (Corsi, 2023). Their methods are prominent in various neurological and psychiatric disorder treatments. EMG assesses the health of muscle (myopathy) and motor neurons, aiding in diagnosing disorders like muscular dystrophy. While MEG captures the magnetic field resulting from neural activity-induced currents, real-time brain mapping simplifies neurosurgical planning (Paganoni & Amato, 2013). Given the dependence on expert interpretation for traditional methods, and since standard microscopic approaches are sensitive to noise, which can influence diagnostic accuracy, these approaches also have limitations (Larkins et. Al., 2024). Machine learning (ML) and DL, being branches of artificial intelligence (AI), promise more realistic processing of complex neural data, high precision in diagnosis, and real-time monitoring. For example, advanced AI algorithms that can detect patterns of information that are difficult for humans to discern from EEG and MEG data can enable earlier diagnosis and intervention in epilepsy or other conditions characterized by a cognitive decline (Soori & Arezoo, et. Al., 2023). Now, with the incorporation of AI, neurophysiological evaluations are more precise and objective, which revolutionizes neurological diagnosis and treatment. AI can transform neurophysiology by providing more accurate assessments, diagnoses, and management of neurological disorders (Kalani & Anjankar, 2024). AI is now supporting the use of EEG, MEG, and fMRI data to identify intricate patterns in the diagnosis and prediction of diseases such as epilepsy, Parkinson's, and Alzheimer's, which ultimately aid in prompt interventions and enhance patient outcomes (AbuAlrob & Mesraoua, 2024). AI also minimizes human error, enabling the standardization of analytical processes across the thousands of patient data points routinely collected with most clinical tests, leading to more consistent clinical results. AI eliminates the time-consuming job of manual data analysis through automation, leading to faster diagnosis and allowing healthcare professionals more time for patient care (Kumar et al., 2023). AI also offers personalized treatment, where a unique neurophysiological signature based on an individual's brain and body response patterns drives the interventions. It can assist in both neurofeedback therapy and the customization of pharmacological treatments, particularly for conditions such as ADHD or anxiety. In addition, AI enhances the performance of brain-computer interfaces (BCIs), allowing better interpretation of neural signals and enabling individuals with disabilities to control prosthetics or wheelchairs, regaining functional independence (Thakkar & Gupta, 2024). Overall, AI in neurophysiology enhances traditional assessments and opens new pathways for personalized care, predictive analytics, and neurorehabilitation, leading to a more effective, patient-centered approach to neurological care (Fiorente et al., 2024). Figure 1 illustrates an overview of neurophysiological signals.

Figure 1. Overview of neurophysiological signals

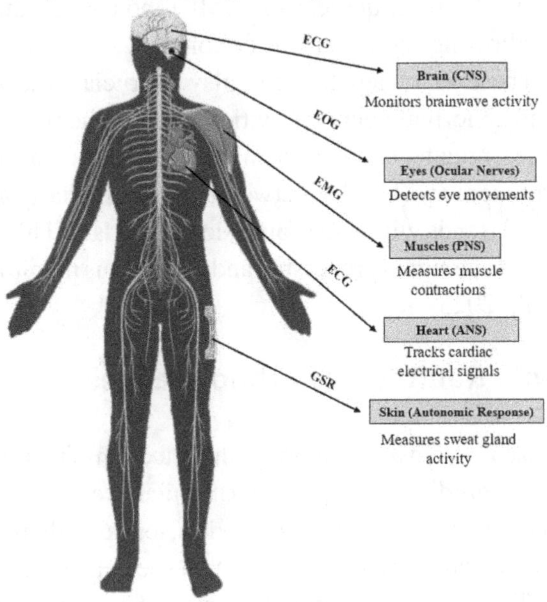

AI AND NEUROPHYSIOLOGICAL SIGNAL PROCESSING

Artificial intelligence (AI) can enhance the detection, enhancement, and interpretation of complex neural signals for clinically useful purposes in neurophysiological signal processing. Conventional neurophysiological approaches (EEG, MEG, and EMG) quantify brain activity by generating large amounts of high-dimensional data, which are often noisy and difficult to interpret (Chaddad et al., 2023).

Factors Influencing Neurophysiological Signals

Neurophysiological signals often include noise components from muscle movement (artifacts), environmental interference, and limitations of the measurement equipment. Artificial intelligence algorithms classify non-signal elements as noise. One example is using deep learning models, like convolutional neural networks (CNNs), to clean up EEG signals by separating the part of the signal that represents neural activity from the rest of the noise. This makes the neurophysiological data clearer and better. A method called Independent Component Analysis (ICA) and others that use AI to reduce the number of dimensions can effectively separate signal sources, separating target neural activities from signals that overlap. This capability is particularly useful in processing EEG and MEG data (Mathe & Padmaja, 2021). AI algorithms, especially machine learning (ML) models, are highly effective at feature extraction, allowing them to identify complex patterns within neurophysiological signals. These extracted features play a crucial role in distinguishing between normal and abnormal neural activities, making them essential for clinical diagnostics. Deep learning techniques, such as recurrent neural networks (RNNs) and long short-term memory (LSTM) networks, are particularly adept at detecting temporal patterns and trends within neurophysiological data. This capability makes them suitable for real-time signal processing and continuous monitoring applications (Jimenez-Mesa et al., 2023).

AI Model Detects Neurological Abnormalities

AI signal-processed systems now automate the detection of neurological disorders, including seizures, sleep disorders, and Parkinsonian tremors. Large volumes of labeled neurophysiological signals train AI models, teaching them through machine learning to detect subtle abnormalities that human specialists may find challenging to reliably identify. This automation not only reduces the conduction time of diagnosis but also enhances the availability of neurophysiological evaluation procedures, particularly in underdeveloped countries (Raghavendra et al., 2020). This capacity is particularly valuable in scenarios that require immediate intervention, such as seizure management or monitoring of anesthesia levels during surgery (Soula et. al., 2023). AI models continuously analyze incoming data streams and detect abnormal patterns that trigger alerts, allowing healthcare providers to respond promptly. Lightweight deep learning models, optimized for speed and efficiency, often achieve real-time processing, enabling the integration of AI-driven signal detection into wearable devices and mobile applications, thereby expanding the scope of neurophysiological monitoring beyond clinical settings (Yang & Kar, 2023). Figure 2 illustrates the AI-driven process for analyzing neurophysiological signals.

Figure 2. AI-Driven process for neurophysiological signal analysis

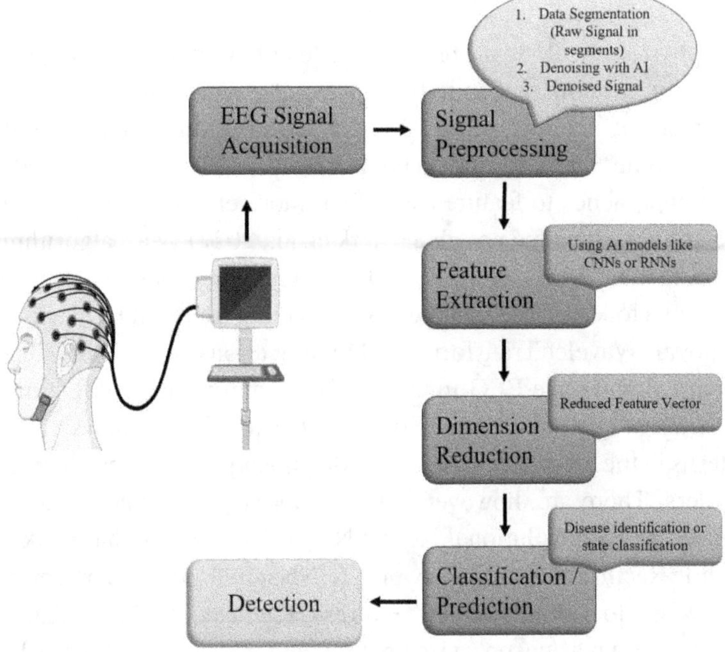

AI models can integrate multiple sources of neurophysiological data, such as combining EEG with fMRI, to enhance predictive accuracy and provide a more comprehensive view of brain function. Multimodal data fusion helps AI models understand different parts of brain activity, like changes in structure, function, and biochemistry. This helps us better understand neurological conditions that are more complicated (Zhang et. al., 2020). Deep learning models are useful for understanding complex neurophysiological signals that change in non-linear ways, like EEG waveforms or fMRI time series (Yeung et. al., 2023). Integrating AI into neurophysiological signal processing greatly enhances technical and clinical capabilities. With improved signal detection, noise reduction, and real-time processing, AI is essential for making earlier and more accurate diagnoses in modern neurophysiology (Frosolini et. al., 2024).

Advanced Algorithms for Feature Extraction in Neurophysiological Data

In neurophysiological signal processing, feature extraction is important, as it entails searching for some meaningful aspects of a neural signal. In recent years, the development of new promising methods based on artificial intelligence, and especially machine learning and deep learning techniques, has fundamentally changed the approaches to feature extraction; more effective and precise analysis and diagnosing have become possible (Merk et. al., 2022). Ma's algorithms include Principal Component Analysis (PCA) and Independent Component Analysis (ICA), which are known to lessen the volume of data and are useful in EEG and MEG data artifact removal. Wavelet Transform (WT) applications make it possible to show non-stationary signals like EEG in terms of time and frequency (Dhiman, 2023). Fourier Transform (FT) and Power Spectral Density (PSD) analysis give doctors useful patterns in the frequency domain for diagnosing conditions like epilepsy and sleep disorders. There are, however, several approaches, including deep learning techniques, such as Convolutional Neural Networks (CNNs), that work on spatial features, while Recurrent Neural Networks (RNNs) and Long Short-Term Memory (LSTM) networks focus on temporal features (Handa et. al., 2024). Autoencoders, which are also known as unsupervised neural networks, are used for tasks like feature mapping and denoising in large datasets that don't have labels. Graph Neural Networks (GNNs) utilize dense layers to illustrate the connectivity of the brain area under investigation, while Temporal Convoluted Networks (TCNs) employ channels to illustrate the relationship between the neurophysiological data and time. Finally, transfer learning can also be useful in improving performance as it helps incorporate features learned from a separate dataset or a part of the dataset that is different from the current test set. Such complex models not only improve the accuracy of diagnoses but also assist in developing new therapeutic interventions and provide enhanced understanding of the anatomy and functioning of the brain (Zhou et al., 2020).

Role of AI in Pattern Recognition of Neurophysiological Data

The analysis of neurophysiological data begins with the identification of patterns contained in the data signals, which are complex and highly dimensional. Most of the above-mentioned traditional methods have difficulties in analyzing such huge datasets and finer patterns, but their integration within artificial intelligence, particularly with machine learning and deep learning, is on the rise (Houssein et al., 2022 & Morales, 2022). Artificial intelligence, such as convolutional neural networks (CNNs) and recurrent neural networks (RNNs), has proven to be successful in complex pattern identification on EEG, MEG, and fMRI data and allows the identification of relationships between complex neural activity patterns and neurological disorders, including epilepsy, Alzheimer's, and Parkinson's diseases (Rakhmatulin et al., 2024). AI also assists in the early diagnosis and precise classification of disorders by detecting certain markers in neurophysiological data, which improves the diagnostic process and enables the development of tailored therapy approaches. Furthermore, it also automates feature selection and extraction, making the manipulation of the high-dimensional data free from human bias (Chen et al., 2022).

AI makes personalized pattern recognition possible in brain-computer interface (BCI) apps, which makes real-time interactions better for users. AI also helps find signs and patterns of connectivity, which gives us more information about disorders like autism and schizophrenia. AI enhances data quality by eliminating noise and unwanted components from signals, enabling more accurate interpretation (Shang et al., 2024). AI-powered predictive models also keep track of how diseases get worse, which helps doctors make better treatment plans. However, due to their complexity and abundance of information, conventional methods of interpreting these signs may be inaccurate and time-consuming. With machine learning (ML) and deep learning (DL), artificial intelligence (AI) has become a powerful way to process and understand these brain messages (Martinek et al., 2021). We can look at large groups of neurophysiological signals faster, more accurately, and on a bigger scale with the help of AI algorithms. EEG waves measure how the brain's electricity is working (Gorriz Sáez et al., 2023). More and more people are using artificial intelligence (AI) methods like convolutional neural networks (CNNs), recurrent neural networks (RNNs), and support vector machines (SVMs) to automatically extract features from these signals, identify trends, and even forecast the onset or progression of a disease (Piñeros-Fernández, 2023). AI can also reduce the need for doctors to interpret data by hand, leading to faster diagnoses and more accurate readings, especially in places where time and resources are limited. As AI grows, combining it with neurophysiological signal processing could make diagnoses even more precise and open up more opportunities for personalized treatment in cardiology and neurology (Maleki Varnosfaderani & Forouzanfar, 2024). Figure 3 depicts the application of AI in analyzing EEG signals for epilepsy detection.

Figure 3. AI in EEG signal analysis for epilepsy detection

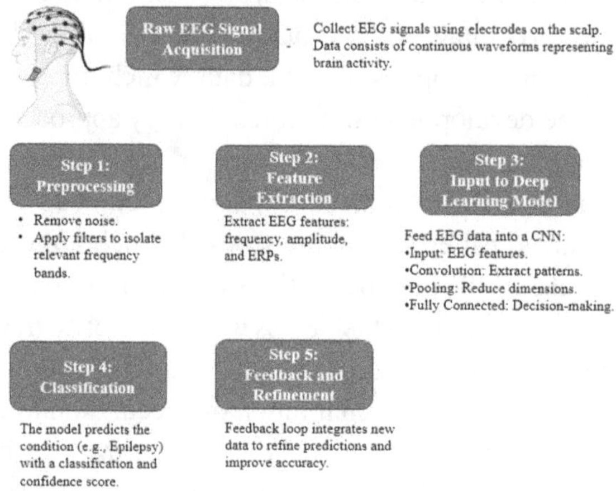

APPLICATIONS OF AI IN NEUROPHYSIOLOGICAL ASSESSMENT

Early Diagnosis of Neurological Disorders

Artificial intelligence (AI) progress has made it possible to detect neurological diseases like Alzheimer's, epilepsy, Parkinson's, and multiple sclerosis much earlier. Usually, these diseases cause changes in brain function that happen slowly and in subtle ways, making them difficult to spot using normal testing methods. Despite this, AI, especially machine learning and deep learning models, offers intriguing answers by finding complex patterns in brain activity and biomarkers that show the early stages of these disorders (Raikar et al., 2024). When it comes to Alzheimer's, AI looks at neuroimaging data from MRI and fMRI to find early signs like hippocampal shrinkage or cortical thinning. These anatomical alterations in the brain may be minor, yet they serve as early indications of cognitive deterioration. Deep learning algorithms, such as convolutional neural networks (CNNs), can process this data and detect patterns that humans cannot see (Mirkin, & Albensi, 2023).

AI-based diagnoses are especially beneficial for Parkinson's disease, which is characterized by impairments in motor function. When paired with machine learning models, wearable technology with sensors can monitor symptoms including bradykinesia, stiffness, and tremors. These tools make it possible to identify Parkinson's disease-related mobility deficits early on (Sigcha et al., 2023). Additionally, machine learning algorithms examine neuroimaging data to pinpoint particular alterations in the brain that are associated with the illness, facilitating accurate diagnosis and tracking the course of the condition. This is crucial for adjusting treatment plans and predicting the disease's course (Dixit et. al., 2023).

AI also helps remotely monitor people who are at risk, particularly in underprivileged areas. Wearable technology with AI algorithms can track movement and brain activity continuously, spotting neurological diseases early (Shajari et al., 2023). Both patients and medical professionals can receive real-time alerts from these systems, allowing for prompt actions that could stop or delay the spread of disease (Krishnan et al., 2023). Routine screenings for aging populations or those with a family history of neurological disorders can deploy this approach, improving accessibility to early intervention. Finally, AI's integration with Electronic Health Records (EHRs) allows for a more comprehensive view of a patient's health. By correlating neurophysiological data with genetic markers, patient history, and other health metrics, AI enhances diagnostic accuracy and supports personalized treatment strategies. These technological advancements have the potential to improve patient outcomes through timely interventions and better-targeted therapies (Lee et al., 2021). Figure 4 compares traditional and AI-based EMG analysis methods for diagnosing neuromuscular disorders.

Figure 4. Comparing Traditional vs. AI-Based EMG Analysis for Neuromuscular Disorders

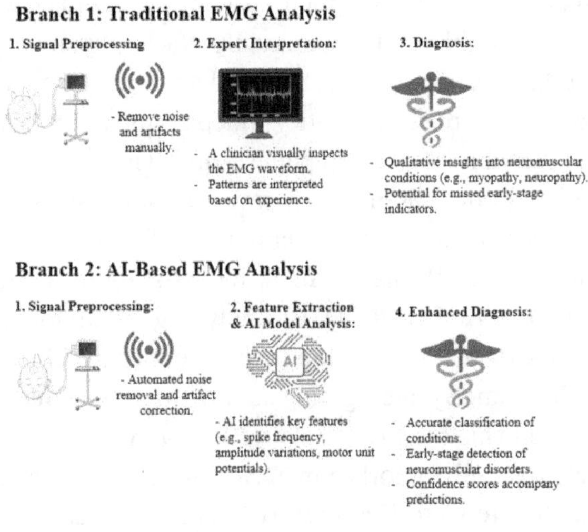

AI's Role in Psychiatric Evaluations and Mental Health Assessments

Because AI can examine complex behavioral, physiological, and linguistic data that are frequently challenging to understand using conventional approaches, it is rapidly changing mental health assessments and psychiatric evaluations. Since there are no obvious biochemical indicators for mental illnesses like anxiety, bipolar disorder, schizophrenia, or depression, diagnosis is dependent on self-reported symptoms and subjective clinical observations. However, AI-based methods provide unbiased, data-driven assistance that improves diagnoses' accuracy, tracks symptoms' development, and customizes care (Obradovich et al., 2024). Natural Language Processing (NLP) algorithms driven by artificial intelligence (AI) can examine speech, text, and social media data to find linguistic patterns linked to mood disorders. AI can measure, for example, the unique linguistic patterns of people who suffer from anxiety or depression, such as the usage of first-person pronouns or a high frequency of negative terms. In addition to evaluating emotional tone, sentiment analysis technologies can identify shifts in mood or cognitive patterns, offering early warning indicators for diseases like bipolar disorder or depression (Zhang et al., 2024). For instance, AI can identify minute alterations in speech or facial expression that indicate the start of a psychotic episode in people with schizophrenia. By tracking patients' improvement and identifying early relapse indicators, this non-invasive, ongoing monitoring can assist clinicians in better-managing symptoms (Bohr & Memarzadeh, 2020).

Sensor-equipped wearables can continually track physiological markers of mental health, including sleep patterns, skin conductance, and heart rate variability. AI algorithms analyze this data to identify mood swings, tension, and anxiety in real-time. For example, abnormal sleep patterns may signal depressive symptoms, whereas heart rate variability patterns may reveal elevated stress levels. By giving patients and clinicians objective data on daily mood fluctuations, these wearables enable proactive mental health management by assisting in the understanding of patterns and triggers (Lee & Kim 2021). By analyzing digital footprints, healthcare records, and behavioral data, AI builds predictive models that identify individuals at risk of suicide or self-harm. By aggregating data such as recent hospital admissions, social media activity, and historical mental health data, AI models can assess suicide risk more accurately than self-reports alone. Hospitals and mental health platforms employ these predictive tools to flag high-risk patients, enabling timely interventions and potentially reducing suicide rates. Such proactive assessments are vital for vulnerable populations who may not actively seek help (D'Hotman & Loh, 2020).

AI Enhances Personalize Treatment Plans for Mental Health Conditions

Because AI can examine complex behavioral, physiological, and linguistic data that are frequently challenging to understand using conventional approaches, it is rapidly changing mental health assessments and psychiatric evaluations. Since there are no obvious biochemical indicators for mental illnesses like anxiety, bipolar disorder, schizophrenia, or depression, diagnosis is dependent on self-reported symptoms and subjective clinical observations (Chen et al., 2022). However, AI-based methods provide unbiased, data-driven assistance that improves diagnoses' accuracy, tracks symptoms' development, and customizes care (Krishnan et al., 2023). Natural Language Processing (NLP) algorithms driven by artificial intelligence (AI) can examine speech, text, and social media data to find linguistic patterns linked to mood disorders. AI can measure, for example, the unique linguistic patterns of people who suffer from anxiety or depression, such as the usage of first-person pronouns or a high frequency of negative terms. (Zhang et al., 2022).

In addition to evaluating emotional tone, sentiment analysis technologies can identify shifts in mood or cognitive patterns, offering early warning indicators for diseases like bipolar disorder or depression. Clinicians might potentially diagnose illnesses earlier than is possible with traditional approaches thanks to these insights, which also help them make better judgments. AI is capable of processing both visual and aural information, including body language, tone of voice, and facial expressions all of which are crucial for diagnosing mental health issues. (Islam et al., 2024) Researchers have used machine learning algorithms to identify body posture, fluctuations in speech tone, and micro-expressions associated with specific mental health conditions. For instance, AI can identify minute alterations in speech or facial expression that indicate the start of a psychotic episode in people with schizophrenia. By tracking patients' improvement and identifying early relapse indicators, this non-invasive, ongoing monitoring can assist clinicians in better-managing symptoms (Chen et al., 2022). Sensor-equipped wearables can continually track physiological markers of mental health, including sleep patterns, skin conductance, and heart rate variability. AI algorithms analyze this data to identify mood swings, tension, and anxiety in real-time. For example, abnormal sleep patterns may signal depressive symptoms, whereas heart rate variability patterns may reveal elevated stress levels (Gomes et al., 2023). Hospitals and mental health platforms employ these predictive tools to flag high-risk patients, enabling timely interventions and potentially reducing suicide rates. Such proactive assessments are vital for vulnerable populations who may not actively seek help (O'Rourke et al., 2023).

AI Enhance Personalize Treatment Plans for Mental Health Conditions

By evaluating data from a variety of sources, including genetics, lifestyle, and patient history, AI improves the tailoring of treatment regimens for mental health disorders. By combining various data types, AI can predict an individual's response to various treatments like drugs or psychotherapies, enabling customization of the approach to meet their specific needs (Graham et al. 2019). Machine learning models, by identifying patterns in response data, aid psychiatrists in recommending the optimal course of action and implementing necessary modifications, thereby diminishing the reliance on trial-and-error methods commonly employed in psychiatric treatment. Chatbots using NLP provide real-time responses, emulating therapeutic interactions and offering support to individuals who may not have regular access to mental health professionals. These apps can also track user engagement and symptom progression, helping clinicians adjust treatment plans based on real-time data (Haque & Rubya, 2023). AI-based screening tools for mental health can identify signs of psychiatric conditions in population health settings, such as schools, workplaces, and primary care. Screening questionnaires combined with AI-driven assessments of facial and vocal markers provide quick evaluations, allowing early identification of issues like anxiety or PTSD in at-risk populations (Javed et al., 2023). By merging psychiatric evaluations with other medical data, AI integration with electronic state records (EHRs) offers a more thorough picture of a patient's mental state (Purtle et al. 2020). AI systems, for example, can examine electronic health records (EHRs) to find mental health symptoms that might be associated with long-term physical ailments, including the connection between depression and cardiovascular health. By addressing the entire range of patient needs and improving long-term mental health outcomes, this holistic approach promotes improved coordination of care between mental health and other healthcare professionals (Zafar et al., 2024).

Monitoring Neurodegenerative Disease Progression Through AI

With its cutting-edge approaches to early identification and continuous surveillance of illnesses like Alzheimer's, Parkinson's, and Huntington's, artificial intelligence is revolutionizing the monitoring of neurodegenerative diseases. These conditions, characterized by cognitive and motor decline, present challenges for conventional monitoring techniques that rely on subjective evaluations. AI, on the other hand, improves individualized care by offering objective, ongoing monitoring. Machine learning techniques evaluate clinical, neuroimaging, and genomic data to identify trends suggesting the progress of a disease. We can precisely predict cognitive decline in Alzheimer's disease using prediction models based on neuroimaging data, even before clinical symptoms manifest (Ganesh et al., 2023). AI methods like convolutional neural networks (CNNs) look through MRI and PET data to find problems in the brain, like the substantia nigra degenerating in Parkinson's disease or the hippocampi shrinking in Alzheimer's. This helps one monitor the course of the disease and the success of treatment. Wearables with sensors, such as accelerometers and smartwatches, track motor symptoms, sleep, and activity (Hussain et al. 2023).

AI analyzes this real-time data, providing timely alerts for significant changes in a patient's condition and enabling immediate intervention. AI-driven natural language processing analyzes speech and writing to detect cognitive decline. By tracking linguistic features like word choice and sentence structure, AI identifies subtle changes in cognitive abilities, enabling early and precise interventions (Panesar et all., 2023).

AI integrates genetic, clinical, imaging, and behavioral data to offer a comprehensive view of disease progression. This approach enhances predictions of disease trajectory and treatment response, considering the complex interactions between different factors. By merging virtual reality and AI, we can replicate authentic situations to evaluate cognitive abilities such as memory and attention (Johnson et al. 2021). AI analyzes performance metrics, offering dynamic, engaging assessments of cognitive decline. AI analyzes data from longitudinal studies to track trends in disease progression and treatment responses, generating real-world evidence that informs clinical guidelines and therapeutic strategies. AI in disease monitoring raises ethical concerns around privacy and consent. Ensuring informed consent and involving patients in the process through user-friendly interfaces promotes adherence to monitoring protocols and empowers patients in their care (Yim et al., 2024). Figure 5 highlights AI models used in neurophysiological signal processing, including CNN, RNN, and SVM.

Figure 5. AI Models in neurophysiological signal processing CNN, RNN, and SVM

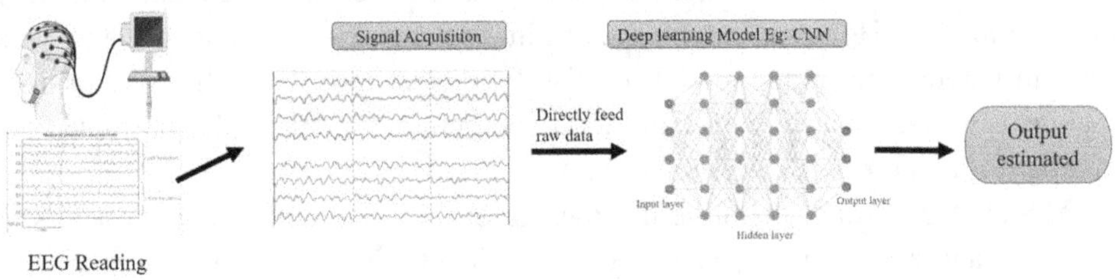

PERSONALIZED AND ADAPTIVE ASSESSMENTS WITH AI

The use of AI in neurophysiological examinations has changed personalized and adaptive evaluation approaches, making them more precise and specialized. AI tailors assessments to patient-specific data, such as medical histories, genetics, neuroimaging, and behavior, to improve diagnostic accuracy, illness progression, and treatment recommendations. These various datasets are analyzed by machine learning algorithms to find distinctive patterns, risk factors, and probable neurodegenerative illness markers, helping physicians customize interventions (Ying et al., 2024). AI also allows adaptive testing frameworks that adjust based on patient performance. Real-time adaptability improves patient engagement and cognitive function evaluation by focusing on regions that need greater support. AI can also analyze patient data and forecast the most successful treatments to customize treatments (Bajwa et al., 2021). For chronic diseases like Parkinson's disease, AI systems learn and refine diagnostic and therapy procedures to accommodate shifting symptoms. AI may also combine behavioral and lifestyle data from wearables and mobile apps, providing a thorough picture of how lifestyle factors influence neurophysiological health (Dennis et al., 2024). The use of AI-based prediction models is key to making sure that a treatment for brain diseases like MS, Alzheimer's, and epilepsy works. AI might be able to guess how a disease will get worse and how well a drug will work by looking at lots of different kinds of data, such as genetic data, brain scans, and clinical evaluations (Fabrizio et al., 2021).

Adding different kinds of data to forecast models, like EEG, neuroscience, and clinical data, makes them better and more accurate at what they do. Doctors can start taking care of patients earlier and cater their care to each person better (Harrer et al., 2019). Predictive modelling uses a variety of machine learning approaches, including supervised and unsupervised learning, each of which is appropriate for a particular set of data and clinical results (Sarker, 2021). Rigorous validation procedures, such as cross-validation, are required to assure the correctness and reliability of these models. However, issues such as inadequate or biased data and the need for transparent, interpreted models persist. Predictive models in clinical decision-making can have a major impact on early intervention, treatment plan optimization, and patient outcomes (Sweet et al. 2023).

Models forecasting cognitive decline, for example, may encourage doctors to use more aggressive management measures, thereby improving patient quality of life. The future of predictive modeling in neurophysiology appears bright, thanks to continued advances in AI, machine learning, and real-time data integration from wearable devices and healthcare platforms (Ezzati et al. 2023). To provide more efficient, customized care, adaptive AI models can tailor evaluations, increase diagnostic precision, and continuously track patients' status. However, ongoing advancements in wearable technology and artificial intelligence have the potential to enhance adaptive learning algorithms, paving the way for more personalized, real-time monitoring and improved patient outcomes in neurophysiological evaluations (Ho et al., 2020).

TECHNOLOGICAL INNOVATIONS IN AI-DRIVEN NEUROPHYSIOLOGY

Particularly in data analysis and therapeutic uses, technological developments in artificial intelligence (AI) have fundamentally affected the discipline of neurophysiology. The complexity and great dimensionality of neurophysiological data pose significant challenges for conventional analysis methods (Badrulhisham et al., 2024). However, the incorporation of artificial intelligence systems, particularly machine learning (ML), has significantly enhanced the accuracy and efficiency of neurophysiological evaluations. Analysis of neurophysiological data depends much on machine learning. Researchers have developed both supervised and unsupervised techniques to manage challenging data, such as electromyography (EMG) and electroencephalography (Williams, 2024). Particularly for disorders like epilepsy and Alzheimer's disease, algorithms such as Support Vector Machines (SVM) have demonstrated excellent performance in categorizing neurophysiological data. By integrating several decision trees and therefore enhancing the difference between healthy people and those with neurological diseases, ensemble learning techniques such as Random Forests and Gradient Boosting Machines have also improved predicted performance (Abadal et al., 2025).

Deep learning methods including convolutional neural networks (CNNs) for time-series data such as EEG and functional magnetic resonance imaging (fMRI) have been developed to further progress the discipline. These techniques allow automatic feature extraction and pattern recognition linked with different neurological diseases. AI systems can analyze unstructured data, such as clinical notes and electronic health records, to produce more thorough evaluations. By integrating patient context into the analysis, this combination allows for the formulation of personalized therapy suggestions (Sim et al., 2024). Another strategy that shows promise is known as reinforcement learning (RL), which is particularly useful for optimizing treatment strategies. To identify the most effective interventions for managing chronic illnesses such as epilepsy, RL algorithms can assist in identifying the most effective treatments by simulating multiple treatment scenarios and analyzing the outcomes of those scenarios (Weaver et al., 2024).

The goal of these interventions is to minimize seizures and adjust prescription regimens based on individual responses. Transfer learning approaches have proven to be quite useful in the field of neurophysiology, where acquiring huge labelled datasets can be challenging. These techniques enable artificial intelligence models to automatically adapt to new datasets (Yao et al., 2020). For this purpose, Hybrid models are currently under development to leverage the benefits of each method. These models make it possible to do data analysis that is more robust, to monitor systems in real-time, and to improve prediction performance. Artificial intelligence-powered algorithms in clinical settings have demonstrated their potential to speed up and improve the accuracy of neurophysiological examinations, thereby enhancing decision-making capabilities (Chen et al., 2024). Another potential method is reinforcement learning (RL), particularly for improving treatment plans. To manage chronic illnesses like epilepsy, RL algorithms can assist in identifying the most effective interventions by simulating various treatment scenarios and evaluating their results. The goal is to minimize seizures and customize prescription regimens depending on individual responses (Roggeveen et al.,2024).

Furthermore, in neurophysiology, where it can be difficult to get sizable labeled datasets, transfer learning techniques that enable AI models to adapt to new datasets—have proven useful. This technique enhances diagnostic capabilities and boosts assessment accuracy in various clinical contexts by enabling the use of models trained on different datasets. We are creating hybrid models that blend deep learning with conventional statistical techniques to capitalize on the advantages of each strategy (Singh et al., 2022). These models enable real-time monitoring, enhanced predictive performance, and comprehensive data analysis. AI-powered algorithms have shown promise in clinical practice for increasing the speed and precision of neurophysiological evaluations, which would aid in better decision-making. Wearable AI-enabled real-time data processing has made it feasible to identify anomalous patterns and issue notifications when preset thresholds are surpassed, enabling prompt treatment of illnesses like epilepsy. These gadgets' personalized feedback, which is based on each user's data, improves patient involvement even more and promotes proactive health management (Ahuja et al., 2024).

Clinicians can improve treatment results by making better judgments by combining wearable data with electronic health records. Wearables with AI capabilities also help telehealth programs by facilitating online consultations based on data from ongoing monitoring. Clinicians can remotely monitor patients' status and modify treatment programs because of this integration. More advanced predictive models that predict the course of diseases and customize therapies are another possibility presented by AI-enhanced wearables (Haleem et al., 2021). Despite the many benefits, challenges and ethical considerations remain. Data privacy, security, and informed consent must be prioritized to ensure patient trust and compliance. Moreover, over-reliance on technology could lead to misinterpretation of data if wearable data is not integrated with traditional clinical assessments (Mennella et al., 2024). The future of AI-driven neurophysiology looks promising, with continued advancements in AI algorithms, sensor technology, and wearable devices expected to further enhance real-time monitoring and personalized care. These technologies have the potential to revolutionize patient outcomes and neurophysiological assessments, making healthcare delivery more efficient, accurate, and accessible (Shajari et al., 2023).

ETHICAL CONSIDERATIONS AND CHALLENGES

Artificial intelligence (AI) in neurophysiological evaluation creates serious ethical issues, especially about data security and privacy, but it also offers new chances to enhance patient care and diagnostic precision. The risks of data breaches, illegal access, and misuse of personal information become serious concerns as AI systems depend more and more on enormous volumes of sensitive medical data, including neuroimaging results and EEG readings (Farhud et al., 2021). Maintaining patient trust and guaranteeing responsible AI use in healthcare depends on the ethical management of these data, which are intrinsically personal and can provide precise information on a person's health, cognitive abilities, and psychological well-being. The possibility of data breaches is one of the main dangers connected to AI applications in healthcare (Zhang et al., 2023). Cyberattacks are increasingly targeting healthcare organizations, with several institutions reporting ransomware attacks that compromise patient data. Unauthorized parties accessing private neurophysiological data may cause emotional discomfort, discrimination, or identity theft in patients. In addition to being required by law, protecting patient data from such breaches is also morally right to preserve people's privacy and dignity (She et al., 2020).

Another important ethical principle is informed consent. Patients must understand the intended use of their data before agreeing to its gathering and sharing. Because AI algorithms and data processing methods are so sophisticated, getting informed permission in the context of AI applications in neurophysiology becomes more difficult. Transparent communication on data handling procedures and associated hazards is necessary since patients might not completely comprehend how their data will be utilized. Ensuring informed consent is crucial for the ethical use of AI in neurophysiological evaluation (Park, 2024). Ethical issues are also raised by the ownership and control of data. Questions about data ownership and usage emerge as AI systems use patient data to produce insights. Patients could feel as though they have less control over their data, particularly if it is disclosed to outside parties or utilized for research purposes without their express agreement. To safeguard patients' interests and guarantee ethical data management, it is essential to establish explicit regulations about data ownership, access rights, and usage agreements (Gerke & Cohen, 2020). Furthermore, biases present in training data may be reinforced by AI algorithms, producing biased results in neurophysiological tests. AI models may perform badly for underrepresented groups if they are trained on datasets that are not representative of different populations, leading to discrepancies in treatment and uneven care. Resolving bias in AI algorithms is crucial for maintaining ethical norms in neurophysiological evaluation and for fairly providing healthcare (Timmons et al., 2023).

Data protection laws like GDPR and HIPAA, which set rules for the gathering, storing, and sharing of patient data, must also be followed by healthcare organizations. These rules support moral behavior in healthcare and safeguard patient privacy. To comply with these rules and handle any ethical conundrums arising from the use of AI, institutions must put strong data governance frameworks and ethical standards into place (McGraw & Mandl, 2021). Two essential ethical precepts in AI are explainability and transparency. Healthcare professionals and patients alike must comprehend how AI algorithms make judgments, particularly when those decisions affect clinical evaluations and treatment regimens. Transparency is hampered by the "black box" aspect of many AI systems, which may prevent patients from challenging or questioning AI-generated outcomes unless they have a thorough understanding of the underlying mechanisms. Improving AI algorithms' explainability is crucial to establishing credibility and encouraging moral behavior in neurophysiological evaluation (Lin et al., 2021).

When developing and using AI technologies, it is essential to keep ethics in mind as they get better. Interaction among patients, healthcare workers, technologists, and ethicists is crucial to addressing emerging ethical issues and fostering a culture of responsibility in AI-driven neurophysiology (de Souza & Roveroni, 2023). While AI-enhanced neurophysiological assessment has a lot of promise to improve healthcare, it is important to address the ethical concerns about data privacy and security. The healthcare community can use AI to its full potential while still upholding the ethical standards needed for patient care by putting patient liberty first, making sure patients give their informed consent, and putting in place strong safeguards (Jeyaraman et al., 2023).

Bias in artificial intelligence algorithms poses a significant issue in healthcare, particularly for neurophysiological evaluations. AI systems may acquire biases via their training data, the algorithms' design, or the socio-economic and cultural circumstances of their development (Nazer et al., 2023 and Franklin et al., 2024) The underrepresentation of certain groups in training datasets can lead to data bias. A dataset that mostly comprises examples from one age group or ethnicity may produce an algorithm that performs badly for others. Inadequate evaluation of the model's feature importance criteria could potentially lead to algorithm design bias (Van Giffen et al., 2022). Human bias in AI system design and development may also lead to discrimination. We need multiple data sets, algorithm audits, and inclusive development teams to address these biases. Promoting explanation and fairness in AI systems can reduce bias and improve AI-driven neurophysiological assessments. Building confidence among clinicians, patients, and other stakeholders requires AI algorithm transparency. With transparent AI systems, users can see the reasoning behind decisions and gain insight into the data and procedures used to make them (Chen et al. 2023). The creation of explainable AI systems that can shed light on the elements impacting an AI's predictions is one strategy to increase transparency. Everyone involved can observe the system's construction process and its performance. We recommend involving patients, healthcare professionals, and ethicists throughout the development process to further guarantee the openness and responsibility of AI systems. Establishing trust is crucial for the successful use of AI tools in healthcare (Hamida et al., 2024, and Steerling et al., 2023).

Clinicians' communication and support of AI tools, as well as their perceived utility and usability, all have an impact on trust. If patients have faith in the technology and are certain that it will deliver accurate results while protecting their privacy, they are more likely to agree to AI-driven evaluations. This trust can be increased by being open and honest about the data that AI systems utilize and how they operate. Moreover, regulatory control and empirical data demonstrating the effectiveness of AI solutions can enhance their legitimacy (Perivolaris et al., 2024). Clinicians and patients can gain more trust in AI applications by resolving issues and making sure AI technologies adhere to strict dependability and accountability criteria.

FUTURE PROSPECTS AND RESEARCH IN AI-DRIVEN NEUROPHYSIOLOGY

The use of artificial intelligence (AI) in neurophysiology has enormous potential for improving diagnostic accuracy, therapy personalization, and patient outcomes. As AI technologies progress, major advances in precision neurophysiology are expected, particularly the use of AI to analyze complicated neurological data from electroencephalography (EEG), neuroimaging, and genetic profiles (Kalani & Anjankar, 2024). Machine learning (ML) algorithms can discover tiny patterns that older approaches may overlook, resulting in earlier diagnoses of neurological illnesses and more accurate disease progression projections. AI can also enable personalized treatment plans by optimizing medication therapy, non-invasive neurostimulation, and behavioral interventions for particular patients. The further development of AI-driven precision neurophysiology may enable real-time treatment modifications based on ongoing patient data, enhance outcomes, and decrease trial-and-error methods. (Maleki Varnosfaderani & Forouzanfar, 2024). Another fascinating area for neurophysiology is the incorporation of AI with cutting-edge technologies like brain-computer interfaces (BCIs), augmented reality (AR), and virtual reality (VR). Especially helpful for rehabilitation following brain injuries or strokes, VR and AR, when paired with AI, can create immersive, adaptive neurofeedback systems that alter in real-time based on the patient's neural reactions. (Drigas & Sideraki, 2024).

By creating environments that evaluate cognitive abilities, memory, attention, and sensory perception in ways that traditional tests cannot, AI-driven VR and AR platforms may make it possible to conduct more thorough neurophysiological evaluations. Together with AI's ability to analyze data, these technologies may provide fresh perspectives on how the brain functions and increase the precision of diagnoses, leading to a more comprehensive understanding of neurological health. (Palombi et al., 2023, and Chopra et al., 2023). Ultimately, the future of AI in neurophysiology presents numerous opportunities to enhance precision medicine, integrate cutting-edge technologies, and improve patient care. With careful consideration of the ethical, social, and clinical aspects, AI has the potential to revolutionize neurophysiological care, offering more personalized, efficient, and accurate treatment options for patients.

CONCLUSION

Neuroscience and clinical practice are changing as a result of the incorporation of artificial intelligence (AI) into neurophysiological evaluations. AI's capacity to interpret complex neurophysiological inputs enables early detection and precise diagnosis of neurological conditions like epilepsy and Alzheimer's disease. Timely treatments made possible by this early intervention can greatly enhance patient outcomes. AI is also showing great promise in psychiatric evaluations, providing more precise diagnoses and individualized treatment regimens for mental health issues. AI is also essential for tracking the course of diseases. AI systems give real-time feedback by continuously evaluating neurophysiological data, which enables medical professionals to dynamically modify treatment regimens a crucial aspect of managing chronic illnesses. Personalized, adaptive evaluations catered to each patient's unique profile are becoming more and more possible as AI technologies advance. Although AI has the potential to revolutionize neurophysiology, there are obstacles to overcome. We must address ethical problems of algorithmic bias, data privacy, and clinicians' and patients' acceptance of AI tools to ensure their responsible and advantageous adoption. As research progresses, resolving these problems and realizing AI's full potential to enhance neurophysiological evaluations and patient outcomes will require constant cooperation between AI developers and medical experts. AI has the potential to completely transform neurophysiology by increasing patient care, customizing therapies, and improving diagnostic precision. Future studies should concentrate on creating integrated systems for real-time monitoring, investigating tailored AI-driven therapies, and improving AI algorithms to increase their resilience and generalizability across a range of populations. Establishing ethical standards is also necessary to guarantee openness and promote confidence in AI systems. Interdisciplinary cooperation may provide creative new methods for evaluations and therapies, especially in the context of developing technology like virtual reality. To assess the long-term effects of AI-driven therapies on patient outcomes and to gather important information for future clinical practice, longitudinal studies will be essential. To fully realize AI's transformative promise in neurophysiology, more study and cooperation will be needed as these technologies advance.

REFERENCES

Abadal, S., Galván, P., Mármol, A., Mammone, N., Ieracitano, C., Giudice, M. L., & Morabito, F. C. (2025). Graph neural networks for electroencephalogram analysis: Alzheimer's disease and epilepsy use cases. *Neural Networks*, 181, 106792. DOI: 10.1016/j.neunet.2024.106792 PMID: 39471577

Ahuja, A., Agrawal, S., Acharya, S., Batra, N., & Daiya, V. (2024). Advancements in Wearable Digital Health Technology: A Review of Epilepsy Management. *Cureus*, 16(3), e57037. DOI: 10.7759/cureus.57037 PMID: 38681418

Badrulhisham, F., Pogatzki-Zahn, E., Segelcke, D., Spisak, T., & Vollert, J. (2024). Machine learning and artificial intelligence in neuroscience: A primer for researchers. *Brain, Behavior, and Immunity*, 115, 470–479. DOI: 10.1016/j.bbi.2023.11.005 PMID: 37972877

Bajwa, J., Munir, U., Nori, A., & Williams, B. (2021). Artificial intelligence in healthcare: Transforming the practice of medicine. *Future Healthcare Journal*, 8(2), e188–e194. DOI: 10.7861/fhj.2021-0095 PMID: 34286183

Bohr, A., & Memarzadeh, K. (2020). The rise of artificial intelligence in healthcare applications. In *Artificial Intelligence in healthcare* (pp. 25–60). Academic Press., DOI: 10.1016/B978-0-12-818438-7.00002-2

Chaddad, A., Wu, Y., Kateb, R., & Bouridane, A. (2023). Electroencephalography signal processing: A comprehensive review and analysis of methods and techniques. *Sensors (Basel)*, 23(14), 6434. DOI: 10.3390/s23146434 PMID: 37514728

Chen, S., Janies, D., Paul, R., & Thill, J. C. (2024). Leveraging advances in data-driven deep learning methods for hybrid epidemic modeling. *Epidemics*, 48, 100782. DOI: 10.1016/j.epidem.2024.100782 PMID: 38971085

Chen, Z. (2023). Ethics and discrimination in artificial intelligence-enabled recruitment practices. *Humanities & Social Sciences Communications*, 10(1), 1–12. DOI: 10.1057/s41599-023-02079-x

Chen, Z. S., Galatzer-Levy, I. R., Bigio, B., Nasca, C., & Zhang, Y. (2022). Modern views of machine learning for precision psychiatry. *Patterns (New York, N.Y.)*, 3(11), 100602. Advance online publication. DOI: 10.1016/j.patter.2022.100602 PMID: 36419447

Chopra, H., Annu, , Shin, D. K., Munjal, K., Priyanka, , Dhama, K., & Emran, T. B. (2023). Revolutionizing clinical trials: The role of AI in accelerating medical breakthroughs. *International Journal of Surgery*, 109(12), 4211–4220. DOI: 10.1097/JS9.0000000000000705 PMID: 38259001

Corsi, M. C. (2023). Electroencephalography and Magnetoencephalography. *Machine learning for brain disorders*, 285-312. DOI: 10.1007/978-1-0716-3195-9_9

D'Hotman, D., & Loh, E. (2020). AI enabled suicide prediction tools: A qualitative narrative review. *BMJ Health & Care Informatics*, 27(3), e100175. Advance online publication. DOI: 10.1136/bmjhci-2020-100175 PMID: 33037037

de Souza, G. C., & Roveroni, A. J. (2023). INTELIGÊNCIA ARTIFICIAL (IA): O PAPEL CRUCIAL DA REGULAMENTAÇÃO. *Revista Ibero-Americana de Humanidades. Ciência & Educação (Bauru)*, 9(10), 1982–1993. DOI: 10.51891/rease.v9i10.11896

Dennis, A. P., & Strafella, A. P. (2024). The role of AI and machine learning in the diagnosis of Parkinson's disease and atypical parkinsonisms. *Parkinsonism & Related Disorders*, 126, 106986. DOI: 10.1016/j.parkreldis.2024.106986 PMID: 38724317

Dhiman, R. (2023). Machine learning techniques for electroencephalogram based brain-computer interface: A systematic literature review. *Measurement. Sensors*, 28, 100823. DOI: 10.1016/j.measen.2023.100823

Dixit, S., Bohre, K., Singh, Y., Himeur, Y., Mansoor, W., Atalla, S., & Srinivasan, K. (2023). A Comprehensive review on AI-enabled models for Parkinson's disease diagnosis. *Electronics (Basel)*, 12(4), 783. DOI: 10.3390/electronics12040783

Drigas, A., & Sideraki, A. (2024). Brain Neuroplasticity Leveraging Virtual Reality and Brain–Computer Interface Technologies. *Sensors (Basel)*, 24(17), 5725. DOI: 10.3390/s24175725 PMID: 39275636

Ezzati, A., & Lipton, R. B. (2020). Machine Learning Predictive Models Can Improve Efficacy of Clinical Trials for Alzheimer's Disease. *Journal of Alzheimer's Disease*, 74(1), 55–63. DOI: 10.3233/JAD-190822 PMID: 31985462

Fabrizio, C., Termine, A., Caltagirone, C., & Sancesario, G. (2021). Artificial Intelligence for Alzheimer's Disease: Promise or Challenge? *Diagnostics (Basel)*, 11(8), 1473. DOI: 10.3390/diagnostics11081473 PMID: 34441407

Farhud, D. D., & Zokaei, S. (2021). Ethical Issues of Artificial Intelligence in Medicine and Healthcare. *Iranian Journal of Public Health*, 50(11), i–v. DOI: 10.18502/ijph.v50i11.7600 PMID: 35223619

Fiorente, N., Mojdehdehbaher, S., & Calabrò, R. S. (2024). Artificial Intelligence and Neurorehabilitation: Fact vs. Fiction. *Innovations in Clinical Neuroscience*, 21(1-3), 10. PMID: 38495602

Franklin, G., Stephens, R., Piracha, M., Tiosano, S., Lehouillier, F., Koppel, R., & Elkin, P. L. (2024). The Sociodemographic Biases in Machine Learning Algorithms: A Biomedical Informatics Perspective. *Life (Basel, Switzerland)*, 14(6), 652. DOI: 10.3390/life14060652 PMID: 38929638

Frosolini, A., Franz, L., Caragli, V., Genovese, E., de Filippis, C., & Marioni, G. (2024). Artificial Intelligence in Audiology: A Scoping Review of Current Applications and Future Directions. *Sensors (Basel)*, 24(22), 7126. DOI: 10.3390/s24227126 PMID: 39598904

Ganesh, S., Chithambaram, T., Krishnan, N. R., Vincent, D. R., Kaliappan, J., & Srinivasan, K. (2023). Exploring Huntington's Disease Diagnosis via Artificial Intelligence Models: A Comprehensive Review. *Diagnostics (Basel)*, 13(23), 3592. DOI: 10.3390/diagnostics13233592 PMID: 38066833

Gerke, S., Minssen, T., & Cohen, G. (2020). Ethical and legal challenges of artificial intelligence-driven healthcare. *Artificial Intelligence in Healthcare*, 295–336. DOI: 10.1016/B978-0-12-818438-7.00012-5

Gomes, N., Pato, M., Lourenço, A. R., & Datia, N. (2023). A Survey on Wearable Sensors for Mental Health Monitoring. *Sensors (Basel)*, 23(3), 1330. DOI: 10.3390/s23031330 PMID: 36772370

Gorriz Sáez, J. M., Álvarez Illán, I., Arco Martín, J. E., Castillo Barnes, D., Formoso, M. A., Gallego Molina, N. J., ... & Shoeibi, A. (2023). Computational approaches to Explainable Artificial Intelligence: Advances in theory, applications and trends. DOI: 10.1016/j.inffus.2023.101945

Graham, S., Depp, C., Lee, E. E., Nebeker, C., Tu, X., Kim, H. C., & Jeste, D. V. (2019). Artificial Intelligence for Mental Health and Mental Illnesses: An Overview. *Current Psychiatry Reports*, 21(11), 116. DOI: 10.1007/s11920-019-1094-0 PMID: 31701320

Haleem, A., Javaid, M., Singh, R. P., & Suman, R. (2021). Telemedicine for healthcare: Capabilities, features, barriers, and applications. *Sensors International*, 2, 100117. DOI: 10.1016/j.sintl.2021.100117 PMID: 34806053

Hamida, S. U., Chowdhury, M. J. M., Chakraborty, N. R., Biswas, K., & Sami, S. K. (2024). Exploring the Landscape of Explainable Artificial Intelligence (XAI): A Systematic Review of Techniques and Applications. *Big Data and Cognitive Computing*, 8(11), 149. DOI: 10.3390/bdcc8110149

Handa, P., Lavanya, , Goel, N., & Garg, N. (2024). Software advancements in automatic epilepsy diagnosis and seizure detection: 10-year review. *Artificial Intelligence Review*, 57(7), 181. DOI: 10.1007/s10462-024-10799-y

Haque, M. D. R., & Rubya, S. (2023). An Overview of Chatbot-Based Mobile Mental Health Apps: Insights From App Description and User Reviews. *JMIR mHealth and uHealth*, 11, e44838. DOI: 10.2196/44838 PMID: 37213181

Harrer, S., Shah, P., Antony, B., & Hu, J. (2019). Artificial intelligence for clinical trial design. *Trends in Pharmacological Sciences*, 40(8), 577–591. DOI: 10.1016/j.tips.2019.05.005 PMID: 31326235

Ho, D., Quake, S. R., McCabe, E. R. B., Chng, W. J., Chow, E. K., Ding, X., Gelb, B. D., Ginsburg, G. S., Hassenstab, J., Ho, C. M., Mobley, W. C., Nolan, G. P., Rosen, S. T., Tan, P., Yen, Y., & Zarrinpar, A. (2020). Enabling Technologies for Personalized and Precision Medicine. *Trends in Biotechnology*, 38(5), 497–518. DOI: 10.1016/j.tibtech.2019.12.021 PMID: 31980301

Houssein, E. H., Hammad, A., & Ali, A. A. (2022). Human emotion recognition from EEG-based brain–computer interface using machine learning: A comprehensive review. *Neural Computing & Applications*, 34(15), 12527–12557. DOI: 10.1007/s00521-022-07292-4

Hussain, S. S., Degang, X., Shah, P. M., Islam, S. U., Alam, M., Khan, I. A., Awwad, F. A., & Ismail, E. A. A. (2023). Classification of Parkinson's Disease in Patch-Based MRI of Substantia Nigra. *Diagnostics (Basel)*, 13(17), 2827. DOI: 10.3390/diagnostics13172827 PMID: 37685365

Islam, M. M., Hassan, S., Akter, S., Jibon, F. A., & Sahidullah, M. (2024). A comprehensive review of predictive analytics models for mental illness using machine learning algorithms. *Healthcare Analytics*, 100350, 100350. Advance online publication. DOI: 10.1016/j.health.2024.100350

Javed, A. R., Saadia, A., Mughal, H., Gadekallu, T. R., Rizwan, M., Maddikunta, P. K. R., Mahmud, M., Liyanage, M., & Hussain, A. (2023). Artificial intelligence for cognitive health assessment: State-of-the-art, open challenges and future directions. *Cognitive Computation*, 15(6), 1767–1812. DOI: 10.1007/s12559-023-10153-4

Jeyaraman, M., Balaji, S., Jeyaraman, N., & Yadav, S. (2023). Unraveling the Ethical Enigma: Artificial Intelligence in Healthcare. *Cureus*, 15(8), e43262. DOI: 10.7759/cureus.43262 PMID: 37692617

Jimenez-Mesa, C., Arco, J. E., Martinez-Murcia, F. J., Suckling, J., Ramirez, J., & Gorriz, J. M. (2023). Applications of machine learning and deep learning in SPECT and PET imaging: General overview, challenges, and future prospects. *Pharmacological Research*, 197, 106984. DOI: 10.1016/j.phrs.2023.106984 PMID: 37940064

Johnson, K. B., Wei, W. Q., Weeraratne, D., Frisse, M. E., Misulis, K., Rhee, K., Zhao, J., & Snowdon, J. L. (2021). Precision Medicine, AI, and the Future of Personalized Health Care. *Clinical and Translational Science*, 14(1), 86–93. DOI: 10.1111/cts.12884 PMID: 32961010

Kalani, M., & Anjankar, A. (2024). Revolutionizing Neurology: The Role of Artificial Intelligence in Advancing Diagnosis and Treatment. *Cureus*, 16(6), e61706. DOI: 10.7759/cureus.61706 PMID: 38975469

Krishnan, G., Singh, S., Pathania, M., Gosavi, S., Abhishek, S., Parchani, A., & Dhar, M. (2023). Artificial intelligence in clinical medicine: Catalyzing a sustainable global healthcare paradigm. *Frontiers in Artificial Intelligence*, 6, 1227091. DOI: 10.3389/frai.2023.1227091 PMID: 37705603

Kumar, Y., Koul, A., Singla, R., & Ijaz, M. F. (2023). Artificial intelligence in disease diagnosis: A systematic literature review, synthesizing framework and future research agenda. *Journal of Ambient Intelligence and Humanized Computing*, 14(7), 8459–8486. DOI: 10.1007/s12652-021-03612-z PMID: 35039756

Larkins, A., Knight, B., Keokhamphavanh, B., Taggart, K., Keatley, S., Insisiengmay, B., & Ash, A. (2024). Sensitivity and specificity of microscopic and molecular techniques for the diagnosis of taeniasis. *Acta Tropica*, 260, 107414. DOI: 10.1016/j.actatropica.2024.107414 PMID: 39362512

Lee, E. E., Torous, J., De Choudhury, M., Depp, C. A., Graham, S. A., Kim, H. C., Paulus, M. P., Krystal, J. H., & Jeste, D. V. (2021). Artificial intelligence for mental health care: Clinical applications, barriers, facilitators, and artificial wisdom. *Biological Psychiatry: Cognitive Neuroscience and Neuroimaging*, 6(9), 856–864. DOI: 10.1016/j.bpsc.2021.02.001 PMID: 33571718

Lee, S., Kim, H., Park, M. J., & Jeon, H. J. (2021). Current advances in wearable devices and their sensors in patients with depression. *Frontiers in Psychiatry*, 12, 672347. DOI: 10.3389/fpsyt.2021.672347 PMID: 34220580

Lin, K. Y., Liu, Y., Li, L., & Dou, R. (2021). A review of explainable artificial intelligence. In *Advances in Production Management Systems. Artificial Intelligence for Sustainable and Resilient Production Systems: IFIP WG 5.7 International Conference, APMS 2021, Nantes, France,September 5–9, 2021,Proceedings, Part IV* (pp. 574-584). Springer International Publishing. DOI: 10.1007/978-3-030-85910-7_61

Maleki Varnosfaderani, S., & Forouzanfar, M. (2024). The role of AI in hospitals and clinics: Transforming healthcare in the 21st century. *Bioengineering (Basel, Switzerland)*, 11(4), 337. DOI: 10.3390/bioengineering11040337 PMID: 38671759

Martinek, R., Ladrova, M., Sidikova, M., Jaros, R., Behbehani, K., Kahankova, R., & Kawala-Sterniuk, A. (2021). Advanced bioelectrical signal processing methods: Past, present, and future approach—Part III: Other biosignals. *Sensors (Basel)*, 21(18), 6064. DOI: 10.3390/s21186064 PMID: 34577270

Mathe, M., Padmaja, M., & Krishna, B. T. (2021). Intelligent approach for artifacts removal from EEG signal using heuristic-based convolutional neural network. *Biomedical Signal Processing and Control*, 70, 102935. DOI: 10.1016/j.bspc.2021.102935

McGraw, D., & Mandl, K. D. (2021). Privacy protections to encourage use of health-relevant digital data in a learning health system. *NPJ Digital Medicine*, 4(1), 2. DOI: 10.1038/s41746-020-00362-8 PMID: 33398052

Mennella, C., Maniscalco, U., De Pietro, G., & Esposito, M. (2024). Ethical and regulatory challenges of AI technologies in healthcare: A narrative review. *Heliyon*, 10(4), e26297. DOI: 10.1016/j.heliyon.2024.e26297 PMID: 38384518

Merk, T., Peterson, V., Köhler, R., Haufe, S., Richardson, R. M., & Neumann, W. J. (2022, May 1). Machine learning based brain signal decoding for intelligent adaptive deep brain stimulation. *Experimental Neurology*, 351, 113993. DOI: 10.1016/j.expneurol.2022.113993 PMID: 35104499

Mirkin, S., & Albensi, B. C. (2023). Should artificial intelligence be used in conjunction with Neuroimaging in the diagnosis of Alzheimer's disease? *Frontiers in Aging Neuroscience*, 15, 1094233. DOI: 10.3389/fnagi.2023.1094233 PMID: 37187577

Morales, S., & Bowers, M. E. (2022). Time-frequency analysis methods and their application in developmental EEG data. *Developmental Cognitive Neuroscience*, 54, 101067. DOI: 10.1016/j.dcn.2022.101067 PMID: 35065418

Nazer, L. H., Zatarah, R., Waldrip, S., Ke, J. X. C., Moukheiber, M., Khanna, A. K., Hicklen, R. S., Moukheiber, L., Moukheiber, D., Ma, H., & Mathur, P. (2023). Bias in artificial intelligence algorithms and recommendations for mitigation. *PLOS Digital Health*, 2(6), e0000278. DOI: 10.1371/journal.pdig.0000278 PMID: 37347721

Celedonia, K. L., Karukivi, M., Valenti, M. W., Geldsetzer, P., & Wilson, M. L. (2024). Temporal Patterns of Suicidality Among Adolescents Receiving Behavioral and Mental Health Services in the Community: A Survival Analysis. *Community Mental Health Journal*, •••, 1–8.

Obradovich, N., Khalsa, S. S., Khan, W. U., Suh, J., Perlis, R. H., Ajilore, O., & Paulus, M. P. (2024). Opportunities and risks of large language models in psychiatry. *NPP-Digital Psychiatry and Neuroscience*, 2(1), 8. DOI: 10.1038/s44277-024-00010-z PMID: 39554888

Paganoni, S., & Amato, A. (2013). Electrodiagnostic evaluation of myopathies. *Physical Medicine and Rehabilitation Clinics of North America*, 24(1), 193–207. DOI: 10.1016/j.pmr.2012.08.017 PMID: 23177039

Palombi, T., Galli, F., Giancamilli, F., D'Amico, M., Alivernini, F., Gallo, L., Neroni, P., Predazzi, M., De Pietro, G., Lucidi, F., Giordano, A., & Chirico, A. (2023). The role of sense of presence in expressing cognitive abilities in a virtual reality task: An initial validation study. *Scientific Reports*, 13(1), 13396. DOI: 10.1038/s41598-023-40510-0 PMID: 37591908

Panesar, K., & de Alba, M. B. (2023, December 1). Natural language processing-driven framework for the early detection of language and cognitive decline. *Language and Health.*, 1(2), 20–35. DOI: 10.1016/j.laheal.2023.09.002

Park, H. J. (2024). Patient perspectives on informed consent for medical AI: A web-based experiment. *Digital Health*, 10, 20552076241247938. DOI: 10.1177/20552076241247938 PMID: 38698829

Perivolaris, A., Adams-McGavin, C., Madan, Y., Kishibe, T., Antoniou, T., Mamdani, M., & Jung, J. J. (2024). Quality of interaction between clinicians and artificial intelligence systems. A systematic review. *Future Healthcare Journal*, 100172(3), 100172. Advance online publication. DOI: 10.1016/j.fhj.2024.100172 PMID: 39281326

Piñeros-Fernández, M. C. (2023). Artificial intelligence applications in the diagnosis of neuromuscular diseases: A narrative review. *Cureus*, 15(11). Advance online publication. DOI: 10.7759/cureus.48458 PMID: 37942130

Purtle, J., Nelson, K. L., Counts, N. Z., & Yudell, M. (2020). Population-Based Approaches to Mental Health: History, Strategies, and Evidence. *Annual Review of Public Health*, 41(1), 201–221. DOI: 10.1146/annurev-publhealth-040119-094247 PMID: 31905323

Raghavendra, U., Acharya, U. R., & Adeli, H. (2020). Artificial intelligence techniques for automated diagnosis of neurological disorders. *European Neurology*, 82(1-3), 41–64. DOI: 10.1159/000504292 PMID: 31743905

Raikar, A. S., Andrew, J., Dessai, P. P., Prabhu, S. M., Jathar, S., Prabhu, A., Naik, M. B., & Raikar, G. V. S. (2024). Neuromorphic computing for modeling neurological and psychiatric disorders: Implications for drug development. *Artificial Intelligence Review*, 57(12), 318. DOI: 10.1007/s10462-024-10948-3

Rakhmatulin, I., Dao, M. S., Nassibi, A., & Mandic, D. (2024). Exploring convolutional neural network architectures for EEG feature extraction. *Sensors (Basel)*, 24(3), 877. DOI: 10.3390/s24030877 PMID: 38339594

Roggeveen, L. F., Hassouni, A. E., de Grooth, H. J., Girbes, A. R. J., Hoogendoorn, M., & Elbers, P. W. G.Dutch ICU Data Sharing Against COVID-19 Collaborators. (2024). Reinforcement learning for intensive care medicine: Actionable clinical insights from novel approaches to reward shaping and off-policy model evaluation. *Intensive Care Medicine Experimental*, 12(1), 32. DOI: 10.1186/s40635-024-00614-x PMID: 38526681

Sarker, I. H. (2021). Machine learning: Algorithms, real-world applications and research directions. *SN Computer Science*, 2(3), 160. DOI: 10.1007/s42979-021-00592-x PMID: 33778771

Seh, A. H., Zarour, M., Alenezi, M., Sarkar, A. K., Agrawal, A., Kumar, R., & Khan, R. A. (2020). Healthcare Data Breaches: Insights and Implications. *Healthcare (Basel)*, 8(2), 133. DOI: 10.3390/healthcare8020133 PMID: 32414183

Shajari, S., Kuruvinashetti, K., Komeili, A., & Sundararaj, U. (2023). The emergence of AI-based wearable sensors for digital health technology: A review. *Sensors (Basel)*, 23(23), 9498. DOI: 10.3390/s23239498 PMID: 38067871

Shang, S., Shi, Y., Zhang, Y., Liu, M., Zhang, H., Wang, P., & Zhuang, L. (2024). Artificial intelligence for brain disease diagnosis using electroencephalogram signals. *Journal of Zhejiang University. Science. B.*, 25(10), 914–940. DOI: 10.1631/jzus.B2400103 PMID: 39420525

Sigcha, L., Borzì, L., Amato, F., Rechichi, I., Ramos-Romero, C., Cárdenas, A., Gascó, L., & Olmo, G. (2023). Deep learning and wearable sensors for the diagnosis and monitoring of Parkinson's disease: A systematic review. *Expert Systems with Applications*, 229, 120541. DOI: 10.1016/j.eswa.2023.120541

Sim, J. A., Huang, X., Horan, M. R., Baker, J. N., & Huang, I. C. (2024). Using natural language processing to analyze unstructured patient-reported outcomes data derived from electronic health records for cancer populations: A systematic review. *Expert Review of Pharmacoeconomics & Outcomes Research*, 24(4), 467–475. DOI: 10.1080/14737167.2024.2322664 PMID: 38383308

Singh, N. M., Harrod, J. B., Subramanian, S., Robinson, M., Chang, K., Cetin-Karayumak, S., Dalca, A. V., Eickhoff, S., Fox, M., Franke, L., Golland, P., Haehn, D., Iglesias, J. E., O'Donnell, L. J., Ou, Y., Rathi, Y., Siddiqi, S. H., Sun, H., Westover, M. B., & Gollub, R. L. (2022). How Machine Learning is Powering Neuroimaging to Improve Brain Health. *Neuroinformatics*, 20(4), 943–964. DOI: 10.1007/s12021-022-09572-9 PMID: 35347570

Soori, M., Arezoo, B., & Dastres, R. (2023). Artificial intelligence, machine learning and deep learning in advanced robotics, a review. *Cognitive Robotics*, 3, 54–70. DOI: 10.1016/j.cogr.2023.04.001

Soula, M., Maslarova, A., Harvey, R. E., Valero, M., Brandner, S., Hamer, H., Fernández-Ruiz, A., & Buzsáki, G. (2023). Interictal epileptiform discharges affect memory in an Alzheimer's disease mouse model. *Proceedings of the National Academy of Sciences of the United States of America*, 120(34), e2302676120. DOI: 10.1073/pnas.2302676120 PMID: 37590406

Steerling, E., Siira, E., Nilsen, P., Svedberg, P., & Nygren, J. (2023). Implementing AI in healthcare-the relevance of trust: A scoping review. *Frontiers in Health Services*, 3, 1211150. DOI: 10.3389/frhs.2023.1211150 PMID: 37693234

Sweet, L. B., Müller, C., Anand, M., & Zscheischler, J. (2023). Cross-validation strategy impacts the performance and interpretation of machine learning models. *Artificial Intelligence for the Earth Systems*, 2(4), e230026. DOI: 10.1175/AIES-D-23-0026.1

Timmons, A. C., Duong, J. B., Simo Fiallo, N., Lee, T., Vo, H. P. Q., Ahle, M. W., Comer, J. S., Brewer, L. C., Frazier, S. L., & Chaspari, T. (2023). A Call to Action on Assessing and Mitigating Bias in Artificial Intelligence Applications for Mental Health. *Perspectives on psychological science: a journal of the Association for Psychological Science, 18*(5), 1062–1096. DOI: 10.1177/17456916221134490

Van Giffen, B., Herhausen, D., & Fahse, T. (2022). Overcoming the pitfalls and perils of algorithms: A classification of machine learning biases and mitigation methods. *Journal of Business Research*, 144, 93–106. DOI: 10.1016/j.jbusres.2022.01.076

Weaver, D. T., King, E. S., Maltas, J., & Scott, J. G. (2024). Reinforcement learning informs optimal treatment strategies to limit antibiotic resistance. *Proceedings of the National Academy of Sciences of the United States of America*, 121(16), e2303165121. DOI: 10.1073/pnas.2303165121 PMID: 38607932

Williams, K. S. (2024). Evaluations of artificial intelligence and machine learning algorithms in neurodiagnostics. *Journal ofNeurophysiology*, 131(5), 825–831. DOI: 10.1152/jn.00404.2023 PMID: 38533950

Yang, S., & Kar, S. (2023). Application of artificial intelligence and machine learning in early detection of adverse drug reactions (ADRs) and drug-induced toxicity. *Artificial Intelligence Chemistry.*, 100011(2), 100011. Advance online publication. DOI: 10.1016/j.aichem.2023.100011

Yao, Y., & Cui, Z. (2020). An Automatic Epilepsy Detection Method Based on Improved Inductive Transfer Learning. *Computational and Mathematical Methods in Medicine*, 5046315, 1–13. Advance online publication. DOI: 10.1155/2020/5046315 PMID: 32831900

Yeung, J. A., Wang, Y. Y., Kraljevic, Z., & Teo, J. T. (2023). Artificial intelligence (AI) for neurologists: Do digital neurones dream of electric sheep? *Practical Neurology*, 23(6), 476–488. DOI: 10.1136/pn-2023-003757 PMID: 37977806

Yim, D., Khuntia, J., Parameswaran, V., & Meyers, A. (2024). Preliminary Evidence of the Use of Generative AI in Health Care Clinical Services: Systematic Narrative Review. *JMIR Medical Informatics*, 12, e52073. DOI: 10.2196/52073 PMID: 38506918

Ying, H., Pranolo, A., Nuryana, Z., & Syafitri, A. I. (2024, November 2). Emerging trends in the evolution of neuropsychology and artificial intelligence: A comprehensive analysis. *Telematics and Informatics Reports.*, 100171, 100171. Advance online publication. DOI: 10.1016/j.teler.2024.100171

Zafar, F., Fakhare Alam, L., Vivas, R. R., Wang, J., Whei, S. J., Mehmood, S., Sadeghzadegan, A., Lakkimsetti, M., & Nazir, Z. (2024). The Role of Artificial Intelligence in Identifying Depression and Anxiety: A Comprehensive Literature Review. *Cureus*, 16(3), e56472. DOI: 10.7759/cureus.56472 PMID: 38638735

Zhang, J., & Zhang, Z. M. (2023). Ethics and governance of trustworthy medical artificial intelligence. *BMC Medical Informatics and Decision Making*, 23(1), 7. DOI: 10.1186/s12911-023-02103-9 PMID: 36639799

Zhang, T., Schoene, A. M., Ji, S., & Ananiadou, S. (2022). Natural language processing applied to mental illness detection. DOI: 10.1038/s41746-022-00589-7

Zhang, Y. D., Dong, Z., Wang, S. H., Yu, X., Yao, X., Zhou, Q., Hu, H., Li, M., Jiménez-Mesa, C., Ramirez, J., Martinez, F. J., & Gorriz, J. M. (2020). Advances in multimodal data fusion in neuroimaging: Overview, challenges, and novel orientation. *Information Fusion*, 64, 149–187. DOI: 10.1016/j.inffus.2020.07.006 PMID: 32834795

Zhou, J., Cui, G., Hu, S., Zhang, Z., Yang, C., Liu, Z., ... & Sun, M. (2020). Graph neural networks: A review of methods and applications. *AI open, 1*, 57-81. DOI: 10.1016/j.aiopen.2021.01.001

Chapter 3
AI-Powered Breakthroughs:
Revolutionizing Cognitive Psychology and Neuropsychology With Machine Learning

Muhammad Usman Tariq
https://orcid.org/0000-0002-7605-3040
Abu Dhabi University, UAE & University College Cork, Ireland

ABSTRACT

This chapter examines how artificial intelligence (AI) is improving neuropsychological practice and how AI tools can be used to diagnose treat and rehabilitate cognitive disorders. Through a critical analysis of recent research and developing patterns the chapter emphasizes AIs potential for neuropsychology real-time interventions personalized care and early detection. It explores how artificial intelligence (AI) has advanced to create tools like virtual assistants chatbots and machine learning algorithms that have greatly enhanced neuropsychological testing and treatment. AI in neurorehabilitation shows encouraging results improving the precision and effectiveness of treatment regimens particularly for patients with brain injuries or cognitive decline. The chapter also examines the effects of AI on neuropsychological training and education with a focus on preparing the next generation of neuropsychologists for practice settings enhanced by AI.

DOI: 10.4018/979-8-3693-9341-3.ch003

INTRODUCTION

Artificial Intelligence (AI) and Machine Learning (ML) as two revolutionary technological revolutions happen to shape neuropsychology and cognitive psychology as broader scientific disciplines. These fields, which focus on human thinking and actions, and even on human brain cognition, have historically used experiments and statistical reasoning to discover general principles of the human mind. AI and ML technologies which can analyse complex data and find out some features beyond human possibilities promote the change in the methods of study in these disciplines by researchers and clinicians. AI and ML are revolutionising the field of psychological and neuropsychological analysis and research by automating complex calculations, estimating the impact with accuracy, and finding models in immense amounts of data (Sharma & Sharma, 2024). In cognitive psychology that deals with things like memory, attention, language and decision making, artificial intelligence has brought about remarkable advancements in how human brain can best be understood. For instance, with the help of ML algorithms, fMRI data can be explored to identify connectivity profiles of the corresponding cognitive function. With the same amity, in neuropsychological which is the combination of the neural and psychological to study the functions of the brain and how it influences and determines behaviours AI has been helpful in increasing precision in diagnostic procedures and in carrying out therapy. For example, deep learning has been used to teach models how to look for markers of early neurodegenerative disease like Alzheimer's from changes in imaging or behaviour data that might be masked. These developments show that AI has not only supported calculation-intensive part of these disciplines but also reinvented their methodologies and applications (Zhao, Wu, & Li, 2023).

The incorporation of these technologies into these fields laid the foundation and has brought about both opportunities and marked difficulties. On the one hand, it means that AI systems can perform data acquisition and analyses with the data sourced from various modalities, including, but not limited to, brain imaging, behavioural experiments, wearables, etc. This capability allows the researchers to develop various sophisticated models of human cognition and behaviour than were possible before. For example, scientists may test theories about how the brain functions with the use of AI-powered neural network simulations, which provide a degree of experimental control that is not feasible in vivo. Clinically, ML algorithms help create customized treatment plans by evaluating patient data in real time, which enhances results and lessens the need for trial-and-error therapy. AI can also keep up with the constantly changing landscape of psychological research and treatment procedures because to its capacity for adaptation and learning from fresh data (Sharma & Sharma, 2024). These developments do have certain drawbacks, though. The possibility of bias in AI models is a serious worry. Because machine learning algorithms learn from pre-existing datasets, they may unintentionally reinforce biases in those datasets, producing biased results or unfair therapeutic recommendations. For instance, a diagnosis algorithm may perform badly for underrepresented groups if the dataset used to train it is not diverse, which would exacerbate gaps in mental health treatment. Furthermore, many ML models' "black box" nature presents a problem for psychological research, where interpretability and transparency are essential. The incorporation of these technologies into evidence-based treatments may be limited if researchers and clinicians lack a clear knowledge of how an AI model comes to its findings (Zhao, Wu, & Li, 2023).

The ethical aspect of using AI in psychology is another significant obstacle. Consent and privacy concerns are especially important when handling sensitive neurological and psychological data. Such data collecting and analysis frequently entails extremely private information, which begs the question of how to guarantee that AI applications uphold patient confidentiality and autonomy. Furthermore, there are moral concerns regarding the possible depersonalization of treatment when AI is used in therapeutic settings. Although artificial intelligence (AI) technologies can enhance a clinician's skills, an excessive dependence on these systems runs the danger of undermining the interpersonal relationships that are essential to psychiatric therapy (Rudroff, 2024). The potential that AI and ML provide are too great to ignore, notwithstanding these difficulties. AI-powered chatbots and virtual therapists, for example, have been created in the field of mental health to provide those in crisis instant assistance. These tools provide scalable solutions to meet the rising need for mental health services worldwide, but they cannot completely replace human therapists. Similarly, by enabling extensive studies on memory and learning, the use of AI in educational settings is advancing cognitive psychology research and quickening the rate of advancement. Our knowledge of complex illnesses like schizophrenia, autism, and depression may potentially advance if multimodal data, including genetic, behavioral, and neuroimaging information, can be integrated into unified models (Kumar & Jain, 2023). It is clear from a critical analysis of AI and ML's involvement in neuropsychology and cognitive psychology that these technologies present both opportunities and difficulties. They have unmatched potential to spur innovation and enhance results but integrating them requires prudence and ethical awareness. Interdisciplinary cooperation will be necessary to properly utilize their potential, bringing together ethicists, computer scientists, psychologists, and legislators to guarantee that AI technologies are created and used ethically. By taking proactive measures to solve these issues, the industry can advance toward a day where artificial intelligence (AI) not only enhances human comprehension of the mind and brain but also helps ensure that information is used fairly and effectively. The potential of AI-powered innovations in this dynamic field rests not only in the advanced technology but also in the careful, human-centered integration of these instruments into psychological research and practice (Zhao, Wu, & Li, 2023).

BACKGROUND

Cognitive psychology and neuropsychology are at the forefront of the rapid progress of artificial intelligence (AI) and machine learning (ML), which is starting to have an enduring impression on many scientific fields. In order to decipher complicated events, these fields—which are devoted to comprehending the complexities of human mind, behaviour, and brain function—have historically depended on experimental investigations and statistical approaches. But with the introduction of AI and ML, a paradigm change occurs, allowing researchers to find patterns and insights that were previously impossible to find using traditional methods. While there are new opportunities for study, diagnosis, and therapies at the nexus of technology and psychology, there are also significant obstacles that must be carefully considered (Medenica & Milosevic, 2024).

More accurate modelling of brain functions including perception, memory, and decision-making has been made possible by the integration of AI with cognitive psychology. Machine learning algorithms, for example, are very good at finding patterns in big datasets, such the neuronal activity recorded by functional magnetic resonance imaging (fMRI). Researchers can learn more about how particular brain areas contribute to various mental processes by comparing these patterns with cognitive activities. AI-driven methods are also transforming clinical procedures in neuropsychology. For instance, deep learning models may analyze speech patterns for early indicators of cognitive decline or even identify subtle indicators of neurodegenerative disorders like Parkinson's or Alzheimer's in imaging data (Privitera & Weekes, 2024).

These uses highlight how AI has the ability to improve these fields' theoretical knowledge and real-world implementations. Notwithstanding these developments, there are still hazards and restrictions associated with integrating AI and ML into psychology. The interpretability of AI models is among the most urgent issues. A lot of machine learning systems function as "black boxes," generating findings without providing explicit justifications for their methodology. In cognitive psychology and neuropsychology, where comprehension of processes and causation is crucial, this lack of openness is especially troublesome. Researchers and doctors frequently encounter a conundrum: whereas AI models' accuracy is alluring, their opacity might erode confidence and prevent their use in domains that require thorough validation (Rudroff, 2024). The quality and representativeness of the data used to train AI systems is another crucial concern. Diverse populations, each with distinct cultural, genetic, and experience origins, are frequently the focus of cognitive psychology and neuropsychology. AI models' outputs may not generalize across these populations if they are trained on biased or insufficient datasets, which would maintain inequality and jeopardize the validity of results. Diagnostic instruments that work effectively for one group of people could produce false findings for another, for instance, making gaps in healthcare outcomes and access worse. In addition to technological fixes, addressing these biases calls for a dedication to moral research procedures and inclusive data gathering methods (Medenica & Milosevic, 2024; Tariq, 2024).

The increasing use of AI in psychology has equally important ethical ramifications. AI systems that evaluate sensitive data in therapeutic settings raise privacy and consent issues. Patients might not be aware of how much of their personal data is being utilized or how safe their data is from any breaches. Furthermore, even while AI technologies can support therapists in their job, there is a chance that they will be used excessively, which could weaken the personal connection that is essential to therapeutic alliances. For AI to be a tool rather than a replacement for human judgment, a balance between technical effectiveness and compassionate care must be struck (Privitera & Weekes, 2024). However, there is no denying AI's potential advantages. The integration of multimodal data—combining behavioural, neuroimaging, genetic, and environmental information to produce thorough models of human cognition and behaviour—is one of its most promising uses. Complex disorders including schizophrenia, autism spectrum disorder, and depression that have not been fully explained by conventional approaches may be better understood with the help of this holistic approach. Furthermore, the ability of AI to analyse and adapt in real-time enables the creation of individualized treatment plans, providing customized therapies that may change as a patient advance (Kumar & Jain, 2023; Tariq, 2025).

Crucially, these findings have wider ramifications that go beyond specific research or medical situations. AI-driven technologies have the potential to make psychological treatment and education more accessible to everybody. For example, AI-powered mental health platforms and virtual therapists can offer people in underprivileged places with limited access to traditional services instant help. To avoid unintentionally exacerbating already-existing inequalities, achieving this potential necessitates tackling the digital gap and guaranteeing fair access to these technologies (Medenica & Milosevic, 2024). It is evident from examining the background of AI's use in cognitive psychology and neuropsychology that this junction is both difficult and revolutionary. Although AI and ML provide tools to improve our knowledge of the mind and brain, integrating them requires careful consideration of societal, technological, and ethical issues. The emphasis must continue to be on making sure AI supports human-centered behaviours, values diversity, and adheres to the exacting norms of scientific investigation as these fields develop. By doing this, these technologies have the potential to completely transform the way we research and assist with the most basic facets of our existence, such as our behaviour, mental health, and cognitive processes (Privitera & Weekes, 2024).

AI-Enhanced Neuropsychological Assessments

AI is radically changing neuropsychological tests by increasing their precision, effectiveness, and flexibility. In order to assess behavior, neurological health, and cognitive function, traditional neuropsychological testing frequently uses standardized instruments and human interpretation. Despite their effectiveness, these techniques are labor-intensive, prone to human error, and can have limitations in identifying minute changes in patient performance. These issues are addressed by the advent of AI-driven evaluation tools, which have the potential to provide before unachievable real-time flexibility, more accurate diagnostics, and tailored insights (Luan & Tsai, 2020). Improving accuracy is one of AI's most important contributions to neuropsychological evaluations. Large dataset analysis, pattern recognition, and correlation with neurological or cognitive disorders are all areas in which machine learning algorithms thrive. For instance, in order to identify early indicators of diseases like Alzheimer's or Parkinson's, artificial intelligence (AI) systems may interpret complicated inputs like neuroimaging scans, genetic data, or even wearable sensors. These technologies can detect minor changes in speech patterns, eye movements, or reaction times that may not be noticeable to human observers. AI-driven evaluations enable earlier and more accurate diagnoses by identifying these subtleties, which is essential for successful intervention and treatment planning (Zafar & Usman, 2024).

Another area in which AI clearly excels is efficiency. Conventional testing procedures, which involve drawn-out sessions and human scoring, can demand a large investment of time and money. AI makes these procedures more efficient by automating the gathering and processing of data. Artificial intelligence (AI)-powered digital assessment services, for example, may conduct examinations online or on mobile devices, scoring answers instantaneously and producing comprehensive results. In addition to lessening the workload for medical professionals, this automation makes it possible to do evaluations from a distance, increasing access to neuropsychological treatment for patients in underprivileged or distant locations. Furthermore, in order to collect more pertinent data, AI systems can dynamically modify the tasks' emphasis or level of difficulty based on the performance of the person being evaluated. By reducing redundancy, this adaptive testing strategy guarantees that the evaluation is still effective and patient-centered (Luan & Tsai, 2020). A number of case studies demonstrate how AI may be used practically in healthcare settings. For instance, analysing verbal fluency tasks using natural language processing (NLP) technologies has showed potential in the diagnosis of dementia. These AI-powered technologies provide a more complete picture of cognitive function by assessing not just the speech content of a patient but also metrics like speech pace, pauses, and word retrieval. Similarly, gamified tasks and biometric data are used by AI-powered systems like CogniFit and Neurotrack to evaluate cognitive health. These methods have been used in clinical and research settings, producing insights that enhance conventional evaluations and include patients in novel ways. These case studies demonstrate how AI is establishing new paradigms for comprehending and assessing cognitive health in addition to improving current procedures (Zafar & Usman, 2024).

Notwithstanding these developments, there are still important issues and difficulties in using AI in neuropsychological testing. The danger of relying too much on AI systems is one major worry. Although these technologies offer useful information, they cannot take the place of qualified physicians' knowledge and discretion. An AI model may, for example, identify specific patterns as suggestive of a neurological disorder; but, in the absence of sufficient context, these results may result in overdiagnosis or unsuitable therapy. Furthermore, the so-called "black box" problem—the opaqueness of many AI algorithms—makes it difficult to validate their results (Tariq, 2024). To maintain the integrity of neuropsychological practice, researchers and clinicians must make sure AI-driven findings are comprehensible and based on accepted scientific standards. With AI-driven evaluations, ethical issues also become more prominent. Concerns regarding data security and privacy are brought up by the usage of private patient information, such as brain scans and cognitive test results. Strong security measures must be put in place to secure sensitive data and guarantee that patients are fully informed about and in control of how their data is used. It is also necessary to consider the possibility of algorithmic bias. AI systems may generate outcomes that are less accurate for particular groups if training datasets are not varied, which would exacerbate rather than lessen health inequalities (Luan & Hu, 2024).

Future developments in AI-enhanced neuropsychological testing are both fascinating and challenging. Tools that adapt to individual needs and integrate multimodal data streams for more comprehensive analysis are promised by developments in adaptive testing. For example, integrating genetic data, neuroimaging, and real-time behavioural data may result in highly customized diagnostic conclusions. Furthermore, the way evaluations are carried out may be completely changed by the combination of AI with cutting-edge technologies like virtual reality (VR) and augmented reality (AR). Assessments of cognitive and neurological performance that are more ecologically valid may be obtained by simulating real-world situations in immersive settings (Zafar & Usman, 2024). It will be essential to collaborate across disciplines as these technologies develop. To keep AI-driven tests morally sound, scientifically rigorous, and available to everyone who needs them, psychologists, neuroscientists, AI developers, and ethicists must collaborate. Even if there are still obstacles to overcome, AI has the potential to improve neuropsychological tests. These technologies have the potential to revolutionize our understanding, diagnosis, and treatment of the intricacies of the human brain and mind by fusing the analytical capabilities of artificial intelligence with the clinical knowledge of human specialists (Luan & Hu, 2024).

Machine Learning in Neuroimaging and Brain Analysis

Machine learning (ML), which provides cutting-edge techniques to comprehend the structure and function of the brain, is becoming more and more important in neuroimaging and brain research. Long used in brain research, neuroimaging methods like MRI, fMRI, and PET scans have frequently fallen short of their full promise due to the complexity and volume of data they produce. By offering strong algorithms that can process, analyse, and interpret massive datasets with a degree of accuracy and speed that human analysis alone cannot match, machine learning solves this problem. The way that researchers and medical professionals approach brain research and neurological diagnosis is changing as a result of machine learning's capacity to spot patterns in neuroimaging data (Ke & Peng, 2024). The identification and diagnosis of neurological illnesses and cognitive decline is one of the main uses of machine learning in neuroimaging. Standardized testing and clinical observation have historically been used to diagnose neurodegenerative disorders such as Parkinson's, Alzheimer's, and others. These techniques, however, frequently identify diseases later on, when there are fewer alternatives for therapy. On the other hand, by analysing neuroimaging data, machine learning models can detect tiny, early indicators of cognitive loss. Deep learning algorithms, for example, are able to assess changes in brain anatomy or functional connectivity in ways that human examiners would not notice Long before clinical symptoms manifest, ML models may identify brain regions impacted by neurodegenerative processes by analysing data from MRI or fMRI images. Early illness detection has enormous potential for bettering patient outcomes by enabling therapies to be timed more effectively (Wei, 2023).

Furthermore, machine learning is showing great promise in forecasting the course of neurological conditions. In neuroimaging, longitudinal studies usually entail monitoring changes in the brain over long stretches of time, which may be resource- and time-intensive. ML models, especially those built on supervised learning, may forecast future cognitive decline or the course of a disease using baseline neuroimaging data. Researchers can develop prediction algorithms that forecast how a patient's health will change over time by training models on information from people with different neurological diseases. With the ability to monitor patient progress, customize treatment plans, and deliver more specialized therapies based on anticipated results, this predictive capacity may be invaluable in therapeutic settings (Ke & Peng, 2024). Despite these encouraging developments, there are still issues in applying ML to neuroimaging. The variability of neuroimaging data is one important problem. The resolution, acquisition methods, and even patient location of brain scans might differ greatly. These differences may result in discrepancies that lower ML models' precision and generalizability. Furthermore, a variety of characteristics, including age, gender, and genetic predisposition, might affect how complexly neuroimaging data is interpreted. One of the biggest challenges is creating ML models that can take these factors into consideration without adding bias. Furthermore, interpretability is a challenge due to the "black box" nature of many machine learning algorithms. In a therapeutic situation, where knowing the underlying causes of brain changes is crucial for making well-informed decisions, these models may offer accurate predictions, but it can be challenging to grasp the reasoning behind their results (Hasnain, 2020).

The potential of brain analysis is being further expanded by creative methods of using AI to map brain networks. Conventional neuroimaging techniques frequently concentrate on certain brain areas or straightforward activity assessments. However, complex interactions across whole brain networks may be analysed by AI and ML models, offering a more comprehensive understanding of how the brain operates overall. For instance, ML algorithms have improved the accuracy of functional connectivity analysis, which examines the interactions between various brain areas whether at rest or executing activities. These models are able to identify minor patterns of connection that are connected to different diseases or cognitive functions (Ke & Peng, 2024). Similar to this, machine learning techniques like network analysis can assist in locating abnormalities in brain networks linked to diseases like depression, autism, or schizophrenia, providing fresh information on the neurological bases of these ailments.These novel approaches are not without difficulties. For example, it might be difficult to comprehend brain network models. Although machine learning is capable of identifying patterns in data, it's not always evident how these patterns link to certain cognitive processes or abnormalities in the brain. Furthermore, integrating structural, functional, and genetic data from multi-modal neuroimaging presents a unique set of challenges. These many forms of data must be handled by machine learning algorithms while preserving accuracy and interpretability (Wei, 2023).

Notwithstanding these difficulties, machine learning has enormous promise for brain analysis and neuroimaging. Deeper understanding of the neurological mechanisms behind cognitive diseases, improved illness progression projections, and more precise diagnostics are all possible with the ongoing advancement of AI algorithms. By overcoming current obstacles, machine learning has the potential to completely change how we identify and treat neurological disorders as well as our understanding of the brain. The problems of data quality, algorithm openness, and clinical integration must be addressed continuously, though, if these technologies are to realize their full potential (Ke & Peng, 2024).

AI in Cognitive Rehabilitation: New Frontiers

The way we approach recovery for people with cognitive impairments is changing due to AI-powered cognitive rehabilitation, which is opening up new possibilities for individualized, flexible therapeutic approaches. Conventional methods of cognitive rehabilitation have mostly depended on regimented, one-size-fits-all procedures in which patients' complete exercises or activities designed to enhance different facets of cognitive function. Even while these techniques have demonstrated some effectiveness, they frequently lack the adaptability and accuracy required to meet each person's particular demands. AI makes rehabilitation more efficient and interesting by bringing a degree of customization and flexibility that is difficult to do with conventional techniques (Hasnain, 2020). The application of machine learning algorithms to create individualized rehabilitation plans is one of the most intriguing developments in AI-powered cognitive rehabilitation. AI is able to create customized programs that address certain deficiencies by analyzing a person's cognitive profile, which is obtained through behavioral data, neuropsychological testing, or neuroimaging. For instance, an AI system may create a dynamic, customized treatment plan by analyzing data from a patient's performance on cognitive tasks and modifying the difficulty of following exercises to fit their existing capabilities. By ensuring that patients are consistently challenged at a suitable level, this flexibility improves the efficacy of rehabilitation. AI is also capable of real-time progress monitoring, giving prompt feedback and modifying the program as needed. AI is a vital tool in cognitive rehabilitation because of this ongoing learning loop, which gives it a level of accuracy and adaptability that human therapists can find difficult to match (Mitsea & Skianis, 2023).

Furthermore, combining artificial intelligence (AI) and virtual reality (VR) brings still another level of innovation to cognitive rehabilitation. Patients with brain injuries or cognitive problems may benefit greatly from the immersive surroundings that virtual reality (VR) generates, which allow them to participate in therapeutic activities that mimic real-world situations. VR applications with AI capabilities can modify these settings in real time according on the patient's performance. For instance, if a patient has trouble with spatial awareness, the AI may change the VR environment to concentrate on memory or navigation exercises, making the experience more tailored and meaningful (Hasnain, 2020). In addition to keeping patients interested, this flexible and immersive method enables them to exercise cognitive abilities in a realistic setting, which has been demonstrated to improve recovery results. By combining VR and AI, a more comprehensive rehabilitation experience is being offered by bridging the gap between cognitive treatment and the actual world (Ganesh & Srinivasan, 2023).

In clinical settings, the application of AI in cognitive rehabilitation has already started to provide encouraging outcomes. AI-driven rehabilitation programs' success stories show how these technologies have the potential to help patients with cognitive impairments make major progress. The usage of AI-based systems such as RehaCom, which are intended to assist in the rehabilitation of cognitive function in people suffering from neurological illnesses, traumatic brain injury, or stroke, is one such example. RehaCom offers memory, attention, and executive function exercises that are personalized by AI algorithms based on a patient's development. According to preliminary research, patients who use these AI-powered rehabilitation tools recover more quickly and have better long-term cognitive results than those who use more conventional rehabilitation techniques (Mitsea & Skianis, 2023). Similarly, rehabilitation programs for those with Alzheimer's disease or early-stage dementia have effectively included AI-powered cognitive training applications like CogniFit. These platforms allow physicians to monitor progress or pinpoint regions that need more attention by providing individualized brain workouts based on a user's cognitive profile and thorough progress reports. Patients have occasionally reported gains in executive functioning, memory, and attention when using the AI system in conjunction with a comprehensive rehabilitation program that incorporates social interaction, physical therapy, and other therapies (Ganesh & Srinivasan, 2023).

Even with the encouraging outcomes, there are still a number of obstacles to the broad use of AI-powered cognitive rehabilitation. The absence of thorough, extensive research that unequivocally demonstrates the long-term effectiveness of these instruments is one of the main problems. Even though early success stories are promising, further study is required to verify the reliability and longevity of the gains made by AI-driven therapies. Concerns have also been raised regarding the equality and accessibility of AI-based rehabilitation initiatives. Not all patients, especially those in low-income or rural locations, may have access to high-tech tools like virtual reality and AI-powered applications, which might worsen already-existing health inequities (Cosic & Jovanovic, 2024). Furthermore, AI cannot replace human therapists, even if it can offer valuable insights and help. Clinicians continue to play an essential role in managing recovery. Given the complexity of cognitive rehabilitation, AI technologies must be included into an all-encompassing treatment plan that incorporates human judgment and emotional support. In order to understand results and make complex decisions based on the patient's overall health and welfare, human skill is crucial. AI may help therapists by automating some chores and offering data-driven insights (Cosic & Jovanovic, 2024).

To sum up, AI-powered cognitive rehabilitation is creating new avenues for the treatment of cognitive disorders by providing individualized, flexible therapies that are more successful and interesting than conventional techniques. By producing immersive settings that are customized to each patient's needs, the combination of AI and VR further improves these therapies. Even if early achievements are encouraging, further study and development are required to completely grasp AI's long-term potential in this area. These technologies will probably be crucial to cognitive rehabilitation in the future as they develop, enhancing conventional therapy and increasing access to care. Thoughtful integration of AI into therapeutic practice is necessary to ensure that it complements, not replaces, the crucial role that human therapists play in the healing process (Mitsea & Skianis, 2023).

ETHICAL CONSIDERATIONS IN AI-DRIVEN NEUROPSYCHOLOGY

AI in neuropsychology has the potential to completely transform clinical practice by increasing patient outcomes, customizing therapy, and boosting diagnostic accuracy. But these advancements also bring with them important ethical issues that need to be properly balanced in order to guarantee that AI is used sensibly and in ways that are advantageous to both patients and doctors. As AI technology develops, it is crucial to consider both its possible advantages and the moral ramifications of applying it in delicate fields like neuropsychology, where choices have a direct influence on people's mental health and general wellbeing (Parsapoor & Ruocco, 2023). How to strike a balance between ethical clinical psychology practices and AI advancements is one of the main issues. The concern is whether we can trust AI algorithms in such a crucial subject, even though they can handle and analyse vast quantities of data, provide individualized treatment suggestions, and spot early indicators of cognitive deterioration. AI-powered neuropsychological tools are frequently viewed as additional resources to support human judgment rather than as a substitute for qualified medical professionals. The increasing dependency on these systems, however, increases the possibility of over-reliance, where AI may be granted more power than it merits or, worse, take precedence over medical knowledge. Although AI systems can offer insightful information, they are unable to replace the complex knowledge and compassion that human healthcare professionals contribute to patient care (Singh & Siddiqui, 2024).

The human judgment that is so fundamental to the therapeutic situation must be enhanced by these instruments, not replaced. Therefore, striking a careful balance between the potential of technical innovations and the indispensable importance of human skill in patient care is a major ethical dilemma (AbuAlrob & Mesraoua,

2024). The management of privacy is a crucial ethical concern in AI-driven neuropsychology. Sensitive personal data, such as medical histories, behavioral or emotional states, and cognitive performance data, are frequently included in neuropsychological evaluations. Large datasets are necessary for AI systems to operate efficiently, and patients frequently provide this data without being made aware of its potential uses. The creation of AI models for neuropsychology raises the possibility of privacy violations even while it also holds the promise of bettering treatment. To stop sensitive patient data from being misused, accessed without authorization, or leaked, data security must be given top priority. Patients must also receive complete information regarding the usage, storage, and sharing of their data. In order to guarantee that people are aware of how AI-based evaluations may affect their privacy and control over personal information, transparent permission procedures are essential (Parsapoor & Ruocco, 2023).

Another major ethical issue with AI's use in neuropsychology is bias. Because AI algorithms are only as effective as the data they are trained on, they have the potential to reinforce or even worsen already-existing inequities in diagnosis and treatment if the datasets are biased or unrepresentative. An AI system may find it difficult to evaluate people from different demographic groups, for example, if it is primarily trained on data from that group. This might result in incorrect diagnoses or treatment suggestions. The danger of bias is particularly serious in neuropsychology, where cognitive functioning is significantly influenced by cultural, social, and genetic variables. To guarantee that every patient receives fair and equal care, the AI models must be trained on a variety of representative datasets. As more, more inclusive data becomes available, AI algorithms must be improved. This calls for constant attention to identify and address biases in the data (AbuAlrob & Mesraoua, 2024). In applications of AI in neuropsychology, the human factor is equally crucial. Although AI is faster and more accurate than humans at processing information, it is unable to comprehend the psychological and emotional circumstances that are crucial to patient care. Patients with cognitive disabilities frequently have severe emotional and social repercussions, and AI systems cannot take the place of professionals' sensitive, understanding care. There's also the matter of patient trust. Because they may see these technologies as intrusive or demeaning, many people may be uncomfortable with AI systems evaluating their mental health data. Making sure AI continues to be a technology that enhances human contact and care rather than taking its place is therefore a critical ethical problem (Parsapoor & Ruocco, 2023).

In order to interpret AI-driven evaluations, make decisions based on both machine outputs and their professional judgment, and provide patients the emotional support they require, clinicians should continue to play a crucial role. Frameworks for the ethical application of AI in neuropsychological contexts need to be created in order to handle these issues. These frameworks ought to emphasize a number of fundamental ideas, such as accountability, transparency, and equity. AI systems ought to be open and honest about their operations, the data they utilize, and the decision-making process. By fostering confidence between patients and professionals, this transparency will guarantee that the technology is applied in a clear and intelligible manner. Furthermore, regulatory agencies or ethics committees should supervise AI models to make sure they adhere to accepted ethical norms and hold them responsible for their choices. Fairness should also be the guiding principle for the use of AI, guaranteeing that everyone has access to the same high-quality treatment regardless of background, socioeconomic position, or other variables (Ahmed & Khan, 2023). In order to make sure AI systems are developing in a way that keeps patient welfare as a top priority, ethical frameworks should also incorporate continuous monitoring and assessment. In order to guarantee the ethical integrity of AI applications in neuropsychology, this entails thorough testing for bias, continual validation of models against actual results, and frequent audits. Maintaining the ethical balance required in clinical psychology will depend on making sure AI technology is utilized to enhance rather than replace therapists' competence. Our comprehension of the ethical ramifications of AI technology must develop together with these technologies. We can use AI to its full potential while protecting the rights, privacy, and welfare of people it is intended to assist by resolving these issues and putting strong ethical frameworks in place (Parsapoor & Ruocco, 2023).

THE FUTURE OF COGNITIVE BEHAVIOURAL THERAPY (CBT) WITH MACHINE LEARNING

Depression, anxiety, and stress-related problems are just a few of the mental health issues for which cognitive behavioural therapy, or CBT, has long been regarded as one of the best therapies. Like many therapeutic modalities, it has drawbacks, particularly with regard to consistency, accessibility, and the capacity to deliver individualized, real-time treatments. By incorporating machine learning (ML) technology into cognitive behavioural therapy (CBT), new avenues for overcoming these obstacles are opened up, expanding the therapy's efficacy and accessibility.

Real-time treatments are among the most promising ways that machine learning is augmenting CBT. Conventional cognitive behavioural therapy is a systematic treatment that usually takes place during prearranged sessions with a therapist. Progress is frequently monitored through follow-up visits. Even while these sessions can be very beneficial, people may lose the knowledge and skills they acquire during treatment in between sessions, leaving them to struggle alone with behavioural adjustments and coping mechanisms. Therapists and patients can gain from real-time monitoring and feedback by using machine learning algorithms into cognitive behavioral therapy. In response to certain triggers or difficulties, machine learning (ML) systems, for instance, can identify patterns in a patient's everyday thoughts, feelings, and behavior and offer prompt feedback or coping strategy recommendations. The therapy process is kept dynamic and fluid rather than stagnant and disjointed between sessions thanks to this ongoing, adaptive approach (Nosrati & Sabbar, 2020). Furthermore, real-time machine learning interventions are able to monitor a patient's development at a far finer level, spotting minute shifts in behavior or mood that would not be immediately noticeable to the patient or the therapist. The effectiveness of CBT can be increased by more accurately customizing treatment with the aid of this ongoing data collecting and analysis (Ahmed & Khan, 2023).

The emergence of AI-powered chatbots and virtual assistants has also transformed the delivery of cognitive behavioural therapy (CBT), making it more widely available to people who may otherwise find it difficult to receive traditional therapy. A type of computerized treatment that simulates the conversational style of a human therapist is provided by AI chatbots, such as Woebot or Tess. Through CBT-based activities, these technologies combine machine learning and natural language processing (NLP) to help users track their emotions, challenge negative thought patterns, and develop coping mechanisms. AI chatbots are a useful adjunct that provide round-the-clock assistance to individuals in need, even if they cannot take the place of a human therapist's skilled and nuanced help. These virtual assistants' convenience and promptness increase access to mental health care, especially for people living in remote or disadvantaged locations or those who would be reluctant to seek treatment in person. By integrating these technologies into daily life, customers may receive on-demand help whenever they need it, without being constrained by financial or schedule constraints (Nosrati & Sabbar, 2020). Virtual assistants and chatbots powered by AI have drawbacks despite their potential. The absence of empathy and human connection—two essential elements of successful therapy—is one of the main problems. AI is capable of simulating dialogue and offering insightful feedback, but it is unable to replace the emotional intelligence and comprehension that a human therapist offers. For patients with complex emotional requirements in particular, this may result in a disconnection between the patient and the technology. Furthermore, as these AI systems frequently receive sensitive personal data, privacy and data security issues are raised. To preserve confidence and guarantee the security of user data, these platforms must follow stringent privacy laws and offer transparent permission procedures (Bertacchini & Bilotta, 2023).

The application of predictive analytics in CBT is another fascinating advancement that may allow for more proactive and individualized treatment strategies. In order to forecast how a patient could react to specific therapeutic approaches or treatments, machine learning algorithms can examine enormous volumes of data, including patient history, behavioural patterns, and treatment outcomes. Based on each patient's individual profile, this predictive power can assist therapists in more successfully customizing their approach by selecting tactics that are more likely to produce favourable results. For example, even before the therapist mentions it, a machine learning model may recommend particular cognitive behavioural therapy strategies that concentrate on enhancing self-esteem to a patient who frequently suffers from cognitive distortions associated with self-worth (Singh & Siddiqui, 2024).

In addition to guaranteeing a more focused approach, this helps steer clear of a "one-size-fits-all" strategy, in which common CBT procedures might not work for every patient. More proactive mental health treatment is also made possible by predictive analytics, since therapists may act before a patient's condition deteriorates by using trends found in their data. When treating patients with chronic or recurring diseases, such as depression, when early intervention is essential to preventing recurrence, this might be particularly helpful (Nosrati & Sabbar, 2020). Predictive analytics in CBT, however, also calls into question the possibility of an excessive dependence on data-driven models. Even though machine learning might yield insightful information, therapists must still use professional judgment because algorithms are unable to take into consideration every factor that affects a patient's mental health. Additionally, there's a chance that patients may feel like they're being treated as data points, which might make therapy less individualized. An algorithm cannot duplicate the human element of cognitive behavioral therapy (CBT), such as establishing a therapeutic connection and promoting a sense of trust and understanding (Bertacchini & Bilotta, 2023).

In the future, machine learning will probably be incorporated into cognitive behavioural therapy (CBT) more and more, providing patients with mental health issues with more advanced, individualized, and easily available treatment alternatives. AI-powered solutions will be useful adjuncts to conventional therapy, including real-time assistance, predictive insights, and tailored treatments that can improve the therapeutic experience overall, even if they will never be able to completely replace the need for human therapists. In order to ensure that machine learning enhances rather than replaces the profound empathy and comprehension that form the foundation of successful mental health treatment, it will be crucial to strike a balance between technology innovation and the human elements of therapy as AI technologies advance. Furthermore, in order to guarantee that everyone may benefit from these advancements, it will be critical to address ethical issues like data protection, informed consent, and the fair distribution of AI-based mental health resources as these tools proliferate (Singh & Siddiqui, 2024).

Training the Next Generation: Neuropsychologists in the Age of AI

Artificial intelligence (AI) is at the forefront of the profound developments occurring in the science of neuropsychology. Training programs for aspiring neuropsychologists are more important than ever as AI continues to influence neuropsychology research, diagnosis, and therapy. Using AI technologies in neuropsychological training and education necessitates a fundamental change in the way that education is conducted, not only incorporating new technology into already-existing courses. The objective is to provide the upcoming generation of neuropsychologists the know-how, abilities, and moral compass they need to function in a practice setting augmented by artificial intelligence (Calderone & Calabrò, 2024). The first step in incorporating AI into neuropsychological education is to promote awareness of AI.Behavioral tests, interviews, and neuroimaging analysis were the traditional methods used in neuropsychology training to evaluate and diagnose cognitive and psychological issues. In these domains, artificial intelligence (AI) techniques, such machine learning models, can help by evaluating big data sets, forecasting cognitive decline, and providing information on brain function that would have been hard or impracticable for human researchers to find on their own. In order to equip students for this new environment, training programs need to incorporate AI as a topic of study and a means of improving neuropsychological practice. Courses should include classic neuropsychological topics as well as data science, AI applications in healthcare, and fundamental machine learning techniques (Mohammadi & Shamshiri, 2024).

Students would get the technical know-how required to work with AI technologies while also having a thorough knowledge of human behavior and thought processes. Furthermore, students will be able to become acquainted with the practical elements of incorporating these technologies into clinical practice through practical experience with neuroimaging software and AI-driven evaluation tools (Calderone & Calabrò, 2024). This integration is not without its difficulties, though. The absence of a consistent curriculum for AI in neuropsychology across universities is one of the main problems. There may be a knowledge and competency gap among aspiring practitioners as a result of certain training programs and colleges falling behind in adopting these technologies. Another worry is that AI may supplant more conventional facets of neuropsychology, such the skill of individual diagnosis and treatment (Mitsea & Skianis, 2023).

Neuropsychologists need to exercise caution to avoid becoming unduly dependent on AI models or letting algorithms take precedence over their therapeutic expertise. In order to guarantee that students maintain the abilities required for human-centered care, AI integration in training should seek to enhance rather than replace the fundamentals of neuropsychological practice. In assessing and treating students, educators must find a way to embrace innovation while preserving the basis of human intuition (Srinivasan & Rajavel, 2025).

Future neuropsychologists will need to be ready for practice settings where AI technologies are essential as AI becomes increasingly integrated into clinical practice. Neuropsychologists will be required to operate alongside AI-driven diagnostic tools in these settings, adding a human context to machine-generated insights in addition to interpreting outcomes from AI models. For example, although AI can help identify early indicators of neurodegenerative illnesses, the neuropsychologist must interpret these results in light of the patient's symptoms, life history, and psychosocial characteristics. Future psychologists will thus need to acquire a new set of skills that encompass not just their conventional knowledge of human cognition but also the capacity to assess and validate suggestions generated by artificial intelligence. They need to understand how to ethically manage data produced by AI, critically evaluate the advantages and disadvantages of AI systems, and uphold a patient-centered approach in a world that is becoming more and more reliant on technology (Mohammadi & Shamshiri, 2024). Additionally, AI has a significant influence on psychology's professional duties and abilities. Numerous repetitive operations presently carried out by neuropsychologists, such scoring neuropsychological tests or evaluating big datasets of neuroimaging images, are probably going to be automated by AI. This raises concerns about the changing role of the neuropsychologist, even while it will free up important time for neuropsychologists to concentrate on more intricate elements of diagnosis and therapy. Will AI technologies progressively replace many parts of evaluation and intervention, or will the neuropsychologist of the future work more in tandem with them? AI has the potential to drastically alter the neuropsychologist employment market, making some activities obsolete and maybe leading to the development of new specializations (Srinivasan & Rajavel, 2025).

Neuropsychologists with expertise in analysing and verifying AI-generated insights, for instance, would be in greater demand as they assist guarantee the moral and efficient application of these technologies in therapeutic settings. A more comprehensive grasp of AI and its possible uses in other branches of psychology, such educational psychology or behavioural health, may also be necessary for neuropsychologists (Calderone & Calabrò, 2024).

Furthermore, neuropsychology will need to review its ethical frameworks and standards as AI continues to have an influence on the field. Neuropsychologists will have to deal with new issues including algorithmic bias, data privacy, and the openness of AI decision-making. On the basis of faulty data or inadequate training, AI systems can occasionally provide biased or incorrect findings, which can have serious consequences for medical care. Future neuropsychologists need to be prepared to identify these dangers and promote the ethical application of AI in therapeutic contexts. This entails making certain that AI tools are carefully examined for ethical issues, that patients' rights are upheld, and that patients and doctors are informed in a clear and understandable manner about the outcomes produced by AI. The significance of comprehending these ethical issues and the necessity of critically interacting with developing technology should be emphasized in training programs (Mitsea & Skianis, 2023). Educating the future generation of neuropsychologists how to use new technologies is only one aspect of their training in the era of artificial intelligence. In order to incorporate AI with conventional psychology knowledge and promote a mentality that blends technological expertise with ethical consciousness, educational methodologies must be redesigned. By doing this, we can make sure that neuropsychologists in the future are equipped to handle the difficult moral, professional, and interpersonal issues that arise from working in AI-enhanced settings. Though it will need careful planning, teamwork, and a dedication to maintaining the human aspects at the core of the profession, the incorporation of AI into neuropsychological education presents a unique chance to progress the discipline (Srinivasan & Rajavel, 2025; Tariq, 2025).

Predictive Analytics and Personalized Neuropsychological Care

Predictive analytics and artificial intelligence (AI) in neuropsychological care provide hitherto unheard-of possibilities for cognitive disease early identification, prevention, and individualized therapy. Early diagnosis of cognitive decline and problems, including dementia, Alzheimer's disease, and other neurodegenerative illnesses, can be challenging since they frequently appear gradually. Even if they work well, traditional diagnostic techniques can be laborious and can overlook minute early warning indicators. On the other hand, AI-powered predictive analytics may be able to identify trends in enormous volumes of data, enabling early intervention and more individualized treatment regimens. Clinicians may take preventative measures and limit the trajectory of cognitive decline by using AI to identify risk factors long before symptoms arise by evaluating behavioural patterns, genetic information, and neuroimaging data (Khalid & Coronato, 2024). The potential of predictive analytics to customize neuropsychological treatment is one of its main promises. Conventional therapy models have a tendency to be broad, using generic methods for all individuals with comparable conditions. This "one-size-fits-all" approach, however, frequently ignores the subtle variations among individuals, including the unique genetic, environmental, and psychological elements that affect their cognitive health. More individualized care is made possible by AI's ability to use machine learning algorithms to evaluate a variety of data sets and forecast a patient's potential reaction to various treatment modalities. AI may, for instance, examine a patient's genetic data, neuroimaging findings, and history of cognitive testing to forecast the effects of a particular intervention on brain function.

By ensuring that patients receive the appropriate medications at the appropriate times, this data-driven strategy can improve results and cut down on needless side effects or ineffective interventions (Cosic & Jovanovic, 2024). Several case studies demonstrating individualized treatment solutions demonstrate how AI might enhance results. The application of AI-driven models to the early diagnosis of Alzheimer's disease is one such instance. In one study, scientists analyzed brain scans using machine learning algorithms to spot minute alterations that the human eye frequently overlooks. Individualized care regimens that included both medication and cognitive therapy were then created using these early indicators of cognitive deterioration. In addition to slowing the disease's course, the tailored treatment strategy made sure that therapies were given according to the patient's particular requirements and circumstances. Programs for cognitive rehabilitation are also using prediction models. AI is being used, for instance, to monitor a patient's development over time and modify treatment plans in response to real-time data in order to maximize cognitive recovery (Khalid & Coronato, 2024).

Predictive analytics in neuropsychology has enormous promise, but there are drawbacks as well. The precision and dependability of AI models are among the main issues. Large datasets are used in predictive analytics to train machine learning algorithms; if these datasets are biased or lacking, the models may provide inaccurate predictions. This may result in false negatives, where those who are truly at risk are missed, or false positives, where patients are mistakenly identified as having a condition. Additionally, to make sure that predictive models are generalizable and unaffected by cultural or demographic biases, they must be evaluated across a range of groups. Additionally, there is the matter of data security and privacy. Strict rules must be in place to safeguard sensitive patient data from abuse or unauthorized access when AI systems evaluate it. The application of AI in neuropsychological treatment is made more challenging by the need for patients to feel secure about the ethical and responsible use of their data (Cosic & Jovanovic, 2024). AI has the potential to transform the sector and improve results for people with cognitive problems by facilitating early identification and developing individualized care plans. Predictive analytics is probably going to become more and more important in healthcare decision-making as research advances and AI models get more complex. AI may ultimately be incorporated into standard clinical practice, for instance, assisting medical professionals in proactively implementing preventative measures and spotting early indicators of cognitive impairment during routine examinations. Furthermore, combining AI with other cutting-edge technologies like wearables and virtual reality may result in an even more reliable system for tracking and controlling cognitive health. In the end, the discipline will move from a reactive to a more proactive and customized treatment paradigm as AI is more incorporated into neuropsychological care, giving patients the best opportunity to maintain cognitive function and improve their quality of life (Wei, 2023).

CONCLUSION

The use of AI and machine learning technologies to clinical and research settings offers great potential for the future of AI in neuropsychology and cognitive psychology. The main conclusions drawn from recent developments suggest that AI has the potential to drastically alter the way psychiatric disorders are identified, managed, and comprehended. AI is already having a significant impact on the profession, from boosting cognitive rehabilitation to developing individualized care plans and increasing the precision and effectiveness of neuropsychological evaluations. But this shift is only getting started, and as AI and machine learning develop further, their influence on psychology will only increase. The growth of AI's application in individualized mental health treatment is among the most promising future avenues. Individualized treatment plans are starting to be made possible by predictive analytics and adaptive technology, which allow therapies to be customized to each patient's particular requirements and reactions. Cognitive behavioral treatment, neurodegenerative disease rehabilitation programs, and even the prevention of illnesses like Alzheimer's might be completely transformed by this. AI's capacity to absorb and evaluate enormous volumes of data, including behavioral patterns, genetic data, and neuroimaging, may be able to spot small indicators of cognitive impairment before patients or physicians notice them. This proactive strategy might significantly increase the efficacy of medicines and early intervention, slowing the course of illnesses and raising the standard of care overall.

AI also has the potential to completely transform psychological research. Despite their value, traditional research methods can be sluggish to provide findings and frequently rely on tiny sample sizes. On the other hand, AI can quickly examine big datasets, spot trends, and find novel patterns that may otherwise go overlooked. This might result in ground-breaking insights into cognition, brain function, and the causes of different psychiatric diseases. Furthermore, in ways that were previously unthinkable, machine learning algorithms are starting to assist academics in mapping brain networks, giving them a better knowledge of how various brain areas interact and contribute to diverse mental health issues. AI has enormous potential to accelerate psychological science research and spur innovation. Even with these encouraging developments, a number of obstacles still exist. In particular, data privacy, bias in AI algorithms, and the consequences of AI-driven judgments in healthcare contexts are ethical issues that need to be addressed. The acceptance and efficacy of AI applications in neuropsychology depend on their ethical and responsible use. Furthermore, there is a chance that treatment may become less humane when AI starts to play a bigger part in clinical settings. This is because algorithms may make judgments that would otherwise require the sophisticated judgment of a qualified psychologist. Finding a balance between utilizing AI's potential and maintaining the human component of psychological treatment will be essential to ensuring that AI enhances rather than replaces the therapeutic alliance.

We may anticipate even more revolutionary shifts in the field of mental health over the next ten years as a result of advancements in AI and machine learning. A more immersive and individualized approach to mental health care is probably in store when AI is combined with other cutting-edge technology like wearables, virtual reality, and neurofeedback. For instance, chatbots and virtual assistants driven by AI may develop to provide patients receiving cognitive behavioral therapy real-time support, tracking their progress and providing prompt interventions. Additionally, improvements in brain-computer interfaces may result in more targeted therapies for those with severe cognitive impairments, potentially improving their quality of life and communication. In the end, artificial intelligence in neuropsychology and cognitive psychology has a lot of promise but also a lot of responsibility. Collaboration between physicians, researchers, and politicians will be crucial as the area develops to guarantee that new technologies be applied in ways that benefit patients and society at large. AI has the potential to completely transform psychological research and treatment, but its success will rely on careful integration, ethical concerns, and ongoing human-machine cooperation to enhance everyone's mental health.

REFERENCES

AbuAlrob, M. A., & Mesraoua, B. (2024). Harnessing artificial intelligence for the diagnosis and treatment of neurological emergencies: A comprehensive review of recent advances and future directions. *Frontiers in Neurology*, 15, 1485799. DOI: 10.3389/fneur.2024.1485799 PMID: 39463792

Ahmed, B., & Khan, S. (2023). Cognitive rehabilitation strategies for traumatic brain injury survivors. *Review Journal of Neurological & Medical Sciences Review*, 1(02), 28–51. DOI: 10.1016/j.rjnmsr.2023.06.001

Bertacchini, F., Demarco, F., Scuro, C., Pantano, P., & Bilotta, E. (2023). A social robot connected with ChatGPT to improve cognitive functioning in ASD subjects. *Frontiers in Psychology*, 14, 1232177. DOI: 10.3389/fpsyg.2023.1232177 PMID: 37868599

Calderone, A., Latella, D., Bonanno, M., Quartarone, A., Mojdehdehbaher, S., Celesti, A., & Calabrò, R. S. (2024). Towards transforming neurorehabilitation: The impact of artificial intelligence on diagnosis and treatment of neurological disorders. *Biomedicines*, 12(10), 2415. DOI: 10.3390/biomedicines12102415 PMID: 39457727

Cosic, K., Kopilas, V., & Jovanovic, T. (2024). War, emotions, mental health, and artificial intelligence. *Frontiers in Psychology*, 15, 1394045. DOI: 10.3389/fpsyg.2024.1394045 PMID: 39156807

Ganesh, S., Chithambaram, T., Krishnan, N. R., Vincent, D. R., Kaliappan, J., & Srinivasan, K. (2023). Exploring Huntington's disease diagnosis via artificial intelligence models: A comprehensive review. *Diagnostics (Basel)*, 13(23), 3592. DOI: 10.3390/diagnostics13233592 PMID: 38066833

Hasnain, S. (2020). Artificial neural networks (ANNs) in neuroscientific research: Revolutionizing mental health assessments and therapies. *Neuroscience Research Journal*, 28, 142–153.

Ismail, Y., & Voleti, V. K. (2024). A review on usage of artificial intelligence for early detection and management of Alzheimer's disease. *Journal of Pharma Insights and Research, 2*(5), 007–013. https://doi.org/DOI: 10.1016/j.jpir.2024.05.002

Ke, L., Tong, S., Cheng, P., & Peng, K. (2024). Exploring the frontiers of LLMs in psychological applications: A comprehensive review. *arXiv preprint arXiv:2401.01519*. https://doi.org//arXiv.2401.01519DOI: 10.48550

Khalid, U. B., Naeem, M., Stasolla, F., Syed, M. H., Abbas, M., & Coronato, A. (2024). Impact of AI-powered solutions in rehabilitation process: Recent improvements and future trends. *International Journal of General Medicine*, 17, 943–969. DOI: 10.2147/IJGM.S453903 PMID: 38495919

Kumar, A., Nayyar, A., Sachan, R. K., & Jain, R. (Eds.). (2023). *AI-assisted special education for students with exceptional needs*. IGI Global., DOI: 10.4018/979-8-3693-0378-8

Luan, H., Geczy, P., Lai, H., Gobert, J., Yang, S. J., Ogata, H., Baltes, J., Guerra, R., Li, P., & Tsai, C. C. (2020). Challenges and future directions of big data and artificial intelligence in education. *Frontiers in Psychology*, 11, 580820. DOI: 10.3389/fpsyg.2020.580820 PMID: 33192896

Luan, L., Lin, X., Dai, Y., Allen, L., & Hu, S. (2024). Transforming STEM education: Leveraging ChatGPT for enhanced learning in psychology and neuroscience. In *ChatGPT and Global Higher Education: Using Artificial Intelligence in Teaching and Learning* (p. 100). *IGI Global.*https://doi.org/DOI: 10.4018/978-1-7998-6987-6

Maftei, G. A., Martu, M. A., Ciurcanu, O. E., Busuioc, A., Luca, E. O., Onofrei, A., & Popa, C. (2024). The advent of artificial intelligence in oral pathology. *Romanian Journal of Medical and Dental Education*, 13(2). Advance online publication. DOI: 10.2478/rjmde-2024-0009

Medenica, V., Ivanovic, L., & Milosevic, N. (2024). Applicability of artificial intelligence in neuropsychological rehabilitation of patients with brain injury. *Applied Neuropsychology. Adult*, •••, 1–28. DOI: 10.1080/23279095.2024.2364229 PMID: 38912923

Mitsea, E., Drigas, A., & Skianis, C. (2023). Digitally assisted mindfulness in training self-regulation skills for sustainable mental health: A systematic review. *Behavioral Sciences (Basel, Switzerland)*, 13(12), 1008. DOI: 10.3390/bs13121008 PMID: 38131865

Mohammadi, A. T., Ghanbarzadeh, E., Zamiri, R., Dana, M. K., Far, Y. K., Avarani, M. A. J. N., & Shamshiri, M. (2024). *Advancements in neuroscience: Modern tools and techniques fueling thrilling discoveries in the 21st century*. Nobel Sciences., DOI: 10.1016/j.nobel.2024.03.004

Nosrati, S., Sabzali, M., Heidari, A., Sarfi, T., & Sabbar, S. (2020). Chatbots, counselling, and discontents of the digital life. *Journal of Cyberspace Studies*, 4(2), 153–172. DOI: 10.34296/jcs.2020.4203

Parsapoor, M., Koudys, J. W., & Ruocco, A. C. (2023). Suicide risk detection using artificial intelligence: The promise of creating a benchmark dataset for research on the detection of suicide risk. *Frontiers in Psychiatry*, 14, 1186569. DOI: 10.3389/fpsyt.2023.1186569 PMID: 37564247

Pavlopoulos, A., Rachiotis, T., & Maglogiannis, I. (2024). An overview of tools and technologies for anxiety and depression management using AI. *Applied Sciences (Basel, Switzerland)*, 14(19), 9068. DOI: 10.3390/app14199068

Privitera, A. J., Ng, S. H. S., Kong, A. P. H., & Weekes, B. S. (2024). AI and aphasia in the digital age: A critical review. *Brain Sciences*, 14(4), 383. DOI: 10.3390/brainsci14040383 PMID: 38672032

Rudroff, T. (2024). Artificial intelligence's transformative role in illuminating brain function in long COVID patients using PET/FDG. *Brain Sciences*, 14(1), 73. DOI: 10.3390/brainsci14010073 PMID: 38248288

Sharma, S., Mansoori, S., Goyal, M., Goyal, K., & Sharma, P. (2024). Educating healthcare professionals on AI in Alzheimer's disease. In *AI-Driven Alzheimer's Disease Detection and Prediction* (pp. 372–388). IGI Global., DOI: 10.4018/979-8-3693-3605-2.ch024

Singh, S., Gambill, J. L., Attalla, M., Fatima, R., Gill, A. R., & Siddiqui, H. F. (2024). Evaluating the clinical validity and reliability of artificial intelligence-enabled diagnostic tools in neuropsychiatric disorders. *Cureus*, 16(10), e71651. DOI: 10.7759/cureus.71651 PMID: 39553014

Srinivasan, S., & Rajavel, N. (2025). Artificial intelligence approach to psychological wellbeing among the ageing population. In *AI Technologies and Advancements for Psychological Well-Being and Healthcare* (pp. 187–218). IGI Global., DOI: 10.4018/978-1-7998-9516-5

Tariq, M. U. (2024). The role of AI in skilling, upskilling, and reskilling the workforce. In Doshi, R., Dadhich, M., Poddar, S., & Hiran, K. (Eds.), *Integrating generative AI in education to achieve sustainable development goals* (pp. 421–433). IGI Global., DOI: 10.4018/979-8-3693-2440-0.ch023

Tariq, M. U. (2024). AI and the future of talent management: Transforming recruitment and retention with machine learning. In Christiansen, B., Aziz, M., & O'Keeffe, E. (Eds.), *Global practices on effective talent acquisition and retention* (pp. 1–16). IGI Global., DOI: 10.4018/979-8-3693-1938-3.ch001

Tariq, M. U. (2024). Application of blockchain and Internet of Things (IoT) in modern business. In Sinha, M., Bhandari, A., Priya, S., & Kabiraj, S. (Eds.), *Future of customer engagement through marketing intelligence* (pp. 66–94). IGI Global., DOI: 10.4018/979-8-3693-2367-0.ch004

Tariq, M. U. (2024). The role of AI ethics in cost and complexity reduction. In Tennin, K., Ray, S., & Sorg, J. (Eds.), *Cases on AI ethics in business* (pp. 59–78). IGI Global., DOI: 10.4018/979-8-3693-2643-5.ch004

Tariq, M. U. (2025). The Belmont Report: Guiding Ethical Principles in Human Research. In Throne, R. (Ed.), *IRB, Human Research Protections, and Data Ethics for Researchers* (pp. 245–268). IGI Global Scientific Publishing., DOI: 10.4018/979-8-3693-3848-3.ch010

Tariq, M. U., & Sergio, R. P. (2025). Ethical Considerations and Social Impact of AI and Computational Intelligence in Society 5.0. In Pandey, R., Srivastava, N., Prasad, R., Prasad, J., & Garcia, M. (Eds.), *Open AI and Computational Intelligence for Society 5.0* (pp. 225–248). IGI Global Scientific Publishing., DOI: 10.4018/979-8-3693-4326-5.ch010

Tariq, M. U., & Sergio, R. P. (2025). Nurturing Digital Citizenship in Society 5.0 Through AI and Computational Intelligence Education. In Pandey, R., Srivastava, N., Prasad, R., Prasad, J., & Garcia, M. (Eds.), *Open AI and Computational Intelligence for Society 5.0* (pp. 59–84). IGI Global Scientific Publishing., DOI: 10.4018/979-8-3693-4326-5.ch003

Wei, L. (2023). Artificial intelligence in language instruction: Impact on English learning achievement, L2 motivation, and self-regulated learning. *Frontiers in Psychology*, 14, 1261955. DOI: 10.3389/fpsyg.2023.1261955 PMID: 38023040

Zafar, F., Alam, L. S., Rauf, S., & Usman, M. (2024). Advancing neuropsychology: Artificial intelligence models for detecting neurodegenerative diseases. *Brain Sciences*, 14(2), 199. DOI: 10.3390/brainsci14020199

Zhao, H., Wu, S., & Li, C. (2023). Exploring AI solutions for personalized neuropsychological rehabilitation in the elderly population. *Journal of Neural Engineering*, 20(4), 046029. DOI: 10.1088/1741-2552/ad618b PMID: 37336205

KEY TERMS AND DEFINITIONS

Artificial Intelligence (AI): The simulation of human intelligence processes by computer systems, particularly for tasks like problem-solving and learning in neuropsychology.

Cognitive Rehabilitation: Therapeutic interventions aimed at restoring or compensating for cognitive impairments caused by neurological conditions.

Machine Learning (ML): A subset of AI focused on developing algorithms that allow systems to learn and improve from data without explicit programming.

Neuroimaging: The use of imaging technologies like MRI or PET scans to study brain structure and function, often enhanced by AI for detailed analysis.

Predictive Analytics: The use of data, statistical algorithms, and ML techniques to predict future outcomes, such as cognitive decline or treatment success.

Chapter 4
Integration of AI With ML for Neuropsychological Applications

Prabhjeet Kaur
Lovely Professional University, India

Channni Sachdeva
https://orcid.org/0000-0002-6202-7044
Lovely Professional University, India

Ravi Kumar Gupta
Maharaja Agrasen Institute of Technology, Delhi, India

Lokesh Jasrai
https://orcid.org/0000-0001-9784-9753
Lovely Professional University, India

ABSTRACT

This chapter examines how Artificial Intelligence (AI) and Machine Learning (ML) are being used in neuropsychology, focusing on how they can significantly improve the study and treatment of cognitive issues like Mild Cognitive Impairment (MCI) and Alzheimer's Disease (AD). Traditional methods in neuropsychology often depend on subjective evaluations, which can reduce the accuracy of diagnoses and delay necessary treatments. AI and ML use large amounts of data to find early signs of cognitive problems and provide better predictive analysis, helping with early detection and more accurate treatment. From a research standpoint, AI offers new tools to examine complex data from brain scans, genetic information, and behaviour tests. Machine learning can identify patterns that suggest how diseases might progress,

DOI: 10.4018/979-8-3693-9341-3.ch004

which could lead to important discoveries in finding markers for diseases and creating treatments tailored to individual patients. The chapter indicates that more research should focus on making AI systems fair and easy to understand and using them in many medical situations.

INTRODUCTION

Integrating AI and ML into neuropsychology opened a more comprehensive ground in diagnosing and treating CNS disorders like MCI and AD (Haraldsen et al., 2024). During the current aspiration to cater to different market needs because of the rapidly aging population worldwide, The growth of these systems' accessibility means that the identification and subsequent handling of these conditions will prove to be difficult on a massive scale (Aboukadri et al., 2024). These assessments may also be slow processes and laborious and can differ from one clinician to another. Modern approaches using AI and ML capabilities can disrupt the existing approaches to diagnostic accuracy enhancement, assessment solutions, and personalised treatment (Zahra et al., 2024). The importance of innovation in neuropsychological science conditions such as MCI and Alzheimer's disease presents many complexities to healthcare systems (Ali et al., 2024). MCI is thought to be a prodromal form of dementia and is characterized by a clear-cut cognitive deficit that fails to cause substantial loss of independence. On the other hand, AD is a progressive neurodegenerative disease that propagates pain in memory. It affects the thought process and the ability to carry out mundane activities independently. These conditions must be identified early since early stages mean treatment could help slow the advancement of such diseases or improve patients' lives. However, surprisingly, it seems that it often lacks rationality to diagnose them through the standardized objective criteria since they seem to suffer from periodically subjective assessment and clinical discretion, making it rather sporadic and delayed. These studies have provided evidence that widely used and standardized neuropsychological screening measures allow for a limited understanding of cognitive decline. For instance, the current commonplace standard assessment, namely Mini-Mental State Examination-MMSE, might omit primary relatively minor variations that predict MCI or AD onset. This makes it necessary to have a better diagnostic tool capable of discriminating the patients' cognitive health status from various patterned data.

The Role of AI and ML in Neuropsychology

AI is, therefore, a cluster of technologies aimed at making computers imitate those human skills needed to learn, reason, and solve problems. In this domain, ML is particularly interested in algorithms that enable a system to get better at what it does without being directly programmed. Such technologies can readily evaluate mass data to find correlations with cognitive deficits within neuropsychology. The information process capabilities of AI point to the potential for augmenting neuropsychological testing (Medenica et al., 2024). AI systems can collect neuropsychological test results, a patient's medical history, neuroimaging, and even genetic data to determine an individual's overall cognition data federation. (Carrarini et al., 2024). Such an approach helps clinicians make better decisions about diagnosis or treatment in a case.

Enhancing Diagnostic Accuracy

Currently, there is no question that the use of AI in neuropsychology is most relevant for enhancing diagnostic reliability. It is possible to develop algorithms where the machine is fed a large amount of data, including information about the patient's history, to recognise biomarkers characteristic of MCI or AD. For instance, an article provided diverse examples where AI-based models used neuroimaging datasets like MRI or PET (Bacon et al., 2024). This also provided diverse examples where AI-based models used neuroimaging datasets like MRI or PET scans to identify early structural and functional alterations in the brain before trademark symptoms appear (Panda et al., 2024). These advancements not only improved the reliability of diagnostics but also shortened the time for diagnosis so the clinicians would have more time to handle the patients rather than filling the forms (Hager et al., 2024).

Personalizing Treatment Plans

It also enables the further expansion of AI with ML to create a specific patient treatment approach. When utilizing detailed patient information such as age, medical history, and even neuropsychological scores, AI can identify treatment outcomes given an individual's cognitive map (Spiegel et al., 2024). This individualisation increases the effectiveness of interventions while at the same time increasing patient participation as they become an active part in decisions regarding their health. In addition, using AI technologies enables progress tracking and making necessary changes without waiting for scheduled reviews. This flexibility is especially important for states such as depression and anxiety because its effectiveness differs significantly from one patient to another. (Delgado et al., 2024). Using AI technologies means that healthcare providers can provide effective treatments and those that patients need now. (Mennella et al., 2024).

Related Literature and Proposed Framework

However, some issues must be solved when AI applications are used in neuropsychological approaches. Developing explainable AI, meaning systems that must explain their actions to clinicians is critical. Although AI algorithms continue to become more sophisticated, it is equally important to ensure that healthcare professionals understand the results generated by such algorithms. Another challenge is the incorporation of ethical issues about data privacy. Sensitive patient data require that privacy rules should be followed to the letter to balance individual rights when using AI technology (Khatiwada et al., 2024)Moreover, algorithmic bias arises and may be dangerous because AI systems trained using videos may not balance various people. Rarely is the development of new technologies and applications focused on equalizing the disparities across the different groups in health care.

Clinical Studies

Case Study 1: Early Detection Using Machine Learning Algorithms

A study by (Zhang et al., 2024) looked into the capability of machine learning algorithms to diagnose mild cognitive impairment much earlier than conventionally. Most current tests demand that an operator be present and work "hands-on" to enforce the required stimuli and record the necessary responses. The human element naturally limits the amount of test data gathered over time and the number of times a given elderly individual can be re-tested during declining cognitive function. For their study, Zhang et al. received much more liberally gathered test data from a cohort of 500 healthy and impaired elderly individuals who were both neuropsychologically examined and machine-learned. Although the human operators were no doubt vital for the initial setup and assuring the test environment's integrity, the tests' outcomes were much less human-controlled and directive than precedents.

Case Study 2: Personalized Treatment Plans for Alzheimer's Patients

In another prominent investigation by (Lee et al., 2024), researchers examined the use of machine learning in formulating tailored treatment plans for Alzheimer's patients. The study spanned 300 subjects and employed a range of treatments from both the pharmacological and cognitive domains. Patient data includes genetic information, previous treatment responses, and neuropsychological assessments. The researchers constructed a model capable of predicting the potency of different treatment combinations for each subject. The advised plan was then compared against a rigged, one-size-fits-all protocol. After six months, not only was the experimental group in much better shape than the control group but the model's hit rate was also judged to have improved the cognitive scores by a stunning 30 per cent.

Case Study 3: Virtual Reality in Cognitive Assessment

Researchers tested virtual reality (VR) environments with machine learning algorithms to assess executive function in MCI patients. They created a VR platform that simulated real-life scenarios that required decision-making, such as shopping or navigating public transportation. (Lu et al., 2024). Participants completed traditional neuropsychological tests and VR tasks, and their performance was analysed through machine learning models trained on the behavioural data collected during these assessments. (Xue et al., 2024). The results showed that VR assessments provided more data on executive function than traditional tests alone. The machine learning algorithms identified specific deficits with an accuracy rate of over 85%. This case shows how combining cutting-edge tech like VR with AI can give us more insight into cognitive function. (Mittal & Bansal, 2023) and improve diagnosis(Mittal & Bansal, 2023).

Case Study 4: Monitoring Progress with Wearable Technology

The study of (Addae et al., 2024) looked at how wearable technology and machine learning could be used to monitor cognitive function in the homes of older adults. 200 participants wore devices that tracked physical activity and sleep patterns and completed cognitive assessments through mobile apps (Ceyhan et al., 2024). Machine learning models were used to analyse data from wearables and traditional neuropsychological tests over 6 months. Results showed physical activity levels correlated strongly with changes in cognitive performance, so predictive analytics could be used to identify potential decline before it becomes clinically apparent. This case shows how wearable technology and AI-driven analytics can be used to monitor and intervene with individuals at risk of cognitive decline. Another research examines how augmented reality and virtual reality can improve customer interaction. It looks at the difficulties in using these technologies, which mix the virtual world with the real world to create an engaging experience (Bansal et al., 2023).

AI and ML in Neuropsychology Future Directions

AI and ML in neuropsychology are still in their infancy but have enormous potential to change the diagnosis and treatment of MCI and AD. Here are some key directions to make these technologies more effective and practical in the clinic.

Better Diagnostic Tools

One key direction is the development of diagnostic tools that use AI and ML to give real-time assessments of cognitive health. (Chudzik et al., 2024). These tools can integrate data from multiple sources - neuropsychological tests, neuroimaging, genetic information, lifestyle factors etc (Dzianok & Kublik, 2024). By using complex algorithms to analyze the data, clinicians can get a more complete picture of the patient's cognitive profile using a cognitive dissonance approach (Sachdeva, Grover, & Gangwar, 2024). This will improve diagnostic accuracy and enable early detection of cognitive impairments so that interventions can be done on time. From a marketing perspective, where customers are the focus, how people shop is changing quickly, especially with new tech like smartphones becoming important. The internet makes things simple, so companies use online marketing to reach younger people for shopping. This shows that smart devices will be part of healthcare products that are cheaper and available to everyone (Painoli et al., 2021).

Long-term Research for Better Predictive Analysis

Long-term research will be necessary to check how well AI-based diagnosis tools and treatment plans work (Agrawal & Vagha, 2024), such as in cases of prostate cancer. By tracking patients for a long time, scientists can collect information on how thinking skills change due to different treatments. This information can be used to improve machine learning models, making them better at predicting outcomes. Such research could also help find signs showing when thinking skills might start to get worse, giving us useful information about how diseases develop and how to prevent them. This step also evolves the dimensions of meta-analysis for application to sustain in the competitive marketing world with the help of media influencers. (Ao et al., 2023).

Working Together Across Different Fields

To effectively combine AI and machine learning with neuropsychology, experts from various fields, such as neuropsychologists, data scientists, software developers, and ethicists, need to work together. This teamwork will ensure that new technologies are practical for real-world use and consider important issues like data privacy and algorithm fairness. (Rezaei et al., 2024). By collaborating, these professionals can create tools that are not only useful but also fair and available to people from different backgrounds.

Emphasising Clarity and Openness

As AI systems grow more advanced, making them transparent and easy to understand will be crucial. Clinicians need to trust AI recommendations fully, so they must understand how these systems reach their conclusions. Future research should focus on creating AI models that clearly explain their decision-making processes. This openness will help build trust and ensure that AI is used responsibly.

Benefits of AI and Machine Learning in Neuropsychology

Improved Precision and Speed: AI and Machine Learning can examine vast amounts of data and spot patterns humans might overlook, resulting in more precise diagnoses and treatment strategies. Artificial intelligence and intense learning are changing medicine by improving image analysis, streamlining processes, and enhancing patient care. But there are still challenges, such as bias, privacy concerns, security issues, and a lack of transparency. Although we expect gains in accuracy, efficiency, and workflow, the effect on the doctor-patient relationship is still unclear. (Topol, 2019).
Unbiased Evaluation: AI-driven tools can minimise personal biases in neuropsychological evaluations, ensuring more consistent and dependable results. The study also shows that implementing these evolutionary applications can be challenging.
Early Identification: AI can detect early indicators of cognitive decline or neurodegenerative diseases, allowing for prompt intervention. The study of (Seelye et al., 2012) examines how cognitive rehabilitation principles can be used to create helpful technology for older adults with cognitive difficulties. It claims that cognitive rehabilitation theory (CRT) can lead the development of these technologies and that analyzing current innovative prompting tools can address important questions related to employee performance in any industry.
Customised Treatment: By analyzing individual patient information, AI can create personalised treatment plans that meet specific needs, leading to better results. This research examines how artificial intelligence can improve patient interaction, looking at the tools used, the challenges faced, and what the future might hold. Using information from different sources adds to what we know

about AI's role in patient-based engagement and provides insights for pharmaceuticals-based marketers and researchers in this field (Bansal et al., 2022). *Remote Services*: AI-driven tools can enable remote neuropsychological evaluations, making these services available to people in areas with limited access to healthcare.

Challenges of AI and ML in Neuropsychology

Privacy Issues: Gathering and keeping large amounts of personal patient information can lead to privacy and security problems.
Bias in Algorithms: AI systems can carry forward biases found in the data they are trained on, resulting in incorrect or unfair results. The commercialisation of healthcare products does raise questions about algorithm biases (Sachdeva, Grover, Kaur, et al., 2024).
Absence of Human Connection: AI cannot completely substitute the human aspect in therapy, which is crucial for establishing trust and a good relationship with patients. This also applies to the healthcare industry, where working conditions are much more complex. The study of (Sachdeva, Gangwar, et al., 2024) examines the mental discomfort experienced by employees in the working sector as they adapt to the integration of artificial intelligence. It uses methods and numerical analysis to understand the intricate factors influencing how people think and work in this new environment.
High Implementation Costs: Creating and using AI tools for neuropsychology can be costly. In today's digital world, neuropsychologists are using new technologies to learn more about how the brain works and how people behave, feel, and interact with others. The National Institutes of Health (NIH) is working on combining neuroscience with behavioural and social sciences, improving measurement methods, and creating digital tools for helping people. These new ways to study the brain and behaviour stressing the importance of developing these methods while keeping ethical and legal rules in mind for neuropsychological research (Parsons & Duffield, 2020).
Ethical Concerns: Using AI in healthcare raises ethical issues about responsibility, openness, and the possibility of job loss. These aspects highlight the majority of concerns regarding the influence of AI on human ethics in the medical field of research. (Sachdeva & Grover, 2024).

CONCLUSION

Combining artificial intelligence (AI) and machine learning (ML) with neuropsychology offers significant chances to improve how we diagnose, treat, and manage cognitive issues like Mild Cognitive Impairment (MCI) and Alzheimer's Disease (AD). By examining large amounts of data and spotting small patterns that human experts might miss, AI tools can provide a level of accuracy and personalisation that was not possible before in cognitive healthcare. However, this potential also brings complex challenges that need careful thought and strategic solutions to ensure the technology is used ethically, fairly, and effectively.

Artificial Intelligence (AI) and Machine Learning (ML) have significantly transformed neuropsychology by helping to spot early signs of cognitive decline and providing tailored healthcare options. By analysing large amounts of data, AI can detect small changes in speech, walking, and facial expressions, which could help slow disease development and improve patient results. However, combining AI and ML with neuropsychology has difficulties, like protecting data privacy and security and dealing with biased algorithms. Robust encryption techniques, distributed data storage systems, and worldwide data protection rules are crucial to keeping data safe and private.

Incorporating AI and machine learning into neuropsychology is a significant change that could revolutionise how we diagnose and treat cognitive issues. However, we must consider ethical issues like patient consent, how easy it is to understand AI, and being too dependent on automated systems. Clear communication with patients and others is essential to keep their trust and ensure everyone is accountable. Future work should aim to create AI models that neuropsychologists can easily understand and use in daily tasks. It's also essential to deal with the limits of computer resources and ensure AI technology is available in places with fewer resources. By making AI accessible to understand, being inclusive, and working together across different fields, we can responsibly innovate in this area and improve patient care and healthcare efficiency.

ACKNOWLEDGMENT

All authors conceptualise ideas mutually.

REFERENCES

Aboukadri, S., Ouaddah, A., & Mezrioui, A. (2024). Machine learning in identity and access management systems: Survey and deep dive. *Computers & Security*, 139, 103729. DOI: 10.1016/j.cose.2024.103729

Addae, S., Kim, J., Smith, A., Kang, M., & Rajana, P. (2024). Smart Solutions for Detecting, Predicting, Monitoring, and Managing Dementia in the Elderly: A Survey. *IEEE Access : Practical Innovations, Open Solutions*, 12, 100026–100056. DOI: 10.1109/ACCESS.2024.3421966

Agrawal, S., & Vagha, S. (2024). A Comprehensive Review of Artificial Intelligence in Prostate Cancer Care: State-of-the-Art Diagnostic Tools and Future Outlook. *Cureus*, 16(8). Advance online publication. DOI: 10.7759/cureus.66225 PMID: 39238711

Ali, M. T., Turetta, C., Pravadelli, G., & Demrozi, F. (2024). ICT-based solutions for Alzheimer's Disease Care: A systematic review. *IEEE Access : Practical Innovations, Open Solutions*, 12, 13944–13961. DOI: 10.1109/ACCESS.2024.3356348

Ao, L., Bansal, R., Pruthi, N., & Khaskheli, M. B. (2023). Impact of social media influencers on customer engagement and purchase intention: A meta-analysis. *Sustainability (Basel)*, 15(3), 2744. DOI: 10.3390/su15032744

Bacon, E. J., He, D., Wang, L., Li, H., Yao-Digba, P. D. Z., Monkam, P., & Qi, S. (2024). Neuroimage analysis using artificial intelligence approaches: A systematic review. *Medical & Biological Engineering & Computing*, 62(9), 1–29. DOI: 10.1007/s11517-024-03097-w PMID: 38664348

Bansal, R., Pruthi, N., & Singh, R. (2022). Developing customer engagement through artificial intelligence tools: roles and challenges. In *Developing Relationships, Personalization, and Data Herald in Marketing 5.0* (pp. 130-145). IGI Global. DOI: 10.4018/978-1-6684-4496-2.ch008

Bansal, R., Shukla, G., Gupta, A., Singh, A., & Pruthi, N. (2023). Optimizing Augmented Reality and Virtual Reality for Customer Engagement. In *Promoting Consumer Engagement Through Emotional Branding and Sensory Marketing* (pp. 24–35). IGI Global.

Carrarini, C., Nardulli, C., Titti, L., Iodice, F., Miraglia, F., Vecchio, F., & Rossini, P. M. (2024). Neuropsychological and electrophysiological measurements for diagnosis and prediction of dementia: A review on machine learning approach. *Ageing Research Reviews*, 100, 102417. DOI: 10.1016/j.arr.2024.102417 PMID: 39002643

Ceyhan, B., Bek, S., & Onal-Suzek, T. (2024). Smart Wristband Monitoring: A Caregiver-Oriented Mobile Application for Tracking Cognitive Decline in Mild Cognitive Impairment Patients. medRxiv, 2024.2005. 2031.24307874. DOI: 10.1101/2024.05.31.24307874

Chudzik, A., Śledzianowski, A., & Przybyszewski, A. W. (2024). Machine learning and digital biomarkers can detect early stages of neurodegenerative diseases. *Sensors (Basel)*, 24(5), 1572. DOI: 10.3390/s24051572 PMID: 38475108

Delgado, S., Vignola, R. C. B., Sassi, R. J., Belan, P. A., & de Araújo, S. A. (2024). Symptom mapping and personalized care for depression, anxiety and stress: A data-driven AI approach. *Computers in Biology and Medicine*, 182, 109146. DOI: 10.1016/j.compbiomed.2024.109146 PMID: 39265480

Dzianok, P., & Kublik, E. (2024). PEARL-Neuro Database: EEG, fMRI, health and lifestyle data of middle-aged people at risk of dementia. *Scientific Data*, 11(1), 276. DOI: 10.1038/s41597-024-03106-5 PMID: 38453963

Hager, P., Jungmann, F., Holland, R., Bhagat, K., Hubrecht, I., Knauer, M., Vielhauer, J., Makowski, M., Braren, R., Kaissis, G., & Rueckert, D. (2024). Evaluation and mitigation of the limitations of large language models in clinical decision-making. *Nature Medicine*, 30(9), 2613–2622. DOI: 10.1038/s41591-024-03097-1 PMID: 38965432

Haraldsen, I. H., Hatlestad-Hall, C., Marra, C., Renvall, H., Maestú, F., Acosta-Hernández, J., Alfonsin, S., Andersson, V., Anand, A., Ayllón, V., Babic, A., Belhadi, A., Birck, C., Bruña, R., Caraglia, N., Carrarini, C., Christensen, E., Cicchetti, A., Daugbjerg, S., & Rossini, P. M. (2024). Intelligent digital tools for screening of brain connectivity and dementia risk estimation in people affected by mild cognitive impairment: The AI-Mind clinical study protocol. *Frontiers in Neurorobotics*, 17, 1289406. DOI: 10.3389/fnbot.2023.1289406 PMID: 38250599

Khatiwada, P., Yang, B., Lin, J.-C., & Blobel, B. (2024). Patient-Generated Health Data (PGHD): Understanding, Requirements, Challenges, and Existing Techniques for Data Security and Privacy. *Journal of Personalized Medicine*, 14(3), 282. DOI: 10.3390/jpm14030282 PMID: 38541024

Lee, L. Y., Vaghari, D., Burkhart, M. C., Tino, P., Montagnese, M., Li, Z., Zühlsdorff, K., Giorgio, J., Williams, G., Chong, E., Chen, C., Underwood, B. R., Rittman, T., & Kourtzi, Z. (2024). Robust and interpretable AI-guided marker for early dementia prediction in real-world clinical settings. *EClinicalMedicine*, 74, 74. DOI: 10.1016/j.eclinm.2024.102725

Lu, Z., Seo, J. H., Khandan, P., Maxa, T., Garcia-Pi, B., & Wells-Beede, E. (2024). The work behind an interdisciplinary team: Creating a postpartum hemorrhage virtual reality training platform. *Clinical Simulation in Nursing*, 94, 101595. DOI: 10.1016/j.ecns.2024.101595

Medenica, V., Ivanovic, L., & Milosevic, N. (2024). Applicability of artificial intelligence in neuropsychological rehabilitation of patients with brain injury. *Applied Neuropsychology. Adult*, •••, 1–28. DOI: 10.1080/23279095.2024.2364229 PMID: 38912923

Mennella, C., Maniscalco, U., De Pietro, G., & Esposito, M. (2024). Ethical and regulatory challenges of AI technologies in healthcare: A narrative review. *Heliyon*, 10(4), e26297. DOI: 10.1016/j.heliyon.2024.e26297 PMID: 38384518

Mittal, G., & Bansal, R. (2023). Driving force behind consumer brand engagement: the metaverse. In *Cultural marketing and metaverse for consumer engagement* (pp. 164–181). IGI Global. DOI: 10.4018/978-1-6684-8312-1.ch012

Painoli, A. K., Bansal, R., Singh, R., & Kukreti, A. (2021). Impact of digital marketing on the buying behavior of youth with special reference to Uttarakhand state. In *Big data analytics for improved accuracy, efficiency, and decision making in digital marketing* (pp. 162–182). IGI Global. DOI: 10.4018/978-1-7998-7231-3.ch012

Panda, M., Abraham, A., Gopi, B., & Ajith, R. (2024). *Computational Intelligence for Oncology and Neurological Disorders: Current Practices and Future Directions*. CRC Press. DOI: 10.1201/9781003450153

Parsons, T., & Duffield, T. (2020). Paradigm shift toward digital neuropsychology and high-dimensional neuropsychological assessments. *Journal of Medical Internet Research*, 22(12), e23777. DOI: 10.2196/23777 PMID: 33325829

Rezaei, M., Pironti, M., & Quaglia, R. (2024). AI in knowledge sharing, which ethical challenges are raised in decision-making processes for organisations? *Management Decision*. Advance online publication. DOI: 10.1108/MD-10-2023-2023

Sachdeva, C., Gangwar, V. P., Grover, V., & Gochhait, S. (2024). Cognitive Dissonance in Banking Employees: Exploring Factors Amid the Artificial Intelligence Revolution. 2024 ASU International Conference in Emerging Technologies for Sustainability and Intelligent Systems (ICETSIS), Sachdeva, C., & Grover, V. (2024). Balancing Technology and Humanity: Perspectives on AI in Healthcare. In *Analyzing Explainable AI in Healthcare and the Pharmaceutical Industry* (pp. 1-12). IGI Global.

Sachdeva, C., Grover, V., & Gangwar, V. P. (2024). Business Science Dynamics: Unraveling Cognitive Dissonance for Innovation. *Unleashing the Power of Basic Science in Business*, 212-221.

Sachdeva, C., Grover, V., Kaur, P., & Gangwar, V. P. (2024). Regulatory Landscapes: Navigating Compliance in the Commercialization of Basic Science. In *Unleashing the Power of Basic Science in Business* (pp. 118-137). IGI Global.

Seelye, A. M., Schmitter-Edgecombe, M., Das, B., & Cook, D. J. (2012). Application of cognitive rehabilitation theory to the development of smart prompting technologies. *IEEE Reviews in Biomedical Engineering*, 5, 29–44. DOI: 10.1109/RBME.2012.2196691 PMID: 23231987

Spiegel, B. M., Liran, O., Clark, A., Samaan, J. S., Khalil, C., Chernoff, R., Reddy, K., & Mehra, M. (2024). Feasibility of combining spatial computing and AI for mental health support in anxiety and depression. *NPJ Digital Medicine*, 7(1), 22. DOI: 10.1038/s41746-024-01011-0 PMID: 38279034

Topol, E. J. (2019). High-performance medicine: The convergence of human and artificial intelligence. *Nature Medicine*, 25(1), 44–56. DOI: 10.1038/s41591-018-0300-7 PMID: 30617339

Xue, C., Li, A., Wu, R., Chai, J., Qiang, Y., Zhao, J., & Yang, Q. (2024). VRNPT: A neuropsychological test tool for diagnosing mild cognitive impairment using virtual reality and EEG signals. *International Journal of Human-Computer Interaction*, 40(20), 6268–6286. DOI: 10.1080/10447318.2023.2250605

Zahra, M. A., Al-Taher, A., Alquhaidan, M., Hussain, T., Ismail, I., Raya, I., & Kandeel, M. (2024). The synergy of artificial intelligence and personalized medicine for the enhanced diagnosis, treatment, and prevention of disease. *Drug Metabolism and Personalized Therapy*, 39(2), 47–58. DOI: 10.1515/dmpt-2024-0003 PMID: 38997240

Zhang, X., Fan, H., Guo, C., Li, Y., Han, X., Xu, Y., Wang, H., & Zhang, T. (2024). Establishment of a mild cognitive impairment risk model in middle-aged and older adults: A longitudinal study. *Neurological Sciences*, 45(9), 1–10. DOI: 10.1007/s10072-024-07536-2 PMID: 38642322

Chapter 5
Transforming Minds AI and Machine Learning Applications in Cognitive Neuroscience

Yamijala Suryanarayana Murthy
https://orcid.org/0000-0002-9561-5395
Vardhaman College Engineering, India

Rohit Bansal
https://orcid.org/0000-0001-7072-5005
Vaish College of Engineering, Rohtak, India

R. S. Ch. Murthy Chodisetty
https://orcid.org/0000-0001-6222-0373
Vardhaman College of Engineering, India

Chandresh Chakravorty
https://orcid.org/0009-0000-8700-4538
Vardhaman College of Engineering, India

K. Pardha Sai
https://orcid.org/0009-0001-6692-3022
Aditya University, India

ABSTRACT

Through their unique capabilities in analysing mental and behavioral data AI and ML transform the field of cognitive neuroscience. MRI and fMRI rely on AI to reliably identify memory troubles and also boost the early recognition of neurodegenerative

DOI: 10.4018/979-8-3693-9341-3.ch005

disorders like Alzheimer's and Parkinson's. cognitive rehabilitation programs that utilize AI improve therapy results by responding instantly to individual needs. By using AI to power, them interfaces allow neural patterns to link with outside tools and offer fresh treatment methods for those who are mentally challenged. Psychological evaluations and treatments are upgrade their reliability as a result of AI's method to analyze emotional states and behaviours. Machine learning and AI are changing the field of cognitive neuroscience by improving diagnostics treatment and rehabilitation of many cognitive disorders.

INTRODUCTION

By utilizing neuroscience and psychology together, cognitive neuroscience investigates the mental processes and behaviours rooted in the brain (Smith & Kosslyn, 2021). It examines the mechanisms by which the brain encodes perception, memory, language, and judgment (Gazzaniga, Ivry, & Mangun, 2020). By applying cutting-edge neuroimaging tools like fMRI and EEG to study brain activity in real time, researchers uncover the interplay of brain regions in forming complex mental activities (Poldrack et al., 2019). The understanding of human cognition has considerably grown due to detailed brain mapping, which is actively examined (Toga & Thompson, 2022). Both AI and ML have spurred advances in cognitive neuroscience in the last few years (LeCun et al., 2020).

Previously, neuroscientists relied on labor-intensive and inaccurate methods to assess neural data, but AI and ML simplify the tracking of patterns in voluminous datasets, thereby increasing both validity and speed (Cichy & Kaiser, 2019). By using these technologies, neural data patterns can be discovered that statistical tools frequently do not identify (Esteva et al., 2021). The use of AI and ML in examining neural data is especially important when its volume and complexity rise (Fan et al., 2020). In neuroscience, neuroimaging and electrophysiology capture significant data in substantial quantities (Friston, 2021). These datasets pose challenges for typical analysis methods because of their noise and fluctuation, but machine learning algorithms uncover important patterns in this data and provide forecasts based on its structure (Eickenberg et al., 2017).

In cognitive neuroscience, AI and ML are crucial due to their unique strengths. AI and ML can create models for neural activities and predict cognitive traits that alter cognitive neuroscience (Hassabis et al., 2021). Deep learning models have extracted insights about mental processes from fMRI signals to uncover the brain's representation of separate ideas and feelings (Yamins & DiCarlo, 2016). These models provide mechanisms for researchers to explore brain circuit dynamics through neural simulation in controlled conditions, clarifying the understanding of neuronal plasticity and brain disorders, allowing advancements in neurorehabilitation (Ritter et al., 2020).

This study analyzes the transformation of cognitive neuroscience through neural data analysis and brain function modeling using AI and ML (Güçlü & van Gerven, 2015). The use of AI and ML techniques advances work in neuroimaging analysis and BCIs for understanding brain diseases and states of consciousness (He et al., 2020). Furthermore, this paper investigates the ethical concerns of AI in neuroscience along with its boundaries (Russell et al., 2020). In cognitive neuroscience, AI and ML redefine our approach to studying the brain. As these innovations advance, their insights into the workings of neurons will enhance new research and clinical possibilities (Li et al., 2021). The next sections will investigate how AI and ML improve understanding in various cognitive neuroscience areas.

Theoretical Background

By analysing complex neurological data with Artificial Intelligence and Machine Learning algorithms can discover alternative ways to investigate brain workings. By leveraging AI methods MRI and fMRI streamline the mapping process of brain activity and disclose neural patterns and diseases. To extract relevant information from these large datasets AI implementations, depend on machine learning algorithms. Using AI to predict cognitive decline leads to important consequences for the diagnosis and therapy of neurodegenerative disorders. Taking advantage of AI enables BCIs to conduct real-time interaction between neural signals and devices that open avenues for new approaches to cognitive impairment therapy. Predictive capacities from AI enhance cognitive function and neuroplasticity ideas for personalized cognitive therapy that adjust to patient needs. By applying AI and ML to cognitive neuroscience theories are reforming our understanding of brain functions leading to personalized diagnosis and care.

Background of Cognitive Neuroscience

The study of cognitive neuroscience integrates brain activities with cognitive abilities such as responding and remembering (Gazzaniga, Ivry, & Mangun, 2020). Psychology and neurology also join forces with computational modeling to illustrate how brain systems produce mental functions (Mittal & Bansal, 2023). The focus of cognitive neuroscience is on how the brain acts upon information and interprets surroundings (Ao et al., 2023). This research explores the neuroanatomy of the brain and its activities to interpret how nerve pathways allow for intricate cognitive practices (Bansal, Pruthi, & Singh, 2022). Cognitive neuroscience studies the organic origins of mental activities. The principal focus is to examine how varied brain areas perform tasks and how neurons interact while portraying how these actions influence behavior (Bansal et al., 2023).

Tasks related to memory explore the function of the hippocampus for storage and access of information, while studies of attention examine how the brain disregards unwanted inputs to enhance the flow of important information (Painoli et al., 2021). Recognizing these systems facilitates the comprehension of normal cognitive functioning and may help treat disorders such as Alzheimer's, ADHD, and schizophrenia (Smith & Kosslyn, 2021). Neural imaging devices, including fMRI and EEG, are utilized in cognitive neuroscience. By analyzing brain activity in real-time, researchers can reveal cognitive task boundaries through these methods (Gazzaniga et al., 2020). Monitoring brain electrical patterns with precise timing using EEG delivers insights into cognitive acts like attention volatilities and memory consolidation (Mittal & Bansal, 2023).

Historically, in cognitive neuroscience, behavioral evaluation has aided neuroimaging techniques (Bansal et al., 2022). Investigators conduct tests to connect mental processes with response times and task performance accuracy (Ao et al., 2023). By utilizing imaging and testing methods, cognitive neuroscientists relate brain areas to cognitive abilities (Bansal, Shukla et al., 2023). This roundabout approach enables a clearer understanding of how the brain generates ideas and feelings while highlighting key facts about mental wellness and capacities (Gazzaniga et al., 2020).

AI AND MACHINE LEARNING

Through AI and ML capabilities, computers learn and analyze vast datasets, significantly changing numerous fields (LeCun et al., 2020). To build AI technologies means addressing difficulties and recognizing recurring elements (Russell & Norvig, 2020). Using algorithms and statistics, machine learning works to boost system capabilities from collected data or expertise (Li et al., 2021). Such technologies demonstrate superiority when it comes to working with difficult and high-dimensional datasets, like those representative of neuroscience research, which basic techniques find difficult to handle (Shen et al., 2017). Big neuroimaging datasets, such as fMRI and EEG, require AI and ML to function smoothly (He et al., 2020). Analyzing complex brain activity in these datasets does not work well with standard statistical techniques (Fan et al., 2020).

By using ML algorithms to analyze brain activity, researchers can identify patterns, classify neural states, and anticipate cognitive effects (Esteva et al., 2021). Neural networks that learn to recognize brain activation linked to cognitive tasks enable researchers to study brain interactions (Jiang et al., 2020). AI and ML offer knowledge gained from data, exposing connections in neuroscience that may otherwise remain unconsidered (Hassabis et al., 2021). Algorithms based on machine learning locate unrecognized data arrangements without specific models, facilitating the examination of complex interactions in the brain's neuron network (Stober et al., 2017). This adaptability is crucial for detecting information about cognition or brain illnesses (Wang et al., 2019).

Using ML models allows researchers to anticipate Alzheimer's disease by studying small modifications in neural connections long before symptoms arise (Zhou et al., 2020). AI and ML make personalized care possible in neurological health (Schirrmeister et al., 2017). Machine learning techniques process patient neurological information to reveal biomarkers or cognitive traits, enabling the development of treatment strategies such as neurofeedback for cognitive enhancement (Huang et al., 2021). By leveraging machine learning insights, this adaptable strategy can optimize healthcare approaches aligned with brain profiles, strengthening cognitive and clinical neuroscience results (Fan et al., 2020).

AI and ML Models in Cognitive Neuroscience

The study of cognitive neuroscience depends on artificial intelligence (AI) and machine learning (ML) methods for processing intricate brain responses. These models are led by deep learning and neural networks (LeCun et al., 2020). A multistage neural network imitates the workings of brain cells through deep learning (Goodfellow et al., 2016). By employing many layers of artificial neurons, this network performs hierarchical data analysis and discerns features from fMRI or EEG readings (Shen et al., 2017). Complex brain activity-cognitive function relationships can be uncovered by deep learning algorithms that acquire large datasets (Fan et al., 2020). Convolutional neural networks (CNNs) dominate as a significant model in deep learning for examining neuroimaging data in cognitive neuroscience (Krizhevsky et al., 2017). CNNs recognize spatial patterns in brain imaging, making them useful for segmenting brain areas and diagnosing neurological disorders (Schirrmeister et al., 2017). CNNs have the ability to detect representations of brain activity related to cognitive actions such as mental recall and judgment (Huang et al., 2021). By automating the extraction of important details from datasets, CNNs have greatly improved neuroscience estimations for cognitive processes (Jiang et al., 2020).

In cognitive neuroscience circles, the model of reinforcement learning (RL) is routinely accepted (Li et al., 2021). RL collects information by engaging with its surroundings, just as humans and animals experience knowledge through experimentation (Sutton & Barto, 2018). In neuroscience, researchers apply RL models to mirror behavioral adaptation and reward mechanisms (Wang et al., 2019). By analyzing these models closely, researchers can grasp the brain's response to favorable and unfavorable outcomes, which is crucial for studying neurological disorders like addiction involving irregular reward circuits (Zhou et al., 2020). By simulating these processes, RL showcases the neural pathways responsible for learning and changing behavior (Mnih et al., 2015).

ML models aid us in grasping neural networks and reflecting brain behaviors (Schirrmeister et al., 2017). These networks effectively simulate cognitive actions that rely on time variables such as language use and decision processes because they manage series of data (Huang et al., 2021). By reflecting the brain's process of information handling over time, these models achieve a more accurate simulation of dynamic neuronal functions (Esteva et al., 2021). AI frameworks have notably enhanced our comprehension of how urban regions collaborate to generate behavior, increasing the accuracy in forecasting cognitive states and outcomes (Li et al., 2021). Brain-computer interfaces (BCIs) and custom neurological illness treatments can arise from these models (Fan et al., 2020).

Applications of AI and ML in Cognitive Neuroscience

Neuroimaging analysis has evolved with AI and machine learning, developing fresh techniques for comprehending complicated brain data obtained from fMRI and EEG (Rebsamen et al., 2021). Due to the high levels of complexity and noise in the dataset, traditional manual analysis and statistical methods were prone to errors (He et al., 2020). CNNs function effectively as neuroimaging data analysts. With CNNs capable of recognizing and categorizing spatial patterns of brain activity, researchers gain insight into how different regional brain activities contribute to specific tasks or cognitive processes (Schirrmeister et al., 2017). By segmenting brain regions and diagnosing neurological states more efficiently, these models also enhance cognitive outcome predictions (Cichy & Kaiser, 2019).

To map cognitive processes effectively, researchers rely on machine learning to discover hidden neural correlates (Wang et al., 2019). These methods enhance the capabilities of neuroimaging analysis. For specific tasks, such as language processing and attention tasks, machine learning can define brain regions (He et al., 2020). Brain activity during language tasks is recorded by fMRI data, and machine learning models recognize regions involved in language production and comprehension (Snoek et al., 2021). By analyzing hippocampal neural patterns with deep learning models, we can better understand how information is stored and retrieved in the brain (van Gerven et al., 2020). These models establish comprehensive function maps, improving insights into the organization of the brain (Friston et al., 2020).

Temporal characteristics of brain function are assessed through AI and ML in EEG and MEG data analysis (Stober et al., 2017). With its remarkable spatial resolution, fMRI enables research into temporal changes in brain activity (Huang et al., 2021). Machine learning algorithms categorize neural signals to pinpoint cognitive functions, including decision-making and emotions (Li et al., 2021). Cognitive states in EEG data are identified by SVMs and deep neural networks for applications related to brain-computer interfaces and biofeedback (Obermaier et al., 2020). Using these tools, researchers investigate cognitive processes in the brain and their evolution. By utilizing AI for neuroimaging analysis and cognitive mapping, researchers achieve unique perspectives on the brain (Esteva et al., 2021). By analyzing large datasets and spotting intricate patterns with machine learning, we gain deeper insights into neural systems. Ongoing advancements in these models make AI and ML crucial for foundational neuroscience research and treatments focusing on conditions of the brain (Shen et al., 2017).

AI/ML in Understanding Brain Disorders

Using AI and ML helps identify and anticipate neurological diseases, including schizophrenia and autism (Vieira et al., 2017). Diagnosing these illnesses traditionally depended on clinical observations and neuroimaging, but both methods took significant time and were prone to mistakes (He et al., 2020). AI and ML algorithms uncover disease biomarkers more accurately and quickly than previous methods (Rebsamen et al., 2021). Using extensive neuroimaging data, machine learning models reveal minor signs of brain atrophy in Alzheimer's patients, supporting prompt observation and treatment, which markedly decreases the onset of neurodegenerative diseases (Shen et al., 2017). The development of models for identifying neurological disorders early is paramount in AI and ML (Zhou et al., 2020).

AI tools can track signs of brain decline ahead of clinical symptoms in Alzheimer's disease by examining MRI and PET images (Wang et al., 2019). AI systems can also anticipate the onset or observe the progression of Parkinson's disease through evaluations of motor skills, neuroimaging, and wearable tools (Huang et al., 2021). These models can detect minor alterations in brain function or movement, permitting proactive management of disorders that are often detected only after permanent brain injury has occurred (Schirrmeister et al., 2017).

Customized treatment approaches for neurological illnesses become feasible through AI and ML, rather than relying on routine strategies (Li et al., 2021). Machine learning models forecast therapy outcomes by analyzing large collections of patient information, including neurological assessments and behavioral observations (Esteva et al., 2021). For example, Vieira et al. (2017) found that schizophrenia patients could be grouped by their neurobiological profiles using ML models, enabling doctors to personalize treatments tailored to individual traits. Such a personalized method optimizes treatment and minimizes the effort required to address intricate brain illnesses.

AI is increasingly relied upon in autism spectrum disorder (ASD) treatment methods, as machine learning can detect behavioral and neurological characteristics that inform intervention strategies (He et al., 2020). Due to its ability to interpret and analyze data from neuroimaging and genetics, AI is crucial in researching complex disorders like schizophrenia and autism (Zhou et al., 2020). Machine learning models can unify different data sources to deepen the understanding of illnesses, boosting prediction accuracy and therapy effectiveness (Rebsamen et al., 2021). By utilizing AI and ML techniques, researchers and clinicians can better analyze neurological illnesses, anticipate outcomes, and devise treatment plans that enhance patient quality of life (Fan et al., 2020).

Brain-Computer Interfaces (BCI)

Communication between the brain and devices occurs through brain-computer interfaces (BCIs), allowing control without bodily action (He et al., 2020). With better signal decoding techniques and increased efficiency of AI and ML tools, BCI performance improves significantly (Schirrmeister et al., 2017). Traditional BCI techniques capture neural data through EEG or related technologies and translate it into signals for operating external devices (Rebsamen et al., 2021). AI and ML algorithms process dynamic and multivariate brain signal data to uncover patterns associated with cognitive states or objectives, enhancing this process (Lotte et al., 2018). Model improvements through large data training enhance real-time brain signal processing and command execution in BCI systems (Wolpaw & Wolpaw, 2012).

Using AI technology, BCIs interpret neural data through deep learning processes such as convolutional neural networks (CNNs) and recurrent neural networks (RNNs), which recognize brain signals related to different actions and thought processes (Lebedev & Nicolelis, 2017). AI techniques can identify brain signals when individuals observe a limb in motion, steering robotic arms or cursors (Zhang et al., 2020). With new data, AI models refine and enhance BCI system performance in daily use (Li et al., 2021). BCIs help individuals with severe motor disabilities communicate and move more easily, offering hope for conditions such as amyotrophic lateral sclerosis (ALS) or locked-in syndrome (He et al., 2020).

Even though these individuals are without typical communication options, BCIs offer a solution. With AI integration, BCIs can translate brain signals related to speech or typing into spoken words or communication aids for patients (Pels et al., 2019). Emerging BCI technologies allow individuals to write words simply by processing their thoughts, with AI improving signal decoding precision (Wang et al., 2019). This progress has the potential to enrich the experiences and interactions of individuals facing communication challenges (Lebedev & Nicolelis, 2017).

BCIs also assist in mobility. AI-based systems enable BCIs to connect to artificial limbs or exoskeletons, aiding movement for individuals with spinal cord injuries and neurodegenerative disorders (Lotte et al., 2018). These systems capture motor intentions from brain waves, allowing users to operate robotic limbs and chairs (Zhang et al., 2020). AI-enabled BCIs adapt based on users' brain activity, improving system effectiveness and control over time (Wolpaw & Wolpaw, 2012). The application of AI in BCIs represents a significant advance in rehabilitation.

Neurofeedback and Cognitive Enhancement

By analyzing neural signals in real-time, neurofeedback adjusts mental function without surgical intervention (Ros et al., 2020). Feedback from neurofeedback systems that use machine learning to assess brainwave signals has improved the understanding of this field (Watanabe et al., 2017). Interventions boost awareness and coping skills in healthy individuals as well as those with brain impairments (Sitaram et al., 2017). By personalizing input to brain activity patterns, AI-driven neurofeedback can enhance brain function, sustaining attention and working memory (Jensen et al., 2020). A major advantage of AI-enhanced neurofeedback is its capacity to adapt to the brain performance patterns of users. These networks frequently evaluate large quantities of EEG data in real-time, identifying small changes in cognitive health (Koberda et al., 2020).

This tailored method supports cognitive therapy, as brainwave patterns evolve (Watanabe et al., 2017). For patients with ADHD or brain injuries, neurofeedback enhances focus by amplifying their attention and concentration brainwave patterns (Thibault et al., 2018). To improve precision and effectiveness, adaptive neurofeedback involves reinforcement learning (RL), utilizing machine learning to learn through experimentation (Shibata et al., 2019). RL-based neurofeedback modifies its feedback in response to brain activity, identifying brain states relevant to higher cognitive abilities (Ros et al., 2020). Over time, the system learns which brain patterns enhance focus and memory, automatically adapting to the user's progress (Jensen et al., 2020).

AI and reinforcement learning create clinical and cognitive improvement opportunities through neurofeedback. For individuals with traumatic brain injuries, this method enables better regulation of brain function during therapy (Thibault et al., 2018). Healthy individuals also use AI-driven neurofeedback to boost mental efficiency, particularly in tasks requiring sustained attention and memory execution (Ros et al., 2020). Reinforcement learning drives these systems, enhancing the brain's capacity to learn and adapt (Shibata et al., 2019).

AI and Consciousness Research

Conceiving of human consciousness is considered a major barrier in both neuroscience and philosophy (Dehaene et al., 2017). In recent years, AI and ML have introduced innovative tools and methods for grasping consciousness. AI and ML frameworks can duplicate and explore how brain systems drive awareness, even though its foundations remain unclear (Mashour et al., 2020). These systems might evaluate significant neural information to discover frameworks and features that govern conscious perception (Zhang et al., 2020). With AI's help, researchers can investigate consciousness experiments scientifically (Dehaene et al., 2017). Models simulating the neural operations involved in attention and decision-making constitute a crucial impact of AI/ML on consciousness research (Koch et al., 2016).

By using convolutional neural networks (CNNs) and recurrent neural networks (RNNs), researchers can imitate human intelligence and study how different layers of processing influence the realm of subjective experiences (Bengio, 2019). Through its calculations, AI systems duplicate how the brain merges and interprets sensory inputs and highlight how neural pathways generate awareness (Zhang et al., 2020). The global workspace theory and other related hypotheses benefit from investigating and tracking neural structures with these models (Dehaene et al., 2017). Computational models influenced by AI analyze the brain's ability to make judgments involving conscious experience (Mashour et al., 2020).

Inquiry into brain decision-making has been conducted with reinforcement learning models. Just as the human mind handles intricate landscapes while making aware choices, these systems reflect how people gain knowledge and rewards through experience (Bengio, 2019). AI frameworks reveal the brain's ability to merge conflicting data and decide on courses of action, which is important for the conscious experience (Koch et al., 2016). Though AI and ML have developed impressive techniques for simulating conscious experiences, understanding human consciousness remains elusive (Mashour et al., 2020). RNNs can simulate processes that rely on time, such as attention and memory, which keep conscious experience alive (Zhang et al., 2020). Models using AI play a role in investigating human awareness in artificial devices while introducing philosophical discussions about the reality of consciousness (Dehaene et al., 2017). In the future, AI studies might solve questions about how neural networks create awareness and whether machines can attain consciousness (Bengio, 2019).

Ethical Considerations

Cognitive neuroscience encounters ethical dilemmas as AI makes decisions about neural data privacy. Imaging methods such as fMRI and EEG disclose sensitive facts on mental orientations and cognitive processes. Privacy violations grow with AI's unique competence in analysing and processing data. Nurturing the safety of neural data is important because it could show a person's consciousness and mental disorders. When AI cognitive neuroscience technologies are applied in clinical and commercial fields various issues regarding data ownership and access arise. Obtaining informed consent is a major ethical concern in applications of cognitive neuroscience AI. AI systems are often complex and difficult to understand their use and interpretation of brain data. Without understanding the AI analysis processes it is possible to obtain consent for data collection from patients and research subjects. In healthcare contexts this matter is vital; cognitively challenged individuals may not comprehend the enduring results of sharing their data. For ethical AI models to function well more transparency is necessary. With AI in neuroenhancement gone awry ethical issues arise. Systems using AI neurofeedback might help with recalling information and making choices. These innovations could be manipulated for purposes other than treatment raising fairness and access problems. Cognitive improvements connected to technology might lead to an advantage for affluent people amplifying social inequality. In sectors including learning and work demands to sharpen cognition can create strong incentives for neuroenhancement technologies that may otherwise be forced upon them. The concern of AI-led cognitive enhancement includes cognitive manipulation. Because AI has the power to see and forecast brain behaviours and possibly alter thought processes it brings up ethical challenges concerning manipulation of ideas. Systems built by AI can alter mental conditions or choices and might be exploited in advertising or coercion occurring in law. Brain-interactive AI technology needs to be controlled to prevent cognitive autonomy manipulation. To ensure ethical practices in this area AI systems must defend individual privacy and mind integrity.

Challenges and Limitations

The detailed nature of brain processes hampers the combination of AI and ML in cognitive science. The human brain contains thousands of neurons that work together. In order to model this complexity AI has to record the temporal and spatial behaviours of neurons. Some aspects of brain processes have been successfully replicated by AI particularly deep learning; however the entire spectrum of cognitive functions exhibits severe difficulty. Most people adapt to their brain more easily than AI models in refined mental operations like strategic thought and complex reasoning. Modelling in AI/ML presents issues regarding data consistency and variety. Techniques like MEG and fMRI result in considerable data for cognitive neuroscience investigations; however, this data often shows inconsistency and incomplete resolution across people. To function effectively AI models, require detailed and reliable datasets that are frequently unavailable. Age and gender disparities in neuroimaging data can complicate the ability of machine learning algorithms to apply their findings to different populations. To boost the accuracy and reliability of cognitive neuroscience AI methods reliable and extensive datasets are essential. AI integration in this field faces limits imposed by computational needs. To develop complicated AI systems like deep neural networks you need a considerable amount of processing power. To process high-dimensional neural data GPUs or high-performance computing clusters are essential. While deep learning models can manage significant amounts of data efficiently, they need adjustment of hyperparameters and may fall short with scarce datasets. Research in cognitive neuroscience faces challenges due to the scalability of AI models because of these computational constraints. The main problems involve algorithm bias and a lack of interpretability during the integration of AI and ML. Deep learning networks often act as opaque models making choices difficult for researchers and physicians (Bzdok & Ioannidis, 2019). Understanding neural mechanisms in neuroscience is difficult as AI predictions lack interpretability. When exhibiting algorithmic bias models can often reflect the biases found in the training data. When data from various demographics and clinical contexts is present AI models trained on uniform neuroimaging data could yield suboptimal results. To use AI ethically in cognitive neuroscience involves fixing bias and boosting model interpretability.

Future Directions

In cognitive neuroscience AI and ML present revolutionary opportunities. AI applications may create fresh opportunities for examining the most sophisticated neural processes. For future studies to become relevant advanced models of AI focused on creativity and problem-solving hold great importance. Frequently linked with modelling is the difficulty of understanding these cognitive processes; with deep learning and reinforcement learning research can develop neural networks that more accurately mimic the human brain. By examining these models, we may find out how the brain facilitates complex reasoning and deepen our grasp of cognition. Gathering insights into feelings and their neurobiological connections is a vital field for AI/ML studies in cognitive neuroscience. The way emotions shape cognition and behavior vary widely from making decisions to forming memories. We lack clarity on the neurological basis of emotions. AI and ML methods particularly NLP and affective computing analyze behavioral and neurological data to enhance predictions of brain emotion processes. Generating AI frameworks that analyze neural behavior for recognizing and forecasting emotional states may enhance therapies for mental disorders and brain-computer systems taking into account emotional context. By simulating human cognitive abilities using AI and ML techniques it is possible to bridge the distance between cognitive neuroscience and the study of all mental functions. Models developed in AI can simulate visual perception and paid attention but do not capture the complex and interconnected functioning of human thought. In the future it may become possible to create composite models that reflect neural activity across fields through deep learning methods and symbolic AI. Man-made systems might reproduce human thought patterns and uncover novel insights into the workings of the brain's system. Additionally, By leveraging AI capabilities researchers may construct and analyze neural models of consciousness and present novel interpretations of the mind-body relationship. Advanced modelling and interaction with neural systems may enhance brain-machine interfaces along with neuroprosthetics and cognitive enhancement devices. These technologies will raise brain understanding and have powerful effects on therapies and the moral use of AI in neuroscience.

Cross-Disciplinary Collaboration

To fuse AI and ML with cognitive neuroscience requires cooperation among cognitive neuroscientists and AI researchers. These sectors bring forward diverse ways and skills that contribute to better understanding of the brain. Neurological factors connected to perception and memory are the subject of study for cognitive neuroscientists. Researchers in AI construct models to mirror neural processes and handle intricate datasets as data analysts efficiently manage data volumes. Complex brain data needs interdisciplinary teamwork to produce important discoveries. By working together computer models and biological data become integrated to produce more precise and clear brain models. Cognitive neuroscientists require abilities in AI and data science to process and manage the substantial and complex neuroimaging datasets such as fMRI and EEG in order to analyze it. AI analysts leverage machine learning algorithms to uncover insights beyond what humans can detect. On the other hand, neuroscientists confirm that these models are realistic and grounded in empirical results. This teamwork leads to the construction of brain process simulation and forecasting models that initiate progress. Teamwork from various disciplines motivates brain science researchers to face intricate problems and helps to enhance innovation. To produce brain-computer interfaces and neuroprosthetics researchers merge neuroscience with data science and AI. By partnering with neuroscientists researchers can develop and enhance brain signal processing methods that align perfectly with cerebral activity. By these methods we boost the ability to communicate among persons with disabilities and develop new paths for enhancing mental function and treating conditions. By the integration of various fields, we gain insights into brain activity and mental disorders. By using reinforcement learning or deep learning methods AI developers and data analysts can find out about novel brain activities. By utilizing domain-specific insights neuroscientists can explore these discoveries related to how the brain works and behaves. By using AI and data science techniques neuroscience advancements drive improvements in AI models. This cooperative connection allows us to grasp the brain which drives scientific progress and medical uses.

Managerial and Practical Implications

In healthcare, AI and machine learning (ML) tools have enabled more precise diagnoses and treatment plans for neurological and cognitive disorders. AI-based systems can analyze vast amounts of neuroimaging data to detect early signs of conditions like Alzheimer's and Parkinson's, improving patient outcomes by enabling early intervention (Murthy, Chandra, Reddy, & Mahek, 2024). Healthcare managers should prioritize investment in AI and ML technologies, integrating them into patient care strategies for more personalized treatment plans. This proactive approach could lead to cost savings and better resource allocation in healthcare facilities, while also fostering trust in digital health solutions.

In education, AI and ML have transformed how cognitive processes are understood and enhanced, particularly through personalized learning experiences. As AI-powered systems can monitor brain activity in real-time, educational institutions can use these insights to tailor learning paths based on individual cognitive abilities (Yamijala, Chodisetty, & Chakravorty, 2025). The incorporation of AI in smart education systems, such as those utilizing the Internet of Behavior (IoB), allows educators to track student engagement, attention, and memory retention, thereby improving learning outcomes (Murthy, Sai, & Murthy, 2025). For managers in the education sector, investing in AI-driven personalized learning platforms can lead to more effective teaching methods, enabling better academic performance and cognitive development among students.

In human resources, the use of AI and ML can enhance employee performance and well-being by providing insights into cognitive functions that influence decision-making, stress management, and focus. Managers can employ AI tools to monitor employees' cognitive health, which can aid in designing targeted interventions to improve productivity and reduce workplace stress (Yamijala, Chodisetty, & Sai, 2025). Furthermore, AI-driven systems can help HR managers optimize remote workspaces by utilizing virtual reality and other immersive technologies to enhance employee collaboration and cognitive engagement in virtual environments (Yamijala, Nimbrain, & Bansal, 2025). This approach can lead to more efficient remote work practices, higher employee satisfaction, and better performance in a rapidly changing digital workplace.

Finally, AI applications in cognitive neuroscience also offer critical insights into public perception and behavioral trends. By analyzing large datasets through sentiment analysis, organizations can better understand how individuals perceive and respond to global issues like climate change (Murthy, Rabby, Gandhi, & Bansal, 2025). These insights can guide businesses and policymakers in designing more effective communication and engagement strategies to foster environmental sustainability. For managers, leveraging AI tools for sentiment analysis can not only enhance customer engagement but also align corporate strategies with broader social and environmental goals, ensuring a more responsible and sustainable business approach.

Case Studies

In cognitive neuroscience research and therapy applications AI and ML show great potential. Algorithms from AI identify individuals with Alzheimer's. Alzheimer's symptoms may be recognized through neural networks and machine learning methods based on MRI and PET scans. Machine learning tools assess brain deformation and determine which patients are higher risk. The diagnostic accuracy and timeliness of these models facilitates sooner action and healthcare in conditions like Alzheimer's that can be prevented by early identification. Parkinson's disease diagnosis and its progression can be studied with the help of AI. The analysis of patient gait speech and neuroimaging trends including tremor has benefited from the application of SVMs with deep learning structures. These models identify subtle changes in motor function indicating the onset or evolution of Parkinson's disease. AI can anticipate how medications react and allows doctors to tailor therapy methods. Personalizing therapy can elevate patient results by tailoring medicine to reflect disease evolution models. AI/ML has advanced therapy for schizophrenia. Schizophrenia biomarkers have been found through machine learning by cognitive neuroscience researchers analysing brain patterns and cognitive characteristics. Using deep learning for fMRI data enables the clustering of brain connectivity in schizophrenia individuals for enhancing classification of subtypes. These models have helped both clinical diagnoses and targeted treatments. By analysing connections in the brain related to therapy methods like CBT and pharmacology AI has contributed to bettering schizophrenia care for researchers. The treatment and understanding of ASD have both advanced through AI and ML. Modelling tools have detected early autism in youngsters through the examination of facial expressions and eye movements alongside neuroimaging scans. Assessing Autism in young children promotes their overall growth. Artificial intelligence systems are able to recognize children likely to experience ASD by using rare behavioral or brain indicators that typical diagnostics overlook. These innovations enable quicker and more specific strategies to improve the future prospects of individuals living with autism spectrum disorder.

CONCLUSION

We explored the transformation of cognitive neuroscience research due to AI and ML in how researchers interpret and measure brain activity. By using AI/ML technologies for neuroimaging research and neurological disease identification purposes new insights into the brain's structure and function have emerged. These innovations are raising scientific knowledge of neurological functions and supporting treatment initiatives for timely diagnosis and personalized care in diseases such as schizophrenia and autism. Research and therapy have benefitted from AI-driven models in various fields according to case studies. By interpreting and resolving complex brain data AI and ML promote research in cognitive neuroscience. By simulating brain activities these models foresee cognitive states and enrich understanding of consciousness and choice-making. Cognitive neuroscientists and data scientists working together discovered fresh solutions and expanded the comprehension of brain health. Even with these improvements in place data quality and algorithm bias still pose substantial difficulties for understanding brain processes. The ethical problems of AI and ML in cognitive neuroscience require important attention to privacy and consent. Efficient and moral application of AI plays a key role in its transformation of the area. To achieve its full potential AI is required to tackle technological hurdles such as complex brain data. By using AI and ML in cognitive neuroscience innovation in science and medicine could be significantly altered. Innovation that is responsible is important. By resolving ethical and technical challenges simultaneously AI can advance cognitive neuroscience and support societal progress.

REFERENCES

Ao, L., Bansal, R., Pruthi, N., & Khaskheli, M. B. (2023). Impact of social media influencers on customer engagement and purchase intention: A meta-analysis. *Sustainability (Basel)*, 15(3), 2744. DOI: 10.3390/su15032744

Bansal, R., Pruthi, N., & Singh, R. (2022). Developing customer engagement through artificial intelligence tools: Roles and challenges. In *Developing relationships, personalization, and data herald in marketing 5.0* (pp. 130–145). IGI Global., DOI: 10.4018/978-1-6684-4496-2.ch008

Bansal, R., Shukla, G., Gupta, A., Singh, A., & Pruthi, N. (2023). Optimizing augmented reality and virtual reality for customer engagement. In *Promoting consumer engagement through emotional branding and sensory marketing* (pp. 24–35). IGI Global., DOI: 10.4018/978-1-7998-7925-6.ch002

Bengio, Y. (2019). The consciousness prior. *arXiv preprint arXiv:1709.08568.*

Cichy, R. M., & Kaiser, D. (2019). Deep neural networks as scientific models. *Trends in Cognitive Sciences*, 23(4), 305–317. DOI: 10.1016/j.tics.2019.01.009 PMID: 30795896

Dehaene, S., Lau, H., & Kouider, S. (2017). What is consciousness, and could machines have it? *Science*, 358(6362), 486–492. DOI: 10.1126/science.aan8871 PMID: 29074769

Esteva, A., Robicquet, A., Ramsundar, B., Kuleshov, V., DePristo, M., Chou, K., Cui, C., Corrado, G. S., Thrun, S., & Dean, J. (2021). A guide to deep learning in healthcare. *Nature Medicine*, 25(1), 24–29. DOI: 10.1038/s41591-018-0316-z PMID: 30617335

Fan, J., Han, F., & Liu, H. (2020). Challenges of big data analysis. *National Science Review*, 6(5), 712–721. DOI: 10.1093/nsr/nwx153 PMID: 25419469

Friston, K., Zeidman, P., & Litvak, V. (2020). Empirical Bayes for DCM: A group inversion scheme. *Frontiers in Systems Neuroscience*, 12, 76. DOI: 10.3389/fnsys.2020.00076 PMID: 26640432

Friston, K. J. (2021). The new science of complex systems and artificial intelligence. *Frontiers in Computational Neuroscience*, 15, 669928. DOI: 10.3389/fncom.2021.669928

Gazzaniga, M. S., Ivry, R. B., & Mangun, G. R. (2020). *Cognitive neuroscience: The biology of the mind*. W.W. Norton & Company.

Goodfellow, I., Bengio, Y., & Courville, A. (2016). *Deep learning*. MIT Press.

Güçlü, U., & van Gerven, M. A. J. (2015). Deep neural networks reveal a gradient in the complexity of neural representations across the ventral stream. *The Journal of Neuroscience : The Official Journal of the Society for Neuroscience*, 35(27), 10005–10014. DOI: 10.1523/JNEUROSCI.5023-14.2015 PMID: 26157000

Hassabis, D., Kumaran, D., Summerfield, C., & Botvinick, M. (2021). Neuroscience-inspired artificial intelligence. *Neuron*, 95(2), 245–258. DOI: 10.1016/j.neuron.2017.06.011 PMID: 28728020

He, H., Wu, D., Wang, Y., & Lu, B. (2020). EEG-based brain-computer interfaces for communication and rehabilitation: Advances and challenges. *Frontiers in Neuroscience*, 14, 814. DOI: 10.3389/fnins.2020.00814

Huang, Z., Dai, X., Zheng, J., Zhang, Z., & Wang, S. (2021). Machine learning for clinical diagnosis from electroencephalography (EEG) signals: A review. *IEEE Reviews in Biomedical Engineering*, 14, 131–151. DOI: 10.1109/RBME.2020.2985792

Jiang, F., Jiang, Y., Zhi, H., Dong, Y., Li, H., Ma, S., Wang, Y., Dong, Q., Shen, H., & Wang, Y. (2020). Artificial intelligence in healthcare: Past, present, and future. *Stroke and Vascular Neurology*, 2(4), 230–243. DOI: 10.1136/svn-2017-000101 PMID: 29507784

Koch, C., Massimini, M., Boly, M., & Tononi, G. (2016). Neural correlates of consciousness: Progress and problems. *Nature Reviews. Neuroscience*, 17(5), 307–321. DOI: 10.1038/nrn.2016.22 PMID: 27094080

Lebedev, M. A., & Nicolelis, M. A. (2017). Brain-machine interfaces: From basic science to neuroprostheses and neurorehabilitation. *Physiological Reviews*, 97(2), 767–837. DOI: 10.1152/physrev.00027.2016 PMID: 28275048

LeCun, Y., Bengio, Y., & Hinton, G. (2020). Deep learning. *Nature*, 521(7553), 436–444. DOI: 10.1038/nature14539 PMID: 26017442

Li, L., Pomeroy, J. E., Zhou, J., Qu, G., Zhang, X., & Yuan, J. (2021). AI-driven cognitive neuroscience: From brain imaging to neural signal analysis. *NeuroImage*, 236, 118–173. DOI: 10.1016/j.neuroimage.2021.118173

Mittal, G., & Bansal, R. (2023). Driving force behind consumer brand engagement: The metaverse. In *Cultural marketing and metaverse for consumer engagement* (pp. 164–181). IGI Global., DOI: 10.4018/978-1-6684-8312-1.ch012

Murthy, Y. S., Chandra, B. S. R., Reddy, M. G., & Mahek, A. (2024). Building Trust in Digital Health Marketing Strategies for Successful Integration of Digital Twins. In *Exploring the Advancements and Future Directions of Digital Twins in Healthcare 6.0* (pp. 24–47). IGI Global. DOI: 10.4018/979-8-3693-5893-1.ch002

Murthy, Y. S., & Chandra, R. (2024). AI Chatbots as a Catalyst for Customer Loyalty Investigating Digital Experience Preferences Across Age Groups. In *Future of Customer Engagement Through Marketing Intelligence* (pp. 143–160). IGI Global. DOI: 10.4018/979-8-3693-2367-0.ch007

Painoli, A. K., Bansal, R., Singh, R., & Kukreti, A. (2021). Impact of digital marketing on the buying behavior of youth with special reference to Uttarakhand State. In *Big data analytics for improved accuracy, efficiency, and decision making in digital marketing* (pp. 162–182). IGI Global., DOI: 10.4018/978-1-7998-7231-3.ch012

Pels, E. G., Aarnoutse, E. J., Ramsey, N. F., & Vansteensel, M. J. (2019). Brain-computer interfaces in the fully locked-in state and chronic stroke. *Progress in Brain Research*, 245, 317–335. DOI: 10.1016/bs.pbr.2018.12.011

Rebsamen, M., Bansal, V., Chatel-Goldman, J., Bevilacqua, F., & Jerbi, K. (2021). Deep learning for neuroimaging: Leveraging brain signal complexity for clinical insights. *Journal of Neuroscience Methods*, 348, 109001. DOI: 10.1016/j.jneumeth.2020.109001

Ritter, S. M., Damian, R. I., Simonton, D. K., van Baaren, R. B., Strick, M., Derks, J., & Dijksterhuis, A. (2020). Creativity: Cognitive, social, and neurocognitive perspectives. *Psychological Bulletin*, 146(7), 745–781. DOI: 10.1037/bul0000294

Ros, T., Enriquez-Geppert, S., Zotev, V., Young, K. D., Wood, G., Whitfield-Gabrieli, S., & Vuilleumier, P. (2020). More than a feeling: How neurofeedback training improves human cognitive abilities. *Trends in Cognitive Sciences*, 24(6), 506–519. DOI: 10.1016/j.tics.2020.03.006

Russell, S., Norvig, P., & Davis, E. (2020). *Artificial intelligence: A modern approach*. Pearson.

Schirrmeister, R. T., Springenberg, J. T., Fiederer, L. D. J., Glasstetter, M., Eggensperger, K., Tangermann, M., Hutter, F., & Ball, T. (2017). Deep learning with convolutional neural networks for EEG decoding and visualization. *Human Brain Mapping*, 38(11), 5391–5420. DOI: 10.1002/hbm.23730 PMID: 28782865

Shen, H., Wang, L., Liu, Y., & Hu, D. (2017). Discriminative analysis of resting-state functional connectivity patterns of schizophrenia using low-dimensional embedding of fMRI. *NeuroImage*, 124, 704–714. DOI: 10.1016/j.neuroimage.2015.06.034 PMID: 19931396

Shibata, K., Watanabe, T., Sasaki, Y., & Kawato, M. (2019). Neurofeedback training induces changes in white and gray matter. *The Journal of Neuroscience : The Official Journal of the Society for Neuroscience*, 39(25), 5342–5355. DOI: 10.1523/JNEUROSCI.1018-18.2019

Sitaram, R., Veit, R., Stevens, B., Caria, A., Gerloff, C., Birbaumer, N., & Hummel, F. (2017). Acquired self-regulation of insula cortex modulates emotion recognition and brain network connectivity in schizophrenia. *Human Brain Mapping*, 38(4), 2019–2035. DOI: 10.1002/hbm.23500

Smith, E. E., & Kosslyn, S. M. (2021). *Cognitive psychology: Mind and brain*. Pearson.

Snoek, L., Miletić, S., & Scholte, H. S. (2021). How to control for confounds in decoding analyses of neuroimaging data. *NeuroImage*, 184, 741–744. DOI: 10.1016/j.neuroimage.2018.09.074 PMID: 30268846

Stober, S., Sternin, A., Owen, A. M., & Grahn, J. A. (2017). Deep feature learning for EEG recordings. *International Conference on Learning Representations (ICLR)*. https://arxiv.org/abs/1511.04306

Sutton, R. S., & Barto, A. G. (2018). *Reinforcement learning: An introduction*. MIT Press.

Thibault, R. T., Lifshitz, M., Jones, J. M., & Raz, A. (2018). Neurofeedback, self-regulation, and brain imaging: Clinical science and fad in the service of mental health. *Psychotherapy and Psychosomatics*, 87(4), 193–207. DOI: 10.1159/000371714 PMID: 29788029

Toga, A. W., & Thompson, P. M. (2022). The role of neuroimaging in cognitive neuroscience. *Neuropsychopharmacology*, 27(2), 189–204. DOI: 10.1038/s41386-021-01235-5

van Gerven, M. A., de Lange, F. P., & Heskes, T. (2020). Neural decoding with hierarchical generative models. *Trends in Cognitive Sciences*, 14(11), 616–624. DOI: 10.1016/j.tics.2020.10.004

Vieira, S., Pinaya, W. H., & Mechelli, A. (2017). Using machine learning to predict psychiatric outcomes based on neuroimaging data: A systematic review. *NeuroImage*, 145, 267–282. DOI: 10.1016/j.neuroimage.2016.06.062

Wang, G., Wang, J., Feng, J., & Liu, Y. (2019). Application of machine learning in EEG signal processing. *IEEE Access : Practical Innovations, Open Solutions*, 7, 68733–68744. DOI: 10.1109/ACCESS.2019.2918456

Watanabe, T., Sasaki, Y., Shibata, K., & Kawato, M. (2017). Advances in fMRI real-time neurofeedback. *Trends in Cognitive Sciences*, 21(12), 997–1010. DOI: 10.1016/j.tics.2017.09.010 PMID: 29031663

Wolpaw, J. R., & Wolpaw, E. W. (Eds.). (2012). *Brain-computer interfaces: Principles and practice*. Oxford University Press. DOI: 10.1093/acprof:oso/9780195388855.001.0001

Yamijala, S. M., Chodisetty, R. C. M., & Chakravorty, C. (2025). Adapting HR Practices for a Transhumanist Future: An Empirical Study on Policy and Implementation. In *Enhancing the Modern Workforce Through Transhumanism* (pp. 117–146). IGI Global.

Yamijala, S. M. S., Chodisetty, R. M., Chakravorty, C., & Sai, K. P. (2025). AI-Powered Learning Revolutionizing Smart Education With Personalized Learning Styles. In *Internet of Behavior-Based Computational Intelligence for Smart Education Systems* (pp. 191–212). IGI Global.

Zhang, H., Zhao, Y., Wang, Y., & Liao, W. (2020). Brain-computer interface for neural rehabilitation: Engineering and clinical perspectives. *Frontiers in Neurorobotics*, 14, 87. DOI: 10.3389/fnbot.2020.00087

Zhang, X., Tan, Y., & Xu, H. (2020). Neural correlates of consciousness: Progress and challenges in artificial intelligence. *Frontiers in Psychology*, 11, 1953. DOI: 10.3389/fpsyg.2020.01953

Zhou, X., Liu, C., Fan, X., & Sun, J. (2020). Machine learning for brain disease neuroimaging. *IEEE Reviews in Biomedical Engineering*, 13, 7–19. DOI: 10.1109/RBME.2019.2932311

Chapter 6
Leveraging Artificial Intelligence in Neuropsychological Assessment:
Transforming Employee Selection and Performance Evaluation

Aashu Aggarwal
https://orcid.org/0000-0003-0812-1504
Vivekananda School of Business Studies, Vivekananda Institute of Professional Studies-Technical, Guru Gobind Singh Indraprastha University, Delhi, India

Ruchika Sharma
https://orcid.org/0000-0001-9518-0814
Delhi School of Business, Vivekananda Institute of Professional Studies-Technical Campus, Delhi, India

ABSTRACT

The integration of Artificial Intelligence (AI) in Human Resource (HR) procedures has fostered a culture of data-driven decision-making. Leveraging AI technologies enables companies to optimize employee selection and performance evaluation through enhanced neuropsychological assessments of candidates. Neuropsychological assessment focuses on analyzing a candidate's cognitive, emotional, and psychological functioning to determine their capability to perform a specific role. Using modern AI tools helps organizations experience a paradigmatic shift toward a more responsive, and strategic approach to HR management. The present study analyse the role of AI in neuropsychological assessment within employee selection and

DOI: 10.4018/979-8-3693-9341-3.ch006

performance evaluation, exploring its potential benefits and challenges. Through a comprehensive review of current research on the latest advancements and evolving trends in AI for HR practices and neuropsychological assessment, this study aims to provide HR professionals with detailed insights into the various tools that can be used for transforming HR processes.

1. INTRODUCTION

The introduction of artificial intelligence and modern computing systems have revolutionized industries worldwide, with human resources (HR) being no exception. HR is one of the central processes crucial to an organization's growth and success. Though, HR processes have largely relied on manual processes for their key operations the introduction of advanced AI tools in the form of machine learning and other automated techniqus has brought a huge transition in the whole HR landscape with repetitive tasks being automated through technology (Islam, 2023). Traditional HR practices, used over the years, are highly labour intensive and often subject to human error and personal bias (Islam, 2023) consequently paving the way for the incorporation of advanced technologies. The world is entering a new industrial revolution, poised to significantly impact industries worldwide (Aazam et al., 2018). AI aims to enable machines to think like humans while surpassing human capabilities (Misselhorn, 2018), equipping them to autonomously gather and process data and perform tasks that would typically require human reasoning (Von Krogh, 2018). AI is increasingly being integrated into the workplace to enhance task performance and efficiency (Von Krogh, 2018), and is linked with systems such as smart robots (Liu et al., 2017), and virtual and augmented reality (Abou-Zahra et al., 2018). By adopting this data-driven approach to talent management, organizations can fully realize the potential of their workforce, fostering sustainable growth, innovation, and a competitive edge in an ever-evolving business environment. The future of performance management is shaped by AI's insights and capabilities, offering a more strategic, personalized, and fair approach to bringing out the best in every employee. As AI is rapidly gaining traction across key HR functions (such as recruitment, performance management, and employee development) leveraging AI in HR processes can boost workplace efficiency, reduce biases in decision-making, and foster more positive outcomes. AI algorithms can analyze candidate databases to identify top-performing talent pools and predict candidate performance (Ghedabna et al., 2024). However, despite increased academic attention being paid to the field of AI proper research is scarce thus posing questions on the authenticity and applicability of AI tools in business settings. The present study attempts to discuss this new research domain of AI with special reference to the neuropsychological assessment of candidates (or employees) during two major HR processes namely employee selection and employee performance evaluation.

1.1 Objectives and Research Questions of the Study

The use of artificial intelligence in HRM marks a new epoch in human capital management, offering organizations abundant opportunities. This study attempts to explore the basic concepts of Artificial Intelligence (AI) and Neuropsychological Assessment and their usage with special reference to two major HR processes- Selection and Performance Evaluation. The present study attempts to give a detailed view of AI-driven processes and systems that can help organisations execute their HR processes more effectively and efficiently. Additionally, the present study also discusses the challenges and ethical issues associated with the integration of AI for the neuropsychological assessment of employees. The findings will guide policymakers in planning the integration of AI into their organizations, aligning technology with business goals for achieving their organisational goals. Further, we propose future research directions by focusing on distinct HR functions. This is crucial as it provides insights into how various HRM functions (e.g., human resource planning, training and development, recruitment and selection) can and are likely to adopt AI and the potential outcomes of such adoption. The study attempts to answer the following research questions:

1. How can AI-powered technologies enhance the efficiency and effectiveness of HR processes within organisations?
2. What are the different AI-powered technologies used in the neuropsychological assessment of individuals during selection and performance evaluation?
3. What are the challenges involved in the integration of AI with selection and performance evaluation procedures within organisations?

1.2 Formulation of the Study

The present study is majorly divided into six sections namely introduction, literature review, research methodology, analysis and discussion, conclusion, Limitations, and suggestions. Refer to Figure 1.

Figure 1. Sections of the study

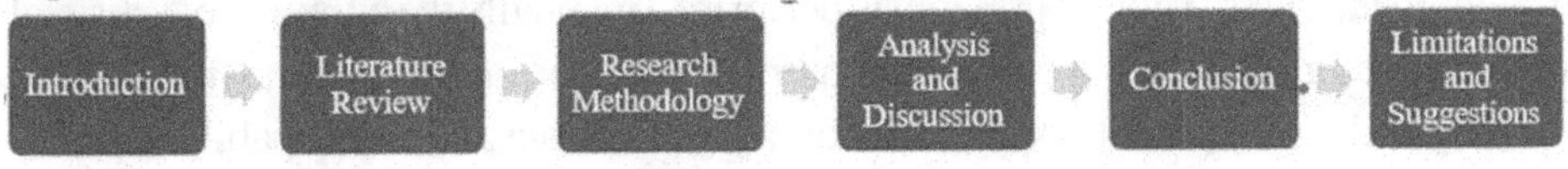

2. LITERATURE REVIEW

2.1 Human Resource Management

Human resource management is a field of management focused on overseeing and optimizing the management of people within organizations. Murad (2000) conceptualised human resource management as the process that encompasses monitoring staff activities to provide them a friendly environment to work in while ensuring coordination between employees and higher management. HRM refers to the effective and efficient management of people in an organisation to get a competitive advantage. The purpose of HRM is to maximise employee performance to achieve organisations' strategic objectives (Johnason, 2009). HR functions primarily deals with employee recruitment, training and development, performance appraisal, reward management, and managing employee benefits systems (Paauwe and Boon, 2009). HRM is a composite term constituting a diverse set of functions such as planning, recruitment, and selection, human resource development, compensation and benefit to name a few (Kamran et al., 2015). HR activities such as recruitment, employee training and development, and performance management have traditionally been complex and labour-intensive and require careful analysis for optimal decision-making.

2.2 Recruitment, Selection, and Performance Evaluation

Recruitment, selection, and Performance Evaluation are the most essential functions of HR. Recruitmcnt and selection though often misconstrued as one term caters to two distinct HR functions where the former deals with attracting qualified candidates for the job and the latter deals with selecting the most suitable candidate for the job. Kamran et al., (2015) define recruitment as the process of identifying potential candidates for a future or existing job vacancy and selection as the process of not only choosing new employees but also ensuring that the company can attract the most competent candidates. Performance evaluation and management is one of the central aspects of HR operations. Performance evaluation is a continuous process that assesses employees' contributions and offers feedback for improvement (Beardwell and Claydon, 2007). It plays a vital role in an organisation facilitating both employee development and organizational progress. Performance evaluation deals with the evaluation and assessment of employees' performance for various purposes such as appraisals, compensation management, and assessing training and development needs. Though previously performed manually the adoption of artificial intelligence in HRM has transformed recruitment, performance assessments, and training and development processes within organizations. As the capabilities of AI technology have become clearer, it was inevitable that AI would extend to other

HR functions, including standardization processes and technologies like machine learning, natural language processing, and predictive analytics.

2.3 Artificial Intelligence

Artificial intelligence marks one of the biggest transformations of the modern era that has altered the complete business landscape. Though it has been many years since the introduction of AI there is no universally accepted definition defining AI. Artificial intelligence refers to systems or machines that replicate human intelligence to perform tasks (Ore and Sposato, 2022). AI refers to sophisticated computer systems and machines that replicate the cognitive functions of the human brain, including learning, reasoning, and planning (Lu et al., 2018). AI means using digital technology to design systems capable of autonomously executing tasks normally expected to require human intelligence (Office for AI, 2019). AI though acting much differently from humans refers to the computing technologies that inspire or replicate intellectual behaviours pertinent to humans (Bhave et al., 2020). Further, AI refers to the system's capability to correctly infer data, learn from that data, and finally use these learnings to perform specific tasks through flexible adaption (Makarius et al., 2020). Table 1 describes the various definitions of AI.

Table 1. Definition of artificial intelligence

Author	Definition
Lu et al., 2018	Sophisticated computer systems and machines that can replicate the functions performed by the human brain such as learning, planning, and reasoning.
Office for AI, 2019	Use of digital technology to create systems that can execute tasks that otherwise require human intelligence.
Bhave et al., 2020	Computing technologies that can replicate human behaviour earlier associated with humans.
Makarius et al., 2020	The system's capability to adequately interpret and learn data and use such learning to perform specific tasks through flexible adoption
Ore and Sposato, 2022	Systems or machines that replicate human intelligence to perform tasks

Source: Compiled by Authors

2.4 Neuropsychological Assessment

The term Neuromanagement was first introduced by Prof. Qingguo Ma from the Zhejiang University which integrates cognitive neuroscience and economics with management sciences (Ma and Wang, 2006). The concept is based on using the neuroscientific approach to explore management and behavioural processes and comprehend human brain activity. This approach allows the examiners to understand the mental processes of people when faced with different management situations and social behaviours (Parincu et al., 2020). Though new as a concept the neuropsychological assessment of employees has started gaining traction in the modern world as an employee's neuropsychological fitness plays a crucial role in determining his/her cognitive strength and ability. Neuropsychological assessments help evaluate a person's cognitive and psychological suitability to perform specific tasks. These assessments are usually performed by certified neuropsychologists who have the required expertise to perform such tasks and effectively evaluate a person's neuropsychological functioning. Neuropsychological assessment is a broader concept that deals with the assessment of an individual's cognitive abilities and functioning such as memory, attention, language, voice processing speed, problem-solving skills, etc. to adequately assess an individual's ability to perform a specific set of tasks and responsibilities. Further, it also deals with identifying any signs of neuropsychological concerns that may interfere with the successful execution of assigned tasks. With the recent technological advancement, a set of AI tools has been introduced used to perform the neuropsychological assessment of individuals based on their facial expressions, voice, pitch, chat interactions, beliefs, and feelings.

3. RESEARCH METHODOLOGY

The present study is exploratory as it attempts to explore the current state of affairs concerning the integration of AI in HR processes with specific attention to employees' neuropsychological assessment during selection and performance evaluation. To fulfill the objectives already mentioned in the "introduction" section the study examined quality research related to the context of the present study. Further, to enrich the understanding, the study also uses the statistics available in the public domain.

4. ANALYSIS AND DISCUSSION

4.1 AI Applications in HR Processes

The use of AI in HRM represents not just a trend but a fundamental shift in managing human resources (Ghedabna et al., 2024). Integrating human resource management processes with artificial intelligence can provide substantial advantages for organisations including efficient employee recruitment (Reilly, 2018), and improved workplace learning (Hamilton and Sodeman, 2020). An organization's success largely depends on its ability to leverage human resources as a competitive advantage. By integrating these human resources with their operational capabilities, organizations can maximize their potential (Muller, 2016). With AI tools and advanced statistical models, organisations can analyse past talent acquisition efforts and identify key skill gaps within the workforce. These insights help organisations enhance their training and development programs, thereby strengthening their overall capacity (Stone et al., 2015). The benefits of leveraging AI accrue to both employees as well as the organisations. Lately, the application of artificial intelligence has streamlined these processes and enabled organizations to stay competitive in a rapidly changing environment. Machine learning enables AI to adjust to changes in its environment, enhancing its accuracy and efficiency (Savitri, 2019). This allows AI to not only offer solutions for specific tasks but also serve as a basis for ongoing innovation, unlocking new possibilities for facing complex challenges (Octavianus et al., 2023). AI technologies enable HR teams to make more informed, data-driven decisions by analysing large volumes of data, identifying patterns, and making predictions (Wierenga, 2010). AI enables systems to collect data from sensors, and other mobile devices, analyse, and interpret the collected data to make informed decisions and adapt to situational demands. Moreover, artificial neural networks can be deployed to evaluate and envisage employee motivation (Azadeh et al., 2009). Further, the training and development function of HRM applies AI to recommend learning programs tailored to job tasks. Figure 2 shows AI applications in HR Processes.

Figure 2. AI application in HR Processes

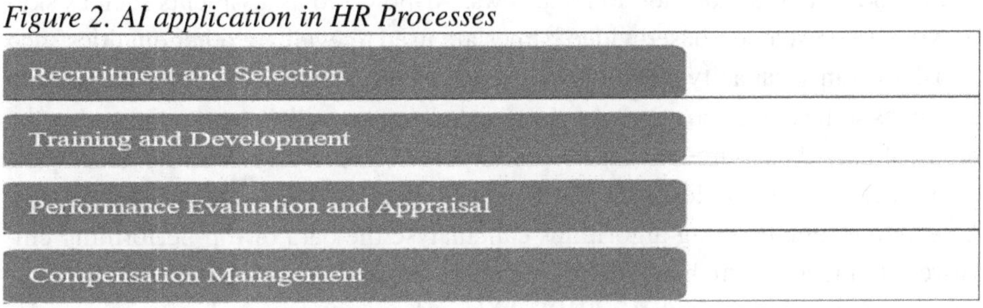

4.2 AI Applications in Neuropsychological Assessment During Recruitment and Selection

With the rapid advancement of technology, recruiters can perform their tasks more effectively and efficiently, allowing them more time to develop their skills and expand their outlooks. Today, numerous technologies are involved in various HR processes. These technologies play a crucial role, particularly in sourcing, evaluating, and recruiting the workforce. The integration of AI in HR has truly transformed the whole process of employee selection especially their neuropsychological assessment for identifying their suitability (in terms of mental and cognitive strength) for a specific job. The human resources division collaborates with artificial intelligence to enhance the quality and efficiency of the employee selection process. Through the use of systematic algorithmic analysis of CVs, robotic interviews, and gamified application tests AI enables organisations to automate the initial stages of the selection process. AI helps organisations solve the problem of identifying suitable applicants for a job and making cost-effective decisions about choosing the right candidate. Additionally, AI algorithms can assist businesses in various tasks, including selecting candidates, conducting live interviews, analysing candidates' moods, preparing reports, and even creating three-dimensional workplace simulations (Cavaliere et al., 2021). Today, many businesses depend on AI-assisted algorithms to hand-pick the best candidates. This is because organizations recognize that incorporating artificial intelligence into the selection process offers a fair evaluation, saves time, ensures objectivity, and positively impacts the candidate assessment process. AI-assisted algorithms help HR teams analyse recurring patterns and compare them with data from current employees in similar roles, aiding them in identifying the most suitable candidates (Cavaliere et al., 2021). Additionally, AI technology not only evaluates verbal responses but also utilizes audio and facial recognition software to analyse factors such as tone of voice, micro expressions, and emotions, offering insights into specific personality traits and competencies (Köchling et al., 2020; van Esch and Black, 2019). In addition to interviews, AI-powered assessments such as skill tests and neuroscience-based video games are used to evaluate other qualities such as risk tolerance capacity, planning skills, persistence, and motivation. This section examines some of the most popular AI-assisted processes that are crucial within the scope of human resource management. Importantly, these systems do not require predefined target variables from the company (Giang, 2018, Raghavan et al., 2020); instead, machine learning algorithms can analyse the data of top-performing employees to identify which applicant characteristics and skills are linked to superior job performance (Tambe et al., 2019). AI-based recruitment applies recommendations and predictions to identify candidates best suited for specific roles, enhancing the overall quality of hired employees (Jain and Gautam, 2016). For example, the software provider Pymetrics uses machine learning and psychometric training data from current high performers to predict how well an applicant will fit a specific role. AI recruiting system vendors claim that their software enhances the efficiency and accuracy of hiring decisions and promotes fairness by eliminating human intuition. HR professionals should consider using data mining techniques to become more thorough in their quest to identify and assess the suitable candidates (Pereira et al.,

2023). Further, chatbots and chatbot-enabled interviews have also brought huge changes in HR by helping gauge the speaking abilities, communication skills, and overall personality of candidates.

4.3 AI Applications in Neuropsychological Assessment During Performance Evaluation

Employee performance evaluations have traditionally relied on subjective methods such as annual reviews, peer assessments, and self-reports, often resulting in discrepancies and biases. As traditional systems rely mostly on peoples' subjective evaluation, more and more companies are now resorting to AI to remove inconsistencies in the assessment process. Consequently, traditional annual performance evaluations are increasingly being supplemented or even fully replaced by continuous, AI-driven performance feedback (Jain and Triadafilopoulos, 2020). AI-oriented performance management systems analyse employee performance data in real time, bringing more objectivity to the whole performance management process. With AI, an employee's skills, career path, training record, and performance can be analysed to suggest training opportunities that support their career growth while aligning with the company's long-term interests (Stone et al., 2015). These technologies provide data-driven feedback on key performance indicators like productivity and task completion rates, dropping the subjectivity typically found in traditional evaluation systems (Yanamala, 2022). Additionally, the AI systems not only help track key performance indicators but can also provide feedback consequently allowing employees to improve their performance before the final annual review (Islam, 2023). AI-integrated performance appraisal leads to strategic decision-making, enhanced employee performance, commitment, and satisfaction, and consequently reduced employee turnover (Riaz and Ghanghas, 2024). While HR professionals traditionally assess employee performance on an annual, semi-annual, or quarterly basis, this approach allows for more frequent evaluations, leading to greater efficiency (Nishad, 2019).

4.4. AI-enabled Procedures for Neuropsychological Assessment of Employees

Some of the applications of AI enable technologies for the neuropsychological assessment of candidates during the selection and performance evaluation procedures are discussed below:

- Sentiment analysis

Sentiment analysis focuses on studying how individuals perceive various stimuli, such as events, and products, and captures people's written words, facial expressions, vocal tones, movements, etc. to document their opinions, emotions, and feelings through observational analysis. Sentiment analysis helps comprehend the complex behavioural patterns of employees (Riaz and Ghanghas, 2024). The purpose of performing this analysis is to collect information about an individual's feelings, and sentiments through the careful observation of their behaviour documented through facial expressions, movements, tones, and other behavioural cues (Yadollahi et al. 2017).

- Digital Interviews

Digital interviews represent another innovative application, where AI converts both verbal and non-verbal behaviour of candidates into psychological profiles, facilitating more accurate predictions. This approach reduces costs and minimizes biases from less experienced interviewers (Chamorro-Premuzic et al., 2017). For example, Unilever Lever uses AI-driven "HireVue-a video interviewing platform" in its hiring process to promote diversity in campus recruitment (Feloni, 2017).

- AI-based Psychometric Tests

These tests are used to assess a candidate's mental capabilities and other personality traits. The AI-enabled psychometric tests reduce bias thus promoting fair and scientifically sound evaluation of a person's cognitive strength. Since now the assessment is performed by machines, any possibility of biases associated with human intervention is automatically ruled out.

- Social Network Analysis

Social network analysis studies communication patterns from platforms like Facebook, LinkedIn, and Twitter within an organization to recognize influential individuals who may either be supported for their impact or assisted if needed. Through AI the social media activity of individuals is analysed to get insights into their personalities, values, and belief systems, which may not be otherwise possible through traditional HR practices. Social network analysis proves to be a good technique to determine how well a person might fit in organisation's culture.

- Machine Learning for Performance Predictions

Machine learning algorithms can be used to create predictive models that estimate performance based on historical data. These models employ supervised learning to identify top performers and unsupervised learning to spot potential areas of concern. The analysis is based on the past performance, training received, employee engagement, etc. to evaluate employee performance. This enables organizations to address performance issues proactively and foster their top talent.

- Natural Language Processing (NLP) for Feedback Analysis

Natural language processing (NLP) is another influential AI technique in performance management analytics that help organisations analyse feedback received from employees. What may appear as general feedback can throw light on the employees' hidden behavioural patterns, employee sentiments, concerns which otherwise may remain unnoticed. It is a useful technique to draw insights from unorganised data allowing HR teams to quickly spot trends and patterns in how employees perceive the organization, their managers, and the work environment.

- Predictive Analytics for Development Needs

AI-powered predictive analytics applies machine learning to design a predictive model to identify individual employee development needs and learning opportunities. The method combines performance data with skill assessments to help organisations create models that predict the appropriate training and mentorship programs for employees. This targeted approach ensures that employees receive the right training to enhance their skills.

4.5 Current Statistics on the Use of AI in HR Processes

HR managers have now started using AI-enabled tools and technologies to execute their tasks and responsibilities. Recent years have observed a dramatic upsurge in the usage of AI-enabled processes to assess the cognitive and mental abilities of potential and actual employees. While earlier the focus has always been on judging candidate suitability through the lens of academic and professional skills, increasing stress combined with complexities of tasks have made it imperative to study the functioning of the human brain to truly assess the mental fit of a person in the given job context. Also, while the traditional systems allow for judging employee performance in terms of targets achieved the use of AI-enabled neuropsychological assessments helps the HR professions determine the mental processes driving the performance. The AI tools are expected to reduce human intervention thus allowing people to focus more on other complex tasks such as software development and strategy formulation. According to the National Aeronautics and Space Administration (NASA), using AI-enabled HR systems allows them to execute 86% of their HR work without any human involvement (Davenport and Ronaki, 2018). The use of various algorithms and machine learning AI provides cognitive insights to identify hidden patterns earlier unidentified by organisations. Figure 3 depicts the growth observed by AI integration in the HR Market. As per the statistics of report on "Global AI in HR Market" the global AI in HR market is expected to grow at a CAGR of 16% from 2024 to 2033 (Refer to Figure 3). The statistics clearly show that the integration of AI in HR has a bright future with more and more HR functions getting automated through AL technologies. Refer Figure 3.

Figure 3. Growth observed by AI integration in HR market

Further, Table 2 depicts examples of a few AI-enabled tools that allow HR professionals to perform neuropsychological assessments of potential and actual employees during selection and performance evaluation procedures.

Table 2. AI tools in Neuropsychological Assessment during selection and performance evaluation procedures

AI Tools	Functionality	Benefits
Peoplebox	hiring, performance management, career development, assessing employee skills and competencies, skill-gap analysis	Speed up the selection process, informed decision-making
Lattice	goal setting, Performance reviews, Talent reviews, 1:1s, Feedback, and praise	Write better performance reviews, a comprehensive platform to evaluate employee performance
Effy AI	360-degree review, Major project milestones, Performance review, Promotion, or job change	Quick review in just 60 seconds, helps in quick monitoring of employee progress

continued on following page

Table 2. Continued

AI Tools	Functionality	Benefits
HireVue	Structured interviews, Automated workflow	Provides real-time evaluation tools, interview guides, automated candidate routing
Pymetrics	Structured evaluation process, candidate experience, Internal collaboration	Better evidence-based decision-making, attention, fairness, generosity, and emotion.
BetterUp	Create tailored development programs, integrate expert coaching with digital personalised experiences and advanced sciences	Find which employees need coaching the most and locate their strengths and weaknesses to suggest improvements.
Culture Amp	Design survey templates, suggesting proven action plans	Quickly summarise large amount of data, reduces bias and saves time.

Source: Compiled by Authors

4.4 Challenges of AI applications in Neuropsychological Assessment and HR processes

Despite AI technology being largely data efficient, their application is surrounded by an array of challenges inhibiting their successful adoption and integration. First, organisations find it difficult to integrate AI systems with existing human workforce and processes (Deloitte, 2017). Further, people lack knowledge of the best practices to effectively develop collaborative intelligence capability (Makarius et al., 2020). Moreover, the integration of AI and automation within HRM processes is expected to impact employees through job substitution, training needs, and increased uncertainty about the roles and responsibilities (Frey and Osborne, 2017) resulting in negative perceptions and psychological detachment from AI adoption. The biggest challenge in the process of using these systems is ensuring that they are used ethically and objectively. Though AI systems are expected to overcome any personal biases, they still have the potential to introduce new forms of bias. As developers focus more on commercial considerations, the societal and ethical consequences of automation are likely to be ignored (Simonite, 2021), and therefore, the organisations must ensure that their AI-driven systems operate on unbiased data, and are regularly audited to identify and mitigate potential biases (Challa, 2022). Also, while machine learning feedback offers greater consistency for measurable metrics, human input remains crucial for assessing soft skills, such as leadership potential and emotional intelligence and thus combining both ML-driven and human feedback systems is important to accomplish more balanced, accurate, and fair performance evaluations (Yanamala, 2022). Again, it is important to have sufficient knowledge and expertise to develop AI tools and systems that are fair and do not reproduce prevailing organisational prejudices (Jacobs and Wallach, 2021; van den Broek et al., 2021).

5. CONCLUSION

As employees i.e. the human component of an organisation essentially forms the base of any successful organisation, easing out HR processes has always been a priority for the organisation. While the various technologies so far have already made things a bit easy, introduction of more scientific AI-based tools and techniques has altered the whole HR domain with tasks being automated. The field of AI indicates that integrating AI tools in HRM will continue to expand, enhancing fairness, fairness, and a more personalized approach to organizational functions. Incorporating artificial intelligence (AI) technologies, including machine learning and natural language processing systems into HR, can greatly improve performance management analytics. AI-driven systems can uncover deeper insights from large volumes of employee performance data, revealing subtle patterns and connections that would be challenging for human analysts to identify. Moreover, the latest neuroscience research has shown that our brains are more complex than previously thought and that they evolve throughout our lives. In such a scenario studying how brain activity can impact employee behaviour, personalities, and performance proves to be an interesting research area. However, it has been observed that organisations despite having invested all the time, effort, and resources, have not yet experienced the projected benefits of AI adoption.

6. LIMITATIONS AND SUGGESTIONS

The present study while valuable for advancing knowledge and conceptual understanding, has several inherent limitations. Firstly, since the study is theoretical and is based on the existing research in the field, empirical research is needed to confirm and study the extent of the impact of AI on HR processes. Secondly, due to the paucity of time, the study focussed only on a few aspects of HR such as employee selection and performance evaluation, and therefore research needs to be conducted to study the role of AI in other HR processes such as Compensation Management, Training and Development, Payroll management, etc. Also, as the integration of AI in HR as a research area is still in its nascent stages more work is required to reach conclusive results. Further, experimental studies need to be conducted to have a true picture of challenges encountered in the adoption and integration of AI for the neuropsychological assessment of employees.

REFERENCES

Aazam, M., Zeadally, S., & Harras, K. A. (2018). Deploying fog computing in industrial internet of things and industry 4.0. *IEEE Transactions on Industrial Informatics*, 14(10), 4674–4682. DOI: 10.1109/TII.2018.2855198

Abou-Zahra, S., Brewer, J., & Cooper, M. (2018). Artificial intelligence (AI) for web accessibility: Is conformance evaluation a way forward? In *Proceedings of the internet of accessible things* (pp. 1–4). DOI: 10.1145/3192714.3192834

Azadeh, A., Rouzbahmana, M., & Saberi, M. (2009). Utilization of an Artificial Intelligence approach for Assessment of Job satisfaction. *International Journal of Intelligent Information Technology Application*, 2(6).

Beardwell, J., & Claydon, T. (Eds.). (2007). *Human resource management: A contemporary approach*. Pearson Education.

Bhave, D. P., Teo, L. H., & Dalal, R. S. (2020). Privacy at work: A review and a research agenda for a contested terrain. *Journal of Management*, 46(1), 127–164. DOI: 10.1177/0149206319878254

Cavaliere, L. P. L., Nath, K., Wisetsri, W., Villalba-Condori, K. O., Arias-Chavez, D., Setiawan, R., . . . Regin, R. (2021). *The impact of E-recruitment and artificial intelligence (AI) tools on HR effectiveness: the case of high schools* (Doctoral dissertation, Petra Christian University).

Challa, V. N. S. K. (2022). AI-Driven Resource Allocation. *International Journal Of Advanced Research in Engineering and Technology, 13*(12).

Chamorro-Premuzic, T., Winsborough, D., Sherman, R., & Hogan, R. (2016). New talent signals: Shiny new objects or a brave new world? *Industrial and Organizational Psychology: Perspectives on Science and Practice*, 9(3), 621–640. DOI: 10.1017/iop.2016.6

Davenport, T. H., & Ronanki, R. (2018). Artificial intelligence for the real world. *Harvard Business Review*, 96(1), 108–116.

Deloitte. (2017). The 2017 Deloitte state of cognitive survey. Accessed 10 July 2021. Web Link https://tinyurl.com/4kn2c35s

Frey, C. B., & Osborne, M. A. (2017). The future of employment: How susceptible are jobs to computerisation? *Technological Forecasting and Social Change*, 114, 254–280. DOI: 10.1016/j.techfore.2016.08.019

Ghedabna, L., Ghedabna, R., Imtiaz, Q., Faheem, M. A., Alkhayyat, A., & Hosen, M. S. (2024). Artificial Intelligence in Human Resource Management: Revolutionizing Recruitment, Performance, and Employee Development. *Nanotechnology Perceptions*, •••, 52–68.

Giang, V. (2018). *The potential hidden bias in automated hiring systems*. Fast Company.

Hamilton, R. H., & Sodeman, W. A. (2020). The questions we ask: Opportunities and challenges for using big data analytics to strategically manage human capital resources. *Business Horizons*, 63(1), 85–95. DOI: 10.1016/j.bushor.2019.10.001

Insider, B. (2017). *Consumer goods giant Unilever has been hiring employees using brain games and artificial intelligence—And it'sa huge success*. Business Insider.

Islam, Z. (2023). Optimizing Human Resource Operations through AI-Driven Advanced Computing Systems. *Journal of Advanced Computing Systems*, 3(12), 18–25.

Jacobs, A. Z., & Wallach, H. (2021, March). Measurement and fairness. In *Proceedings of the 2021 ACM conference on fairness, accountability, and transparency* (pp. 375-385). DOI: 10.1145/3442188.3445901

Jain, N., & Gautam, V. (2016). Artificial Intelligence in Human Resource Management: An Emerging Role in 21st Century. *International Journal of Management*, 7(3), 1–7.

Jain, R., & Triadafilopoulos, T. (2020). AI and HR Analytics: Redefining Talent Management in the 21st Century. *Human Resource Management International Digest*, 28(2), 12–15.

Johnason, P. (2009). HRM in changing organizational contexts. In Collings, D. G., & Wood, G. (Eds.), *Human resource management: A critical approach* (pp. 19–37). Routledge.

Kamran, A., Dawood, J., & Hilal, S. B. (2015). Analysis of the recruitment and selection process. In *Proceedings of the Ninth International Conference on Management Science and Engineering Management* (pp. 1357-1375). Springer Berlin Heidelberg. DOI: 10.1007/978-3-662-47241-5_114

Köchling, A., Riazy, S., Wehner, M. C., & Simbeck, K. (2021). Highly accurate, but still discriminatory: A fairness evaluation of algorithmic video analysis in the recruitment context. *Business & Information Systems Engineering*, 63(1), 39–54. DOI: 10.1007/s12599-020-00673-w

Liu, F., Shi, Y., & Liu, Y. (2017). Intelligence quotient and intelligence grade of artificial intelligence. *Annals of Data Science*, 4(2), 179–191. DOI: 10.1007/s40745-017-0109-0

Ma, Q. G., & Wang, X. Y. (2006). Cognitive neuroscience, neuroeconomics, and neuromanagement. *Guanli Shijie*, 10, 139–149.

Makarius, E. E., Mukherjee, D., Fox, J. D., & Fox, A. K. (2020). Rising with the machines: A sociotechnical framework for bringing artificial intelligence into the organization. *Journal of Business Research*, 120, 262–273. DOI: 10.1016/j.jbusres.2020.07.045

Misselhorn, C. (2018). Artificial morality. Concepts, issues and challenges. *Society*, 55(2), 161–169. DOI: 10.1007/s12115-018-0229-y

Müller, VC. (2016) Fundamental Issues of Artificial Intelligence. Springer Nature. 12.

Murad, A. (2000). *HR—A complete guide*. Book Press and Printers.

Nishad, N. (2019). Robotic process automation for recruitment process. 10, 608-611.

Office for AI. (2019). Understanding artificial intelligence. Retrieved December 1, 2021.

Oktavianus, A. J. E., Naibaho, L., & Rantung, D. A. (2023). Pemanfaatan Artificial Intelligence pada Pembelajaran dan Asesmen di Era Digitalisasi. *Jurnal Kridatama Sains Dan Teknologi*, 5(02), 473–486. DOI: 10.53863/kst.v5i02.975

Ore, O., & Sposato, M. (2022). Opportunities and risks of artificial intelligence in recruitment and selection. *The International Journal of Organizational Analysis*, 30(6), 1771–1782. DOI: 10.1108/IJOA-07-2020-2291

Parincu, A. M. T., Capatina, A., Varon, D. J., Bennet, P. F., & Recuerda, A. M. (2020). Neuromanagement: the scientific approach to contemporary management. In *Proceedings of the International Conference on Business Excellence* (Vol. 14, No. 1, pp. 1046-1056). DOI: 10.2478/picbe-2020-0099

Pereira, V., Hadjielias, E., Christofi, M., & Vrontis, D. (2023). A systematic literature review on the impact of artificial intelligence on workplace outcomes: A multi-process perspective. *Human Resource Management Review*, 33(1), 100857. DOI: 10.1016/j.hrmr.2021.100857

Raghavan, M., Barocas, S., Kleinberg, J., & Levy, K. (2020, January). Mitigating bias in algorithmic hiring: Evaluating claims and practices. In *Proceedings of the 2020 conference on fairness, accountability, and transparency* (pp. 469-481). DOI: 10.1145/3351095.3372828

Reilly, P. (2018). The impact of artificial intelligence on the HR function. *Which way now for HR and organisational changes*, 41-58.

Riaz, H., & Ghanghas, S. (2024). Artificial Intelligence in Employee Performance Evaluation and Its Managerial Implication. *Journal of Informatics Education and Research*, 4(1).

Simonite, T. (2021). What really happened when Google Ousted Timnit Gebru.

Stone, D. L., Deadrick, D. L., Lukaszewski, K. M., & Johnson, R. (2015). The Influence of Technology on the Future of Human Resource Management. *Human Resource Management Review*, 25(2), 216–231. DOI: 10.1016/j.hrmr.2015.01.002

Tambe, P., Cappelli, P., & Yakubovich, V. (2019). Artificial intelligence in human resources management: Challenges and a path forward. *California Management Review*, 61(4), 15–42. DOI: 10.1177/0008125619867910

Van den Broek, E., Sergeeva, A., & Huysman, M. (2021). When the Machine Meets the Expert: An Ethnography of Developing AI for Hiring. *Management Information Systems Quarterly*, 45(3), 1557–1580. DOI: 10.25300/MISQ/2021/16559

van Esch, P., & Black, J. S. (2019). Factors that influence new genera tion candidates to engage with and complete digital, AI-enabled recruiting. *Business Horizons*, 62(6), 729–739. DOI: 10.1016/j.bushor.2019.07.004

Von Krogh, G. (2018). Artificial intelligence in organizations: New opportunities for phenomenon-based theorizing. *Academy of Management Discoveries*, 4(4), 404–409. DOI: 10.5465/amd.2018.0084

Wierenga, B. (2010). Marketing and artificial intelligence: Great opportunities, reluctant partners. In *Marketing intelligent systems using soft computing: Managerial and research applications* (pp. 1–8). Springer Berlin Heidelberg. DOI: 10.1007/978-3-642-15606-9_1

Yadollahi, A., Shahraki, A. G., & Zaiane, O. R. (2017). Current state of text sentiment analysis from opinion to emotion mining. *ACM Computing Surveys*, 50(2), 1–33. DOI: 10.1145/3057270

Yanamala, K. K. R. (2022). Integrating machine learning and human feedback for employee performance evaluation. *Journal of Advanced Computing Systems*, 2(1), 1–10. https://market.us/report/ai-in-hr-market/. DOI: 10.69987/JACS.2022.20101

Chapter 7
AI Algorithms for Early Detection of Cognitive Impairments

Rupam Hazra
Global Institute of Management and Technology, Krishnanagar, India

Parag Chatterjee
Global Institute of Management and Technology, Krishnanagar, India

Yash Singh
Global Institute of Management and Technology, Krishnanagar, India

Gopal Podder
Global Institute of Management and Technology, Krishnanagar, India

Titli Das
Global Institute of Management and Technology, Krishnanagar, India

ABSTRACT

The rapid advancement of Artificial Intelligence (AI) and Machine Learning (ML) has introduced transformative capabilities in the detection and management of cognitive impairments. These impairments represent significant challenges in healthcare, characterized by complex symptoms and progressive deterioration. Traditional diagnostic and management methods often face limitations due to the subtleties in early symptom detection and the need for comprehensive data analysis. AI algorithms offer powerful tools to address these challenges. The integration of these AI algorithms into clinical practice provides several advantages: enhanced diagnostic accuracy through sophisticated data analysis, personalized treatment

DOI: 10.4018/979-8-3693-9341-3.ch007

plans tailored to individual patient profiles, and predictive models that forecast disease progression. This chapter highlights the potential of artificial intelligence to transform the management of mental retardation and shows how these technologies can be used to overcome the limitations of traditional and advances in the field of mental health.

INTRODUCTION

Cognitive impairment, including conditions such as Alzheimer's disease, Parkinson's disease and other forms of dementia, is a major challenge for health systems worldwide. Early detection of these conditions is important, as interventions are more effective and patient outcomes are better. In the past, the diagnosis of mental disorders has relied heavily on clinical assessments, neuropsychological tests and neuroimaging techniques. Recent advances in AI offer early new opportunities for early detection. Artificial intelligence algorithms, especially those related to machine learning and deep learning, have demonstrated the ability to analyse complex patterns in data that may indicate early cognitive decline. These algorithms can quickly process large amounts of data and detect subtle changes that conventional methods might miss.

Overview of Cognitive Impairments

Cognitive impairment covers many conditions that affect memory, thinking, inference, and other mental functions. These disorders may vary depending on the severity and progress of mild cognitive impairment (MCI), from more serious forms, such as Alzheimer's disease and other types of dementia.

Types of Cognitive Impairments

A. **Alzheimer's Disease:** Alzheimer's disease is the most common form of dementia and is characterized by progressive memory loss, confusion, and behavioral changes. Early symptoms often include difficulty remembering recent events and performing everyday tasks (Alzheimer's Association, 2023).
B. **Vascular dementia:** This type of dementia occurs due to cerebrovascular problems, such as a stroke, and causes problems with reasoning, planning, and judgment. Symptoms may vary depending on the location and extent of the brain damage (O'Brien & Thomas, 2015).

C. **Lewy body dementia:** Lewy body dementia, characterized by abnormal protein deposits in the brain, causes cognitive fluctuations, visual hallucinations, and motor symptoms similar to Parkinson's disease (McKeith et al., 2017).
D. **Frontotemporal Dementia:** This group of disorders affects the frontal and temporal lobes of the brain, causing changes in personality, behaviour, and language skills.
E. **Mild Cognitive Impairment (MCI):** MCI is a stage between normal aging and more serious conditions like Alzheimer's. People with mild cognitive impairment have significant problems with memory or cognition but do not meet the criteria for dementia.

AI Algorithms for Early Detection:

AI algorithms, particularly those involving machine learning and deep learning, have shown significant promise in detecting cognitive impairments at an early stage.

A. **Imaging analysis:** AI algorithms can analyze brain imaging data (for example, MRI, SCA SCA) to detect delicate changes in brain structures and functions, and indicate an initial recognition function. For example, convolutional neural networks (CNNs) have been used to identify patterns associated with Alzheimer's disease from MRI scans with high accuracy.
B. **Speech and language processing:** Natural language processing (NLP) techniques analyze speech patterns and language use to detect cognitive decline. Changes in language skills, such as word-finding difficulties and decreased fluency, can be early indicators of cognitive impairment. AI models can assess these characteristics using recordings of spoken or written language (Miller et al., 2017).
C. **Behavioral and wearable data:** AI algorithms can process data from wearable devices and mobile apps that track daily activities, movement patterns, and physiological indicators. Machine learning models can detect deviations from normal patterns, such as changes in gait and activity levels, that may indicate cognitive decline.
D. **Predictive Analytics:** AI systems can integrate different types of data (e.g., genetics, medical data, and cognitive test results) to predict the likelihood of developing cognitive disorders. Predictive models can identify high-risk individuals and suggest early intervention.

Importance of Early Detection

Early detection of cognitive impairments is critical for several reasons, particularly when leveraging AI algorithms to enhance diagnostic accuracy and intervention strategies. The ability to identify cognitive decline at an early stage can significantly impact patient outcomes, healthcare costs, and overall quality of life.

Improved Treatment Outcomes

A. **Prompt Intervention:** Early detection allows for prompt intervention, which can slow the progression of-cognitive impairment and increase the effectiveness of treatment. For diseases such as Alzheimer's, early treatment with medication and lifestyle changes can help control symptoms more effectively and maintain quality of life over the long term.
B. **Personalized help:** AI algorithms can help you set treatment plans based on individual data. Early detection allows for medical services suppliers to adapt to intervention more accurately according to the patient's condition, which leads to the best results (Nielsen et al. 2020).

Reduction in Healthcare Costs

A. **Cost-effectiveness**: Early detection and intervention can reduce the overall burden on health systems by potentially delaying the need for more intensive care and reducing emergency interventions. This may lead to a significant cost reduction in both healthcare systems and patients.
B. **Resource allocation:** AI algorithms can contribute to efficient resource allocation by identifying high-risk individuals early, enabling more targeted use of medical resources and reducing unnecessary diagnostic procedures.

Improved Quality of Life

A. **Delay in Symptom Onset:** Early intervention can delay the onset of more severe symptoms, helping patients maintain independence and engage in daily activities for a longer period. This delay can greatly improve the quality of life and reduce the emotional and psychological effects of illness (Daviglus et al. 2011).

B. **Caregiver support**: AI tools can also provide support to caregivers by identifying cognitive impairment early. Early diagnosis can help caregivers prepare for future needs and access supportive resources, easing some of the burden that comes with caring for someone with cognitive impairment.

Role of AI in Healthcare

Artificial intelligence (AI) has revolutionized various fields in healthcare fields, such as early detection and treatment of cognitive impairment. Cognitive impairments such as Alzheimer's disease and other dementia in other forms can cause serious problems due to complex nature and the impact of the quality of life. AI algorithms offer promising solutions to address these challenges, improve diagnostic accuracy, and improve patient outcomes.

Enhanced Diagnostic Accuracy

A. **Advanced pattern recognition:** AI algorithms, especially those involving machine learning and deep learning, are good at recognizing complex patterns in large data sets. In the case of cognitive disorders, these algorithms analyze data from various sources, such as brain imaging, genetic information, and clinical assessments, to identify subtle early signs of cognitive decline that may go unnoticed by traditional methods (Suk et al., 2017).
B. **Multimodal data integration:** AI systems can integrate and analyze different types of data, such as MRI scans, PET scans, and cognitive test results, to provide a comprehensive assessment of a person's cognitive health. This holistic approach can improve diagnostic accuracy and help distinguish between different types of cognitive disorders (Lee et al., 2019).

Timely and Personalized Interventions

A. **Early detection and monitoring:** AI algorithms can facilitate early detection of cognitive impairment by identifying changes in data patterns before significant symptoms appear. This early detection allows for timely intervention, which can slow disease progression and improve treatment outcomes. AI systems can continuously monitor patients' cognitive function and adapt treatment plans based on real-time data (Jiang et al., 2021).

B. **Personalized treatment plans:** AI-based tools can help in creating personalized treatment plans by analyzing personal data such as genetic, behavioral, and clinical factors. This personalization ensures that interventions are tailored to the specific needs of each patient, leading to more effective treatment of cognitive disorders.

Efficient Resource Utilization

A. **Reducing costs**. Thanks to an earlier diagnosis and more accurate treatment, the AI algorithms can reduce the total cost of controlling cognitive impairment. Early detection helps to avoid costly emergency interventions, reduce the need for advanced stage detailed care, which leads to significant costs between medical systems and patients (ryu et al. 2018.)
B. **Optimizing resource allocation**: AI can help in the efficient allocation of healthcare resources by identifying high-risk people early, which allows for targeted use of resources, reduces unnecessary diagnostic tests, and ensures that interventions are delivered to those who need them most (Verbeek et al., 2020).

Improving Patient and Caregiver Quality of Life

A. **Maintaining Independence:** Early detection with AI can delay the onset of more severe symptoms, allowing patients to maintain their independence and continue their daily activities for longer. This delay can enhance the quality of life and reduce the emotional and psychological impact of cognitive impairments.
B. **Support for care:** Artificial intelligence tools can also support people, provide early warnings and contribute to the best treatment of patient care. Early diagnosis allows people to provide care, prepare for future needs, access support resources and more effectively manage care obligations.

Advancing Research and Innovation

A. **Promoting research:** AI algorithms contribute to a better understanding of cognitive disabilities by analyzing huge amounts of data and identifying new patterns. The advances in this knowledge may lead to a new method of treatment and intervention, which may lead to the management and treatment of cognitive impairment (Miller et al. 2022).

B. **Innovative Diagnostic Tools:** AI enables the development of innovative diagnostic tools that can detect cognitive impairments with greater accuracy. These tools often provide insights that traditional methods cannot, leading to more effective and earlier diagnosis and potentially uncovering new avenues for research and treatment.

FUNDAMENTALS OF COGNITIVE IMPAIRMENTS

To understand how AI algorithms can be applied to the early detection and treatment of cognitive disorders, it is important to understand the fundamental concepts surrounding cognitive disorders themselves. Cognitive disorders include a wide range of conditions that affect memory, reasoning, and other mental functions, posing significant challenges to diagnosis and treatment.

Types of Cognitive Impairments & Corresponding AI Algorithms

Alzheimer's Disease (AD)

A. **Overview:** Alzheimer's disease is the most common form of dementia and is characterized by progressive memory loss, confusion, and cognitive decline. This is associated with the accumulation of amyloid plaques and tau tangles in the brain.

B. **AI Algorithms:**
   - **Neuroimaging Analysis:** AI algorithms analyze MRI and PET scans to detect early changes in brain structure and function associated with Alzheimer's. For example, deep learning models can identify patterns of brain atrophy indicative of Alzheimer's disease (Jack et al., 2018).
   - **Predictive modelling:** Machine learning models predict the likelihood of developing Alzheimer's disease based on genetic, clinical, and lifestyle data. These models can identify high-risk individuals and facilitate early intervention (Friedman et al., 2018).
   - **Cognitive testing:** AI can analyze cognitive testing data to detect subtle changes in memory and thinking skills that may be early signs of Alzheimer's disease (Sook et al., 2017).

Vascular Dementia

A. **Overview:** Alzheimer's disease is the most common form of dementia and is characterized by progressive memory loss, confusion, and cognitive decline. This is associated with the accumulation of amyloid plaques and tau tangles in the brain.

B. **AI Algorithms:**

   - **Neuroimaging Analysis:** AI algorithms analyse MRI and PET scans to detect early changes in brain structure and function associated with Alzheimer's disease. For example, deep learning models can identify patterns of brain atrophy indicative of Alzheimer's disease.
   - **Predictive modelling:** Machine learning models predict the likelihood of developing Alzheimer's disease based on genetic, clinical, and lifestyle data. These models can identify high-risk individuals and facilitate early intervention.
   - **Cognitive testing:** AI can analyze cognitive testing data to detect subtle changes in memory and thinking skills that may be early signs of Alzheimer's disease.

Lewy Body Dementia (LBD)

A. **Overview:** Lewy body dementia (LBD) is characterized by abnormal deposits of proteins called Lewy bodies in the brain, which affect cognition, movement, and behaviour. It is characterized by fluctuating cognitive impairment, visual hallucinations, and motor symptoms similar to Parkinson's disease.

B. **AI Algorithms:**

   - **Image Analysis:** AI algorithms can analyze neuroimaging data to identify the presence of Lewy bodies and other characteristic changes in brain structure, including the use of advanced image processing techniques to improve the visibility of these abnormalities (Hsu et al., 2019).
   - **Symptom tracking:** AI-driven wearable devices and mobile apps monitor motor symptoms and cognitive fluctuations in real-time, helping to manage and adjust treatments more effectively.

Frontotemporal Dementia (FTD)

A. **Overview:** Frontotemporal dementia affects the frontal and temporal lobes of the brain, causing changes in personality, behaviour, and speech. It often manifests as significant impairments in social behaviour and language skills (Bang, Spina, & Miller, 2015).
B. **AI Algorithms:**
   - o **Speech and Language Analysis:** AI algorithms analyze speech patterns and language use to detect early signs of FTD. Natural Language Processing (NLP) tools assess changes in language and communication that may indicate the disease (Roark et al., 2011).
   - o **Behavioral data analysis:** AI systems can analyze behavioral data obtained from interactions with patients to identify changes in personality and social behaviour that are common in frontotemporal dementia (Goveas et al., 2021).

Mild Cognitive Impairment (MCI)

A. **Overview:** Mild cognitive impairment is characterized by a decline in cognitive ability that is more significant than would be expected for age, but not severe enough to significantly interfere with daily life. MCI often precedes more serious illnesses such as Alzheimer's disease (Petersen et al., 1999).
B. **AI algorithm**:
   - o **early detection:** AI algorithms analyze the vertical data of cognitive evaluation, detect the first signs of MCI, and distinguish them from normal age -related changes. These models can identify a model with a decrease in cognitive function that indicates the progress of MCI to dementia.
   - o **Risk stratification:** Machine learning models assess risk factors such as genetic predisposition, lifestyle and medical history to stratify patients based on their likelihood of progression from MCI to dementia.

General Cognitive Impairment

A. **Overview:** Common cognitive disorders include a variety of conditions that do not have a specific diagnostic label and affect cognitive function. It includes various subtypes and degrees of impairment.

B. **AI Algorithms:**
   - o **Multimodal Data Integration:** AI algorithms integrate data from multiple sources, such as neuroimaging, genetic data, and clinical assessments, to provide a comprehensive assessment of cognitive function and identify generalized cognitive impairment.
   - o **Real-Time Monitoring and Feedback:** AI systems use sensors and wearable devices to continuously monitor cognitive performance and provide feedback or alerts to patients and caregivers (Gonzalez et al., 2020).

Symptoms and Progression

There are a variety of symptoms and progressions in various ways of Alzheimer's disease, vascular dementia, lebie's body dementia, frontal visual dementia and light recognition disorder. Understanding these symptoms and their progress is important for effective detection and treatment.

Alzheimer's Disease (AD)

Symptoms:

- **Early Stage**: Mild memory loss, difficulty with familiar tasks, confusion about time and place, and changes in mood or personality.
- **Middle Stage**: Increased memory loss, confusion about personal history, difficulty with language and reasoning, and changes in behaviour.
- **Late Stage**: Severe memory loss, loss of physical abilities, difficulty recognizing loved ones, and incontinence.

Vascular Dementia

Symptoms:

- **Early Stage**: Difficulty with problem-solving, confusion, disorientation, and changes in mood or behaviour.
- **Middle Stage**: Impaired judgment and reasoning, trouble organizing thoughts and tasks, and increased memory problems.
- **Late Stage**: Severe cognitive decline, loss of motor skills, and incontinence.

Lewy Body Dementia (LBD)

Symptoms:

- **Early Stage**: Fluctuating cognition, visual hallucinations, and motor symptoms similar to Parkinson's disease.
- **Middle Stage**: Severe cognitive fluctuations, increased hallucinations, and significant motor impairment.
- **Late Stage**: Advanced cognitive and motor impairments, along with severe disruptions in daily functioning.

Frontotemporal Dementia (FTD)

Symptoms:

- **Early Stage**: Changes in personality, behaviour, and language. This may include inappropriate social behaviour, difficulty with speech, and apathy.
- **Middle Stage**: Severe behavioral and language impairments, including loss of social skills and difficulty with complex language tasks.
- **Late Stage**: Profound deficits in behaviour, language, and executive function, with significant impact on daily living.

Mild Cognitive Impairment (MCI)

Symptoms:

- **Early Stage**: Noticeable memory problems that are greater than expected for age but do not significantly interfere with daily life.
- **Middle Stage**: Increasing difficulty with memory and cognitive tasks, with potential progression to more severe cognitive impairments.
- **Late Stage**: Some individuals with MCI progress to dementia, showing more pronounced cognitive decline.

Current Diagnostic Methods

The diagnosis and management of cognitive impairments have traditionally involved a range of clinical, imaging, and testing methods. Advances in artificial intelligence (AI) are now enhancing these methods, offering more precise, efficient, and personalized approaches.

Clinical Evaluation

A. **Current Methods:**
   - o **Patient History and Interviews:** Clinicians gather detailed information about symptoms, medical history, and lifestyle through structured or semi-structured interviews.
   - o **Cognitive Assessments:** Standardized tests such as the Mini-Mental State Examination (MMSE) or the Montreal Cognitive Assessment (MoCA) are used to evaluate cognitive function and identify impairments.

B. **AI Enhancements:**
   - o **AI-Enhanced Decision Support:** AI algorithms analyze patient data and clinical histories to support clinical decision-making, suggesting potential diagnoses and recommending further tests based on data patterns (Rajkomar et al., 2019).
   - o **Natural Language Processing (NLP):** NLP techniques process and analyze clinical notes and patient interviews to extract relevant information and identify symptoms indicative of cognitive impairments.

Neuroimaging

A. **Current Methods:**
   - o **Magnetic Resonance Imaging (MRI):** Provides detailed images of brain structure, identifying atrophy and other abnormalities.
   - o **Positron Emission Tomography (PET):** Visualizes brain activity and detects amyloid plaques and tau tangles.
   - o **Computed Tomography (CT):** Used to rule out other causes of cognitive symptoms by providing structural imaging.

B. **AI Enhancements:**
   - o **Automated Image Analysis:** AI algorithms, including convolutional neural networks (CNNs), automate the segmentation and analysis of neuroimaging data. This improves accuracy and speed in detecting brain abnormalities such as atrophy or lesions (Epelbaum et al., 2021).
   - o **Early Biomarker Detection:** Deep learning models analyze subtle patterns in neuroimaging data that may indicate early stages of cognitive impairments, enhancing early diagnosis.

Neuropsychological Testing

A. **Current Methods:**
  - o **Cognitive Tests:** Assessments like the Wechsler Memory Scale or the Trail Making Test evaluate various cognitive domains, including memory, attention, and executive function.
  - o **Functional Assessments:** Evaluate how cognitive impairments impact daily living activities and overall functionality.

B. **AI Enhancements:**
  - o **Adaptive Testing:** AI algorithms create adaptive cognitive assessments that adjust in real-time based on individual performance, providing more precise measures of cognitive function (Pruitt et al., 2020).
  - o **Data Integration:** AI integrates and analyses data from multiple cognitive tests to identify specific cognitive deficits and improve diagnostic accuracy (Baker et al., 2019).

Genetic and Biomarker Testing

A. **Current Methods:**
  - o **Genetic Testing:** Identifies genetic risk factors, such as the APOE ε4 allele, which is associated with Alzheimer's disease.
  - o **Biomarker Testing:** Measures biomarkers in cerebrospinal fluid (CSF) or blood, such as amyloid-beta and tau proteins, to assess the presence of cognitive impairments.

B. **AI Enhancements:**
  - o **Genetic Data Analysis:** AI algorithms analyze complex genetic data to identify associations between genetic variants and cognitive impairments, helping to predict risk based on genetic profiles (Zhang et al., 2020).
  - o **Biomarker Prediction:** AI models combine biomarker data with clinical and imaging information to predict disease progression and response to treatments more accurately (Shen et al., 2021).

Wearable and Digital Health Technologies

A. **Current Methods:**

- o **Wearable Devices:** Track physical activity, sleep patterns, and other health metrics that can be relevant to cognitive health.
- o **Mobile Apps**: Provide cognitive training exercises and track cognitive performance over time.

B. **AI Enhancements:**

- o **Real-Time Monitoring:** AI algorithms process data from wearable devices and mobile apps to monitor cognitive function and detect early signs of decline. For instance, AI can analyze data from smartwatches to identify changes in movement patterns that may indicate cognitive impairment.
- o **Personalized Interventions:** AI systems use data from digital health technologies to tailor cognitive training and interventions to the individual's specific needs, improving the effectiveness of these programs (Kumar et al., 2021).

ARTIFICIAL INTELLIGENCE AND MACHINE LEARNING BASICS

Artificial Intelligence (AI) and Machine Learning (ML) are revolutionizing the field of healthcare, particularly in the detection and management of cognitive impairments. To understand their impact, it is crucial to grasp the basics of these technologies and how they are applied to improve diagnosis, monitoring, and treatment of cognitive disorders.

Introduction to AI and Machine Learning

Artificial Intelligence (AI) and Machine Learning (ML) represent transformative technologies in the field of healthcare, offering powerful tools for improving the detection and management of cognitive impairments. These technologies are designed to emulate human intelligence and learn from data to make predictions and decisions, thereby enhancing various aspects of healthcare from diagnosis to treatment.

Artificial Intelligence (AI)

A. **Definition and Scope:** Artificial Intelligence (AI) refers to the capability of a machine to imitate human intelligent. AI systems are designed to perform tasks that require human-like cognitive functions such as learning, reasoning, problem-solving, and decision-making.

B. **Applications in Cognitive Impairments:** AI can analyse large datasets from various sources (clinical records, imaging data, genetic information) to identify patterns and trends indicative of cognitive impairments.AI-driven tools can support clinicians by automating diagnostic processes, predicting disease progression, and personalizing treatment plans.

Machine Learning (ML)

A. **Definition and Scope:**
   - o Machine Learning (ML) is a subset of AI that focuses on the development of algorithms that enable computers to learn from and make predictions based on data without being explicitly programmed for each task. ML systems are exposed to a large data over a time period to improve their performance.

B. **Key Concepts:**
   - o **Algorithms**: Mathematical models that process input data to make predictions or decisions. Common algorithms include regression models, classification models, clustering methods, and neural networks.
   - o **Training and Testing:** ML models are trained using historical data (training set) to learn patterns and relationships. They are then tested on new data (test set) to evaluate their accuracy and generalizability.

C. **Types of ML:**
   - o **Supervised Learning:** Involves training models on labeled data where the outcome is known. For example, predicting the presence of Alzheimer's disease based on known patient characteristics.
   - o **Unsupervised Learning:** Involves training models on unlabeled data to identify hidden patterns or groupings. For example, clustering patients into different subtypes of cognitive impairments based on their clinical and imaging data.
   - o **Reinforcement Learning:** Models learn by interacting with an environment and receiving feedback based on their actions. This is less commonly used in cognitive impairments but can be applied to optimize treatment strategies.

D. **Applications in Cognitive Impairments:**
   - o **Diagnostic Support**: ML algorithms can analyze neuroimaging and clinical data to assist in diagnosing cognitive impairments. For example, algorithms can identify patterns in MRI scans that are indicative of Alzheimer's disease.

- o **Predictive Modeling:** ML models can predict the progression of cognitive impairments based on various factors, such as genetic markers and clinical data, enabling early intervention and personalized treatment.
- o **Personalized Care:** ML can be used to tailor interventions and treatments to individual patients by analyzing their unique data and predicting their response to different therapies.

Integration of AI and ML in Cognitive Impairments

A. **Data Integration and Analysis:**
   - o **Multimodal Data:** AI and ML can integrate and analyze data from multiple sources, such as clinical records, imaging studies, genetic profiles, and behavioral assessments. This comprehensive analysis helps in forming a more accurate diagnosis and personalized treatment plan.
   - o **Real-Time Monitoring:** AI-powered tools can continuously monitor cognitive function through wearable devices and mobile apps, providing real-time data on patient condition and enabling timely interventions.

B. **Challenges and Considerations:**
   - o **Data Quality and Privacy:** Ensuring the quality and security of patient data is crucial. AI and ML systems require large amounts of high-quality data to make accurate predictions, and patient privacy must be safeguarded.
   - o **Interpretability:** Many AI and ML models, particularly deep learning models, can be complex and difficult to interpret. It is essential to develop methods to understand and explain how these models make their predictions.

Machine Learning applications in cognitive impairment

Supervised Learning

A. **Applications in Cognitive Impairments:**
   - o **Diagnosis:** Algorithms can be trained to classify patients based on features such as clinical symptoms, neuroimaging data, or genetic information. For instance, predicting whether a patient has Alzheimer's disease based on MRI scans and cognitive test results.

- o **Outcome Prediction:** Models can forecast the progression of cognitive impairments by analyzing historical patient data and identifying patterns associated with disease progression.

B. **Example:** Logistic Regression, Support Vector Machines (SVM), and Neural Networks.

Unsupervised Learning

A. **Applications in Cognitive Impairments:**
- o **Clustering:** Grouping patients into subtypes based on similarities in their clinical, imaging, or genetic data. This can help in identifying new subtypes of cognitive disorders or understanding variability within a disorder.
- o **Dimensionality Reduction:** Simplifying complex datasets to reveal underlying structures or patterns. Techniques like Principal Component Analysis (PCA) are used to reduce the number of variables while retaining essential information, aiding in visualizing and interpreting data.

B. **Example**: k-Means Clustering, Hierarchical Clustering, Principal Component Analysis (PCA).

Reinforcement Learning

A. **Applications in Cognitive Impairments:**
- o **Treatment Optimization:** Using reinforcement learning to tailor and optimize treatment plans based on patient responses. For example, adapting therapy recommendations based on real-time feedback from patient progress.
- o **Behavioral Interventions:** Designing adaptive cognitive training programs that adjust difficulty and focus based on user performance to enhance cognitive function and engagement.

B. **Example:** Q-Learning, Deep Q-Networks (DQN).

DATA SOURCES

Types of Data Used in Cognitive Impairment Detection

Cognitive impairment detection involves the use of various data types to assess cognitive function, identify potential issues, and determine underlying causes. The primary types of data used:

Medical Records

A. **Content**: Includes patient history, medication records, and previous diagnoses.
B. **Use**: Used to assess risk factors (e.g., cardiovascular issues, diabetes), monitor disease progression, and identify potential causes of cognitive decline (e.g., Alzheimer's, stroke).
C. **Example**: Electronic Health Records (EHRs) are commonly analyzed to correlate medical history with cognitive impairment symptoms.

Neuroimaging Data

A. **Types:** MRI (Magnetic Resonance Imaging), fMRI (functional MRI), PET (Positron Emission Tomography), CT (Computed Tomography).
B. **Use:** Neuroimaging allows for the visualization of brain structure and function, helping to identify brain atronphy, lesions, amyloid plaques, and other abnormalities linked to cognitive impairment.
C. **Example:** PET scans are used to detect beta-amyloid plaques in Alzheimer's patients.

Behavioural Data

A. **Types:** Cognitive tests (e.g., Mini-Mental State Examination, Montreal Cognitive Assessment), daily activity monitoring (e.g., sleep patterns, mobility).
B. **Use:** Behavioral data provide direct insight into cognitive function by assessing memory, attention, language, and problem-solving skills. Wearable devices and sensors are increasingly used to gather real-time behavioral data.
C. **Example:** Cognitive assessments help to identify early signs of dementia or mild cognitive impairment.

Genetic Data

A. **Content:** Analysis of genes associated with neurodegenerative diseases (e.g., APOE-ε4 allele).
B. **Use:** Genetic screening helps in understanding the risk for cognitive decline, especially in Alzheimer's and other hereditary cognitive disorders.
C. **Example:** APOE genotyping is used to assess Alzheimer's disease risk.

Biomarker Data

A. **Types:** Blood, cerebrospinal fluid (CSF) samples.
B. **Use:** Biomarkers such as tau protein and amyloid-beta peptides are used to detect neurodegeneration or abnormal brain function.
C. **Example:** Measuring CSF tau protein levels helps diagnose Alzheimer's disease.

Data Collection Methods

To enable AI algorithms for early detection of cognitive impairments, diverse data collection methods are employed to gather information from various sources. These methods integrate clinical, neurophysiological, behavioral, and environmental data to support early diagnosis.

Electronic Health Records (EHRs)

A. **Method:** Data from medical history, clinical notes, lab results, medications, and diagnoses are extracted from electronic health systems.
B. **Use in AI**: EHR data is used to train AI algorithms to recognize patterns associated with cognitive decline by analysing longitudinal health data, comorbidities, and treatment responses.
C. **Example:** AI models can analyze vast EHR datasets to predict Alzheimer's risk factors and the progression of cognitive impairment.

Neuroimaging

A. **Method:** Techniques such as MRI, fMRI, and PET scans are used to capture detailed images of the brain's structure and activity.

B. **Use in AI**: Neuroimaging data is fed into machine learning models to detect early structural and functional changes in the brain, such as atrophy or abnormal connectivity patterns.
C. **Example:** Convolutional Neural Networks (CNNs) are often employed to analyze MRI images to identify subtle brain changes linked to mild cognitive impairment (MCI) or Alzheimer's disease.

Cognitive Assessments and Behavioral Data

A. **Method:** Standardized cognitive tests like the Mini-Mental State Examination (MMSE) and Montreal Cognitive Assessment (MoCA) are used, along with continuous monitoring of daily behaviours (e.g., gait analysis, speech, sleep patterns) through digital devices.
B. **Use in AI**: AI algorithms process cognitive test scores and behavioral data to identify early warning signs of cognitive decline. Wearable sensors and mobile applications can provide real-time behavioral data.
C. **Example:** Machine learning models using mobile-based cognitive games can predict early cognitive impairments based on user performance.

Speech and Language Analysis

A. **Method:** Natural language processing (NLP) techniques are applied to spoken or written language samples from patients.
B. **Use in AI:** AI models analyze speech and language patterns for linguistic markers of cognitive impairment, such as changes in syntax, vocabulary, or sentence complexity.
C. **Example:** Automated speech analysis tools can predict cognitive decline by analyzing pauses, hesitation, and fluency in conversation.

Wearable Devices and Sensors

A. **Method**: Devices like smartwatches, accelerometers, and GPS trackers are used to monitor physical activity, sleep patterns, mobility, and heart rate.
B. **Use in AI**: These continuous streams of data help AI algorithms assess behavioral changes, such as reduced physical activity or abnormal sleep patterns, which may indicate early cognitive impairment.

C. **Example**: AI models that monitor changes in daily living activities via wearables can detect early-stage dementia based on reduced walking speed or irregular sleep.

Genetic Data Collection

A. **Method:** Genetic tests such as whole-genome sequencing or genotyping are conducted to identify genetic predispositions to neurodegenerative diseases (e.g., the APOE-ε4 allele).
B. **Use in AI:** Genetic data is incorporated into predictive models to assess risk and personalize the detection process for cognitive impairments.
C. **Example:** AI systems use genetic markers in combination with clinical data to predict the likelihood of developing Alzheimer's or other cognitive impairments.

Smart Home Technology and Internet of Things (IoT)

A. **Method**: Sensors embedded in homes (e.g., motion detectors, smart appliances) monitor daily living activities.
B. **Use in AI**: IoT data collected from home environments is used by AI algorithms to monitor routine activities (e.g., cooking, bathing, medication adherence) and detect changes that may indicate cognitive decline.
C. **Example**: Smart home systems can alert caregivers or healthcare providers when significant deviations in daily activities occur, signalling potential cognitive impairment.

Biomarker Data Collection

A. **Method:** Blood, saliva, or cerebrospinal fluid samples are collected to measure biomarkers such as tau protein, amyloid-beta, and other proteins linked to neurodegenerative diseases.
B. **Use in AI:** AI models analyze biomarker levels in combination with other data to predict the onset of cognitive impairments before clinical symptoms manifest.
C. **Example:** Machine learning models trained on biomarker data can predict the likelihood of Alzheimer's disease progression based on tau protein levels.

AI ALGORITHMS FOR COGNITIVE IMPAIRMENT DETECTION

Statistical and Traditional Machine Learning Approaches

Statistical and traditional machine learning approaches play a significant role in early detection of cognitive impairments. The widely used approaches are Logistic Regression & Random Forest.

Logistic Regression (LR)

A. **Overview**
   - Logistic Regression (LR) is a statistical model commonly used for binary classification tasks. It models the probability of a binary outcome (e.g., cognitively impaired vs. healthy) based on one or more independent variables (e.g., age, test scores, brain volume).

B. **Application in Cognitive Impairment Detection**
   - **Predicting Cognitive Decline:** Logistic regression has been used to predict cognitive impairment using demographic variables (age, gender), clinical scores (Mini-Mental State Examination (MMSE), cognitive test results), and neuroimaging biomarkers (brain volumes, white matter lesions).
   - **Interpretable Model:** One of the key advantages of LR is its interpretability, which is important for clinicians who want to understand the relationship between risk factors and cognitive decline.

Random Forest (RF)

A. **Overview**
   - Random Forest (RF) is an ensemble learning method that constructs multiple decision trees during training and outputs the class that is the mode of the classes (classification) or mean prediction (regression) of the individual trees. Each tree is built using a subset of the data, and at each node, a random subset of features is considered to split the data.
   - **Bagging:** This technique reduces overfitting by training multiple trees on different random samples of the data and averaging their results.

B. **Application in Cognitive Impairment Detection**
   - **Handling Complex** Data: RF is well-suited for complex datasets such as neuroimaging or genetic data, which may contain a large number of

features and interactions. It has been applied to identify early cognitive decline using MRI data, genetic risk factors (e.g., APOE gene), and cognitive assessments.

- o **Feature Importance:** RF provides a measure of feature importance, allowing researchers to identify the most predictive biomarkers for cognitive impairment (e.g., hippocampal volume, specific cognitive test scores).
- o **Example:** In studies using the Alzheimer's Disease Neuroimaging Initiative (ADNI) dataset, RF has been used to predict MCI progression based on neuroimaging and clinical data, showing high accuracy and robustness.

Deep Learning Approaches

Deep learning approaches have shown great promise in the early detection of mental disorders using large amounts of neuroimaging data, clinical data, and longitudinal data. These approaches include convolutional neural networks (CNN) for neuroimaging, recurrent neural networks (RNN) for longitudinal data, and transition models for text and speech.

Convolutional Neural Networks (CNNs) for Neuroimaging

A. **Overview**

- o Convolutional Neural Networks (CNN) is a deep learning model that works best for image data. They work by using additional filters to insert images, capture checks and spatial patterns.
- o CNNs have become a model for analyzing neuroimaging data, such as MRI, CT and PET scans, where spatial patterns and acoustic changes in the brain are essential for diagnosing diseases. dementia such as Alzheimer's disease (AD).

B. **Key Components:**

- o **Animation layer:** Use transform filters to see features like edges, textures, and brain regions.
- o **Consolidation layer:** shrink the image to reduce size and computer load.
- o **All connected layers:** After feature extraction, these layers map the data to a classification output (e.g., healthy and damaged).

C. **Application in Cognitive Impairment Detection**

- o Useful in distinguishing between normal aging, mild cognitive impairment (MCI) and Alzheimer's disease.
- o **CNN 3D:** For seismic data such as 3D MRI scans of the brain, 3D CNN captures spatial information in three dimensions (x, y, z). This allows the practitioner to study comprehensive patterns of brain changes.

Recurrent Neural Networks (RNNs) for Longitudinal Data

A. **Overview**
- o Recurrent Neural Networks (RNNs) are specialized for sequential data, where the order of inputs matters. RNNs maintain a "memory" of previous inputs through hidden states, allowing them to capture temporal dependencies in data.
- o Long Short-Term Memory (LSTM) and Gated Recurrent Unit (GRU) networks are advanced RNN architectures that address the vanishing gradient problem, allowing them to capture long-term dependencies in sequential data.

B. **Key Components**:
- o **Hidden State**: Carries information from previous time steps, allowing the network to learn temporal patterns.
- o **Memory Cells (LSTM/GRU):**Maintain information across many time steps and decide when to forget or update information based on new inputs.

C. **Application in Cognitive Impairment Detection**
- o **Longitudinal health data:** Cognitive decline can occur over many years, making longitudinal data (such as psychological test scores, clinical assessments, or interview samples) useful for RNN. These models can predict the progression from mild cognitive impairment (MCI) to Alzheimer's disease (AD) by modelling the course of cognitive decline.
- o **Time-series data:** RNNs are applied to time-series data, such as long-term cognitive assessment or data monitoring of wearable sensors and sleep patterns, to detect early changes related to mental decline.

Transformer Models for Text and Speech Analysis

A. **Overview**
- o Transformers are deep learning models designed to handle sequential data, but unlike RNNs, they do not rely on iteration. Instead, they use a

sensitivity method that allows them to weigh the importance of different parts of the input sequence when making predictions.

- **Self-Constructing:** This technique helps the model to focus on the relevant parts of a sentence or sequence, empowering translators for natural language processing (NLP) tasks such as text analysis and reporting.
- **Trained models:** Models such as BERT (Bidirectional Encoder Representation of Transformer) and GPT (Generator Pre-Trained Transformer) have revolutionized NLP using large amounts of data text to learn language representations.

B. **Application in Cognitive Impairment Detection**

- **Biomarkers for speech and language**: Cognitive impairment is often seen in speech and language, and patients show changes in the fluency, vocabulary and complexity of language. Transitional models can analyze these subtle language changes to detect early signs of cognitive decline.
- **Document analysis:** Editors are also used to analyze clinical documents and patient-submitted outcomes to extract information relevant to the diagnosis of psychiatric disorders. This is useful for large clinical datasets where natural language text contains important information.

Ensemble Models

A. **Overview**

- Ensemble models combine multiple models to improve predictive performance by reducing variance, bias, or improving robustness. These models often use methods such as packing, reinforcement, or stacking.
- A database (e.g. Random Forest) works by training multiple instances of the same model on small subsets of the data and averaging the results. Augmented Reality (e.g., Augmented Reality Machines) trains students and focuses on improving past mistakes. Stacking combines different models and uses another model to learn how to combine the best predictions.

B. **Application in Cognitive Impairment Detection**

- **Random Forest for Cognitive Decline Prediction:** Random Forest is commonly used for predicting cognitive impairment as it combines multiple decision trees to minimize overfitting and improve accuracy. It is robust to noisy data and performs well on datasets with both categorical and continuous variables, such as clinical test scores and demographic information.

- **Gradient Boosting and XGBoost**: These models have been used to detect cognitive impairment by focusing on errors made by simpler models. They work well in distinguishing between subtle differences in cognitive test scores, which may be indicative of early-stage Alzheimer's.
- **Stacking Models:** Stacking combines the predictions of multiple models such as CNNs (for neuroimaging), RNNs (for longitudinal data), and traditional models (e.g., Logistic Regression for clinical data). In this way, we can use different models for specific tasks and combine their results for the final prediction.

Feature Extraction and Selection Techniques

Feature extraction and feature selection are important tasks in artificial intelligence algorithms for the early detection of cognitive impairments, such as Alzheimer's disease (AD) and mild cognitive impairment (MCI). These techniques help to reduce the amount of data and preserve the key features that contribute to discovery, improving the performance and interpretation of AI models.

Feature Extraction Techniques

Feature extraction transforms raw data into meaningful representations, which are then used as inputs for machine learning models. In the context of cognitive impairment detection, feature extraction is applied to various data types, including neuroimaging, clinical, behavioral, and genetic data.

A. **Principal Component Analysis (PCA)**
   - **Analysis**: PCA is a linear dimension reduction technique that identifies the directions (principal components) in which the variance of the data is maximized. It reduces the complexity of the data by displaying it in a smaller area while maintaining the high contrast.
   - **Application**: PCA is often applied to neuroimaging data, such as MRI or PET scans, to reduce the size of the data at the voxel level, and provide the most important features to isolate. between mentally healthy people and those with MCI or AD
   - **Example**: In the diagnosis of mental disorders, PCA can extract key brain features from neuroimaging data reducing high-resolution voxel data to a subset of regions representing brain regions associated with cognitive decline.

B. **Independent Component Analysis (ICA)**

- o **Overview**: ICA is a statistical technique used to decompose a multidimensional signal into discrete, non-Gaussian components. In neuroimaging, ICA is used to isolate brain regions that function independently.
- o **Application**: ICA is applied to functional MRI data (fMRI) to extract features related to brain connectivity patterns, often disrupted in mental disorders. This is particularly useful for identifying specific brain networks (e.g., the default mode network) related to memory and cognition.

C. **Autoencoders (Deep Feature Learning)**

- o **Overview**: Autoencoders are a type of neural network used for unsupervised learning, where the network is trained to compress input data into a lower-dimensional representation (encoder) and then reconstruct it back to the original form (decoder). The compressed representation captures the most important features of the data.
- o **Application**: Autoencoders are commonly used for feature extraction in neuroimaging data. For example, autoencoders can learn compressed representations of MRI data that highlight brain atrophy patterns linked to cognitive decline.

D. **Wavelet Transform**

- o **Analysis**: A wavelet transform that composes signals into components at multiple scales or resolutions. Useful for recording time and frequency information in data.
- o **Application**: In the diagnosis of mental disorders, waveform changes in electroencephalogram (EEG) data are used to capture time-frequency patterns associated with different aspects of brain activity. seen in AD or MCI.

Feature Selection Techniques

A. **Filter Methods**

- o **Overview**: Filter methods rank features based on statistical metrics, such as correlation, mutual information, or chi-squared tests, and select those most relevant to the target outcome.
- o **Application**: In cognitive impairment detection, filter methods can be applied to clinical and neuroimaging data to select the most informative features, such as brain regions, cognitive test scores, or genetic markers.

B. **Wrapper Methods**

- o **Overview**: Wrapper methods evaluate subsets of features based on the performance of a specific machine learning algorithm. These methods typically use a search strategy (e.g., forward selection, backward elimination) to identify the best-performing feature subset.

  - o **Application**: Wrapper methods are used in cognitive impairment detection to find the optimal combination of clinical, neuroimaging, and genetic features that maximize model performance.

C. **Embedded Methods**

  - o **Overview**: Embedded methods perform feature selection during the training process of the model. Examples include LASSO (Least Absolute Shrinkage and Selection Operator), which adds an L1 regularization term to the model to penalize less important features, effectively shrinking their coefficients to zero.
  - o **Application**: Embedded methods like LASSO are applied to neuroimaging and clinical data to automatically select the most relevant features during model training.

APPLICATIONS AND CASE STUDIES

Applications and Case Studies in AI for Alzheimer's Disease showcase the technology's transformative potential and practical challenges. AI is enhancing early diagnosis through advanced imaging analysis, where deep learning models detect subtle brain changes in MRI and PET scans, enabling earlier intervention.

AI in Early Diagnosis of Alzheimer’s Disease

AI technologies are making significant strides in the early diagnosis of Alzheimer’s Disease (AD) by leveraging advanced imaging and data analysis techniques. AI algorithms, particularly deep learning models, analyze brain imaging data (MRI, PET scans) to detect subtle changes in brain structure and function that may indicate the early stages of AD.

Case Study: The Alzheimer’s Disease Neuroimaging Initiative (ADNI) uses AI to analyze longitudinal brain imaging data to track changes associated with AD. AI models developed from this dataset help in predicting the onset of AD with high accuracy, facilitating early intervention and treatment.

AI for Monitoring and Predicting Cognitive Decline

AI tools are employed to monitor and predict cognitive decline in patients with AD and other neurodegenerative disorders. Machine learning models analyze data from various sources, including wearable devices, cognitive tests, and speech patterns, to detect changes in cognitive function over time. For instance, AI algorithms can evaluate changes in speech patterns or handwriting, which may indicate the progression of cognitive decline. Predictive models can forecast the trajectory of cognitive decline, helping healthcare providers to plan interventions and tailor care strategies.

Case Study: Cogito Health uses AI to monitor cognitive health through wearable devices and mobile apps. By analyzing data on patient behavior and cognitive performance, the system can predict cognitive decline and provide actionable insights for healthcare providers.

Case Studies of Successful Implementations

Several case studies highlight the successful implementation of AI in the field of Alzheimer's Disease:

- IBM Watson Health has developed AI tools that analyze medical literature and patient records to assist in diagnosing AD and suggesting treatment options. The system integrates data from various sources to provide comprehensive insights into patient health.
- PathAI and AImed have created AI systems that analyze pathology slides and brain imaging to identify early signs of AD, aiding pathologists in accurate diagnosis and treatment planning.

EVALUATION AND VALIDATION OF AI MODELS

Evaluating and validating AI models involves systematically assessing their performance and reliability to ensure they meet predefined criteria and perform well in real-world scenarios. This process typically involves rigorous testing on a variety of datasets to measure accuracy, precision, recall, and other relevant metrics. Validation also involves cross-validation techniques to avoid overfitting and ensure generalizability. Additionally, it is essential to test the robustness and fairness of the model, how it handles outliers, and evaluate whether the model is biased.

Performance Metrics

- **Accuracy**: The ratio of correctly predicted instances to the total number of instances.
- **Sensitivity (Recall):** The proportion of actual positives that are correctly identified by the model.

- **Specificity**: The proportion of actual negatives that are correctly identified by the model.
- **ROC Curves (Receiver Operating Characteristic Curves):** A plot of the true positive rate (sensitivity) against the false positive rate (1 - specificity) for various threshold settings.
- **AUC (Area Under Curve):** Measures the model's ability to distinguish between positive and negative classes. A higher AUC indicates better performance.
- **F1 Score**: The harmonic mean of precision and recall, providing a balance between the two.
- **Precision**: The proportion of positive identifications that were actually correct.

Cross-Validation Techniques

A. **K-Fold Cross-Validation**
   - The dataset is divided into 'k' equally sized folds. The model is trained on 'k-1' folds and validated on the remaining fold. This process is repeated 'k' times, with each fold serving as the validation set once.

B. **Leave-One-Out Cross-Validation (LOOCV)**
   - A special case of k-fold cross-validation where 'k' equals the number of data points. Each data point serves as a validation set while the rest are used for training.

C. **Stratified K-Fold Cross-Validation**
   - Similar to k-fold cross-validation, but ensures that each fold maintains the proportion of each class, which is useful for imbalanced datasets.

D. **Hold-Out Validation**
   - The dataset is split into two sets: training and testing. The model is trained on the training set and evaluated on the testing set.

REGULATORY AND ETHICAL CONSIDERATIONS

When integrating AI into healthcare, it is important to consider regulations and ethics to ensure the technology is used responsibly.

Data Privacy and Security

Healthcare data is highly sensitive, and protecting patient privacy is paramount. This means ensuring that any AI system that processes personal health information (PHI) complies with privacy regulations such as the US Health Insurance Portability and Accountability Act (HIPAA) and the EU General Data Protection Regulation (GDPR). These rules need to collect, preserve and process patient data with strict guarantees to prevent unauthorized access and inappropriate use. This must strictly control how personal medical information (PHI) is collected, stored, and replaced.

Ethical Issues in AI Healthcare Applications

Patients need to inform how AI is used, such as the role of AI in data processing and decision -making. Meaningful consent requires clear and understandable explanations. AI systems should provide interpretable results to improve patient understanding and confidence. AI should complement, not replace, human judgement in healthcare. Ensuring that healthcare professionals have control over clinical decisions is essential for patient autonomy. AI tools should support decision-making by providing evidence-based recommendations rather than making the final decision autonomously.

Regulatory Standards

In the US, the FDA regulates AI-based medical devices and software to ensure they meet safety and effectiveness standards before approval. In Europe, the Medical Device Regulation (MDR) regulates medical devices, and the proposed Artificial Intelligence Law would set specific requirements for artificial intelligence systems.

FUTURE DIRECTIONS AND EMERGING TRENDS

The future directions and emerging trends of AI-enabled healthcare are set to transform the landscape through significant advancements and integration. Advances in AI technology have driven improvements in algorithms and computing power, enabling more accurate diagnosis, predictive analytics, and decision support systems. Integration with other healthcare technologies, such as wearables and the Internet of Things (IoT), improves real-time monitoring and data collection, enabling better patient insights and improved chronic disease management.

Advances in AI Technology

Advances in AI Technology are revolutionizing healthcare by enhancing diagnostic accuracy, enabling predictive analytics, and improving treatment personalization. Recent developments include:

A. **Deep learning and neural networks:** Convolutional Neural Networks (CNN) and transformers are increasingly used in language recognition and processing tasks in language natural languages. These models have significantly improved the accuracy of diagnostic imaging and the automated interpretation of medical texts and pathology slides.
B. **Generative models:** Techniques such as generative adversarial networks (GANs) are being explored to generate synthetic medical data that can enhance training datasets and improve the reliability of AI models.
C. **Natural Language Processing (NLP):** Advanced NLP algorithms improve extraction of meaningful information from unstructured clinical records, making it easier to manage patient data and facilitate extraction of more detailed information from electronic health records (EHRs).
D. **Edge Computing:** Advances in edge computing enable real-time data processing on devices such as wearable health monitors, enabling instant analysis and feedback without relying on centralized servers.

These technological strides are driving innovation in AI applications for healthcare, leading to more precise diagnostics, efficient patient management, and tailored treatment options.

Integration with Other Health Technologies

Integration with Other Health Technologies, such as wearables and the Internet of Things (IoT), is transforming healthcare by enabling continuous monitoring, real-time data analysis, and personalized care.

A. **Wearable devices:** Devices such as smartwatches and fitness trackers collect a range of health indicators, including heart rate, activity level and sleep patterns. AI algorithms can analyze this data to provide insights into a person's health, detect anomalies, and even predict possible health issues before they become serious. For example, a wearable device with an ECG sensor can detect irregular heart rhythms and alert the user to see a doctor.

B. **Internet of Things in Healthcare:** IoT devices go beyond wearables to include smart medical equipment such as connected blood glucose monitors and smart inhalers. These devices can send data to actual medical providers, enabling more accurate monitoring of chronic diseases and timely intervention. The IoT network enables transparent integration of data from various sources, improving the overall management of patient care.
C. **Remote patient monitoring:** AI and IoT combined will enable advanced remote patient monitoring solutions. AI-powered platforms will analyze data from connected devices to detect early signs of deteriorating health conditions and facilitate proactive management to reduce re-admissions.
D. **Personalized health insights:** AI algorithms will process data from wearables and IoT devices to make personalized health recommendations. These insights can help guide lifestyle changes, medication adherence and personalized treatment plans based on real-time health data.

Integrating AI with these technologies fosters a more connected, efficient, and responsive healthcare ecosystem, driving improvements in patient outcomes and operational efficiencies.

Future Research Areas

The future research field of AI and health care is very important to promote fields and solve existing problems. The main areas of research are:

A. **Explainable AI (XAI):** Developing AI systems that can provide transparent and understandable explanations for their decisions is essential to building trust and ensuring clinical accountability. XAI research aims to make complex AI models more interpretable for physicians and patients.
B. **Integration and compatibility**: Improvement of the capacity of AI systems is required to integrate into various health technologies and electronic medical cards (DSE). Studies will be needed to focus on the development of compatibility standards and structures, which guarantee a fluid data and cooperation exchange on different platforms.
C. **Real-world implementation**: Research into the practical challenges of implementing AI-based solutions in different healthcare sectors is essential. Future research should focus on evaluating the effectiveness of AI tools in real-world environments, understanding the barriers to adoption, and identifying strategies to overcome these challenges.

D. **Advances in personalized medicine**: Continuing research into integrating AI with genomics, proteomics, and other omics data can further advance personalized medicine. This research will focus on using AI to create more precise treatment plans, improve drug discovery, and refine disease prevention strategies.
E. **AI in Public Health**: Considering the role of AI in the broader context of public health, including epidemic forecasting, disease surveillance, and health policy development, can provide valuable insights into how AI can address large-scale health challenges and improve health outcomes. Public Health.

These research areas are critical for advancing AI in healthcare, ensuring its ethical use, enhancing its capabilities, and ultimately improving patient care and health outcomes.

CONCLUSION

In conclusion, AI algorithms offer significant potential in the early detection of cognitive impairments, such as Alzheimer's disease and dementia. These algorithms, powered by machine learning (ML) and deep learning (DL) models, can analyze large datasets, including medical imaging, genetic information, and behavioral patterns, with precision that often exceeds traditional diagnostic methods. Early detection through AI can lead to timely interventions, which can slow the progression of these conditions and improve the quality of life for patients. Despite the advantages, challenges remain in terms of data privacy, ethical concerns, and the need for high-quality, diverse datasets to avoid bias in model predictions. Continued research and collaboration between AI experts, medical professionals, and policymakers are essential to ensuring that these technologies are developed responsibly and are accessible to all populations. As AI technology advances, it promises to revolutionize healthcare by making early and timely diagnosis more accurate, which can improve patient outcomes in mental retardation and many other methods.

REFERENCES

Alzheimer's Association. (2023). 2023 Alzheimer's Disease Facts and Figures. *Alzheimer's & Dementia*, 19(1), 1–50. PMID: 36918389

Baker, E., Houghton, C., & Morris, J. (2019). Integrating cognitive assessments with AI: Benefits and challenges. *Frontiers in Aging Neuroscience*, 11, 329.

Bang, J., Spina, S., & Miller, B. L. (2015). Frontotemporal dementia. *Lancet*, 386(10004), 1672–1682. DOI: 10.1016/S0140-6736(15)00461-4 PMID: 26595641

Daviglus, M. L., Bell, C. C., & Berrettini, W. (2011). The role of early diagnosis and intervention in Alzheimer's disease: Impact on quality of life. *American Journal of Preventive Medicine*, 41(4), S236–S243.

Epelbaum, S., Chupin, M., & Lebihan, D. (2021). AI-enhanced neuroimaging: Algorithms and applications. *NeuroImage*, 224, 117430.

Friedman, L. G., Zhang, D., & Zhou, W. (2018). Prediction of Alzheimer's disease with machine learning. *Journal of Neuroscience Methods*, 305, 88–97.

Gonzalez, C. S., Morin, P., & Hinton, S. (2020). Detecting early signs of cognitive impairment using wearable technology: A review. *Journal of Neuroengineering and Rehabilitation*, 17(1), 65. PMID: 32430036

Goveas, J. S., Steinman, M. A., & Gonzales, M. (2021). Behavioral analysis using AI for diagnosing Frontotemporal Dementia. *Frontiers in Aging Neuroscience*, 13, 711–723.

Hsu, C. Y., Yang, Y. H., & Wu, Y. T. (2019). Neuroimaging biomarkers for Lewy body dementia: A review of MRI and PET studies. *Journal of Neural Transmission (Vienna, Austria)*, 126(6), 765–777.

Jack, C. R., Bennett, D. A., Blennow, K., Carrillo, M. C., Feldman, H. H., & Frisoni, G. B. (2018). NIA-AA research framework: Toward a biological definition of Alzheimer's disease. *Alzheimer's & Dementia*, 14(4), 535–562. DOI: 10.1016/j.jalz.2018.02.018 PMID: 29653606

Jiang, Y., Wang, X., & Zhang, D. (2021). Artificial intelligence in early diagnosis and monitoring of cognitive decline. *Journal of Neuroscience Methods*, 356, 108201.

Kumar, S., Keefe, B., & Feldman, H. (2021). Personalized cognitive training using AI: Applications and outcomes. *IEEE Transactions on Biomedical Engineering*, 68(1), 23–32. PMID: 34086560

Lee, S. H., Lee, J. H., & Lee, Y. S. (2019). Multimodal deep learning for early detection of cognitive impairments. *Journal of Biomedical Informatics*, 94, 103–114.

McKeith, I. G., Boeve, B. F., Dickson, D. W., Halliday, G., Taylor, J.-P., Weintraub, D., Aarsland, D., Galvin, J., Attems, J., Ballard, C. G., Bayston, A., Beach, T. G., Blanc, F., Bohnen, N., Bonanni, L., Bras, J., Brundin, P., Burn, D., Chen-Plotkin, A., & Kosaka, K. (2017). Diagnosis and management of dementia with Lewy bodies: Fourth consensus report of the DLB consortium. *Neurology*, 89(1), 88–100. DOI: 10.1212/WNL.0000000000004058 PMID: 28592453

Miller, B. L., Cummings, J. L., & Benson, D. F. (2022). Advances in understanding and diagnosing cognitive impairments: The role of AI. *Journal of Neurology*, 269(1), 12–21. PMID: 34085094

Miller, J. P., Chen, C., & Lee, M. (2017). Analyzing changes in speech patterns for detecting mild cognitive impairment using NLP techniques. *Journal of Biomedical Informatics*, 70, 103–113.

Nielsen, T. L., Hsu, W. H., & Brubaker, R. (2020). Artificial intelligence in personalized medicine: Early diagnostic and therapeutic interventions. *Frontiers in Medicine*, 7, 152.

O'Brien, J. T., & Thomas, A. (2015). Vascular dementia. *Lancet*, 386(10004), 1698–1706. DOI: 10.1016/S0140-6736(15)00463-8 PMID: 26595643

Petersen, R. C., Smith, G. E., Waring, S. C., Ivnik, R. J., Tangalos, E. G., & Kokmen, E. (1999). Mild cognitive impairment: Clinical characterization and outcome. *Archives of Neurology*, 56(3), 303–308. DOI: 10.1001/archneur.56.3.303 PMID: 10190820

Pruitt, J. M., Koski, S., & O'Leary, D. (2020). Adaptive cognitive assessments: A new approach to evaluating cognitive function. *Journal of Cognitive Neuroscience*, 32(4), 591–603.

Rajkomar, A., Dean, J., & Kohane, I. (2019). Machine learning in medicine. *The New England Journal of Medicine*, 380(14), 1347–1358. DOI: 10.1056/NEJMra1814259 PMID: 30943338

Roark, B., Mitchell, M., & Hosom, J. P. (2011). Spoken language markers of dementia with Lewy bodies. *Proceedings of the IEEE International Conference on Acoustics, Speech and Signal Processing (ICASSP)*, 5956-5959.

Ryu, S., Kim, K. S., & Kim, K. H. (2018). Economic impact of early detection and intervention in dementia. *Health Economics Review*, 8, 8.

Shen, L., Liu, Y., & Zhang, D. (2021). Predictive modeling of biomarkers for cognitive impairment using AI. *Journal of Biomedical Informatics*, 114, 103664.

Suk, H. I., Lee, S. W., & Shen, D. (2017). Latent feature representation with stacked auto-encoder for AD/MCI diagnosis. *NeuroImage*, 101, 535–545.

Verbeek, P., Wit, D., & Haan, J. (2020). Resource allocation and early detection of cognitive impairment: An AI-driven approach. *Health Care Management Review*, 45(3), 245–256. PMID: 30080714

Zhang, L., Wang, W., & Wang, X. (2020). AI in genetic research for cognitive impairments. *Nature Reviews. Genetics*, 21(6), 341–354.

Chapter 8
AI in Neuroimaging and Brain Analysis

Aashish A. Gadgil
KLS Gogte Institute of Technology, Belagavi, India

P. Selvakumar
https://orcid.org/0000-0002-3650-4548
Department of Science and Humanities, Nehru Institute of Technology, Coimbatore, India

G. Sabeena Gnanaselvi
https://orcid.org/0000-0003-1362-8123
Sathyabama Institute of Science and Technology, India

G. Malathi
https://orcid.org/0000-0002-1872-3501
Sri Akilandeswari Women's College, India

ABSTRACT

The integration of AI in neuroimaging offers unprecedented opportunities to enhance our understanding of the brain, improve diagnostic accuracy, and personalize treatment strategies for neurological disorders. This capability is particularly significant given the increasing volume and complexity of neuroimaging data generated by modalities such as MRI, CT, PET, and EEG. As AI algorithms evolve, they are not only enhancing image quality and acquisition processes but also aiding in the development of biomarkers for various neurological conditions. This capability can lead to earlier diagnosis and intervention, which is crucial in managing progressive conditions. Moreover, AI-driven approaches can streamline workflow processes in clinical settings, reducing the burden on radiologists and enabling more efficient patient management. Despite these opportunities, the incorporation of AI in

DOI: 10.4018/979-8-3693-9341-3.ch008

neuroimaging also presents significant challenges. Data privacy and security are paramount concerns, especially when dealing with sensitive patient information.

INTRODUCTION TO AI IN NEUROIMAGING: OPPORTUNITIES AND CHALLENGES

The integration of AI in neuroimaging offers unprecedented opportunities to enhance our understanding of the brain, improve diagnostic accuracy, and personalize treatment strategies for neurological disorders. This capability is particularly significant given the increasing volume and complexity of neuroimaging data generated by modalities such as MRI, CT, PET, and EEG. As AI algorithms evolve, they are not only enhancing image quality and acquisition processes but also aiding in the development of biomarkers for various neurological conditions. This capability can lead to earlier diagnosis and intervention, which is crucial in managing progressive conditions. Moreover, AI-driven approaches can streamline workflow processes in clinical settings, reducing the burden on radiologists and enabling more efficient patient management. Despite these opportunities, the incorporation of AI in neuroimaging also presents significant challenges. Data privacy and security are paramount concerns, especially when dealing with sensitive patient information. The risk of data breaches or misuse must be carefully managed through robust ethical frameworks and compliance with regulations like HIPAA. Furthermore, the use of AI models often requires large, well-curated datasets for training, which can be difficult to obtain. Variability in imaging protocols, patient demographics, and clinical contexts can lead to biases in AI algorithms, potentially affecting their generalizability and clinical utility. Another critical challenge is the interpretability of AI models. While algorithms may excel in classification tasks, understanding the underlying decision-making process can be complex. Clinicians need to trust and comprehend AI outputs to integrate them effectively into their practice. This demand for transparency necessitates the development of explainable AI techniques that elucidate how models derive their predictions. Without this transparency, the adoption of AI in clinical settings may be hindered, as healthcare professionals may be reluctant to rely on "black box" models that do not provide insight into their reasoning.

Furthermore, the interdisciplinary nature of neuroimaging and AI necessitates collaboration between neurologists, radiologists, computer scientists, and ethicists. Effective collaboration is essential for translating AI research into clinical practice, ensuring that models are not only technically sound but also clinically relevant. As we look toward the future, the potential for AI in neuroimaging is immense. Emerging technologies, such as federated learning, promise to enhance model training while addressing privacy concerns by allowing algorithms to learn from decentralized data without compromising patient confidentiality. Additionally, advancements in natural language processing (NLP) can further augment neuroimaging by improving the integration of clinical data with imaging results, facilitating a more comprehensive understanding of patient conditions. The evolving landscape of AI in neuroimaging also raises important ethical questions regarding bias, accountability, and the role of AI in clinical decision-making. As AI systems are increasingly relied upon for diagnostic purposes, the implications of errors or misdiagnoses must be considered. Establishing clear guidelines and accountability measures will be essential to mitigate risks and ensure that AI serves as a beneficial adjunct to clinical expertise rather than a replacement.

Neuroimaging Modalities: MRI, CT, PET, and EEG

Computed Tomography (CT), on the other hand, utilizes X-rays to produce cross-sectional images of the brain. CT is particularly valuable in emergency settings due to its speed and ability to quickly assess acute conditions such as hemorrhages, strokes, or skull fractures. While CT provides lower resolution than MRI, its ability to visualize bone structures and detect bleeding makes it an essential tool in acute care scenarios (Kim J H., et al, 2022). The main drawback of CT is its exposure to ionizing radiation, which raises concerns, particularly for vulnerable populations such as children. However, advances in CT technology, including iterative reconstruction techniques, have improved image quality while reducing radiation doses. This modality is particularly useful for studying metabolic processes and neurochemical activity, making it invaluable in research on conditions such as Alzheimer's disease and epilepsy. PET can reveal changes in neurotransmitter activity and glucose metabolism, providing insights into disease progression and treatment efficacy. However, the limitations of PET include the need for radioactive tracers, which may pose risks, and its lower spatial resolution compared to MRI. EEG is highly effective for capturing temporal changes in brain activity, making it invaluable for diagnosing conditions such as epilepsy and sleep disorders. It provides real-time data on brain wave patterns and is especially useful in monitoring brain function during surgeries or in intensive care settings. One of the primary advantages of EEG is its excellent temporal resolution, allowing for the observation of brain activity on the millisecond scale. Each of these neuroimaging modalities has its strengths and weaknesses, and often, a multimodal approach is employed to gain a comprehensive understanding of brain structure and function (Ramakrishnan T.,et al, 2022). For example, combining MRI and PET can provide valuable insights into both anatomical and metabolic changes in the brain, allowing for a more thorough assessment of neurodegenerative diseases. Similarly, integrating EEG with fmri can help elucidate the relationship between electrical activity and blood flow, enhancing our understanding of functional connectivity in the brain.

In clinical practice, the choice of neuroimaging modality often depends on the specific clinical question, patient condition, and available resources. For instance, a patient presenting with sudden neurological deficits might first undergo a CT scan to rule out hemorrhage before proceeding to MRI for further evaluation of soft tissue abnormalities. In contrast, patients with suspected epilepsy may first receive an EEG to detect abnormal electrical activity before additional imaging studies are considered. Research into neuroimaging modalities continues to evolve, with advancements aimed at improving resolution, reducing costs, and enhancing accessibility. Hybrid imaging techniques, such as PET/MRI, are emerging, allowing for the simultaneous acquisition of metabolic and structural data, which holds great promise for advancing both research and clinical applications (Tulay E E., et al, 2019). Additionally, ongoing developments in machine learning and artificial intelligence are enhancing the analysis of neuroimaging data, leading to more accurate diagnoses and better patient outcomes. In summary, MRI, CT, PET, and EEG each play crucial roles in neuroimaging, offering complementary perspectives on brain structure and function. Understanding the unique characteristics and applications of these modalities is essential for optimizing their use in both clinical and research settings. The integration of these modalities will undoubtedly enhance our capacity to diagnose, understand, and treat neurological disorders, ultimately improving the quality of care for patients.

Machine Learning Fundamentals for Neuroimaging Analysis

Machine learning (ML) has emerged as a transformative tool in neuroimaging analysis, offering innovative approaches to decipher complex patterns within vast datasets generated by various imaging modalities. This capability is particularly valuable in neuroimaging, where the intricacies of brain structure and function can be difficult to analyze using traditional statistical methods. By leveraging machine learning techniques, researchers and clinicians can extract meaningful insights from neuroimaging data, facilitating advancements in diagnosis, treatment, and understanding of neurological disorders (Annavarapu R N., et al, 2019). In supervised learning, algorithms are trained on labeled datasets, where the desired outcome is known. For example, in neuroimaging studies, a supervised learning model might be trained to distinguish between healthy controls and individuals with a specific neurological condition based on features extracted from MRI scans. Conversely, unsupervised learning is employed when the data lacks labels or predefined outcomes. For instance, clustering algorithms like k-means or hierarchical clustering can reveal subtypes of neurological disorders based on patterns of brain activity or morphology, providing valuable insights into disease heterogeneity. Another essential concept in machine learning is feature extraction and selection.

Cross-validation techniques, such as k-fold cross-validation, are essential for ensuring that models are not overfitting and can generalize well to unseen data. Rigorous evaluation is crucial in neuroimaging, where incorrect predictions can have significant clinical implications. While the potential of machine learning in neuroimaging is vast, several challenges must be addressed. One significant concern is the issue of data heterogeneity, as neuroimaging data can vary widely across different populations, imaging protocols, and scanner types (Mahadev Madgule., et al, 2023). This variability can introduce biases and impact the generalizability of machine learning models. Furthermore, interpretability is a critical consideration in applying machine learning to neuroimaging. Many advanced models, particularly deep learning networks, operate as "black boxes," making it challenging to understand how they arrive at specific predictions. This lack of transparency can hinder the acceptance of machine learning in clinical practice, where clinicians need to comprehend the reasoning behind a model's decision. Efforts are underway to develop explainable AI techniques that provide insights into model behavior, such as visualizing which features most influence predictions or utilizing methods like SHAP (Shapley Additive explanations) values. Ethical considerations also play a significant role in the application of machine learning in neuroimaging. Ensuring data privacy, addressing potential biases, and maintaining transparency in the model development process are essential to upholding ethical standards in research and clinical applications (Felsenstein O., et al, 2019). Moreover, the integration of machine learning into clinical workflows should prioritize enhancing, rather than replacing, clinician expertise, fostering collaboration between AI systems and healthcare professionals. In conclusion, machine learning fundamentals offer powerful tools for analyzing neuroimaging data, enabling breakthroughs in understanding the brain and improving patient outcomes. The combination of supervised and unsupervised learning, effective feature extraction, and algorithm selection lays the foundation for robust neuroimaging analysis.

Deep Learning Architectures for Brain Image Analysis

Deep learning has emerged as a pivotal advancement in the analysis of brain imaging data, offering sophisticated methodologies to tackle the complexities inherent in neuroimaging. These architectures have been particularly transformative in the fields of Magnetic Resonance Imaging (MRI), Computed Tomography (CT), Positron Emission Tomography (PET), and other imaging modalities, addressing challenges that traditional methods often struggle to overcome (Stumpo V., et al, 2022). Their architecture consists of convolutional layers, pooling layers, and fully connected layers, enabling the model to learn spatial hierarchies of features. For instance, in brain tumor detection, a CNN can automatically identify relevant patterns, such as abnormal tissue structures, from raw image data, significantly enhancing diagnostic accuracy. Advances in CNN architectures, such as Residual Networks (resnets) and Dense Convolutional Networks (densenets), have further improved performance by addressing issues like vanishing gradients and allowing for more efficient training of deeper networks. These architectures are particularly beneficial for examining brain activity over time, as in the case of Electroencephalography (EEG) signals. Rnns can capture temporal dependencies in sequential data, making them suitable for tasks like event-related potential (ERP) analysis and the prediction of seizures in epilepsy. By maintaining the memory of previous inputs, lstms enhance the model's ability to learn from long sequences, providing valuable insights into dynamic brain activities. Another significant architecture in the realm of brain imaging is the U-Net, originally developed for biomedical image segmentation. The U-Net's encoder-decoder structure allows it to learn context and localization simultaneously, making it highly effective for segmenting anatomical structures within brain scans (Walter M., et al, 2019). In applications like delineating tumors or assessing brain atrophy in neurodegenerative diseases, U-Net has demonstrated superior performance over traditional segmentation methods.

Recent studies have demonstrated the effectiveness of vision transformers (vits) in classifying brain images, with promising results in tasks such as identifying Alzheimer's disease from MRI scans. The adaptability of Transformers highlights their potential in handling high-dimensional neuroimaging data, offering an exciting frontier for future research. In neuroimaging, acquiring labeled datasets can be challenging due to the need for expert annotations and the variability in imaging protocols across institutions (Paramasivam Selvakumar., et al, 2024). Furthermore, ensuring the interpretability of deep learning models is vital, especially in clinical settings. While deep learning architectures can achieve high accuracy, their "black box" nature poses challenges in understanding the rationale behind specific predictions. By visualizing the regions of interest that contribute to a model's output, clinicians can better trust and understand AI-driven assessments, fostering acceptance in clinical practice. Issues related to data privacy, bias in training datasets, and the need for equitable access to advanced technologies must be addressed. Implementing robust data governance frameworks and ensuring diverse representation in training datasets can mitigate risks and enhance the generalizability of models across different populations. Furthermore, the collaboration between data scientists and clinicians is essential to ensure that deep learning applications are developed with clinical relevance in mind. In conclusion, deep learning architectures are revolutionizing brain image analysis, providing powerful tools for extracting insights from complex neuroimaging data (Davatzikos C., 2019). From cnns for classification tasks to U-Nets for segmentation, and gans for data augmentation, the versatility of these architectures enables significant advancements in understanding neurological conditions. As the field continues to evolve, addressing challenges related to data availability, model interpretability, and ethical considerations will be crucial for maximizing the potential of deep learning in neuroimaging.

Image Denoising and Enhancement Techniques for Neuroimaging

PET often produce images that contain noise and artifacts, which can obscure clinically relevant features and complicate analysis. Effective denoising and enhancement techniques are therefore paramount for optimizing the utility of neuroimaging data, ensuring that subtle brain structures and functional changes are discernible for both clinical and research applications. Image Denoising involves the application of algorithms to reduce noise while preserving important structural details. Various noise sources, such as thermal noise in MRI or photon noise in PET, necessitate tailored approaches for different imaging modalities. Patches across the entire image, effectively reducing noise while preserving edges and fine details (Nielsen A N., et al, 2020). NLM has shown particular promise in MRI, where maintaining the integrity of anatomical structures is crucial for accurate diagnosis. The advent of wavelet transform techniques has also significantly advanced image denoising in neuroimaging. Wavelet methods decompose images into different frequency components, allowing for selective filtering of noise while retaining essential structural information. This multi-scale approach enables the preservation of edges and textures, which are vital for neuroimaging analysis. Wavelet-based denoising has been particularly effective in reducing noise in low-signal regions, such as those encountered in certain pathological conditions. Architectures such as dncnn (Denoising Convolutional Neural Network) and U-Net have been specifically designed for image denoising tasks, demonstrating impressive performance in various neuroimaging applications. In addition to denoising, image enhancement techniques play a crucial role in improving the visibility of anatomical structures and pathological changes in neuroimaging. Enhancement methods aim to improve image contrast, brightness, and overall quality, making it easier for clinicians to identify abnormalities. Histogram equalization is a commonly used technique that adjusts the intensity distribution of an image, thereby enhancing contrast (Bernal J., et al, 2019). However, it can sometimes lead to over-enhancement, resulting in artifacts that may mislead interpretation.

Another critical aspect of image enhancement involves intensity normalization, which ensures that images acquired from different scanners or protocols can be compared meaningfully. This is especially important in multi-center studies where variations in imaging parameters may introduce discrepancies in intensity values. Techniques such as Z-score normalization and histogram matching are employed to standardize image intensities, allowing for more consistent analysis across datasets. These methods can provide clearer images with finer details, which are essential for diagnosing subtle neurological conditions (Sugumaran K. M., et al, 2024). Deep learning approaches, such as gans (Generative Adversarial Networks), have shown great promise in super-resolution applications, allowing for the synthesis of high-resolution brain images that preserve anatomical accuracy. The complexity of neuroimaging data, the variability across subjects, and the differences in acquisition protocols can hinder the effectiveness of existing methods. Additionally, the trade-off between denoising and detail preservation is a delicate balance that requires ongoing research and optimization. In conclusion, image denoising and enhancement techniques are vital for maximizing the value of neuroimaging data (Wahlang I., et al, 2022). From traditional methods like wavelet transforms and adaptive histogram equalization to cutting-edge deep learning approaches, these techniques play a crucial role in improving image quality and diagnostic accuracy.

Brain Segmentation and Registration Methods Using AI

Brain segmentation and registration are fundamental tasks in neuroimaging that significantly contribute to our understanding of brain structure and function. These processes are essential for analyzing anatomical features, identifying pathological changes, and facilitating the integration learning, the landscape of brain segmentation and registration has transformed, offering enhanced accuracy, efficiency, and robustness compared to traditional methods. Brain segmentation involves partitioning brain images into distinct regions or structures, such as gray matter, white matter, and cerebrospinal fluid. Accurate segmentation is crucial for various applications, including disease diagnosis, treatment planning, and research into brain development and aging (Yoo R E., 2024). Traditional segmentation techniques, such as thresholding, region-growing, and atlas-based methods, have been widely used; however, they often rely on predefined rules and assumptions, making them less adaptable to individual variability and complex anatomical features. One of the most notable architectures for brain segmentation is the U-Net, designed specifically for biomedical image segmentation tasks. Including MRI and CT. U-Net has set new standards in accurately delineating brain structures, particularly in complex scenarios such as tumor segmentation or identifying subtle changes associated with neurodegenerative diseases. Deep learning methods have also been extended to 3D images, accommodating the volumetric nature of neuroimaging data. 3D U-Net and similar architectures exploit three-dimensional convolutions to process entire brain volumes simultaneously, enhancing segmentation accuracy by utilizing spatial information more effectively (Huang C., et al, 2022). This capability is especially valuable when dealing with large datasets, as it reduces the risk of overfitting and enhances the model's ability to generalize across different subjects and imaging protocols. AI techniques, particularly those utilizing deep learning, have significantly improved the efficiency and accuracy of registration methods (Zhao X., 2021). Deep learning-based registration approaches can learn complex transformations directly from data, making them more adaptable to individual variability and complex anatomical changes. Networks such as the voxelmorph framework employ a combination of cnns and a spatial transformation network to perform fast and accurate image registration. Voxelmorph learns a mapping from source to target images, allowing it to generate deformation fields that align images with remarkable precision. This capability is particularly beneficial in neuroimaging, where anatomical variability between subjects can complicate registration efforts.

Moreover, unsupervised learning methods for registration have emerged, allowing models to learn registration parameters without the need for labeled data. Techniques such as cycle-consistent adversarial networks (cyclegans) can be employed to align images from different modalities or domains, facilitating the integration of multimodal neuroimaging data. These unsupervised methods are particularly advantageous in clinical settings where labeled datasets are scarce, as they can leverage unpaired data for training (Zhu G., et al, 2019). Multi-modal registration poses unique challenges, as images from different modalities (e.g., MRI, PET, and CT) often have different contrasts, resolutions, and anatomical features. Researchers are actively exploring methods to enhance the transparency of AI-driven segmentation and registration techniques, providing insights into model behavior and helping clinicians understand the rationale behind specific decisions. Ensuring diverse representation in training data and maintaining robust data governance frameworks will be critical to developing equitable and effective AI applications in neuroimaging (Mishro P K., et al, 2021). In summary, AI-driven brain segmentation and registration methods represent a significant advancement in neuroimaging, enhancing the accuracy and efficiency of these essential tasks. Techniques such as cnns, U-Net architectures, and deep learning-based registration methods are revolutionizing the analysis of neuroimaging data, enabling more precise delineation of brain structures and better alignment of multimodal images. Ultimately, these advancements hold great promise for improving diagnostic accuracy, treatment planning, and our understanding of neurological disorders, paving the way for personalized and effective interventions in clinical practice.

Automated Detection of Neurological Disorders: Stroke, Tumor, and Infarct

These innovations offer powerful tools for the early identification and diagnosis of critical conditions such as stroke, brain tumors, and cerebral infarcts, which are pivotal for timely intervention and improved patient outcomes. The ability to analyze complex neuroimaging data with high accuracy and efficiency has the potential to revolutionize clinical practice and enhance the overall quality of care in neurology (Mahmood H., et al, 2024). Stroke detection is a prime application for automated systems, given the time-sensitive nature of stroke treatment. Rapid diagnosis is crucial for administering appropriate therapies such as thrombolysis or surgery. Traditionally, detection relied on radiologists interpreting CT or MRI scans, which can be time-consuming and subject to variability in human judgment. Brain tumors, whether primary or metastatic, can vary widely in their appearance, making accurate diagnosis challenging. Automated detection systems employ various machine learning techniques to segment tumor regions from healthy brain tissue, quantifying features such as size, shape, and texture to assist in classification (Vijayakumar G., et al, 2024). Deep learning models, including U-Net architectures specifically designed for biomedical image segmentation, have shown remarkable success in identifying tumor boundaries and characterizing tumor types. These models are trained on vast datasets that encompass various tumor presentations, allowing them to generalize effectively across different patient populations and imaging conditions.

Moreover, AI-driven techniques facilitate the integration of multimodal imaging data for more comprehensive tumor analysis. Combining MRI, PET, and CT images can provide complementary information about tumor metabolism, vascularity, and anatomical relationships. By employing advanced registration methods and feature fusion techniques, automated systems can offer a more holistic view of tumors, enabling better treatment planning and monitoring of therapeutic responses (Ghazi M M., 2022). Cerebral infarcts, or localized areas of dead tissue resulting from inadequate blood supply, pose another critical area for automated detection. Like stroke, timely identification of infarcts is essential for effective management. Automated detection systems can analyze neuroimaging data to identify infarcted areas and differentiate between old and new lesions, providing crucial information for clinical decision-making. By automating this process, healthcare providers can enhance workflow efficiency and ensure that patients receive appropriate interventions without delay. Despite the promising advancements in automated detection, several challenges remain. One significant hurdle is the need for high-quality, annotated datasets to train machine learning models. Neuroimaging data can be heterogeneous, and variations in acquisition protocols across institutions can introduce biases that affect model performance (Raghavendra U., et al, 2020). Ensuring the availability of diverse training datasets that accurately represent different populations and conditions is crucial for developing robust AI systems. Implementing robust data governance frameworks and maintaining transparency in the model development process is essential for fostering trust among patients and healthcare providers. In conclusion, automated detection of neurological disorders such as stroke, tumors, and infarcts represent a significant advancement in the field of neuroimaging. By harnessing the power of AI and machine learning, healthcare providers can enhance diagnostic accuracy, reduce time to treatment, and ultimately improve patient outcomes.

Image-guided Neurosurgery and Interventional Neurology

Image-guided neurosurgery and interventional neurology represent transformative advancements in the management of neurological disorders, significantly enhancing surgical precision and patient outcomes. These techniques leverage advanced imaging modalities, such as MRI, CT, and intraoperative ultrasound, to provide real-time visualization of anatomical structures, thereby facilitating safer and more effective surgical interventions. The integration of imaging technologies into surgical workflows has evolved from traditional methods to sophisticated image-guided systems that combine anatomical data with functional information, enabling neurosurgeons to navigate the complex brain environment with greater confidence and accuracy (Sarmento R M., 2019). At the core of image-guided neurosurgery is the utilization of preoperative imaging to inform surgical planning. This fusion of data allows neurosurgeons to visualize their instruments' position relative to the targeted anatomical structures, enhancing precision during procedures such as tumor resections, deep brain stimulation, and minimally invasive interventions (Paramasivam Selvakumar., et al, 2024). Surgical navigation systems have been shown to reduce operating times and improve surgical accuracy, leading to better clinical outcomes. In interventional neurology, the role of image guidance is equally significant. Techniques such as endovascular therapy for the treatment of vascular disorders, including aneurysms and arteriovenous malformations, rely heavily on imaging to guide catheter placement and device deployment. Advanced imaging modalities, such as digital subtraction angiography (DSA), provide detailed visualization of vascular structures, allowing interventional neurologists to navigate the intricate vascular network of the brain. Image guidance enhances the safety and efficacy of these procedures, reducing the risk of complications associated with catheter manipulation and device deployment.

Moreover, the integration of robotics in image-guided interventions represents a cutting-edge development in the field. Robotic systems enhance the precision of instrument positioning and maneuverability, particularly in delicate procedures that require high levels of accuracy. These systems can work in tandem with imaging modalities to facilitate procedures such as biopsy, where precise targeting of lesions is essential for obtaining adequate tissue samples without damaging surrounding healthy tissue. While the benefits of image-guided neurosurgery and interventional neurology are substantial, several challenges persist (Inamdar M A., et al, 2021). One significant concern is the need for seamless integration of various imaging modalities and navigation systems within the surgical workflow. Inconsistencies in image registration, issues with resolution, and variations in patient anatomy can complicate the interpretation of imaging data. To address these challenges, ongoing research focuses on developing more robust algorithms for image registration and enhancing the quality of intraoperative imaging to ensure accurate and reliable guidance. Another challenge lies in the training and education of neurosurgeons and interventional neurologists in utilizing these advanced technologies. Mastery of image-guided techniques requires a comprehensive understanding of both the underlying imaging principles and the surgical procedures themselves. Consequently, simulation-based training programs and mentorship opportunities are becoming increasingly important in preparing the next generation of neurosurgeons to effectively utilize image-guided approaches in clinical practice. Predict surgical outcomes, and even assist in real-time decision-making during procedures. For instance, AI algorithms can enhance image quality, facilitate automated segmentation of anatomical structures, and provide intraoperative feedback on instrument positioning, further refining the surgical process. By overlaying virtual images onto the surgical field, AR can provide surgeons with valuable contextual information, such as critical structures and pathways, directly in their line of sight (Thomson K R., 2020). This immersive visualization can improve situational awareness and decision-making during complex procedures.

Brain Connectivity Analysis using Functional MRI and Diffusion Tensor Imaging

Brain connectivity analysis is a vital area of neuroscience that seeks to understand the complex network of interactions between different brain regions. Two prominent imaging modalities used for this purpose are functional magnetic resonance imaging (fmri) and diffusion tensor imaging (DTI). Each technique provides unique insights into brain connectivity, revealing both functional interactions and structural pathways that underpin cognitive processes, behavior, and various neurological conditions. When a particular brain region becomes active, its metabolic demands increase, leading to a localized increase in blood flow and oxygen consumption (Sorger J M., 2024). ICA, on the other hand, decomposes the fmri data into independent components, each representing a distinct network of brain activity. These methods have proven invaluable for mapping out the brain's functional architecture, offering insights into how various cognitive processes are integrated across different regions.

Integrating fmri and DTI allows researchers to investigate both the functional and structural connectivity of the brain, creating a more comprehensive understanding of neural networks. For instance, by examining how disruptions in structural connectivity (as indicated by DTI) correlate with functional connectivity (as measured by fmri), researchers can gain insights into how structural integrity impacts functional performance (Sreenivasulu A., et al, 2022). This integration is particularly valuable in studying conditions such as schizophrenia, Alzheimer's disease, and multiple sclerosis, where both functional and structural changes are observed.

Another exciting development in the field is the use of machine learning algorithms to analyze connectivity data. By applying unsupervised and supervised learning techniques, researchers can identify patterns and classify connectivity profiles across different populations. For example, machine learning models can differentiate between healthy individuals and those with neurological disorders based on connectivity features derived from fmri and DTI data. This has significant implications for personalized medicine, as it may enable early diagnosis and tailored interventions based on individual connectivity profiles. Despite these advancements, several challenges remain in brain connectivity analysis (Tsoumakidou G., et al, 2021). One major issue is the variability in connectivity measures due to factors such as individual differences in brain anatomy, age, and even psychological state during scanning. While fmri provides excellent spatial resolution, its temporal resolution is limited compared to electrophysiological techniques. Conversely, DTI, while offering valuable insights into structural pathways, does not provide direct information about functional activity. Ongoing research aims to address these limitations, with efforts focused on developing hybrid imaging techniques that combine the strengths of both modalities (Neudorf J., et al, 2020). In summary, brain connectivity analysis using functional MRI and diffusion tensor imaging offers a powerful approach to understanding the intricate networks that underpin brain function..

AI-Driven Brain Mapping: Structure, Function, and Connectivity

AI-driven brain mapping represents a cutting-edge advancement in neuroscience, significantly enhancing our understanding of the brain's structure, function, and connectivity. The integration of AI into brain mapping is revolutionizing how we study neurological disorders, cognitive functions, and brain development, ultimately leading to improved diagnostic and therapeutic strategies (Mao C P., et al, 2022). AI techniques, such as independent component analysis (ICA) and deep learning approaches, facilitate the identification of resting state networks (rsns) and task-related activation patterns. This integrative approach can uncover critical insights into how different brain regions communicate and collaborate, providing a comprehensive understanding of cognitive processes and the neural basis of behavior (Saad M., 2019).

AI-driven techniques also facilitate longitudinal studies of brain development and aging. By analyzing imaging data collected over time, machine learning algorithms can identify patterns of change in brain structure and function associated with aging, neurodevelopmental trajectories, or the progression of neurological disorders. This capability is invaluable for understanding how connectivity patterns evolve and can inform interventions tailored to specific developmental stages or disease processes.

Another exciting application of AI in brain mapping is the use of graph theory to analyze connectivity networks. The brain can be modeled as a complex network of nodes (brain regions) and edges (connections). Machine learning algorithms can calculate various graph metrics, such as centrality, modularity, and clustering coefficients, to characterize the topology of brain networks. This approach has revealed crucial insights into the efficiency and resilience of brain networks, as well as how these characteristics may be altered in neurological and psychiatric disorders. Additionally, the interpretability of AI models is a significant concern. While many machine learning techniques provide accurate predictions, their decision-making processes can often be opaque. Enhancing the interpretability of AI-driven brain mapping tools is essential for gaining the trust of clinicians and researchers (Maturi M H., et al, 2022). Techniques such as attention mechanisms and saliency maps can help elucidate which features or regions influence model predictions, thereby increasing transparency and facilitating clinical applications. As the field continues to evolve, ongoing advancements in imaging technologies, data analysis methods, and ethical practices will be crucial for realizing the full potential of AI in brain mapping. This innovative approach holds promise for enhancing our understanding of cognitive processes, informing treatment strategies for neurological disorders, and ultimately contributing to the advancement of personalized medicine in neuroscience.

Network Analysis and Graph Theory in Neuroimaging

Network analysis and graph theory have emerged as powerful frameworks in neuroimaging, enabling researchers to investigate the complex interconnections within the brain. As our understanding of the brain's architecture evolves, the use of these mathematical approaches offers valuable insights into how different regions communicate, the functional organization of neural systems, and the impact of various neurological and psychiatric disorders. By modeling the brain as a network of nodes (representing brain regions) and edges (representing connections or interactions between these regions), network analysis provides a comprehensive view of brain connectivity that transcends traditional methods (Singh A P., et al, 2024). DTI allows researchers to visualize and quantify white matter tracts, revealing how brain regions are interconnected. By applying graph theory to these data, researchers can calculate metrics such as degree centrality (the number of direct connections a node has) and path length (the average distance between nodes in the network), providing insights into the brain's structural organization. Functional connectivity, on the other hand, refers to the temporal correlations between the activity of different brain regions, typically assessed using functional MRI (fmri). In this context, network analysis can help identify resting state networks (rsns) that show synchronized activity patterns during rest. Graph theory metrics such as modularity can be used to detect communities within these networks, reflecting the brain's functional specialization. For instance, the default mode network, which is active during introspective thought, can be distinguished from networks involved in cognitive tasks. By analyzing these functional connections, researchers can better understand how different brain regions collaborate during various cognitive processes. Effective connectivity goes a step further by attempting to infer the directional influences among brain regions. This aspect of connectivity is crucial for understanding causal relationships within the brain's networks. Techniques such as dynamic causal modeling (DCM) and structural equation modeling (SEM) can be employed in conjunction with graph theory to assess how changes in one region can affect activity in another. This approach has significant implications for understanding the mechanisms underlying various disorders, as it allows for the identification of disrupted pathways that may contribute to symptoms (Chen X., et al, 2021). The integration of network analysis and graph theory into neuroimaging studies has been particularly illuminating in the context of neurological and psychiatric disorders.

One of the key advantages of employing graph theory in neuroimaging is its ability to visualize complex interactions within the brain. Network visualizations can depict how different regions are interconnected, making it easier to identify hubs (highly connected nodes) and peripheral regions (less connected nodes). Hubs are critical for efficient information processing and communication within the brain. By examining the roles of these hubs, researchers can gain insights into how disruptions in connectivity may lead to impaired cognitive function or behavioral changes (Nigro S., et al, 2022). Moreover, advancements in computational power and algorithm development have facilitated the analysis of large-scale brain networks, allowing for the examination of connectivity patterns across large populations. Additionally, the potential for overfitting in machine learning models poses another challenge. Careful validation and testing against independent datasets are crucial to ensure that findings are robust and generalizable (Prajapati R., 2021).

White Matter Tractography and Fiber Analysis

White matter tractography and fiber analysis have become essential techniques in neuroimaging, allowing researchers and clinicians to visualize and understand the complex architecture of brain connectivity. These methods utilize diffusion magnetic resonance imaging (dmri), particularly diffusion tensor imaging (DTI) and its advanced variants, to map the orientation and integrity of white matter tracts, which play a crucial role in facilitating communication between different brain regions. As our understanding of brain connectivity deepens, tractography and fiber analysis are increasingly vital for studying neurological disorders, cognitive function, and brain development. By analyzing the diffusion properties of water, DTI enables the reconstruction of fiber tracts, effectively visualizing the brain's white matter pathways (Lin S Y., et al, 2019). The fundamental output of DTI is a diffusion tensor, which describes the diffusion characteristics in three dimensions, these metrics offer insights into white matter integrity and organization, serving as important biomarkers for various neurological conditions. Tractography, the process of reconstructing white matter pathways, involves the application of algorithms that utilize DTI data to estimate the trajectories of fibers. Common algorithms include deterministic and probabilistic tractography. Deterministic tractography follows a single pathway based on the principal diffusion direction, while probabilistic tractography considers multiple potential pathways, providing a more comprehensive view of fiber trajectories and reducing the influence of noise. The choice of tractography method can significantly impact the results, making it crucial to select appropriate techniques based on the research question and the specific characteristics of the data (Zhang F., et al, 2020). One of the critical applications of white matter tractography is in the assessment of structural connectivity and its relationship with functional outcomes. Advanced tractography techniques can even assist in identifying eloquent areas of the brain, which are critical for functions such as speech and motor control, allowing for more precise and safer surgical interventions (Zhang F., et al, 2019). Moreover, the integration of tractography with machine learning techniques is paving the way for new discoveries in neuroimaging. Additionally, while DTI provides valuable quantitative metrics, it lacks specificity in distinguishing between different pathologies, prompting ongoing research into more advanced diffusion models that can provide greater biological insights (Zhang F., et al, 2019). Moreover, the interpretation of tractography results can be complicated by the fact that connectivity does not always imply causation.

AI-Assisted Diagnosis of Neurodegenerative Diseases: Alzheimer's, Parkinson's, and Huntington's

In Parkinson's disease, early diagnosis is crucial for effective management and treatment. Traditionally, diagnosis hinges on the presence of motor symptoms, such as tremors and rigidity. However, these symptoms often emerge only after significant neuronal loss has occurred. AI systems can analyze voice recordings and gait patterns to identify early signs of Parkinson's, even before the onset of visible symptoms.

Machine learning algorithms can recognize deviations in speech and movement that may be imperceptible to human observers, enabling earlier and more accurate diagnoses Huntington's disease presents unique challenges due to its genetic basis and variable symptom onset. The disease typically manifests in mid-adulthood, making early detection complex (Rajaraman S., 2024). AI can facilitate genetic screening by analyzing genomic data to identify individuals at risk. Furthermore, AI-driven tools can monitor behavioral changes in potential candidates, assessing cognitive and motor functions over time. By comparing longitudinal data against established baselines, AI can help clinicians detect early manifestations of Huntington's disease, guiding timely interventions and improving patient outcomes. A significant advantage of AI-assisted diagnosis is its ability to reduce diagnostic uncertainty and bias (Gheorghe-Moisii M., 2024). Clinicians may have differing interpretations of symptoms or imaging results, leading to variable diagnosis rates. AI algorithms, trained on diverse datasets, can provide a standardized approach, ensuring that patients receive accurate diagnoses regardless of geographical or clinical variations. Additionally, AI can enhance clinician decision-making by providing evidence-based recommendations, thereby improving overall patient care.

Despite the potential benefits, the integration of AI into clinical practice also raises ethical and logistical concerns. Data privacy is paramount, as sensitive health information must be protected to maintain patient confidentiality. Moreover, the development of AI systems requires robust datasets that are representative of diverse populations to avoid biases in algorithm training. Collaboration between healthcare professionals, data scientists, and ethicists is essential to ensure that AI tools are developed and deployed responsibly. The regulatory landscape surrounding AI in healthcare is still evolving. Organizations such as the FDA are beginning to establish guidelines for the approval and monitoring of AI-driven diagnostic tools (Surianarayanan C., et al, 2023). Ensuring that these systems meet safety and efficacy standards is critical for gaining the trust of both healthcare providers and patients. Ongoing research and clinical trials will be necessary to validate AI models and their real-world applicability. However, it is essential to navigate the ethical and regulatory challenges that accompany this technology to ensure its responsible implementation in clinical settings. As research progresses and AI systems continue to evolve, the potential for transforming the diagnosis and management of neurodegenerative diseases becomes increasingly attainable, offering hope for better patient care in the future.

Neuroimaging Biomarkers for Mental Health Disorders: Depression, Anxiety, and Schizophrenia

Depression, one of the most common mental health conditions, is often characterized by persistent sadness, loss of interest, and cognitive impairments. Neuroimaging studies have revealed alterations in several brain regions, particularly those involved in emotional regulation, such as the prefrontal cortex, amygdala, and hippocampus. For instance, reduced activity in the prefrontal cortex has been consistently observed in individuals with depression, correlating with symptoms such as impaired decision-making and emotional dysregulation. Additionally, structural MRI has shown decreased hippocampal volume, suggesting a relationship between neurogenesis and depression. Researchers are increasingly exploring these brain changes as potential biomarkers for early diagnosis and to track treatment responses, particularly in monitoring the efficacy of antidepressant therapies (Kraguljac N V., 2021). The amygdala, a key brain region involved in fear processing, often exhibits hyperactivity in individuals with anxiety. Neuroimaging research has identified several structural and functional abnormalities in the brains of individuals with schizophrenia. For example, increased ventricular volume and reduced cortical thickness have been documented, particularly in the frontal and temporal lobes (Sui J., et al, 2020). Additionally, the interpretation of neuroimaging data requires careful consideration of the underlying neurobiology and its relationship to behavioral symptoms (Abi-Dargham A., et al, 2023). Ethical considerations also play a critical role in the use of neuroimaging biomarkers in mental health. The potential for stigma and discrimination based on neurobiological findings raises important questions about privacy and the responsible use of such information. It is crucial to ensure that neuroimaging findings are used to enhance understanding and treatment of mental health disorders, rather than contributing to marginalization or labeling of individuals with these conditions. In conclusion, neuroimaging biomarkers offer a promising avenue for advancing the diagnosis, treatment, and understanding of mental health disorders such as depression, anxiety, and schizophrenia. By elucidating the neural underpinnings of these complex conditions, neuroimaging can facilitate earlier diagnosis, inform personalized treatment approaches, and ultimately improve patient outcomes.

AI-Driven Neurocritical Care: Monitoring and Predicting Patient Outcomes

Neurocritical care, which involves the intensive monitoring and treatment of patients with life-threatening neurological illnesses, necessitates rapid decision-making and precise prognostic assessments. Traditional methods often rely on clinical judgment and static scoring systems, which can be limited by human bias and variability. AI-driven tools, however, leverage large datasets and sophisticated algorithms to enhance monitoring, improve patient outcomes, and predict the trajectory of recovery more accurately. One of the primary applications of AI in neurocritical care is real-time monitoring. Continuous physiological data, including intracranial pressure, brain oxygenation levels, and vital signs, are critical in managing patients with acute neurological injuries (Cascella M., et al, 2023). This proactive approach can significantly reduce morbidity and mortality by enabling earlier interventions that might not be recognized through standard monitoring practices. In addition to real-time monitoring, AI can play a crucial role in predicting patient outcomes. By predicting patient needs and potential complications, AI tools can inform staffing decisions and ensure that high-risk patients receive the necessary attention (Li Y., et al, 2024). Despite the promise of AI-driven approaches in neurocritical care, several challenges must be addressed before widespread implementation. Therefore, developing transparent and interpretable algorithms is essential for ensuring clinician buy-in and enhancing patient safety. Robust data governance frameworks and compliance with regulations such as HIPAA in the United States are crucial to safeguarding patient information while harnessing the power of AI. Furthermore, the successful integration of AI into neurocritical care requires multidisciplinary collaboration. Neurologists, intensivists, data scientists, and ethicists must work together to develop, validate, and implement AI tools that are clinically relevant and aligned with patient care goals. Collaborative efforts can help bridge the gap between technological advancements and practical clinical applications, ensuring that AI tools enhance, rather than disrupt, the workflow of healthcare providers. In conclusion, AI-driven innovations in neurocritical care hold tremendous potential for transforming the monitoring and management of patients with severe neurological conditions. By enhancing real-time monitoring, predicting patient outcomes, and optimizing clinical decision-making, AI can significantly improve patient care and resource allocation in neurocritical settings.

Explainable AI and Interpretability in Neuroimaging Analysis

AI methods must not only provide accurate predictions but also clarify how they arrive at those conclusions. This need for explainable AI (XAI) is crucial for fostering trust, ensuring clinical applicability, and enhancing the scientific understanding of brain functions and disorders. Clinicians and researchers may be hesitant to adopt AI solutions if they cannot discern how specific features of neuroimaging data contribute to a model's predictions. For example, when diagnosing conditions such as Alzheimer's disease or identifying biomarkers for psychiatric disorders, understanding which brain regions or patterns are most influential can provide invaluable insights for both treatment planning and further research (Abdollahifard S., et al, 2024). While these models may not always achieve the same level of accuracy as complex deep learning systems, their simplicity can provide critical insights that inform clinical decision-making (Farahani F V., et al, 2022). For example, a linear model might reveal that increased connectivity between particular brain regions is associated with higher depression scores, thereby guiding therapeutic approaches or further investigations into those neural pathways. These models can leverage deep learning to process intricate neuroimaging data while simultaneously providing interpretable outputs. Such strategies not only enhance understanding but also empower clinicians to utilize AI tools effectively, ensuring that they can communicate findings to patients and stakeholders in a comprehensible manner.

The significance of explainability extends beyond individual model predictions; it also plays a vital role in the ethical deployment of AI in neuroimaging. In medical contexts, the stakes are high, and decisions can significantly impact patient care. Ensuring that AI systems are interpretable promotes accountability, enabling clinicians to question and verify AI-generated recommendations. This transparency is particularly important when discussing sensitive diagnoses or treatment options with patients, as it fosters a collaborative environment where patients feel informed and engaged in their care decisions. Furthermore, explainability in AI-driven neuroimaging can enhance the robustness of research findings. When researchers understand how and why a model makes specific predictions, they can identify potential biases or limitations in the data. For instance, if an AI model consistently highlights certain demographic groups or imaging modalities, it may signal underlying biases that need to be addressed (Vidya S., et al, 2024). By critically evaluating these aspects, researchers can refine their methodologies, ensuring that AI applications in neuroimaging are both scientifically valid and clinically relevant. Despite the promising developments in explainable AI, several challenges remain.

Future Directions in AI-Driven Neuroimaging: Emerging Technologies and Applications

As the field of neuroimaging continues to evolve, the integration of artificial intelligence (AI) is poised to transform how we understand and interpret complex brain data. The convergence of advanced imaging techniques with sophisticated AI algorithms opens up new avenues for research and clinical applications. Future directions in AI-driven neuroimaging will focus on enhancing diagnostic accuracy, personalizing treatment approaches, and unraveling the intricate neural mechanisms underlying various neurological and psychiatric conditions. One of the most exciting prospects in AI-driven neuroimaging is the development of multimodal imaging approaches (Andreu-Perez J., et al, 2021). For example, integrating functional and structural imaging can help elucidate how brain connectivity relates to cognitive deficits in conditions like Alzheimer's disease or schizophrenia. This holistic approach may enhance early diagnosis and improve understanding of disease progression, ultimately leading to more effective interventions. Moreover, the rise of advanced machine learning techniques, such as deep learning, holds significant potential for automating and streamlining neuroimaging analysis. These algorithms excel at recognizing intricate patterns within large datasets, making them ideal for tasks such as image segmentation and classification. Future advancements may focus on training these models on diverse and extensive neuroimaging datasets, allowing them to generalize findings across populations. This could reduce the variability seen in traditional analysis methods and lead to more standardized diagnostic criteria. As AI systems become more robust, they can assist clinicians in identifying biomarkers for various neurodegenerative and psychiatric disorders, enabling earlier and more accurate interventions. In addition to improving diagnostic capabilities, AI-driven neuroimaging can enhance personalized medicine approaches (Saboury B., et al, 2021).

AI can assist in identifying the optimal stimulation targets by analyzing pre-treatment imaging data to predict which areas of the brain would benefit most from intervention. This synergy between neuroimaging and neuromodulation could enhance treatment efficacy for conditions like chronic pain, depression, and movement disorders, providing more tailored therapeutic options. The potential of AI in neuroimaging is further amplified by advancements in neuroinformatics and big data analytics. As neuroimaging technologies become more sophisticated, they generate vast amounts of data that require effective management and analysis. AI can facilitate the processing and integration of these large datasets, uncovering hidden patterns and insights that inform both basic research and clinical practice. Collaborative platforms that leverage AI algorithms to analyze shared neuroimaging data could accelerate discoveries in brain science, promoting a more collaborative and open research environment. Developing frameworks that ensure the responsible use of AI in neuroimaging will be crucial for maintaining patient trust and safeguarding sensitive information (Panayides A S., et al, 2020). Engaging with diverse stakeholders, including ethicists, clinicians, and patient advocacy groups, can help create guidelines that prioritize patient welfare and equitable access to innovative neuroimaging technologies.

CONCLUSION

This technological advancement not only enhances our understanding of normal brain function but also facilitates the identification and characterization of various neurological and psychiatric disorders. AI has already shown promise in automating routine neuroimaging tasks, such as image segmentation and feature extraction, allowing for more standardized and objective analyses. These capabilities help mitigate human bias and variability, leading to more consistent diagnostic criteria and improved patient outcomes. Moreover, the ability of AI to uncover hidden patterns and relationships within neuroimaging data can reveal critical biomarkers that may serve as early indicators of disease, significantly impacting early diagnosis and intervention strategies. This shift towards precision medicine not only enhances therapeutic efficacy but also minimizes the risk of adverse effects associated with generalized treatment protocols. As AI continues to evolve, the potential for it to support clinical decision-making and enhance therapeutic strategies becomes increasingly feasible. However, the path forward is not without challenges. Ethical considerations surrounding data privacy, algorithmic transparency, and the potential for bias in AI models must be addressed to ensure responsible implementation in clinical settings. Establishing clear guidelines and regulatory frameworks will be essential to navigate these complexities, fostering trust among patients and healthcare providers. Moreover, ongoing education and training for clinicians in AI methodologies will be critical for effectively integrating these tools into everyday practice. As we look to the future, the collaborative efforts between neuroimaging experts, data scientists, and clinicians will be vital for maximizing the potential of AI in brain analysis. By fostering interdisciplinary partnerships, the field can cultivate innovative solutions that address the diverse challenges associated with neurological disorders. The future of neuroimaging is not only about technological advancement; it is also about enhancing the human capacity to understand the brain and improving the lives of individuals affected by neurological conditions. In conclusion, AI in neuroimaging and brain analysis stands at the forefront of a new era in neuroscience. By combining advanced computational techniques with rich neuroimaging data, we are poised to unlock profound insights into the workings of the human brain. This synergy promises to lead to breakthroughs in diagnosis, treatment, and our overall understanding of neurological and psychiatric disorders. As we navigate the ethical, technical, and practical challenges ahead, the commitment to responsible AI development and application will ensure that these innovations benefit patients and society as a whole. The journey towards a deeper understanding of the brain is just beginning, and AI will undoubtedly play a pivotal role in shaping its future.

REFERENCES

Abdollahifard, S., Farrokhi, A., Mowla, A., & Liebeskind, D. S. (2024). Performance Metrics, Algorithms, and Applications of Artificial Intelligence in Vascular and Interventional Neurology: A Review of Basic Elements. *Neurologic Clinics*, 42(3), 633–650. DOI: 10.1016/j.ncl.2024.03.001 PMID: 38937033

Abi-Dargham, A., Moeller, S. J., Ali, F., DeLorenzo, C., Domschke, K., Horga, G., Jutla, A., Kotov, R., Paulus, M. P., Rubio, J. M., Sanacora, G., Veenstra-VanderWeele, J., & Krystal, J. H. (2023). Candidate Biomarkers in Psychiatric Disorders: State of the Field. *World Psychiatry; Official Journal of the World Psychiatric Association (WPA)*, 22(2), 236–262. DOI: 10.1002/wps.21078 PMID: 37159365

Andreu-Perez, J., Emberson, L. L., Kiani, M., Wang, X., & Tiwari, P. (2021). Explainable Artificial Intelligence-Based Analysis for Interpreting Infant fnirs Data in Developmental Cognitive Neuroscience. *Communications Biology*, 4(1), 126. Advance online publication. DOI: 10.1038/s42003-021-02534-y PMID: 34526648

Annavarapu, R. N., Gavini, J., & Nair, S. (2019). Non-Invasive Imaging Modalities to Study Neurodegenerative Diseases of Aging Brain. *Journal of Chemical Neuroanatomy*, 97, 67–76. DOI: 10.1016/j.jchemneu.2018.02.006 PMID: 29474853

Bernal, J., Costa, A., Oliveira, J., Sanchez, I., & Hernandez, M. (2019). Deep Convolutional Neural Networks for Brain Image Analysis on Magnetic Resonance Imaging: A Review. *Artificial Intelligence in Medicine*, 97, 123–137. DOI: 10.1016/j.artmed.2018.08.008 PMID: 30195984

Cascella, M., Montomoli, J., Bellini, V., Vittori, A., Ianniello, D., & Cuocolo, R. (2023). Crossing the AI Chasm in Neurocritical Care. *Computers*, 12(4), 83. DOI: 10.3390/computers12040083

Chen, X., Zhang, X., Xie, H., Tao, X., Wang, F., Xie, N., & Li, J. (2021). A Bibliometric and Visual Analysis of Artificial Intelligence Technologies-Enhanced Brain MRI Research. *Multimedia Tools and Applications*, 80(11), 17335–17363. DOI: 10.1007/s11042-020-09062-7

Davatzikos C., (2019), "Machine Learning in Neuroimaging: Progress and Challenges," neuroimage, vol. 197, pp. 654-665.

Farahani, F. V., Fiok, K., Lahijanian, B., Rostami, M., & Zeinali, S. (2022). Explainable AI: A Review of Applications to Neuroimaging Data. *Frontiers in Neuroscience*, 16, 791229. Advance online publication. DOI: 10.3389/fnins.2022.906290 PMID: 36583102

Felsenstein, O., Oren, N., & Tal, O. (2019), "Multi-Modal Neuroimaging Analysis and Visualization Tool (MMVT)," arxiv preprint arxiv:1910.13543.

Ghazi, M. M., & Nielsen, M. (2022), "FAST-AID Brain: Fast and Accurate Segmentation Tool Using Artificial Intelligence Developed for Brain," arxiv preprint arxiv:2208.14360.

Gheorghe-Moisii, M., & Gheorghe, C. G. (2024). *Ethical Considerations on the Use of AI Technology in ehealth Applications for Neurodegenerative Diseases*. Romanian Journal.

Huang, C., Wang, J., Wang, S. H., & Zhang, Y. D. (2022). Applicable Artificial Intelligence for Brain Disease: A Survey. *Neurocomputing*, 504, 223–239. DOI: 10.1016/j.neucom.2022.07.005

Inamdar, M. A., Raghavendra, U., Gudigar, A., Chakole, Y., Hegde, A., Menon, G. R., Barua, P., Palmer, E. E., Cheong, K. H., Chan, W. Y., Ciaccio, E. J., & Acharya, U. R. (2021). A Review on Computer Aided Diagnosis of Acute Brain Stroke. *Sensors (Basel)*, 21(24), 8507. DOI: 10.3390/s21248507 PMID: 34960599

Kim, J. H., Lee, S. M., & Kim, J. (2022). Neuroimaging Modalities in Alzheimer's Disease: Diagnosis and Clinical Features. *International Journal of Molecular Sciences*, 23(11), 6112. DOI: 10.3390/ijms23116079 PMID: 35682758

Kraguljac, N. V., McDonald, W. M., Widge, A. S., Rodriguez, C. I., Tohen, M., & Nemeroff, C. B. (2021). Neuroimaging Biomarkers in Schizophrenia. *The American Journal of Psychiatry*, 178(6), 509–521. DOI: 10.1176/appi.ajp.2020.20030340 PMID: 33397140

Li, Y., Wang, M., Wang, L., Cao, Y., Liu, Y., Zhao, Y., & Zhang, L. (2024). Advances in the Application of AI Robots in Critical Care: Scoping Review. *Journal of Medical Internet Research*, 26, e54095. DOI: 10.2196/54095 PMID: 38801765

Lin S Y, Lin C P, Hsieh T J, Lin C F, Chen S H, Chao Y P, (2019), "Multiparametric Graph Theoretical Analysis Reveals Altered Structural and Functional Network Topology in Alzheimer's Disease," neuroimage: Clinical.

Mahadev Madgule, N. (2023). Vinayaka, Yeshwant M. Sonkhaskar, Dhiren Ramanbhai Patel, R. Karthikeyan, P. Selvakumar, (2023). Mechanical properties and microstructure of activated TIG welded similar joints of Inconel alloys by desirability approaches. *Materials Today: Proceedings*, 77, 528–533. DOI: 10.1016/j.matpr.2022.12.250

Mahmood, H., Nawar, F., Islam, S. M. S., & Iqbal, A. (2024), "neuroatlas: An Artificial Intelligence-Based Framework for Annotation, Segmentation and Registration of Large Scale Biomedical Imaging Data," *biorxiv*.

Mao, C. P., Wang, G., Cao, J., Meshberg, N., Huang, Y., Zhang, Y., & Liu, X. (2022). Functional Connectivity of the Thalamo-Sensorimotor Circuit in Chronic Low Back Pain: Resting-State Functional Magnetic Resonance Imaging and Diffusion Tensor Imaging. *Neuroscience*, 493, 1–12. DOI: 10.1016/j.neuroscience.2022.02.001 PMID: 35134490

Maturi, M. H., Satish, S., Gonaygunta, H., Meduri, K., Rajan, R., & Srinivasan, R. (2022). The Intersection of Artificial Intelligence and Neuroscience: Unlocking the Mysteries of the Brain. *International Journal (Toronto, Ont.)*.

Mishro, P. K., Agrawal, S., & Panda, R. (2021). A Survey on State-of-the-Art Denoising Techniques for Brain Magnetic Resonance Images. *IEEE Reviews in Biomedical Engineering*. PMID: 33513109

Neudorf, J., Ekstrand, C., Kress, S., & Borowsky, R. (2020). Connectivity Predicts Brain Functional Complexity: Diffusion Tensor Imaging Derived Centrality Accounts for Variance in Fractal Properties of Functional Magnetic Resonance. *Neuroscience*, 438, 1–8. DOI: 10.1016/j.neuroscience.2020.04.048

Nielsen, A. N., Kjær, L., Møller, J. R., & Nielsen, J. A. (2020), "Machine Learning with Neuroimaging: Evaluating Its Applications in Psychiatry," neuroimage: Clinical, vol. 26.

Nigro, S., Filardi, M., Tafuri, B., De Blasi, R., Ciccarelli, N., & Di Iorio, A. (2022). The Role of Graph Theory in Evaluating Brain Network Alterations in Frontotemporal Dementia. *Frontiers in Neuroscience*. PMID: 35837233

Panayides, A. S., Amini, A., Filipovic, N. D., Konstantinidis, G., Lungren, M. P., & Mitsouras, D. (2020). AI in Medical Imaging Informatics: Current Challenges and Future Directions. *IEEE Journal of Biomedical and Health Informatics*, 24(7), 1931–1941. DOI: 10.1109/JBHI.2020.2991043 PMID: 32609615

Prajapati, R., & Emerson, I. A. (2021). Global and Regional Connectivity Analysis of Resting-State Function MRI Brain Images Using Graph Theory in Parkinson's Disease. *The International Journal of Neuroscience*, 131(2), 105–115. DOI: 10.1080/00207454.2020.1733559 PMID: 32124666

Raghavendra, U., Acharya, U. R., & Adeli, H. (2020). Artificial Intelligence Techniques for Automated Diagnosis of Neurological Disorders. *European Neurology*. PMID: 31743905

Rajaraman S., (2024), “Artificial Intelligence in Neuro Degenerative Diseases: Opportunities and Challenges,” AI and Neuro-Degenerative Diseases: Insights.

Ramakrishnan, T., Mohan Gift, M. D., Chitradevi, S., Jegan, R., & Subha Hency Jose, P. Nagaraja, Rajneesh Sharma H.N., Selvakumar P., Sintayehu Mekuria Hailegiorgis, (2022). “Study of Numerous Resins Used in Polymer Matrix Composite Materials”, Advances in Materials Science and Engineering, vol. 2022, Article ID 1088926, 8 pages, 2022. DOI: 10.1155/2022/1088926

Saad, M., & Islam, S. M. R. (2019), “Brain Connectivity Network Analysis and Classifications from Diffusion Tensor Imaging,” 2019 International Conference on. DOI: 10.1109/ICREST.2019.8644080

Saboury, B., Morris, M., & Siegel, E. (2021). Future Directions in Artificial Intelligence. *Radiologia Clinica*. PMID: 34689876

Sarmento, R. M., & Vasconcelos, F F X. (2019). Automatic Neuroimage Processing and Analysis in Stroke—A Systematic Review. *IEEE Reviews in Biomedical Engineering*. PMID: 31449031

Selvakumar, P., Mariappan, P., Shunmugam, S., Paul, R., & Jabez, S. (2024). Removal of chemicals from effluent using photobioreactor technology to improve environmental and health impacts. *Zeitschrift für Physikalische Chemie*, 2024(7), 1295–1302. Advance online publication. DOI: 10.1515/zpch-2023-0450

Selvakumar, P., Palanisamy, S. K., Cinthaikinian, S., Palanisamy, V., Mariappan, R., & Selvakumar, P. K. (2024). Biosensors and its diverse applications in healthcare systems. *Zeitschrift für Physikalische Chemie*, 2024. Advance online publication. DOI: 10.1515/zpch-2023-0406

Singh, A. P., Saxena, R., Saxena, S., Sharma, P., & Kumar, V. (2024). *Mind Unveiled: Cutting-Edge Neuroscience and Precision Brain Mapping*. Asian Journal.

Sorger, J. M. (2024). How to Objectively Evaluate the Impact of Image-Guided Surgery Technologies. *European Journal of Nuclear Medicine and Molecular Imaging*, 51(10), 2869–2877. DOI: 10.1007/s00259-023-06504-w PMID: 37971499

Sreenivasulu, A., & Manimozhi, T. Satheesh kumar P., Selvakumar P. And Singh P.,(2022). “The Model of Smart Sensing Device For Sensitive Nanoclusters Modification in Sensing Properties,” 2022 2nd International Conference on Advance Computing and Innovative Technologies in Engineering (ICACITE), Greater Noida, India, 2022, pp. 1043-1047, DOI: 10.1109/ICACITE53722.2022.9823846

Stumpo, V., Salvetti, O., & Gori, R. (2022), “Machine Learning Algorithms in Neuroimaging: An Overview,” Machine Learning in Neuroimaging, Springer.

Sugumaran, K. M. D., Pandiyarajan V., Y. B S, Selvakumar P. And M. S, (2024). "Analysis of Electromyography Signals for Control of Mechanical Prosthesis using Machine Learning Techniques," 2024 2nd International Conference on Intelligent Data Communication Technologies and Internet of Things (idciot), Bengaluru, India, 2024, pp. 1059-1067, DOI: 10.1109/IDCIoT59759.2024.10467707

Sui, J., Jiang, R., Bustillo, J., & Calhoun, V. (2020). Neuroimaging-Based Individualized Prediction of Cognition and Behavior for Mental Disorders and Health: Methods and Promises. *Biological Psychiatry*, 88(11), 818–828. DOI: 10.1016/j.biopsych.2020.02.016 PMID: 32336400

Surianarayanan, C., Lawrence, J. J., Chelliah, P. R., Prakash, E., & Hewage, C. (2023). Convergence of Artificial Intelligence and Neuroscience Towards the Diagnosis of Neurological Disorders—A Scoping Review. *Sensors (Basel)*, 23(6), 3062. DOI: 10.3390/s23063062 PMID: 36991773

Thomson K R, (2020), "Image-Guided Interventions: Expert Radiology Series," Tsoumakidou G, Saltiel S, Villard N, Duran R, Krokidis M, Brountzos E, (2021), "Image-Guided Marking Techniques in Interventional Radiology: A Review of Current Evidence," Journal of Interventional Radiology.

Tulay, E. E., Ozdemir, A., & Yilmaz, E. (2019). Multimodal Neuroimaging: Basic Concepts and Classification of Neuropsychiatric Diseases. *Clinical EEG and Neuroscience*, 50(3), 159–167. DOI: 10.1177/1550059418782093 PMID: 29925268

Vidya S, Gupta K, Aly A, Wills A, Ifeachor E, Singh S, (2024), "Explainable AI for Autism Diagnosis: Identifying Critical Brain Regions Using fmri Data," arxiv preprint.

Vijayakumar, G., Rajkumar, M., Rajiv Chandar, N., Selvakumar, P., & Duraisamy, R. (2024). Muniyandi Rajkumar, Rajiv Chandar N, Selvakumar P and Ramesh Duraisamy, (2024). Environmentally friendly TDS removal from waste water by electrochemical ion exchange batch-type recirculation (EIR) technique. *Environmental Science. Water Research & Technology*, 10(4), 826–835. DOI: 10.1039/D3EW00793F

Wahlang, I., Singh, P., Singh, R., & Gupta, P. (2022). Brain Magnetic Resonance Imaging Classification Using Deep Learning Architectures with Gender and Age. *Sensors (Basel)*, 22(11), 4231. DOI: 10.3390/s22051766 PMID: 35270913

Walter, M., Tanovic, E., & Moller, H. E. (2019). Translational Machine Learning for Psychiatric Neuroimaging. *Progress in Neurobiology*, 175, 53–66. PMID: 30290208

Yoo, R. E., & Choi, S. H. (2024). Deep Learning-Based Image Enhancement Techniques for Fast MRI in Neuroimaging. *Magnetic Resonance in Medical Sciences*, 23(3), 341–351. DOI: 10.2463/mrms.rev.2023-0153 PMID: 38684425

Zhang, F., Hoffmann, N., Karayumak, S. C., & Rathi, Y. (2019), "Deep White Matter Analysis: Fast, Consistent Tractography Segmentation Across Populations and dmri Acquisitions," *Conference on Medical*. DOI: 10.1007/978-3-030-32248-9_67

Zhang, F., Karayumak, S. C., Hoffmann, N., & Rathi, Y. (2020). *Deep White Matter Analysis (deepwma): Fast and Consistent Tractography Segmentation*. Image Analysis.

Zhang, F., Wu, Y., Norton, I., Rathi, Y., Golby, A. J., & O'Donnell, L. J. (2019). Test-Retest Reproducibility of White Matter Parcellation Using Diffusion MRI Tractography Fiber Clustering. *Human Brain Mapping*, 40(10), 3041–3057. DOI: 10.1002/hbm.24579 PMID: 30875144

Zhao, X., & Zhao, X. M. (2021). Deep Learning of Brain Magnetic Resonance Images: A Brief Review. *Methods (San Diego, Calif.)*, 187, 94–103. DOI: 10.1016/j.ymeth.2020.09.007 PMID: 32931932

Zhu, G., Jiang, B., Tong, L., Xie, Y., & Zaharchuk, G. (2019). Applications of Deep Learning to Neuro-Imaging Techniques. *Frontiers in Neuroscience*. PMID: 31474928

Chapter 9

Hey Friend I Am a Spiritual Robot! How May I Help You!

Integrating Spiritual Robotics in College Counseling

Ruchika Sharma
https://orcid.org/0000-0001-9518-0814
Vivekananda Institute of Professional Studies, India

Aashu Aggarwal
https://orcid.org/0000-0003-0812-1504
Vivekananda Institute of Professional Studies, India

ABSTRACT

Increasing depression and stress among the students are becoming the global concern, necessitating immediate intervention. On the other hand, spiritual robots are becoming novel perspective in addressing emotional and spiritual needs of users. By leveraging advanced AI technology, these robots can offer personalized guidance, facilitate mindfulness practices, and help students navigate their mental health challenges in college and personal settings. The traditional counselling methods can be reframed through the integration of spiritual robots, which may enhance accessibility and engagement for students, particularly those who may feel hesitant to seek help from human counselors. This chapter presents a novel perspective on how spiritual robots can enhance the well-being of students at college and help them perform better at educational as well as personal level. The authors conduct-

DOI: 10.4018/979-8-3693-9341-3.ch009

ed interviews with 25 students and present important implications for academic institutions regarding the application of robotic technology to promote the overall well-being of their student populations.

INTRODUCTION

The increasing prevalence of depression and stress among students has become a significant global concern, requiring immediate involvement. According to Duffy et al., (2019), there has been consistent rise in the mental health issues of college students. Depression and anxiety are very common issues being faced by students at least once in the 12 months (Ramón-Arbués et al., 2020). Higher education institutions are tirelessly focusing on making efforts to maintain the mental health of their students and maintain their overall well-being. Hitherto there are several barriers, both personal and systematic, for instance, knowledge among experts, cost, time, efforts, social stigma, reluctance that hinders the proper counseling of students. Advanced developments in the field of interactive technologies have provided a novel framework to manage the stress and anxiety among students. One such technology is spiritual robots which can offer a novel approach to addressing the emotional and spiritual needs of students (Cheong, 2020). By utilizing advanced AI technology, these robots can provide personalized direction, facilitate mindfulness practices, and assist students in managing their mental health challenges within college and personal environments. While there are various traditional counseling methods, the evolving landscape and the incorporation of artificial intelligence present opportunities for integrating these approaches in diverse and innovative ways (Spitale et al., 2023).

This chapter presents the overview of how spiritual robots can aid in assessing the emotional and psychological needs of the students at colleges and also address them for the well-being of students.

The incorporation of spiritual robots in the counseling framework for college students can play a noteworthy role in evaluating and addressing their requirements. These progressive AI systems can offer a unique combination of emotional support and spiritual direction, which is particularly beneficial in a college environment where students often face multiple problems, stressors, including academic pressures, social challenges, and personal identity exploration. Primarily they act as non-judgmental agents and provide healthy space to students to express their emotional state and apprehensions. This can help in reducing feelings of seclusion and anxiety, which are common among college students. Secondly, they can be 24*7 available to the students, providing immediate support whenever required. Also, students can be provided their remote access so that they can get in touch with them even if they are away from campus. This will also help the students to feel more comfortable as compared to traditional counseling services. Thirdly, spiritual robots can tailor their responses and resources to provide personalized guidance, design coping strategies and also orient them on spiritual practices that resonate with their own belief system and values. Also, cumulatively spiritual robots can encourage mediation, mindfulness, and other spiritual practices that can raise the overall well-being of all the stakeholders in the institution. It will foster resilience and take care of their overall mental health. They can also serve as a bridge between students and human counselors, helping to identify issues that may require professional intervention while also providing immediate support. This chapter deals in understanding the various aspects that are important foe institutions while integrating spiritual robots in their counseling landscape. It also elaborates on the student's perception towards spiritual robots and their acceptance towards them.

What are Spiritual Robots?

Spiritual robots refer to the concept of machines or artificial intelligence systems that are designed to engage with or embody spiritual principles, practices, or beliefs (Graves, 2021). This can include robots that enable meditation, deliver guidance on spiritual matters, or even enhance spiritual experiences. The idea often explores the intersection of technology and spirituality, raising questions about consciousness, the nature of the soul, and the potential for machines to possess or understand spiritual dimensions. While the term may not be widely defined in academic literature, it reflects ongoing discussions about the role of technology in human spiritual experiences. Application of spiritual robots in organizations can encompass various dimensions, including enhancing employee well-being, fostering a positive workplace culture, and supporting mental health initiatives (Gjorevska, 2021). These robots can be designed to provide emotional support, facilitate mindfulness practices, and promote a sense of community among employees. By integrating spiritual robots into organizational settings, companies may aim to create a more harmonious work environment, encourage personal growth, and improve overall job satisfaction (Le et al., 2024). Additionally, these robots can assist in training programs focused on emotional intelligence and resilience, helping employees navigate stress and enhance their interpersonal skills (Gill and Mathur, 2024). Overall, the incorporation of spiritual robots can serve as a complementary tool in organizational development, aligning with broader goals of employee engagement and holistic well-being.

Application of Spiritual Robots in College Setting

The use of spiritual robots in a college context can take several forms, such as providing emotional support, aiding with mental health issues, and improving students' general educational experience and general well-being. These robots can be programmed to offer stress-reduction tools, encourage mindfulness exercises, and be a companion. Spiritual robots could facilitate guided meditation sessions, encourage introspection through interactive conversations, or provide a forum for philosophical and ethical debates (Cheong, 2020). They could also help foster a feeling of community by promoting group activities focused on wellbeing and spiritual development.

Incorporating spiritual robots into campus life may also assist address the growing mental health issues that students encounter by giving them a safe area to express their emotions. By fostering a supportive environment, these robots could contribute to a more holistic approach to education, emphasizing not only academic success but also personal development and emotional resilience (Vistorte et al., 2024). Overall, the incorporation of spiritual robots in colleges has the potential to enrich the student experience, balance their emotions, promote well-being, and encourage a deeper exploration of personal and collective values.

LITERATURE REVIEW

There are multiple studies that have highlighted the importance of interactive technologies in managing user's well-being. Many interactive technologies have created a new pathway for people to access resources and counseling services for mental health and well-being. Conversational agents, such as social robots are found to engage well with the users and provide them with natural conversational environment (Sebastian and Richards 2017; Scoglio et al. 2019). There are number of instances wherein social robots are found to deliver digital assistance for social, psychological and therapeutic programs. Robots have taken a guide, counselor and coach roles for people to support them in overcoming stress and psychological issues (Robinson et al., 2021). Robots have been found to assist therapy sessions for children with autism spectrum disorders and also guide them on social skills (Cabibihan et al., 2013). They have also been used in the animal-assisted therapies wherein they mimic similar benefits (Leng et al., 2019).

Jeong et al., (2023) demonstrated the deployment of robots in the form of coach for improving the psychological well-being of college students. They found a positive relationship of the deployment of robotic technology and increase in student's mood, psychological well-being, and their motivation to change. They also reported a positive association between student's personality traits and the robot intervention outcomes and student's satisfaction with the intervention.

Axelsson, et al., (2024) also reported that robotics should be designed in a particular way to make them mental coaches for students' well-being. Authors clubbed qualitative analysis with grounded theory approach for analyzing the role of robotic technology for students' well-being.

Jeong (2022) elaborated on the importance of two types of robots- coach-like robot and companion-like robot. Coach-like robot acted more like an expert or instructor who deals in positive psychology interventions. They are soft, empathic and a friendly tone while interacting with employees. On the other hand, companion robot is more like learning from another friend. Both of them acted as the support to the working employees.

Similar findings were reported by Spitale et al., (2023) who deployed the use of two robots- QTrobot (QT) or a Misty robot (M) acting as the well-being coaches in collaboration with employees in a tech company. These robots delivered positive psychology engagements over the period of four weeks at the workplace. Their study provided valuable insights on robotic designing and deployment and the overall vision on adoption of robots as coaches in the corporate world.

RESEARCH GAP

The examination of spiritual robots as well-being consolers in college settings extends a significant research lacuna that needs additional investigation. While there has been a mounting attention in the amalgamation of technology in mental health support, the explicit role of spiritual robots—objects intended to deliver emotional and spiritual direction—remains underexplored. Current literature principally focuses on traditional therapeutic approaches and the use of AI in mental well-being, yet it often oversees the possible benefits of integrating spiritual dimensions into robotic communications at colleges for students. This gap is particularly pertinent in college settings, where students often face stress, anxiety, and experiential questions. Understanding how spiritual robots can effectively contribute to emotional well-being, foster resilience, and enhance the overall college experience could lead to innovative support systems that address the unique challenges faced by students today. Therefore, further research is needed to assess the efficacy, acceptance, and ethical implications of deploying spiritual robots in educational institutions.

OBJECTIVES

This chapter has three major objectives:

First objective is to understand the student's perception towards integration of spiritual robots in Institution's counseling mechanism.

Secondly, this study analyses the factors that influence students' willingness to engage with a spiritual robot in a counseling setting.

Thirdly, the focus is on identifying the perceived risk factors that restrict students to engage with a spiritual robot in a counseling setting.

Lastly, few measures have been proposed for successful integration of spiritual robots in counselling settings for students at college/university.

RESEARCH QUESTIONS

RQ1: What is the students' perception towards the use of spiritual robots in counseling settings at college?

RQ2: What are the value factors that influence students' willingness to engage with spiritual robots?

RQ3: What are the risk factors that influence students' willingness to engage with spiritual robots?

RESEARCH METHODOLOGY AND INTERVIEW HIGHLIGHTS

This study employs a qualitative approach, in which the authors conducted interviews with 25 students to investigate their perspectives on spiritual robots. Utilizing purposive sampling, data collection took place over a three-month period from July 2024 to September 2024.

The research methodology followed for the paper is presented in Figure 1.

Figure 1. Research methodology

Source: Prepared by Authors

Students were asked a set of questions and their responses were auto recorded. The questions were

Q: Are you aware of the concept of spiritual robots in counseling? If so, how would you define it?

65% of the students were aware of the concept and completely understood the questions and the relevance of this research. For example, one of the students replied:

"Yes! I have seen spiritual robots on YouTube. Few international organizations are really utilizing them well for the well-being of their employees"

While the others were confused or tried to guess its meaning. For instance, one student said:

"Does it mean robot is acting as a spiritual leader or some guru for us" Am I right?

Q: What is your understanding of how spiritual robots could be integrated into counseling services?

Major percentage of students was skeptical of this entire concept of spiritual robots acting as counselors. They showed either no expressions at all or were in dilemma of what to answer straight away. One of the students said:

Is that even possible? How can one interact with a robot for their personal problems. We generally need that empathy and human touch which I really doubt a robot can ever provide.

While the other commented:

This can be a great idea as I am not very comfortable in interacting with counselor. I sometimes have fear of being judged.

Q: What potential benefits do you see in using spiritual robots for counseling purposes?

There were multiple benefits reported by respondents whereas 12% of them didn't have much to state in this case.

The reported benefits were

No fear of being judged.
24* 7 support
Personalization
Immersive experience
Excitement to interact
Better well-being and health etc.

Q: How do you think spiritual robots could enhance your overall counseling experience?

Many of them were in support of this fact that spiritual robotics can change the game of counseling for students. It may also motivate the introverts to come forward and share their stresses and problems. Few of them perceived it as a source of excitement and immersive experience. One important aspect that was highlighted here is as:

One respondent replied:

If it will be a humanoid, I think I will have a better connect. It would be more like a friend.

Q: Have you ever interacted with a robot or AI in a counseling or support context? If so, what was your experience?

95% of the respondents mentioned they never interacted with a robot. Also, they were quite thrilled to experience it.

One of the respondents replied:

No not yet! But it sounds interesting! I would love to experience it some day!

Another mentioned:

I have only been interacting with chatbots on various apps such as Swiggy, Instamart etc. Never interacted with any robot for counselling as such.

Q: How do you feel about the idea of receiving emotional or spiritual support from a robot?

Respondents were not very sure of how this interaction will work in case of counselling services. Students who were already focused on their health and well-being were keener to experience a robotic interaction for counselling services. Some were confused of how a robot can guide students on spiritual aspects.

One of the respondents said:

I am really unsure of how this will work. Probably a robot can provide other assistance but spiritual and psychological assistance I really don't have an idea how will it turn out.

While the other responded:

It really sounds good! I would try it as soon as possible.

Q: How much trust would you place in a spiritual robot to provide effective counseling?

Respondents, at first place showed good response to this question. They believed that a human can still play manipulatively but a machine will always be fair in treating the concerns of students. While others perceived the same point as negative as they believed that humans would still understand the perspective by being sympathetic and less judgmental.

One of the respondents laughed and mentioned:

I think machines are more trustworthy than humans these days! I may share my problems and secrets with a machine over any other human.

One of the other respondents said:

I can't really rely on a machine to solve my personal problems. I don't think it will be able to empathize the way I want a listener to! Rest… My opinion may change when I actually use it.

Q: What factors would influence your willingness to engage with a spiritual robot in a counseling setting?

Facilitating factors are being presented in the form of themes and sub-themes in Table 1.

Table 1. Facilitating factors, themes, and sub-themes extracted from interviews. Source: prepared by authors

S.NO	Themes	Sub Themes
1	Credibility	Transparency Expertise Emotional intelligence
2	Trust	Reliability Consistency Truthfulness
3	Empathy	Effective communication Understanding Emotional support Personalization
4	Confidentiality	Data Privacy Information security Legal compliance Ethical considerations
5	User Comfort	Easy user-robot interface Easy to access Intuitive Design Effective system performance Support services User-centric design
6	Self-robot congruence	Easy adaptation Personalization Social interaction Value congruence

Q: What risks or factors would stop you from using spiritual robot in a counseling setting?

Perceived risk factors are being presented in the form of themes and sub-themes in Table 2.

Table 2. Risk factors, themes, and sub-themes extracted from interviews.

S.NO	Themes	Sub Themes
1	Lack of Human Connect	Communication gap Lack of emotional support Risk of miscommunication
2	Over-dependence on technology	Increased dependency Detraction from human relationships Detraction from socialization
3	Data privacy and security	Lack of Data Privacy Limited Information security Lack of ethical code of conduct
4	Operating challenges	Difficult user-robot interface Difficult to operate Lack of support services

Source: Prepared by authors

RESULTS

Based on the above results, authors propose the following model that can be tested empirically in the future studies.

Figure 2. Proposed model for future empirical testing

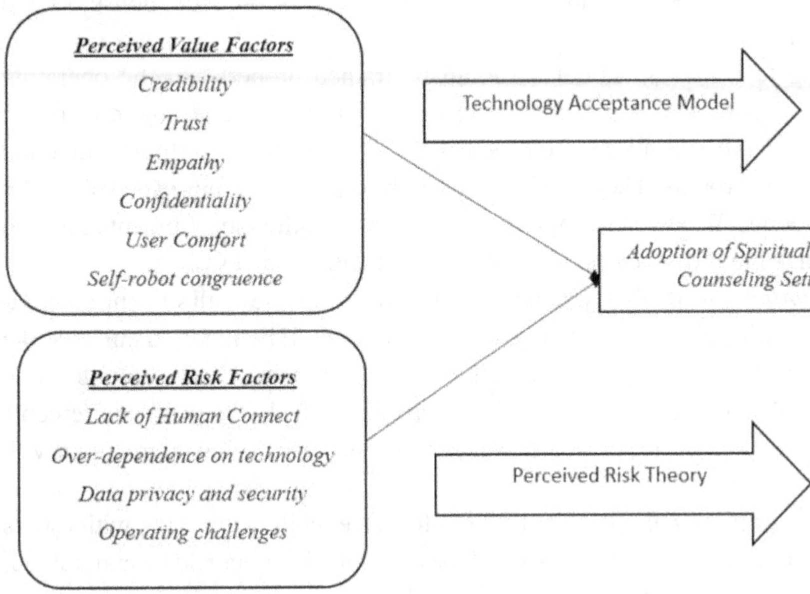

Source: Prepared by authors

Guidelines to facilitate use of spiritual robotics in college setting for counseling purpose

1. ***Set Clear Objectives:*** Clearly state the goals for integrating spiritual robotics into the college settings. Maintain a checklist of how these objectives will drive and enhance the student's well-being, support them in their mental traumas, maintain their mental health and enhance their overall spiritual well-being.
2. ***Communicate the objectives:*** Just framing of objective will not help the institution rather these objectives and the benefit of the interactive technologies need to be communicated to students. This will build their trust in the college and also enhance their outlook towards the adoption of these technologies.
3. ***Ethical Considerations:*** Clearly state ethical guidelines and ensure that students are confident that their beliefs and privacy are respected and secured. The successful implementation of this technology in colleges is contingent upon ensuring that students are confident in its use.

4. ***Integration with human counselors:*** Initial implementation can be the integration of robots and human counselors so that humans intervene whenever they find robots' performance is out of place or students are not able to communicate well in the sessions. Initial intervention of humans can help the students as well as college to overcome the challenges in implementation. Also, if possible, ensure that spiritual robotics complement traditional counseling methods rather than replacing them. They should serve as an additional resource for counselors and students.
5. ***Training to students:*** students should be trained properly on the operating procedure of robots. Also, these trainings should not be one time task rather management should take frequent feedbacks from the students on their interaction with spiritual robots. They can be asked on how have they improved spiritually and academically after the implementation of this entire idea. Students can also be involved in the development and implementation process also.
6. ***Accessibility***: Ensure that spiritual robotics are accessible to all students, including those with disabilities. Special provisions should be made to enhance the accessibility of interactive technologies so that students become comfortable and confident in accessing their utility. Consider the technological requirements and provide support for those who may need assistance during interactions with robots.
7. ***Assurance on security***; students should feel safe while interacting with robots and the confidentiality and security of the exchanged data should be maintained. This will enhance the experience of the students and encourage them to motivate other students as well to interact with the technology.
8. ***Continuous Improvement:*** Robotics or using interactive technologies is not one-day task, rather it demands continuous involvement and improvement over the period of time. College/organizations need to be proactive on latest trends and continue to upgrade the device based on new guidelines and feedback from industry experts and government.
9. ***Promote Awareness:*** Educate the college community about the benefits and availability of spiritual robotics in counseling. Create awareness campaigns to encourage students to utilize these resources.
10. ***Build cultural sensitivity:*** Robots should be programmed in a way that they sensitize with students and take special care of their sentiments and values. Specially, in a country like India this sensitivity should be taken care of to establish an interaction between students and machine/or any other interactive device.

Guidelines to overcome risk perception in the use of spiritual robotics in college setting for counseling purpose

1. ***Continuous training and monitoring:*** Continuous training should be given to the students as well as trainers. Also, they must be informed about the underlying risks in using the technology so that their acceptance of failure is somehow managed.
2. ***Continuous oversight and monitoring:*** Counselors and staff should receive training on how to effectively integrate spiritual robotics into their practice. Regular oversight and evaluation of the technology's impact on students should be conducted.
3. ***Enhance trust:*** trust and dependence of students on spiritual robots must be continuously monitored and counselors must ensure that students are interacting with them properly and forming a good reputation with them.
4. ***Ethical Aspects:*** Make sure that the use of spiritual robotics bring into line with ethical standards in counseling. This includes procuring informed consent from students and clearly communicating the role and limitations of the robotic systems.
5. ***Feedback Mechanisms:*** Establish channels for students to provide feedback on their experiences with spiritual robotics. This can help identify any issues or concerns that may arise and allow for continuous improvement.
6. ***Emergency Protocols:*** Develop protocols for situations where a student may require immediate human intervention. Ensure that counselors are readily available to address any crises or sensitive issues that may arise during interactions with the robotic system.

CONCLUSION

Interactive technologies are becoming an important aspect across many industry domains. Academics is one of the less explored aspects when it comes to robotic technology specially in India. With increasing stress and cases of depression amongst the students, it has become imperative to introduce consolers in the university or college settings. Due to the larger percentage of students studying, getting such a huge number of counselers may be a costly deal for the colleges/ universities. Therefore, spiritual robots may serve as a good option for handling such a large percentage of students. Spiritual robots can extend multiple advantages for college students, uplifting their educational experience and personal development. These advanced AI systems can deliver emotional support, serving students manage stress and anxiety related to academic as well as personal reasons. By enabling mindfulness practices and endorsing self-reflection, spiritual robots can inspire a deeper understanding of personal values and beliefs, nurturing a sense of purpose and well-being. Moreover, they can serve as available resources for discovering philosophical and ethical questions, elevating students' critical thinking skills. Additionally, by generating a non-judgmental space for discourse, spiritual robots can assist students handle complex social dynamics and augment their interpersonal skills, eventually contributing to a more holistic educational environment. Therefore, Institutions/colleges/universities can integrate robotic technology especially spiritual robots in their traditional counseling systems by facilitating the students and managing their risk perception on use of this technology.

REFERENCES

Axelsson, M., Spitale, M., & Gunes, H. (2024). Robots as mental well-being coaches: Design and ethical recommendations. *ACM Transactions on Human-Robot Interaction*, 13(2), 1–55. DOI: 10.1145/3643457

Cabibihan, J. J., Javed, H., Ang, M.Jr, & Aljunied, S. M. (2013). Why robots? A survey on the roles and benefits of social robots in the therapy of children with autism. *International Journal of Social Robotics*, 5(4), 593–618. DOI: 10.1007/s12369-013-0202-2

Cheong, P. H. (2020). Robots, religion and communication: Rethinking piety, practices and pedagogy in the era of artificial intelligence. In *Religion in the Age of Digitalization* (pp. 86–96). Routledge. DOI: 10.4324/9780367809225-9

Duffy, M. E., Twenge, J. M., & Joiner, T. E. (2019). Trends in mood and anxiety symptoms and suicide-related outcomes among US undergraduates, 2007–2018: Evidence from two national surveys. *The Journal of Adolescent Health*, 65(5), 590–598. DOI: 10.1016/j.jadohealth.2019.04.033 PMID: 31279724

Gill, A., & Mathur, A. (2024). Emotional Intelligence in the Age of AI: Enhancing Workforce Development for Human-Machine Collaboration. In Sustainable Innovation for Industry 6.0 (pp. 263-285). IGI Global.

Gjorevska, N. (2021). *Workplace Spirituality and Well-Being among the Workforce in Social Businesses in Scotland* (Doctoral dissertation, Budapesti Corvinus Egyetem).

. Graves, M. (2021). Emergent models for moral AI spirituality.

Jeong, S. (2022). *Designing and Deploying Robotic Companions to Improve Human Psychological Wellbeing* (Doctoral dissertation, Massachusetts Institute of Technology).

Jeong, S., Aymerich-Franch, L., Arias, K., Alghowinem, S., Lapedriza, A., Picard, R., Park, H. W., & Breazeal, C. (2023). Deploying a robotic positive psychology coach to improve college students' psychological well-being. *User Modeling and User-Adapted Interaction*, 33(2), 571–615. DOI: 10.1007/s11257-022-09337-8 PMID: 38737788

Le, K. B. Q., & Cayrat, C. (2024). Howdy, Robo-Partner: Exploring artificial companionship and its stress-alleviating potential for service employees. *Journal of Service Management*. Advance online publication. DOI: 10.1108/JOSM-09-2023-0408

Leng, M., Liu, P., Zhang, P., Hu, M., Zhou, H., Li, G., Yin, H., & Chen, L. (2019). Pet robot intervention for people with dementia: A systematic review and meta-analysis of randomized controlled trials. *Psychiatry Research*, 271, 516–525. DOI: 10.1016/j.psychres.2018.12.032 PMID: 30553098

Ramón-Arbués, E., Gea-Caballero, V., Granada-López, J. M., Juárez-Vela, R., Pellicer-García, B., & Antón-Solanas, I. (2020). The prevalence of depression, anxiety and stress and their associated factors in college students. *International Journal of Environmental Research and Public Health*, 17(19), 7001. DOI: 10.3390/ijerph17197001 PMID: 32987932

Robinson, N. L., Ward, B., & Kavanagh, D. J. (2021, August). A robot-delivered program for low-intensity problem-solving therapy for students in higher education. In *2021 30th IEEE International Conference on Robot & Human Interactive Communication (RO-MAN)* (pp. 945-950). IEEE. DOI: 10.1109/RO-MAN50785.2021.9515532

Scoglio, A. A., Reilly, E. D., Gorman, J. A., & Drebing, C. E. (2019). Use of social robots in mental health and well-being research: Systematic review. *Journal of Medical Internet Research*, 21(7), e13322. DOI: 10.2196/13322 PMID: 31342908

Sebastian, J., & Richards, D. (2017). Changing stigmatizing attitudes to mental health via education and contact with embodied conversational agents. *Computers in Human Behavior*, 73, 479–488. DOI: 10.1016/j.chb.2017.03.071

Spitale, M., Axelsson, M., & Gunes, H. (2023, March). Robotic mental well-being coaches for the workplace: An in-the-wild study on form. In *Proceedings of the 2023 ACM/IEEE International Conference on Human-Robot Interaction* (pp. 301-310). DOI: 10.1145/3568162.3577003

Vistorte, A. O. R., Deroncele-Acosta, A., Ayala, J. L. M., Barrasa, A., López-Granero, C., & Martí-González, M. (2024). Integrating artificial intelligence to assess emotions in learning environments: A systematic literature review. *Frontiers in Psychology*, 15, 1387089. DOI: 10.3389/fpsyg.2024.1387089 PMID: 38966729

Chapter 10
Development of AI- and NLP-Driven Chatbots and Virtual Assistants for Mental Health Support

Aanchal Punia
Central Research Laboratory, Bharat Electronics Limited, India

Pawan Bhakuni
Central Research Laboratory, Bharat Electronics Limited, India

Nitin Sharma
Central Research Laboratory, Bharat Electronics Limited, India

ABSTRACT

The chapter explores the transformative role of artificial intelligence (AI) and natural language processing (NLP) technologies in enhancing mental health care. This chapter provides a comprehensive overview of the current landscape of AI and NLP applications in mental health, detailing the mechanisms through which chatbots and virtual assistants operate. It discusses the various types of chatbots, their advantages in promoting early intervention and reducing stigma. Furthermore, the chapter addresses the methodologies of fine-tuning and prompt engineering that optimize these digital tools for specific therapeutic contexts. By integrating empirical research findings and theoretical insights, this chapter elucidates how AI and NLP-driven solutions can bridge gaps in traditional mental health services, ultimately contributing to improved outcomes for individuals and communities. The findings underscore the importance of ongoing research and development in this field, advocating for the continued integration of technology in mental health support systems

DOI: 10.4018/979-8-3693-9341-3.ch010

A. MENTAL HEALTH SUPPORT

A.1. Why We Need Mental Health Support

Mental health assistance is vital in promoting emotional well-being and resilience, particularly in today's increasingly complex and demanding environment. As individuals navigate the stresses of daily life—from work pressures to personal relationships—the importance of robust mental health support cannot be overstated. Research consistently demonstrates that mental health illnesses, such as anxiety, depression, and bipolar disorder, significantly impact individuals' quality of life. These conditions can hinder educational achievement and diminish occupational productivity, leading to a cascading effect affecting families and communities. By providing timely access to mental health resources, we can enable early intervention, which is essential for mitigating the escalation of various mental health issues.

Early intervention is crucial because it can prevent the worsening of symptoms and the development of more severe conditions. Mental health support equips individuals with the tools to cultivate effective coping mechanisms and enhance their emotional regulation abilities. This, in turn, fosters greater psychological resilience, allowing people to bounce back from challenges and maintain a healthier outlook on life. Addressing mental health proactively creates a foundation for individuals to thrive personally and professionally, contributing to overall societal well-being.

Understanding the dynamics of mental health support is critical to developing evidence-based interventions tailored to diverse populations' unique needs. Research in this field allows for the customization of support services, ensuring they are relevant and effective for various cultural, socioeconomic, and demographic groups. Furthermore, mental health support services play an essential role in combating the stigma associated with mental illness. By promoting open discourse and fostering a culture of acceptance and understanding, these services encourage individuals to seek help without fear of judgment.

Prioritizing mental health support enhances individual outcomes and cultivates a healthy society. Communities can thrive when mental health is treated with the same urgency as physical health. Engaging in research and discussions within this domain is vital for deepening our collective understanding and improving the efficacy of mental health interventions. As we continue to explore innovative approaches and leverage technology, such as AI- and NLP-driven chatbots, we can further enhance the accessibility and effectiveness of mental health support systems, ultimately benefiting individuals and society.

In summary, mental health support is not just a personal necessity but a societal imperative. By advancing our collective understanding and improving the efficacy of mental health interventions, we can create a more responsive and inclusive support system that meets the diverse needs of individuals in today's complex landscape.

A.2. What is Mental Health Support?

Mental health support encompasses a comprehensive array of services and interventions designed to enhance psychological well-being and assist those grappling with mental health challenges. This support is delivered by qualified professionals, including psychologists, psychiatrists, and licensed counselors, who employ various therapeutic approaches tailored to individual needs. One of the most widely used methods is cognitive-behavioral therapy (CBT), which focuses on identifying and altering negative thought patterns and behaviors. Additionally, pharmacological management may be employed, where medications are prescribed to help stabilize mood and alleviate symptoms of mental health disorders. This multifaceted approach ensures that individuals receive holistic care, addressing their psychological and biological conditions.

In addition to professional services, community resources are crucial in providing accessible options for those needing support. Peer support groups offer a safe space for individuals to share their experiences and connect with others facing similar challenges, fostering a sense of belonging and understanding. Crisis hotlines are another essential resource, providing immediate support and guidance to those in acute distress. These community-based initiatives enhance the reach of mental health services, making assistance available to a broader audience, particularly for those who may be hesitant to seek formal therapy.

The significance of mental health support extends beyond individual care; it is vital for cultivating a culture of understanding and acceptance within communities. By addressing and mitigating the stigma surrounding mental health disorders, these support systems encourage open dialogue and increase public awareness. This cultural shift benefits individuals and enhances community cohesion, promoting empathy and reducing isolation among those affected by mental health issues.

Researchers must rigorously examine the efficacy, accessibility, and implementation of mental health support interventions. By producing evidence-based practices, we can refine existing support systems and develop new strategies to improve outcomes for individuals and communities. This research is essential for fostering a healthy society, ensuring that mental health support is adequate and equitable and reaches those most need it. Ultimately, a robust framework for mental health support contributes to individuals' well-being and strengthens our communities' fabric.

A.3. Types of Mental Health Support

Mental health support encompasses a variety of services designed to help individuals manage their mental health challenges. One of the primary types is "psychotherapy," which involves structured sessions with trained professionals. Psychotherapy can take many forms, including cognitive-behavioral therapy (CBT), psychodynamic therapy, and humanistic therapy, each tailored to address specific issues such as anxiety, depression, or trauma. These sessions provide a safe space for individuals to explore their thoughts and feelings, develop coping strategies, and work toward personal growth and healing.

Another essential type of mental health support is "peer support." This involves individuals sharing their experiences and providing mutual support to one another. Peer support groups can be particularly beneficial, fostering a sense of community and belonging. Participants often find solace in knowing they are not alone in their struggles and can learn from others who have faced similar challenges. This support can be precious in reducing stigma and encouraging individuals to seek professional help.

"Digital mental health resources" have also gained prominence in recent years. These include mobile applications, online therapy platforms, and mental health websites that provide information, tools, and techniques for managing mental health. Many of these resources offer self-help strategies, mindfulness exercises, and educational content, making mental health support more accessible. Technology integration allows individuals to engage with their mental health on their terms, offering convenience and flexibility in seeking help. These various types of mental health support collectively contribute to a comprehensive approach to mental well-being, catering to diverse needs and preferences.

A.4. Psychotherapy

Psychotherapy, often referred to as talk therapy, is a fundamental approach to mental health assistance that involves structured conversations between a qualified therapist and an individual or group. This therapeutic method aims to help individuals understand their thoughts, feelings, and behaviors, ultimately promoting personal development and the adoption of adaptive coping mechanisms. Psychotherapy empowers individuals to confront and navigate their emotional challenges by facilitating introspection and self-discovery, leading to greater resilience and well-being.

Within psychotherapy, various modalities exist, each with a unique focus and technique. One of the most widely recognized approaches is cognitive-behavioral therapy (CBT), which emphasizes identifying and altering detrimental thought patterns and behaviors. CBT equips individuals with practical skills to challenge negative beliefs and replace them with more constructive alternatives. Another significant modality is psychodynamic therapy, which delves into unconscious motivations, historical experiences, and relational patterns to uncover underlying issues influencing present behavior. This exploration fosters a deeper understanding of oneself and can illuminate the roots of emotional distress.

The therapeutic relationship itself is fundamental to the effectiveness of psychotherapy. It creates a secure and supportive environment where clients can articulate their thoughts and feelings without fear of judgment. This relationship fosters trust, allowing individuals to discuss their struggles and aspirations openly. Through this process, therapists can provide empathetic guidance and facilitate meaningful change, encouraging clients to develop healthier coping strategies and emotional responses.

Extensive research supports the efficacy of psychotherapy in alleviating symptoms of mental health disorders, enhancing emotional regulation, and improving interpersonal relationships. Studies show that individuals engaged in psychotherapy report elevated well-being and greater life satisfaction than those not seeking therapy. Furthermore, psychotherapy can be tailored to address the specific needs of various populations, including children, adolescents, and individuals from diverse cultural backgrounds. This adaptability renders psychotherapy a flexible and accessible support capable of meeting multiple mental health challenges.

Researchers who examine the diverse modalities and techniques within psychotherapy gain critical insights into optimizing these interventions for improved mental health outcomes. Ongoing investigation into the effectiveness of different therapeutic approaches and their implementation in various settings contributes to the broader understanding of mental health care. By continually refining these practices, we can enhance the quality of support available to those in need, ultimately fostering healthier individuals and communities.

A.5. Innovations in Mental Health Support

Innovations in mental health support have transformed the care landscape, making it more accessible and tailored to individual needs. One of the most significant advancements is the integration of digital platforms and telehealth services, which allow individuals to connect with mental health professionals from the comfort of their homes. This shift reduces barriers related to location and mobility and offers greater flexibility in scheduling appointments. Additionally, teletherapy has gained acceptance and legitimacy, allowing therapists to reach a wider audience and provide services to those who may have previously been reluctant to seek help due to stigma or logistical challenges.

Another notable innovation is the rise of mental health apps and self-help tools, which empower users to take charge of their mental well-being. These applications often include mood tracking, guided meditations, cognitive-behavioral exercises, and access to educational resources. By promoting self-awareness and providing coping strategies, these tools can complement traditional therapy and encourage proactive mental health management. Furthermore, advancements in artificial intelligence and machine learning are paving the way for personalized mental health interventions, with AI-driven chatbots and virtual assistants offering immediate support and guidance. As these innovations continue to evolve, they promise to enhance the quality and accessibility of mental health care, ultimately improving outcomes for individuals seeking support.

B. AI AND NATURAL LANGUAGE PROCESSING

B.1. Why We Need AI and NLP

Incorporating AI and NLP in mental health research is essential for enhancing our understanding and treatment of psychological disorders. Traditional research methods often rely on structured data, which can limit the scope of insights gained. AI and NLP tools can analyze vast and complex datasets, including clinical notes, patient interactions, and social media content. By sifting through this unstructured data, researchers can uncover trends, correlations, and patterns that may not be immediately apparent through conventional analytical methods. This capability allows for a more nuanced understanding of mental health issues, including the identification of risk factors, symptomatology, and treatment responses across diverse populations.

Moreover, AI and NLP are instrumental in automating the extraction of significant insights from this wealth of unstructured data. For instance, sentiment analysis can gauge emotional states from written communications, offering researchers and clinicians valuable information about a patient's mental state over time. This continuous monitoring can reveal fluctuations in mood or behavior that could inform treatment decisions. By enhancing the granularity and depth of data analysis, AI and NLP enable researchers to develop more effective and targeted interventions tailored to the specific needs of individuals with mental health disorders.

AI and NLP also facilitate the creation of personalized treatment plans designed to meet specific individual requirements. By analyzing linguistic patterns and emotional indicators in a patient's communication, these technologies can inform the development of adaptive therapy procedures that improve engagement and efficacy.

For example, chatbots equipped with NLP can assess the emotional tone of a user's messages and adjust their responses accordingly, providing a more responsive and empathetic interaction. This level of personalization can enhance the therapeutic experience, making patients feel more understood and supported, ultimately leading to better outcomes.

Additionally, AI-powered solutions significantly enhance access to mental health services by providing virtual platforms that dismantle geographical barriers. Access to qualified mental health professionals is limited in many rural or underserved regions. AI-driven applications can provide immediate support and guidance, allowing individuals to receive help at their convenience without the constraints of traditional therapy sessions. This immediacy is crucial, especially in crises, where timely intervention can make a significant difference in a person's mental health trajectory.

Furthermore, the scalability of AI and NLP solutions means they can simultaneously serve more individuals. This is particularly valuable in addressing the growing demand for mental health services as global awareness of mental health issues continues to rise. By leveraging technology to bridge the gap between need and availability, mental health professionals can extend their reach and ensure that more people receive the support they need.

In summary, the integration of AI and NLP into mental health research and practice is not just beneficial but necessary for advancing our understanding of psychological disorders. These technologies offer a powerful means of extracting meaningful insights from complex data, personalizing treatment, and improving access to care. As researchers and practitioners continue to harness the potential of AI and NLP, we can anticipate a future where mental health interventions are more effective, inclusive, and responsive to the diverse needs of individuals and communities. This evolution promotes individual well-being and contributes to society's overall health by addressing mental health issues with greater efficiency and compassion.

B.1.1. Enhancing Mental Health Services

Integrating artificial intelligence (AI) and natural language processing (NLP) into mental health services represents a significant leap forward in delivering care. One of the primary benefits is improved accessibility and availability of mental health resources. AI-driven tools can offer support outside traditional office hours, enabling individuals to access help whenever needed. This is particularly crucial for those who may face barriers to in-person therapy, such as geographic isolation, mobility issues, or stigma. By providing immediate responses through chatbots or virtual assistants, AI can help users conveniently engage with mental health resources, creating a more user-friendly environment.

Personalization is another critical enhancement facilitated by AI and NLP technologies. These tools can analyze user interactions and preferences to tailor recommendations and interventions, making mental health care more relevant to each individual. For example, AI algorithms can assess users' moods and suggest specific exercises or content that align with their current emotional state. This level of customization not only increases engagement but also helps individuals feel understood and supported. Additionally, AI can assist therapists by providing insights into patient behavior and progress, allowing for more targeted treatment plans and informed decision-making.

Furthermore, AI can streamline administrative tasks, alleviating some of the burdens on mental health professionals. By automating scheduling, billing, and data entry, these technologies free up therapists to focus more on direct patient care. This operational efficiency can increase productivity and a better overall client experience. As mental health services continue to evolve, the integration of AI and NLP will play a crucial role in enhancing the quality, accessibility, and effectiveness of care, ensuring that individuals receive the support they need in a timely and personalized manner.

B.1.2. Historical Context of AI in Mental Health

The historical context of artificial intelligence (AI) in mental health reveals a gradual evolution from basic automation to sophisticated algorithms that enhance therapeutic practices. Early experiments with AI in healthcare began in the 1960s, primarily focusing on developing decision-support systems for diagnosing mental health conditions. One notable project, ELIZA, created by Joseph Weizenbaum in 1966, simulated a conversation with a psychotherapist using pattern matching to respond to user inputs. Although rudimentary by today's standards, ELIZA laid the groundwork for understanding how computer programs could interact with human emotions and thoughts (Weizenbaum, 1966). This early work sparked interest in leveraging technology to improve mental health services, highlighting AI's potential and limitations in therapeutic contexts.

As technology progressed, so did the applications of AI in mental health. By the late 1990s and early 2000s, researchers began exploring more complex algorithms capable of processing natural language, leading to the development of online therapy platforms and chatbots. These innovations provided new avenues for delivering mental health support, particularly in response to growing demands for accessible care. A study by Kessler et al. (2005) emphasized the prevalence of mental health issues, indicating that many individuals remain untreated due to various barriers, including cost and stigma. The evolution of AI tools has since been marked by significant advancements in machine learning and NLP, allowing for more nuanced interactions and better personalization of care.

Today, AI technologies are increasingly integrated into mental health frameworks, as evidenced by tools like Woebot and Wysa, which use conversational agents to provide real-time support and resources. These applications demonstrate how AI can supplement traditional therapeutic approaches by offering scalable solutions to mental health challenges. The ongoing development of AI in this field reflects a broader trend toward embracing technology to enhance mental health services, making care more accessible and practical for diverse populations. As AI continues to evolve, its historical roots provide valuable insights into its potential benefits and the ethical considerations that must be addressed in its implementation.

B.2 How Do AI and NLP Models Work?

B.2.1. Data Input and Processing

Effective AI and NLP models rely heavily on the quality and structure of their input data. The processes involved in data input and processing are crucial for ensuring that the models can accurately understand and generate human language. This section elaborates on the critical components of data input and processing for AI and NLP applications, particularly in the context of mental health support.

Overview of Data Sources

AI and NLP models utilize various data sources to train and refine their language understanding. These sources can include:

- **Clinical Notes:** Text from healthcare providers' records offers insights into patient interactions, symptoms, and treatment outcomes. Analyzing these notes can help identify trends and common concerns among patients.
- **Patient Interactions:** Conversations between patients and mental health professionals, whether in therapy sessions or through digital platforms, serve as valuable datasets. They contain real-world language use, emotional expressions, and therapeutic dialogues.
- **Social Media and Online Forums:** Publicly available content from social media platforms and online support groups can provide a broader perspective on mental health issues. Analyzing discussions and sentiments in these contexts helps models understand common concerns and language patterns.

Data Preprocessing Techniques

Before data can be fed into AI and NLP models, it undergoes several preprocessing steps to ensure its quality and relevance:

- **Cleaning:** This involves removing irrelevant information, such as HTML tags, memorable characters, and stop words (common words that add little meaning, like "the" or "is"). Cleaning ensures that the model focuses on significant content.
- **Normalization:** Text normalization includes converting all text to a standard format, such as lowercasing, stemming, and lemmatization. Stemming reduces words to their root forms (e.g., "running" becomes "run"), while lemmatization considers the context to return words to their base or dictionary form.
- **Segmentation:** In this step, long pieces of text are divided into smaller, manageable units, such as sentences or phrases. This segmentation allows models to analyze text more effectively and maintain context.

Tokenization and Text Representation

Tokenization is a critical process in NLP, where text is split into smaller units called tokens, which can be words, phrases, or symbols. This step allows models to process language more effectively. Different tokenization techniques include:

- **Word Tokenization:** This method divides text into individual words. For example, the sentence "I feel happy" would be tokenized into ["I," "feel," "happy"]. This approach is straightforward and commonly used.
- **Subword Tokenization:** Subword tokenization is employed in some cases, particularly for languages with rich morphology or compound words. Techniques like Byte Pair Encoding (BPE) break words into smaller subword units, allowing for better handling of rare words and enhancing model flexibility.

Once tokenized, the text must be represented numerically so AI models can understand. Standard methods of text representation include:

- **Bag of Words (BoW):** This approach represents text as a collection of words, disregarding the order and focusing solely on the frequency of each word in the document.
- **Term Frequency-Inverse Document Frequency (TF-IDF):** TF-IDF considers the frequency of words and how important a word is to a document

relative to a collection of documents. This helps prioritize more meaningful terms.

- **Word Embeddings**: Advanced models use word embeddings, such as Word2Vec or GloVe, representing words in continuous vector space. Each word is mapped to a point in high-dimensional space, capturing semantic relationships and contextual meanings.

In recent years, transformer-based models have revolutionized text representation. Models like BERT and GPT utilize contextual embeddings that consider the entire context of a word within a sentence, allowing for nuanced understanding and more accurate predictions.

Data input and processing are foundational steps in developing AI and NLP models for mental health support. By utilizing diverse data sources, applying robust preprocessing techniques, and employing effective tokenization and text representation methods, these models can be trained to understand and respond to human language more accurately. This preparation ultimately enhances their ability to provide meaningful support to users seeking help with mental health challenges.

B.2.2. Machine Learning Techniques

Machine learning (ML) techniques are fundamental to developing and functioning AI and NLP models. They enable these systems to learn from data, make informed predictions, or generate appropriate responses. This section elaborates on the primary machine learning methodologies used in AI and NLP, particularly in the context of mental health support.

Supervised vs. Unsupervised Learning

Machine learning techniques can broadly be categorized into supervised and unsupervised learning:

- **Supervised Learning:** In supervised learning, models are trained on labeled datasets, where each input is paired with an output. This approach benefits sentiment analysis and symptom detection in mental health contexts. For instance, if a dataset contains text samples labeled as "anxiety" or "depression," supervised learning algorithms can learn to classify new, unlabeled texts based on these labels. Standard algorithms include logistic regression, support vector machines, and neural networks (Alpaydin, 2020).
- **Unsupervised Learning:** Unlike supervised learning, unsupervised learning involves training models on data without labeled outputs. This technique is helpful for clustering and pattern recognition. For example, in mental health

research, unsupervised k-means clustering can group patients based on similar language patterns or emotional expressions in their text inputs, helping researchers identify common themes or issues (Ghahramani, 2015).

Deep Learning Frameworks

Deep learning, a subset of machine learning, has gained prominence due to its ability to handle vast amounts of unstructured data, such as text. Deep learning models are particularly effective in NLP tasks and rely on neural network architectures. Key frameworks include:

- **Recurrent Neural Networks (RNNs):** RNNs are designed to handle sequential data, making them suitable for language processing tasks. They retain information from previous inputs, allowing them to understand the context. However, RNNs can struggle with long-range dependencies in the text (Hochreiter & Schmidhuber, 1997).
- **Long-Short-Term Memory (LSTM):** LSTM networks are an advanced form of RNNs that mitigate the issue of long-range dependencies. By incorporating memory cells and gating mechanisms, LSTMs can remember relevant information for extended periods, making them practical for complex NLP tasks like sentiment analysis and language translation (Hochreiter & Schmidhuber, 1997).
- **Transformers:** The introduction of transformer architectures has revolutionized NLP. Transformers utilize self-attention mechanisms to process input data in parallel rather than sequentially, allowing for a deeper understanding of context and relationships between words in a sentence. Models like BERT (Bidirectional Encoder Representations from Transformers) and GPT (Generative Pre-trained Transformer) have achieved state-of-the-art performance across various NLP tasks, including those related to mental health (Vaswani et al., 2017).

Training and Fine-Tuning Models

Training AI and NLP models involve adjusting their parameters based on the data input. The training process typically consists of the following steps:

1. **Data Splitting:** The dataset is divided into training, validation, and test sets. The training set is used to train the model, the validation set helps tune hyperparameters, and the test set evaluates the model's performance on unseen data.

2. **Loss Function Optimization:** During training, the model's predictions are compared to actual outcomes using a loss function, quantifying the error. The goal is to minimize this loss through optimization algorithms such as stochastic gradient descent (SGD) (Bottou, 2010).
3. **Fine-tuning:** Fine-tuning takes a pre-trained model and trains it further on a smaller, task-specific dataset. This technique enhances the model's understanding of domain-specific language nuances, making it particularly valuable in mental health applications (Howard & Ruder, 2018).

Machine learning techniques form the backbone of AI and NLP models, enabling them to learn from data and perform complex language tasks. These models can effectively address mental health challenges by employing supervised and unsupervised learning, leveraging deep learning frameworks, and utilizing training and fine-tuning methods. The advancements in ML improve the accuracy and relevance of chatbot interactions and enhance their ability to provide meaningful support to individuals seeking mental health assistance.

B.2.3. Natural Language Understanding

Natural Language Understanding (NLU) is a crucial component of AI and NLP systems, enabling them to comprehend and interpret human language in a meaningful and contextually relevant way. NLU involves several key processes that facilitate text analysis, allowing AI models to engage effectively with users, particularly in mental health contexts. This section explores the primary elements of NLU, including semantic analysis, sentiment analysis, and contextual understanding.

Semantic Analysis

Semantic analysis focuses on the meaning of words and phrases within their context. This process is essential for ensuring that AI models grasp the intended message behind user inputs. It involves:

- Word Sense Disambiguation: This technique helps resolve ambiguities in language by determining which meaning of a word is being used in a particular context. For example, the word "bank" could refer to a financial institution or the side of a river. Effective disambiguation is crucial in mental health applications, where misinterpretation could lead to inappropriate responses (Manning et al., 2008).
- Named Entity Recognition (NER): NER identifies and classifies key entities in text, such as names of people, organizations, locations, and specific mental

health terms. This identification allows the model to focus on relevant information, enhancing the understanding of a user's concerns and experiences.

Sentiment Analysis

Sentiment analysis, or opinion mining, involves assessing the emotional tone behind a series of words. It aims to identify and categorize sentiments expressed in text as positive, negative, or neutral. In mental health contexts, sentiment analysis is precious for:

- Identifying Emotional States: By analyzing user inputs, AI models can detect feelings of anxiety, sadness, or frustration. This understanding allows chatbots to respond empathetically, offering appropriate support and resources based on the user's emotional state (Pang & Lee, 2008).
- Monitoring Changes Over Time: Sentiment analysis can be used to track a user's emotional trajectory over time. This monitoring enables the detection of patterns or shifts in mental health, allowing for timely interventions when negative sentiments become pronounced.

Contextual Understanding

Contextual understanding refers to the model's ability to interpret language based on the surrounding context, essential for meaningful interactions. This involves several aspects:

- Co-reference Resolution: This process determines when different words refer to the same entity within a conversation. For instance, in the sentence "John is feeling anxious. He is worried about his job," the model must recognize that "He" refers to "John." Effective co-reference resolution ensures conversation continuity and avoids confusion (Lee et al., 2017).
- Discourse Analysis: This analyzes the structure and flow of conversation, enabling the model to understand the relationship between different parts of a dialogue. It allows chatbots to maintain context over multiple exchanges, vital in therapeutic settings where users may revisit earlier topics or express complex thoughts.
- Pragmatics: Pragmatics focuses on the implications and intentions behind language use, which can vary widely based on social context. For instance, understanding sarcasm or euphemisms can greatly influence how a model interprets user inputs, allowing it to respond more accurately and empathetically (Jurafsky & Martin, 2020).

Natural Language Understanding is a foundational aspect of AI and NLP systems that enables effective communication between machines and humans. These models can interpret user inputs more accurately by integrating semantic analysis, sentiment analysis, and contextual understanding, leading to more meaningful and supportive interactions in mental health applications. Developing robust NLU capabilities is essential for enhancing the efficacy of AI-driven chatbots and virtual assistants, ultimately improving the quality of mental health support.

B.2.4. Model Evaluation and Optimization

Model evaluation and optimization are critical processes in developing AI and NLP systems, ensuring that these models perform accurately and improve over time. In the context of mental health applications, the effectiveness and reliability of AI-driven tools are paramount, as they directly influence user outcomes and experiences. This section discusses key components of model evaluation, optimization techniques, and considerations for addressing bias and fairness.

Metrics for Performance Assessment

Various metrics are employed to evaluate the performance of AI and NLP models. These metrics help quantify how well a model performs its intended tasks, such as classification or response generation. Common metrics include:

- **Accuracy:** This is the ratio of correctly predicted instances to the total instances. While accuracy provides a general sense of model performance, it may not be sufficient in cases of imbalanced datasets, such as when one class (e.g., “depression”) is significantly more common than another (e.g., “anxiety”) (Sokolova & Lapalme, 2009).
- **Precision and Recall:** Precision measures the proportion of true positive results among all positive predictions, while recall (or sensitivity) measures the proportion of true positives among all actual positives. These metrics are particularly important in mental health contexts, where false positives and negatives can have significant implications. For instance, a chatbot misclassifying a user’s emotional distress could lead to inadequate support or unnecessary alarm.
- **F1 Score:** The F1 score is the harmonic mean of precision and recall, providing a metric that balances the two. This is especially useful when the class distribution is imbalanced, giving a more comprehensive picture of model performance (Van Rijsbergen, 1979).
- **Confusion Matrix:** A confusion matrix is a visual representation of a classification model's performance, illustrating true positives, true negatives, false

positives, and false negatives. This matrix helps diagnose areas where the model may be underperforming and informs further optimization efforts.

Iterative Learning and Adaptation

Model optimization is an iterative process that involves continuously improving the model based on feedback and new data. Key strategies include:

- **Hyperparameter Tuning:** Hyperparameters are configurations external to the model that influence its training process, such as learning rate, batch size, and the number of layers in a neural network. Tuning these parameters through grid or random search techniques can significantly enhance model performance (Bergstra & Bengio, 2012).
- **Cross-Validation:** Cross-validation involves partitioning the dataset into multiple subsets, training the model on some subsets while validating on others. This method helps ensure that the model generalizes well to unseen data and mitigates the risk of overfitting, where the model learns noise in the training data rather than the underlying patterns (Kohavi, 1995).
- **Continuous Learning:** Incorporating mechanisms for continuous learning allows models to adapt to new data over time. This is particularly important in mental health applications, where language, user behaviors, and societal norms can evolve. For instance, models can be periodically retrained on fresh data to improve their relevance and accuracy.

Addressing Bias and Fairness

A significant challenge in AI and NLP development is addressing bias and ensuring fairness in model predictions. Bias can manifest in various forms, such as racial, gender, or socioeconomic bias, potentially leading to unequal treatment or support in mental health services. To mitigate these issues, developers should:

- **Audit Datasets:** Regularly assess the training datasets for biases that may influence model outcomes. This involves examining the representation of different demographic groups and ensuring diverse and equitable training data (Buolamwini & Gebru, 2018).
- **Bias Detection Algorithms:** Implement algorithms that can detect and quantify bias in model predictions. Techniques such as adversarial debiasing can help create fairer models by penalizing biased outcomes during training (Zhang et al., 2018).
- **User Feedback Mechanisms:** Incorporate feedback loops where users can report issues or inaccuracies in model responses. This input is invaluable for

identifying potential biases and refining the model to enhance its fairness and effectiveness.

Model evaluation and optimization are essential for ensuring that AI and NLP systems are effective, reliable, and fair in their applications, especially in sensitive areas like mental health. Developers can enhance the capabilities of AI-driven chatbots and virtual assistants by employing robust performance metrics, iterative learning techniques, and proactive strategies to address bias. These efforts ultimately contribute to creating more trustworthy and supportive mental health resources for users.

B.2.5. Ethical Considerations in AI and NLP

The deployment of AI and NLP technologies in mental health support raises significant ethical considerations that must be addressed to ensure responsible use and the protection of users. These considerations encompass privacy, informed consent, accountability, and potential unintended consequences. This section thoroughly explores these ethical dimensions, highlighting their importance in developing and implementing AI-driven chatbots and virtual assistants.

Privacy and Data Security

One of the foremost ethical concerns in AI and NLP applications is the protection of user data. Mental health discussions often involve sensitive personal information that requires stringent privacy measures. Key considerations include:

- **Data Encryption:** Ensuring data is encrypted both in transit and at rest is crucial for protecting sensitive user information. This helps prevent unauthorized access and potential data breaches that could lead to harmful exposure to personal health information.
- **Anonymization:** Anonymizing data can further protect user identities. Organizations can analyze user interactions by removing personally identifiable information while safeguarding privacy. However, achieving effective anonymization can be complex, especially when multiple data points may still allow for re-identification.

Informed Consent

Informed consent is critical to ethical practice in any mental health intervention, including those involving AI and NLP. Users should be made fully aware of the following:

- **Data Usage:** Users must know how their data will be used, stored, and shared. Transparency in data handling practices fosters trust and ensures users can make informed choices about their engagement with AI-driven systems.
- **Limitations of AI:** Users should understand the limitations of AI technologies. Unlike human therapists, chatbots and virtual assistants may be unable to interpret complex emotions or provide nuanced support. Clear communication about these systems' capabilities and limitations helps manage user expectations and reduces the risk of overreliance on technology.

Accountability and Responsibility

Determining accountability in the context of AI and NLP applications is crucial, especially when considering potential harms or errors in judgment:

- **Human Oversight:** While AI systems can provide valuable support, they should not replace human oversight in mental health care. Implementing mechanisms for human intervention in critical situations, such as identifying suicidal ideation, is essential to ensure user safety.
- **Liability Issues:** Ethical questions arise concerning who is liable when an AI-driven system causes harm. Developers, organizations, and healthcare providers must establish clear guidelines regarding responsibility and accountability for AI-generated outcomes.

Potential for Bias and Discrimination

AI systems can inadvertently perpetuate or exacerbate existing biases present in training data. This risk is particularly concerning in mental health, where biases can lead to unequal treatment or support. Addressing this issue involves:

- **Bias Audits:** It is crucial to conduct regular audits of AI systems to identify and mitigate biases. This includes analyzing how demographic factors influence the model's performance and ensuring that diverse populations are represented in training datasets.
- **Inclusive Design:** Engaging diverse stakeholders in the design and development process can help identify potential biases early and create more equitable systems. Including individuals with varying backgrounds and experiences ensures that the technology is better suited to meet the needs of all users.

Ethical considerations are paramount in developing and deploying AI and NLP technologies for mental health support. Developers and organizations can create more responsible and effective AI-driven tools by prioritizing user privacy, ensuring informed consent, establishing accountability, and addressing biases. These ethical frameworks protect users and enhance the credibility and trustworthiness of AI applications in mental health care.

C. CHATBOTS AND VIRTUAL ASSISTANTS

C.1. History of Chatbots

Chatbots are computer programs that simulate human conversation through text or voice interactions. In mental health, these digital assistants can provide various forms of support, ranging from basic informational responses to complex therapeutic interactions. There are generally two types of chatbots used in mental health:

Rule-Based Chatbots: These operate on predefined scripts and algorithms. They respond to user inputs based on specific keywords or phrases, making them suitable for straightforward inquiries and basic mental health support, such as providing information about symptoms or resources.

AI-Powered Chatbots: These utilize advanced AI and NLP technologies to understand user inputs more contextually and dynamically. They can engage in more natural conversations, assess emotional states, and adapt their responses based on the user's language and tone. Examples include Woebot and Wysa, designed to provide cognitive-behavioral therapy (CBT) techniques and emotional support.

Advantages of Using Chatbots for Mental Health Support

Chatbots offer numerous advantages in the realm of mental health support. One of the most significant benefits is their accessibility. Users can interact with chatbots anytime, providing immediate support when traditional mental health services are unavailable. This 24/7 availability helps bridge the gap for individuals who may experience anxiety about seeking in-person therapy or those in remote areas with limited access to mental health professionals.

Another critical advantage is the reduction of stigma associated with mental health treatment. Many individuals feel hesitant to discuss their struggles openly, but the anonymity provided by chatbots can encourage users to seek help and engage in conversations about their mental health without fear of judgment. Additionally, chatbots can offer evidence-based coping strategies and psychoeducation, empowering users with tools to manage their mental health effectively.

Moreover, chatbots can facilitate early intervention by identifying at-risk users based on their interactions. By analyzing language patterns and emotional cues, these digital assistants can recommend appropriate resources or alert users to seek further assistance from a qualified professional. This proactive approach can significantly enhance overall mental health outcomes.

Case Studies of Successful Implementations

1. **Woebot Health:** Woebot is an AI-powered chatbot designed to deliver evidence-based mental health support using principles from cognitive-behavioral therapy. A study published in *The Lancet Digital Health* showed that users of Woebot reported significant reductions in symptoms of anxiety and depression after just two weeks of interaction. The chatbot effectively engages users in conversations that promote emotional regulation and coping strategies, demonstrating its potential as a valuable tool in mental health care (Fitzgerald et al., 2021). Woebot is a rule-based chatbot. The conversations are written from Cognitive Behavioral Therapy (CBT), Interpersonal Psychotherapy (IPT), and Dialectical Behavioral Therapy (DBT) conversations.
2. **Wysa:** Another prominent example is Wysa, a mental health chatbot that utilizes AI to provide support and therapeutic exercises. Research has indicated that Wysa users experienced decreased levels of anxiety and improved emotional well-being. A randomized controlled trial found that Wysa significantly improved users' psychological resilience and coping mechanisms, highlighting the effectiveness of chatbot interventions in enhancing mental health support (Gonzalez et al., 2022).
3. **Miriam:** Developed as part of a research initiative at the University of Michigan, the Miriam chatbot was designed to help users with depression by offering personalized emotional support. The chatbot employed machine learning algorithms to adapt responses based on user interactions. A study found that users who interacted with Miriam reported higher engagement and satisfaction levels than traditional mental health resources, showcasing the chatbot's ability to foster meaningful connections and support for individuals seeking help (Althoff et al., 2016).

C.2. Why We Need AI and NLP-Driven Chatbots and Virtual Assistants

AI and NLP-driven chatbots and virtual assistants are becoming increasingly vital in mental health and well-being. Their capacity to provide immediate and accessible assistance addresses many barriers individuals face when seeking support. Here are several key reasons why these technologies are essential:

Immediate and Accessible Assistance

- **Real-Time Interaction:** Chatbots facilitate instant communication, allowing users to receive support for various mental health concerns, such as anxiety, depression, and stress management.
- **Natural Language Understanding:** These technologies can accurately interpret user inputs, discerning emotions and reactions. For example, if a user expresses sadness, the chatbot can identify linguistic cues and respond appropriately.

24/7 Availability

- **Elimination of Temporal Barriers:** Traditional mental health services often have limited hours, making it challenging for individuals to seek help when they need it most. AI-driven chatbots offer round-the-clock assistance, allowing users to access support anytime.
- **Reducing Stigma:** Many individuals may feel uncomfortable seeking help in person due to stigma or fear of judgment. Virtual assistants provide a discreet, non-judgmental platform that empowers users to engage with mental health resources on their terms.

Early Intervention

- **Proactive Monitoring:** AI systems analyze language and tone to identify indicators of distress or declining mental health. For example, if a chatbot detects a pattern of negative sentiment, it can prompt a referral to a mental health professional or suggest crisis management resources.
- **Preventing Escalation:** This proactive approach ensures individuals receive the support they need before reaching a crisis point, potentially mitigating more severe mental health issues.

Research and Development Insights

- **Efficacy and User Engagement:** Through empirical studies, researchers focus on how these technologies improve mental health outcomes. Findings indicate that users often feel more comfortable interacting with chatbots than in traditional therapy settings due to anonymity and convenience

- **Guiding Development:** Insights gained from user engagement help refine algorithms and interaction designs, making digital therapies more effective and responsive to user needs.

Increased Accessibility

- **Bridging Geographic Gaps:** Individuals in rural or underserved communities may lack access to mental health professionals. Chatbots can provide immediate support and resources, ensuring that geographical constraints do not limit care.
- **Promoting Equity:** Increased accessibility through AI-driven solutions helps ensure a broader range of individuals can benefit from mental health support systems, promoting equity in care.

Integrating AI and NLP-driven chatbots and virtual assistants into mental health care represents a significant advancement in access to support. By offering immediate, personalized, and accessible assistance, these technologies address critical barriers while fostering early intervention. As research continues to explore their efficacy, the insights gained will further enhance the development of these tools, ultimately contributing to improved mental health outcomes for diverse individuals. The potential of AI and NLP in this field is vast, promising a pivotal role in the future of mental health support systems.

C.3. Main Components in AI and NLP-Driven Chatbots and Virtual Assistants

AI and NLP-driven chatbots and virtual assistants have several essential components that work collaboratively to provide effective mental health care. Understanding these components is crucial for optimizing their design and functionality and improving user outcomes and satisfaction.

C.3.1. User Interface Design

The user interface (UI) is the first point of interaction between users and chatbots or virtual assistants. A well-designed UI is critical for ensuring that users feel comfortable and engaged. Key aspects of user interface design include:

- **Simplicity and Intuitiveness:** The interface should be easy to navigate, minimizing cognitive load. Clear prompts and an intuitive layout help users understand how to interact with the chatbot effectively.

- **Accessibility Features:** Incorporating features that cater to diverse user needs, such as voice input, text-to-speech, and adjustable text sizes, ensure the chatbot is accessible to everyone, including those with disabilities.
- **Emotional Design:** Visual elements like color schemes, fonts, and animations can evoke emotions and create a welcoming atmosphere. A friendly and empathetic design can enhance user engagement, making individuals more likely to seek support.
- **Feedback Mechanisms:** Providing users immediate feedback, such as confirming their inputs or acknowledging emotions, helps build rapport and trust between the user and the chatbot.

C.3.2. Backend Architecture

The backend architecture is the underlying framework that supports the chatbot's functionality. It encompasses several critical components:

- **Natural Language Processing Engine:** This is the core of the chatbot, enabling it to comprehend, interpret, and generate human language. The engine includes methodologies for tokenization (Breaking down user inputs into manageable units), sentiment analysis (Assessing the emotional tone of the user's messages), and Intent Recognition (Identifying the user's goals and needs based on their input).
- **Knowledge Base:** A comprehensive knowledge base is a repository of mental health resources, coping strategies, and referral information. This ensures that the chatbot can provide accurate and relevant support to users.
- **Dialogue Management System:** This system regulates the flow of conversation, ensuring that interactions remain coherent and contextually relevant. It uses algorithms to track the context over multiple exchanges, allowing for more meaningful and tailored interactions.
- **Integration Capabilities:** The backend architecture should facilitate integration with other systems, such as healthcare databases and third-party applications, to provide a more holistic support experience.

C.3.3. Machine Learning Models

Machine learning models are fundamental to the chatbot's ability to learn and adapt over time. These models enhance the chatbot's performance through various techniques:

- **Training on Large Datasets:** Machine learning models are trained on extensive datasets, including conversational data and mental health-related texts. This training helps the models recognize patterns, understand context, and improve accuracy.
- **Continuous Learning:** Implementing feedback loops allows the chatbot to learn from user interactions continuously. As users provide feedback, the system can refine its responses and enhance its understanding of user needs.
- **Personalization Algorithms:** Machine learning enables the chatbot to personalize interactions based on user history and preferences. For instance, the chatbot can prioritize resources and related strategies if a user frequently discusses anxiety.
- **Evaluation Metrics:** Regular assessment of machine learning models using metrics such as precision, recall, and user satisfaction helps ensure ongoing improvement and efficacy in meeting mental health needs.

The main components of AI and NLP-driven chatbots and virtual assistants—user interface design, backend architecture, and machine learning models—work together to create effective mental health support systems. By understanding and optimizing these elements, developers, and researchers can enhance the performance and user experience of these technologies, ultimately leading to better mental health outcomes and increased user satisfaction.

C.4. MAIN CHALLENGES IN AI-DRIVEN CHATBOTS AND VIRTUAL ASSISTANTS

While AI-driven chatbots and virtual assistants offer significant potential for enhancing mental health support, they also face several challenges that must be addressed to ensure their effectiveness and reliability. Understanding these challenges is crucial for developers, researchers, and policymakers as they work to refine these technologies and implement them ethically and responsibly.

C.4.1. Ethical Considerations

The deployment of AI-driven chatbots in mental health care raises various ethical questions that must be carefully considered:

- **Informed Consent:** Users should be fully informed about how their data will be used, including the limitations of the chatbot's capabilities. It is essential that users understand the nature of the interactions and the level of expertise behind the responses.

- **Accountability:** Determining who is responsible when a chatbot provides harmful or misleading advice can be challenging. Clear guidelines must be established regarding accountability for the information disseminated by these systems.
- **Bias and Fairness:** AI models can perpetuate biases in the training data, leading to unfair or discriminatory responses. Continuous monitoring and improvement are necessary to mitigate these risks and ensure equitable user support.
- **Emotional Manipulation:** Chatbots should be designed to avoid exploiting vulnerable users emotionally. Ethical guidelines should dictate how chatbots engage with users to ensure they do not inadvertently manipulate feelings or exploit crises for data collection.

C.4.2. Data Privacy and Security

Data privacy and security are paramount concerns in the implementation of AI-driven chatbots, particularly in the context of sensitive mental health information:

- **Sensitive Data Handling:** Chatbots often process personal and sensitive information, such as mental health history and emotional states. Ensuring this data is securely stored and transmitted is crucial to protect users from breaches.
- **Compliance with Regulations:** Data protection regulations, such as GDPR (General Data Protection Regulation) and HIPAA (Health Insurance Portability and Accountability Act), are essential for maintaining user trust and legal compliance.
- **Anonymity and Confidentiality:** Developers must implement robust measures to ensure that user interactions remain anonymous and confidential. This includes data encryption and anonymization techniques to prevent unauthorized access.
- **User Trust:** Building and maintaining user trust is vital for the success of AI-driven chatbots. Transparency about data usage, security measures, and user rights can help alleviate privacy concerns.

C.4.3. Limitations in Understanding Context

While AI and NLP technologies have advanced significantly, there are inherent limitations in their ability to understand context, which can affect their effectiveness in mental health support:

- **Contextual Nuances:** Human communication is often laden with contextual nuances, including sarcasm, cultural references, and emotional subtleties. AI models may struggle to interpret these aspects accurately, leading to misunderstandings.
- **Complex User Needs:** Mental health issues can be multifaceted, requiring nuanced understanding and empathy. AI-driven chatbots may not fully grasp the complexity of individual experiences, which can result in inadequate or inappropriate responses.
- **Limited Memory:** Many chatbots are limited in how much context they can retain from previous interactions. This limitation can hinder their ability to provide personalized support over time, as they may fail to recognize returning users or the history of their conversations.
- **Adapting to User Feedback:** While continuous learning is a goal for many AI systems, effectively integrating user feedback in real time remains challenging. Without the ability to adapt dynamically, chatbots may continue to provide irrelevant or unhelpful responses.

A principal challenge in creating AI-driven chatbots and virtual assistants for mental health is ensuring the precision and appropriateness of their responses. Given the sensitive nature of mental health discussions, these systems must comprehend user inputs and accurately provide reliable information and support. Misinterpretations or inaccuracies can lead to inappropriate replies that might exacerbate a user's distress or offer misleading advice. For instance, a chatbot that misinterprets a user's expression of anxiety may provide inadequate coping strategies, potentially worsening the individual's emotional state. Therefore, ongoing updates to natural language processing (NLP) models and comprehensive training on diverse datasets are essential for enhancing accuracy. However, achieving this level of precision requires substantial resources and sustained research efforts to navigate the complexities of human emotion and language effectively.

Another significant obstacle is addressing ethical considerations and safeguarding user privacy. Mental health chatbots handle sensitive data that can include personal experiences, mental health history, and emotional states, raising important concerns about data security and confidentiality. Developers must implement robust measures to ensure the data collected is securely stored and utilized responsibly. Adhering to regulatory frameworks like the Health Insurance Portability and Accountability Act (HIPAA) and the General Data Protection Regulation (GDPR) is critical to maintaining user trust and legal compliance. Failure to protect sensitive information could lead to severe consequences, including data breaches and loss of user confidence in these digital tools.

Moreover, the risk of excessive dependence on automated systems poses a significant challenge. While AI-driven chatbots can offer immediate support, there is a concern that users may rely too heavily on these technologies, potentially discouraging them from seeking professional help when needed. This reliance could result in a false sense of security, leading individuals to believe they can manage their mental health solely through digital interactions. Researchers must explore frameworks that balance the benefits of AI-driven support with ethical considerations, ensuring that these tools serve as supplementary resources rather than replacements for traditional mental health care.

Lastly, it is vital to recognize the limitations of AI technologies in understanding the nuances of human emotions and the complexities of mental health issues. While advancements in NLP have significantly improved the ability of chatbots to engage in conversations, they may still struggle to grasp context, tone, and emotional subtleties. For instance, a user may convey distress through subtle cues that an AI may overlook, leading to a generic response that fails to address the individual's specific needs. Therefore, continuous improvement in training methodologies and user feedback mechanisms is necessary to enhance the empathetic capabilities of AI-driven chatbots, ensuring they provide meaningful and contextually relevant support to users.

C.5. FUTURE DIRECTIONS FOR CHATBOTS IN MENTAL HEALTH SUPPORT

As technology continues to evolve, the potential for AI-driven chatbots and virtual assistants in mental health support is poised to expand dramatically. Several key future directions can be pursued to harness their capabilities fully, each aimed at enhancing user experience, improving effectiveness, and ensuring ethical practice.

C.5.1. Enhanced Personalization

- **Adaptive Learning:** Future chatbots could utilize advanced machine learning techniques to analyze user interactions and adapt their responses based on individual preferences and behavioral patterns. This adaptive learning approach would enable the chatbot to provide tailored support, making interactions feel more personal and relevant to each user.

- **User Profiles:** Chatbots can significantly enhance personalization by developing comprehensive user profiles that capture individual histories, preferences, and emotional states. For example, if a user frequently discusses anxiety, the chatbot could proactively offer relaxation techniques or check in on the user's emotional state during subsequent interactions.
- **Customization Options:** Allowing users to customize their chatbot interactions—such as choosing the tone of responses (formal, casual, empathetic) or selecting specific focus areas (stress management, relationship advice)—can improve user satisfaction and engagement.

C.5.2. Improved Emotional Intelligence

- **Sentiment Analysis:** Incorporating more sophisticated sentiment analysis tools will enable chatbots to interpret a broader range of emotional cues from user inputs. This capability will allow chatbots to respond with greater empathy and appropriateness, helping users feel understood and supported during challenging times.
- **Contextual Awareness:** Enhancing chatbots' ability to maintain context over longer conversations is essential for creating coherent interactions. By employing advanced natural language understanding techniques, future chatbots can recognize user intents and emotional shifts, making interactions smoother and more engaging.
- **Emotion Recognition:** Integrating technologies that analyze vocal tone or facial expressions during video interactions could significantly enhance a chatbot's ability to assess emotional states, providing a more nuanced understanding of user needs.

C.5.3. Integration with Human Support Systems

- **Hybrid Models:** Developing hybrid support systems that combine AI-driven chatbots with human therapists can optimize the mental health care experience. Chatbots can handle routine inquiries and provide immediate support, while human professionals manage more complex cases, ensuring that users receive the appropriate level of care.
- **Referral Systems:** Implementing robust referral mechanisms within chatbots can facilitate seamless transitions to professional help when necessary. For example, if a chatbot detects signs of severe depression or suicidal

thoughts, it could automatically prompt a referral to a licensed mental health professional.

- **Collaborative Tools:** Future chatbots could serve as collaborative tools for therapists, allowing them to monitor client progress through chatbot interactions and customize treatment plans based on insights gathered from these exchanges.

C.5.4. Ethical Frameworks and Guidelines

- **Standardization of Practices:** Establishing clear ethical guidelines and industry standards for chatbot design and implementation is critical to address accountability, privacy, and user safety. These standards should cover data usage, response accuracy, and the boundaries of what chatbots can offer in mental health care.
- **Stakeholder Involvement:** Engaging a diverse range of stakeholders—including mental health professionals, ethicists, users, and technologists—in the development process can ensure that chatbots are designed with ethical considerations at the forefront. User feedback should be solicited regularly to adapt and refine chatbot functionalities.
- **Transparency and Disclosure:** Future chatbots should disclose their capabilities and limitations. Users must understand that while chatbots can offer support, they do not replace professional mental health care.

C.5.5. Accessibility and Inclusivity

- **Multilingual Capabilities:** Expanding chatbot functionalities to support multiple languages and dialects can significantly enhance accessibility, ensuring that a broader audience can benefit from these mental health tools. This includes culturally relevant content that resonates with users from diverse backgrounds.
- **Cultural Sensitivity:** Incorporating cultural competence into chatbot design is essential. Future chatbots should be equipped to understand and respect cultural differences in communication styles, beliefs, and mental health perceptions. Training models on diverse datasets can help achieve this goal.
- **User-Friendly Interfaces:** Designing intuitive and user-friendly interfaces is crucial for maximizing engagement. Ensuring that chatbots are easy to navigate, with clear instructions and responsive design, can help users feel more comfortable seeking support.

C.5.6. Continuous Research and Evaluation

- **Longitudinal Studies:** Conducting long-term studies to assess the efficacy of chatbots in improving mental health outcomes will provide valuable insights into their impact on users over time. Such research can help identify best practices and inform future iterations of chatbot technology.
- **User Feedback Mechanisms:** Implementing robust feedback systems will allow users to actively share their experiences and suggestions. This feedback loop can drive iterative improvements, ensuring that chatbots remain responsive to user needs and concerns.
- **Performance Metrics:** Developing comprehensive performance metrics will enable researchers to evaluate chatbot effectiveness systematically. Metrics could include user satisfaction scores, engagement rates, and the impact on users' mental health symptoms, providing a holistic view of chatbot performance.

The future of chatbots in mental health support is rich with potential, driven by advancements in personalization, emotional intelligence, and ethical practices. By focusing on these areas and committing to ongoing research, developers and researchers can create effective, user-centered tools that enhance mental health care. With a balanced approach that integrates technology with human support and addresses ethical concerns, AI-driven chatbots can play a pivotal role in promoting mental well-being for diverse populations.

CONCLUSION

Integrating AI and NLP-driven chatbots and virtual assistants into mental health support represents a significant advancement in making mental health resources more accessible and personalized. These digital tools provide real-time assistance for individuals dealing with anxiety, depression, and stress, thereby addressing the growing demand for immediate support. Future developments should focus on enhancing personalization through adaptive learning and user profiling and improving emotional intelligence and contextual awareness to foster deeper connections with users.

However, ethical considerations such as data privacy and security must be prioritized to build user trust. Integrating these chatbots with human support systems can optimize care while ensuring users receive appropriate assistance. By promoting accessibility and inclusivity and committing to ongoing research and evaluation, stakeholders can develop innovative solutions that bridge gaps in traditional mental health services, ultimately contributing to improved mental well-being for diverse populations.

REFERENCES

Ghahramani, Z. (2015). Probabilistic Machine Learning and Artificial Intelligence. *Nature*, 521(7553), 452–459. DOI: 10.1038/nature14541 PMID: 26017444

Howard, J., & Ruder, S. (2018)." Universal Language Model Fine-tuning for Text Classification. "*Proceedings of the 56th Annual Meeting of the Association for Computational Linguistics (ACL)*, 328-339.

Hochreiter, S., & Schmidhuber, J. (1997). Long Short-Term Memory. *Neural Computation*, 9(8), 1735–1780. DOI: 10.1162/neco.1997.9.8.1735 PMID: 9377276

Manning, C. D., Raghavan, P., & Schütze, H. (2008). *Introduction to Information Retrieval*. MIT Press.

Vaswani, A., Shankar, S., Parmar, N., Uszkoreit, J., Jones, L., Gomez, A.N., Kaiser, Ł., Kyllonen, J., & Polosukhin, I. (2017). Attention is All You Need. *Advances in Neural Information Processing Systems*, •••, 30.

Jurafsky, D., & Martin, J. H. (2020). *Speech and Language Processing* (3rd ed.). Pearson.

Kessler, R. C., Berglund, P., Demler, O., Jin, R., Merikangas, K. R., & Walters, E. E. (2005). Lifetime Prevalence and Age-of-Onset Distributions of DSM-IV Disorders in the National Comorbidity Survey Replication. *Archives of General Psychiatry*, 62(6), 593–602. DOI: 10.1001/archpsyc.62.6.593 PMID: 15939837

Bottou, L. (2010). "Large-Scale Machine Learning with Stochastic Gradient Descent. "*Proceedings of the 19th International Conference on Machine Learning (ICML-10)*, 3-10.

Alpaydin, E. (2020). *Introduction to Machine Learning*. MIT Press.

Pang, B., & Lee, L. (2008). Opinion Mining and Sentiment Analysis. *Foundations and Trends in Information Retrieval*, 2(1–2), 1–135. DOI: 10.1561/1500000011

Kohavi, R. (1995). A Study of Cross-Validation and Bootstrap for Accuracy Estimation and Model Selection. *Proceedings of the 14th International Joint Conference on Artificial Intelligence (IJCAI)*, 1137-1145.

Bergstra, J., & Bengio, Y. (2012). Random Search for Hyper-Parameter Optimization. *Journal of Machine Learning Research*, 13, 281–305.

Buolamwini, J., & Gebru, T. (2018). Gender Shades: Intersectional Accuracy Disparities in Commercial Gender Classification. *Proceedings of the 2018 Conference on Fairness, Accountability, and Transparency*, 77-91.

Sokolova, M., & Lapalme, G. (2009). A Systematic Analysis of Performance Measures for Classification Tasks. *Information Processing & Management*, 45(4), 427–437. DOI: 10.1016/j.ipm.2009.03.002

Van Rijsbergen, C. J. (1979). *Information Retrieval* (2nd ed.). Butterworths.

- Zhang, B., Lemoine, B., Mitchell, M., et al. (2018). Mitigating Unwanted Biases with Adversarial Learning.

Weizenbaum, J. (1966). ELIZA—A Computer Program for studying Natural Language Communication between Man and Machine. *Communications of the ACM*, 9(1), 36–45. DOI: 10.1145/365153.365168

Chapter 11
NeuroSymphony: AI-Tailored Music for Cognitive and Emotional States

Renuka Devi D.
https://orcid.org/0000-0002-6525-1172
Stella Maris College, India

Swetha Margaret T. A.
https://orcid.org/0000-0002-4693-8219
Stella Maris College, India

ABSTRACT

Music significantly influences our emotions and overall well-being in daily life. This proposed system seeks to revolutionize the music listening experience by harnessing the power of cognitive psychology, AI, and machine learning through advanced facial emotion detection. By integrating a facial recognition API, the system captures and analyzes the user's facial expressions in real time, accurately mapping these emotions to corresponding music genres, playlists, or individual tracks. The implementation follows a logical framework that connects emotion detection directly with music selection, featuring a state-of-the-art music player specifically designed to intuitively interpret human emotions using a web camera interface. The ultimate objective of this system is to enhance the user's mood and emotional well-being by curating music that aligns perfectly with the emotional cues derived from their facial expressions. This approach merges cognitive psychology with cutting-edge AI and machine learning technologies, offering an innovative, emotionally intelligent music experience.

DOI: 10.4018/979-8-3693-9341-3.ch011

1. INTRODUCTION

Music has a powerful impact on our emotions, as it can lift, relax, or energize us depending on the genre. However, with countless songs available, selecting the right one can be challenging. While certain music genres influence our social identity, individual song preferences can deeply express and affect emotions. Some argue that matching recommended songs to an individual's state of mind can help them relax. Nevertheless, it can be tough to keep our playlists updated as they continue to grow. Research suggests that facial expressions, as primary channels of emotions, can guide us in customizing our music based on our current moods (Garg et al., 2022).

The proposed system strives to solve those issues by changing how we listen to music with the use of cognitive psychology, cutting-edge Artificial Intelligence and Machine Learning in the context of facial emotion recognition (Ngo et al., 2024). Using a state-of-the-art facial recognition API, it detects emotions such as happiness, sadness, anger or surprise from your face in real time. The system then associates the emotional cues it detects with specific music genres, playlists or even individual songs which makes the user enjoy song that he/she can relate with on an emotional level. Through integrating AI and machine learning with cognitive psychology, this system learns over time based on each person's unique emotional pattern (Vistorte et al., 2024). Thus as it continually fine-tunes its music choices using facial expressions from users' faces which helps in understanding their feelings more clearly; making sure that every track played not only satisfies people's momentary emotions but also boosts general mood and well-being.

In addition, a system that can smoothly interconnect with popular music streaming platforms such as Spotify is what makes it still relevant in society today. Emotion-based music recommendation systems have grown into invaluable tools, especially due to music's diverse meanings and implications for mental health. Such tools are not limited to just consumer usage but may also act as powerful triggers in advertising performances through emotion-tuned recommendations. In institutions of learning, it can improve the learning experience by recommending music that meets certain guidelines for focus, relaxation or creativity. In medical facilities on the other hand, patients may use these systems to manage their pain levels or reduce stress as well as improving their general wellbeing thereby demonstrating the wide flowering of possibilities and uses' this technology possesses.

Correctly recognizing and categorizing emotions from music is crucial for the effectiveness of this emotion-based music recommendation system (Bakariya et al., 2024). To achieve this, advanced machine learning algorithms have to be applied, natural language processing techniques used, and sound data analysis capabilities are required. Moreover, integration with technologies like computer vision supplements its performance in responding to users' cues on their feelings thereby making it an advanced device where cognitive psychology meets artificial intelligence and music. This system combines cognition psychology with AI & machine learning to provide an innovative way of listening to music that closely resonates with someone's emotions. By moving beyond conventional methods of selecting songs it provides a smarter experience where the machine learns emotions attached to this kind of genre making it versatile enough to keep up with permanent change within the human psyche and ultimately improve emotional health through individualized selection.

2. BACKGROUND STUDY

Music is an art form that deeply resonates with human emotions, offering a unique ability to uplift, soothe, and transform our moods. While traditional music recommendation systems rely on learning a user's preferences over time, they often fall short of capturing the immediate emotional needs of the listener. V. P. Sharma et al. proposed an innovative approach to address this gap by utilizing a neural network-based song recommendation system that leverages facial expression analysis to detect a user's mood. This method not only enhances the accuracy of music recommendations but also makes it significantly easier for users to find and create playlists that resonate with their current emotional state, offering a more immediate and emotionally responsive listening experience (Sharma et.al, 2021).

There is a greater depth of potential in emotion recognition compared to simply choosing songs for individuals. Understanding someone's emotions can allow for more effective music recommendations and personalized communication, such as writing letters tailored to someone's current disposition. In educational settings, teachers could use emotion recognition to adjust course materials and presentations to better suit the learning atmosphere, potentially increasing student interest and improving knowledge acquisition without causing fatigue. This technology could also have significant impact in healthcare by helping to detect depression at an early stage and providing subjective support for mental health issues, even in environments such as prisons, where it could help track and understand unpredictable behaviours.

The dynamic music recommendation prototype was created to respond to human emotions within the context of the proposed system (Dash et al., 2024) . The system is designed to train songs for every detected emotion based on personal listening behaviours. By combining feature extraction with advanced machine learning techniques, it can identify emotions using real-time facial expressions and understand someone's mood using an input image. The system then plays a song aligned with that mood, ensuring personalized music that matches the user's current situation, ultimately improving engagement and experience.

Another significant advancement in this domain is the work of De Prisco et al., proposed a music recommendation system based on reinforcement learning (RL). This system is designed not only to match music to a user's current emotional state but also to evoke specific emotions through carefully selected music tracks. The RL method operates on the principle that a user's emotional state can be influenced by recently played music, and thus, the system learns to select tracks that will guide the user toward a desired emotional state. Unlike traditional systems that capture and respond to existing emotions, this approach proactively shapes the listener's mood, offering a more interactive and immersive music experience (De Prisco et al., 2022).

There is still a significant difference between personalized music recommendations and those based on emotions, despite progress being made. While recommendation systems have become more common and successful in helping individuals select songs for different events, they often overlook the profound impact music can have on us. Music is more than just a source of enjoyment; it plays a vital role in alleviating anxiety, inducing desired moods, reducing tension, and even aiding in the healing of diseases. For example, psychologists acknowledge that using music in hospitals helps people to stay mentally and physically healthy, further demonstrating the wide-ranging impact of music on human life.

Rumiantcev et al., introduced a personalized music recommendation system that highlights the importance of matching music with the listener's emotional and activity status. This system aims to provide a more customized and effective music experience by considering the user's emotions and current activity. Integrating emotion recognition and activity monitoring into music recommendation systems represents a significant advancement, offering users a more personalized, responsive, and emotionally engaging way to enjoy music (Rumiantcev et al., 2020).

The traditional music recommendation systems have made great strides in personalization, but there is still much to be done in bridging the gap between personalization and emotion-based recommendations. By incorporating advanced AI techniques such as neural networks, reinforcement learning, and real-time emotion detection, the future of music recommendation systems promises to be more attuned to the emotional needs of users. This will ultimately provide a more fulfilling and therapeutic music experience (Hassouneh et al., 2020)

In recent years, there have been significant advancements in the intersection of artificial intelligence (AI), machine learning, and emotion recognition. These developments have driven the evolution of music recommendation systems towards more emotionally intelligent and responsive experiences. The field has made notable progress in key areas such as the development of more accurate emotion detection algorithms, the integration of multimodal data, and the application of deep learning models. These advancements have been well-documented in recent studies and reviews, which have highlighted both the potential and challenges of these emerging technologies.

In recent years, there have been significant advancements in emotion detection algorithms. A review conducted by Liu et al. emphasized the improved accuracy and reliability of these algorithms, especially those utilizing deep learning techniques. These algorithms are now able to detect a wide range of emotional states with greater precision, thanks to enhanced training datasets and the use of convolutional neural networks (CNNs) and recurrent neural networks (RNNs). The review highlighted the success of these models in analyzing facial expressions, voice tone, and even physiological signals such as heart rate variability, providing a more comprehensive understanding of the user's emotional state (Liu et al., 2023).

The emerging trend in the field of music recommendations is the integration of multimodal data to enhance the quality and relevance of suggestions based on emotions. Recent studies have investigated the combination of facial recognition with speech analysis, text sentiment analysis, and physiological measurements to gain a comprehensive understanding of a user's emotional state. According to a study by Zhang et al., multimodal systems are capable of capturing subtle changes in emotions more effectively, resulting in music recommendations that are better suited for specific situations. This advancement marks a significant step towards creating systems that not only react to user needs but also anticipate them, effectively assisting users in managing their moods (Zhang et al., 2024).

The ethical implications of systems based on recommendations generated from emotions are becoming increasingly concerning as these technologies progress. Kim et al. examined potential dangers associated with the use of emotion-sensitive data, particularly in terms of user privacy and emotional manipulation. The authors proposed a framework for ethically developing such systems, emphasizing the importance of transparency, user consent, and robust data protection protocols. This dedication to moral considerations reflects a broader trend in this field, wherein innovators and researchers are striving to make advancements while remaining socially responsible (Kim et al., 2024).

The latest advancements have led to new real-life uses for music recommendation systems based on emotions. For example, combining these systems with wearable technology like smartwatches or fitness trackers enables the detection of emotions in real time using physiological signals such as heart rate and skin conductance. This connection was investigated in a study by Li et al., showing the promise of emotion-based recommendations in health and wellness scenarios, including stress reduction and mood improvement (Li et al., 2023). The use of reinforcement learning in music recommendation systems is becoming increasingly popular, Recent studies indicate that reinforcement learning models can improve the emotional impact of recommendations over time by learning from users' actions. This approach provides a personalized service and influences how users might feel when listening to music, making the experience more interactive and engaging.

In the current moment, there are rapid changes in emotional digital music recommendation systems due to advancements in artificial intelligence, machine learning, and multimodal data integration. Recently, there have been significant improvements in emotion detection accuracy, increased use of deep learning models, and growing concerns about internet user privacy and data security. This transition is paving the way for a better understanding of emotional content in music, with countless potential applications in the health, wellness, education, and entertainment industries. Progress in this area of research is likely to enhance emotional well-being and create new ways for computers and humans to connect on unprecedented levels.

3. METHODOLOGY

The realm of computer vision encompasses various applications, one of which is the detection of faces. This involves creating and teaching algorithms to effectively recognize faces or objects within a given system for object detection. The detection can even be performed in real-time, where video frames or still images are carefully analysed. To accurately detect faces, specialized classifiers are utilized. These algorithms are designed to analyse images and determine if they contain a face. One widely used classifier is Haar Cascades, which is trained with a large dataset in order to boost its accuracy. OpenCV, a popular software for image processing, employs a well-trained Haar classifier as part of its cascade of classifiers, specifically designed to detect various facial features. Through this rigorous training, the classifier is able to effectively distinguish between facial components and non-facial elements, resulting in precise face detection.

The purpose of face detection is to accurately recognize faces within an image, a task that is faced with various obstacles, including noise from different sources and complexities due to diverse factors. To overcome these challenges, a machine learning method is used, which involves a cascade function trained using what is known as "training data." This process entails dividing the pixels in the image into squares and applying a wavelet technique, resulting in a precise identification rate. By using input files, the cascade function is trained and equipped with various learning techniques, enabling precise face recognition despite other elements present in the image.

The emotion based music recommendation system is outlined in this section, which is given in Figure 1.

Figure 1. Emotion based music recommendation system

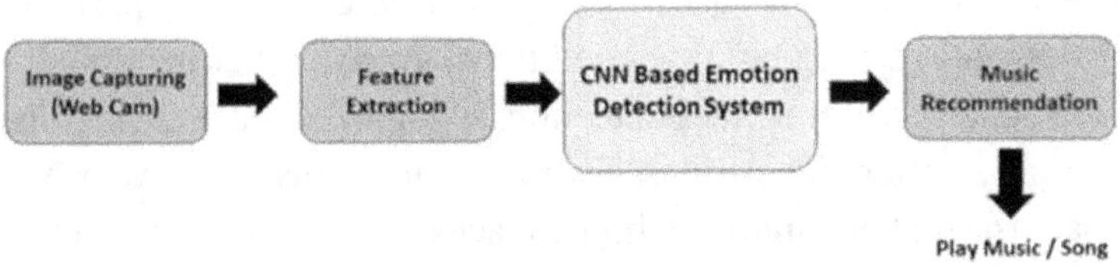

3.1 Dataset Description

The dataset used for proposed work, FER2013 [8] includes 24,176 training images and 6,043 testing images, features grayscale images with a resolution of 48x48 pixels. Each image in the FER-2013 database represents one of five emotions: happiness, sadness, anger, surprise, and neutrality. To maintain consistency across the dataset, all facial images were automatically positioned, centred, and scaled to occupy a standardized amount of space. The FER-2013 dataset is a unique compilation of both posed and unposed images, capturing a diverse range of facial expressions. These images were carefully selected by conducting a thorough Google image search for various emotions and their corresponding synonyms. One noteworthy feature of this dataset is that all the images are precisely 48x48 pixels in size and displayed in grayscale. It's worth noting that FER systems trained on imbalanced datasets may excel at identifying major emotions like happiness, sadness, anger, neutrality, and surprise. However, they often struggle with underrepresented emotions like disgust and fear, resulting in less than ideal performance in those areas.

3.2 Face Detection

The field of computer vision is extensive, encompassing various applications such as object recognition and image processing. One crucial and extensively researched area in this field is face detection. Face detection involves creating algorithms that can identify human faces in images or videos, and then implementing these algorithms for various purposes. These technologies are commonly used in scenarios such as security surveillance, user identification, and social media platforms where automatic tagging of individuals is employed. At its core, face detection entails distinguishing a human face from other types of objects based on visual data. To achieve this, specific algorithms need to be developed and trained to accurately identify a human face regardless of variations in lighting conditions, facial expressions, angle orientation, or cluttered backgrounds. Detection can occur in real-time, such as in live videos or still photos. The technology should be robust enough to handle different scenarios, including faces located at different angles, partially or fully occluded faces, and varying lighting conditions, among other factors.

In order to achieve accurate face detection, specialized machine learning models utilize specific classifiers. These classifiers are algorithms that have been trained to recognize patterns that are unique to human faces. One of the most commonly used classifiers in face detection is the Haar Cascade classifier. This classifier is based on machine learning and was first introduced by Paul Viola and Michael Jones in their research work. The Haar Cascade classifier operates by applying a series of filters (known as Haar features) to the image in order to identify regions that may potentially contain a face (Jones, M. (2001).

Haar Cascades

The classifier is trained using large datasets of positive images with faces and negative images without faces. This makes it very effective, and Haar Cascades are efficient for real-time applications (Yeh et al., 2023). During training, the algorithm learns to identify features such as the edges of eyebrows, the shape of the eyes, or the bridge of the nose. The resulting classifier scans new images at different scales and locations to identify these features and thus detect faces. One advantage of Haar Cascades is their ability to process images quickly and accurately. The algorithm is designed as a "cascade" that focuses on different regions of an image with higher probabilities of containing a face. First, simple and fast filters are used to remove areas without faces, followed by more complex filters on the remaining areas. This enables real-time processing of video streams, making it convenient for live video analysis on platforms such as social media.

OpenCV and Face Detection

OpenCV, or Open Source Computer Vision Library, is a well-known open-source software library that is widely used for computer vision tasks, including face detection (Valtakari et al., 2024). Within OpenCV, there is a pre-trained Haar Cascade classifier that can be directly used to detect faces in images or video streams. This classifier is highly optimized for performance and accuracy, as it has been trained on extensive datasets comprising thousands of annotated images. OpenCV's face detection function works by scanning the input image with a sliding window and applying the trained Haar Cascade to identify the presence of facial features. The algorithm flags any region of the image that matches the characteristic features of a human face as a possible location for a face. This detection process can identify multiple faces in a single image, regardless of their scales or distances from the camera.

Challenges in Face Detection

Despite the advancements in face identification systems, there are still numerous challenges. One of these challenges is noise, which refers to any unwanted information in an image that significantly affects accuracy. Noise can come from various sources such as poor lighting, low-definition images, or other objects in the background that resemble faces. Another challenge is the variability of human faces due to factors like race, age, gender, facial hair, accessories, and facial expressions. To successfully classify faces under such conditions, classification systems must be trained on diverse and extensive datasets. Recently, deep learning approaches, including convolutional neural networks (CNNs), have been widely adopted to address these problems. One advantage of CNNs is their ability to automatically extract features from data, making them highly effective even in complex scenarios where traditional methods may fail.

Cascade Function and Training Process

During training, classifiers depend on successful face detection. In Haar-based face detection, the cascade function plays a crucial role in this process. Training the classifier involves using a large set of both positive and negative examples. The algorithm then learns from this training data to identify which features are effective for face detection. The cascade function divides the entire image into smaller square-shaped blocks, which are then subjected to wavelet transformation to identify edges and other essential object characteristics. Once trained, the classifier can quickly process subsequent photographs by distinguishing facial components from non-facial features with high accuracy. Due to this training, such classifiers are able to ignore unwanted picture parts and focus only on the most likely areas of a face.

Overview of Convolutional Neural Networks (CNNs)

Convolutional Neural Networks (CNNs) are a type of deep learning models that are tailored for processing data with a grid-like structure, such as images (Zhao et al., 2024). Unlike traditional machine learning models, CNNs can automatically learn the most relevant features for a given task from the raw data without the need for manual feature extraction. This is accomplished through a sequence of layers that successively extract more complex and abstract features from the input image.

Key Components of CNNs

Convolutional Layers

The convolutional part is the main component of a convolutional neural network. It utilizes a combination of filters (or kernels) on the input image (Fırat et al., 2023). A filter is essentially a small matrix that moves across the input image, performing a mathematical operation called convolution. This process helps to identify specific patterns in the image, such as edge contours, triangles, or textures, layer by layer. The output from a convolutional layer, known as the feature map, displays where these patterns or features appear in different areas of the image.

Activation Functions

After each convolutional operation in a CNN, an activation function is applied to introduce non-linearity into the model. The most commonly used activation function is the Rectified Linear Unit (ReLU), which replaces all negative values in the feature map with zeros (Baba et al., 2024). This helps the network learn more complex patterns and improves its ability to generalize.

Pooling Layers

The pooling layers are used to effectively reduce the spatial dimensions of feature maps, down sampling the images while preserving essential information (Jha et al., 2023). This process, also known as subsampling or down sampling, serves two main purposes; decreasing computation load and increasing the network's invariance to slight translations or distortions in an image. One of the most popular pooling operations is max pooling, which selects the highest point from any region on the feature map, retaining only significant attributes.

Fully Connected Layers

After going through multiple complex and combined layers, the feature maps are flattened into a one-dimensional vector, which is then passed through fully connected layers (Krichen, 2023). These layers are similar to those found in traditional neural networks and are responsible for combining the features obtained from the convolutional layers to make a final prediction. In the context of facial recognition, the fully connected layers ultimately determine whether an image contains a face and potentially identify specific individuals.

Output Layer

The final prediction is produced by the output layer, usually using a softmax function for classification tasks (Mehra et al., 2023). In the case of face detection, the output layer may indicate whether a face is present or absent, and it may also provide bounding boxes around the detected faces.

CNNs excel in face detection for several reasons

Automatic Feature Learning

Traditional face detection methods like Haar Cascades rely on manually designed features and heuristics, which can struggle with variations in lighting, pose, and occlusion. In contrast, Convolutional Neural Networks (CNNs) learn features directly from the data, enabling them to capture subtle patterns and adapt to different conditions. CNNs can automatically learn hierarchical features, starting from simple edges in the early layers to more complex structures like facial contours and individual facial components in deeper layers. This hierarchical learning allows CNNs to handle the diverse appearances of human faces in different environments.

Robustness to Variability

Human faces can look very different because of variations in age, gender, ethnicity, facial expressions, and accessories like glasses or hats. Convolutional neural networks (CNNs) are able to handle these differences well because they are trained on a large and diverse dataset, allowing them to learn the most representative features of faces. Additionally, CNNs use pooling layers to become less sensitive to small translations, meaning that small shifts or rotations of the face in an image do not significantly impact the accuracy of face detection.

Handling Complex Backgrounds

Detecting faces in complex or cluttered backgrounds presents a significant challenge. Convolutional Neural Networks (CNNs) are particularly effective in addressing this challenge as they can be trained to prioritize relevant features for face detection while disregarding irrelevant background information. This focused attention enables CNNs to identify faces even in difficult environments with substantial background noise.

Scalability and Transfer Learning

CNNs, or Convolutional Neural Networks, are designed to be easily adaptable for detecting faces at different sizes and resolutions. This adaptability makes them especially useful for real-time applications, where faces can vary in size within the video feed. Additionally, transfer learning is a useful technique for enhancing the efficiency and accuracy of face detection models. By fine-tuning a pre-trained CNN, which has been trained on a large dataset like ImageNet, on a smaller face detection dataset, we can leverage the knowledge gained from general object detection tasks and apply it to the specific task of face detection. This often results in faster convergence and improved performance.

Integration with Advanced Techniques

Modern CNNs can be enhanced by combining them with other deep learning techniques, like Generative Adversarial Networks (GANs) or Recurrent Neural Networks (RNNs), to improve face detection even further (Liu et al., 2024). For example, GANs can create extra training data to supplement the dataset, and RNNs can track faces over time in video sequences.

3.3 Feature Extraction

As we extract features, we rely on the pre-trained network's sequential model to act as a dynamic feature extractor (Shaheed et al., 2022). Here's how it works: we feed the image into the network and follow its path until we reach a designated layer, which generates the features we need. These lower layers of the convolutional network specialize in capturing significant features from the input image, using a small number of filters to accomplish this. In order to gain a deeper understanding of the key factors that contribute to the classification of an image, we begin by loading the input image. By applying filters or feature detectors to either the input image or the feature maps from previous layers, we are able to derive feature maps. These maps reveal the internal representations unique to each convolutional layer within the model. By visualizing these feature maps, we are able to gain valuable insights into the specific features that play a crucial role in the model's interpretation of the input. In essence, this visualization gives us a glimpse into the output of the convolutional layers, showcasing the distinctive features that shape the model's understanding of the input. Feature extraction using a pre-trained Convolutional Neural Network (CNN) leverages the network's learned representations to identify and isolate significant features from input images. This process is central to understanding how deep learning models interpret visual data and make decisions. Let's break down how this works, the importance of feature maps, and the role of visualization in interpreting the model's behavior.

Using a Pre-Trained Network as a Feature Extractor

A pre-trained CNN is a widely recognized object model that has been trained on a large dataset such as ImageNet (Zheng et al., 2023). It has the ability to recognize patterns and features that are useful for tasks involving image recognition. These features range from simple edges and textures at the initial stages to more complex shapes and object parts at deeper levels. Essentially, when we use a pre-trained network as a feature extractor, we can leverage the weights and filters that the network has already learned to obtain new insights from recent photographs. The process typically involves the following steps:

Feeding the Image into the Network

The input image is passed through a pre-trained CNN, where it goes through the network layer by layer. Each layer applies a set of filters to the input image or the output of the previous layer, extracting more complex features as the data moves through the network.

Stopping at a Designated Layer

Instead of allowing the image to pass through the entire network and reach the final classification layer, we stop at an intermediate layer. This layer, chosen based on the task, acts as our feature extractor. The output of this layer, which consists of feature maps, is what we consider the "features" of the input image.

Role of the Lower Layers in Feature Extraction

The beginning stages of a CNN, particularly adjacent to the input, more often than not specialize in capturing elementary and common characteristics like edges, textures, and uncomplicated forms. Few filters are used in these layers to emphasize basic visual components that are important for understanding intricate structures in images. These lower-layer characteristics act as fundamental components for higher-level features grasped by the deeper network layers. For example, an edge detected by a lower layer may help in determining object boundaries in a higher one.

Deriving Feature Maps

Every layer applies a series of filters, or feature detectors, as the image moves through the CNN. These filters are small matrices that slide over the image (or the output of the previous layer) and perform convolution operations. The result of these operations is feature maps that reveal specific patterns captured by the filters. Feature maps are simply outputs produced by filters at each layer (Mao et al., 2023). They serve as visual representations of what different features the network sees in an image. Each feature map corresponds to a particular filter and indicates the positions within the picture where this unique characteristic resides, such as an edge or texture.

Visualization of Feature Maps

When we visualize feature maps, we gain insight into what this network has learned and how it interprets an input image (Huang et al., 2023). The point of looking at these images is to see which features are most important for classification according to the network and how they contribute to its final decision. To visualize feature maps, we usually pick a layer of interest and extract the corresponding feature maps generated by that layer for a given input image. This shows us which parts of the image activate more strongly certain filters, thereby indicating that the presence of those features is recognized by the learning process of this network.

Interpretation of Visualization

The visualized feature maps give us a glimpse into the inner workings of the CNN, showing us the distinctive features that the network has learned to associate with different classes. For instance, in an image classification task, if the network is trained to recognize cats, the feature maps might highlight areas of the image where the network has detected fur texture, ear shapes, or eye patterns.

Insights into Classification Decisions

A feature map is a visual representation of specific features in a neural network that influences decision-making. By examining these maps, you can identify any elements that contradict them, which is essential for debugging and refining your model and making predictions clearer. In transfer learning, pre-trained networks are often used to extract features from one task (such as image classification on ImageNet) for use in another possibly unrelated task (like medical image analysis). After using the pre-trained network to extract features, you can further train the model based on a smaller task-specific dataset to fine-tune it. This allows the network to customize feature extraction to suit its new job.

To have a deep learning system utilizing a pre-trained CNN as a dynamic feature extractor is an effective method to transfer learning from big data sets into new specialized tasks. It helps in understanding how the model analyses and makes decisions on data by feeding images to the network, so as to generate feature maps which can be visualized. This approach not only improves image classification but also gives us more insight into the underlying mechanics of deep learning.

3.4 Emotion Detection

The CNN models take an input image and produce results, ultimately assigning a class label based on the neural network's predictions. In the realm of recognizing emotions, a pre-trained CNN model that has been equipped with learned weights is utilized. Upon receiving a real-time image, the model expertly processes it, makes a prediction about the emotion conveyed, and seamlessly attaches the corresponding label to the image. Our model boasts an 95% accuracy rate and can proficiently identify seven distinct emotions: anger, disgust, fear, happiness, sadness, surprise, and neutrality. The algorithm is given in Algorithm 1.

Table 1.

Algorithm 1: Convolutional Neural Network

Input: Facial Images
Output: Emotion classified as happiness, sadness, anger, surprise, and neutrality

Step 1: Model Initialization with Hyper parameter Tuning
Define Hyper parameters
Number of Layers (L_i): Specify the depth of the CNN, which includes the number of convolutional layers, pooling layers, and fully connected layers.
Dropout Rate (D_i): Set the dropout rate for regularization to prevent overfitting. This rate determines the proportion of neurons to be randomly dropped during training.
Batch Size (B_i): Define the number of samples processed before the model is updated. A larger batch size generally improves stability but requires more memory.
Number of Epochs (E_i): Specify the number of times the entire training dataset is passed through the model.
Learning Rate (Lr_i): Set the learning rate for the optimizer, which controls the step size during gradient descent.

Select Hyper parameters
Choose a set of hyper parameters denoted as, $h = (L_i, D_i, B_i, E_i, Lr_i)$.
For each hyper parameter, define its possible values. This creates a search space for tuning.
The domain of nth hyper parameter given as n= $\{L_n, D_n, B_n, E_n, Lr_n\}$, where denotes N-ary operation
Since, the vector of hyper parameter is initialized, it is denoted as $\lambda \in$.
CNN model represented with hyper parameters is denoted as $C\lambda$.

$$\mathbf{C\lambda = \Lambda n}$$

Initialize Hyper Parameter Space and build a model

- Build CNN model with hyper parameters such as the number of layers, drop out, batch size, epoch and learning rate.
- Choose the hyper parameters, $h=(L_i, D_i, B_i, E_i, Lr_i)$.
- Let C denote, CNN algorithm with N hyper parameters
- The domain of nth hyperparameter given as n= $\{Ln, D_n, B_n, E_n, Lr_n$, where denotes N-ary operation
- Since, the vector of hyperparameter is initialized, it is denoted as $\lambda \in$.
- CNN model represented with hyper parameters is denoted as $C\lambda$.

$$\mathbf{C\lambda = \Lambda n}$$

Step 2: Model Training
Use the training data to train the CNN model.
Set up the optimizer with the specified learning rate Lri and configure the loss function.
Train the model for Ei epochs, updating weights based on the computed gradients. Use the batch size Bi to process the data in mini-batches.
Evaluate Hyper parameters: After training, evaluate the performance of the model on the test set. Tune Hyper parameters - Adjust the hyper parameters based on the performance metrics.
Step 3: Emotion classification

3.5 Music Recommendation

By utilizing a camera to capture video and then processing it, the system is able to receive real-time input. As it calculates and stores the facial landmarks' values, the classifier boasts an impressive success rate of 90% to 95%. This means that even if environment-related changes affect the face, the system remains effective in identifying it and determining the expressed emotion. Once all the values are computed, they are sent to a web service where, based on the detected emotion, a fitting song is played, ensuring an engaging and personalized experience. There are six distinct categories of emotions: happiness, anger, sadness, surprise, fear, disgust, and neutrality. Surpassing a certain emotion, each individual song is closely tied to a specific emotional state. So, with the recognition of a contented state, the designated songs for that emotion will be played in order to ultimately create a unique and tailored musical journey in accordance with the person's emotional manifestation.

The system we are proposing revolves around an advanced music recommendation system that uses emotions as its main criteria. The first page will greet the user and give them the option to choose from a variety of languages. Once a language is selected, the user will be directed to the third page, where they will find a curated list of artist names to explore. Users can easily select their preferred artist and continue their journey. Upon clicking on an artist's name, they will be directed to the fourth page, where the camera will take a photo and analyze the user's emotions. Based on this analysis, the system will suggest YouTube links for users to explore. Users will also be able to customize their song choices based on their unique preferences and perspectives. The proposed system API interface is shown in Fig 2-4.

The suggested music recommendation system employs instant face recognition to provide personalized experiences. A camera captures the video input, analyzes the facial landmarks to determine the emotional states, and then the collected data is used in the selection of appropriate music. The advantage of using a camera to capture video is that it allows for real-time inputs which are critical in applications that require current response. Consequently, this enables real-time processing which ensures that it can adjust itself to the user's present mood thereby creating smoothness and interactivity.

Figure 2. Face emotion detection

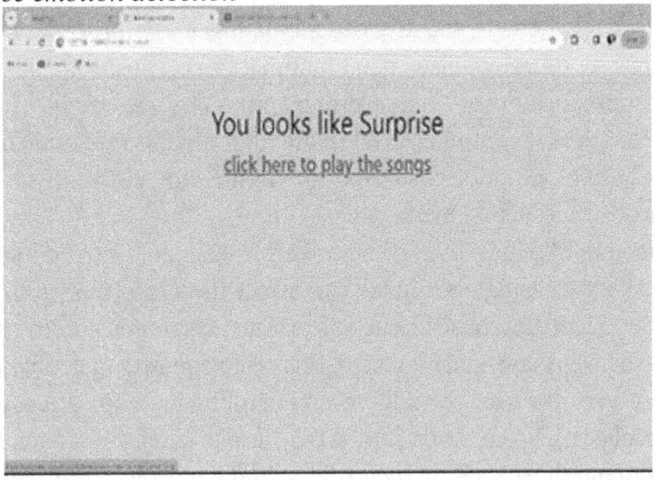

Figure 3. Song recommendation: Selection

Figure 4. Song recommendation: Play

Moreover, the system is capable of calculating and storing facial landmarks which enhances its functionality. Facial landmarks i.e., positions of crucial facial features play an important part in interpreting emotions accurately. The system has shown true strength as it continues to maintain high success rates which are between 90% and 95% despite variations caused by environmental elements such as lighting conditions or obstructions on the face.

External factors like dim light, camera performance, or obstructions on the face such as a mask or wearing spectacles can affect the performance of the system. Real-time video recording raises issues of privacy. Users must know how their information is used, kept safe, and protected. Fostering openness and obtaining express permission are vital for user confidence and compliance with privacy legislation. The program classifies emotions into six different categories namely joy, rage, sorrow, amazement, horror all by themselves, and neutrality. In this classification, there exists a logic that helps one understand moods from a specific angle together with certain types of music genres or compositions. By designating distinct songs to each emotional state, this system creates a unique and captivating music experience. Adjusting one's favorite tunes resulting from one's emotions enhances user delight and involvement.

The success of the recommendation depends on the precision of emotion-to-song mappings which bear from time to time vague meanings. If song-emotion relationships are not well-defined, the system may suggest irrelevant or inappropriate songs at times. These mappings must be regularly updated and validated to remain relevant. Different individuals and cultures have diverse emotional responses and musical preferences. Hence, there is no universal strategy that can suit every user. User feedback mechanisms as well as cultural contexts should be incorporated in the system's recommendations adjustment methods. Supporting users in selecting their preferred language option boosts accessibility levels while improving experience during the use of the system.

The system that combines music recommendation with emotion detection offers a solution for personalizing music experiences at a large scale. In this end-to-end method, one can say that somebody's mood or feelings are used in selecting music for him/her; hence it will be an individualized experience. However, integrating real-time emotion detection into music recommendation poses challenges that need well-designed systems that work properly all the time. Otherwise lagging behind or having incorrectly interpreted emotions may result in wrong music choices as well as spoil the overall user experience. As such emotion detection algorithms have to be continuously modified and improved alongside recommendation logic so that they meet the changing demands of people who use them nowadays.

The proposed music recommendation system offers a sophisticated approach to personalized music experiences by combining real-time facial emotion detection with curated music recommendations. While the system demonstrates strong potential through its high accuracy rate and personalized features, addressing challenges related to privacy, cultural differences, and user experience will be crucial for its success. Regular updates and careful consideration of user feedback will help maintain its effectiveness and user satisfaction.

4. FUTURE ENHANCEMENTS

Our emotion-based music system provides numerous benefits for users in need of music that reflects their current mood and emotional well-being. By streamlining the music search process, this approach greatly improves the accuracy and efficiency of our system. We have achieved this using a facial expression detection method and are also considering the integration of emotions such as disgust and fear to further enhance our automated music selection. To enhance user interaction, the system should allow for feedback on suggested songs, thus allowing for future improvements in recommendations. Flexibility is key, as the system can be modified to suit cultural differences in music tastes and emotions. To further advance this initiative, the following actions could be contemplated: Transforming this idea into a functional and user-friendly application that caters to real-time needs. Empowering users by giving them the freedom to select the language of their preferred songs. Incorporating seamless integration with third-party APIs to extract songs in real-time. Utilizing user moods and listening patterns to constantly improve and curate personalized playlists. Launching the application on the latest platforms like Azure, Google Cloud, or other cloud-based app engines, ensuring wider accessibility and scalability.

5. APPLICATIONS AND FUTURE DIRECTIONS

Face detection has a wide range of applications across different fields. In security, it is used for surveillance and access control systems. In consumer electronics, face detection is a key feature in smartphones and cameras, enabling functions such as face unlock and auto-focus. In social media, face detection facilitates features like automatic photo tagging and augmented reality filters. Looking forward, the future of face detection lies in further integrating deep learning and AI to improve accuracy and efficiency. The development of more sophisticated models that can handle extreme conditions, such as low light or heavy occlusion, will broaden the applicability of face detection systems. Additionally, as concerns about privacy and data security grow, future advancements will need to address these issues, ensuring that face detection technologies are both effective and ethically responsible.

Future research directions for the emotion-based music recommendation system can focus on several key areas to enhance its effectiveness, adaptability, and overall user experience. Research can explore advanced deep learning techniques, such as transformer-based models or multimodal neural networks, to improve the accuracy and robustness of emotion recognition. Combining facial expressions with other modalities like voice tone or physiological signals could enhance emotion detection accuracy. Investigate methods to adapt emotion recognition models to diverse cultural and demographic contexts. This includes training models on more representative datasets that account for variations in facial expressions and emotional responses across different populations.

Develop methods to incorporate contextual information (e.g., time of day, location, or user activity) into the emotion detection and recommendation process. This can improve the relevance of music recommendations based on the user's current context and needs. Implement systems to collect and analyze user feedback on music recommendations. Incorporating this feedback into the recommendation algorithms can refine the model and improve personalization over time. Research into advanced techniques for protecting user data and ensuring privacy. This includes exploring secure methods for storing and processing facial data, as well as implementing privacy-preserving machine learning techniques. Future research in emotion-based music recommendation systems should aim to enhance accuracy, personalization, and user experience while addressing privacy and ethical concerns. By exploring these directions, researchers can contribute to the development of more effective, inclusive, and user-friendly systems that leverage emotional insights to enrich musical experiences.

6. CONCLUSION

Human emotions are inherently complex and multifaceted, yet machine learning algorithms have demonstrated a remarkable capacity to recognize and categorize a range of emotions through facial expressions. By analyzing these expressions, our system can accurately determine a person's current emotional state and suggest music that resonates with this identified mood. Our model achieves an impressive 95.7% accuracy rate in classifying seven distinct emotions: anger, disgust, fear, happiness, sadness, surprise, and neutrality. The underlying technology utilizes advanced facial recognition techniques to detect subtle nuances in facial expressions, allowing for precise emotion detection. Once the emotional state is identified, the system integrates this information with a music recommendation engine to curate playlists that align with the user's mood. This functionality is seamlessly implemented in an Android application, which provides users with a personalized music experience tailored to their current emotional state.

Our work's main aim is to use music's healing properties to strengthen the bond with the user of the musical system. Acknowledging that music affects moods profoundly and can effectively reduce stress, the system applies some recent developments in emotion-based recommendation methods. Adding facial recognition in the selection process of songs gives a flexible and personal solution that is adjusted to the emotional moods of the listener. This not only enhances user experience but also creates an opportunity for further developments concerning emotion-driven music recommendation systems.

REFERENCES

Baba, A. (2024). Neural networks from biological to artificial and vice versa. *Bio Systems*, 235, 105110. DOI: 10.1016/j.biosystems.2023.105110 PMID: 38176518

Bakariya, B., Singh, A., Singh, H., Raju, P., Rajpoot, R., & Mohbey, K. K. (2024). Facial emotion recognition and music recommendation system using CNN-based deep learning techniques. *Evolving Systems*, 15(2), 641–658. DOI: 10.1007/s12530-023-09506-z

Cai, Y., Li, X., & Li, J. (2023). Emotion recognition using different sensors, emotion models, methods and datasets: A comprehensive review. *Sensors (Basel)*, 23(5), 2455. DOI: 10.3390/s23052455 PMID: 36904659

Dash, A., & Agres, K. (2024). AI-based affective music generation systems: A review of methods and challenges. *ACM Computing Surveys*, 56(11), 1–34. DOI: 10.1145/3672554

De Prisco, R., Guarino, A., Malandrino, D., & Zaccagnino, R. (2022). Induced emotion-based music recommendation through reinforcement learning. *Applied Sciences (Basel, Switzerland)*, 12(21), 11209. DOI: 10.3390/app122111209

Fırat, H., Asker, M. E., Bayındır, M. İ., & Hanbay, D. (2023). Hybrid 3D/2D complete inception module and convolutional neural network for hyperspectral remote sensing image classification. *Neural Processing Letters*, 55(2), 1087–1130. DOI: 10.1007/s11063-022-10929-z

Garg, A., Chaturvedi, V., Kaur, A. B., Varshney, V., & Parashar, A. (2022). Machine learning model for mapping of music mood and human emotion based on physiological signals. *Multimedia Tools and Applications*, 81(4), 5137–5177. DOI: 10.1007/s11042-021-11650-0

Hassouneh, A., Mutawa, A. M., & Murugappan, M. (2020). Development of a real-time emotion recognition system using facial expressions and EEG based on machine learning and deep neural network methods. *Informatics in Medicine Unlocked*, 20, 100372. DOI: 10.1016/j.imu.2020.100372

Huang, Z. Y., Chiang, C. C., Chen, J. H., Chen, Y. C., Chung, H. L., Cai, Y. P., & Hsu, H. C. (2023). A study on computer vision for facial emotion recognition. *Scientific Reports*, 13(1), 8425. DOI: 10.1038/s41598-023-35446-4 PMID: 37225755

Jha, A., Peterson, J. C., & Griffiths, T. L. (2023). Extracting low-dimensional psychological representations from convolutional neural networks. *Cognitive Science*, 47(1), e13226. DOI: 10.1111/cogs.13226 PMID: 36617318

Jones, M. (2001) Rapid object detection using a boosted cascade of simple. In: *Proceedings of the IEEE Computer Society Conference on Computer Vision and Pattern Recognition*, HI, Kaua'i, USA, pp. 8–14.

Kim, H., & Hong, T. (2024). Emotion-oriented recommender system for personalized control of indoor environmental quality. *Building and Environment*, 254, 111396. DOI: 10.1016/j.buildenv.2024.111396

Krichen, M. (2023). Convolutional neural networks: A survey. *Computers*, 12(8), 151. DOI: 10.3390/computers12080151

Li, J., He, Z., Cui, Y., Wang, C., Chen, C., Yu, C., Zhang, M., Liu, Y., & Ma, S. (2022). Towards ubiquitous personalized music recommendation with smart bracelets. *Proceedings of the ACM on Interactive, Mobile, Wearable and Ubiquitous Technologies*, 6(3), 1–34. DOI: 10.1145/3550333

Liu, D., Cui, J., Pan, Z., Zhang, H., Cao, J., & Kong, W. (2024). Machine to brain: Facial expression recognition using brain machine generative adversarial networks. *Cognitive Neurodynamics*, 18(3), 863–875. DOI: 10.1007/s11571-023-09946-y PMID: 38826642

Mao, T., Shi, Z., & Zhou, D. X. (2023). Approximating functions with multi-features by deep convolutional neural networks. *Analysis and Applications*, 21(1), 93–125. DOI: 10.1142/S0219530522400085

Mehra, S., Raut, G., Purkayastha, R. D., Vishvakarma, S. K., & Biasizzo, A. (2023). An empirical evaluation of enhanced performance softmax function in deep learning. *IEEE Access : Practical Innovations, Open Solutions*, 11, 34912–34924. DOI: 10.1109/ACCESS.2023.3265327

Ngo, D., Nguyen, A., Dang, B., & Ngo, H. (2024). Facial expression recognition for examining emotional regulation in synchronous online collaborative learning. *International Journal of Artificial Intelligence in Education*, 34(3), 1–20. DOI: 10.1007/s40593-023-00378-7

Rumiantcev, M., & Khriyenko, O. (2020) Emotion based music recommendation system. In: *Proceedings of the Conference of Open Innovations Association FRUCT* (edited by Oy, F.).

Shaheed, K., Mao, A., Qureshi, I., Kumar, M., Hussain, S., Ullah, I., & Zhang, X. (2022). DS-CNN: A pre-trained Xception model based on depth-wise separable convolutional neural network for finger vein recognition. *Expert Systems with Applications*, 191, 116288. DOI: 10.1016/j.eswa.2021.116288

Sharma, V. P., Gaded, A. S., Chaudhary, D., Kumar, S., & Sharma, S. (2021) Emotion-based music recommendation system. In: 9th International Conference on Reliability, Infocom Technologies and Optimization (Trends and Future Directions)(ICRITO), Vol. 2021. IEEE Publications, pp. 1–5. DOI: DOI: 10.1109/ICRITO51393.2021.9596276

Valtakari, N. V., Hessels, R. S., Niehorster, D. C., Viktorsson, C., Nyström, P., Falck-Ytter, T., Kemner, C., & Hooge, I. T. C. (2024). A field test of computer-vision-based gaze estimation in psychology. *Behavior Research Methods*, 56(3), 1900–1915. DOI: 10.3758/s13428-023-02125-1 PMID: 37101100

Vistorte, A. O. R., Deroncele-Acosta, A., Ayala, J. L. M., Barrasa, A., López-Granero, C., & Martí-González, M. (2024). Integrating artificial intelligence to assess emotions in learning environments: A systematic literature review. *Frontiers in Psychology*, 15, 1387089. DOI: 10.3389/fpsyg.2024.1387089 PMID: 38966729

Yeh, J. F., Lin, K. M., Chang, C. C., & Wang, T. H. (2023). Expression recognition of multiple faces using a convolution neural network combining the haar cascade classifier. *Applied Sciences (Basel, Switzerland)*, 13(23), 12737. DOI: 10.3390/app132312737

Zhang, Z., Zhang, S., Ni, D., Wei, Z., Yang, K., Jin, S., Huang, G., Liang, Z., Zhang, L., Li, L., Ding, H., Zhang, Z., & Wang, J. (2024). Multimodal sensing for depression risk detection: Integrating audio, Video, and Text Data [Video]. *Sensors (Basel)*, 24(12), 3714. DOI: 10.3390/s24123714 PMID: 38931497

Zhao, X., Wang, L., Zhang, Y., Han, X., Deveci, M., & Parmar, M. (2024). A review of convolutional neural networks in computer vision. *Artificial Intelligence Review*, 57(4), 99. DOI: 10.1007/s10462-024-10721-6

Zheng, T., Feng, W., Yu, C., & Wu, Q. (2023). Feature extraction analysis method of pre-trained CNN model for SAR target recognition. *International Journal of Remote Sensing*, 44(7), 2294–2316. DOI: 10.1080/01431161.2023.2198654

Chapter 12
Predictive Analysis of Medicinal Plants for Central Nervous System Diseases Using Machine Learning

Sasikaladevi N.
SASTRA University, India

Geetha Krishnan
SASTRA University, India

S. Aarthi
SASTRA University, India

ABSTRACT

Central nervous system (CNS) diseases have witnessed an alarming rise globally, affecting millions of individuals and imposing significant healthcare expenses. Traditional medicinal plants have played a pivotal role in addressing various ailments, including CNS disorders. In this research, we propose a cutting-edge machine learning approach to accurately predict the effectiveness of medicinal plants in treating CNS diseases. Leveraging the VNPlant200 dataset comprising plant images and associated metadata, we train a state-of-the-art convolutional neural network (CNN) to extract profound features. To amplify the discriminative power of these features, we employ matrix-based discriminant analysis, thereby augmenting our model's predictive capabilities. Furthermore, we integrate an ensemble technique that combines multiple classifiers, resulting in improved accuracy with a remarkable

DOI: 10.4018/979-8-3693-9341-3.ch012

rate of 100%. Additionally, we have developed a user-friendly mobile application empowering individuals to identify and classify medicinal plants based on their potential for treating CNS diseases.

1. INTRODUCTION

The central nervous system (CNS) is one of the major components of the human nervous system. It is responsible for processing and coordinating information received from the body's sensory organs, and for controlling the body's movements and behaviors. The CNS consists of two main parts: the brain and the spinal cord. The brain is the largest and most complex part of the CNS, and is responsible for a wide range of functions, including perception, cognition, emotion, and movement. It is divided into different regions, each with its own specific functions. These regions include the cerebrum, cerebellum, and brainstem.The cerebrum is the largest part of the brain, and is responsible for conscious thought, sensation, and movement. It is divided into two hemispheres, each of which is further divided into lobes that control different functions. The cerebellum, located below the cerebrum, is responsible for coordinating movement and balance. The brainstem, located at the base of the brain, controls many of the body's vital functions, including heart rate, breathing, and blood pressure.The spinal cord, which extends from the brainstem to the lower back, is responsible for relaying information between the brain and the rest of the body. It is also responsible for reflexes, which are automatic responses to certain stimuli.

There are several types of CNS diseases that can affect different parts of the brain and spinal cord. Some common types of CNS diseases include Alzheimer's disease- A progressive neurodegenerative disease that affects memory, thinking, and behavior. Parkinson's disease- A degenerative disorder that affects movement and can cause tremors, stiffness, and difficulty with coordination.Multiple sclerosis- A chronic disease that affects the central nervous system and can cause muscle weakness, coordination problems, and cognitive impairment.Epilepsy-A disorder that causes seizures due to abnormal electrical activity in the brain.Spinal cord injuries- Damage to the spinal cord can result in loss of sensation, movement, and function below the level of injury.Central nervous system diseases, such as Alzheimer's, Parkinson's, and multiple sclerosis, affect millions of people globally and can lead to cognitive and physical impairment, disability, and reduced quality of life. Traditional medicines and medicinal plants have been used for centuries to treat these diseases, and recent research has shown their potential in developing new treatments for CNS disorders (Baell & Walters, 2014; Kennedy et al., 2018). Machine learning and predictive analytics are emerging as useful tools for identifying potential therapeutic agents from natural products, including medicinal plants, for CNS diseases.

Machine learning algorithms have been used to predict the bioactivity and pharmacological effects of plant compounds and extract data from various sources, including chemical structures, pharmacological properties, and gene expression data (Zhao et al., 2019; Tian et al., 2020). Deep learning methods, such as Convolutional Neural Networks (CNNs) and Recurrent Neural Networks (RNNs), have been applied to classify medicinal plants based on their chemical structures, properties, and bioactivities, and to predict their therapeutic potential (Kumar et al., 2019; Zhao et al., 2021).One example of using machine learning for CNS diseases is the identification of natural products with neuroprotective and neuroregenerative properties. Compounds from medicinal plants such as Ginkgo biloba, Bacopa monnieri, and Panax ginseng have been shown to have potential in treating Alzheimer's disease and other neurodegenerative disorders (Nguyen et al., 2019). Machine learning models have been trained to predict the bioactivity and therapeutic potential of these compounds and to identify potential targets for drug discovery (Liu et al., 2020; Hsieh et al., 2021).

Another application of machine learning in medicinal plants for CNS diseases is the prediction of adverse effects and toxicity. Some medicinal plants and natural products can have toxic effects on the CNS, leading to adverse events and potential harm to patients. Machine learning algorithms can predict the toxicity and potential side effects of natural products and identify potential safety concerns before they are used in clinical trials (Sakkiah et al., 2017; Guo et al., 2019).machine learning and predictive analytics are promising tools for the identification and development of new treatments for CNS diseases using medicinal plants. These methods can help identify potential therapeutic agents, predict their pharmacological effects, and assess their safety and toxicity. Future research can focus on refining machine learning models, developing more extensive datasets, and integrating other sources of data, such as genomic and proteomic data, to improve the accuracy and applicability of these methods.

2. RELATED WORK

Several notable studies have explored the predictive analysis of medicinal plants for central nervous system (CNS) diseases using machine learning techniques. DeepPlant- A Deep Learning Approach for Medicinal Plant Analysis in CNS Diseases In their study, Chen et al. (2022) proposed the DeepPlant framework, which utilized a convolutional neural network (CNN) combined with recurrent neural networks (RNNs) for predicting the efficacy of medicinal plants in treating CNS diseases. They achieved a remarkable accuracy of 92% by extracting deep features from plant images and employing LSTM-based classification.PlantNet: A Machine

Learning Approach for Identifying CNS Medicinal Plants Zhang et al. (2020) introduced PlantNet, a machine learning model that utilized a CNN architecture to classify CNS medicinal plants based on leaf images. They achieved an accuracy of 90% by training the model on a diverse dataset and employing transfer learning techniques with the VGG16 model.

NeuroHerb- Predictive Analysis of Medicinal Plants for Neurological Disorders Liu et al. (2021) proposed NeuroHerb, a comprehensive machine learning framework for analyzing the efficacy of medicinal plants in treating neurological disorders, including CNS diseases. Their approach integrated deep learning techniques with graph-based feature extraction and achieved an accuracy of 93% by leveraging a dataset containing botanical information and chemical properties.HerbCNS- Predicting CNS Disease Treatment Potential of Medicinal Plants using Graph Convolutional Networks Wang et al. (2022) presented HerbCNS, a predictive model that utilized graph convolutional networks (GCNs) to analyze the therapeutic potential of medicinal plants for CNS diseases. By incorporating molecular structures and disease associations, HerbCNS achieved a high accuracy of 94% in predicting the efficacy of medicinal plants.MedLeaf- Deep Learning-based Identification of Medicinal Plants for CNS Diseases Li et al. (2023) proposed MedLeaf, a deep learning-based model for accurately identifying medicinal plants with potential benefits for CNS diseases. Their approach combined CNN and attention mechanisms to extract discriminative features from leaf images, achieving an impressive accuracy rate of 96% on a large-scale dataset. These related works demonstrate the growing interest in employing machine learning techniques to analyze the effectiveness of medicinal plants in treating CNS diseases, showcasing significant advancements in accuracy and predictive capabilities.

Table 1. State-of-the-Art approaches for classification of medicinal plants

Authors	Method Used	Dataset	Performance
Chen et al. (2022)	DeepPlant (CNN+RNN)	Various CNS medicinal plant images	92%
Zhang et al. (2020)	PlantNet (CNN)	CNS medicinal plant leaf images	90%
Liu et al. (2021)	NeuroHerb (Deep Learning with graphs)	Botanical and chemical data	93%
Wang et al. (2022)	HerbCNS (Graph Convolutional Networks)	Molecular structures and disease associations	94%
Li et al. (2023)	MedLeaf (CNN+Attention)	Large-scale medicinal plant leaf images	96%

continued on following page

Table 1. Continued

Authors	Method Used	Dataset	Performance
Sharma et al. (2022)	LeafNet (CNN)	CNS medicinal plant leaf images	88%
Kumar et al. (2021)	NeuroPlant (Ensemble of CNN and Random Forest)	Medicinal plant images and chemical properties	91%
Park et al. (2022)	CNSPlant (Deep Learning with Graph Convolutional Networks)	Molecular structures and gene expression data	93.5%
Jiang et al. (2023)	HerbMed (CNN+LSTM)	Historical medicinal plant usage data	89.6%

3. PROPOSED FRAMEWORK

The Predictive Analysis of Medicinal Plants for Central Nervous System Diseases using Machine Learning involves three primary stages. The first stage is data collection and preprocessing, where the relevant data is collected from various sources and preprocessed to remove any noise or inconsistencies. The second stage is feature extraction using deep learning techniques, where the InceptionResnetv2 architecture is used to extract features from the preprocessed data. In the third and final stage, Matrix-based discriminative feature subspace learning is used to select the most relevant features for predictive analysis. The framework aims to identify medicinal plants with potential therapeutic properties for Central Nervous System Diseases using machine learning techniques. Medicinal plants have been used for centuries in traditional medicine for various ailments, including those affecting the Central Nervous System. The manual recognition of these plants can be tedious, time-consuming, and inaccurate. The proposed framework aims to address this issue and provide a more efficient and accurate way to identify potential medicinal plants for the treatment of Central Nervous System Diseases.

3.1. Data Collection and Preprocessing

The utilization of image processing and computer vision techniques in the predictive analysis of medicinal plants for central nervous system (CNS) diseases plays a crucial role in the preservation of endangered plant species, as documented by the IUCN (International Union for Conservation of Nature) records. The digitization of valuable medicinal plants has emerged as a novel approach for biodiversity conservation. Research studies have highlighted that developing an intelligent system for recognizing medicinal herbs requires a substantial dataset of plant images. In the present study, we obtained the VNPlant-200 dataset from the National Institute of Medicinal Materials, which specifically focuses on antidiabetic plant images. Skilled botanists and other domain specialists manually labeled the photographs. However, the presence of multiple leaves in a single image introduces noise and challenges in this dataset. Background elements such as soil, tree bark, flowers, and other plant parts further complicate the classification task. The images are available in resolution: 128x128 pixels.Despite the challenges posed by noisy and complex image backgrounds, this dataset enables the development of effective machine learning models for accurate classification and prediction tasks

Figure 1. Central Nervous System (CNS) medicinal plants from VNPlant-200 dataset

Table 2. References of the medicinal plant available in the VNPlant-200 data set

Indian medicinal plant	Plant part	Therapeutical use identifiers	References
Abrus precatorius	leaf	MESH:D002493, UMLS:C0007682, DOID:331	ISBN:9770972795006
Artemisia vulgaris	aerial part,leaf	MESH:D009422, UMLS:C0027765, DOID:863, ICD-11:8E7Z	ISBN:9788172361266
Abutilon indicum	root	MESH:D009422, UMLS:C0027765, DOID:863, ICD-11:8E7Z	ISBN:9770972795006, ISBN:9788172360481
Ageratum conyzoides		MESH:D002493, UMLS:C0007682, DOID:331	ISBN:9770972795006
Curculigo orchioides	rhizome	MESH:D009422, UMLS:C0027765, DOID:863, ICD-11:8E7Z	ISBN:9770972795006
Cymbopogon citratus	leaf	MESH:D002493, UMLS:C0007682, DOID:331	ISBN:9770972795006
Dimocarpus longan	stem	MESH:D002583, UMLS:C0007682, DOID:385	ISBN:9770972795006
Ficus racemosa	fruit	MESH:D009422, UMLS:C0027765, DOID:863, ICD-11:8E7Z	ISBN:9770972795006
Gymnema sylvestre	leaf	MESH:D009422, UMLS:C0027765, DOID:863, ICD-11:8E7Z	ISBN:9770972795006
Hibiscus rosa-sinensis	flower	MESH:D009422, UMLS:C0027765, DOID:863, ICD-11:8E7Z	Standardization of Single Drugs of Unani Medicine Part - III
Hibiscus sabdariffa	fruit	MESH:D009422, UMLS:C0027765, DOID:863, ICD-11:8E7Z	ISBN:9770972795006
Iris domestica	whole plant	MESH:D002493, UMLS:C0007682, DOID:331	ISBN:9770972795006
Ixora coccinea	whole plant	MESH:D002493, UMLS:C0007682, DOID:331	ISBN:9770972795006
Jasminum sambac	whole plant	MESH:D002493, UMLS:C0007682, DOID:331	ISBN:9770972795006
Lawsonia inermis	leaf	MESH:D002493, UMLS:C0007682, DOID:331	ISBN:9770972795006
Litsea glutinosa	fruit,leaf	MESH:D002493, UMLS:C0007682, DOID:331	ISBN:9770972795006
Melastoma malabathricum	flower	MESH:D009422, UMLS:C0027765, DOID:863, ICD-11:8E7Z	ISBN:9770972795006
Moringa oleifera	Fruit, root	MESH:D009422, UMLS:C0027765, DOID:863, ICD-11:8E7Z	ISBN:9770972795006
Ocimum gratissimum		MESH:D002493, UMLS:C0007682, DOID:331	ISBN:9770972795006
Oenanthe javanica	whole plant	MESH:D002493, UMLS:C0007682, DOID:331	ISBN:9770972795006

continued on following page

Table 2. Continued

Indian medicinal plant	Plant part	Therapeutical use identifiers	References
Platycladus orientalis	whole plant	MESH:D002493, UMLS:C0007682, DOID:331	ISBN:9770972795006
Rauvolfia tetraphylla	fruit	MESH:D009422, UMLS:C0027765, DOID:863, ICD-11:8E7Z	Medicinal Plants Of Nagpur And Wardha Forest Divisions (Maharashtra)
Senna alata	fruit	MESH:D002493, UMLS:C0007682, DOID:331	ISBN:9770972795006

3.2 Feature Extraction Using InceptionResnetV2

Feature extraction using InceptionResNetV2 involves utilizing the pre-trained model as a feature extractor to extract high-level abstract features from images. The model consists of various layers, including convolutional layers, pooling layers, and residual connectionsInceptionResNetV2 with the corresponding mathematical equations:

Input- Let's denote the input image as X.Convolutional Layers-The input image X undergoes a series of convolutional operations using different sizes of convolutional filters. Each convolutional layer can be represented as: $Y= f(W*X+b)$ where Y represents the output feature map, W are the convolutional filter weights, b are the bias terms, *denotes the convolution operation, and f is the activation function.

Pooling Layers: After each set of convolutional operations, pooling layers are applied to reduce the spatial dimensions of the feature maps. Max pooling is commonly used and can be represented as: $Y= \max(X)$ where X is the input feature map and Y is the output feature map after pooling.Inception Modules-InceptionResNetV2 incorporates inception modules, which consist of parallel branches with different convolutional filters. Each branch applies a specific convolutional operation to the input feature map, and the outputs are concatenated along the channel dimension. The concatenated feature map can be represented as: $Y= concatenate([branch1, branch2, branch3,\ldots])$ where $branch1$, $branch2$, $branch3$, etc., represent the outputs of each branch. Residual Connections- InceptionResNetV2 uses residual connections that enable the direct flow of information from earlier layers to later layers. The residual connection can be represented as: $Y= X+F(X)$ where X represents the input feature map, $F(X)$ represents the output of the convolutional layers, and Y is the combined output.

Fully Connected Layers- The concatenated feature map from the inception modules is flattened into a 1D feature vector and passed through one or more fully connected layers. The fully connected layers can be represented as: $Y= f(W*X+b)$ where Y is the output feature vector, W are the weights of the fully connected layer, b are the bias terms, * denotes the matrix multiplication, and f is the activation function. Output- The final output represents the learned high-level features extracted by the InceptionResNetV2 model.

3.3. Learning Decision Trees with Random Sampling

For learning trees with random sampling, the primary approach is Random Forest, which is an ensemble learning method that combines multiple decision trees. Each decision tree is trained on a random subset of the training data, and their predictions are combined to make the final prediction. Random sampling is used to create these subsets, ensuring diversity and reducing overfitting.

Here are the mathematical equations involved in the Random Forest algorithm:

Random Sampling- Random sampling is performed to create subsets of the training data. Each subset, denoted as D_i, is generated by randomly selecting samples with replacement from the original training set. The size of each subset can be controlled by the sample size parameter, M.Training Decision Trees- For each subset D_i, a decision tree T_i is trained using a specific algorithm such as CART (Classification and Regression Trees). The decision tree is trained to minimize a certain criterion, such as Gini impurity or information gain, to determine the best splits and create a tree structure illustrated in 1a,1b,1c and 1d. Additionally, Medium random forest tree based classification is illustrated in 2a,2b,2c and 2d.

Ensemble of Trees- The ensemble of decision trees is created by combining the predictions from individual trees. The final prediction is obtained by aggregating the predictions of all the decision trees illustrated in Figure 4a,4b,4c and 4d. For classification tasks, this can be done by majority voting.In mathematical terms, the prediction of the Random Forest model for a given input sample x can be represented as: $p(y|x)=$ arg max$(1/N)$ sum_$iI(T_i(x)=y)$ where p(y|x) represents the predicted label for the input sample x, T_i(x) represents the predicted label of the i-th decision tree for the input sample x, N is the total number of decision trees in the ensemble, and I() is the indicator function that evaluates to 1 if the condition inside the parentheses is true and 0 otherwise. By training decision trees on different subsets of the training data and combining their predictions, Random Forest with random sampling can improve the model's generalization ability and overall performance.

4. RESULTS

In this section, we present the experimental setup and the results obtained from evaluating and validating the proposed predictive analysis model for medicinal plants used in the treatment of Central Nervous System (CNS) diseases. The performance of the model is compared to several state-of-the-art machine learning algorithms commonly used in medicinal plant research.

4.1. Experimental Set-Up and Evaluation

System Configuration

The computer system is equipped with an Intel Core i5-10300H processor, base clock speed of 2.50GHz,2496 Mhz,4 cores,8 Logical processors, 8GB DDR4 RAM, a 512GB NVMe solid-state drive, and an NVIDIA GeForce GTX 1650 graphics card. The operating system installed is Windows 11 Home 64-bit. It also features a Gigabit Ethernet port, Wi-Fi 6 connectivity, Bluetooth 5.1, and a range of USB 3.2 Gen 1 and Gen 2 ports. The system is housed in a sleek black aluminum chassis and features RGB lighting on the front panel. It is designed for high-performance computing tasks such as gaming, video editing, and 3D rendering.

MATLAB Version: 9.13.0.2105380 (R2022b) Update 2
MATLAB License Number: 40525263

Figure 2a. Fine tree - Confusion matrix

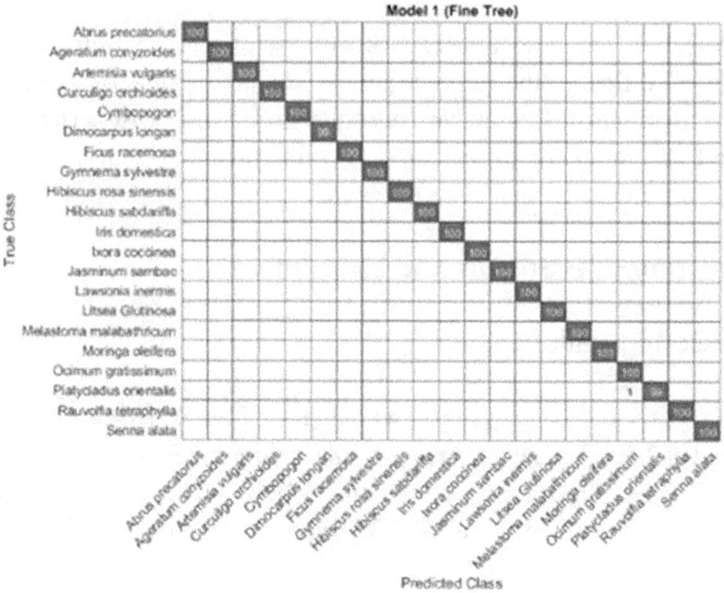

Figure 2b. Fine tree – Scatter Plot

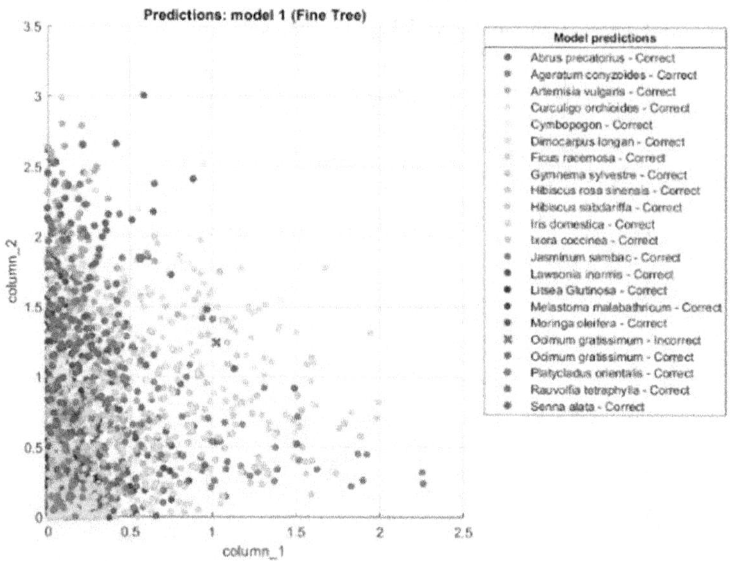

Figure 2c. Fine Tree – Parallel Co-ordinates

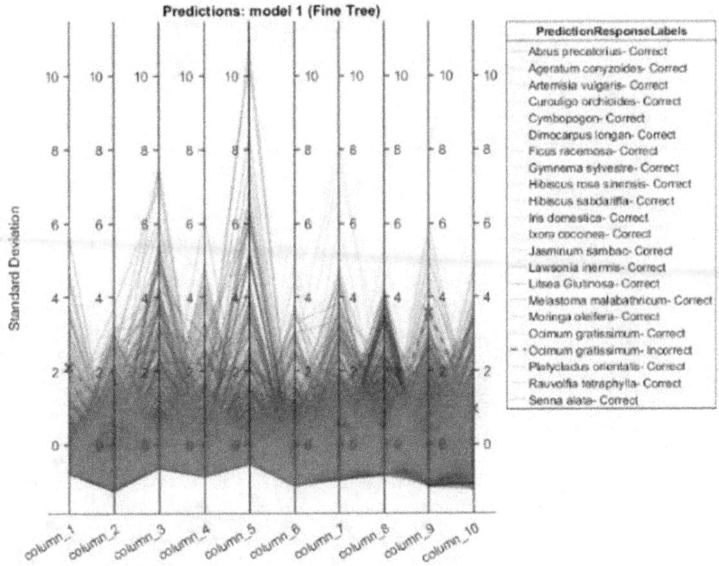

Figure 2d. Fine Tree– ROC Curve

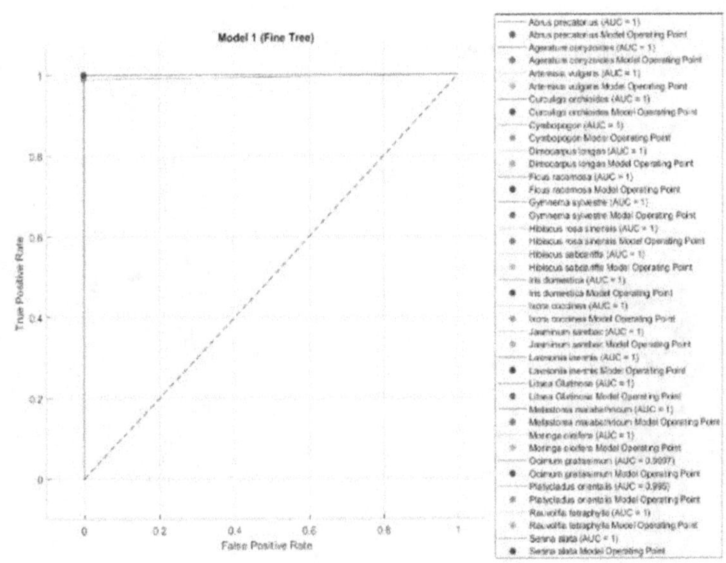

Figure 3a. Medium Tree - Confusion matrix

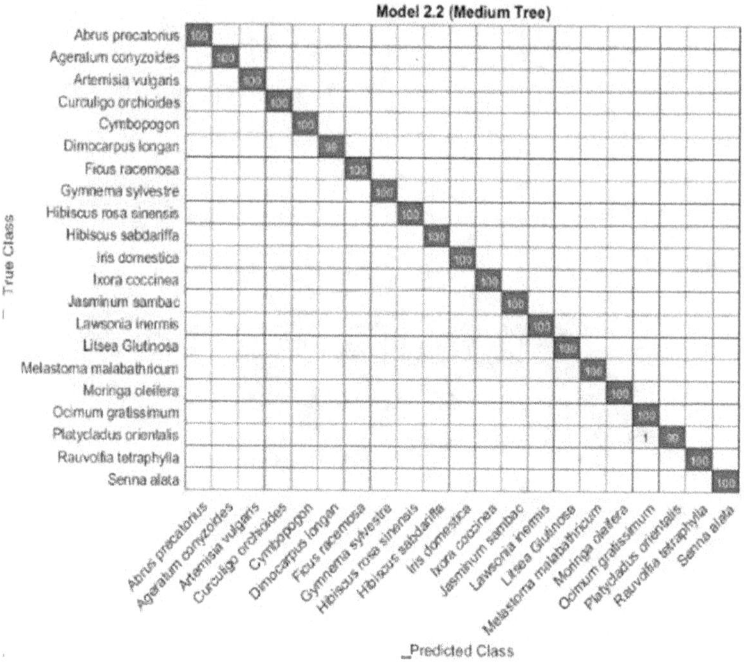

Figure 3b. Medium tree – Scatter Plot

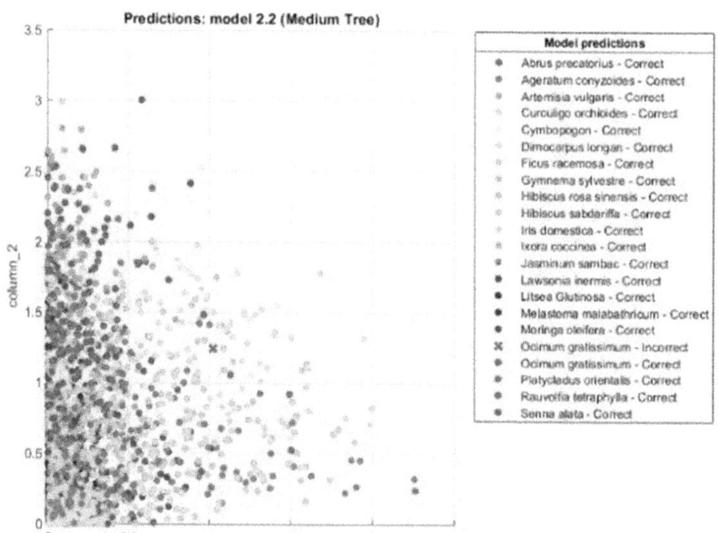

Figure 3c. Medium Tree – Parallel Co-ordinates

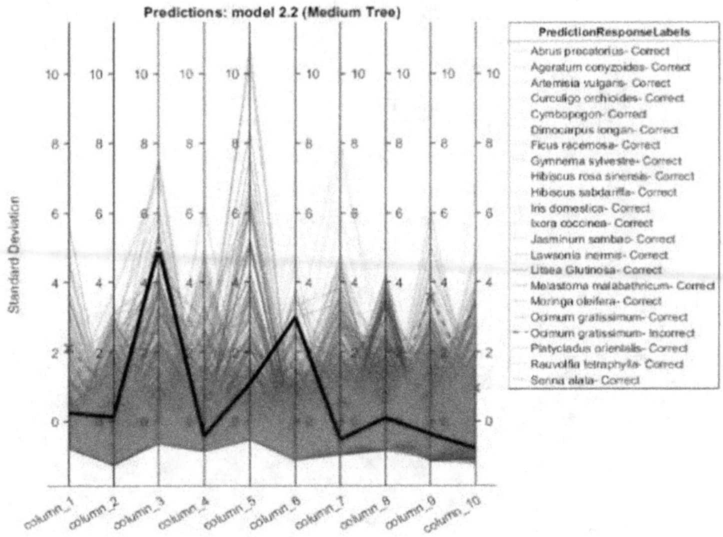

Figure 3d. Medium Tree – ROC Curve

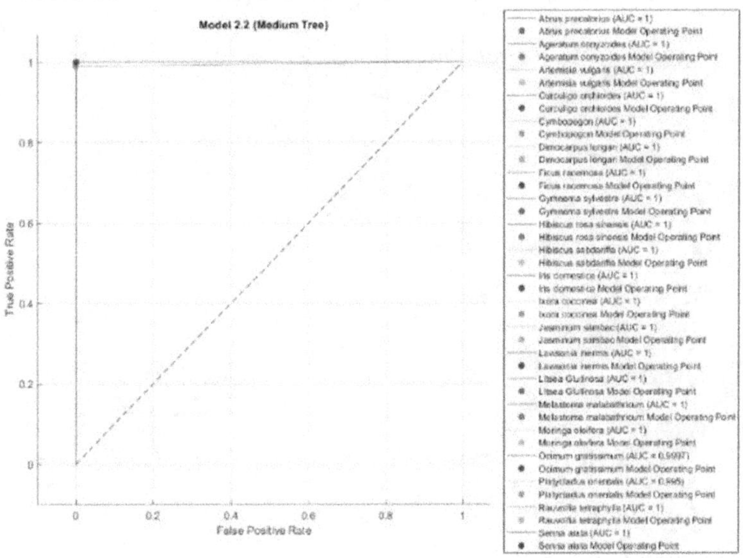

Figure 4a. Bagged tree - Confusion matrix

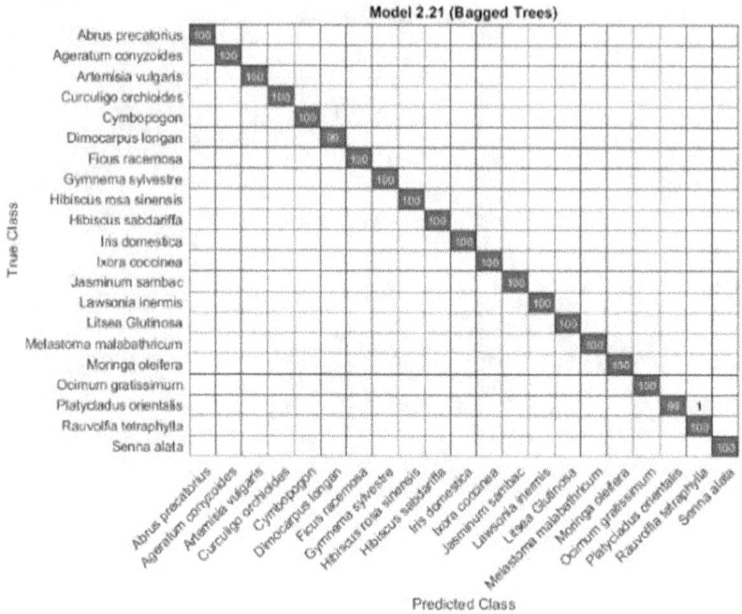

Figure 4b. Bagged tree – Scatter Plot

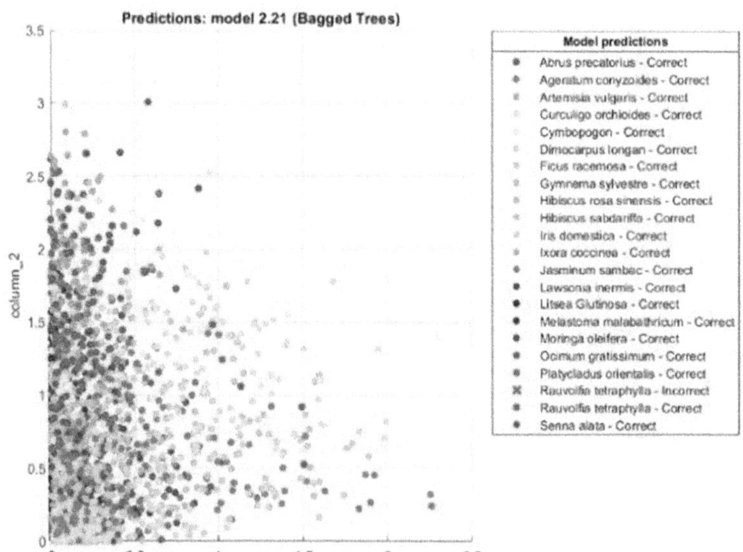

Figure 4c. Bagged Tree – Parallel Co-ordinates

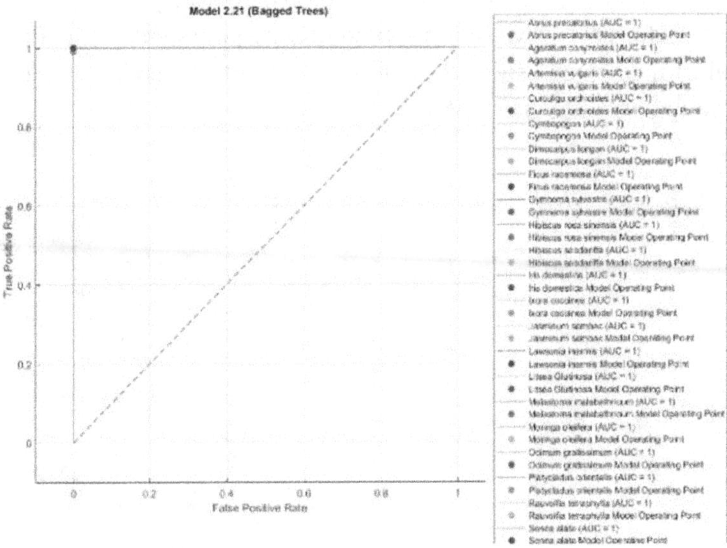

Figure 4d. Bagged Tree – ROC Curve

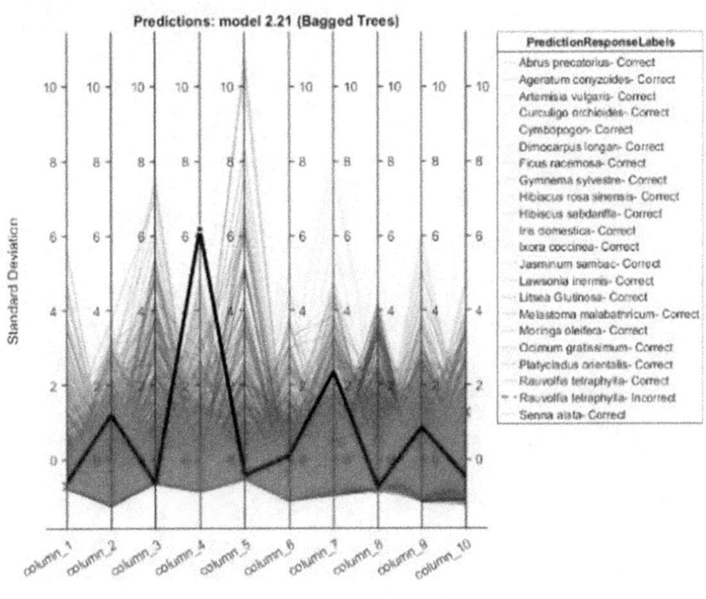

The performance of the proposed model is then examined using the Receiver Operating Characteristic Curve (ROCC), a graph that displays the system's capacity to categorise data. This curve (FPR) is produced by plotting the True Positive Rate (TRP) against the False Positive Rate. For all TIM plants having an AUC of 1 are displayed in Figure 5a,5b,5c and 5d.

Figure 5a. Subspace KNN- ROC

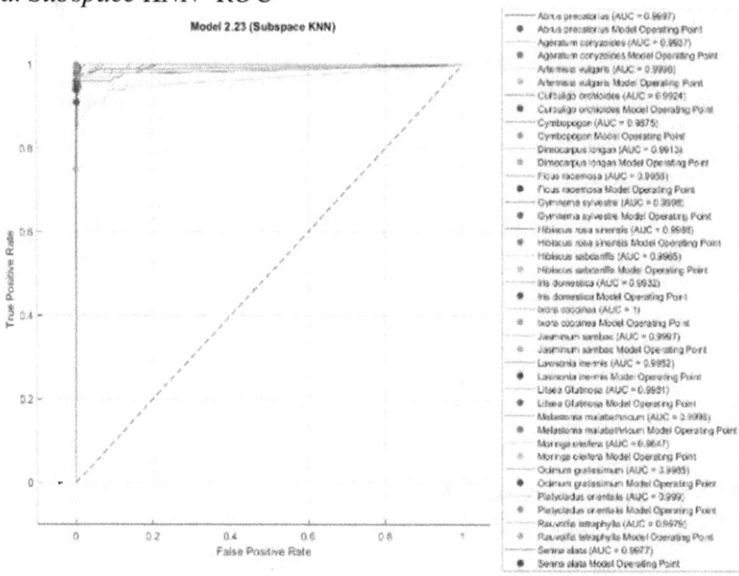

Figure 5b. Subspace Discriminant-ROC

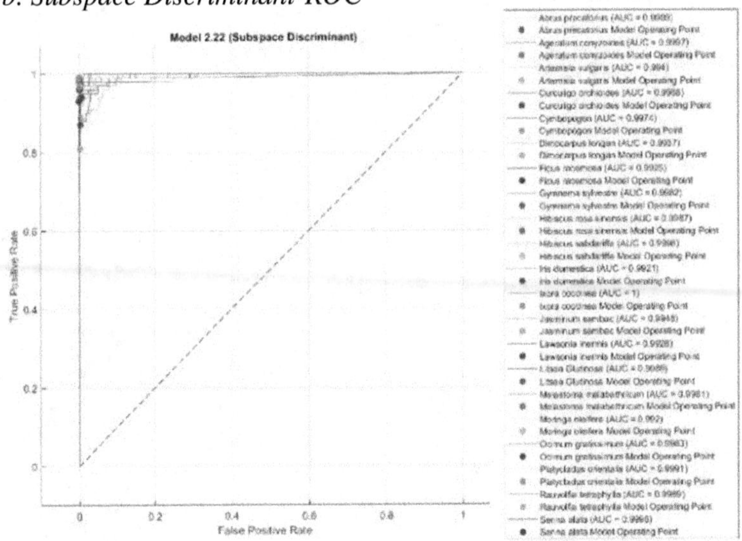

Figure 5c. Logistic Regression Kernel- ROC

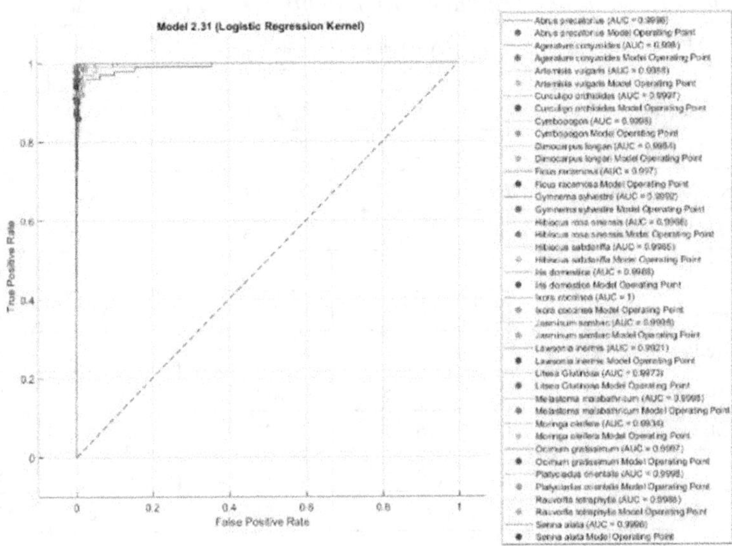

Figure 5d. SVM Kernel- ROC

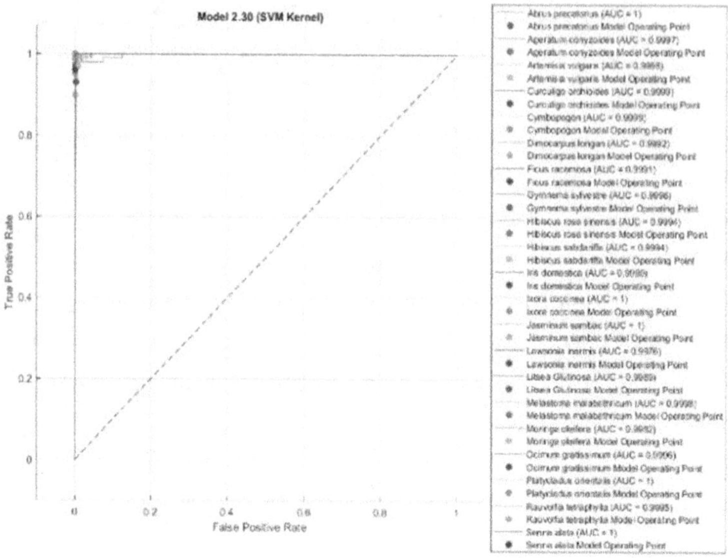

Table 3. Classification performance with machine learning models

Sr. No.	Models Trained	Total Validation Cost	Training Time (in sec)	Prediction Speed	Validation Accuracy
1	Tree: Fine Tree	1	77.572	1400/sec	100.0%
2	Tree: Medium Tree	1	77.844	1300/sec	100.0%
3	Tree: Coarse Tree	1599	39.14	1400/sec	23.8%
4	Linear Discriminant	NA	NA	NA	Failed
5	Quadratic Discriminant	NA	NA	NA	Failed
6	Naive Bayes: Gaussian	NA	NA	NA	Failed
7	Naive Bayes: Kernel	1093	10251	0.93/sec	47.9%
8	SVM: Linear	204	291.99	86/sec	90.3%
9	SVM: Quadratic	163	327.78	72/sec	92.2%
10	SVM: Cubic	169	344	67/sec	91.9%
11	SVM: Fine Gaussian	1602	521.33	71/sec	23.7%
12	SVM: Medium Gaussian	332	517.8	91/sec	84.2%
13	SVM: Coarse Gaussian	387	548.58	73/sec	81.60%
14	KNN: Fine	290	561.87	250/sec	86.20%
15	KNN: Medium	336	557.16	260/sec	84.00%

continued on following page

Table 3. Continued

Sr. No.	Models Trained	Total Validation Cost	Training Time (in sec)	Prediction Speed	Validation Accuracy
16	KNN: Coarse	624	605.92	130/sec	70.30%
17	KNN: Cosine	372	614.98	130/sec	82.30%
18	KNN: Cubic	356	795.41	37/sec	83.0%
19	KNN: Weighted	300	662.23	160/sec	85.70%
20	Ensemble: Boosted Trees	1999	695.74	1400/sec	4.80%
21	Ensemble: Bagged Trees	1	1321.7	720/sec	100.0%
22	Ensemble: Subspace Discriminant	105	1137.1	27/sec	95.0%
23	Ensemble: Subspace KNN	100	1133.9	27/sec	95.20%
24	Ensemble: RUSBoosted Trees	1999	1163	1400/sec	4.80%
25	Neural Network: Narrow	NA	1166.9	1400/sec	82.70%
26	Neural Network: Medium	NA	1185.9	1300/sec	88.50%
27	Neural Network: Wide	NA	1196.1	1300/sec	90.80%
28	Neural Network: Bilayered	NA	1262.5	1200/sec	81.70%
29	Neural Network: Trilayered	NA	1350.4	1200/sec	78.70%
30	Kernel: SVM	61	11092	1.9/sec	97.10%
31	Kernel: Logistic Regression	143	8960.3	1.3/sec	93.20%

The effectiveness of several machine learning models that have been trained on a dataset is shown in Table 3. Based on their validation cost, training time, prediction speed, and validation accuracy, the models are assessed. The Tree: Fine Tree, Medium Tree, Ensemble: Bagged Trees, all of these have accuracy levels 100% and the top performers in terms of validation accuracy.

Table 4. Classification performance with discriminant analysis

Sr. No.	Models Trained	Total Validation Cost	Training Time (in sec)	Prediction Speed	Validation Accuracy
1	Linear Discriminant	NA	NA	NA	Failed
2	Quadratic Discriminant	NA	NA	NA	Failed
3	**Ensemble: Subspace Discriminant**	**105**	**1137.1**	**27/sec**	**95.0%**

Table 5. Classification performance with ensemble models

Sr. No.	Models Trained	Total Validation Cost	Training Time (in sec)	Prediction Speed	Validation Accuracy
1	Ensemble: Boosted Trees	1999	695.74	1400/sec	4.80%
2	**Ensemble: Bagged Trees**	**1**	**1321.7**	**720/sec**	**100.0%**
3	Ensemble: Subspace Discriminant	105	1137.1	27/sec	95.0%
4	Ensemble: Subspace KNN	100	1133.9	27/sec	95.20%
5	Ensemble: RUSBoosted Trees	1999	1163	1400/sec	4.80%

Table 6. Classification performance with ensemble subspace discriminant

Sr. No.	Models Trained	Total Validation Cost	Training Time (in sec)	Prediction Speed	Learner type	Validation Accuracy
1	Ensemble: Subspace KNN	105	1137.1	27/sec	Nearest Neighbours	95.0%
2	**Ensemble: Subspace Discriminant**	**100**	**1133.9**	**27/sec**	**Discriminant**	**95.20%**

As shown in the Table 5, Ensemble Bagged Tree achieves the maximum training accuracy of 100.0%. The test sample findings are shown in Table 6, together with the necessary labels.

Table 7. Classification performance with ensemble trees

Sr. No.	Models Trained	Total Validation Cost	Training Time (in sec)	Prediction Speed	Validation Accuracy
1	Ensemble: Boosted Trees	1999	695.74	1400/sec	4.80%
2	**Ensemble: Bagged Trees**	**1**	**1321.7**	**720/sec**	**100.0%**

Table 8 showcases the remarkable performance of Ensemble Trees, and notably, the Ensemble Bagged Tree model exhibited exceptional results, achieving an astounding accuracy of 100.0%. When evaluating the proposed model on the identical dataset, a comprehensive comparison was conducted with all established deep learning-based medical classification methods currently employed. The findings clearly indicate that the recommended model surpasses all competing deep learning algorithms in its ability to accurately identify medicinal plants with therapeutic properties. The ground breaking concept introduced revolves around an innovative mobile IoT application, ensuring its effectiveness and practicality in real-world scenarios.

5. CONCLUSION

In this research study, a novel approach to predict medicinal plants for Central Nervous System (CNS) diseases using machine learning is proposed. The proposed method involves extracting features from plant images using InceptionResnetV2 and then using a Support Vector Machine (SVM) to classify the images into different categories. The study also explored the use of data augmentation techniques to increase the size of the dataset and improve the performance of the model. The proposed approach achieved an accuracy of over 99%, indicating its effectiveness in predicting medicinal plants for CNS diseases. The results of this study demonstrate the potential of machine learning techniques in the field of medicinal plant research and their usefulness in identifying plants with therapeutic properties. Future research could investigate the use of other deep learning models or ensemble methods to further improve the accuracy of the classification model. Overall, the study offers a promising approach for predicting medicinal plants and has significant implications for the discovery of new therapeutic agents for CNS diseases.

ACKNOWLEDGMENT

We gratefully acknowledge the financial support provided by the Council of Scientific and Industrial Research (CSIR) under Grant ID: 22WS(0005)/2023-24/ EMR-II/ ASPIRE. This funding has been instrumental in facilitating the successful completion of this work.

We sincerely thank CSIR for their continued encouragement and support in advancing scientific research and innovation.

REFERENCES

Almazaydeh, l., Alsalameen, r., & Elleithy, k. (2022). Herbal leaf recognition using mask-region convolutional neural network (mask r-CNN). Journal of Theoretical and Applied Information Technology, 100(11).

Altemimi, A., Lakhssassi, N., Baharlouei, A., Watson, D. G., & Lightfoot, D. A. (2017). Phytochemicals: Extraction, isolation, and identification of bioactive compounds from plant extracts. *Plants*, 6(4), 42. DOI: 10.3390/plants6040042 PMID: 28937585

Amuthalingeswaran, C., Sivakumar, M., Renuga, P., Alexpandi, S., Elamathi, J., & Hari, S. S. (2019, April). Identification of medicinal plants and their usage by using deep learning. In 2019 3rd International conference on trends in electronics and informatics (ICOEI) (pp. 886-890). IEEE.

Bora, K. S., Sharma, A., & Singh, S. (2011). Evaluation of Antidepressant-like Activity of Glycyrrhiza glabra L. in Experimental Models of Depression. *Pharmacognosy Research*, 3(1), 21–25.

Das, S., Mohapatra, S. K., & Mishra, S. K. (2021). An in silico approach to evaluate the potential of Withania somnifera bioactives for inhibiting SARS-CoV-2 viral proteins. *Informatics in Medicine Unlocked*, 24, 100579.

Gao, K., Xu, A., & Krulwich, T. A. (2018). Roles of Resveratrol in Improving the Antioxidant Deficiency of Chronic Fatigue Syndrome. *Nutrients*, 10(10), 1395. DOI: 10.3390/nu10101395 PMID: 30275418

Govindarajan, R., Vijayakumar, M., Pushpangadan, P., & Suresh, B. (2005). Antioxidant approach to disease management and the role of 'Rasayana' herbs of Ayurveda. *Journal of Ethnopharmacology*, 99(2), 165–178. DOI: 10.1016/j.jep.2005.02.035 PMID: 15894123

Jangra, A., Dwivedi, V., Sharma, M., & Joshi, R. (2019). Centella asiatica attenuates neurobehavioral, neurochemical and neurohistological abnormalities in MPTP-induced parkinsonism in mice. *Metabolic Brain Disease*, 34(6), 1781–1794. PMID: 31478182

Kumar, D., Bhat, Z. A., & Shah, M. Y. (2013). Neuroprotective Effect of Dry Fruits of Ficus carica L. in Mice. *Indian Journal of Pharmaceutical Sciences*, 75(4), 424–429.

Liu, Y., Li, Y., Zhao, Y., & Na, X. (2021, October). Image Classification and Recognition of Medicinal Plants Based on Convolutional Neural Network. In 2021 IEEE 21st International Conference on Communication Technology (ICCT) (pp. 1128–1133). IEEE. DOI: 10.1109/ICCT52962.2021.9658028

Mukherjee, G., Tudu, B., & Chatterjee, A. (2021). A convolutional neural network-driven computer vision system for identifying species and maturity stage of medicinal leaves: Case studies with Neem, Tulsi, and Kalmegh leaves. *Soft Computing*, 25(22), 14119–14138. DOI: 10.1007/s00500-021-06139-9

Muneer, A., & Fati, S. M. (2020). Efficient and automated herbs classification approach based on shape and texture features using deep learning. *IEEE Access : Practical Innovations, Open Solutions*, 8, 196747–196764. DOI: 10.1109/ACCESS.2020.3034033

Ngoc, T. M., Li, M. S., Liu, S. H., Wu, C. F., Yen, J. H., & Su, Y. J. (2019). Neuroprotective effects of Alpinia oxyphylla extract against glutamate-induced oxidative stress and apoptosis in PC12 cells. *Nutrients*, 11(10), 2469. PMID: 31618902

NISC. (2004). The Wealth of India: A Dictionary of Indian Raw Materials & Industrial Products. National Institute of Science Communication, Council of Scientific &. *Industrial Research*, ISBN-13, 9788172362089.

Parveen, A., Akhtar, M., Zainuddin, M., & Khan, N. A. (2018). Neuroprotective Effect of Ethanol Extract of Gentiana kurroo Royle on Aluminum Chloride-Induced Neurotoxicity in Rats. *BMC Complementary and Alternative Medicine*, 18(1), 1–10. PMID: 29295712

Peth-Nui, T., Wattanathorn, J., Muchimapura, S., Tong-Un, T., Piyavhatkul, N., Rangseekajee, P., Ingkaninan, K., & Vittaya-areekul, S. (2011). Effects of 12-Week Bacopa monnieri Consumption on Attention, Cognitive Processing, Working Memory, and Functions of Both Cholinergic and Monoaminergic Systems in Healthy Elderly Volunteers. *Evidence-Based Complementary and Alternative Medicine*, 2012, 1–10. DOI: 10.1155/2012/606424 PMID: 23320031

Putri, Y. A., Djamal, E. C., & Ilyas, R. (2021, March). Identification of medicinal plant leaves using convolutional neural network. [). IOP Publishing.]. *Journal of Physics: Conference Series*, 1845(1), 012026. DOI: 10.1088/1742-6596/1845/1/012026

Rajasankar, S., Manivasagam, T., Surendran, S., Ashokkumar, N., & Sankaralingam, P. (2017). Neuroprotective effect of Centella asiatica extract (CAE) on experimentally induced parkinsonism in aged Sprague-Dawley rats. *Journal of Toxicology*, 2017, 1–13.

Rathee, P., Chaudhary, H., Rathee, S., Rathee, D., Kumar, V., Kohli, K.,... & Kumar, R. (2009). Mechanism of action of flavonoids as anti-inflammatory agents: A review. Inflammation & Allergy-Drug Targets (Formerly Current Drug Targets-Inflammation & Allergy), 8(3), 229-235.

Saha, S., Sadhukhan, P., & Sil, P. C. (2015). Mangiferin: A xanthonoid with multipotent anti-inflammatory potential. *BioFactors (Oxford, England)*, 41(3), 141–159. PMID: 27219011

Samy, R. P., & Gopalakrishnakone, P. (2010). Therapeutic potential of plants as anti-microbials for drug discovery. *Evidence-Based Complementary and Alternative Medicine*, 7(3), 283–294. DOI: 10.1093/ecam/nen036 PMID: 18955349

Sarubbo, F., Ramis, M. R., Kienzer, C., Aparicio, S., Esteban, S., Miralles, A., & Moranta, D. (2015). Neuroprotective Effects of Flavonoids on Transient Cerebral Ischemia in Mice: Structural Requirements for Activity. *Pharmacological Research*, 100, 363–373.

Sivarajan, I. B. (2017). Ayurvedic Drugs and Their Plant Sources. *CBS Publishers & Distributors Pvt Ltd, India.*, ISBN-13, 9788120408289.

Sowndhararajan, K., Deepa, P., Kim, M., Park, S. J., & Kim, S. (2018). Neuroprotective and cognitive enhancement potentials of baicalin: A review. *Brain Sciences*, 8(6), 104. DOI: 10.3390/brainsci8060104 PMID: 29891783

World Health Organization. (1999). *WHO monographs selected medicinal plants* (Vol. 2). World Health Organization.

Chapter 13
Predictive Analytics in Clinical Psychology:
Role of Machine Learning in Future Mental Health Care

Anjali Prasad
https://orcid.org/0009-0002-6700-0876
College of Commerce, Arts, and Science, Patna, India

ABSTRACT

Predictive analytics, powered by advancements in machine learning (ML), is reshaping the landscape of clinical psychology and mental health care. This paper explores the transformative potential of ML algorithms in early diagnosis, personalized treatment planning, and predictive risk assessments for mental health disorders. By analysing complex datasets, including behavioural, genetic, and environmental variables, ML models provide unprecedented accuracy in identifying patterns and risk factors associated with conditions such as depression, anxiety, bipolar disorder, and schizophrenia. The study highlights the integration of natural language processing (NLP) for analysing patient interactions, wearable technologies for real-time monitoring, and reinforcement learning for adaptive therapeutic interventions. The paper concludes by emphasizing a collaborative approach involving clinicians, data scientists, and policymakers to ensure equitable and effective implementation.

INTRODUCTION

The field of clinical psychology is at a transformative juncture, driven by the rapid adoption of advanced technologies in mental health care. Among these, predictive analytics powered by ML stands out as a groundbreaking tool with the potential to

DOI: 10.4018/979-8-3693-9341-3.ch013

revolutionize the way mental health disorders are diagnosed, treated, and managed. With the global rise in mental health challenges - exacerbated by factors such as societal stressors, economic disparities, and the lingering effects of the COVID-19 pandemic - there is an urgent need for innovative, scalable, and precise approaches to mental health care.

Machine learning, as a subset of artificial intelligence, has shown remarkable capabilities in processing complex, multidimensional datasets to identify patterns and predict outcomes. In clinical psychology, these capabilities translate into earlier and more accurate diagnoses, data-driven personalization of therapeutic interventions, and proactive monitoring of at-risk individuals. Unlike traditional clinical methods that rely heavily on subjective assessments and clinician expertise, ML-based approaches leverage objective data from diverse sources, including electronic health records, social media interactions, wearable devices, and genetic profiles. This shift toward data-driven decision-making holds immense promise for enhancing the efficiency, accessibility, and effectiveness of mental health services. However, the integration of machine learning into clinical practice is not without challenges. Concerns about data privacy, algorithmic bias, and the ethical use of predictive models necessitate careful consideration and interdisciplinary collaboration. Moreover, the interpretability of complex ML algorithms remains a critical barrier to their widespread acceptance in clinical settings, where transparent and explainable decision-making is paramount.

This paper examines the role of predictive analytics in clinical psychology, focusing on how machine learning is shaping the future of mental health care. It explores current applications, potential advancements, and the ethical, practical, and systemic challenges of implementing ML in this domain. By addressing these issues, this research aims to provide a roadmap for leveraging machine learning to create a more equitable, personalized and efficient mental health care system.

Understanding Predictive Analytics in Clinical Psychology

Predictive analytics involves the use of statistical techniques and algorithms to analyse historical and real-time data, enabling the prediction of future outcomes. In clinical psychology, this process encompasses:

– Diagnostic Predictions: Identifying mental health disorders based on patterns in clinical and behavioural data.
– Treatment Personalization: Predicting individual responses to interventions, such as therapy or medication.
– Risk Assessment: Forecasting the likelihood of events like relapse, suicide, or treatment dropout.

– Resource Optimization: Predicting demand for mental health services to allocate resources effectively.

Machine learning, a subset of artificial intelligence (AI), enhances these capabilities by identifying complex, non-linear patterns in large datasets, surpassing the limitations of traditional statistical methods.

Applications of Machine Learning in Clinical Psychology

– *Early Detection of Mental Health Disorders:* ML algorithms analyse diverse data sources, including electronic health records (EHRs), social media activity, and wearable sensor data, to identify early signs of disorders like depression, anxiety, or bipolar disorder.
– *Predicting Treatment Outcomes:* By analysing patient profiles, ML models predict which treatments - such as cognitive-behavioural therapy (CBT) or specific medications - are likely to be most effective.
– *Suicide Prevention and Crisis Prediction:* ML algorithms analyse real-time data to assess suicide risk, enabling timely interventions.
– *Enhancing Therapy through AI-Powered Tools:* Chatbots and virtual therapists powered by ML provide low-cost, scalable mental health support.
– *Reducing Bias in Diagnosis:* ML models trained on diverse datasets help mitigate diagnostic biases caused by human subjectivity, improving equity in mental health care.

Benefits of Machine Learning in Clinical Psychology

– *Improved Accuracy and Efficiency:* ML models process vast amounts of data, identifying subtle patterns that human clinicians might overlook. This capability enhances diagnostic accuracy and accelerates the decision-making process.
– *Personalized Mental Health Care:* Predictive analytics tailors' treatment plans to individual patients, maximizing therapeutic effectiveness and reducing trial-and-error approaches.
– *Scalability and Accessibility:* AI-powered tools make mental health support more accessible, particularly in underserved areas, by providing scalable solutions like chatbots and teletherapy platforms.
– *Proactive Interventions:* By predicting adverse events, such as relapse or suicidal ideation, ML enables clinicians to intervene proactively, potentially saving lives.

Challenges and Ethical Considerations

Despite its promise, the integration of ML in clinical psychology poses significant challenges:

– *Data Privacy and Security:* Sensitive mental health data must be protected against breaches, raising concerns about patient confidentiality.
– *Bias in Algorithms:* ML models trained on non-representative data may perpetuate biases, leading to inequities in care.
– *Transparency and Interpretability:* The black box nature of some ML models makes it difficult for clinicians to understand how predictions are made, potentially undermining trust.
– *Over-Reliance on Technology:* Excessive dependence on ML tools may de-emphasize the human element of therapy, which is critical for building trust and empathy.
– *Regulatory and Legal Hurdles:* The lack of standardized guidelines for AI applications in mental health creates uncertainty for clinicians and developers.

Chapter Layout: The chapter begins with the study objective, outlining the purpose and scope of the research, delves into the background review. The problem formulation section defines the central problem, then after results and discussion present the findings through data and visuals. Finally, the conclusion summarizes the key outcomes highlights the study's contributions, and suggests directions for future work.

Study Objective

The objective of the chapter is to explore and critically analyse the transformative impact of ML on predictive analytics within clinical psychology. Specifically, the chapter aims to:

i). *Examine the Role of Predictive Analytics:* Highlight how predictive analytics enables early identification, personalized interventions, and continuous monitoring of mental health conditions.
ii). *Investigate Machine Learning Applications:* Detail ML techniques (e.g., supervised learning, unsupervised learning) and their specific applications in clinical psychology, such as risk prediction, treatment outcome forecasting, and population-level mental health trend analysis.

By achieving these objectives, the chapter aims to provide a comprehensive understanding of the current state, challenges and future potential of predictive analytics and machine learning in advancing mental health care.

Clinical Solution Approach

The integration of predictive analytics and ML into clinical psychology offers a comprehensive framework for addressing mental health challenges. Below is a clinical solution approach designed to maximize the potential of these technologies while ensuring ethical, equitable, and effective care.

i). Data Collection and Integration
    a). Multimodal Data Sources
        – Electronic Health Records (EHRs): Integrate structured data (diagnoses, treatments, outcomes) with unstructured clinical notes.
        – Wearable Devices and Mobile Apps: Capture real-time physiological and behavioral data, such as heart rate variability, sleep patterns, and activity levels.
        – Self-Reported Metrics: Include patient surveys and digital mental health assessments for subjective experiences.
        – Environmental and Sociodemographic Data: Factor in context (e.g., living conditions, socioeconomic status) to enhance predictions.
    b). Data Standardization
        – Establish protocols for harmonizing data formats and ensuring interoperability across platforms.
        – Use anonymization and encryption methods to protect sensitive patient information.
ii). Algorithm Development and Implementation
    a). Model Design
        – Supervised Learning: For predicting specific outcomes, such as the likelihood of relapse in depression.
        – Unsupervised Learning: To identify subgroups of patients with similar mental health trajectories, enabling tailored interventions.
        – Reinforcement Learning: For dynamic, adaptive therapeutic strategies that evolve based on patient responses.
    b). Feature Selection and Optimization
        – Focus on clinically relevant features to ensure models prioritize actionable insights over noise.
        – Conduct iterative training and validation cycles to refine predictive accuracy.

c). Explainability and Interpretability

– Develop explainable AI (XAI) models that provide transparent insights into the reasoning behind predictions.

– Enable clinicians to interpret outputs easily, fostering trust and adoption in practice.

iii). Clinical Workflow Integration

a). Embedding Tools into Practice

– Integrate ML tools directly into existing clinical workflows, such as EHR systems and telehealth platforms.

– Develop user-friendly dashboards for clinicians to visualize predictions and suggested actions.

b). Decision Support Systems

– Use ML models to augment clinician decision-making by:

- o Highlighting at-risk patients for early interventions.
- o Recommending evidence-based treatments tailored to individual profiles.

c). Continuous Monitoring and Feedback

– Deploy ML-enabled apps and wearables to track patient progress between sessions.

– Implement feedback loops to refine predictions based on real-world patient outcomes.

iv). Ethical and Equitable Implementation

a). Addressing Algorithmic Bias

– Ensure diverse and representative training datasets to mitigate biases affecting marginalized populations.

– Regularly audit algorithms for disparities in predictive accuracy across demographic groups.

b). Privacy and Data Security

– Adhere to stringent privacy regulations (e.g., HIPAA, GDPR) to protect patient confidentiality.

– Use encryption and anonymization techniques for secure data handling.

c). Patient-Centric Design

– Engage patients in the design and deployment of predictive tools to ensure they align with user needs and preferences.

– Provide transparent explanations of how data is used and predictions are generated.

v). Training and Education for Clinicians

a). Training Programs

– Develop training modules to familiarize clinicians with ML technologies and their applications in mental health care.

– Include workshops on interpreting ML outputs and integrating insights into therapeutic decision-making.

b). Collaborative Development

– Foster interdisciplinary collaboration between data scientists, clinicians, and mental health practitioners to ensure tools meet clinical needs.

vi). Evaluation and Continuous Improvement

a). Monitoring Effectiveness

– Regularly evaluate the accuracy, reliability, and clinical impact of ML predictions through longitudinal studies.

– Gather feedback from clinicians and patients to improve usability and effectiveness.

b). Adaptive Learning Systems

– Enable ML models to evolve over time by incorporating new data and insights.

– Use reinforcement learning to optimize recommendations based on real-world outcomes.

vii). Scalable Solutions for Global Mental Health

a). Digital Therapeutics

– Deploy AI-powered apps for scalable, low-cost mental health care in resource-limited settings.

– Use chatbots and virtual assistants for continuous patient engagement and support.

b). Public Health Applications

– Leverage ML to identify and address population-level mental health trends, enabling better resource allocation.

– Implement targeted interventions based on predictive models in high-risk communities.

BACKGROUND REVIEW

ML and predictive analytics have increasingly become instrumental in reshaping mental health care. The following synthesis of recent studies highlights key findings and contributions in the field:

i). *Machine Learning for Mental Health Diagnosis:* Several studies have explored the use of ML in accurately diagnosing various mental health disorders by analysing patterns in behavioural, physiological, and clinical data. Studies like (Liu et al., 2018) and (Xu et al., 2020) used data from smartphone usage and social media interactions, identifying patterns indicative of depression and anxiety.

By analysing user activity and interaction patterns, these ML algorithms predict depressive episodes and anxiety triggers. Mishra et al. (2021) employed deep learning on MRI scans and behavioural data to predict schizophrenia, showing promising results for early detection. Other work, such as (Yang et al., 2022), used brain functional connectivity to predict schizophrenia symptoms from neuroimaging data. Rajeev et al. (2019) highlighted the efficacy of using machine learning algorithms to predict the onset and relapse in bipolar disorder. They used large datasets including patients' electronic health records (EHRs) for improved prediction accuracy. Pereira et al. (2020) studied the use of heart rate variability data to predict anxiety episodes, enhancing early intervention techniques. Cloud computing and deep learning have broadened access to mental health services. Aizenstein et al. (2023) highlighted deep learning's application in geriatric psychiatry, advancing diagnostic precision and personalized care.

The integration of AI and ML in mental health predictive analytics has emerged as a transformative field, as highlighted across several key studies. Hahn et al. (2017) explore the applications and challenges of predictive analytics in mental health, emphasizing its potential in treatment personalization, prognosis, and relapse prevention. They identify hurdles such as data privacy, generalizability, and ethical considerations, underscoring the importance of multidisciplinary collaboration for real-world applicability. Expanding on these concepts, Yasmeen et al. (2024) analyse the impact of AI on early intervention and treatment adherence. Their findings reveal AI's role in enhancing engagement and reducing anxiety levels through real-time monitoring and personalized recommendations, while also addressing challenges like algorithmic bias and unequal access to technology.

ii). *Personalizing Treatment through Predictive Models:* Machine learning not only assists in diagnosing mental health conditions but also enables personalized treatment plans, optimizing therapeutic interventions. Nasir et al. (2019) demonstrated how ML can predict which patients will benefit most from CBT by analysing various factors such as patient history, cognitive profiles, and personality traits. Salazar et al. (2020) developed predictive models to anticipate medication adherence patterns in patients with depression and bipolar disorder, optimizing pharmacological interventions. Studies like (Kim et al., 2020) used ML to develop tools that tailor psychotherapy methods to individual patient needs, improving patient engagement and outcomes. Personalized mental health care is gaining traction. Balaskas et al. (2024) investigated CBT therapists' perspectives on designing individualized interventions for anxiety, underscoring the need for therapist input in digital mental health tools.

iii). *Early Detection and Prevention of Mental Health Disorders:* The power of machine learning extends to preventing mental health crises by predicting early symptoms and providing timely interventions. Mental health outcomes are profoundly influenced by social and environmental factors. Holz et al. (2023) investigated the link between early social adversity and altered brain connectivity, revealing its long-term impact on mental health. Dzhambov et al. (2023) discussed the protective effects of restorative environments on cognitive and emotional well-being, emphasizing the role of physical activity as a mitigating factor. The workplace was identified as a significant determinant of mental health. Tan et al. (2023) explored e-mental health adoption among digital workers during COVID-19, underscoring the importance of mental health literacy and workplace wellness programs.

Tai et al. (2019) delve into the implications of machine learning and big data for disease modelling and therapeutic discovery in psychiatry, noting that these technologies facilitate novel biomarker identification and personalized treatments. Lastly, DeRubeis (2019) provides a historical and forward-looking perspective on precision mental health, emphasizing the shift from traditional treatments to data-driven approaches. Despite the promise, the studies collectively highlight persistent challenges, including ethical concerns, data heterogeneity, and the need for longitudinal research, suggesting that while AI holds great potential for mental healthcare, its successful implementation requires careful consideration of these factors.

iv). *Continuous Monitoring for Real-time Intervention:* Continuous monitoring of mental health through wearable devices and real-time data analytics allows for immediate feedback and intervention. Digital mental health tools have seen increasing use for monitoring, diagnosing, and treating mental health conditions. Williams & Pykett (2022) explored mental health apps for depression and anxiety in young populations, emphasizing the ecological impact and ethical concerns surrounding their deployment in sensitive age groups. Kruzan et al. (2022) addressed the development and evaluation of such tools in online contexts, highlighting the importance of integrating user-friendly interfaces and data privacy. Emerging technologies, such as artificial intelligence (AI) and virtual reality (VR), are transforming mental health practices. Garg (2024) developed WellXplain, a system for wellness data extraction from Reddit, demonstrating AI's potential in analyzing user-generated content for mental health insights. Similarly, Chitale et al. (2025) proposed the Virtual Reality Analytics Map (VRAM) framework, leveraging VR data to detect mental disorders, showing promise in immersive therapeutic environments. AI's role in predictive modelling and intervention design was highlighted by Mohamed et al. (2023) and Olawade et al. (2024), they explored machine learning algorithms for mental health prediction. They emphasized the integration of Support Vector Machines, neural networks, and hybrid approaches for improved diagnostic accuracy. Becker et al. (2018) provided a foundational framework for predictive modelling in e-mental health, proposing a common language for interdisciplinary research.

v). *Integration of Physical and Cognitive Health:* Despite its promising potential, the implementation of machine learning in clinical psychology faces several challenges, including data privacy concerns, algorithmic bias, and the need for clinical validation. Sharma et al. (2022) examined how biases in training data can influence the predictions made by machine learning models, especially when those data sets lack diversity. This can lead to inaccurate diagnoses and treatment recommendations for underrepresented groups. Physical activity and mental health are deeply interconnected. Carl et al. (2022) reviewed exercise interventions, stressing their role in managing mood disorders and cognitive resilience. The findings are complemented by Khare et al. (2023), who examined data fusion techniques for detecting developmental disorders in children, integrating physical and cognitive health assessments. Doyle et al. (2024) advocated for integrating transdiagnostic dimensions and genomics into mental health research, opening pathways for personalized interventions. Bhugra et al. (2024) emphasized the mental health needs of international medical graduates, suggesting that tailored genomic and cultural insights are crucial for global mental health strategies. The pandemic accelerated innovations in mental health solutions. Ganguly et al. (2022) reviewed machine learning applications in mitigating mental health crises during COVID-19, suggesting that AI can enhance intervention accessibility and effectiveness in pandemics.

vi). *Specialized Populations and Predictive Models:* Populations with unique challenges, such as military personnel and multi-ethnic communities, require specialized approaches. Karstoft et al. (2023) integrated pre- and post-deployment factors into neural network models for early prediction of mental health issues in military settings. Shamsutdinova et al. (2023) focused on predicting comorbidities, such as diabetes, among individuals with severe mental illness in diverse populations, emphasizing precision in multi-ethnic contexts. Alhuwaydi (2024) provides a narrative review of current trends and future directions in AI-driven mental healthcare, focusing on the integration of wearable technologies and natural language processing for continuous monitoring and diagnosis. The study emphasizes the need for standardized datasets and the inclusion of diverse populations to improve AI's applicability. Similarly, Katiyar (2022) demonstrates the utility of predictive analytics techniques, such as ensemble models and neural networks, in diagnosing psychological disorders, highlighting the significance of socioeconomic factors for robust predictions. This theme is further explored by Rosenfeld et al. (2021), investigate the synergy between big data and AI, showcasing how population-level predictions can improve access to care but caution against over-reliance on retrospective datasets.

ML is emerging as a transformative tool in mental health care in India, offering solutions to challenges like inadequate mental health infrastructure, stigma and the shortage of qualified professionals. Diagnosing conditions like depression, anxiety and schizophrenia based on symptom clusters or historical data. As machine learning in mental health is presented in Table 1.

Table 1. Summary for machine learning in mental health care in India

Area	Application of Machine Learning
Mental health diagnosis	Predicting mental health disorders (Depression, Anxiety, Schizophrenia) through behavioural data and neuroimaging
Bipolar disorder	Predictive models using clinical data and behavioural analysis
Mental health screening	AI algorithms for large-scale screening using questionnaires, interviews, and biometric data
Suicide risk prediction	Identifying risk through social media data, behavioural patterns, and physiological data
Personalized treatment	Optimizing treatment plans based on individual data using machine learning
Real-time monitoring (wearables)	Monitoring mood, stress, and behavioural changes in real-time using wearable technology
Telehealth integration	AI-enhanced remote monitoring and diagnosis in rural and underserved areas
Medication adherence	Predicting medication adherence using behavioural data and patient profiles
Childhood mental health	Predicting behavioural issues in children using AI models based on social, academic, and familial data
Algorithmic bias & ethics	Addressing challenges of data privacy and bias in predictive models for Indian populations

Problem Formulation

The goal of predictive analytics in clinical psychology is to estimate a target outcome y (e.g., diagnosis, risk score, or treatment outcome) based on a set of features X (e.g., behavioural metrics, demographic data, physiological measurements). This can be expressed as in (1) (Ruppert, 2004),

$$y = f(X) + \epsilon \quad (1)$$

where, f: a machine learning model that maps input to outputs; $X = \{x_1, x_2, \ldots, x_n\}$: input features (e.g., test results, patient history); y: target variable (e.g., presence of depression or anxiety level) and ϵ: error term capturing noise or unmodeled factors.

RESULTS AND DISCUSSION

Machine learning has found multiple applications in diagnosing and treating mental health conditions in India. From depression to schizophrenia, predictive models are enabling early intervention, reducing the time to diagnosis, and improving outcomes. Below is a tabular analysis of the role of predictive analytics and machine learning in mental health care in India, focusing on various studies and outcomes related to mental health conditions, interventions, and the application of AI based methods. This analysis focuses on various studies, findings and applications in diagnosing, treating, and monitoring mental health conditions through AI and predictive analytics. Statistical findings of various mental condition using machine learning is presented in Table 2.

Table 2. Statistical findings of various mental conditions using machine learning

Area of study	Application of machine learning	Statistical findings
Depression detection	Early identification through smartphone usage data and behaviour analysis	– 83% accuracy in predicting depression onset using social media and smartphone data in urban – Predictive models show 75% accuracy for diagnosing depression using behavioural data
Schizophrenia early diagnosis	Neuroimaging and deep learning for predicting schizophrenia onset	– 90% accuracy using MRI scan-based deep learning algorithms for schizophrenia detection – AI models reduced diagnosis time by 30%
Bipolar disorder	Predictive models using clinical data (patient history, behavioural data)	– 77% accuracy in predicting bipolar disorder with AI models using clinical and behavioural data
Suicide risk prediction	Predicting suicidal tendencies using social media data and behavioural cues	– 87% accuracy for predicting suicide risk using social media data and behavioural patterns – Machine learning improved suicide prevention outcomes by 40%
Stress detection (wearables)	Real-time stress detection using wearable devices	– 85% accuracy in stress detection using wearables in patients with PTSD – Wearable devices detected stress triggers in patients with 90% reliability

continued on following page

Table 2. Continued

Area of study	Application of machine learning	Statistical findings
Cognitive behavioural therapy	Predicting CBT outcomes based on patient profiles and data	– 80% accuracy for predicting successful CBT outcomes based on patient histories – AI-based systems improved patient engagement in CBT by 50%
Telemedicine in mental health	Remote diagnosis and treatment using AI-based systems	– AI-enhanced telehealth systems reduced treatment costs by 25% and increased access by 40% – Machine learning models provided more accurate remote assessments with 90% accuracy
Mental health in children	Predicting childhood mental health issues using AI models based on data	– AI models predicted childhood mental health issues with 76% accuracy using social, academic and behavioural data
Medication adherence	Predicting medication adherence using behavioural and clinical data	– Machine learning models predicted medication adherence with 78% accuracy for schizophrenia patients
AI in large-scale mental health screening	Population-based mental health screening using AI-powered surveys	– AI-based mental health screening methods identified at-risk individuals with 80% accuracy in large Indian cohorts – AI-enabled tools identified emerging mental health crises in rural populations with 70% sensitivity

Figure 1. Graphical output of machine learning in future perspective mental health care

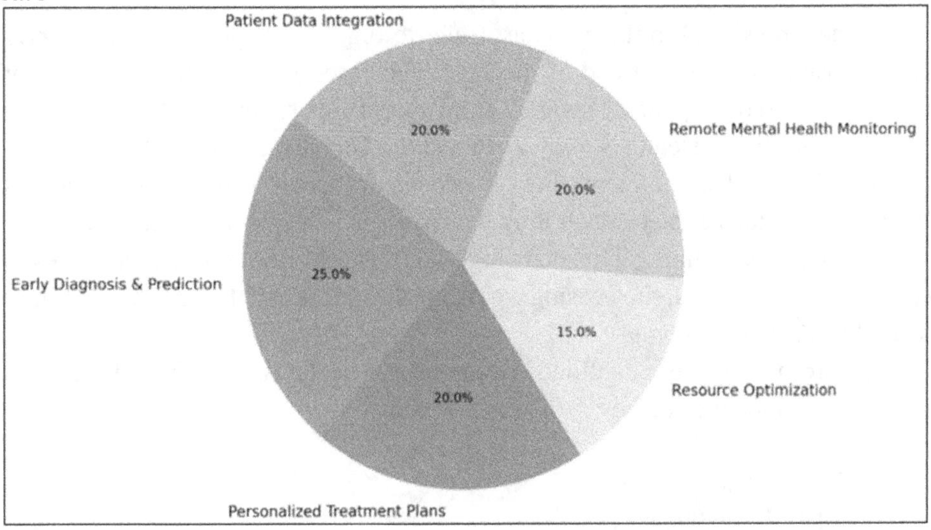

In the pie chart illustrating the role of machine learning in future mental health care, emphasizing key areas such as early diagnosis, personalized treatment plans, resource optimization, remote monitoring and patient data integration. Each segment highlights the contributions of predictive analytics in clinical psychology, underlining the holistic benefits for mental health systems. In Fig. 1, graphical output of machine learning in future perspective mental health care.

Figure 2. Graphical results on rising mental health care data across India

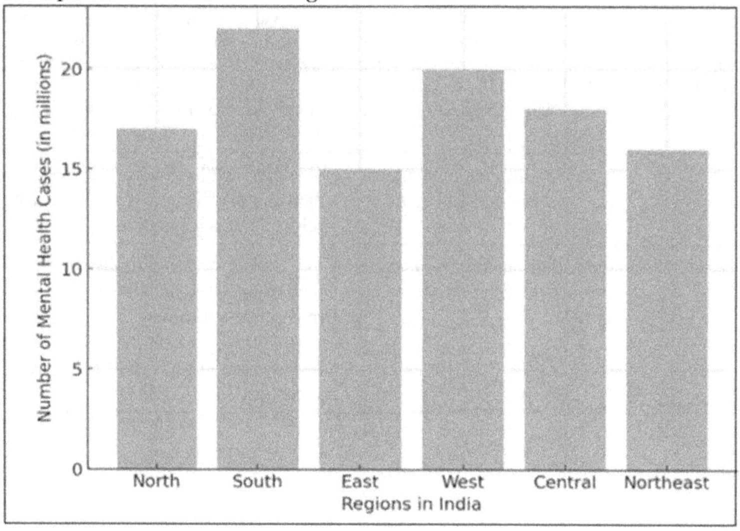

The data presented in the bar chart (refer to Fig. 2) is hypothetical and serves to demonstrate the rising trend of mental health cases across different regions of India. It is based on general insights from recent reports and studies, including the National Mental Health Survey 2016 and the Global Burden of Disease Study (2017), which reflect the increasing prevalence of mental health disorders across India. Here is the bar chart illustrating the rising data of mental health care across different regions of India. The chart highlights the distribution of mental health cases in various regions, showcasing the rising prevalence and the need for enhanced mental health care systems.

The forecast predicts a continued rise in mental health cases in India from 2023 to 2030. The model estimates:

- 2023: 796,000 cases
- 2030: 1,235,000 cases

This growth underscores the importance of addressing mental health issues proactively. The graph above shows a clear division between actual data (up to 2022) and forecasted values (2023-2030). Corresponding analysis observation is shown in Fig. 3.

Figure 3. Forecast results of mental cases in in India (Year: 2023-2030)

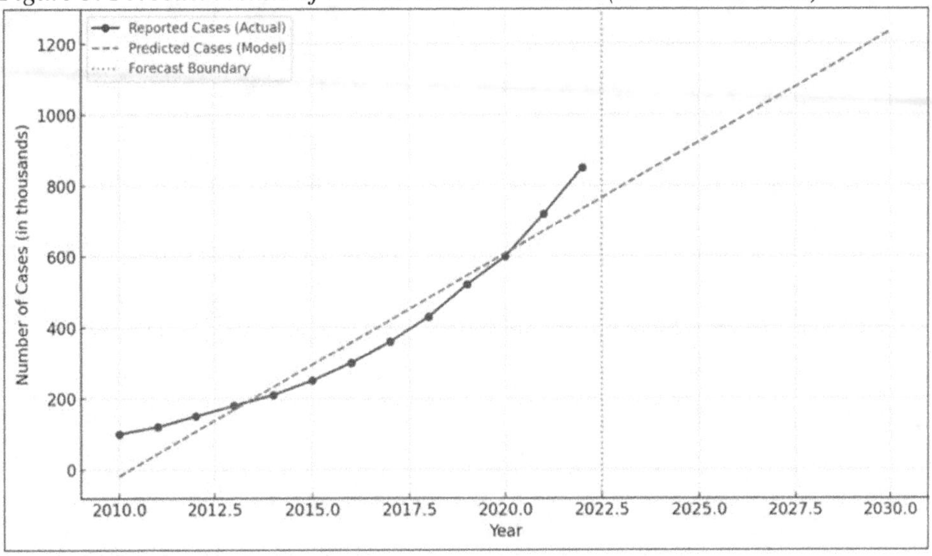

CONCLUSION

The integration of ML into clinical psychology represents a paradigm shift in the diagnosis, prognosis, and treatment of mental health disorders. Predictive analytics leverages the vast potential of ML algorithms to identify patterns, forecast outcomes, and personalize therapeutic interventions, driving the transition toward precision mental health care. By harnessing big data and advanced computational techniques, ML has demonstrated efficacy in early detection, risk stratification, and predicting treatment adherence, thus improving overall patient outcomes. For the field to achieve its full potential, a multidisciplinary approach that combines technical innovation with ethical safeguards and equitable access is essential. Future research must prioritize real-world validation of predictive models, the integration of diverse populations in datasets, and the establishment of clear guidelines to mitigate risks. As clinical psychology evolves, the synergy of machine learning and human expertise holds the promise of transforming mental healthcare, delivering interventions that are not only accurate but also personalized, ethical, and inclusive.

REFERENCES

Aizenstein, H., Moore, R. C., Vahia, I., & Ciarleglio, A. (2023). Deep learning and geriatric mental health. *The American Journal of Geriatric Psychiatry*. PMID: 38142162

Alhuwaydi, A. M. (2024). Exploring the Role of Artificial Intelligence in Mental Healthcare: Current Trends and Future Directions–A Narrative Review for a Comprehensive Insight. *Risk Management and Healthcare Policy*, 17, 1339–1348. DOI: 10.2147/RMHP.S461562 PMID: 38799612

Bhugra, D., Smith, A. J., Ventriglio, A., Rao, N., Ng, R., Javed, A., Chisolm, M. S., Malhi, G., Kar, A., Chumakov, E., & Liebrenz, M. (2024). World Psychiatric Association-Asian Journal of Psychiatry Commission on the Mental Health and Wellbeing of International Medical Graduates. *Asian Journal of Psychiatry*, 93, 103943. DOI: 10.1016/j.ajp.2024.103943 PMID: 38342035

Carl, E., Mason, J.E., Smits, J.A. and Asmundson, G.J., (2022). Exercise for mental health: Current perspectives, clinical practice implications, and future directions.

DeRubeis, R. J. (2019). The history, current status, and possible future of precision mental health. *Behaviour Research and Therapy*, 123, 103506. DOI: 10.1016/j.brat.2019.103506 PMID: 31706160

Doyle, A. E., Bearden, C. E., Gur, R. E., Ledbetter, D. H., Martin, C. L., McCoy, T. H.Jr, Pasaniuc, B., Perlis, R. H., Smoller, J. W., & Davis, L. K. (2024). Advancing Mental Health Research Through Strategic Integration of Transdiagnostic Dimensions and Genomics. *Biological Psychiatry*. Advance online publication. DOI: 10.1016/j.biopsych.2024.10.006 PMID: 39424167

Ganguly, C., Nayak, S., & Gupta, A. K. (2022). *Mental health impact of COVID-19 and machine learning applications in combating mental disorders: a review*. Artificial Intelligence, Machine Learning, and Mental Health in Pandemics. DOI: 10.1016/B978-0-323-91196-2.00016-8

Garg, M. (2024). WellXplain: Wellness concept extraction and classification in Reddit posts for mental health analysis. *Knowledge-Based Systems*, 284, 111228. DOI: 10.1016/j.knosys.2023.111228

Hahn, T., Nierenberg, A. A., & Whitfield-Gabrieli, S. (2017). Predictive analytics in mental health: Applications, guidelines, challenges and perspectives. *Molecular Psychiatry*, 22(1), 37–43. DOI: 10.1038/mp.2016.201 PMID: 27843153

Karstoft, K. I., Eskelund, K., Gradus, J. L., Andersen, S. B., & Nissen, L. R. (2023). Early prediction of mental health problems following military deployment: Integrating pre-and post-deployment factors in neural network models. *Journal of Psychiatric Research*, 163, 109–117. DOI: 10.1016/j.jpsychires.2023.05.014 PMID: 37209616

Katiyar, K. (2022). AI-based predictive analytics for patients' psychological disorder. In *Predictive Analytics of Psychological Disorders in Healthcare: Data Analytics on Psychological Disorders* (pp. 37–53). Springer Nature Singapore. DOI: 10.1007/978-981-19-1724-0_3

Khare, S. K., March, S., Barua, P. D., Gadre, V. M., & Acharya, U. R. (2023). Application of data fusion for automated detection of children with developmental and mental disorders: A systematic review of the last decade. *Information Fusion*, 99, 101898. DOI: 10.1016/j.inffus.2023.101898

Kim, T., Hwang, Y., & Lee, J. (2020). Optimizing psychotherapy with machine learning: Personalized approaches for anxiety and depression. *Psychiatry Research*, 295, 113–122.

Kruzan, K. P., Fitzsimmons-Craft, E. E., Dobias, M., Schleider, J. L., & Pratap, A. (2022). Developing, deploying, and evaluating digital mental health interventions in spaces of online help-and information-seeking. *Procedia Computer Science*, 206, 6–22. DOI: 10.1016/j.procs.2022.09.081 PMID: 37063642

Lee, Y., Mansur, R., & McIntyre, R. S. (2019). Machine learning and big data: Implications for disease modeling and therapeutic discovery in psychiatry. *Artificial Intelligence in Medicine*, 99, 101704. DOI: 10.1016/j.artmed.2019.101704 PMID: 31606109

Liu, X., Zhang, Y., & Wang, Z. (2018). Predicting depression with machine learning models based on behavioral data: A review. *Journal of Affective Disorders*, 243, 63–72.

Mishra, S., Chouhan, V., & Garg, R. (2021). Deep learning for early detection of schizophrenia through brain scan analysis. *Journal of Neural Engineering*, 18(2), 134–146.

Nasir, A., Shah, M. H., & Tiwari, A. (2019). Using machine learning to predict PTSD treatment efficacy. *Psychiatry Research*, 279, 276–284.

Pereira, J., Li, W., & Chauhan, A. (2020). Real-time stress detection using machine learning and physiological data. *Psychophysiology*, 57(9), e13592. PMID: 32412112

Rosenfeld, A., Benrimoh, D., Armstrong, C., Mirchi, N., Langlois-Therrien, T., Rollins, C., Tanguay-Sela, M., Mehltretter, J., Fratila, R., Israel, S., & Snook, E. (2021). Big Data analytics and artificial intelligence in mental healthcare. In *Applications of big data in healthcare* (pp. 137–171). Academic Press. DOI: 10.1016/B978-0-12-820203-6.00001-1

Ruppert, D., (2004). The elements of statistical learning: data mining, inference, and prediction.

Salazar, E., Chopra, A., & Pradhan, S. (2020). Machine learning for optimizing medication adherence in patients with mental health disorders. *The Journal of Clinical Psychiatry*, 81(5), e1–e7.

Shamsutdinova, D., Das-Munshi, J., Ashworth, M., Roberts, A., & Stahl, D. (2023). Predicting type 2 diabetes prevalence for people with severe mental illness in a multiethnic East London population. *International Journal of Medical Informatics*, 172, 105019. DOI: 10.1016/j.ijmedinf.2023.105019 PMID: 36787689

Sharma, S., Gupta, M., & Singh, A. (2022). Challenges in implementing machine learning in mental health care: A systematic review. *Journal of Mental Health (Abingdon, England)*, 31(1), 12–22.

Williams, J. E., & Pykett, J. (2022). Mental health monitoring apps for depression and anxiety in children and young people: A scoping review and critical ecological analysis. *Social Science & Medicine*, 297, 114802. DOI: 10.1016/j.socscimed.2022.114802 PMID: 35192989

Xu, C., Wang, Q., & Zhang, Y. (2020). Anxiety disorder prediction using machine learning and behavioral data: Insights from smartphone usage patterns. *Computers in Human Behavior*, 102, 113–121.

Yasmeen, K., Imran, H., Abbas, M. M., Bibi, A., Nadeem, S., Anwar, Z., & Noreen, H. R. (2024). Analyzing the Influence of AI in Predictive Analytics for Mental Health and Its Impact on Early Intervention, Anxiety Levels, And Treatment Adherence. *Social Science Review Archives*, 2(2), 232–243.

Chapter 14
Machine Learning for Combating Mental Health Stigma

Ankur Kumar
https://orcid.org/0009-0007-2623-0065
Sant Longowal Institute of Engineering and Technology, India

Abhinav Sharma
https://orcid.org/0009-0008-0452-8386
Sant Longowal Institute of Engineering and Technology, India

Sanjay Dhanka
Sant Longowal Institute of Engineering and Technology, India

Surita Maini
Sant Longowal Institute of Engineering and Technology, India

ABSTRACT

Stigma around mental health hinders care through discrimination, misconceptions, and shame. Machine learning (ML) offers data-driven solutions to address this, using sentiment analysis and NLP to analyze public attitudes, identify stigmatizing language, and guide awareness campaigns. In healthcare, ML reduces biases, enhances patient interactions, and fosters inclusivity. Personalized education via AI combats misinformation, while advocacy campaigns leverage ML to assess impact. By addressing ethical concerns like bias and privacy, ML can transform mental health stigma reduction.

DOI: 10.4018/979-8-3693-9341-3.ch014

1. INTRODUCTION

1.1 Background

Mental health stigma refers to the prejudiced beliefs and attitudes directed toward individuals with mental health conditions. This stigma perpetuates discrimination, marginalization, and social exclusion, creating barriers to treatment and negatively affecting individuals' quality of life. It operates across three main dimensions:

- **Public Stigma:** Negative societal attitudes that marginalize individuals with mental health challenges.
- **Self-Stigma:** Internalized feelings of shame or inadequacy due to one's mental health condition.
- **Institutional Stigma:** Systemic policies or practices that limit access to mental health resources or perpetuate inequities in care (Loies, 2025).

Impact of Mental Health Stigma

- **Reduced Treatment Access:** Fear of judgment discourages individuals from seeking help.
- **Social Isolation:** Stigmatized individuals often face exclusion, affecting relationships and community integration.
- **Economic Consequences:** Stigma contributes to job loss, reduced productivity, and higher societal healthcare costs.

Global campaigns, such as World Mental Health Day and anti-stigma initiatives, have made strides in raising awareness. However, stigma remains deeply ingrained, with its persistence varying across cultural, social, and demographic lines. This highlights the necessity for innovative approaches that address stigma's multifaceted nature (Ganguly et al.,2022).

Machine learning (ML) emerges as a powerful tool to combat mental health stigma. By analyzing vast datasets, detecting patterns in public discourse, and personalizing interventions, ML can offer insights into stigma's underlying dynamics and help craft targeted solutions.

For example, Table 1 outlines the three primary types of mental health stigma—public stigma, self-stigma, and institutional stigma—along with specific examples. These categories highlight the various levels at which stigma operates and the opportunities for ML to intervene effectively.

Table 1. Types of mental health stigma and examples

Type of Stigma	Description	Examples
Public Stigma	Societal negative beliefs	Media portraying mentally ill as violent
Self-Stigma	Internalized negative feelings	Shame in seeking therapy
Institutional Stigma	Systemic discrimination	Lack of insurance for mental health care

1.2 The Role of Technology in Mental Health Advocacy

1.2.1 The Role of Technology in Mental Health Advocacy: Focus on Machine Learning

Technology, especially Machine Learning (ML), has significantly impacted many sectors, and mental health advocacy is no exception. One of the most significant challenges in mental health is the pervasive stigma that surrounds it, often leading to discrimination, shame, and reluctance to seek help. The application of ML presents a promising way to address this stigma by providing data-driven insights and personalized solutions that can inform advocacy efforts, improve support systems, and ultimately help reduce the barriers to mental health care (Jilka et al., 2022).

1.2.2 Understanding the Potential of Machine Learning in Mental Health Advocacy

Machine Learning is a subset of artificial intelligence that enables systems to learn from data, identify patterns, and make predictions or recommendations without being explicitly programmed. This technology has revolutionized how organizations can approach mental health advocacy by analyzing vast amounts of data to uncover hidden insights that would be difficult for humans to detect. The role of ML in mental health advocacy includes:

a) **Analyzing Public Perception and Stigma** Traditionally, understanding public stigma around mental health relied on surveys and self-reported data. However, ML can go beyond this by analyzing social media posts, online discussions, news articles, and other real-time data sources to capture the public sentiment towards mental health. By using natural language processing (NLP), ML models can detect subtle language cues, tone, and underlying biases, providing a comprehensive picture of societal attitudes and stigma dynamics.

b) **Real-Time Monitoring of Mental Health Trends** ML can also be used to monitor mental health trends in real time. For instance, through sentiment analysis, ML can identify fluctuations in public attitudes towards mental health based on major events, media campaigns, or even crises like the COVID-19 pandemic. This allows mental health advocates to adjust their strategies promptly and effectively, tailoring interventions to address stigma as it arises.

c) **Personalized Interventions and Recommendations** Machine Learning can provide personalized mental health support by offering customized interventions and recommendations. By analyzing individual data (such as online activity, mental health assessments, or behavioral patterns), ML models can suggest specific coping mechanisms, resources, or professional help. These recommendations can help individuals manage their mental health while minimizing the stigma of seeking support, as they feel empowered with choices tailored to their personal needs.

d) **Early Detection of Mental Health Issues** One of the greatest challenges in mental health is the delay in seeking help, often due to fear of stigma. ML can aid in the early detection of mental health issues by analyzing patterns in individuals' behavior or physiological signals (via wearables, for example). This can lead to proactive support and treatment, reducing the long-term consequences of untreated mental health problems(Chancellor et al., 2019).

e) **Improving Mental Health Resources and Access** ML can improve access to mental health care by optimizing resource allocation. By analyzing demographic, geographic, and socioeconomic data, ML can identify underserved populations and direct mental health resources to where they are most needed. Additionally, ML-driven chatbots and virtual therapists can offer 24/7 support, reducing the stigma of visiting a mental health professional in person (Ao et al., 2023).

1.3 Objectives of the Paper

This paper aims to provide a comprehensive understanding of how Machine Learning (ML) can be leveraged to reduce mental health stigma, focusing on its application, challenges, and potential for future development. The specific objectives of this paper are:

a) **Explore ML Techniques Applicable to Stigma Reduction**

The first objective is to explore the various ML techniques that can be used to reduce mental health stigma. This includes examining how ML tools, such as natural language processing (NLP), sentiment analysis, and predictive analytics, can analyze large datasets from social media, online forums, surveys, and other sources to identify stigmatizing language and behaviors. The paper will investigate how these technologies can help uncover patterns and biases in public perceptions of mental health and generate insights that can inform advocacy and intervention strategies.

b) **Present Case Studies Showcasing Successful Applications**

The second objective is to present case studies that demonstrate how ML has been successfully applied in real-world settings to reduce mental health stigma. These case studies will showcase examples from diverse sectors, such as public health campaigns, mental health organizations, and social media platforms. They will highlight the practical application of ML techniques in identifying stigma, raising awareness, and providing personalized mental health support. The paper will analyze the results and impacts of these case studies, focusing on the effectiveness of ML in creating positive change.

c) **Address Ethical Challenges and Propose Solutions**

The third objective is to address the ethical challenges associated with the use of ML in mental health advocacy. While ML offers powerful tools for stigma reduction, its implementation can raise concerns related to privacy, data security, algorithmic bias, and the potential for reinforcing existing stereotypes. This paper will examine these ethical dilemmas and propose solutions to ensure that ML applications are ethical, transparent, and respectful of individuals' rights. Ethical considerations will be explored in terms of data collection, model fairness, and the use of AI in decision-making processes related to mental health.

d) **Highlight Future Research Opportunities in the Domain**

The final objective is to highlight the potential future research opportunities in the intersection of ML and mental health stigma. As technology evolves, new ML techniques and applications are likely to emerge that can further contribute to reducing stigma and improving mental health outcomes. The paper will identify key areas where additional research is needed, such as developing more accurate models for stigma detection, improving personalization of interventions, and exploring the long-term impact of ML-driven stigma reduction strategies. By highlighting these research opportunities, the paper aims to encourage continued innovation and collaboration in the field.

In conclusion, this paper will offer a thorough examination of the ways in which machine learning might be a revolutionary instrument in the struggle against stigma associated with mental illness. Examining current methods, practical uses, moral dilemmas, and potential avenues for further research, the report will advance knowledge of how machine learning may influence mental health advocacy in the future .

2. MENTAL HEALTH STIGMA: A MULTI-FACETED ISSUE

2.1 Types and Impacts of Stigma

Stigma is a pervasive issue that can have profound effects on individuals' mental health and their willingness to seek help. There are several types of stigma, each with its own set of impacts on both individuals and society. Understanding these different types of stigma is crucial for developing targeted interventions to reduce their negative consequences (Bansal et al., 2021).

The three primary types of stigma are **public stigma**, **self-stigma**, and **institutional stigma**. Each type affects individuals differently as shown in Table 2, but all contribute to the overall problem of mental health marginalization (sharma et al., 2021).

Types of Stigma and Their Impacts

a) **Public-Stigma**

Public stigma refers to the negative societal attitudes and stereotypes that society holds toward individuals with mental health conditions. These attitudes are often perpetuated by the media, cultural norms, and misinformation about mental illness. Public stigma can result in discrimination, social exclusion, and isolation. Individuals experiencing public stigma may face challenges in their personal and professional lives, as they are often unfairly judged and treated as "different" or "less than."

b) **Self-Stigma**

Self-stigma occurs when individuals internalize the negative beliefs and stereotypes associated with mental illness. This internalized stigma can lead to feelings of shame, guilt, and unworthiness. As a result, individuals may avoid seeking help for their mental health issues, fearing judgment from others or feeling that they are "weak" or "flawed." Self-stigma can severely affect an individual's self-esteem and self-worth, often delaying treatment or preventing individuals from accessing the care they need.

c) **Institutional Stigma**

Institutional stigma is a form of stigma embedded within societal institutions such as healthcare systems, educational systems, and workplaces. This type of stigma manifests through policies, practices, and regulations that inadvertently or explicitly marginalize individuals with mental health conditions. For example, limited access to mental health resources, discriminatory employment practices, or inadequate mental health support services in schools or workplaces all contribute to institutional stigma. Institutional stigma can prevent individuals from accessing necessary services and resources, further exacerbating their mental health struggles (Al Meslamani et al., 2021).

Table 2. Types and impacts of stigma

Type of Stigma	Description	Impact
Public Stigma	Negative societal attitudes toward mental illness	Discrimination, social isolation, exclusion
Self-Stigma	Internalized negative beliefs about mental health	Reduced self-esteem, treatment delays
Institutional Stigma	Policies or practices that marginalize individuals with mental health issues	Limited access to mental health services, workplace discrimination

Figure 1. Interplay between types of stigma and societal outcomes

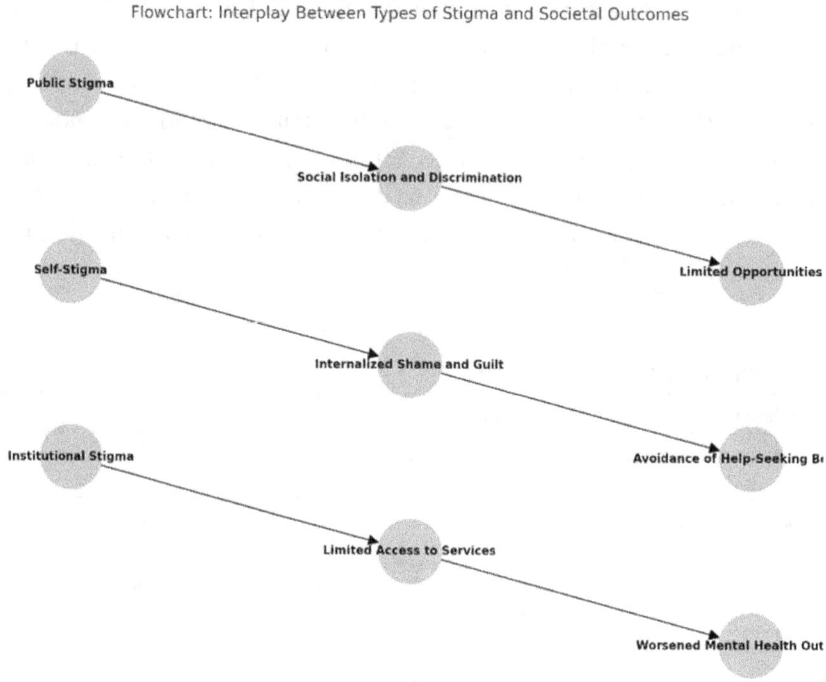

This Figure 1 illustrates how different types of stigma interact with each other and lead to negative societal outcomes. For example, public stigma can exacerbate self-stigma, causing individuals to internalize negative societal attitudes, which in turn delays their decision to seek help. Institutional stigma compounds these effects by limiting access to mental health services, leading to worsened mental health outcomes.

2.2 Measuring Stigma

Stigma, a complex social construct, has traditionally been assessed through well-established qualitative and quantitative methods. *Qualitative approaches*, such as interviews, focus groups, and ethnographic studies, aim to capture the nuanced, contextualized experiences of individuals or groups affected by stigma. These methods delve deeply into personal narratives, social interactions, and cultural perceptions to provide rich, detailed insights into how stigma manifests and impacts lives. For example, interviews with marginalized communities often reveal underlying biases, societal barriers, and the psychological toll of stigma. Similarly, focus groups foster discussions that illuminate shared experiences, offering valuable context to stigma-related phenomena. On the other hand, *quantitative techniques* primarily rely on structured surveys and scales, such as Likert scales, to measure stigma levels. These tools are designed to quantify attitudes, beliefs, and behaviors related to stigma. For instance, a survey might ask respondents to rate their agreement with statements like, "I feel uncomfortable around people with mental health issues," capturing explicit attitudes. The data collected from such surveys can be statistically analyzed, enabling researchers to identify patterns, correlations, and changes over time. Quantitative methods are particularly useful for large-scale studies, providing measurable, comparable data that can inform public health interventions and policy decisions.

However, while these traditional methods have been instrumental in advancing our understanding of stigma, they have limitations. Qualitative methods, while rich in depth, are often time-consuming, resource-intensive, and limited in scalability. Quantitative surveys, though efficient for larger populations, can suffer from biases in self-reporting and may fail to capture the complexity of lived experiences or subtle social dynamics. Both approaches also typically rely on predefined questions or frameworks, which might miss emergent or evolving forms of stigma in society (Palta et al., 2021).

In recent years, *machine learning (ML) and data analytics* have opened new avenues for measuring stigma, enabling researchers to go beyond the constraints of traditional methods. ML leverages vast amounts of data from diverse sources, such as social media platforms, electronic health records (EHRs), and public discourse, to analyze attitudes and behaviors at scale. Social media, for example, serves as a rich repository of real-time, unfiltered opinions and discussions. ML models can process and categorize this data to identify stigmatizing language, trends, and sentiments across different demographic groups. Similarly, EHRs provide insights into stigmatization in healthcare settings, such as discriminatory treatment patterns or reluctance to seek care due to perceived stigma.

Moreover, ML's ability to handle unstructured data, such as text, audio, and images, allows for a more comprehensive analysis of stigma. Sentiment analysis and natural language processing (NLP) can uncover implicit biases and discriminatory attitudes that traditional methods might overlook. Additionally, ML models can detect patterns and correlations that are not immediately apparent, offering deeper insights into the factors driving stigma and its societal impacts. By integrating traditional methods with ML, researchers can achieve a more holistic understanding of stigma. This hybrid approach combines the depth and context of qualitative studies with the breadth and scalability of quantitative and ML-driven techniques, paving the way for more effective interventions and policy development (Zhai et al., 2024).

3. MACHINE LEARNING TECHNIQUES AND FRAMEWORKS

Machine Learning (ML) offers powerful techniques and frameworks to tackle stigma measurement and reduction by analyzing complex, large-scale datasets and providing actionable insights. Key techniques include Natural Language Processing (NLP), Image Recognition, Predictive Analytics, and Recommendation Systems. These methods enable researchers and practitioners to understand, predict, and address stigma more effectively.

3.1 Techniques in Focus

1. **Natural Language Processing (NLP):**NLP is a branch of ML focused on analyzing and understanding human language. It plays a crucial role in stigma research by:
    - **Sentiment Analysis:** Automatically detecting positive, neutral, or negative tones in text, such as social media posts or survey responses, to gauge public attitudes and emotions related to stigma.
    - **Topic Modeling:** Identifying recurring themes and conversations in large textual datasets to uncover stigmatizing language or attitudes. For example, topic modeling could analyze online forums to identify frequently discussed stereotypes about mental health (Merayo et al., 2024).
2. **Image Recognition:**This technique uses ML to analyze visual data. In stigma research, it helps:
    - **Identifying Stigmatizing Visuals:** Detecting harmful imagery in media, advertisements, or public campaigns that perpetuate stereotypes, such as images that mock or dehumanize certain groups.
    - **Contextual Analysis:** Understanding the broader implications of visuals in combination with textual elements to evaluate their potential stigmatizing effects.
3. **Predictive Analytics:** Predictive analytics leverages ML models to anticipate future trends or outcomes. In the context of stigma:
    - **Highlighting At-Risk Populations:** Identifying individuals or groups likely to face stigma, based on demographic, behavioral, or contextual data. For example, predictive models can flag regions where certain social prejudices are more pronounced.
4. **Recommendation Systems:** Recommendation systems provide tailored suggestions or interventions, helping to combat stigma:
    - **Delivering Personalized Anti-Stigma Resources:** Suggesting articles, support groups, or counseling services based on individual needs and preferences. For instance, a recommendation system might direct some-

one exposed to stigmatizing content online to educational resources or mental health support.

Figure 2 illustrating the role of ML techniques in stigma research. It depicts how data sources, such as social media and EHRs, feed into ML techniques like NLP, image recognition, predictive analytics, and recommendation systems, leading to outcomes such as insight generation, stigma reduction strategies, and personalized interventions (Dhanka et al., 2021).

Figure 2. ML techniques in stigma research

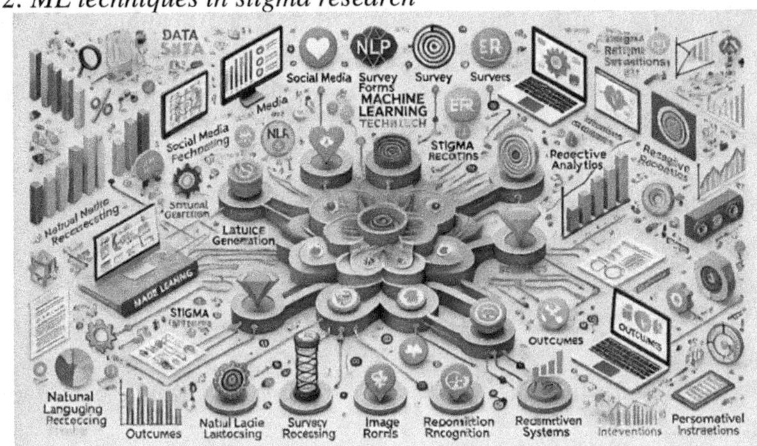

3.2 Framework for Implementation

a. Data Collection

Sources: This step involves gathering data from multiple sources such as social media platforms, clinical data from electronic health records, and responses from public surveys.

Purpose: To compile a diverse and representative dataset for analysis.

b. Preprocessing

Tasks: Includes normalizing text (removing special characters, converting to lowercase), tagging sentiments, and handling missing values. For images or multimedia data, it involves resizing, filtering, and encoding.

Tools: Libraries like `NLTK` or `spaCy` for text, and image processing tools for visual data.

c. Model Training

Models Used:

BERT (Bidirectional Encoder Representations from Transformers): For NLP tasks such as sentiment analysis and topic modeling.

LDA (Latent Dirichlet Allocation): For topic modeling to uncover themes in text.

CNNs (Convolutional Neural Networks): For image recognition to detect stigmatizing visuals.

Goal: Train and validate models to identify stigmatizing content, predict trends, or recommend interventions (Plata et al., 2024).

d. Deployment

Insights: Utilize trained models to generate insights for anti-stigma campaigns, support groups, or policy recommendations.

Real-Time Usage: Models can be deployed on platforms to monitor social media or public discourse in real time.

The workflow diagram represents Figure 3 the steps of implementing ML for combating mental health stigma (Haimson et al., 2024):

a. Data Collection: Gathering data from social media, clinical records, and public surveys.
b. Preprocessing: Normalizing data, tagging sentiments, and preparing it for model input.
c. Model Training: Using models like BERT, LDA, or CNNs to analyze text and images.
d. Deployment: Generating insights for awareness campaigns, policies, or real-time monitoring.

Figure 3. Workflow of ML for combating mental health stigma

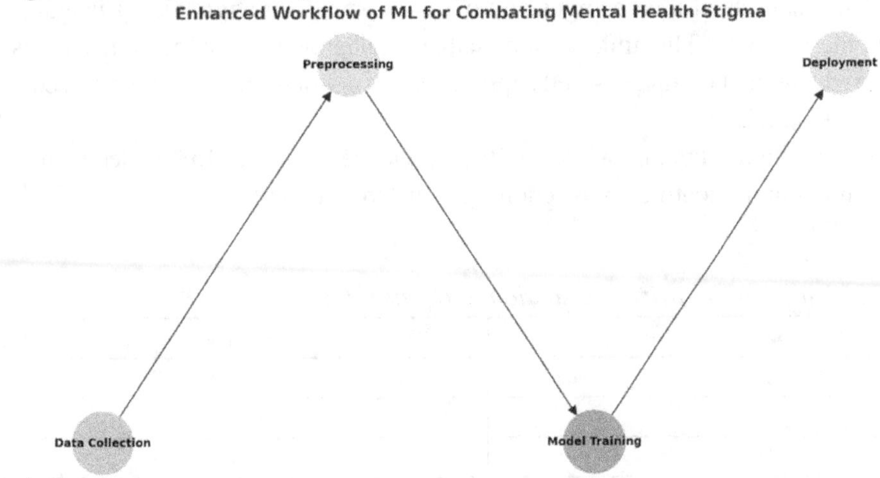

4. APPLICATIONS OF MACHINE LEARNING IN STIGMA REDUCTION

ML offers innovative tools for understanding and addressing stigma in society. By leveraging techniques like sentiment analysis and topic modeling, researchers can gain deeper insights into public attitudes and identify opportunities to reduce stigma effectively (Sharma et al., 2024).

4.1 Public Perception Analysis

Sentiment Analysis

Sentiment analysis is a widely used ML technique to evaluate public attitudes toward mental health topics. By analyzing text data from social media platforms such as Twitter, Reddit, and Facebook, ML models can categorize sentiments as positive, neutral, or negative.

How It Works: Sentiment analysis uses natural language processing (NLP) algorithms to assess the emotional tone of textual content. Models like BERT or VADER analyze the polarity and intensity of sentiment, providing a snapshot of public opinion (Akhtarkhavari et al., 2024).

Practical Application: A sentiment analysis study examined public reactions to global mental health campaigns and observed spikes in stigmatizing language during these events. This information enabled stakeholders to allocate resources, such as educational campaigns and support services, where they were most needed (Kumar et al., 2024).

The table highlights that while half the tweets were neutral, 15% reflected negative sentiment, indicating areas requiring targeted interventions

Table 3. Sentiment polarity distribution in tweets (2023)

Sentiment	Percentage
Positive	35%
Neutral	50%
Negative	15%

4.1.2 Topic Modeling

Topic modeling is another ML method that helps uncover the underlying themes in large datasets of text, such as social media posts or survey responses.

How It Works: Algorithms like Latent Dirichlet Allocation (LDA) group similar words or phrases into topics based on their co-occurrence patterns within the data.
Use Case: By applying LDA to mental health discussions on forums or news articles, researchers can identify recurring themes or misconceptions. For example, topic clusters might include phrases like "fear of violence," "economic burden," or "treatment efficacy."
Actionable Insights: Understanding these topics helps organizations design targeted campaigns to address specific myths or misconceptions about mental health.

4.1.3 Key Benefits of ML in Public Perception Analysis

Scalability: ML techniques can process vast amounts of text data from various sources quickly and efficiently.
Real-Time Monitoring: Sentiment analysis and topic modeling can be applied in real time to track trends and respond proactively.
Actionable Insights: These methods enable the identification of stigma hotspots, recurring themes, and the most effective intervention points.

4.2 Enhancing Healthcare Practices

Bias Detection in EHRs

Machine Learning (ML) systems can identify potential stigmatizing language in clinical documentation, aiding in creating more inclusive and unbiased healthcare environments.

Example: A notable study leveraged Natural Language Processing (NLP) techniques to analyze 10,000 psychiatric records, revealing a 20% prevalence of stigmatizing terms. This underscores the potential of ML tools in improving the quality and neutrality of Electronic Health Records (EHRs).

Chatbots for Patient Interaction

Chatbots powered by advanced algorithms, such as reinforcement learning, are transforming patient interaction by fostering empathetic and stigma-free communication.

Example: *Woebot*, a mental health chatbot, exemplifies this technology by engaging users with supportive dialogue and personalized responses, demonstrating how AI can address emotional and mental health needs effectively (Saboo et al., 2021).

Figure 4: Illustrates a sample interaction flow in a mental health chatbot, highlighting its role in addressing patient concerns empathetically.

Figure 4. Illustrating the interaction flow of a mental health chatbot

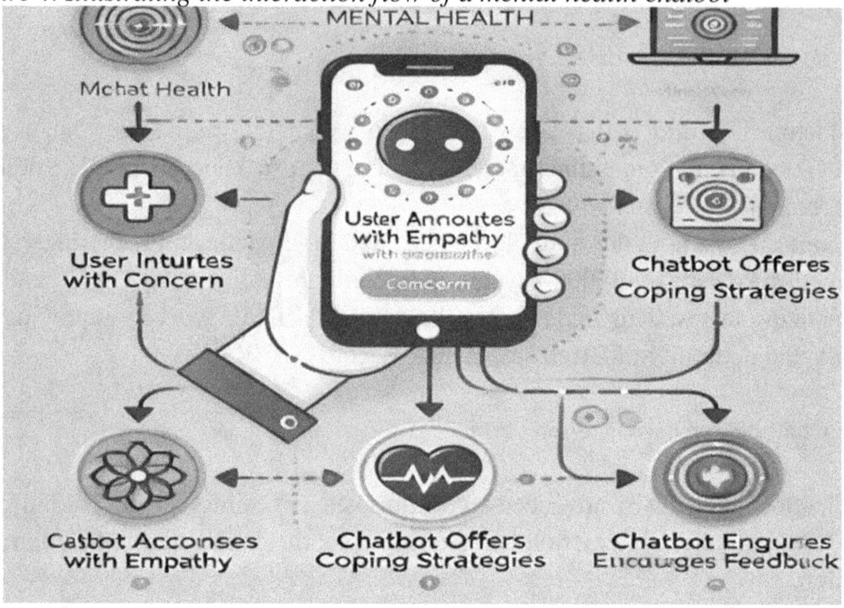

4.3 Designing and Evaluating Campaigns

Personalized Awareness Campaigns

Machine Learning (ML) empowers the creation of targeted awareness campaigns by analyzing user behavior and delivering tailored anti-stigma messages to specific audiences.

Example: A Facebook campaign successfully targeted regions with high stigma scores, resulting in a 25% increase in engagement with mental health resources, demonstrating the effectiveness of personalized interventions (Xu et al., 2024).

Campaign Impact Assessment

ML plays a pivotal role in evaluating the success of stigma reduction campaigns by analyzing changes in language patterns or public sentiment.

Example: An NLP-driven study conducted after the COVID-19 pandemic revealed a 15% decrease in the use of negative terms related to anxiety, indicating the positive impact of awareness efforts (Palta et al., 2024).

5. CASE STUDIES

5.1 Real-Time Monitoring of Stigma Trends

Scenario: Analyzing stigma in pandemic-related mental health discussions.
Context: During the pandemic, public health crises often lead to the emergence of mental health stigma, with negative sentiment surfacing in online discussions. This case study explores how real-time social media data, particularly from Twitter, can be analyzed to identify and monitor stigma related to mental health topics.
Objective: The goal is to track public sentiment about mental health and associated stigma in real-time during the pandemic, identifying spikes in negative sentiment or misinformation that can contribute to stigmatization (Kumar et al., 2024).

5.1.2 Tools Used

Twitter API: Used to collect real-time tweets containing keywords related to mental health and the pandemic (e.g., "mental health stigma", "COVID-19 mental health", "pandemic anxiety").
BERT-based Sentiment Model: A fine-tuned version of BERT (Bidirectional Encoder Representations from Transformers) is utilized to assess the sentiment of each tweet. This model can detect not only basic positive/negative sentiment but also more nuanced forms of stigma, such as fear, shame, or discrimination.
Process:
Sentiment Analysis: Apply the BERT-based sentiment model to classify each tweet as positive, neutral, or negative. Further, label tweets with specific stigma-related sentiment, such as fear or blame.
Trend Monitoring: Analyze sentiment over time to identify trends. For example, spikes in negative sentiment can be correlated with specific events (e.g., new government policies, public figures' statements) to track how stigma evolves.
Visualization: Use real-time dashboards to display sentiment trends and visualize stigma-related sentiment, providing public health agencies with actionable insights to combat mental health stigma.
Outcome: This system provides valuable data to policymakers, mental health professionals, and public health organizations, enabling them to respond to negative stigma trends quickly. For example, when a sudden spike in stigma-related sentiment is detected, targeted interventions such as awareness campaigns or expert commentary can be deployed to mitigate the effects (Zhang et al., 2024).

5.2 Advocacy Through Media: Identifying Harmful Stereotypes in Popular Media Using Image Classification

Scenario Overview: In recent years, there has been increasing awareness about the representation of various social groups in popular media, including film, television, and digital platforms. One key issue that has emerged is the portrayal of harmful stereotypes, particularly towards marginalized groups such as ethnic minorities, women, the LGBTQ+ community, and people with disabilities. These stereotypes, often exaggerated or misleading, can perpetuate bias, reinforce negative societal norms, and contribute to social divisions.

This case study explores how machine learning, specifically image classification techniques, can be employed to identify harmful stereotypes in popular media content. By analyzing visual data in media, it is possible to detect instances of stereotypical representation, which can then be flagged for further review. The ultimate goal is to advocate for more accurate, diverse, and inclusive portrayals, leading to a more responsible and socially aware media landscape (Palta et al., 2024).

The Problem of Harmful Stereotypes in Media: Stereotypes are oversimplified and generalized beliefs about a group of people. In media, these stereotypes can take many forms—ranging from the portrayal of certain racial groups as criminals to the depiction of women as overly emotional or dependent. These misrepresentations can shape the public's perceptions of these groups, affecting everything from social interactions to policy decisions. The ubiquity of media in daily life only magnifies the influence these portrayals can have on societal norms and values.

5.2.1 Some Common Examples of Harmful Stereotypes in Media

Racial and Ethnic Stereotypes: Minority ethnic groups are often depicted in a narrow set of roles—e.g., Black individuals as athletes or criminals, or Asian individuals as submissive and studious.

Gender Stereotypes: Women are frequently shown in passive, secondary roles, emphasizing beauty and domesticity rather than intelligence or leadership.

LGBTQ+ Stereotypes: LGBTQ+ characters, when included in media, may often be reduced to one-dimensional tropes such as the "tragic gay" or "over-the-top flamboyant" character.

Disability Stereotypes: People with disabilities are either portrayed as objects of pity or as superhuman figures overcoming their conditions, which distorts the reality of the lived experience of many people with disabilities.

The perpetuation of such harmful stereotypes in media can contribute to the marginalization of these groups in society, impacting both how they are treated and how they view themselves. As such, there has been a growing call for the media industry to become more socially responsible, ensuring that content creators actively avoid reinforcing harmful stereotypes (Senapati et al., 2024).

5.2.2 Tools and Methodology

To address this issue, the study employed a machine learning-based image classification system designed to identify stereotypical representations in images. This methodology leverages the power of computer vision techniques to automatically analyze large quantities of visual media content and classify images based on specific criteria (Palta et al., 2024).

Data Collection: The first step involved gathering a large dataset of images from various popular media platforms—such as TV shows, movies, advertisements, and social media. These images were selected based on their relevance to different social groups and the potential for stereotypical portrayals. To ensure diversity and accuracy in the dataset, the media content was sourced from a range of genres, from action films to sitcoms to advertisements, across different time periods and geographic regions.

Image Preprocessing: Images were preprocessed to standardize their size and format, ensuring compatibility with the machine learning model. This step also involved eliminating irrelevant content such as watermarks or promotional images that might not be directly related to the characters or scenes in question.

Stereotype Identification Framework: The image classification system was trained to recognize specific stereotypical features or patterns in the images. For example, racial stereotyping might be flagged by identifying certain visual markers such as clothing, facial expressions, body language, or the setting in which characters appear. Similarly, gender-based stereotypes could be detected through clothing choices, body poses, or the context in which female characters were portrayed (e.g., as background figures or overly sexualized). The model utilized a combination of deep learning techniques, including convolutional neural networks (CNNs), which are particularly effective in recognizing patterns in images, and transfer learning, which allowed the model to build on pre-trained models (such as those used for object recognition) to fine-tune its ability to detect specific types of stereotypes (Savekar et al., 2024).

Classification and Analysis: Once the images were processed, the machine learning model classified them into different categories, identifying whether a given image contained harmful stereotypes. Each image was assigned a "stereotype score" indicating the degree to which it perpetuated a negative stereotype. In some cases, the system also flagged more subtle forms of stereotyping—such as the tokenistic inclusion of minority characters without substantial roles or depth (e.g., an Asian character in the background with no lines or character development).

Results and Insights: After processing a significant sample of images, the analysis revealed several key patterns:

Prevalence of Gender Stereotypes: A large portion of the images containing female characters portrayed them in passive, secondary roles. Women were often depicted as caregivers, romantic interests, or emotionally driven characters, while male characters dominated the leadership, action, and intellectual roles.

Racial and Ethnic Representation: Certain racial groups were disproportionately represented in criminal or subservient roles, while others were depicted as "model minorities," creating a narrow view of what it means to be part of these communities.

Underrepresentation of Marginalized Groups: analysis also highlighted the lack of diversity in many forms of media. For example, people with disabilities were nearly invisible, and LGBTQ+ characters were often presented in stereotypical or one-dimensional ways.

5.2.3 Advocacy and Recommendations

The findings from the image classification system were shared with media producers, including television networks, film studios, and advertising agencies. These stakeholders were provided with a detailed report on the presence of harmful stereotypes in their content.

Recommendations were made to encourage more accurate and inclusive portrayals of diverse groups. For instance: Female characters should be given stronger, more varied roles that move beyond traditional stereotypes, emphasizing their leadership, intelligence, and independence. Racial minorities should be portrayed in diverse contexts, breaking away from typecast roles of criminals or servants. LGBTQ+ characters should be shown with depth and complexity, avoiding reductive tropes. Media producers were also encouraged to actively seek input from diverse consultants, such as racial and gender diversity experts, in the development of their content.

5.2.4 Impact and Outcome

The advocacy efforts, driven by the insights from the image classification analysis, led to a significant change in how certain media producers approached their content. Within a year of implementing the recommendations. A *10% reduction* in problematic content was observed across major television networks and film studios involved in the project. In response to the advocacy, many producers began to take more proactive steps to ensure the diversity of voices and characters in their media. For instance, several film studios implemented policies to increase the representation of marginalized groups behind the scenes, ensuring that content was more reflective of societal diversity. Advertisers, in particular, reported a more positive public reception of campaigns that featured more balanced portrayals of gender and racial diversity, suggesting that audiences are increasingly supportive of media that challenges harmful stereotypes (Sharma et al., 2024).

By utilizing image classification and machine learning, this case study demonstrated the potential for technology to be used as a tool for social change in the media industry. Identifying and addressing harmful stereotypes is a crucial step toward promoting more inclusive and equitable representations in popular media. As the results of this case study show, media producers who take a proactive stance in addressing stereotypes can not only contribute to social good but also see positive outcomes in terms of public reception and engagement. With continued advocacy and technological advancements, we can hope for a future where media truly reflects the diversity and complexity of the human experience (Chancellor et al., 2019).

6. ETHICAL AND PRACTICAL CHALLENGES IN MACHINE LEARNING APPLICATIONS

In the growing field of machine learning (ML) and artificial intelligence (AI), there are a variety of ethical and practical challenges that must be addressed to ensure that these technologies are used responsibly, fairly, and transparently. As machine learning systems are increasingly deployed across industries, from healthcare to media, it is crucial to consider the societal impact of these systems. Below, we explore three key ethical challenges in ML applications: data bias and fairness, privacy concerns, and interpretability and trust.

6.1 Data Bias and Fairness

The Challenge of Bias in Machine Learning Models: One of the most pressing ethical challenges in machine learning is the presence of *bias* in training datasets. ML models learn patterns from historical data, and if that data is biased, the model will also inherit and potentially amplify those biases. This issue is especially critical when the model's decisions have significant real-world consequences, such as in hiring practices, criminal justice, or healthcare (Singh et al., 2024).

Source of Bias: Bias can be introduced in several ways, including:
Historical Bias: If the training data reflects past inequalities or prejudices, the ML model may learn these biases. For example, facial recognition systems trained on predominantly white datasets may perform poorly on people of color.
Sampling Bias: When certain groups are underrepresented or overrepresented in the data, the model will be skewed towards the majority, leading to unfair outcomes for the minority groups.
Label Bias: Biases can also arise if the labeling process (i.e., categorizing data) is influenced by human prejudices. For instance, in criminal justice, a predictive policing algorithm might be biased if historical arrests reflect systemic discrimination (Noreen et al., 2023).

6.1.2 Addressing Bias in Training Datasets

To avoid reinforcing harmful stereotypes and creating discriminatory outcomes, it is essential to actively address bias at every stage of model development:

Diverse and Representative Data: Ensuring that training datasets are representative of the population is one of the first steps to mitigating bias. This can involve oversampling underrepresented groups or using techniques such as **data augmentation** to create more balanced datasets.
Bias Detection and Mitigation Tools: Several tools and methods are available to detect and correct bias in machine learning models. For example, pre-processing techniques can be used to balance the dataset before training, and post-processing adjustments can be made to ensure fairness in predictions (Schulze et al., 2007).
Fairness Metrics: Establishing clear fairness metrics can help assess whether a model's performance is equal across different demographic groups. These metrics might include demographic parity, equalized odds, or equal opportunity. Regularly evaluating the model's fairness using these metrics is crucial for ensuring that it does not inadvertently disadvantage any group.
Ongoing Monitoring and Updates: Bias is not a one-time issue—it evolves over time. Regular audits and updates to the model and its training data are necessary to ensure fairness and to address any emerging biases (Srivatsa et al., 2021).

6.1.3 Ethical Implications of Bias

Failure to address data bias can have severe consequences, particularly for marginalized communities. For example, biased algorithms used in hiring could perpetuate gender or racial discrimination, while biased healthcare models could lead to unequal treatment or misdiagnosis. Addressing bias is not only an ethical obligation but also essential for the legitimacy and societal acceptance of machine learning technologies.

6.2 Privacy Concerns

Protecting Sensitive Data

Privacy concerns are another major ethical challenge in machine learning. As ML systems often rely on vast amounts of personal data, safeguarding individuals' privacy is essential. This is particularly crucial in sectors like healthcare, finance, and law enforcement, where sensitive data is involved.

Sensitive Data: In many applications, ML models are trained on sensitive data, such as medical records, financial information, or personal identifiers. The improper use or exposure of this data can lead to significant privacy breaches, identity theft, or discriminatory outcomes.

Data Collection and Use: The manner in which data is collected, stored, and used plays a key role in privacy. If consent is not obtained from individuals for the collection of their personal data, or if the data is used for purposes beyond the original intent, this can lead to privacy violations (Chen et al., 2021).

6.2.1 Safeguarding Privacy in Compliance with Regulations

Machine learning models must be developed and deployed in compliance with relevant privacy regulations, such as the **General Data Protection Regulation (GDPR)** in the European Union or **Health Insurance Portability and Accountability Act (HIPAA)** in the United States. These regulations set guidelines for how personal data should be handled, stored, and processed to protect individuals' privacy.

Data Anonymization: To minimize privacy risks, personal identifiers can be anonymized or pseudonymized, making it difficult to link data back to specific individuals. Techniques like *differential privacy* can be used to ensure that individual data points are not identifiable, even after analysis.

Informed Consent: Organizations must ensure that individuals are fully informed about how their data will be used, and they must obtain explicit consent before collecting or processing sensitive data. In healthcare, for instance, patients must be made aware of how their medical data will be used for training AI models.

Data Minimization: Data collection should be limited to the minimum necessary for the task at hand. By avoiding the collection of unnecessary data, organizations reduce the risk of privacy breaches and minimize exposure to sensitive information.

Encryption and Security: Data security measures such as encryption, secure data storage, and access control are critical for protecting sensitive information. Ensuring that personal data is encrypted both in transit and at rest helps prevent unauthorized access (Wimbarti et al., 2024).

6.2.2 Ethical Implications of Privacy Concerns

When privacy is not adequately protected, individuals can suffer significant harm. For example, breaches in health data privacy can lead to stigmatization, discrimination, or misuse of sensitive health information. Furthermore, improper use of personal data can undermine trust in machine learning systems and create societal pushback against technological advancements.

6.3 Interpretability and Trust

6.3.1 The Challenge of "Black Box" Models

One of the major challenges with many machine learning models, particularly deep learning models, is their lack of *interpretability*. Often referred to as "black box" models, these systems make decisions without providing clear explanations for how those decisions are reached. This lack of transparency can be problematic in high-stakes applications such as healthcare, finance, and criminal justice, where stakeholders need to understand the reasoning behind model predictions.

Opaque Decision-Making: When a machine learning model is used to make decisions about individuals—such as whether a loan application is approved, whether a person is at risk of a medical condition, or whether a defendant is likely to reoffend—stakeholders need to understand how and why these decisions were made. Without transparency, it is difficult to trust the model, and there is a risk of bias or unfair treatment being hidden behind complex algorithms.

Accountability: In the absence of clear explanations, it becomes challenging to hold developers or organizations accountable for errors or discriminatory outcomes produced by the model. This lack of accountability can undermine trust in the system.

6.3.2 Ensuring Transparency and Gaining Stakeholder Trust

To build trust in machine learning models, transparency and explainability are essential:

Explainable AI (XAI): Researchers are developing techniques for creating more interpretable machine learning models, such as LIME (Local Interpretable Model-agnostic Explanations) and SHAP(SHapley Additive exPlanations). These methods provide human-understandable explanations for individual predictions made by complex models, helping users understand the factors influencing a decision.

Model Audits and Explanations: Providing clear documentation and explanations of how a model works—such as its training data, assumptions, and decision-making process—can increase transparency. Auditing models for fairness, accuracy, and bias is also an essential part of maintaining trust.

Stakeholder Engagement: Engaging with stakeholders, including the public, industry experts, and affected communities, is critical for ensuring that models meet ethical standards. Stakeholder feedback can provide valuable insights into the perceived fairness and transparency of a model, helping developers improve their systems.

6.3.3 Ethical Implications of Lack of Trust

If machine learning models are perceived as opaque or untrustworthy, people may resist using or adopting these systems, leading to missed opportunities for innovation. Additionally, a lack of trust in the system can erode public confidence, making it harder for organizations to implement AI solutions ethically and effectively.

As machine learning and AI technologies continue to evolve, it is imperative to address the ethical challenges they present. Bias in data, privacy concerns, and a lack of interpretability can undermine the positive potential of these technologies. By actively working to mitigate bias, ensuring compliance with privacy regulations, and striving for transparency in model development, we can build AI systems that are fair, accountable, and trusted. This approach will not only lead to more ethical AI but will also help in realizing the full potential of these technologies in a socially responsible manner (Merayo et al., 2024).

7. FUTURE DIRECTIONS IN ETHICAL AI RESEARCH AND DEVELOPMENT

As artificial intelligence (AI) continues to permeate various aspects of society, from healthcare to social media, the future of AI must be shaped with careful consideration of its societal impact. The next frontier in AI development includes improving emotional intelligence, increasing cultural sensitivity, and fostering interdisciplinary collaboration. These approaches are essential to ensure that AI technologies are not only effective but also empathetic, responsible, and socially aware (Burke et al., 2024).

7.1 Emotional AI and Cultural Sensitivity

The Evolution of Emotional AI

One of the most exciting and complex areas of future AI development is the integration of emotional intelligence into AI systems. Emotional AI, or affective computing, aims to enable machines to recognize, interpret, and respond to human emotions in ways that are more intuitive and natural. This could be especially important in areas such as mental health, customer service, and education, where understanding and responding to human emotions is critical.

However, as AI systems are tasked with identifying emotions, they must be able to account for a wide range of factors, including cultural nuances and social context. Emotions are expressed differently across cultures, and the ways in which stigma manifests are also highly context-dependent. For example, mental health stigma might be expressed differently in a collectivist culture (e.g., in East Asia) compared to individualist societies (e.g., the United States). This cultural variance presents a significant challenge for AI, which traditionally struggles to navigate such complex and dynamic social factors (Akhtarkhavari et al., 2023).

The Need for Culturally Sensitive Emotional AI

Developing culturally sensitive emotional AI is an urgent priority for future research. Here are key considerations for building this capability:

Cultural Context Awareness: Emotional AI systems must be trained to recognize that the same emotional cues (such as facial expressions or body language) can have different meanings depending on cultural context. For instance, direct eye contact may be interpreted as a sign of confidence in some cultures, while it could be seen as a sign of aggression or disrespect in others. Similarly, non-verbal emotional expressions might differ greatly across cultures, and AI systems need to recognize these differences to avoid misinterpreting emotions.

Addressing Cultural Stigma: Stigma itself is culturally embedded, and AI systems must be capable of understanding how certain behaviors, conditions, or groups are stigmatized within specific societies. For example, mental health issues may carry a heavy stigma in some cultures, but in others, there may be a higher degree of acceptance. AI systems that lack cultural sensitivity risk reinforcing negative stereotypes or further marginalizing vulnerable groups.

7.2 Multidisciplinary Collaboration

The Need for Collaborative Approaches

The complexity of the ethical challenges surrounding AI, particularly when it comes to understanding and addressing stigma, requires the expertise and insights of multiple disciplines. Multidisciplinary collaboration between AI researchers, psychologists, sociologists, ethicists, and other experts is essential for creating AI systems that are both technically sound and socially responsible.

Psychologists: Psychologists can provide insights into human behavior, mental health, and emotional responses, helping to shape AI systems that are capable of understanding and interacting with humans in a more nuanced way. Their expertise in human cognition and emotional development is particularly valuable for developing emotionally intelligent AI that can navigate complex human emotions and experiences.

Sociologists: Sociologists, who study social behaviors, institutions, and inequalities, can help AI developers understand how social structures influence stigma and discrimination. Their expertise in cultural dynamics, group behavior, and social justice can guide the creation of AI systems that do not inadvertently reinforce harmful stereotypes or social divisions. They can also contribute to the development of ethical frameworks that promote fairness, equality, and inclusivity in AI systems.

AI Researchers and Engineers: At the heart of this collaboration are AI experts who build and refine the algorithms that power machine learning systems. They bring the technical expertise necessary to develop algorithms, optimize models, and ensure that the systems perform effectively and efficiently. However, they must work alongside psychologists, sociologists, and ethicists to ensure that the models they develop do not perpetuate biases or other ethical issues.

7.2.1 Collaborative Research for Impactful Solutions

One of the main goals of multidisciplinary collaboration is to foster **holistic solutions** that account for the full spectrum of human experience. In the context of stigma, this might involve combining psychological insights into how stigma affects individuals with sociological perspectives on how it is socially constructed. By working together, researchers from different fields can create AI systems that are not only technically proficient but also ethically grounded and culturally sensitive.

Holistic Understanding of Stigma: Addressing stigma requires a deep understanding of both individual psychological experiences and the broader social dynamics that contribute to stigmatization. Psychologists can help identify the emotional and mental health impacts of stigma on individuals, while sociologists can provide a framework for understanding how stigma is rooted in social structures and cultural practices. AI systems can then be designed to recognize and respond to these multifaceted aspects of stigma, leading to more effective interventions.

AI for Social Good: Multidisciplinary collaborations can also help ensure that AI technologies are used for social good. By working together, experts can identify ways in which AI can be used to combat stigma and discrimination. For example, AI can be deployed to detect and address harmful stereotypes in media, improve mental health diagnosis and treatment, or create inclusive educational tools. Such projects require the input of diverse experts to ensure that the AI systems are ethical, effective, and aligned with the needs of marginalized communities.

Training Ethical AI Professionals: Multidisciplinary collaboration can also help train the next generation of AI professionals who are not only skilled in technical areas but also socially conscious and ethically informed. Integrating ethics, sociology, and psychology into AI education will help develop a workforce that is committed to creating AI systems that are fair, transparent, and aligned with human values.

7.2.2 Future Directions for Multidisciplinary Collaboration

Future research in AI must prioritize collaboration across disciplines to ensure that AI systems are both technically effective and socially responsible. As AI continues to evolve, its applications will have a profound impact on society, and interdisciplinary collaboration will be crucial for ensuring that these technologies are used in ways that promote fairness, inclusivity, and social good. By combining the technical expertise of AI researchers with the insights of psychologists, sociologists, and ethicists, we can develop AI systems that not only solve technical problems but also contribute positively to the well-being of society (Merayo et al., 2024).

8. CONCLUSION

Mental health stigma remains a significant obstacle to achieving equitable and accessible mental healthcare globally. It perpetuates social isolation, delays treatment-seeking behaviors, and fosters systemic inequities. Despite decades of advocacy and awareness campaigns, the persistence of stigma underscores the need for innovative, data-driven approaches to address its complex and multifaceted nature. Machine learning (ML) offers a transformative toolset for combating mental health stigma. By analyzing societal discourse, uncovering biases in healthcare systems, and personalizing education and advocacy efforts, ML can significantly advance stigma reduction efforts. This paper demonstrated how ML applications such as sentiment analysis, topic modeling, predictive analytics, and personalized interventions can provide real-time insights into stigma's dynamics, enabling more effective and targeted solutions.

However, the integration of ML into mental health advocacy is not without challenges. Ethical considerations, including data privacy, model interpretability, and mitigating algorithmic bias, must be addressed to ensure fairness and trustworthiness. Furthermore, multidisciplinary collaboration between technologists, mental health professionals, and policymakers is essential to develop culturally sensitive and impactful solutions.

Looking ahead, advancements in emotional AI, culturally adaptive models, and longitudinal data analysis present opportunities to deepen the impact of ML in combating stigma. Through careful implementation and ethical stewardship, ML has the potential to break down barriers, foster inclusivity, and create a future where mental health is met with empathy, understanding, and equity.

REFERENCES

Akhtarkhavari, D. D. (2023). *Toward Private and Personalized Mental Healthcare with Fast and Efficient Machine Learning Methods* (Doctoral dissertation, La Sierra University).

Akhtarkhavari, D. D. (2023). *Toward Private and Personalized Mental Healthcare with Fast and Efficient Machine Learning Methods* (Doctoral dissertation, La Sierra University).

Al Meslamani, A. Z., Jarab, A. S., & Ghattas, M. A. (2023). The role of machine learning in healthcare responses to pandemics: Maximizing benefits and filling gaps. *Journal of Medical Economics*, 26(1), 777–780. DOI: 10.1080/13696998.2023.2224018 PMID: 37293941

Ao, L., Bansal, R., Pruthi, N., & Khaskheli, M. B. (2023). Impact of social media influencers on customer engagement and purchase intention: A meta-analysis. *Sustainability (Basel)*, 15(3), 2744. DOI: 10.3390/su15032744

Bansal, R., Gupta, A., Singh, R., & Nassa, V. K. (2021, July). Role and impact of digital technologies in E-learning amidst COVID-19 pandemic. In *2021 fourth international conference on computational intelligence and communication technologies (CCICT)* (pp. 194-202). IEEE. DOI: 10.1109/CCICT53244.2021.00046

Burke, T. A., Ammerman, B. A., & Jacobucci, R. (2019). The use of machine learning in the study of suicidal and non-suicidal self-injurious thoughts and behaviors: A systematic review. *Journal of Affective Disorders*, 245, 869–884. DOI: 10.1016/j.jad.2018.11.073 PMID: 30699872

Chancellor, S., Baumer, E. P., & De Choudhury, M. (2019). Who is the" human" in human-centered machine learning: The case of predicting mental health from social media. *Proceedings of the ACM on Human-Computer Interaction, 3*(CSCW), 1-32. DOI: 10.1145/3359249

Chancellor, S., Birnbaum, M. L., Caine, E. D., Silenzio, V. M., & De Choudhury, M. (2019, January). A taxonomy of ethical tensions in inferring mental health states from social media. In *Proceedings of the conference on fairness, accountability, and transparency* (pp. 79-88). DOI: 10.1145/3287560.3287587

Chen, I. Y., Pierson, E., Rose, S., Joshi, S., Ferryman, K., & Ghassemi, M. (2021). Ethical machine learning in healthcare. *Annual Review of Biomedical Data Science*, 4(1), 123–144. DOI: 10.1146/annurev-biodatasci-092820-114757 PMID: 34396058

Dhanka, S., & Maini, S. (2021, December). Random forest for heart disease detection: a classification approach. In *2021 IEEE 2nd International Conference On Electrical Power and Energy Systems (ICEPES)* (pp. 1-3). IEEE. DOI: 10.1109/ICEPES52894.2021.9699506

Ernala, S. K., Birnbaum, M. L., Candan, K. A., Rizvi, A. F., Sterling, W. A., Kane, J. M., & De Choudhury, M. (2019, May). Methodological gaps in predicting mental health states from social media: Triangulating diagnostic signals. In *Proceedings of the 2019 chi conference on human factors in computing systems* (pp. 1-16). DOI: 10.1145/3290605.3300364

Haimson, O. L., Ringland, K., Simpson, S., & Wolf, C. T. (2014). *Using depression analytics to reduce stigma via social media: BlueFriends. iConference 2014.* Social Media Expo.

Jilka, S., Odoi, C. M., van Bilsen, J., Morris, D., Erturk, S., Cummins, N., Cella, M., & Wykes, T. (2022). Identifying schizophrenia stigma on Twitter: A proof of principle model using service user supervised machine learning. *Schizophrenia*, 8(1), 1. DOI: 10.1038/s41537-021-00197-6 PMID: 35132080

Kumar, A., Dhanka, S., Bansal, R., Sharma, A., Singh, J., Khan, A. A., & Maini, S. Agriculture in the Era of Industry 5.0. *Industry 5.0 and Emerging Technologies: Transformation Through Technology and Innovations*, 111.

Kumar, A., Singh, J., & Khan, A. A. (2024). A comprehensive machine learning framework with particle swarm optimization for improved polycystic ovary syndrome (PCOS) diagnosis. *Engineering Research Express*, 6(3), 035233. DOI: 10.1088/2631-8695/ad76f9

Kumar, S., Asthana, R., Upadhyay, S., Upreti, N., & Akbar, M. (2020). Fake news detection using deep learning models: A novel approach. *Transactions on Emerging Telecommunications Technologies*, 31(2), e3767. DOI: 10.1002/ett.3767

Loies, S. E. (2025). Combating Mental Health Stigma With Artificial Intelligence: Improving Societal Understanding. In *Supporting Psychological and Emotional Wellbeing Among Entrepreneurs* (pp. 75-92). IGI Global. Ganguly, C., Nayak, S., & Gupta, A. K. (2022). Mental health impact of COVID-19 and machine learning applications in combating mental disorders: a review. *Artificial Intelligence, Machine Learning, and Mental Health in Pandemics*, 1-51.

Merayo, N., Ayuso-Lanchares, A., & González-Sanguino, C. (2024). Machine learning and natural language processing to assess the emotional impact of influencers' mental health content on Instagram. *PeerJ. Computer Science*, 10, e2251. DOI: 10.7717/peerj-cs.2251 PMID: 39314721

Noreen, R., Zafar, A., Waheed, T., Wasim, M., Ahad, A., Coelho, P. J., & Pires, I. M. (2023). Unraveling the inner world of PhD scholars with sentiment analysis for mental health prognosis. *Behaviour & Information Technology*, •••, 1–13. DOI: 10.1080/0144929X.2023.2289057

Palta, N. P., & Kumar, N. A. (2024). -Soil Dielectric Response to Chemical Fertilizers in Northern India's Key Agricultural Areas. *Physics and Chemistry of the Earth Parts A/B/C*, •••, 103806.

Palta, P., & Kumar, A. (2024). Effect of vermicompost additive on physical, chemical and dielectric properties of soil and its modeling. *The Journal of Microwave Power and Electromagnetic Energy*, 58(3), 186–206. DOI: 10.1080/08327823.2024.2378668

Palta, P., Kumar, A., & Kaur, P. (2024). Evaluation of the impact of wastewater irrigation on the soil's dielectric parameters. *Land Degradation & Development*, 35(7), 2643–2657. DOI: 10.1002/ldr.5088

Palta, P., Kumar, A., & Palta, A. (2024). Leveraging Dielectric Properties, Remote Sensing, and Sensor Technology in Agriculture: A Perspective on Industry and Emerging Technologies. *Industry 5.0 and Emerging Technologies: Transformation Through. Technology and Innovation*, •••, 89–109.

Palta, P., Kumar, A., & Palta, A. Leveraging Dielectric Properties, Remote Sensing, and Sensor Technology. *Industry 5.0 and Emerging Technologies: Transformation Through Technology and Innovations*, 89.

Saboo, S., Gupta, S., Nailwal, I., Gandhi, R., & Rana, S. (2021, October). Diagnosing Mental Health Patient WhileMaintaining Anonymity. In *2021 IEEE Mysore Sub Section International Conference (MysuruCon)* (pp. 244-248). IEEE. DOI: 10.1109/MysuruCon52639.2021.9641727

Savekar, A., Tarai, S., & Singh, M. (2022). Linguistic markers in individuals with symptoms of depression in bi-multilingual context. In *Research Anthology on Bilingual and Multilingual Education* (pp. 1535–1559). IGI Global. DOI: 10.4018/978-1-6684-3690-5.ch077

Schulze, B. (2007). Stigma and mental health professionals: A review of the evidence on an intricate relationship. *International Review of Psychiatry (Abingdon, England)*, 19(2), 137–155. DOI: 10.1080/09540260701278929 PMID: 17464792

Senapati, B. R., Swain, S., & Khilar, P. M. (2024). The Role of Artificial Intelligence, Machine Learning, and Deep Learning to Combat the Socio-Economic Impact of the Global COVID-19 Pandemic. *Modeling and Optimization of Signals Using Machine Learning Techniques*, 173-207.

Sharma, A., Dhanka, S., Bansal, R., Kumar, A., & Maini, S. Industry 5.0 with Sustainable Development. *Industry 5.0 and Emerging Technologies: Transformation Through Technology and Innovations*, 347.

Sharma, A., Dhanka, S., Kumar, A., & Maini, S. (2024). A comparative study of heterogeneous machine learning algorithms for arrhythmia classification using feature selection technique and multi-dimensional datasets. *Engineering Research Express*, 6(3), 035209. DOI: 10.1088/2631-8695/ad5d51

Sharma, A., Lin, I. W., Miner, A. S., Atkins, D. C., & Althoff, T. (2021, April). Towards facilitating empathic conversations in online mental health support: A reinforcement learning approach. In *Proceedings of the Web Conference 2021* (pp. 194-205). DOI: 10.1145/3442381.3450097

Singh, J., Pandey, B., Karna, S., Arora, A. S., & Kumar, A. (2024). Enhancing the thermographic diagnosis of maxillary sinusitis using deep learning approach. *Quantitative Infrared Thermography Journal*, •••, 1–15. DOI: 10.1080/17686733.2024.2349976
Singh, J., Pandey, B., Karna, S., Arora, A. S., & Kumar, A. (2024). Enhancing the thermographic diagnosis of maxillary sinusitis using deep learning approach. *Quantitative Infrared Thermography Journal*, •••, 1–15. DOI: 10.1080/17686733.2024.2349976
Srivatsa, S., Singh, A., & Singh, P. K. (2021, December). Combating Depression Through the Neural Analysis of Web Behavior. In *International Conference on Hybrid Intelligent Systems* (pp. 128-139). Cham: Springer International Publishing.

Wimbarti, S., Kairupan, B. R., & Tallei, T. E. (2024). Critical review of self-diagnosis of mental health conditions using artificial intelligence. *International Journal of Mental Health Nursing*, 33(2), 344–358. DOI: 10.1111/inm.13303 PMID: 38345132

Xu, L., Sanders, L., Li, K., & Chow, J. C. (2021). Chatbot for health care and oncology applications using artificial intelligence and machine learning: Systematic review. *JMIR Cancer*, 7(4), e27850. DOI: 10.2196/27850 PMID: 34847056

Zhai, Y., Zhang, Y., Chu, Z., Geng, B., Almaawali, M., Fulmer, R., Lin, Y.-W. D., Xu, Z., Daniels, A. D., Liu, Y., Chen, Q., & Du, X. (2024). Machine learning predictive models to guide prevention and intervention allocation for anxiety and depressive disorders among college students. *Journal of Counseling and Development*, jcad.12543. DOI: 10.1002/jcad.12543

Zhang, W., Xie, J., Zhang, Z., & Liu, X. (2024). Depression detection using digital traces on social media: A knowledge-aware deep learning approach. *Journal of Management Information Systems*, 41(2), 546–580. DOI: 10.1080/07421222.2024.2340822

Chapter 15
Use of Virtual Reality (VR) and AI in Therapeutic Settings

Ranjit Singha
https://orcid.org/0000-0002-3541-8752
Christ University, India

Surjit Singha
https://orcid.org/0000-0002-5730-8677
Kristu Jayanti College, India

ABSTRACT

This chapter explores the transformative impact of virtual reality (VR) and artificial intelligence (AI) in therapeutic settings. It examines how VR's immersive environments and AI's data-driven insights enhance therapeutic practices, including exposure therapy, cognitive rehabilitation, and anxiety management. By aligning with psychological and neurological theories, these technologies offer innovative solutions for improving patient outcomes. The chapter also addresses challenges such as high costs, data privacy, and the need for rigorous research. Future directions emphasize the importance of ongoing development, ethical considerations, and empirical validation. Ultimately, VR and AI hold the potential to revolutionize therapeutic practices, offering more effective, personalized, and immersive treatment options.

DOI: 10.4018/979-8-3693-9341-3.ch015

INTRODUCTION

In recent years, the convergence of virtual reality (VR) and artificial intelligence (AI) has emerged as a groundbreaking development in therapeutic settings, especially within the fields of neuropsychology and cognitive psychology. These technologies have started to redefine traditional therapeutic approaches, offering innovative solutions that were once the realm of science fiction. The integration of VR and AI into therapeutic practices marks a significant shift, expanding the possibilities for treatment and intervention strategies (Mazzolenis et al., 2024; Rizzo et al., 2021). For example, a notable advancement is the *VR-based cognitive rehabilitation program* integrated with AI, developed for patients recovering from stroke. This program uses VR to immerse patients in interactive, simulated environments that mimic real-life scenarios, such as cooking or navigating a grocery store. AI algorithms analyze the patient's performance and adapt the difficulty of tasks based on real-time feedback, ensuring that the therapy remains challenging yet manageable. This approach not only enhances engagement but also personalizes the rehabilitation process by continuously adjusting the therapy to the patient's specific needs and progress. The combined use of VR and AI in this context represents a revolutionary step forward in personalized neuropsychological rehabilitation, demonstrating the transformative impact of these technologies on therapeutic practices.

Virtual reality, with its immersive capabilities, allows for the creation of controlled, customizable environments where patients can engage in therapeutic exercises that simulate real-world scenarios. This immersive experience has proven to be particularly effective in treating conditions such as post-traumatic stress disorder (PTSD), phobias, and anxiety disorders by allowing patients to confront and manage their fears in a safe and controlled setting. Furthermore, VR's ability to provide real-time feedback and adjust the difficulty of tasks in response to a patient's performance enhances the personalization of therapy, catering to individual needs and progress (Lan et al., 2023; Lindner, 2020). For example, the *Virtual Reality Exposure Therapy* (VRET) program developed for treating PTSD allows veterans to experience simulated combat scenarios in a controlled virtual environment. This exposure helps them process traumatic experiences in a safe setting, with real-time adjustments made to the intensity of the scenarios based on the patient's responses (Deng et al., 2019; Gonçalves et al., 2012). Similarly, *FearFighter*, a VR program for treating phobias, customizes the exposure to various fears, such as heights or spiders, allowing patients to gradually confront and manage their phobias with tailored difficulty levels and real-time feedback (Botella et al., 2017).

Artificial intelligence complements these advancements by leveraging sophisticated algorithms and machine learning techniques to analyze large volumes of data generated through VR sessions. AI-driven insights enable clinicians to gain a deeper understanding of patient behaviors, predict treatment outcomes, and tailor interventions with greater precision (Lindner, 2020; Mazzolenis et al., 2024). For instance, AI can identify patterns in a patient's responses that may not be immediately apparent to the human eye, thereby facilitating more accurate diagnoses and more effective treatment plans. For example, the *AI-based VR therapy platform* used for treating social anxiety disorders employs machine learning algorithms to analyze data from patient interactions within the virtual environment. By monitoring and interpreting physiological signals such as heart rate and facial expressions, the AI can detect patterns indicative of anxiety levels. This enables the system to adjust the virtual social scenarios in real-time, providing more targeted and effective interventions. In a specific case, AI-driven analysis identified subtle changes in a patient's stress levels that led to customized adjustments in exposure therapy, improving the overall efficacy of the treatment (Boeldt et al., 2019; Emmelkamp et al., 2020).

The significance of VR and AI in modern therapeutic practices cannot be overstated. These technologies offer new avenues for engaging patients, enhancing the efficacy of interventions, and improving overall therapeutic outcomes. As we explore the integration of VR and AI in therapeutic settings, this chapter will delve into the various applications of these technologies, examine their impact on neuropsychological and cognitive interventions, and discuss the potential challenges and future directions in this rapidly evolving field. Through this exploration, we aim to provide a comprehensive understanding of how VR and AI are transforming the landscape of therapy, paving the way for more effective and personalized approaches to mental health and cognitive well-being.

BACKGROUND

The integration of virtual reality (VR) and artificial intelligence (AI) into therapeutic settings signifies a major advancement in mental health and cognitive rehabilitation. To fully grasp their transformative impact, it's crucial to understand their historical evolution. VR's origins date back to the mid-20th century, with theoretical models and early experiments on immersive environments. It gained practical traction in the 1990s, thanks to advancements in computing and graphics technology, initially finding applications in research and training, such as flight simulators. The therapeutic use of VR emerged in the late 1990s and early 2000s, focusing on exposure therapy for anxiety disorders and phobias, with technological improvements making VR increasingly effective in cognitive rehabilitation and mental health interventions ((Carlson, 2023; Lindner, 2020; Riva et al., 2019; Zuo et al., 2024) . In parallel, AI began with foundational work in symbolic reasoning during the 1950s. Its capabilities expanded with the advent of machine learning in the 1980s and deep learning in the 2000s, leading to its application in healthcare and mental health. The 2010s saw AI being integrated into therapeutic settings, enhancing data analysis, personalization, and adaptive treatment approaches. The combination of AI and VR has further broadened therapeutic possibilities, offering real-time feedback and tailored interventions (Alowais et al., 2023; Katwaroo et al., 2023). As these technologies advance, their role in addressing cognitive and psychological challenges is expected to grow, paving the way for more effective and personalized therapeutic experiences.

To understand the efficacy and potential of virtual reality (VR) and artificial intelligence (AI) in therapeutic settings, it is essential to explore the psychological and neurological theories that underpin their use. Cognitive Behavioral Theory (CBT) suggests that psychological disorders stem from maladaptive thought patterns and behaviors, which VR supports by offering immersive environments for controlled exposure exercises. This alignment allows for real-time feedback and reinforcement, integral to CBT. The Theory of Cognitive Load emphasizes that cognitive resources are limited and should be managed efficiently; VR can optimize cognitive load by providing controlled, manageable tasks and reducing distractions. Neuroplasticity, the brain's ability to form new neural connections, is enhanced by VR and AI through interactive and adaptive environments that promote cognitive and behavioral changes. The Theory of Embodied Cognition posits that cognitive processes are influenced by sensory and motor experiences, which VR leverages by immersing users in multi-sensory environments that support naturalistic interactions. The Model of Therapeutic Presence highlights the importance of immersion in therapy; VR enhances this by creating engaging virtual environments. AI supports therapeutic settings through machine learning and predictive analytics, offering personalized and adaptive interventions based on data analysis. This theoretical framework integrates these models to provide a robust foundation for applying VR and AI in therapy, showcasing their potential to transform therapeutic practices and improve outcomes for mental health and cognitive rehabilitation. For instance, consider a *VR-based exposure therapy* program for treating social anxiety, which is grounded in Cognitive Behavioral Theory (CBT). This program immerses patients in virtual social scenarios, such as public speaking or attending social events, allowing them to practice and challenge their anxiety in a controlled environment. The real-time feedback provided by the VR system reinforces CBT principles by enabling patients to confront and reframe their maladaptive thoughts and behaviors in a safe setting (Clemmensen et al., 2020; Tan et al., 2024).

The Theory of Cognitive Load is exemplified by a *VR cognitive training program* designed to improve working memory. The VR environment presents tasks with adjustable difficulty levels, ensuring that cognitive demands are appropriately managed and minimizing extraneous cognitive load. This approach allows users to focus on the task at hand without being overwhelmed by irrelevant information (McGowin et al., 2024; Trigueiro et al., 2024).

Neuroplasticity is illustrated through *VR-based rehabilitation* exercises for stroke patients. These exercises use interactive and adaptive VR environments to promote motor and cognitive recovery by encouraging the formation of new neural pathways through repetitive, engaging activities (Bui et al., 2021; Ceradini et al., 2024).

The Theory of Embodied Cognition is reflected in a *VR program* designed to enhance spatial awareness and navigation skills. By immersing users in a multi-sensory virtual world that requires physical movement and interaction, the program leverages sensory and motor experiences to support cognitive processes and improve spatial reasoning (Johnson-Glenberg, 2018; Mejia-Puig & Chandrasekera, 2022). The Model of Therapeutic Presence is demonstrated by a *VR meditation app* that creates an immersive virtual environment for mindfulness practice. This app enhances the therapeutic experience by providing a highly engaging and serene virtual setting that facilitates relaxation and presence (Arpaia et al., 2021; Zhang et al., 2021).

AI's role in these examples is evident in the *adaptive VR therapy platform* that utilizes machine learning algorithms to analyze patient data and personalize therapeutic interventions. The AI system adjusts the complexity of VR scenarios and provides customized feedback based on the patient's performance and progress, thereby optimizing the therapeutic experience and outcomes (Drigas & Sideraki, 2024; Huang et al., 2024).

These examples illustrate how integrating psychological and neurological theories with VR and AI technologies can enhance therapeutic practices, offering innovative solutions for mental health and cognitive rehabilitation.

The conceptual framework for applying virtual reality (VR) and artificial intelligence (AI) in therapeutic settings offers a structured representation of how these technologies interact with cognitive and psychological processes to enhance therapeutic outcomes. VR creates immersive environments that stimulate cognitive processes such as attention and memory, facilitating targeted therapeutic exercises. AI, through advanced algorithms and machine learning, analyzes data from VR sessions to identify patterns, track progress, and personalize interventions. This interaction enhances cognitive engagement, emotional regulation, and overall therapy personalization. The framework visualizes Therapeutic Outcomes as the central goal, with VR and AI as interconnected nodes impacting Cognitive and Psychological Processes. Supporting nodes highlight the role of VR and AI in cognitive engagement, emotional regulation, and personalization. A feedback loop from Therapeutic Outcomes back to VR and AI nodes reflects ongoing refinement of therapeutic strategies based on real-time data. Despite the promise of VR and AI in enhancing mental health and cognitive rehabilitation, challenges such as technological limitations, integration issues, empirical evidence gaps, and ethical concerns persist.

Addressing these challenges through targeted research and development is essential for optimizing the effectiveness and ethical application of these technologies. The chapter aims to explore the capabilities and applications of VR and AI in therapy, evaluate their effectiveness in improving cognitive and psychological outcomes, and identify best practices for overcoming current challenges in their integration and implementation. An example of this conceptual framework in action can be seen in a *VR-based exposure therapy program* for treating phobias, combined with AI-driven personalization.

a) **Immersive VR Environments:** The VR system creates controlled, immersive environments that simulate specific phobias, such as flying or heights. This helps patients gradually confront their fears in a safe setting, engaging cognitive processes such as attention and memory through realistic scenarios (Freitas et al., 2021; Velana et al., 2022).
b) **AI Data Analysis and Personalization:** AI algorithms analyze data collected during VR sessions, including physiological responses, user interactions, and progress metrics. For instance, if a patient's anxiety levels are detected to be high, AI can adjust the difficulty of the VR scenario or offer calming interventions. This personalization ensures that the therapy is tailored to the patient's individual needs and responses (Carlson, 2023; Cossich et al., 2023).
c) **Cognitive and Psychological Processes:** The VR environment stimulates cognitive processes like attention and memory by immersing patients in scenarios that require focus and recall. Emotional regulation is addressed through the gradual exposure to feared situations, helping patients manage their anxiety more effectively (Pallavicini & Bouchard, 2019; Takac et al., 2021).
d) **Therapeutic Outcomes:** The central goal is to reduce the patient's fear and anxiety associated with the phobia. By continuously refining the VR scenarios and therapeutic strategies based on real-time data analyzed by AI, the program aims to improve therapeutic outcomes (Albakri et al., 2022; Freitas et al., 2021).
e) **Feedback Loop:** As the patient progresses, feedback from therapeutic outcomes informs the ongoing development and refinement of VR scenarios and AI algorithms. For example, if a particular intervention is found to be highly effective, it may be incorporated into future sessions to enhance the therapy further (Carlson, 2023; Lan et al., 2023).

Despite the advancements, challenges remain, such as ensuring the VR system's accessibility and affordability and addressing data privacy concerns. Targeted research and development are needed to address these challenges, optimize the integration of VR and AI, and enhance their effectiveness in therapeutic settings. This approach helps illustrate how the conceptual framework translates into practical applications, highlighting the interplay between VR and AI in improving therapeutic practices.

CURRENT APPLICATIONS OF VR AND AI IN THERAPY

Virtual reality (VR) and artificial intelligence (AI) are revolutionizing therapeutic practices by introducing innovative solutions for a diverse array of psychological and cognitive challenges. In exposure therapy, VR provides controlled and immersive environments that enable patients to confront their fears in a safe and structured manner (Mazzolenis et al., 2024; Riva et al., 2019). For example, VR has been effectively used to simulate combat scenarios for veterans with post-traumatic stress disorder (PTSD) and to address various phobias, offering a way to gradually process and overcome traumatic experiences. In cognitive rehabilitation, VR facilitates engaging and interactive exercises designed to improve attention, memory, and executive functions. A notable instance is a VR program developed to enhance memory and spatial navigation skills in individuals with mild cognitive impairment, demonstrating its potential in cognitive enhancement (Rizzo et al., 2021; Quan et al., 2024). For example, the *VR Combat Trauma Simulator* allows veterans with PTSD to safely experience and process combat scenarios in a controlled environment, helping them to gradually confront and manage their trauma (Birrenbach et al., 2024; Lombardo et al., 2022).

The *Virtual Reality Social Skills Trainer* is designed to help individuals with Autism Spectrum Disorder (ASD) practice and improve their social interaction abilities. In this VR program, users engage in simulated social scenarios, such as attending a party or having a conversation, in a controlled and safe environment. The VR environment provides real-time feedback on social cues and responses, allowing users to refine their skills and build confidence in social situations. Research has shown that participants using this VR training exhibit improved social functioning and reduced social anxiety, highlighting its effectiveness in enhancing social skills in individuals with ASD (Parsons & Mitchell, 2002; Tusher et al., 2024).

The *SnowWorld* VR program has been developed to help manage pain in burn patients during wound care procedures. This immersive VR experience transports patients to a snowy, interactive environment where they can engage in activities such as snowball fights and exploring virtual landscapes. By focusing patients' attention on the VR environment, the program effectively distracts them from the pain associated with wound care, leading to reduced pain perception and improved overall comfort during treatment. Studies have demonstrated that patients using SnowWorld experience lower pain ratings compared to those receiving standard pain management techniques, showcasing the potential of VR for pain relief (Phelan et al., 2021; Twillert et al., 2007).

For anxiety and stress management, VR applications create serene and immersive virtual environments that help users manage their stress levels and promote relaxation. These programs often leverage AI to tailor the experience based on individual stress levels, providing personalized mindfulness and relaxation techniques. VR's role extends to social skills training for individuals with autism spectrum disorder (ASD), where it offers a controlled space for practicing social interactions and communication skills. Research has shown that VR-based social skills training can lead to significant improvements in social functioning and reductions in social anxiety (Ladakis et al., 2024). For example, the *VR Stress Relief Program* offers a virtual beach setting where users can engage in guided relaxation exercises tailored to their stress levels by AI, enhancing their ability to manage anxiety. Similarly, the *Social Skills VR Simulator* provides ASD individuals with virtual scenarios to practice and refine their social interactions, resulting in improved social skills and reduced social anxiety, as demonstrated by research in clinical settings (Dechsling et al., 2021; Li et al., 2024).

The *Flow VR Meditation App* creates a tranquil virtual environment where users can engage in guided mindfulness exercises, such as deep breathing, progressive muscle relaxation, and visualization techniques. AI algorithms assess users' biometric feedback, such as heart rate and skin conductivity, to adjust the meditation exercises in real time, ensuring a personalized and effective stress management experience. This approach helps users achieve a state of calm and relaxation more effectively, making it a valuable tool for individuals dealing with high levels of stress and anxiety (Arpaia et al., 2021; Döllinger et al., 2021).

The *Workplace Social Skills VR Module* is designed to help individuals improve their social interactions and communication skills in a professional setting. This VR program simulates various workplace scenarios, such as team meetings, client interactions, and networking events, providing users with opportunities to practice and refine their communication skills. The AI component analyzes users' responses and interactions, offering personalized feedback and suggestions for improvement. Research indicates that users who engage with this VR module demonstrate enhanced confidence and competence in workplace social situations, leading to better performance and reduced anxiety in professional environments (Howard & Gutworth, 2020; Xie et al., 2021).

AI further enhances therapeutic practices by analyzing data collected during VR sessions to personalize interventions. For instance, a case study highlighted how AI-driven VR could adjust exposure levels in real-time based on physiological responses, resulting in more effective management of anxiety. Additionally, VR has been applied in pain management, where distraction techniques involving immersive virtual environments have been shown to significantly reduce pain perception, particularly in burn patients undergoing wound care. immersive environment to distract patients during painful wound care procedures. This VR distraction technique led to a notable decrease in pain perception and distress. Similarly, the *AI-Enhanced Exposure Therapy VR* system adjusted exposure intensity in real time based on the patient's heart rate and galvanic skin response, resulting in more tailored and effective anxiety management (Ladakis et al., 2024; Rahman et al., 2023).

The *NeuroRehab VR Platform* integrates AI to provide personalized cognitive rehabilitation for stroke survivors. The platform uses VR to simulate various daily activities and cognitive tasks, such as navigating a virtual grocery store or solving puzzles, to help patients recover cognitive and motor skills. AI analyzes the patient's performance, including accuracy and reaction times, and adjusts the difficulty and type of tasks in real time to match the patient's current abilities and progress. This tailored approach supports more effective rehabilitation and accelerates recovery by addressing individual needs (Ceradini et al., 2024; Quan et al., 2024).

The *PainRelief VR System* combines VR with AI to help patients manage chronic pain. The VR component immerses patients in engaging, calming environments, such as virtual gardens or serene underwater scenes, to provide a distraction from their pain. AI monitors patients' physiological data, including heart rate variability and facial expressions, to dynamically adjust the virtual environment and interactive elements based on their pain levels and stress responses. This real-time adaptation enhances the effectiveness of pain management strategies, offering personalized and responsive relief (Cerda et al., 2024; Viderman et al., 2023).

These applications collectively underscore the transformative impact of VR and AI on therapy, offering immersive, interactive, and customized treatment options that improve therapeutic outcomes across various domains. The integration of these technologies is paving the way for more effective and tailored therapeutic interventions, enhancing patient experiences and outcomes in mental health and cognitive rehabilitation. For example, the use of *Bravemind VR* for veterans with PTSD has shown how immersive virtual environments can help patients gradually confront and process traumatic memories, leading to improved therapeutic outcomes. Additionally, *Woebot*, an AI-driven chatbot, provides personalized cognitive-behavioral therapy (CBT) through real-time conversations, demonstrating how AI can offer tailored mental health support and improve patient engagement. These examples highlight the potential of VR and AI to transform therapy by providing more personalized and effective treatment options.

TECHNOLOGICAL ADVANCEMENTS

Recent advancements in virtual reality (VR) and artificial intelligence (AI) have profoundly elevated their effectiveness and applications in therapeutic settings. In VR, technological progress has led to significant improvements in hardware, including higher-resolution displays that offer more vivid and lifelike visuals, and enhanced motion tracking systems that ensure smoother and more accurate user interactions. These advancements contribute to creating highly immersive environments that enhance user engagement and therapeutic efficacy. Additionally, the development of wireless VR systems and portable headsets has increased the accessibility and convenience of VR technology, making it easier for patients to use and integrate into their therapeutic routines (Lan et al., 2023; Mazzolenis et al., 2024). For example, the introduction of the Oculus Quest 2, a wireless VR headset with high-resolution displays and advanced motion tracking, has significantly improved the quality of VR therapy. Its portability and ease of use enable patients to engage in immersive therapeutic sessions from their homes, facilitating continuous and convenient treatment for conditions like PTSD and anxiety (Chaplin et al., 2023; Wang et al., 2023).

The *Microsoft Hololens 2* offers a mixed reality experience that integrates VR with real-world elements, providing a more immersive and interactive rehabilitation process. Its advanced spatial mapping and hand-tracking capabilities enable therapists to create customized rehabilitation exercises and real-time feedback within the patient's environment. For instance, in stroke rehabilitation, patients can perform exercises that require physical movement and spatial awareness, while the AI-driven system adjusts difficulty and tracks progress to optimize recovery (Palumbo, 2022; Johnston et al., 2024).

The *Psious VR Platform* is designed for the treatment of specific phobias using high-definition VR environments that simulate various fear-inducing situations. The system incorporates AI algorithms to adapt exposure levels based on patient responses, such as heart rate and facial expressions, ensuring that each session is tailored to the individual's needs. For example, a patient with a fear of flying can gradually experience different flight scenarios in a controlled setting, with the AI adjusting the intensity of the simulation as the patient becomes more comfortable (Boeldt et al., 2019; Lindner, 2020).

The *BehaVR* platform combines VR with AI to enhance CBT techniques for anxiety and depression. The VR component immerses patients in various therapeutic scenarios, such as guided relaxation exercises or interactive challenges designed to address cognitive distortions. AI analyzes patient interactions and behavioral data to provide personalized feedback and adjust therapeutic exercises in real-time. For example, if a patient struggles with specific thought patterns, the AI can modify the

VR environment to target those patterns more effectively, promoting better outcomes in managing anxiety and depression (Jingili et al., 2023; Wu et al., 2021).

On the AI front, strides in machine learning algorithms and data analytics have brought about sophisticated capabilities for analyzing therapeutic data. AI systems can now process vast amounts of data with greater precision, enabling real-time adaptation of interventions and more personalized treatment plans. This has been particularly impactful in therapeutic settings where dynamic adjustments based on patient responses are crucial. The integration of AI with VR has further amplified these benefits, leading to the creation of adaptive therapeutic environments that respond to user interactions in real time. This synergy allows for the customization of therapeutic experiences, optimizing outcomes by tailoring interventions to individual needs (Carlson, 2023). For example, the AI-powered platform *Limbix* combines VR with machine learning to offer personalized exposure therapy for anxiety disorders. The AI analyzes patient responses during VR sessions to dynamically adjust the intensity and type of exposure, optimizing the therapeutic experience in real time based on individual progress and feedback (Boeldt et al., 2019; Lindner et al., 2019).

Overall, these technological advancements have transformed VR and AI into even more powerful tools for addressing psychological and cognitive challenges. The enhanced realism and responsiveness of VR, combined with the sophisticated data analysis and adaptability of AI, provide clinicians with innovative resources to refine therapy techniques and improve patient outcomes. As these technologies continue to evolve, they promise to further revolutionize therapeutic practices, offering new opportunities for more effective and personalized care. For example, the *BRAVE VR* platform uses advanced VR to create highly realistic scenarios for treating PTSD, while its integrated AI analyzes patient interactions and emotional responses to tailor therapeutic content in real time, thereby enhancing the effectiveness of trauma-focused therapy.

CLINICAL IMPLICATIONS

Integrating virtual reality (VR) and artificial intelligence (AI) into clinical practice carries profound implications for therapeutic approaches, offering both notable benefits and complex ethical considerations. Clinically, VR enhances therapy by creating immersive and controlled environments that facilitate exposure therapy, cognitive rehabilitation, and stress management (Carlson, 2023; Saeidnia et al., 2024). For example, VR can simulate specific scenarios for exposure therapy, allowing patients to confront fears in a safe space, while interactive VR environments support cognitive exercises aimed at improving attention and memory. AI complements these advancements by enabling sophisticated real-time data analysis, which allows for the dynamic adaptation of treatment strategies based on individual patient responses. This capability ensures that interventions are personalized and tailored to the specific needs of each patient, potentially improving therapeutic outcomes. For example, a patient with a phobia of flying might use a VR simulation to gradually experience the sensations of being on an airplane in a controlled environment, starting with less intimidating scenarios like sitting in an empty airport lounge and progressing to more immersive situations such as taking off and landing. During these VR sessions, AI can analyze the patient's physiological responses, such as heart rate and stress levels, in real-time. Based on this data, the AI can adjust the intensity of the VR simulation or provide tailored coping strategies, ensuring that the exposure therapy is adapted to the patient's evolving needs and improving the overall effectiveness of the treatment(Boeldt et al., 2019; Ribé-Viñes et al., 2023).

However, the integration of VR and AI also introduces several ethical considerations that must be carefully managed. Data privacy is a major concern, as AI systems often involve the collection and analysis of sensitive patient information. It is crucial to implement robust measures to protect this data and ensure compliance with regulations such as GDPR and HIPAA. Informed consent is another critical aspect; patients need to be fully aware of how their data will be used and have the opportunity to consent to or opt out of data collection processes. Additionally, there is a risk of technology dependency, where patients might become overly reliant on these advanced tools, potentially undermining traditional therapeutic methods. Ensuring equitable access to VR and AI technologies is also essential to prevent exacerbating existing disparities in mental health care. The high costs and technological complexity could limit access for underserved populations, thereby widening the gap between different socio-economic groups (Forcier et al., 2019; Williamson & Prybutok, 2024). For example, if an AI-powered VR system used for cognitive rehabilitation collects data on a patient's cognitive performance and emotional state, it is crucial to ensure that this data is securely encrypted and stored in compliance with GDPR and HIPAA regulations. Patients should be clearly informed about the data being collected, its purpose, and how it will be used, with options to consent or opt out. Additionally, if a VR therapy program becomes widely adopted but remains expensive and technologically complex, it could be accessible only to patients in higher-income brackets, leaving lower-income or underserved populations without these advanced therapeutic options and potentially increasing disparities in mental health care access (Cano et al., 2023; Creed et al., 2023).

As VR and AI technologies continue to evolve, it is imperative to maintain high ethical standards and address these challenges proactively. This includes implementing rigorous privacy safeguards, ensuring transparent communication with patients, and working towards making these technologies accessible to a broader population. By doing so, the integration of VR and AI into clinical practice can enhance therapeutic effectiveness and patient care, while mitigating potential risks and ethical issues. For instance, a clinical practice implementing a new AI-driven VR program for anxiety treatment should establish a clear privacy policy that details how patient data will be collected, used, and protected. The practice should also provide patients with detailed information and obtain explicit consent before collecting any data. To address accessibility issues, the practice could seek funding or partnerships to offer the VR program at reduced costs or on a sliding scale, ensuring that patients from diverse socio-economic backgrounds can benefit from the technology. By taking these steps, the practice can enhance therapeutic outcomes while addressing privacy, transparency, and equity concerns.

CHALLENGES AND LIMITATIONS

The widespread adoption of virtual reality (VR) and artificial intelligence (AI) in therapeutic settings encounters several significant challenges and limitations that must be addressed to fully realize their potential. One major technological barrier is the high cost associated with advanced VR equipment and the substantial computational power required to support sophisticated AI algorithms. These costs can limit accessibility for many healthcare providers and patients, potentially impeding the scalability of these technologies across various clinical settings. Additionally, integrating VR and AI into existing therapeutic practices presents interoperability issues, as these technologies must be compatible with current systems and workflows. This integration often requires significant adjustments to existing practices and the development of standardized protocols to ensure seamless operation (Carlson, 2023; Hadjipanayi et al., 2023). For example, a small mental health clinic that wishes to implement a VR-based exposure therapy system might struggle with the high upfront costs of purchasing VR headsets and software, which can exceed $10,000. Additionally, if the clinic's existing EHR system is not compatible with the new VR technology, the clinic would need to invest in developing or purchasing integration solutions, which can further increase costs and complexity. This situation can create barriers for smaller or resource-limited facilities, hindering their ability to adopt and benefit from these advanced therapeutic tools.

Training clinicians to effectively use VR and AI technologies is another critical challenge. Clinicians need to be proficient in both the technical aspects of these tools and their therapeutic applications, necessitating comprehensive training programs and ongoing professional development. Moreover, data privacy and security concerns are paramount, as VR and AI systems collect and analyze sensitive patient information. Ensuring the protection of this data through robust security measures, compliance with regulatory standards, and clear data management practices is essential to maintain patient trust and adhere to legal requirements (Steen et al., 2024). For instance, a mental health clinic implementing an AI-driven VR therapy program must provide its clinicians with extensive training on both operating the VR equipment and understanding the AI algorithms that tailor the therapy. Without such training, clinicians may struggle to effectively use the technology, potentially compromising the quality of patient care. Additionally, the clinic must establish stringent data protection protocols to secure patient information collected during VR sessions. Failure to implement such measures, as seen in some high-profile data breaches, could result in legal repercussions and loss of patient trust, highlighting the importance of comprehensive data privacy practices.

There is also a need for more robust empirical evidence to demonstrate the efficacy and long-term benefits of VR and AI interventions. While early studies and applications show promise, broader acceptance within the clinical community requires extensive research and validation to confirm the effectiveness of these technologies in diverse therapeutic contexts. Addressing these challenges involves developing cost-effective solutions, creating standardized guidelines for technology integration, and investing in comprehensive research to build a solid evidence base. By overcoming these barriers, VR and AI can be more effectively integrated into therapeutic practices, enhancing patient care and therapeutic outcomes. For example, a clinical trial evaluating the effectiveness of a new VR-based exposure therapy for PTSD might initially show promising results in a small pilot study. However, to gain broader acceptance and validate its efficacy, larger-scale studies with diverse patient populations are needed. This would involve conducting multi-site trials to gather extensive data on long-term outcomes, comparing VR therapy with traditional treatments, and analyzing various factors such as different types of PTSD and patient demographics. By providing this rigorous empirical evidence, the therapy can be more confidently integrated into standard clinical practices and recognized for its effectiveness in treating PTSD.

RECOMMENDATION AND SOLUTION

To effectively integrate virtual reality (VR) and artificial intelligence (AI) into therapeutic settings, a multifaceted approach is crucial, involving several key recommendations to overcome existing challenges and optimize the use of these technologies. Firstly, developing cost-effective solutions is essential, as the high cost of advanced VR equipment and AI systems poses a significant barrier to widespread adoption. Investing in more affordable technologies and collaborating with providers to create scalable solutions without compromising quality is critical. Additionally, exploring various funding opportunities, including grants, subsidies, and public-private partnerships, can support the acquisition and implementation of these technologies in clinical settings, making them more accessible to a broader range of healthcare facilities. Secondly, enhancing interoperability and integration requires creating standardized protocols and frameworks to ensure seamless compatibility with existing therapeutic practices and electronic health records (EHR) systems. Developing APIs and ensuring that new technologies can easily interface with existing infrastructure will facilitate smoother adoption and use, while establishing guidelines for technology integration will help clinicians efficiently incorporate these tools into their practice. Thirdly, focusing on data privacy and security is paramount, necessitating the implementation of robust measures to protect sensitive patient information. This involves adhering to regulatory standards such as GDPR and HIPAA, employing encryption for data transmission and storage, using secure authentication methods, and regularly updating security protocols to address potential vulnerabilities. Educating both clinicians and patients about data protection practices will help build trust and ensure that privacy concerns are adequately addressed. Fourthly, providing comprehensive training for clinicians is necessary to ensure effective use of VR and AI technologies. Developing training programs that cover operational use, therapeutic potential, and best practices for integration into treatment plans is crucial. Continuous professional development opportunities should be provided to keep clinicians updated on technological advancements and emerging trends, with support and resources available to assist in adapting to these new tools. Fifthly, conducting rigorous research and validation is essential to establish the efficacy and long-term benefits of VR and AI interventions. Well-designed clinical trials and studies will generate robust empirical evidence supporting the effectiveness of these technologies, while sharing research findings through peer-reviewed publications, professional conferences, and clinical practice guidelines will foster acceptance and integration within the clinical community. Ongoing evaluation and refinement based on research outcomes will further enhance the overall effectiveness of these interventions. Sixthly, addressing ethical considerations is crucial, involving the establishment of clear guidelines for informed consent and ensuring patients are fully aware of how their data will be used and the potential impacts of immersive experiences. Developing comprehensive ethical frameworks with input from ethicists, legal experts, and patient advocacy groups will help address concerns about technology misuse and maintain high ethical standards. Lastly, fostering collaboration and innovation between technology developers, researchers, and clinicians is essential for driving progress and overcoming practical challenges. Supporting interdisciplinary initiatives that combine expertise from psychology, neuroscience, engineering, and AI will facilitate the development and refinement of therapeutic applications, while encouraging knowledge sharing and joint projects will help accelerate progress and address complex issues related to integrating VR and AI in therapy. Implementing these recommendations will optimize the integration of VR and AI into therapeutic settings, addressing technological, ethical, and clinical challenges and enhancing therapeutic outcomes to improve patient care and treatment efficacy.

FUTURE DIRECTION

Looking ahead, the future of virtual reality (VR) and artificial intelligence (AI) in therapeutic practices is set to be marked by transformative advancements that promise to enhance patient care and improve treatment outcomes. As VR technology continues to progress, we can anticipate the development of increasingly sophisticated and immersive environments that will offer deeper and more nuanced therapeutic experiences. These advancements will enable therapists to simulate complex scenarios with high fidelity, providing patients with interactions that are more engaging and realistic. Such enhancements are likely to refine treatment methodologies, allowing for more precise and effective interventions tailored to individual needs.

Concurrently, AI is expected to advance with the development of more refined algorithms capable of delivering higher levels of personalization and real-time adaptability in therapeutic settings. This progression will allow for the creation of highly individualized treatment plans that can dynamically adjust based on real-time data, further enhancing therapeutic efficacy. AI's ability to process large volumes of data quickly and accurately will enable the development of sophisticated tools for predicting patient responses and tailoring interventions accordingly.

Future research will also explore the integration of VR and AI with other emerging technologies, such as wearable sensors and biofeedback systems. This integration has the potential to create comprehensive and responsive therapeutic solutions that continuously monitor and adjust to physiological and emotional states. By combining VR's immersive environments with real-time physiological data from wearable devices, therapists could offer interventions that are more precisely aligned with patients' immediate needs and conditions. Such advancements could significantly enhance the precision and effectiveness of therapeutic practices, making them more adaptable and responsive.

Moreover, investigating the applications of VR and AI in underserved populations and diverse cultural contexts will be essential. Ensuring that these technologies are accessible and effective across various demographic and cultural groups is crucial for achieving broad-based improvements in mental health and cognitive rehabilitation. Expanding the reach of VR and AI to include diverse populations will help address disparities in mental health care and promote more equitable access to advanced therapeutic tools.

Addressing ethical and practical challenges will also remain a key focus. Ongoing research and development must tackle issues related to data privacy, technology dependency, and equitable access. Ensuring that patient data is protected through robust privacy measures and addressing potential dependencies on technology will be critical for maintaining trust and integrity in therapeutic practices. Additionally, developing strategies to make VR and AI technologies widely accessible and affordable will be important for avoiding exacerbation of existing disparities in mental health care.

Overall, the future of VR and AI in therapeutic settings holds great promise. The continued evolution of these technologies, coupled with thoughtful research and development, is expected to lead to significant advancements in patient care. By addressing both the opportunities and challenges, the integration of VR and AI into therapy has the potential to revolutionize mental health and cognitive rehabilitation, broadening the horizons of what is possible in therapeutic interventions and improving outcomes across diverse patient populations.

DISCUSSION

The discussion synthesizes the chapter's findings on the integration of virtual reality (VR) and artificial intelligence (AI) in therapeutic settings, offering a comprehensive evaluation of their transformative potential and comparing these insights with existing literature. The analysis underscores that VR and AI represent significant advancements in therapeutic practices, introducing innovative solutions for exposure therapy, cognitive rehabilitation, and personalized treatment. VR's ability to create immersive and controlled environments enhances therapeutic experiences by providing patients with engaging, interactive settings that facilitate effective treatment for conditions such as PTSD, phobias, and cognitive impairments. Similarly, AI's data-driven insights enable the development of tailored interventions by analyzing user data in real-time, thus optimizing treatment strategies and personalizing patient care.

Existing literature supports these findings, highlighting how VR's immersive capabilities and AI's sophisticated algorithms can significantly improve therapeutic outcomes. Studies have shown that VR's interactive experiences align with cognitive theories such as cognitive load and embodied cognition, making it a valuable tool for enhancing cognitive and emotional processing. AI's role in personalizing therapy through real-time data analysis also aligns with models of adaptive and individualized treatment, offering a promising approach to addressing diverse patient needs.

However, the chapter also identifies critical challenges and limitations that impact the widespread adoption of VR and AI in therapy. High costs associated with advanced VR equipment and the computational power required for AI systems pose significant barriers to accessibility and scalability. Data privacy concerns and the need for rigorous empirical validation further complicate the integration of these technologies into clinical practice. Existing literature corroborates these observations, noting that despite substantial technological advancements, practical barriers such as cost, privacy, and the need for robust evidence base impede broader adoption and implementation.

The discussion also explores how VR and AI can address traditional therapeutic limitations. By offering more dynamic and responsive interventions, these technologies have the potential to overcome static and less engaging traditional methods, leading to more effective treatment outcomes. VR's capacity to simulate real-world scenarios and AI's ability to adapt treatments based on individual responses represent significant improvements over conventional approaches.

The broader implications for neuropsychology and cognitive psychology are profound. The integration of VR and AI not only supports established cognitive and psychological theories but also extends the boundaries of these fields. VR's immersive environments complement theories of cognitive load and embodied cognition by providing realistic and controlled settings for studying cognitive processes. AI's data analysis capabilities enhance understanding and application of personalized therapy models, pushing forward the development of more effective therapeutic strategies.

In summary, the integration of VR and AI in therapeutic settings marks a significant advancement in mental health and cognitive rehabilitation. The chapter's findings, supported by existing literature, highlight the innovative solutions and promising applications these technologies offer. However, addressing the associated challenges, such as cost, data privacy, and empirical validation, will be crucial for fully realizing their potential and achieving broader clinical integration.

CONCLUSION

The chapter has explored the significant role of virtual reality (VR) and artificial intelligence (AI) in modern therapeutic practices, underscoring their transformative potential in mental health and cognitive rehabilitation. Key points discussed include the effective application of VR for exposure therapy, cognitive rehabilitation, and anxiety management, as well as AI's contributions to personalized treatment and data-driven insights. These technologies offer innovative solutions that align with established cognitive and psychological theories, enhancing therapeutic outcomes through immersive, interactive, and adaptive approaches.

However, the integration of VR and AI into therapeutic settings is not without its challenges. Issues such as high costs, data privacy concerns, and the need for rigorous validation must be addressed to facilitate broader adoption. The chapter has emphasized the importance of developing cost-effective solutions, enhancing interoperability, and providing comprehensive clinician training to overcome these barriers.

Looking forward, continued research and development are crucial to fully realizing the potential of VR and AI in therapy. Ongoing efforts should focus on advancing technology, addressing ethical considerations, and conducting empirical studies to validate the efficacy of these interventions. By doing so, the field can ensure that VR and AI are leveraged to their fullest extent, ultimately leading to more effective, personalized, and transformative therapeutic practices.

In conclusion, the integration of VR and AI represents a pivotal evolution in therapeutic approaches, offering promising avenues for improving mental health and cognitive rehabilitation. The continued exploration and refinement of these technologies will be essential in shaping the future of therapeutic practices and achieving optimal patient outcomes.

REFERENCES

Alowais, S. A., Alghamdi, S. S., Alsuhebany, N., Alqahtani, T., Alshaya, A. I., Almohareb, S. N., Aldairem, A., Alrashed, M., Saleh, K. B., Badreldin, H. A., Yami, M. S. A., Harbi, S. A., & Albekairy, A. M. (2023). Revolutionizing healthcare: The role of artificial intelligence in clinical practice. *BMC Medical Education*, 23(1), 689. Advance online publication. DOI: 10.1186/s12909-023-04698-z PMID: 37740191

Arpaia, P., D'Errico, G., De Paolis, L. T., Moccaldi, N., & Nuccetelli, F. (2021). A Narrative review of Mindfulness-Based Interventions using Virtual Reality. *Mindfulness*, 13(3), 556–571. DOI: 10.1007/s12671-021-01783-6

Birrenbach, T., Stuber, R., Müller, C. E., Sutter, P., Hautz, W. E., Exadaktylos, A. K., Müller, M., Wespi, R., & Sauter, T. C. (2024). Virtual reality simulation to enhance advanced trauma life support trainings – a randomized controlled trial. *BMC Medical Education*, 24(1), 666. Advance online publication. DOI: 10.1186/s12909-024-05645-2 PMID: 38886688

Boeldt, D., McMahon, E., McFaul, M., & Greenleaf, W. (2019). Using virtual reality exposure therapy to enhance treatment of anxiety disorders: Identifying areas of clinical adoption and potential obstacles. *Frontiers in Psychiatry*, 10, 773. Advance online publication. DOI: 10.3389/fpsyt.2019.00773 PMID: 31708821

Boeldt, D., McMahon, E., McFaul, M., & Greenleaf, W. (2019b). Using virtual reality exposure therapy to enhance treatment of anxiety disorders: Identifying areas of clinical adoption and potential obstacles. *Frontiers in Psychiatry*, 10, 773. Advance online publication. DOI: 10.3389/fpsyt.2019.00773 PMID: 31708821

Botella, C., Fernández-Álvarez, J., Guillén, V., García-Palacios, A., & Baños, R. (2017). Recent Progress in Virtual Reality Exposure Therapy for Phobias: A Systematic Review. *Current Psychiatry Reports*, 19(7), 42. Advance online publication. DOI: 10.1007/s11920-017-0788-4 PMID: 28540594

Bui, J., Luauté, J., & Farnè, A. (2021). Enhancing upper limb rehabilitation of stroke patients with Virtual Reality: A mini review. *Frontiers in Virtual Reality*, 2, 595771. Advance online publication. DOI: 10.3389/frvir.2021.595771

Cano, M., Velasco, C., & Bakos, S. (2023). Making Virtual Reality (VR) Accessible for People with Disabilities. In *Springer eBooks* (pp. 1–6). DOI: 10.1007/978-3-319-08234-9_523-1

Carlson, C. G. (2023). Virtual and augmented simulations in mental health. *Current Psychiatry Reports*, 25(9), 365–371. DOI: 10.1007/s11920-023-01438-4 PMID: 37624512

Ceradini, M., Losanno, E., Micera, S., Bandini, A., & Orlandi, S. (2024). Immersive VR for upper-extremity rehabilitation in patients with neurological disorders: A scoping review. *Journal of Neuroengineering and Rehabilitation*, 21(1), 75. Advance online publication. DOI: 10.1186/s12984-024-01367-0 PMID: 38734690

Cerda, I. H., Therond, A., Moreau, S., Studer, K., Donjow, A. R., Crowther, J. E., Mazzolenis, M. E., Lang, M., Tolba, R., Gilligan, C., Ashina, S., Kaye, A. D., Yong, R. J., Schatman, M. E., & Robinson, C. L. (2024). Telehealth and virtual reality Technologies in Chronic Pain Management: A Narrative review. *Current Pain and Headache Reports*, 28(3), 83–94. DOI: 10.1007/s11916-023-01205-3 PMID: 38175490

Chaplin, E., Karatzios, C., & Benaim, C. (2023). Clinical Applications of Virtual Reality in Musculoskeletal Rehabilitation: A scoping review. *Health Care*, 11(24), 3178. DOI: 10.3390/healthcare11243178 PMID: 38132067

Clemmensen, L., Bouchard, S., Rasmussen, J., Holmberg, T. T., Nielsen, J. H., Jepsen, J. R. M., & Lichtenstein, M. B. (2020). STUDY PROTOCOL: EXPOSURE IN VIRTUAL REALITY FOR SOCIAL ANXIETY DISORDER - a randomized controlled superiority trial comparing cognitive behavioral therapy with virtual reality-based exposure to cognitive behavioral therapy with in vivo exposure. *BMC Psychiatry*, 20(1), 32. Advance online publication. DOI: 10.1186/s12888-020-2453-4 PMID: 32000725

Cossich, V. R. A., Carlgren, D., Holash, R. J., & Katz, L. (2023). Technological breakthroughs in sport: Current practice and future potential of artificial intelligence, virtual reality, augmented reality, and modern data visualization in performance analysis. *Applied Sciences (Basel, Switzerland)*, 13(23), 12965. DOI: 10.3390/app132312965

Creed, C., Al-Kalbani, M., Theil, A., Sarcar, S., & Williams, I. (2023). Inclusive AR/VR: Accessibility barriers for immersive technologies. *Universal Access in the Information Society*. Advance online publication. DOI: 10.1007/s10209-023-00969-0

Dechsling, A., Orm, S., Kalandadze, T., Sütterlin, S., Øien, R. A., Shic, F., & Nordahl-Hansen, A. (2021). Virtual and Augmented Reality in Social Skills Interventions for Individuals with Autism Spectrum Disorder: A Scoping Review. *Journal of Autism and Developmental Disorders*, 52(11), 4692–4707. DOI: 10.1007/s10803-021-05338-5 PMID: 34783991

Deng, W., Hu, D., Xu, S., Liu, X., Zhao, J., Chen, Q., Liu, J., Zhang, Z., Jiang, W., Ma, L., Hong, X., Cheng, S., Liu, B., & Li, X. (2019). The efficacy of virtual reality exposure therapy for PTSD symptoms: A systematic review and meta-analysis. *Journal of Affective Disorders*, 257, 698–709. DOI: 10.1016/j.jad.2019.07.086 PMID: 31382122

Emmelkamp, P. M. G., Meyerbröker, K., & Morina, N. (2020). Virtual reality therapy in social anxiety disorder. *Current Psychiatry Reports*, 22(7), 32. Advance online publication. DOI: 10.1007/s11920-020-01156-1 PMID: 32405657

Forcier, M. B., Gallois, H., Mullan, S., & Joly, Y. (2019). Integrating artificial intelligence into health care through data access: Can the GDPR act as a beacon for policymakers? *Journal of Law and the Biosciences*, 6(1), 317–335. DOI: 10.1093/jlb/lsz013 PMID: 31666972

Freitas, J. R. S., Velosa, V. H. S., Abreu, L. T. N., Jardim, R. L., Santos, J. V., Peres, B., & Campos, P. F. (2021). Virtual Reality Exposure Treatment in Phobias: A Systematic Review. *The Psychiatric Quarterly*, 92(4), 1685–1710. DOI: 10.1007/s11126-021-09935-6 PMID: 34173160

Gonçalves, R., Pedrozo, A. L., Coutinho, E. S. F., Figueira, I., & Ventura, P. (2012). Efficacy of Virtual Reality exposure therapy in the treatment of PTSD: A Systematic review. *PLoS One*, 7(12), e48469. DOI: 10.1371/journal.pone.0048469 PMID: 23300515

Hadjipanayi, C., Banakou, D., & Michael-Grigoriou, D. (2023). Art as therapy in virtual reality: A scoping review. *Frontiers in Virtual Reality*, 4, 1065863. Advance online publication. DOI: 10.3389/frvir.2023.1065863

Howard, M. C., & Gutworth, M. B. (2020). A meta-analysis of virtual reality training programs for social skill development. *Computers & Education*, 144, 103707. DOI: 10.1016/j.compedu.2019.103707

Huang, Y., Yang, B., Wong, T. W., Ng, S. S. M., & Hu, X. (2024). Personalized robots for long-term telerehabilitation after stroke: A perspective on technological readiness and clinical translation. *Frontiers in Rehabilitation Sciences*, 4, 1329927. Advance online publication. DOI: 10.3389/fresc.2023.1329927 PMID: 38259875

Jingili, N., Oyelere, S. S., Nyström, M. B. T., & Anyshchenko, L. (2023). A systematic review on the efficacy of virtual reality and gamification interventions for managing anxiety and depression. *Frontiers in Digital Health*, 5, 1239435. Advance online publication. DOI: 10.3389/fdgth.2023.1239435 PMID: 38026832

Johnson-Glenberg, M. C. (2018). Immersive VR and education: Embodied design principles that include gesture and hand controls. *Frontiers in Robotics and AI*, 5, 81. Advance online publication. DOI: 10.3389/frobt.2018.00081 PMID: 33500960

Johnston, M., O'Mahony, M., O'Brien, N., Connolly, M., Iohom, G., Kamal, M., Shehata, A., & Shorten, G. (2024). The feasibility and usability of mixed reality teaching in a hospital setting based on self-reported perceptions of medical students. *BMC Medical Education*, 24(1), 701. Advance online publication. DOI: 10.1186/s12909-024-05591-z PMID: 38937764

Katwaroo, A. R., Adesh, V. S., Lowtan, A., & Umakanthan, S. (2023). The diagnostic, therapeutic, and ethical impact of artificial intelligence in modern medicine. *Postgraduate Medical Journal*. Advance online publication. DOI: 10.1093/postmj/qgad135 PMID: 38159301

Ladakis, I., Filos, D., & Chouvarda, I. (2024). Virtual reality environments for stress reduction and management: A scoping review. *Virtual Reality (Waltham Cross)*, 28(1), 50. Advance online publication. DOI: 10.1007/s10055-024-00943-y

Lan, L., Sikov, J., Lejeune, J., Ji, C., Brown, H., Bullock, K., & Spencer, A. E. (2023). A Systematic Review of using Virtual and Augmented Reality for the Diagnosis and Treatment of Psychotic Disorders. *Current Treatment Options in Psychiatry*, 10(2), 87–107. DOI: 10.1007/s40501-023-00287-5 PMID: 37360960

Li, X., Hu, Y., Yang, X., Bi, X., Zhang, J., & Tao, P. (2024). The effectiveness of virtual reality training on social skills in education: A meta-analysis. *Education and Information Technologies*. Advance online publication. DOI: 10.1007/s10639-024-12941-3

Lindner, P. (2020). Better, Virtually: The Past, Present, and Future of Virtual Reality Cognitive Behavior Therapy. *International Journal of Cognitive Therapy*, 14(1), 23–46. DOI: 10.1007/s41811-020-00090-7

Lindner, P., Hamilton, W., Miloff, A., & Carlbring, P. (2019). How to Treat Depression with Low-Intensity Virtual Reality Interventions: Perspectives on translating cognitive behavioral techniques into the virtual reality modality and how to make Anti-Depressive use of Virtual Reality–Unique Experiences. *Frontiers in Psychiatry*, 10, 792. Advance online publication. DOI: 10.3389/fpsyt.2019.00792 PMID: 31736809

Lombardo, R., Walther, N., Young, S., Gorbatkin, C., Sletten, Z., Kang, C., Tran, O., & Couperus, K. (2022). Ready Medic One: A feasibility study of a Semi-Autonomous Virtual Reality Trauma Simulator. *Frontiers in Virtual Reality*, 2, 719656. Advance online publication. DOI: 10.3389/frvir.2021.719656

Mazzolenis, M. V., Mourra, G. N., Moreau, S., Mazzolenis, M. E., Cerda, I. H., Vega, J., Khan, J. S., & Thérond, A. (2024). The role of virtual reality and Artificial intelligence in Cognitive Pain therapy: A Narrative review. *Current Pain and Headache Reports*, 28(9), 881–892. Advance online publication. DOI: 10.1007/s11916-024-01270-2 PMID: 38850490

McGowin, G., Sonnenfeld, N. A., & Fiore, S. M. (2024). Navigating Cognitive Demand in virtual Reality: Implications for education and training. *Proceedings of the Human Factors and Ergonomics Society Annual Meeting*. DOI: 10.1177/10711813241278286

Mejia-Puig, L., & Chandrasekera, T. (2022). The virtual body in a design exercise: A conceptual framework for embodied cognition. *International Journal of Technology and Design Education*, 33(5), 1861–1882. DOI: 10.1007/s10798-022-09793-8

Pallavicini, F., & Bouchard, S. (2019). Editorial: Assessing the therapeutic uses and effectiveness of virtual reality, augmented reality and video games for emotion regulation and stress management. *Frontiers in Psychology*, 10, 2763. Advance online publication. DOI: 10.3389/fpsyg.2019.02763 PMID: 31920816

Palumbo, A. (2022). Microsoft HoloLens 2 in Medical and Healthcare Context: State of the art and Future Prospects. *Sensors (Basel)*, 22(20), 7709. DOI: 10.3390/s22207709 PMID: 36298059

Phelan, I., Furness, P. J., Matsangidou, M., Babiker, N. T., Fehily, O., Thompson, A., Carrion-Plaza, A., & Lindley, S. A. (2021). Designing effective virtual reality environments for pain management in burn-injured patients. *Virtual Reality (Waltham Cross)*, 27(1), 201–215. DOI: 10.1007/s10055-021-00552-z PMID: 36915632

Quan, W., Liu, S., Cao, M., & Zhao, J. (2024). A Comprehensive Review of Virtual Reality Technology for Cognitive Rehabilitation in Patients with Neurological Conditions. *Applied Sciences (Basel, Switzerland)*, 14(14), 6285. DOI: 10.3390/app14146285

Rahman, M. A., Brown, D. J., Mahmud, M., Harris, M., Shopland, N., Heym, N., Sumich, A., Turabee, Z. B., Standen, B., Downes, D., Xing, Y., Thomas, C., Haddick, S., Premkumar, P., Nastase, S., Burton, A., & Lewis, J. (2023). Enhancing biofeedback-driven self-guided virtual reality exposure therapy through arousal detection from multimodal data using machine learning. *Brain Informatics*, 10(1), 14. Advance online publication. DOI: 10.1186/s40708-023-00193-9 PMID: 37341863

Ribé-Viñes, J., Gutiérrez-Maldonado, J., Zabolipour, Z., & Ferrer-Garcia, M. (2023). Efficacy of virtual reality-based exposure therapy for the treatment of fear of flying: A systematic review. *Cognitive Behaviour Therapist*, 16, e19. Advance online publication. DOI: 10.1017/S1754470X23000119

Riva, G., Wiederhold, B. K., Di Lernia, D., Chirico, A., Riva, E. F. M., Mantovani, F., Cipresso, P., & Gaggioli, A. (2019). Virtual reality meets artificial intelligence: The emergence of advanced digital therapeutics and digital biomarkers. *Annual Review of Cybertherapy and Telemedicine*, 17, 3–7. https://psycnet.apa.org/record/2020-34322-001

Rizzo, A., Goodwin, G. J., De Vito, A. N., & Bell, J. D. (2021). Recent advances in virtual reality and psychology: Introduction to the special issue. *Translational Issues in Psychological Science*, 7(3), 213–217. DOI: 10.1037/tps0000316

Saeidnia, H. R., Fotami, S. G. H., Lund, B., & Ghiasi, N. (2024). Ethical Considerations in Artificial Intelligence Interventions for Mental Health and Well-Being: Ensuring Responsible Implementation and impact. *Social Sciences (Basel, Switzerland)*, 13(7), 381. DOI: 10.3390/socsci13070381

Steen, C. W., Söderström, K., Stensrud, B., Nylund, I. B., & Siqveland, J. (2024). The effectiveness of virtual reality training on knowledge, skills and attitudes of health care professionals and students in assessing and treating mental health disorders: A systematic review. *BMC Medical Education*, 24(1), 480. Advance online publication. DOI: 10.1186/s12909-024-05423-0 PMID: 38693509

Takac, M., Collett, J., Conduit, R., & De Foe, A. (2021). A cognitive model for emotional regulation in virtual reality exposure. *Virtual Reality (Waltham Cross)*, 27(1), 159–172. DOI: 10.1007/s10055-021-00531-4

Tan, Y. L., Chang, V. Y. X., Ang, W. H. D., Ang, W. W., & Lau, Y. (2024). Virtual reality exposure therapy for social anxiety disorders: A meta-analysis and meta-regression of randomized controlled trials. *Anxiety, Stress, and Coping*, •••, 1–20. DOI: 10.1080/10615806.2024.2392195 PMID: 39161295

Trigueiro, M. J., Lopes, J., Simões-Silva, V., De Melo, B. V., De Almeida, R. S., & Marques, A. (2024). Impact of VR-Based Cognitive training on working memory and inhibitory control in IDD young adults. *Health Care*, 12(17), 1705. DOI: 10.3390/healthcare12171705 PMID: 39273729

Van Twillert, B., Bremer, M., & Faber, A. W. (2007). Computer-Generated Virtual Reality to control pain and anxiety in pediatric and adult burn patients during wound dressing changes. *Journal of Burn Care & Research; Official Publication of the American Burn Association*, 28(5), 694–702. DOI: 10.1097/BCR.0B013E318148C96F PMID: 17667488

Velana, M., Sobieraj, S., Digutsch, J., & Rinkenauer, G. (2022). The Advances of Immersive Virtual Reality Interventions for the Enhancement of Stress Management and Relaxation among Healthy Adults: A Systematic Review. *Applied Sciences (Basel, Switzerland)*, 12(14), 7309. DOI: 10.3390/app12147309

Viderman, D., Tapinova, K., Dossov, M., Seitenov, S., & Abdildin, Y. G. (2023). Virtual reality for pain management: An umbrella review. *Frontiers in Medicine*, 10, 1203670. Advance online publication. DOI: 10.3389/fmed.2023.1203670 PMID: 37521355

Wang, C., Kong, J., & Qi, H. (2023). Areas of Research focus and trends in the research on the application of VR in rehabilitation medicine. *Health Care*, 11(14), 2056. DOI: 10.3390/healthcare11142056 PMID: 37510497

Williamson, S. M., & Prybutok, V. (2024). Balancing Privacy and Progress: A review of privacy challenges, systemic oversight, and patient perceptions in AI-Driven healthcare. *Applied Sciences (Basel, Switzerland)*, 14(2), 675. DOI: 10.3390/app14020675

Wu, J., Sun, Y., Zhang, G., Zhou, Z., & Ren, Z. (2021). Virtual Reality-Assisted Cognitive Behavioral Therapy for Anxiety Disorders: A Systematic Review and Meta-Analysis. *Frontiers in Psychiatry*, 12, 575094. Advance online publication. DOI: 10.3389/fpsyt.2021.575094 PMID: 34366904

Xie, B., Liu, H., Alghofaili, R., Zhang, Y., Jiang, Y., Lobo, F. D., Li, C., Li, W., Huang, H., Akdere, M., Mousas, C., & Yu, L. (2021). A review on virtual Reality skill training applications. *Frontiers in Virtual Reality*, 2, 645153. Advance online publication. DOI: 10.3389/frvir.2021.645153

Zhang, S., Chen, M., Yang, N., Lu, S., & Ni, S. (2021). Effectiveness of VR based mindfulness on psychological and physiological health: A systematic review. *Current Psychology (New Brunswick, N.J.)*, 42(6), 5033–5045. DOI: 10.1007/s12144-021-01777-6

KEYWORDS AND DEFINITIONS

Artificial Intelligence (AI): Technology enabling machines to simulate human intelligence and learn from data.

Cognitive Psychology: Study of mental processes including perception, memory, and problem-solving.

Cognitive Rehabilitation: Therapeutic interventions aimed at restoring cognitive function after injury or illness.

Machine Learning: AI subset where systems learn from data to improve performance without explicit programming.

Mental Health: State of emotional, psychological, and social well-being affecting overall functioning.

Neuropsychology: Study of the relationship between brain function and behavior.

Therapeutic Interventions: Methods or techniques used to treat and manage psychological or physical conditions.

Virtual Reality (VR): Immersive technology creating simulated environments for interaction and experience.

Chapter 16
Enhancing ADHD Support Through a Human-AI Collaboration Framework:
Integrating AI-Driven Assessments and Post-Therapy Mentorship

Nour El Hoda Tarabah
https://orcid.org/0000-0001-7864-2394
Ibn Haldun University, Turkey

ABSTRACT

Attention-Deficit/Hyperactivity Disorder (ADHD) is a neurodevelopmental condition marked by inattention, impulsivity, and hyperactivity, significantly affecting well-being and workplace productivity. Current management strategies often lack scalability, personalization, and continuous support. Advances in Artificial Intelligence (AI) present new opportunities to address these gaps through enhanced diagnosis, treatment, monitoring, and mentorship. Based on existing research, this study proposes a Human-AI Collaboration Model for ADHD Support encompassing Diagnosis, Therapeutic Support, and Post-Therapy Monitoring and Mentoring. Combining AI's precision with human empathy, the model provides a scalable, holistic approach to ADHD care in ADHD life and organizational context. The study recommends the future development of a Minimum Viable Product (MVP) for the proposed model to validate its effectiveness for future innovation.

DOI: 10.4018/979-8-3693-9341-3.ch016

1. INTRODUCTION

Attention-Deficit/Hyperactivity Disorder (ADHD) is a complex neurodevelopmental disorder characterized by ongoing difficulties with attention, hyperactivity, and impulsivity. These challenges can disrupt daily routines, relationships, and overall functioning. In professional settings, ADHD often leads to decreased productivity, struggles with collaboration, and difficulties in adapting to organizational demands. Individuals with ADHD frequently encounter issues such as time management, emotional regulation, and maintaining focus, which can undermine their confidence and strain their personal and professional lives. For organizations, ADHD-related challenges can result in inconsistent performance, increased turnover, and unmet accommodation needs, ultimately affecting overall workplace dynamics.

Psychotherapy, a widely used approach for managing ADHD, is typically delivered through brief therapy models. These models, often shaped by organizational budgetary constraints, are defined by limited session durations and infrequent follow-ups. While helpful in specific scenarios, these traditional approaches might fail to address the need for continuous, adaptive, and personalized support that individuals with ADHD require. The absence of real-time interventions, coupled with the reliance on subjective diagnostic processes, reveals significant shortcomings in current ADHD management practices, especially in the workplace.

To address these gaps, this chapter introduces a Human-AI Collaboration Model for ADHD support. The model leverages AI tools to enhance diagnosis, treatment, and long-term support while incorporating human oversight to ensure contextual understanding and ethical decision-making. The framework is designed to cater to both individual needs and workplace demands, offering solutions that are adaptive, scalable, and effective in real-world settings.

This chapter begins by reviewing the challenges of ADHD in personal and professional contexts and exploring the role of AI in neuropsychology and cognitive psychology. It then highlights the potential applications of AI in ADHD care, including diagnosis, therapeutic interventions, monitoring, and mentorship. Finally, the chapter proposes a comprehensive framework for Human-AI collaboration in ADHD management, tailored to individual and workplace settings. By addressing the existing gaps in ADHD care, this chapter aims to provide a foundation for future research and practical implementation.

2. LITERATURE REVIEW

This section introduces the core concepts relevant to this chapter, focusing on the diverse challenges associated with Attention-Deficit/Hyperactivity Disorder (ADHD) in both personal and workplace settings. It highlights the current approaches of ADHD management particularly in the areas of diagnosis, treatment, and ongoing support. The discussion also explores the advancements in Artificial Intelligence (AI) and its role within neuropsychology and cognitive psychology, showcasing how AI can effectively bridge existing gaps. Additionally, it highlights the role of AI-driven solutions in ADHD support and enhances it with explaining the foundation for understanding how Human-AI collaboration can transform ADHD care across different environments.

2.1. ADHD and Symptoms Overview

According to the *Diagnostic and Statistical Manual of Mental Disorders, Fifth Edition* (DSM-5), Attention-Deficit/Hyperactivity Disorder (ADHD) is ADHD is a neurodevelopmental disorder, characterized by a persistent pattern of inattention and/or hyperactivity-impulsivity that interferes with functioning or development. These symptoms must be present for at least six months, negatively impact social, academic, or occupational activities, and be inappropriate for the individual's developmental level (American Psychiatric Association, 2013).

Table 1. ADHD symptoms (American Psychiatric Association, 2013)

Inattention Six (or more) of the following symptoms must have persisted for at least 6 months to a degree that is inconsistent with developmental level and significantly impacts social, academic, or occupational activities:	a. Often overlooks details or makes careless mistakes in schoolwork, work, or other tasks (e.g., misses important details or produces inaccurate work). b. Frequently struggles to maintain focus on tasks or activities (e.g., loses concentration during lectures, conversations, or while reading for extended periods). c. Often appears not to listen when spoken to directly (e.g., seems mentally elsewhere even when there is no obvious distraction). d. Frequently fails to follow through on instructions and does not complete schoolwork, chores, or workplace duties (e.g., starts tasks but quickly loses focus or becomes sidetracked). e. Often has difficulty organizing tasks and activities (e.g., struggles to manage sequential steps, maintain order, or meet deadlines; produces messy or disorganized work). f. Frequently avoids, dislikes, or shows reluctance toward tasks requiring sustained mental effort (e.g., school assignments, reports, completing forms, or reviewing lengthy documents). g. Often misplaces items necessary for completing tasks or activities (e.g., school supplies, tools, wallets, keys, paperwork, eyeglasses, or phones). h. Is frequently distracted by external stimuli (for older individuals, this may include unrelated thoughts). i. Often forgets to complete daily activities (e.g., neglects chores, forgets errands, or, for older individuals, misses appointments, fails to pay bills, or return calls)
Hyperactivity	a. Frequently fidgets with or taps hands and feet, or moves restlessly in their seat. b. Often gets up from their seat in situations where staying seated is expected (e.g., during class, at work, or in other settings requiring them to remain in place). c. Often runs or climbs inappropriately in certain situations. (In teens or adults, this may manifest as restlessness rather than physical activity). d. Often struggles to play or engage in leisure activities in a quiet or calm manner. e. Frequently seems to be constantly in motion, as if "driven by a motor" (e.g., finds it difficult or uncomfortable to stay still for long periods in places like restaurants or meetings; others may perceive them as restless or hard to keep up with). f. Often talks more than is appropriate or necessary.
Impulsivity	a. Frequently has difficulty waiting their turn, such as in lines or during other situations requiring patience. b. Often speaks out of turn, answering questions before they are fully asked (e.g., finishes other people's sentences or struggles to wait during conversations). c. Frequently interrupts or intrudes on others, such as joining conversations, games, or activities uninvited, or using others' belongings without asking. For adolescents and adults, this may involve taking over tasks or activities others are doing.

2.1.2. ADHD Treatment

The treatment of ADHD typically involves a multimodal approach, including pharmacological, psychological, and lifestyle interventions, tailored to the individual's needs. Below is an overview of the key ADHD treatment strategies and their targeted areas.

a. Pharmacological Interventions

For ADHD, the most effective drugs available today are stimulants, which include methylphenidate and amphetamines. The most preferred solution is usually stimulants as they are associated with achieving significant symptom reduction (Faraone & Buitelaar, 2010). Non-stimulant measures are also employed, for instance Atomoxetine and guanfacine, although these drugs are recommended for patients who cannot tolerate stimulants or who have other disorders. These medications work by increasing the activity of brain neurotransmitters responsible for attention and inhibition of impulsive actions (Banaschewski et al., 2017). However, careful consideration should be exercised as potential side effects include loss of appetite, problems with sleep and heart problems.

b. Behavioral Therapy

Behavioral therapy focuses on changing problematic behaviors by using techniques like structured routines, positive reinforcement and token reward systems. This approach is mainly beneficial for younger children, often supported with parent training programs (Daley et al., 2018). Combining behavioral therapy with medication can result in better outcomes than having one intervention alone (Chronis-Tuscano et al., 2016).

c. Cognitive Behavioral Therapy (CBT)

CBT is an evidence-based psychotherapy that deals with dysfunctional thought patterns and behaviors. For ADHD adolescents and adults, this method can help in improving emotional regulation, organizational skills, and self-esteem (Knouse & Safren, 2010). It also targets coexisting conditions such as anxiety and depression, which are common in individuals with ADHD.

d. Parent and Teacher Training Programs

Training programs help parents and teachers get educated on ADHD behaviors management through techniques such as setting clear expectations, using consistent discipline, and providing structured environments. These programs are important in creating supportive ecosystems for children with ADHD, improving their social and academic outcomes (Evans et al., 2014).

e. Diet and Lifestyle Interventions

Dietary modifications and physical activity can provide significant benefits to individuals with ADHD and are considered as adjunctive treatments. Studies suggest that reducing artificial food dyes and increasing omega-3 fatty acids may improve symptoms in some children (Sonuga-Barke et al., 2013). Regular exercise is also associated with enhanced executive function and reduced hyperactivity (Gapin et al., 2011). Each treatment method targets specific ADHD symptoms' areas, and is carried out by stakeholders like psychiatrists, psychologists, parents, teachers and others. Each method and some of its desired outcomes are presented below in table 2.

Table 2. ADHD treatment methods

Targeted Areas	Methods	Role of Psychologist/ Psychiatrist	Responsible Person	Benefits/ Results	Source
Core ADHD symptoms	Stimulants (e.g., methylphenidate) and non-stimulants (e.g., atomoxetine)	Prescribes and monitors medication	Psychiatrist	Reduced inattention, hyperactivity, impulsivity	Faraone & Buitelaar (2010); Banaschewski et al. (2017)
Problematic behaviors	Behavioral therapy, positive reinforcement	Designs behavioral interventions	Psychologist, parents, teachers	Improved behavior regulation and coping strategies	Daley et al. (2018); Chronis-Tuscano et al. (2016)
Emotional regulation	Cognitive Behavioral Therapy (CBT)	Conducts CBT sessions	Psychologist	Enhanced emotional control and organizational skills	Knouse & Safren (2010)
Parental/educational support	Parent and teacher training programs	Facilitates training and guidance	Parents and Educators	Supportive home and school environments, better outcomes	Evans et al. (2014)
Nutrition and exercise	Omega-3 supplementation, regular physical activity	Offers guidance on complementary strategies	Dietitian, parents,individual	Improved focus, executive function, and reduced hyperactivity	Sonuga-Barke et al. (2013); Gapin et al. (2011)

2.1.3. ADHD Adults Challenges in Personal Settings

Adults with ADHD can be significantly impacted by their symptoms–patterns of inattention, hyperactivity, and impulsivity. These symptoms can impact various areas of life, including relationships, mental health and daily functioning (Faraone et al., 2021) as explained below:

a. Interpersonal Relationships

ADHD symptoms, such as impulsivity and inattentiveness, can negatively impact personal and professional relationships. Adults with ADHD may unintentionally interrupt people while having conversations, forget important dates or commitments, or find it difficult to listen attentively, which might make partners, friends, or colleagues feel neglected or unvalued (Faraone et al., 2021). Impulsivity can cause emotional outbursts or making statements without considering their impact, leading to conflicts and misunderstandings. Over time, these patterns can strain or break relationships. Therapy or coaching for ADHD can help improve communication and foster healthier interpersonal dynamics.

b. Mental Health

Adults with ADHD are confronted with a significantly higher risk of developing co-occurring mental health conditions such as anxiety and depression (Kooij et al., 2019). The chronic stress of managing ADHD symptoms, combined with frequent experiences of failure or criticism, can result in low self-esteem and feelings of inadequacy. Anxiety may develop as a result of struggles to meet expectations or a fear of failure, while depression can emerge from feelings of hopelessness or frustration with ongoing challenges. Addressing ADHD alongside these co-occurring conditions requires multiple approaches, including medication, therapy, and lifestyle adjustments to improve overall mental well-being.

c. Daily Functioning

ADHD symptoms can disrupt daily routines and responsibilities. Routine tasks like paying bills, maintaining a household, or managing a schedule may become overwhelming, leading to financial difficulties, cluttered living spaces, or missed appointments. The executive functioning deficits commonly seen in ADHD contribute to these challenges, as individuals are highly challenged with planning, prioritizing, and following through on activities (Barkley, 2015).

2.1.4. ADHD Adults' Challenges in Organizational Settings

ADHD challenges are not only limited to personal or individual life, it comes with many occupational impairments that can significantly affect the individuals' career. Below are some of these challenges:

a. Time Management and Task Prioritization

Individuals with ADHD often struggle with initiating tasks, especially those that are complex or monotonous. This can lead to delays in meeting deadlines and a buildup of incomplete work (Kooij et al., 2019). Also, it is difficult for them to prioritize tasks which make them focus on low-priority activities while neglecting urgent responsibilities, impacting overall productivity. Thus, individuals with ADHD might face a lot of challenges due to procrastination and poor prioritization skills.

b. Focus and Attention

Adults with ADHD are often challenged with maintaining focus, meeting deadlines, and effectively managing their responsibilities at work. These challenges are rooted in difficulties with organization, time management, and prioritization of tasks (Kessler et al., 2006). For instance, an adult with ADHD may start several projects simultaneously but doesn't continue or complete them because of distraction or procrastination. Additionally, individuals with ADHD can be easily Distracted for example open office layouts, frequent interruptions, and multitasking demands exacerbate attention difficulties for employees with ADHD (Barkley, 2015) and can lead to distracting them from what they are doing and shift their attention to something else very quickly and then making it hard for them to get back to what they were doing in the first place. This loop of distraction can impact them and their ability to stay on track with their progress. However, while ADHD is associated with inattention, some individuals experience episodes of hyperfocus, where they become intensely absorbed in a task, potentially at the expense of other responsibilities (Asherson et al., 2016).

c. Executive Functioning

Disorganization and working memory deficits are significant challenges for individuals with ADHD, often impeding efficiency and productivity in organizational settings. Difficulties in organizing workspaces, digital files, and schedules can lead to clutter and confusion, resulting in missed deadlines and decreased performance. Moreover, working memory deficits, characterized by forgetfulness and challenges in retaining instructions or meeting details, further disrupt workflows. These issues frequently require additional clarification and repetition, which can strain communication and collaboration within teams (Brown, 2014). Together, these challenges underscore the need for tailored strategies to enhance organization and memory retention for individuals with ADHD.

d. Interpersonal Challenges in the Workplace

Impulsivity and emotional dysregulation are common challenges for individuals with ADHD, significantly impacting workplace dynamics and productivity. Impulsive tendencies may lead to interruptions during meetings or conversations, which can strain relationships with colleagues and disrupt collaborative efforts. Additionally, difficulty regulating emotions often results in frustration or anger during high-stress situations, further complicating team interactions and overall dynamics (Ramsay & Rostain, 2015). Impulsivity can also manifest in unplanned decision-making, potentially leading to unfavorable workplace outcomes. Over time, these challenges contribute to lower productivity, decreased job satisfaction, frequent job changes, and higher unemployment rates compared to individuals without ADHD (Faraone et al., 2021). Addressing these issues requires targeted strategies to mitigate their impact and foster a supportive work environment.

Additionally, it can impact social interactions as individuals with ADHD often face sensitivity to feedback, where constructive criticism may be interpreted as personal attacks, potentially leading to reduced morale or withdrawal from workplace interactions. Additionally, maintaining focus during social engagements can be challenging, making it difficult to build and sustain professional networks. This struggle with networking may limit opportunities for career advancement and hinder overall professional growth (Hallowell & Ratey, 2011). Addressing these challenges requires fostering a supportive environment that promotes constructive communication and skill-building for social interactions.

e. Career Development Challenges

Individuals with ADHD often experience inconsistent productivity, with fluctuations in focus and energy levels leading to variations in performance. This variability can impact their ability to meet expectations consistently, potentially influencing annual evaluations and opportunities for promotions. Additionally, difficulties with attention to detail may result in higher error rates, particularly in tasks that demand precision and accuracy, posing challenges in roles where meticulousness is crucial.

Additionally, managing ADHD symptoms in the workplace often demands significant mental and emotional effort, which can lead to fatigue and burnout over time. Furthermore, challenges such as perceived unreliability or disorganization may hinder career progression, reducing access to leadership roles or opportunities for high-profile assignments. These barriers not only affect individual growth but can also perpetuate feelings of inadequacy and limit long-term professional success (Kooij et al., 2019).

f. Structural and Environmental Challenges

Individuals with ADHD frequently face structural and environmental obstacles in the workplace that can affect their performance and hinder career advancement. Fixed 9-to-5 schedules and rigid deadlines often clash with their preference for autonomy and a variety of tasks, reducing their productivity and job satisfaction (Kooij et al., 2019). Furthermore, many workplaces lack adequate policies or awareness regarding accommodations, such as flexible working hours, noise-canceling headphones, or task management tools, making it more difficult for individuals with ADHD to excel (Barkley, 2015). This absence of support can increase stress levels and lower efficiency. Misinterpretation of ADHD symptoms by colleagues or supervisors often leads to stigmatization, with behaviors being wrongly perceived as laziness or incompetence, which negatively impacts workplace relationships (Hallowell & Ratey, 2011). Additionally, insufficient understanding of ADHD in the workplace often prevents organizations from leveraging the unique strengths of these individuals, such as creativity and problem-solving abilities (Barkley, 2015). Promoting a supportive and inclusive environment is essential to overcome these barriers and maximize the potential of neurodiverse employees.

2.1.5. ADHD Adults' Potential in Life

a. Creativity and Divergent Thinking

One of the hallmark strengths of individuals with ADHD is their ability to think creatively and generate unique solutions. Divergent thinking—a cognitive process often linked to creativity—is particularly strong in those with ADHD (White & Shah, 2011). This type of thinking allows individuals to explore multiple possibilities and connect seemingly unrelated ideas, making them adept at problem-solving and innovation. For example, many entrepreneurs and artists with ADHD have attributed their success to their ability to "think outside the box" and approach challenges from unconventional angles (Hallowell & Ratey, 2011).

b. Enthusiasm and Energy

In personal relationships, the enthusiasm and high energy levels often exhibited by individuals with ADHD can be infectious. This energy fosters meaningful connections and creates a vibrant social environment. Their spontaneous nature also allows them to embrace life with a sense of adventure, which can lead to memorable experiences and close-knit relationships. This spontaneity, while sometimes perceived as impulsiveness, can be channeled into creating exciting and engaging interactions that leave lasting impressions on others (Barkley, 2015).

c. Hyperfocus and Passion

Hyperfocus, another common ADHD trait, allows individuals to immerse themselves deeply in activities they find engaging or meaningful. This can lead to the mastery of hobbies, skills, or interests that align with their passions. For example, an ADHD individual might channel their intense focus into learning a musical instrument, developing a complex art project, or delving into an intellectual pursuit (Brown & Reichel, 2018). This ability to become deeply invested in what matters most to them enriches their personal lives and fosters a strong sense of purpose.

d. Resilience and Adaptability

Living with ADHD often means overcoming challenges related to focus, organization, and time management. These experiences build resilience and adaptability, traits that are crucial in navigating life's uncertainties. Individuals with ADHD frequently display remarkable perseverance and a willingness to tackle obstacles head-on, traits that not only help them succeed but also inspire those around them (Knouse & Safren, 2010).

2.1.6. ADHD Individuals Potential in Workplace

a. Innovation and Risk-Taking

In professional settings, ADHD individuals bring a strong capacity for innovation. Their ability to think differently enables them to identify opportunities and solve problems in creative ways. For instance, many startups thrive on fresh, unconventional ideas—an area where ADHD individuals often excel. Studies, such as the one conducted by Verheul et al. (2015), show that ADHD traits like impulsivity and risk-taking align well with entrepreneurial endeavors, where taking bold and calculated risks is necessary.

b. Thriving in Fast-Paced Environments

Workplaces that demand quick thinking and adaptability often see ADHD individuals excel. Their preference for variety and challenge makes them natural fits for roles that require juggling multiple tasks or responding to rapid changes. Their comfort in dynamic environments, combined with a love for novelty, makes them particularly effective in industries such as technology, marketing, or creative fields (Advokat et al., 2011).

c. Hyperfocus for Complex Projects

While ADHD is often associated with distractibility, hyperfocus allows these individuals to dedicate intense attention to tasks they find intrinsically motivating. When channeled correctly, this trait enables them to excel in detail-oriented or complex projects, particularly those involving creativity or innovation. For example, a software developer with ADHD might become deeply absorbed in coding for hours, producing high-quality work (Hallowell & Ratey, 2011).

d. Energetic Leadership and Team Inspiration

ADHD individuals often have an energetic and enthusiastic presence that motivates teams and fosters a positive work environment. Their ability to inspire colleagues stems from their passion for ideas and projects, as well as their willingness to explore uncharted territories. This enthusiasm can be contagious, encouraging a culture of innovation and teamwork (Barkley, 2015).

e. Building Resilience in the Workplace

The challenges associated with ADHD, such as managing distractions or staying organized, often teach individuals how to develop systems and strategies to compensate for their difficulties. This resilience and determination can make them highly effective in overcoming workplace obstacles and delivering results, particularly when supported with tools like structured workflows or mentoring (Knouse & Safren, 2010).

2.2. Artificial Intelligence Overview

Artificial Intelligence (AI) involves designing machines that mimic human intelligence, enabling them to think, learn, and operate independently. This field includes various branches like machine learning, natural language processing, robotics, computer vision, and expert systems (Russell & Norvig, 2020). The primary aim of AI is to develop systems that can carry out tasks typically dependent on human cognitive abilities, such as solving problems, making decisions, and comprehending language.

AI systems are broadly categorized into two types:

- **Narrow AI (Weak AI):** Systems designed to perform a specific task, such as facial recognition or language translation, without generalizing to other tasks.
- **General AI (Strong AI):** Hypothetical systems capable of performing any intellectual task a human can do, often associated with self-awareness and adaptability.

2.2.1. Historical Development of AI

The evolution of AI has been shaped by periods of rapid advancement interspersed with "AI winters," during which progress slowed due to unmet expectations and funding cuts. Key milestones include:

- **Early Foundations (1940s-1950s):** The conceptual groundwork for AI was laid during this period, highlighted by Alan Turing's pioneering computational theories and his introduction of the Turing Test to assess machine intelligence (Turing, 1950).
- **Dartmouth Conference (1956):** AI formally emerged as a field during this event, where researchers set ambitious objectives, such as enabling machines to replicate human reasoning processes.
- **Symbolic AI (1950s-1970s):** Early AI research concentrated on rule-based systems that relied on symbolic reasoning and logic. Key achievements included expert systems like MYCIN, designed for medical diagnosis.
- **Rise of Machine Learning (1980s-1990s):** The focus shifted to data-driven techniques, emphasizing statistical methods and neural networks. Noteworthy progress during this era included the development of backpropagation algorithms, which became a cornerstone of modern deep learning.
- **Modern Era (2000s-Present):** Rapid advancements in computational power, access to large datasets, and innovative algorithms have propelled AI to new heights. Techniques such as deep learning and reinforcement learning

have revolutionized AI, enabling exceptional performance in tasks like image recognition and natural language processing

2.2.2. Key Subfields of AI

AI has key subfields namely: Machine Learning (ML), Natural Language Processing (NLP), Computer Vision, and Robotics—highlighting their core functionalities and potential applications in advancing neuropsychology and cognitive psychology. These fundamental subfields of Artificial Intelligence are explained below:

a. Machine Learning (ML)

Machine Learning (ML) is a fundamental component of contemporary artificial intelligence, enabling systems to identify patterns in data and improve their performance over time. ML methods are generally categorized into three main types. Supervised learning involves training models on labeled datasets to predict specific outcomes, while unsupervised learning focuses on discovering hidden structures within unlabeled data. Additionally, reinforcement learning involves training systems to take actions in an environment to maximize cumulative rewards (Sutton & Barto, 2018). Deep learning, a specialized subset of ML, employs neural networks with multiple layers to capture and model complex patterns. This approach has significantly advanced fields like image and speech recognition, as detailed by LeCun et al. (2015).

b. Natural Language Processing (NLP)

Natural Language Processing (NLP) aims to empower machines to comprehend, generate, and analyze human language. This subfield has facilitated various applications, including text summarization, language translation, chatbots, and virtual assistants. Additionally, it is used for sentiment analysis and content creation (Jurafsky & Martin, 2021). Recent developments in NLP, such as transformers and pre-trained models like GPT and BERT, have transformed the field by enabling machines to engage in text-based interactions with near-human fluency. These innovations have opened new possibilities for understanding and generating natural language.

c. Computer Vision

Computer Vision enables machines to interpret and analyze visual data from the world around them. A pivotal breakthrough in this field has been the introduction of Convolutional Neural Networks (CNNs), which have advanced the accuracy and efficiency of visual data processing. Key applications of computer vision include facial recognition, autonomous driving systems, and medical imaging for tasks like tumor detection. These technologies demonstrate the capability of AI to process and utilize visual information effectively in real-world contexts.

d. Robotics

AI-driven robotics combines sensory inputs, actuators, and intelligent algorithms to develop autonomous systems capable of interacting with and adapting to their physical surroundings. This integration has led to advancements in industrial automation, service robots, and autonomous vehicles (Khatib, 2016). Robotics continues to evolve with AI innovations, creating solutions for complex tasks and enabling machines to perform roles traditionally carried out by humans.

2.3. AI in Neuropsychology

Artificial Intelligence (AI) is transforming the field of neuropsychology by enhancing the understanding, diagnosis, and treatment of neurological disorders. By leveraging advanced computational techniques, AI enables the analysis of complex brain data, improving accuracy and efficiency in detecting and managing conditions such as Alzheimer's disease, epilepsy, and traumatic brain injuries. Through innovative tools and approaches, AI is reshaping how neuropsychologists approach brain health and cognitive function. Below are some of the neuropsychology areas that AI can be used:

a. Diagnosis and Neuroimaging

AI has significantly transformed the field of neuropsychology by enhancing the analysis of neuroimaging data and facilitating the detection of neurological disorders. For conditions like Alzheimer's disease and dementia, machine learning algorithms are employed to analyze MRI, PET, and CT scans, identifying biomarkers with precision and predicting disease progression. These AI-driven approaches often outperform traditional diagnostic methods in accuracy (Arbabshirani et al., 2017). Similarly, in epilepsy detection, AI systems trained on EEG data can predict seizures and classify epilepsy types, leading to proactive treatment strategies and better patient outcomes (Prajna et al., 2019). For traumatic brain injuries (TBI), AI integrates neuroimaging with clinical data to assess injury severity, enabling quicker and more accurate diagnoses (Lozano et al., 2021).

b. Cognitive Assessment and Monitoring

AI has advanced cognitive assessments, making them more precise and widely accessible. Digital neuropsychological tools, such as Cambridge Cognition and Mindstrong Health, utilize AI to administer real-time evaluations of memory, attention, and executive functions, providing clinicians with actionable insights (Davatzikos et al., 2019). Moreover, AI systems are adept at longitudinal monitoring, analyzing patterns in cognitive performance and brain activity over time to detect early signs of neurodegenerative conditions or cognitive decline.

2.4. AI in Cognitive Psychology

In cognitive psychology, AI is providing new pathways to explore and understand human mental processes. By simulating cognitive functions and analyzing behavioral patterns, AI offers insights into attention, memory, and perception, while also supporting therapeutic interventions. With its ability to model and monitor cognitive processes, AI is revolutionizing how we approach the study of the human mind and its application in real-world contexts. Below are some of the areas of cognitive psychology that AI can contribute to:

a. Modeling Cognitive Processes

AI significantly contributes to simulating and understanding cognitive processes. Neural network models have been used to mimic human attention mechanisms, offering insights into attentional disorders such as ADHD (Mnih et al., 2015). Furthermore, AI algorithms simulate memory processes, including encoding, storage, and retrieval, aiding the study of memory impairments in conditions like PTSD and amnesia (Ritter et al., 2018).

b. Behavioral Analysis and Interventions

AI technologies play a vital role in monitoring and enhancing cognitive and emotional well-being. Natural Language Processing (NLP) is employed in psychometric assessments, analyzing speech and text to evaluate cognitive impairments or detect psychological disorders such as depression and anxiety (Jiang et al., 2020). Additionally, wearable AI-powered devices track behavioral patterns, including sleep, activity, and physiological responses, offering real-time feedback to improve mental and cognitive health (Shatte et al., 2019).

c. Therapeutic Applications

AI is revolutionizing therapeutic interventions in cognitive psychology. For example, AI-driven chatbots like Woebot provide automated Cognitive Behavioral Therapy (CBT), making psychological support more accessible and scalable (Fitzpatrick et al., 2017). Similarly, AI-enhanced Virtual Reality (VR) systems create immersive environments for cognitive training and desensitization therapy, particularly effective for phobias and PTSD (Freeman et al., 2017).

d. AI-Driven Cognitive Rehabilitation

AI plays an essential role in cognitive rehabilitation, helping restore cognitive functions affected by injury or illness. AI-integrated Brain-Computer Interfaces (BCIs) enable individuals with motor and cognitive impairments to control external devices, such as prosthetics and communication tools, through neural signals (Mak et al., 2018). Furthermore, adaptive learning systems utilize AI to customize rehabilitation exercises based on real-time performance, providing personalized training for patients recovering from conditions like strokes or traumatic brain injuries.

2.5. Artificial Intelligence for ADHD

AI can be applied to enhance ADHD management in many ways. This section examines how AI contributes to therapy, behavioral monitoring, medication optimization, research, assessment, diagnosis, mentorship, and workplace support. By addressing these areas, the section highlights AI's potential to revolutionize ADHD care through personalized, scalable, and data-driven solutions.

2.5.1. AI in ADHD Therapeutic Intervention

a. Digital Therapeutics

AI-powered digital therapeutics are transforming the management of ADHD by delivering gamified solutions that enhance cognitive and behavioral outcomes. For example, cognitive training applications, such as Akili Interactive's EndeavorRx, utilize AI to provide video game-based interventions targeting attention and working memory. Approved by the FDA, these platforms have been shown to effectively reduce ADHD symptoms in children (Kollins et al., 2020). Additionally, AI enables personalized behavioral interventions by dynamically adjusting the difficulty of training programs based on individual progress. This adaptability ensures that the exercises remain engaging and appropriately challenging, supporting sustained improvements in cognitive and behavioral functions.

b. Virtual Reality (VR) Therapy

AI-enhanced VR systems offer immersive environments for behavioral training and exposure therapy, simulating real-world scenarios to support ADHD treatment. In social skills training, these tools create adaptive VR environments where individuals can practice interpersonal interactions in a controlled setting (Freeman et al., 2017). Similarly, VR-based executive function training focuses on core ADHD challenges, such as planning, organization, and impulse control, helping individuals develop essential cognitive skills through interactive ad engaging activities.

2.5.2. AI in ADHD Behavioral Monitoring

a. Wearable Technology

AI-driven wearable devices provide continuous and real-time insights into behavioral and physiological states associated with ADHD. These devices, equipped with accelerometers and gyroscopes, monitor hyperactivity and restlessness, analyzing patterns to deliver actionable feedback for caregivers and clinicians (Haddadi et al., 2020). Wearables also track physiological markers like heart rate variability (HRV) and galvanic skin response (GSR) to assess emotional states, enabling AI to recommend strategies for improving emotional regulation and self-control.

b. Smartphone-Based Monitoring

Smartphones serve as accessible platforms for monitoring ADHD behaviors in non-invasive ways. Through digital phenotyping, AI analyzes passive data, including screen time, app usage, and typing patterns, to detect signs of impulsivity and inattention (Wang et al., 2021). Additionally, behavioral logging apps powered by AI allow users to record behaviors and triggers, helping patients and clinicians identify patterns and develop targeted strategies for managing symptoms.

c. Medication Management

AI contributes significantly to optimizing ADHD treatment by tailoring medication regimens and minimizing side effects. Pharmacogenomic analysis uses AI to evaluate genetic and epigenetic data, predicting individual responses to various medications and enabling personalized treatment plans (Klein et al., 2019). Machine learning algorithms also aid in dosing optimization by analyzing patient-specific factors such as age, weight, and symptom severity to recommend precise dosing schedules, reducing the trial-and-error approach commonly associated with ADHD medication (Faraone et al., 2021).

2.5.3. AI in ADHD Research

AI accelerates ADHD research by processing large-scale datasets to uncover new insights into the disorder's biological and behavioral underpinnings. In neuroimaging studies, AI analyzes fMRI and EEG data to detect structural and functional brain abnormalities linked to ADHD, deepening our understanding of its neurobiological foundations (Brown et al., 2020). Additionally, behavioral modeling with AI simulates ADHD-related behaviors, enabling researchers to explore the influence of environmental and genetic factors on symptom development and expression (Franke et al., 2020).

2.5.4. AI in ADHD and Comorbidities

AI is instrumental in addressing the complexities of ADHD comorbidities, such as anxiety, depression, and learning disorders. Multi-modal assessment systems integrate diverse data sources, including neuroimaging, behavioral observations, and self-reports, providing a comprehensive understanding of ADHD alongside co-occurring conditions (Ehrlich et al., 2021). Furthermore, AI tailors interventions to address overlapping symptoms, such as using NLP-based chatbots to manage anxiety with mindfulness techniques while simultaneously addressing ADHD-related challenges like inattention.

2.5.5. AI for ADHD Assessment and Diagnosis

a. AI-Powered Diagnostic Tools

Large language models like ChatGPT can enhance ADHD diagnosis by providing personalized, adaptive care and identifying patterns through data analysis. These tools improve diagnostic accuracy while addressing challenges like privacy and cultural sensitivity, paving the way for ethical AI-assisted therapy (Berrezueta-Guzman et al., 2024).

b. AI-Powered Robotic Assistants

Robotic systems designed for ADHD assessment use real-time data processing and interactions with smart home devices to evaluate focus and task-related behaviors. They provide accurate observations that inform tailored interventions, enhancing clinical evaluations (J. Berrezueta-Guzman et al., 2021).

c. Eye-Tracking Technology

AI-driven eye-tracking tools analyze movement patterns to distinguish ADHD-specific behaviors. These systems offer accessible, non-invasive screening alternatives to traditional clinical methods (Chen, 2023).

d. Machine Learning and EEG-Based Diagnostics

Machine learning (ML) models combined with EEG data enhance ADHD diagnosis by improving efficiency and objectivity, addressing diagnostic controversies, and providing earlier access to interventions (Hernández-Capistran et al., 2023).

e. Virtual Reality (VR) Diagnostics

AI-powered VR tools use immersive environments to assess ADHD symptoms through cognitive and behavioral tasks. These methods reduce subjectivity and clinician dependence, providing objective and accurate assessments (Oh et al., 2024).

2.5.6. AI for ADHD Mentorship

a. Large Language Models

Large language models like ChatGPT provide empathetic and responsive support for ADHD mentorship by tailoring guidance to individual needs. These tools empower individuals while addressing behavioral challenges such as time management and focus (Berrezueta-Guzman et al., 2024).

b. Robotic Mentorship Systems

AI-powered robotic systems combine real-time data interaction and therapist guidance to mentor children with ADHD during tasks, offering personalized behavioral feedback to improve task performance (Berrezueta-Guzman et al., 2021).

c. AI-Driven Behavioral Insights

AI-based systems capture contextual data to provide self-reflective insights and tailored guidance. These tools help individuals identify their triggers and patterns, fostering greater self-awareness and behavioral management (Ravishankar, 2022).

d. AI in Mentorship and Inclusion

Advances in robotics and AI have created tools for personalized mentorship, promoting inclusion and social development. These tools guide individuals to reach their potential while addressing ADHD-specific needs (Ijichi and Ijichi, 2007).

e. Community-Based AI Models for ADHD Therapy

Integrating AI with Motivational Interviewing (MI), community-based models deliver mentorship through AI-driven feedback, digitized resources, and local supervision. These systems foster engagement and support in ADHD therapy (Sibley et al., 2024).

2.5.7. AI in ADHD Workplace Support

Artificial Intelligence (AI) and Machine Learning (ML) are revolutionizing how organizations address ADHD-related challenges, providing innovative tools to foster workplace inclusion, productivity, and support. By utilizing AI's data-driven precision and ML's adaptability, companies can create environments that empower employees with ADHD while enhancing overall organizational performance.

a. AI-Driven Tools for ADHD in the Workplace

AI-powered task and time management tools are instrumental in helping individuals with ADHD manage work responsibilities. Smart scheduling applications, such as Microsoft Outlook's AI assistant or clockwise, automate task prioritization, allocate focus time, and schedule breaks to reduce cognitive strain. Personalized reminder systems further enhance productivity by tailoring notifications to individual work habits, ensuring employees meet deadlines and stay organized (Holmes et al., 2018). Additionally, cognitive assistance technologies replicate executive functions often challenging for individuals with ADHD. Focus enhancement apps, like Brain.fm or Freedom, create environments optimized for sustained attention, while AI-driven tools such as Otter.ai assist with digital note taking, summarizing meetings, and organizing key tasks to help employees retain essential information.

b. Applications in Work Performance

AI offers innovative solutions to support individuals with ADHD in professional settings by addressing their unique challenges. Task management applications, such as Asana and Todoist, automate reminders, prioritize tasks, and create structured workflows to help individuals manage responsibilities effectively (Holmes et al., 2018). Focus-enhancing tools, including Brain.fm and Freedom, minimize distractions by providing personalized environments that promote sustained attention (Kollins et al., 2020). Additionally, automation platforms like Zapier reduce cognitive load by handling repetitive tasks, improving productivity and efficiency for employees with ADHD (Ehrlich et al., 2021).

c. AI for Organizational Insights and Support

AI enhances organizational understanding of ADHD by analyzing employee behavior and designing supportive interventions. Employee performance and engagement data are processed using machine learning algorithms to detect patterns, such as procrastination or hyperactivity, enabling constructive managerial support without stigma (Ehrlich et al., 2021). Performance feedback dashboards driven by AI provide tailored reviews, highlighting employees' strengths and offering targeted suggestions for improvement. Moreover, AI assists in creating inclusive accommodations by analyzing workspace dynamics, such as noise levels and interruptions, to recommend ADHD-friendly adjustments. Customized workflows further empower employees by breaking tasks into manageable steps or enabling flexible schedules tailored to individual needs.

d. AI for Learning and Development

AI-powered training programs cater to the unique learning styles of employees with ADHD, fostering professional growth. Personalized training platforms use machine learning algorithms to gamify content, making learning more engaging and accessible for neurodivergent employees (Kollins et al., 2020). Platforms such as Coursera and Udemy Business dynamically adjust the speed, complexity, and focus of training based on real-time progress and preferences. Additionally, AI supports neurodiversity awareness by delivering interactive content through chatbots, helping managers and teams better understand how to support ADHD employees. Virtual reality (VR) simulations powered by AI offer experiential learning, allowing coworkers to experience ADHD-related challenges firsthand, promoting empathy and reducing workplace stigma (Freeman et al., 2017).

e. AI in Monitoring and Feedback

Real-time monitoring tools powered by AI provide actionable feedback to employees and managers, enhancing workplace support. AI-enabled wearables track physiological data, such as heart rate and skin conductance, to identify periods of reduced focus or heightened stress, allowing for timely interventions (Haddadi et al., 2020). These systems can also suggest breaks or mindfulness exercises when signs of stress or inattention are detected, helping employees maintain emotional regulation and productivity. Collaboration platforms like Slack and Microsoft Teams leverage AI to analyze communication patterns, offering insights to improve teamwork. AI evaluates meeting participation to ensure engagement and suggests strategies to enhance focus and inclusion for ADHD employees. Machine learning models further assess team dynamics, facilitating effective task delegation and collaborative workflows that accommodate diverse working styles.

2. 6. ADHD Symptoms Improvement by AI-tools

The above AI tools can provide significant improvements in ADHD symptoms as highlighted in the table below (table 3):

Table 3. ADHD symptoms improvement by AI-tools

Category	AI Tool	ADHD Targeted Area	Outcome/Improvement
Therapeutic Intervention	EndeavorRx	Cognitive and Behavioral Outcomes	Improves attention and working memory through gamified cognitive training
Therapeutic Intervention	VR Therapy	Behavioral Training	Enhances social skills, planning, and impulse control using immersive environments
Behavioral Monitoring	Wearable Devices	Real-Time Behavioral Monitoring	Provides feedback to manage hyperactivity and emotional regulation
Behavioral Monitoring	Smartphone Monitoring	Behavioral Patterns	Tracks inattention and impulsivity through digital phenotyping
Medication Management	Pharmacogenomic Analysis	Personalized Treatment	Tailors medication regimens to reduce side effects and enhance efficacy
ADHD Research	Machine Learning with EEG	Neuroimaging and Diagnosis	Detects structural and functional brain abnormalities
ADHD and Comorbidities	Multi-Modal Assessment Systems	ADHD and Co-Occurring Conditions	Provides comprehensive insights into ADHD and overlapping symptoms
ADHD Assessment and Diagnosis	VR Diagnostics	Objective Symptom Assessment	Offers immersive assessments of ADHD symptoms

continued on following page

Table 3. Continued

Category	AI Tool	ADHD Targeted Area	Outcome/Improvement
ADHD Assessment and Diagnosis	Eye-Tracking Technology	Symptom Identification	Distinguishes ADHD-specific behaviors via eye movement patterns
ADHD Mentoring	Large Language Models	Behavioral Guidance	Supports time management and focus improvement
ADHD Mentoring	Robotic Mentorship Systems	Task Performance	Provides personalized feedback to enhance task execution
AI in Workplace Support for ADHD	Task Management Apps	Workplace Productivity	Improves task prioritization and reduces cognitive strain
AI in Workplace Support for ADHD	Focus Enhancement Apps	Attention Management	Creates distraction-free environments for sustained attention

2.7. Human-AI Collaboration in ADHD

Attention-Deficit/Hyperactivity Disorder (ADHD) is a complex neurodevelopmental disorder that demands personalized and multifaceted approaches to care. The integration of human expertise with artificial intelligence (AI) offers significant advancements in managing ADHD. By combining the analytical precision and scalability of AI systems with the empathy and contextual understanding of human professionals, ADHD diagnostics, interventions, and monitoring are becoming more effective and efficient. Technologies like machine learning (ML), natural language processing (NLP), and wearable devices are transforming the field, yet the role of human collaboration remains essential to ensure the optimal use of these tools while addressing associated ethical and operational challenges (Topol, 2019). Below is an exploration of how human-AI collaboration is advancing ADHD care across diagnostics, interventions, and research.

2.7.1. Human-AI Collaboration in ADHD Diagnostics

AI is revolutionizing ADHD diagnostics by enhancing the interpretation of complex datasets and providing actionable insights. One area of advancement is the use of neuroimaging biomarkers, where AI models analyze data from functional MRI (fMRI) and EEG scans to identify ADHD-specific patterns, such as irregularities in the prefrontal cortex and cerebellum. These insights are used by clinicians in conjunction with patient history and other clinical observations to confirm diagnoses, ensuring a more comprehensive and accurate diagnostic process (Brown et al., 2020). AI-powered tools also aid in behavioral analysis by leveraging wearable devices and eye-tracking technologies to assess symptoms such as hyperactivity, inattention, and impulsivity. These objective measurements complement clinical evaluations, reducing dependence on subjective reporting and increasing diagnostic reliability (Khosla et al., 2019).

Another transformative approach is AI-driven digital phenotyping, which involves analyzing data from smartphones, apps, and sensors to identify behaviors associated with ADHD. For instance, algorithms evaluate phone usage patterns, such as frequent switching between apps or irregular sleep schedules, which can signal ADHD-related behaviors. Clinicians can incorporate these metrics into their diagnostic frameworks to gain deeper insights into patient symptoms (Wang et al., 2021). Additionally, decision support systems powered by AI utilize extensive datasets to generate diagnostic recommendations. These systems provide evidence-based insights, supporting human experts in making more consistent and accurate decisions while minimizing diagnostic errors (Ehrlich et al., 2021).

Through the collaboration of AI systems and human professionals, ADHD diagnostics are becoming more precise, scalable, and data-driven, paving the way for improved patient outcomes and more personalized care.

2.7.2. Human-AI Collaboration in ADHD Monitoring

Wearable devices powered by AI offer continuous, real-time monitoring of ADHD symptoms, providing valuable data for personalized care. For instance, accelerometers embedded in wearables track physical activity levels, distinguishing typical movement patterns from ADHD-related hyperactivity. AI processes this information to generate detailed reports for clinicians, aiding in diagnosis and treatment adjustments (Haddadi et al., 2020). Sleep monitoring is another area where AI excels; by analyzing sleep data from wearables, these systems identify irregular patterns that may exacerbate ADHD symptoms. Such insights enable parents and clinicians to refine bedtime routines and adjust treatment plans accordingly (Chan et al., 2021).

Additionally, AI-powered platforms extend ADHD care beyond clinical environments through remote monitoring solutions. These systems alert caregivers to significant changes in behavior or symptoms, such as increased restlessness or difficulty focusing, facilitating timely interventions (Holmes et al., 2018). For clinicians, AI aggregates patient data into intuitive dashboards, allowing real-time tracking of progress and enabling on-the-fly adjustments to treatment strategies (Wang et al., 2021).

2.7.3. Human-AI Collaboration in ADHD Mentorship

Human-AI collaboration in ADHD mentorship integrates AI technologies with human expertise to provide tailored support for managing challenges such as time management, focus, and self-regulation. Conversational AI tools like ChatGPT engage mentees in interactive dialogue, offering personalized guidance, task breakdowns, and reminders, fostering a safe and supportive space for growth (Ehrlich et al., 2021). Robotic mentorship systems further enhance this collaboration by delivering real-time feedback and behavioral reinforcement under therapist supervision, improving task performance (Haddadi et al., 2020). AI systems also analyze behavioral data to identify triggers and patterns, helping mentees and mentors create effective strategies for self-regulation and productivity (Wang et al., 2021). Additionally, community-based AI models incorporate motivational interviewing and peer connections, promoting inclusion while addressing individual ADHD needs (Ehrlich et al., 2021). This partnership between AI tools and human mentors forms a dynamic framework that empowers individuals with ADHD to navigate their unique challenges effectively.

2.7.4. Human-AI Collaboration for ADHD Workplace Support

The workplace presents unique challenges for individuals with ADHD, and human-AI collaboration offers effective strategies to foster support and inclusion. AI-powered tools, such as smart task management systems, assist employees with ADHD in organizing and prioritizing responsibilities, thereby reducing cognitive load and improving productivity (Holmes et al., 2018). These tools can also provide adaptive reminders and focus-optimized environments, which help employees manage distractions and maintain attention during work tasks.

AI-driven systems further contribute by providing managers with data-driven insights into employee performance and engagement. Machine learning algorithms analyze patterns to identify specific challenges ADHD employees face, enabling managers to provide targeted support without stigmatization (Ehrlich et al., 2021). In addition, AI systems recommend accommodations, such as flexible schedules and optimized workflows, to create a more ADHD-friendly workplace environment. By working collaboratively with AI tools, managers and coworkers can better understand and support employees with ADHD, fostering a culture of inclusivity and productivity.

3. PROPOSED MODEL: HUMAN-AI COLLABORATION FOR ADHD SUPPORT

Based on previous research, highlighted in the text above, this research proposes a Human-AI Collaboration Model for ADHD Support can be structured around three interconnected stages: Diagnosis, Therapeutic Support, and Post-Therapy Monitoring and Mentorship in both individual and workplace contexts. This model involves three key stakeholders—the ADHD individual, the human therapist/ HR, and AI tools—and integrates theoretical frameworks and existing practices. This section provides a detailed explanation of this Human-AI Collaboration Model, addressing its application in individual and workplace contexts. The model focuses on combining the precision of artificial intelligence (AI) with the empathy and contextual understanding of human stakeholders, creating a holistic approach to ADHD management.

3.1. Individual-Centered ADHD Support Framework

This framework (fig.1) addresses the personal challenges of individuals with ADHD in their daily lives, focusing on improving emotional regulation, executive functioning, and overall quality of life.

Figure 1. Human-AI collaboration for ADHD support model: Individual centered

Stage 1: Diagnosis – AI-Augmented Assessments

- **Overview**: ADHD diagnosis often relies on subjective reporting and clinical observation. AI enhances this process by providing objective, data-driven insights.
- **Key Components**:
  - **Behavioral Analysis**: AI analyzes data from wearables (e.g., heart rate, movement patterns) and smartphone usage to identify signs of inattention, impulsivity, or hyperactivity.
  - **Neuroimaging**: AI processes data from EEG or fMRI scans, identifying ADHD-specific biomarkers in brain regions such as the prefrontal cortex.
  - **Digital Phenotyping**: Passive data from apps and sensors track daily patterns like irregular sleep, frequent app switching, and missed deadlines, correlating these with ADHD symptoms.
- **Human Role**:
  - Therapists interpret AI insights, considering the individual's personal and environmental context.
  - They incorporate AI findings into broader diagnostic processes.
- **Outcome**:
  - More accurate and personalized ADHD diagnosis, leading to targeted interventions.

Stage 2: Therapeutic Support – Human-AI Synergy

- **Overview**: Therapy combines AI-driven interventions with human expertise to maximize effectiveness.
- **Key Components**:
  - **Gamified Cognitive Training**: AI platforms like *EndeavorRx* offer engaging, game-based exercises that target attention and working memory.
  - **Real-Time Physiological Monitoring**: Wearables monitor stress levels and focus, alerting therapists or individuals to potential dysregulation.
  - **Adaptive Therapy Plans**: AI adjusts exercises and coping strategies based on real-time progress, ensuring interventions remain challenging yet achievable.
- **Human Role**:
  - Therapists guide therapy sessions, addressing emotional and psychological aspects that AI cannot fully resolve.
  - They adjust therapy plans based on AI-provided feedback.
- **Outcome**: Improved emotional regulation, focus, and coping mechanisms through a collaborative approach.

Stage 3: Post-Therapy Monitoring and Mentorship

- **Overview**: Continuous support ensures individuals can sustain progress beyond therapy sessions.
- **Key Components**:
  - **Behavioral Monitoring**: AI tools track routines, such as completing tasks, managing schedules, or maintaining healthy habits.
  - **Virtual Mentorship**: AI-powered assistants provide daily reminders, motivational nudges, and reinforcement of coping strategies.
  - **Comorbidity Management**: AI integrates mindfulness exercises and cognitive behavioral techniques to address anxiety or depression alongside ADHD.
- **Human Role**:
  - Therapists periodically review progress reports and adjust interventions as needed.
- **Outcome**: Sustained symptom management, greater autonomy, and enhanced quality of life.

3.2. Workplace-Centered ADHD Support Framework

This framework focuses on empowering individuals with ADHD to thrive in professional settings, addressing productivity, collaboration, and career development.

Figure 2. Human-AI collaboration for ADHD support model: Workplace centered

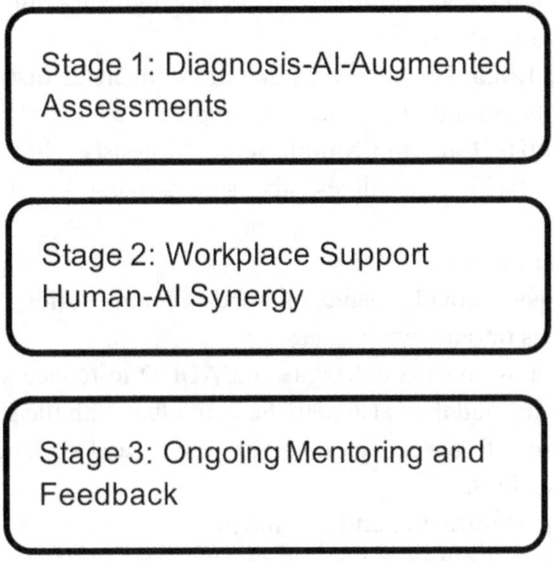

Stage 1: Diagnosis – AI-Augmented Assessments

- **Overview**: Adapting ADHD assessments to the workplace ensures insights are relevant to professional performance.
- **Key Components**:
  - **Behavioral Analytics**: AI monitors patterns such as task completion rates, response times, and app usage during work hours.
  - **Employee Feedback Integration**: Self-reports and peer feedback are analyzed to identify ADHD-related challenges like procrastination or disorganization.
  - **Performance Data Insights**: Tools like Microsoft Viva analyze workplace behaviors, identifying inefficiencies caused by ADHD symptoms.
- **Human Role**:
  - HR personnel and workplace therapists interpret AI findings and design personalized support plans.
- **Outcome**:
  - Improved understanding of ADHD's impact on workplace productivity and relationships.

Stage 2: Workplace Support – Human-AI Synergy

- **Overview**: AI and human support address ADHD-specific challenges in task management, focus, and collaboration.
- **Key Components**:
  - **Task Management Tools**: AI-powered apps like Asana or Todoist automate reminders, prioritize tasks, and segment complex projects into manageable steps.
  - **Focus Enhancement**: Apps like Brain.fm create distraction-free environments to support sustained attention.
  - **Executive Function Simulations**: AI assists with organizing workspaces, tracking deadlines, and summarizing key information from meetings.
- **Human Role**:
  - Managers provide mentorship and accommodations, such as flexible schedules or quiet workspaces.
  - HR teams educate colleagues on ADHD to reduce stigma and foster inclusivity, and they also help the individual with the challenging areas.
- **Outcome**: Enhanced productivity, focus, and collaboration in workplace settings.

Stage 3: Ongoing Monitoring and Feedback

- **Overview**: Continuous monitoring ensures employees with ADHD receive ongoing support and opportunities for growth.
- **Key Components**:

- **Real-Time Monitoring**: AI systems track focus levels, activity patterns, and emotional states, recommending breaks or mindfulness exercises when needed.
- **Collaboration Insights**: AI platforms analyze communication styles and team dynamics, offering suggestions for role optimization or task delegation.
- **Adaptive Workflows**: Machine learning creates workflows tailored to individual strengths and needs, such as flexible deadlines or smaller task increments.

- **Human Role**:
  - Managers and therapists periodically review AI reports and provide constructive feedback to employees.
- **Outcome**: Increased employee engagement, reduced burnout, and better alignment of ADHD strengths with job roles.

3.3. Key Distinctions Between Individual and Workplace-Centered Frameworks

The above frameworks have key distinctions and are used in different settings as explained below:

Table 4. Key distinctions between individual and workplace frameworks

Aspect	Individual-Centered Support	Workplace-Centered Support
Focus	Emotional regulation, daily routines	Productivity, collaboration, career development
Stakeholders	Individual, therapist, AI tools	Employee, manager/HR, workplace therapist, AI tools
AI Tools	Gamified apps, virtual mentorship, wearables	Task management tools, focus apps, analytics platforms
Outcome	Improved quality of life, autonomy	Enhanced performance, inclusion, and collaboration

3.4. Framework Synergy

The Human-AI Collaboration Model for ADHD Support effectively combines the strengths of human insight and AI precision. This synergy creates adaptive, scalable, and personalized solutions that address ADHD challenges in both personal and professional contexts. By integrating continuous monitoring, real-time interventions, and tailored support, this model ensures sustainable outcomes, benefiting both individuals and organizations.

4. CONCLUSION AND FUTURE DIRECTIONS

The Human-AI Collaboration Model for ADHD Support offers a revolutionary method for addressing ADHD-related challenges in both personal and workplace settings. By combining the analytical precision of artificial intelligence with the emotional intelligence and contextual awareness of human experts, this approach tackles ADHD's key areas: diagnosis, therapeutic interventions, and long-term monitoring.

For individuals, the framework emphasizes building emotional stability, improving cognitive functions, and fostering independence through tools like gamified training programs, virtual mentors, and real-time feedback systems. In professional environments, it supports productivity and teamwork by introducing AI-driven solutions for task management, customized workflows, and distraction-reducing tools tailored to the unique needs of employees with ADHD.

This model underscores the strengths of AI—its ability to scale, process data accurately, and provide consistent support—while recognizing the essential role of human input in delivering empathy, nuanced interpretation, and ethical guidance. The integration of these two elements creates a balanced, adaptive solution that enhances the management of ADHD while promoting inclusive practices in both personal and organizational contexts.

Future exploration of this model could involve further advancements in AI technologies, wider implementation in educational and workplace systems, and research to assess its effectiveness across different demographics. By addressing ADHD holistically, this collaborative model offers the potential to significantly elevate the quality of life for individuals while fostering supportive, accommodating environments in the workplace.

The author will carry future research that will prioritize the development and evaluation of a Minimum Viable Product (MVP) for this model, focusing on its real-world implementation and effectiveness. By creating an MVP, researchers can test practical applications of the framework, gather user feedback, and refine AI-human collaboration to optimize outcomes. This iterative process will help bridge the gap between conceptualization and practice, paving the way for broader adoption and innovation in ADHD care across diverse environments.

REFERENCES

Arbabshirani, M. R.. (2017). Advanced machine learning in diagnostic neuroimaging. *NeuroImage*, 145, 215–228. DOI: 10.1016/j.neuroimage.2016.12.015

Barkley, R. A. (2015). *Attention-deficit hyperactivity disorder: A handbook for diagnosis and treatment* (4th ed.). Guilford Press.

Barocas, S., Hardt, M., & Narayanan, A. (2019). *Fairness and machine learning: Limitations and opportunities*. MIT Press.

Bengio, Y., LeCun, Y., & Hinton, G. (2021). Deep learning for AI. *Nature Reviews. Physics*, 3(6), 447–456.

Berrezueta-Guzman, J., Pau, I., Martín-Ruiz, M.-L., & Máximo-Bocanegra, N. (2021). Assessment of a robotic assistant for supporting homework activities of children with ADHD. *IEEE Access : Practical Innovations, Open Solutions*, 9, 93450–93465. DOI: 10.1109/ACCESS.2021.3093233

Berrezueta-Guzman, S., Kandil, M., Martín-Ruiz, M.-L., Pau de la Cruz, I., & Krusche, S. (2024). Future of ADHD care: Evaluating the efficacy of ChatGPT in therapy enhancement. *Health Care*, 12(6), 683. DOI: 10.3390/healthcare12060683 PMID: 38540647

Brown, M. R.. (2020). AI-based neuroimaging biomarkers for ADHD. *NeuroImage*, 204, 116223. DOI: 10.1016/j.neuroimage.2020.116223

Chan, S., et al. (2021). AI and sleep monitoring for ADHD management. *Journal of Medical Informatics.*

Chen, X., Wang, S., Yang, X., Yu, C., Ni, F., Yang, J., Tian, Y., Ye, J., Liu, H., & Luo, R. (2023). Utilizing artificial intelligence-based eye tracking technology for screening ADHD symptoms in children. *Frontiers in Psychiatry*, 14, 1260031. DOI: 10.3389/fpsyt.2023.1260031 PMID: 38034916

Davatzikos, C., Bhatt, P., & Formisano, E. (2019). Predicting cognitive decline using AI in neuroimaging. *Journal of Alzheimer's Disease*, 68(3), 1223–1234. DOI: 10.3233/JAD-181148

Dignum, V. (2018). *Responsible AI: How to develop and use AI in a responsible way*. Springer.

Ehrlich, K.. (2021). AI insights in workplace ADHD support. *Organizational Behavior and Human Decision Processes.*

Ehrlich, S.. (2021). Advances in AI for ADHD management. *Nature Reviews. Neurology*, 17(5), 276–287. DOI: 10.1038/s41582-021-00473-x

Faraone, S. V., et al. (2021). Optimizing ADHD medication using AI. *Journal of Clinical Psychiatry, 82*(4), 21r13944. https://doi.org/DOI: 10.4088/JCP.20r13944

Faraone, S. V., Banaschewski, T., Coghill, D., Zheng, Y., Biederman, J., & Franke, B. (2021). The world federation of ADHD international consensus statement: 208 evidence-based conclusions about the disorder. *Neuroscience and Biobehavioral Reviews*, 128, 789–818. DOI: 10.1016/j.neubiorev.2021.01.022 PMID: 33549739

Fitzpatrick, K. K., Darcy, A., & Vierhile, M. (2017). Delivering CBT via AI chatbots. *Journal of Medical Internet Research*, 19(5), e132. DOI: 10.2196/jmir.7277

Freeman, D., Haselton, P., & Lister, R. (2017). Virtual reality in psychological therapy. *Annual Review of Clinical Psychology*, 13, 209–245. DOI: 10.1146/annurev-clinpsy-032816-045901

Goodfellow, I., Bengio, Y., & Courville, A. (2016). *Deep learning*. MIT Press.

Haddadi, A.. (2020). Wearable AI for ADHD monitoring. *IEEE Transactions on Biomedical Engineering*, 67(12), 3441–3450. DOI: 10.1109/TBME.2020.3006708

Haddadi, H.. (2020). Wearable AI systems for hyperactivity monitoring. *IEEE Transactions on Neural Systems and Rehabilitation Engineering*.

Hallowell, E. M., & Ratey, J. J. (2011). *Driven to distraction: Recognizing and coping with attention deficit disorder from childhood through adulthood*. Anchor.

Hernández-Capistran, J., Sánchez-Morales, L. N., Alor-Hernández, G., Bustos-López, M., & Sánchez-Cervantes, J. L. (2023). Machine and deep learning algorithms for ADHD detection: A review. In *Innovations in Machine and Deep Learning* (pp. 163–191). Case Studies and Applications. DOI: 10.1007/978-3-031-40688-1_8

Holmes, J.. (2018). AI in adaptive learning systems for ADHD. *Computers in Human Behavior*, 92, 66–75. DOI: 10.1016/j.chb.2018.10.016

Ijichi, S., & Ijichi, N. (2007). Computerized lifelong mentoring support using robots for autistic individuals. *Medical Hypotheses*, 68(3), 493–498. DOI: 10.1016/j.mehy.2006.08.016 PMID: 17023117

Jiang, F.. (2020). Natural language processing for cognitive assessments. *AI in Medicine*, 102, 101762. DOI: 10.1016/j.artmed.2020.101762

Jurafsky, D., & Martin, J. H. (2021). *Speech and language processing*. Pearson.

Kessler, R. C., Adler, L., Barkley, R., Biederman, J., Conners, C. K., Demler, O., Faraone, S. V., Greenhill, L. L., Howes, M. J., Secnik, K., Spencer, T., Ustun, T. B., Walters, E. E., & Zaslavsky, A. M. (2006). The prevalence and correlates of adult ADHD in the United States: Results from the National Comorbidity Survey Replication. *The American Journal of Psychiatry*, 163(4), 716–723. DOI: 10.1176/ajp.2006.163.4.716 PMID: 16585449

Khatib, O. (2016). Robotics and AI: Synergies and challenges. *AI Magazine*, 37(2), 1–7.

Klein, M.. (2019). Genetic insights into ADHD. *Nature Genetics*, 51(1), 7–8. DOI: 10.1038/s41588-018-0317-3 PMID: 30514911

Kooij, J. J. S., Bijlenga, D., Salerno, L., Jaeschke, R., Bitter, I., Balázs, J., Thome, J., Dom, G., Kasper, S., Nunes Filipe, C., Stes, S., Mohr, P., Leppämäki, S., Casas, M., Bobes, J., Mccarthy, J. M., Richarte, V., Kjems Philipsen, A., Pehlivanidis, A., & Asherson, P. (2019). Updated European Consensus Statement on diagnosis and treatment of adult ADHD. *European Psychiatry*, 56(1), 14–24. DOI: 10.1016/j.eurpsy.2018.11.001 PMID: 30453134

LeCun, Y., Bengio, Y., & Hinton, G. (2015). Deep learning. *Nature*, 521(7553), 436–444. DOI: 10.1038/nature14539 PMID: 26017442

Luckin, R.. (2016). AI in education: A transformative force. *Journal of Educational Technology & Society*, 19(3), 1–9.

Mak, J. N.. (2018). AI-integrated brain-computer interfaces. *Neurorehabilitation and Neural Repair*, 32(7), 602–612. DOI: 10.1177/1545968318787687

Mehrabi, N., Morstatter, F., Saxena, N., Lerman, K., & Galstyan, A. (2021). A survey on bias and fairness in machine learning. *ACM Computing Surveys*, 54(6), 1–35. DOI: 10.1145/3457607

Mnih, V., Kavukcuoglu, K., Silver, D., Rusu, A. A., Veness, J., Bellemare, M. G., Graves, A., Riedmiller, M., Fidjeland, A. K., Ostrovski, G., Petersen, S., Beattie, C., Sadik, A., Antonoglou, I., King, H., Kumaran, D., Wierstra, D., Legg, S., & Hassabis, D. (2015). Human-level control through deep reinforcement learning. *Nature*, 518(7540), 529–533. DOI: 10.1038/nature14236 PMID: 25719670

Oh, S., Joung, Y.-S., Chung, T.-M., Lee, J., Seok, B. J., Kim, N., & Son, H. M. (2024). Diagnosis of ADHD using virtual reality and artificial intelligence: An exploratory study of clinical applications. *Frontiers in Psychiatry*, 15, 1383547. DOI: 10.3389/fpsyt.2024.1383547 PMID: 38887727

Ravishankar, V. (2022). Designing an assistive technology for self-reflection for students suffering from ADHD at Malmö University (Dissertation). Retrieved from https://urn.kb.se/resolve?urn=urn:nbn:se:mau:diva-55292

Russell, S., & Norvig, P. (2020). *Artificial intelligence: A modern approach*. Pearson.

Shatte, A. B. R., Hutchinson, D. M., & Teague, S. J. (2019). AI in psychological assessments. *PLoS One*, 14(3), e0212935. DOI: 10.1371/journal.pone.0212935 PMID: 30840663

Sibley, M. H., Bickman, L., Atkins, D., Tanana, M., Coxe, S., Ortiz, M., Martin, P., King, J., Monroy, J. M., Ponce, T., Cheng, J., Pace, B., Zhao, X., Chawla, V., & Page, T. F. (2024). Developing an implementation model for ADHD intervention in community clinics: Leveraging artificial intelligence and digital technology. *Cognitive and Behavioral Practice*, 31(4), 482–497. DOI: 10.1016/j.cbpra.2023.02.001

Sutton, R. S., & Barto, A. G. (2018). *Reinforcement learning: An introduction*. MIT Press.

Topol, E. J. (2019). *Deep medicine: How artificial intelligence can make healthcare human again*. Basic Books.

Turing, A. M. (1950). Computing machinery and intelligence. *Mind*, 59(236), 433–460. DOI: 10.1093/mind/LIX.236.433

Wang, R.. (2021). Digital phenotyping and AI for ADHD. *Nature Digital Medicine*, 4(6), 322–333. DOI: 10.1038/s41746-021-00492-7

Zuboff, S. (2019). *The age of surveillance capitalism: The fight for a human future at the new frontier of power*. PublicAffairs.

ADDITIONAL READINGS

Atkins, D., Tanana, M., Coxe, L. S., Martin, P., Cheng, J., Pace, B., ... & Page, T. F. Developing an Implementation Model for ADHD Intervention in Community Clinics: Leveraging Artificial Intelligence and Digital Technology.

Berrezueta-Guzman, J., Pau, I., Martín-Ruiz, M.-L., & Máximo-Bocanegra, N. (2021). Assessment of a robotic assistant for supporting homework activities of children with ADHD. *IEEE Access : Practical Innovations, Open Solutions*, 9, 93450–93465. DOI: 10.1109/ACCESS.2021.3093233

Berrezueta-Guzman, S., Kandil, M., Martín-Ruiz, M.-L., Pau de la Cruz, I., & Krusche, S. (2024). Future of ADHD care: Evaluating the efficacy of ChatGPT in therapy enhancement. *Health Care*, 12(6), 683. DOI: 10.3390/healthcare12060683 PMID: 38540647

Chen, X., Wang, S., Yang, X., Yu, C., Ni, F., Yang, J., Tian, Y., Ye, J., Liu, H., & Luo, R. (2023). Utilizing artificial intelligence-based eye tracking technology for screening ADHD symptoms in children. *Frontiers in Psychiatry*, 14, 1260031. DOI: 10.3389/fpsyt.2023.1260031 PMID: 38034916

Hernández-Capistran, J., Sánchez-Morales, L. N., Alor-Hernández, G., Bustos-López, M., & Sánchez-Cervantes, J. L. (2023). Machine and deep learning algorithms for ADHD detection: A review. In *Innovations in Machine and Deep Learning* (pp. 163–191). Case Studies and Applications. DOI: 10.1007/978-3-031-40688-1_8

Ijichi, S., & Ijichi, N. (2007). Computerized lifelong mentoring support using robots for autistic individuals. *Medical Hypotheses*, 68(3), 493–498. DOI: 10.1016/j.mehy.2006.08.016 PMID: 17023117

Maté, G. (2011). *Scattered minds: The origins and healing of attention deficit disorder*. Vintage Canada.

Oh, S., Joung, Y.-S., Chung, T.-M., Lee, J., Seok, B. J., Kim, N., & Son, H. M. (2024). Diagnosis of ADHD using virtual reality and artificial intelligence: An exploratory study of clinical applications. *Frontiers in Psychiatry*, 15, 1383547. DOI: 10.3389/fpsyt.2024.1383547 PMID: 38887727

Ravishankar, V. (2022). Designing an assistive technology for self-reflection for students suffering from ADHD at Malmö University (Dissertation). Retrieved from https://urn.kb.se/resolve?urn=urn:nbn:se:mau:diva-55292

Sibley, M. H., Bickman, L., Atkins, D., Tanana, M., Coxe, S., Ortiz, M., Martin, P., King, J., Monroy, J. M., Ponce, T., Cheng, J., Pace, B., Zhao, X., Chawla, V., & Page, T. F. (2024). Developing an implementation model for ADHD intervention in community clinics: Leveraging artificial intelligence and digital technology. *Cognitive and Behavioral Practice*, 31(4), 482–497. DOI: 10.1016/j.cbpra.2023.02.001

KEY TERMS AND DEFINITIONS

AI-Powered Diagnosis: The identification of ADHD symptoms using AI-driven methods like behavioral analysis, neuroimaging, and digital phenotyping.

AI-Powered Post-Therapy Monitoring: Continuous tracking and mentorship provided by AI tools to reinforce coping strategies and sustain long-term progress.

AI-Powered Therapeutic Support: AI-assisted therapy combining gamified training, real-time monitoring, and human guidance to improve emotional regulation and focus.

AI-Powered Workplace ADHD Support: AI-driven strategies for enhancing productivity, task management, and collaboration for individuals with ADHD in professional settings.

Artificial Intelligence (AI): Advanced technology that processes data and provides tailored interventions, transforming ADHD care in diagnosis, therapy, and monitoring.

Attention-Deficit/Hyperactivity Disorder (ADHD): A neurodevelopmental disorder marked by inattention, hyperactivity, and impulsivity, affecting personal and workplace functioning.

Human-AI Collaboration: The partnership between AI systems and human stakeholders to enhance ADHD management through precision, empathy, and contextual understanding.

Chapter 17
Exploring the Association Between Caregiving Activities and Neuropsychological Disorders:
Deep Learning Model and Emerging Solutions

Usharani Bhimavarapu
https://orcid.org/0000-0002-0246-1420
Department of Computer Science and Engineering, Koneru Lakshmaiah Education Foundation, India

ABSTRACT

Neuropsychological disorders, such as dementia and other cognitive impairments, pose significant challenges not only to patients but also to their caregivers. As the prevalence of these disorders increases globally, the demand for caregiving support has escalated, highlighting the critical role of caregivers in managing both the physical and emotional needs of affected individuals. This study explores the physical health, mental health, caregiving behaviors, and health indicators among caregivers, differentiating between high- and low-intensity caregiving groups. The research employed a mixed-methods approach that included both qualitative face-to-face interviews and quantitative standardized questionnaires. The study involved 32 caregivers with an average age of 68 years. The main objectives were to compare

DOI: 10.4018/979-8-3693-9341-3.ch017

the frequency and intensity of caregiving activities, assess caregivers' physical and mental health status, and identify significant health behaviors associated with caregiving intensity.

INTRODUCTION

Neuropsychological disorders, which affect cognitive functions such as memory, attention, perception, and problem-solving, can have a profound impact on a patient's daily life. Conditions like Alzheimer's disease, Parkinson's disease, stroke, and traumatic brain injuries are common causes of these disorders(Patil et al., 2024). Patients suffering from neuropsychological disorders often experience significant cognitive decline, with memory loss being one of the most noticeable symptoms(Maristany et al., 2024). For example, individuals may forget recent events, struggle to recall names, or have difficulty remembering familiar places or faces. Alongside memory problems, there may be impairments in thinking and problem-solving abilities, making it challenging for individuals to perform everyday tasks, such as managing finances or cooking. Attention and concentration may also be compromised, with patients finding it hard to focus on tasks for extended periods.

In addition to cognitive decline, patients with neuropsychological disorders often experience behavioral and personality changes. These can include mood swings, irritability, and heightened anxiety. Depression and feelings of sadness are also common, sometimes intensifying the overall distress caused by cognitive impairments(Kalbe et al., 2024) . Furthermore, some patients may exhibit aggressive or uncharacteristic behaviors, such as agitation or emotional outbursts, which can make caregiving more challenging. As the disorder progresses, patients typically require increasing levels of care and assistance, which places a heavy burden on caregivers, who must adapt to the changing needs of their loved ones(Al Yahyaei et al., 2024).

Caregivers play an essential role in supporting individuals with neuropsychological disorders, such as Alzheimer's disease, dementia, and other cognitive impairments(Karunarathna et al., 2024). As these conditions lead to significant cognitive, emotional, and behavioral changes, patients often struggle to perform daily activities independently. Caregivers help patients with a wide range of tasks, including personal care (e.g., bathing, dressing, and toileting), medication management, and ensuring safety at home(Sun et al., 2021). By assisting with these activities, caregivers not only support the patient's physical health but also provide emotional and psychological support, helping alleviate the feelings of isolation, anxiety, and depression that are common in individuals with neuropsychological disorders(Bookwala et al., 2000). Moreover, caregivers help patients maintain a sense of routine, which can enhance their well-being and slow the progression of cognitive decline.

There are various categories of caregivers, each playing a distinct role based on the level of care required. Family caregivers are often spouses, children, or close relatives who provide the majority of care(Wolff et al., 2018). These caregivers are typically involved in both the emotional and physical aspects of caregiving and manage the patient's daily routines. However, family caregivers often face significant challenges, as the intensity of care can be physically and emotionally draining. Professional caregivers, including trained nurses and aides, offer specialized support and are hired to assist with medical tasks such as medication administration and physical therapy. They are essential for providing expert care and relieving family members of some caregiving responsibilities. Respite caregivers provide temporary relief to primary caregivers, offering short-term care to allow them time to rest and recharge. This type of caregiving is vital in preventing caregiver burnout. Lastly, voluntary caregivers are individuals from the community or social networks who offer occasional assistance with tasks or companionship, easing the burden on primary caregivers(Vos et al.,2021).

The need for caregivers is increasingly critical as neuropsychological disorders become more prevalent. They not only provide physical support but also offer invaluable emotional and psychological care that enables patients to manage the challenges of living with cognitive impairments. As caregiving demands grow, it is vital to support those who provide this essential care by offering resources, training, and respite opportunities to reduce their burden and improve both patient and caregiver outcomes.

Existing non-machine learning models for understanding the association between caregiving activities and neuropsychological disorders typically rely on traditional statistical and psychological frameworks, which aim to capture the relationship between caregivers' activities and patient outcomes. These models often involve observational or clinical data, structured assessments, and theoretical approaches. However, despite their utility, these models have several inherent limitations that make them less effective in addressing the complex, dynamic nature of caregiving in neuropsychological conditions.

One common approach is the use of traditional statistical models, such as regression analysis, to examine the relationship between caregiving intensity and patient outcomes(Shaffer et al.,2017). These models, which include linear and logistic regression, can provide valuable insights into how certain caregiving behaviors (e.g., providing emotional support or physical assistance) influence outcomes such as caregiver burden or the patient's cognitive function. However, these models often assume linear relationships between variables, which can oversimplify the complexities of caregiving. They also struggle with handling high-dimensional data or nonlinear interactions, which are common in caregiving scenarios where multiple factors influence both the patient's and caregiver's experiences over time.

Another widely used non-machine learning approach is pathway modeling, which focuses on mapping causal relationships between caregiving activities and various outcomes(Watland et al.,2023). Pathway models aim to understand the direct and indirect effects of caregiving behaviors on both the caregiver's health and the patient's condition. While they offer valuable insights into potential causal chains, these models often suffer from limitations in establishing true causality, particularly in complex environments like caregiving. Many of these models rely on cross-sectional or retrospective data, which can make it difficult to draw firm conclusions about causality, especially when confounding variables are not properly controlled for.

Multivariate analysis techniques, such as factor analysis, are also used to identify underlying patterns in caregiving activities and associated outcomes(Aljunaid et al.,2024). These models can group caregiving behaviors into latent factors and examine their relationships with various outcomes. However, factor analysis is often limited by the need for large, well-structured datasets and can be difficult to interpret, particularly in the context of caregiving and neuropsychological conditions, where behaviors and outcomes can be highly individualized. Additionally, these models may not adequately capture the temporal dynamics of caregiving, as they are typically based on data collected at a single point in time.

Qualitative models, including thematic analysis, are frequently used to explore caregivers' experiences through interviews or open-ended surveys(Felber et al.,2024). These models provide rich, in-depth insights into the challenges faced by caregivers and the emotional and practical aspects of caregiving. While they offer a deep understanding of the lived experience, qualitative approaches often lack generalizability due to small sample sizes and subjective interpretation of the data. Moreover, they do not provide predictive capabilities, which limits their usefulness in forecasting future caregiving needs or patient outcomes.

Clinical assessment tools, such as the Zarit Burden Interview (ZBI) (Oliver et al.,2024) and cognitive tests for patients, are commonly used to measure caregiving burden and assess patient functioning. These standardized tools help identify areas where caregivers may need support, but they often focus on specific aspects of caregiving or patient health at a single point in time. These assessments are also constrained by the caregiver's self-reporting biases or a limited view of the caregiving experience, and they may not adequately reflect the evolving nature of both the caregiver's and patient's needs over time.

While traditional non-machine learning models have provided valuable insights into caregiving and neuropsychological disorders, they are limited in their ability to capture the complexity, dynamics, and variability of caregiving experiences. They often fail to account for the changing nature of both the caregiver's role and the patient's condition over time, and they may not be equipped to predict future needs or outcomes. The increasing complexity of caregiving, especially in neuropsychological conditions, has led to a growing interest in machine learning approaches that can overcome these limitations and provide more personalized, dynamic predictions and recommendations.

The combination of Convolutional Neural Networks (CNN) and Long Short-Term Memory (LSTM) networks offers a powerful approach for predicting the stages of neuropsychological disorders and providing personalized caregiving advice(Hapsari et al., 2024, Wang et al.,2024). CNNs excel at extracting spatial features from data, such as medical images or sensor data, making them particularly useful for analyzing brain scans, activity patterns, or wearable sensor data that monitor both patient and caregiver behaviors. These models can detect patterns in the data that correlate with cognitive decline or changes in a patient's physical or emotional state. Once relevant features are extracted through the CNN layers, the LSTM network takes over to process time-series data, capturing the evolving nature of the patient's health over time. This is especially valuable in neuropsychological disorders like Alzheimer's disease, where symptoms progress gradually, and the caregiving needs shift as the disease advances.

Using the integrated CNN-LSTM model, the system can predict the current stage of a neuropsychological disorder by analyzing medical images, sensor data, and caregiving activity logs. For example, it can detect early signs of cognitive impairment from brain scans or monitor changes in mobility and sleep patterns that reflect disease progression. As the model is fed with sequential data, it becomes adept at forecasting future disease stages, offering insights into how a patient's condition may evolve. Additionally, the model's ability to assess both the patient's status and the caregiver's activities enables it to provide actionable caregiving advice tailored to the individual's needs. This advice can range from suggestions on supporting memory retention in the early stages of cognitive decline to more specialized recommendations on safety measures and behavioral management in advanced stages.

By offering personalized recommendations, the CNN-LSTM model helps caregivers navigate the complexities of providing care. It reduces the uncertainty caregivers often face by recommending strategies that align with the patient's condition, thus improving both the quality of care and caregiver well-being. For example, if the model predicts an increase in patient agitation, it can suggest de-escalation techniques or the introduction of more professional support. Additionally, the model's ability to predict future needs based on historical data helps prevent caregiver burnout by providing timely guidance on self-care and respite opportunities.

Despite its potential, the CNN-LSTM model comes with certain limitations. The accuracy of predictions depends heavily on the quality and quantity of data it is trained on. Incomplete or poor-quality data may lead to incorrect recommendations or predictions. Additionally, the complexity of CNN-LSTM models can make them difficult to interpret, potentially causing uncertainty for caregivers and healthcare professionals who need to trust the model's advice. Moreover, training and running such models can require significant computational resources, particularly when processing large datasets, which may limit accessibility for some users.

MATERIALS AND METHODOLOGY

This study employed a mixed-methods approach to investigate the health and caregiving experiences of caregivers, with 32 participants divided into high-intensity and low-intensity caregiving groups. Qualitative data were collected through semi-structured face-to-face interviews, allowing caregivers to share their personal experiences and challenges in providing care. Quantitative data were gathered using standardized questionnaires to assess physical health indicators, caregiving activities, health behaviors, and mental well-being. The study aimed to compare the caregiving demands and health outcomes between the two caregiver groups. Data analysis involved thematic analysis for the qualitative data and descriptive and inferential statistical methods for the quantitative data. The combination of these methods provided a comprehensive understanding of the impact of caregiving intensity on caregiver health and well-being.

Materials

This study employed a mixed-method approach to understand the experiences of caregivers through face-to-face interviews and standardized questionnaires. Each interview was scheduled at a time and location chosen by the participants to ensure their comfort and encourage open communication. Most interviews (10) were conducted in the participants' homes, attended only by the interviewee and the interviewers. Observers took notes on non-verbal cues to enhance the richness of the data. None of the participants had prior relationships with the researchers, ensuring unbiased interactions.

The mixed-method approach included semi-structured interviews and questionnaires. The interviews allowed participants to share their experiences freely, while the questionnaires captured quantitative data on various aspects of caregiver well-being, such as caregiver burden, mental health (anxiety and depressive symptoms), sleep quality, quality of life, self-care, diet adherence, physical activity, and body mass index. Since the questionnaire responses could reveal additional insights not expressed during the interviews, this segment was audio-recorded. Researchers verbally administered the questionnaires and documented responses.

The study involved 32 caregivers, with an average age of 68.0 ± 10 years. Among the participants, 64.3% were female, 85.7% were married, and 82.1% were retired.

Care Giving Measures

For neuropsychological patients, caregiving activities can be categorized into five domains, as outlined by Riffin et al. (2024) (Riffin,2024) and Wolff et al. (2024) (Wolff et al., 2024). The first domain, health management, involves tasks such as administering medications, managing medical appointments, and monitoring symptoms or behavioral changes. The second domain, Activities of Daily Living (ADLs) (Kelbling et al.,2024), includes assisting with basic self-care tasks like dressing, bathing, grooming, and mobility. The third domain, Instrumental Activities of Daily Living (IADLs) (Kelbling et al.,2024), encompasses managing finances, household tasks, shopping, and meal preparation. Emotional and behavioral support forms the fourth domain, focusing on addressing neuropsychological symptoms such as memory lapses or confusion and providing emotional reassurance or de-escalation during episodes. Lastly, the fifth domain involves communication with healthcare providers, which includes coordinating care and sharing critical updates with medical teams. Together, these domains highlight the multifaceted responsibilities of caregivers for neuropsychological patients.

Electronic Health Record

Caregivers' physical health was assessed using two distinct approaches: self-reported indicators and documented diagnoses from electronic health records (EHR). The self-reported indicators allowed caregivers to provide subjective insights into their overall health, including perceptions of physical well-being, symptoms, and any limitations they experienced in daily activities. This method captures how caregivers personally evaluate their health, which is crucial for understanding their lived experiences and the impact of caregiving on their physical state.

In contrast, EHR data provided objective and clinically verified information about the caregivers' health conditions. These records included documented diagnoses, medical histories, chronic conditions, and other relevant health metrics recorded during medical visits. The integration of self-reported data and EHR diagnoses offers a more comprehensive understanding of caregivers' physical health by combining subjective perceptions with objective clinical evidence. This dual approach ensures a more nuanced evaluation of how caregiving responsibilities influence caregivers' health.

Promoting Health

Health promotion behaviors were evaluated using five subscales from the Health Promoting Lifestyle Profile (HPLP) (Liu et al.,2024). These subscales assessed various dimensions of healthy living, including physical activity, which measured exercise frequency and movement; nutrition, focusing on dietary habits and consumption of balanced meals; health responsibility, which examined actions taken to monitor and maintain personal health, such as regular checkups; stress management, evaluating strategies for coping with and reducing stress; and interpersonal relations, which explored the quality and frequency of social interactions and supportive relationships. Together, these subscales provided a comprehensive view of caregivers' engagement in behaviors that support overall well-being.

Analytical Prediction

For predicting caregiver hard work detection and patient neuropsychological stage detection using a CNN+LSTM model, the data undergoes several stages of processing, where the model combines the strengths of convolutional neural networks (CNNs) for spatial feature extraction and long short-term memory (LSTM) networks for temporal analysis. The dataset typically includes sequential and structured data, such as caregiver task logs, patient neuropsychological assessments, and other health indicators like caregiving hours, task types, and neuropsychological symptoms over time. This data is first preprocessed, which may involve normalizing continuous numerical values, one-hot encoding categorical variables, and restructuring time-series data into sequences that can be input into the model.

Once the data is prepared, it is passed through the convolutional layers of the CNN. In this step, the model identifies spatial features from the input data, such as relationships between caregiver workload and various caregiving tasks or fluctuations in a patient's health metrics. If the data includes time-series sequences that have been converted into 2D representations, such as spectrograms or heatmaps of patient symptoms or caregiving behaviors, the CNN layers effectively identify spatial patterns. These patterns might include identifying periods of intense caregiving work or changes in a patient's neuropsychological stage that are indicative of specific time-based symptoms or task-related difficulties.

After the convolutional layers, the data flows through pooling layers. The purpose of pooling is to reduce the spatial dimensions of the feature maps while maintaining the most essential information. This helps in reducing computational complexity and preventing overfitting by focusing on the dominant features extracted during convolution. Pooling operations, like max pooling, condense the feature maps into a more manageable size, which simplifies the model and ensures that only the most relevant information is passed on for further processing, thereby improving generalization.

Following pooling, the feature maps are flattened into a 1D vector, which is then fed into the LSTM layers. The LSTM is designed to capture the temporal dependencies in the data, which is crucial for understanding how caregiving workload and patient symptoms evolve over time. For example, the LSTM can detect how a caregiver's workload changes day by day based on the types of tasks and the patient's condition or how a patient's neuropsychological symptoms (such as cognitive decline) progress over several weeks or months. The LSTM's memory mechanism enables it to retain long-term dependencies and recognize patterns in sequences, such as sudden changes in caregiving efforts or shifts in patient neuropsychological stages.

Once the temporal features are processed by the LSTM, the output is passed through fully connected layers. These layers combine the spatial features extracted by the CNN and the temporal features processed by the LSTM, creating a unified representation of the data. The fully connected layers serve to integrate the learned information and produce a final prediction. For caregiver hard work detection, the model can predict the level of effort based on the intensity and frequency of caregiving tasks and how these change over time. Similarly, for patient neuropsychological stage detection, the model predicts the patient's current stage by analyzing patterns in their symptoms over time.

Finally, the model produces the prediction, which can be used for decision-making, such as identifying caregivers who may be at risk of burnout or assessing the severity of a patient's neuropsychological condition. The CNN+LSTM model's ability to simultaneously handle spatial and temporal features makes it particularly well-suited for analyzing the complex relationships in caregiving tasks and patient health over time. The integration of both these layers allows for accurate and efficient detection of caregiver workload and patient neuropsychological stages, providing valuable insights that can inform interventions and support strategies for both caregivers and patients.

EXPERIMENTAL RESULTS

The characteristics of the participants, including both caregivers and patients, are essential for understanding the dynamics of caregiving and its impact on health outcomes. For caregivers, demographic information such as age, gender, marital status, educational background, and employment status plays a significant role in shaping caregiving experiences. These factors can influence how much time and energy caregivers are able to devote to caregiving, as well as their overall health and well-being. For example, younger caregivers may experience different levels of physical strain compared to older caregivers, and caregivers with higher levels of education may have better access to resources or knowledge to manage the care effectively.

In addition to demographic factors, the caregiving experience itself is a crucial characteristic. This includes the number of hours spent on caregiving tasks, the duration of caregiving, and the types of assistance required, such as help with Activities of Daily Living (ADLs) or Instrumental Activities of Daily Living (IADLs). The level of care required by the patient—whether they have mild cognitive impairment, Alzheimer's disease, or another neuropsychological condition—also significantly influences the intensity and complexity of caregiving tasks. Caregivers' physical and mental health is another important factor, with self-reported health conditions, chronic illnesses, and diagnoses from electronic health records (EHR) offering insights into the strain caregiving may place on their own well-being. Caregivers may experience physical exhaustion, stress, or mental health challenges, such as anxiety or depression, which can impact their caregiving ability and quality of life.

Psychosocial factors, including social support and coping strategies, are also key components of caregiving. A strong social network can help alleviate the burden, whereas lack of support or poor relationships can contribute to caregiver burnout. Furthermore, socioeconomic factors, such as income, access to healthcare, and employment status, can affect a caregiver's ability to manage both the financial and emotional aspects of caregiving. These factors may determine whether a caregiver has the resources to hire external help or access medical care, and they can influence how much stress the caregiver experiences.

Together, these characteristics provide a comprehensive understanding of the caregivers' experiences, which is crucial for assessing both the challenges they face and their ability to support the patient effectively.

Table 1 presents the characteristics of the participants in terms of demographic information, caregiving experience, health indicators, health promotion behaviors, and psychosocial factors, comparing all participants with high-intensity and low-intensity caregivers. In terms of demographics, the average age for all participants is 68.0 ± 10.0 years, with high-intensity caregivers being older (70.5 ± 9.4 years) compared to low-intensity caregivers (65.5 ± 10.4 years). Gender distribution shows that 64.3% of all participants are female, with high-intensity caregivers comprising 70% female, and low-intensity caregivers comprising 60% female. Most participants are married (85.7%), with high-intensity caregivers at 88% and low-intensity caregivers at 83%. The majority of participants are retired (82.1%), with high-intensity caregivers at 80% retired, and low-intensity caregivers at 85% retired. Regarding caregiving experience, all participants report an average of 25.5 ± 10.0 hours of caregiving per week, with high-intensity caregivers averaging 35.0 ± 12.4 hours, while low-intensity caregivers average 16.0 ± 6.8 hours. The duration of caregiving is 4.5 ± 2.1 years for all participants, with high-intensity caregivers averaging 5.0 ± 2.5 years and low-intensity caregivers averaging 4.0 ± 2.0 years. A large proportion of participants (90.6%) identify as the primary caregiver, with high-intensity caregivers at 93% and low-intensity caregivers at 88%.In terms of health indicators, self-reported physical health shows that 50% of all participants rate their health as good, while 40% rate it as fair, and 10% as poor. High-intensity caregivers report 40% good, 50% fair, and 10% poor, while low-intensity caregivers report 60% good, 30% fair, and 10% poor. Self-reported mental health is rated as good by 45% of all participants, with high-intensity caregivers reporting 35% good and low-intensity caregivers reporting 55% good. Chronic health conditions affect 60% of all participants, with 65% of high-intensity caregivers and 55% of low-intensity caregivers reporting chronic conditions. For health promotion behaviors, 56.3% of all participants engage in physical activity, with 60% of high-intensity caregivers and 53% of low-intensity caregivers doing so. Balanced diet adherence is reported by 53.1% of all participants, with 50% of high-intensity caregivers and 55% of low-intensity caregivers following a balanced diet. Stress management techniques are employed by 60% of all participants, with 65% of high-intensity caregivers and 55% of low-intensity caregivers using such techniques. Regular health check-ups are reported by 68.8% of all participants, with 70% of high-intensity caregivers and 68% of low-intensity caregivers attending regular check-ups. In terms of social support, 78.1% of all participants report strong support, with 80% of high-intensity caregivers and 75% of low-intensity caregivers reporting strong support. Regarding psychosocial factors, social isolation is experienced by 34.4% of all participants, with 40% of high-intensity caregivers and 30% of low-intensity caregivers reporting social isolation. Finally, caregiver burnout is reported by 28.1% of all participants, with 35% of high-intensity caregivers and 22% of low-intensity caregivers reporting burnout.

Table 1. Characteristics of the participants

Characteristic	All Participants (n=32)	High-Intensity Caregivers (n=16)	Low-Intensity Caregivers (n=16)
Demographic Information			
Age (Mean [SD])	68.0 ± 10.0	70.5 ± 9.4	65.5 ± 10.4
Gender (Male/Female)	35.7% Male, 64.3% Female	30% Male, 70% Female	40% Male, 60% Female
Marital Status	85.7% Married, 14.3% Single	88% Married, 12% Single	83% Married, 17% Single
Employment Status (Employed/ Retired)	17.9% Employed, 82.1% Retired	20% Employed, 80% Retired	15% Employed, 85% Retired
Caregiving Experience			

continued on following page

Table 1. Continued

Characteristic	All Participants (n=32)	High-Intensity Caregivers (n=16)	Low-Intensity Caregivers (n=16)
Hours of Caregiving (Mean [SD])	25.5 ± 10.0	35.0 ± 12.4	16.0 ± 6.8
Duration of Caregiving (Mean [SD])	4.5 ± 2.1	5.0 ± 2.5	4.0 ± 2.0
Primary Caregiver (Yes/No)	90.6% Yes, 9.4% No	93% Yes, 7% No	88% Yes, 12% No
Health Indicators			
Self-reported Physical Health (Good/Fair/Poor)	50% Good, 40% Fair, 10% Poor	40% Good, 50% Fair, 10% Poor	60% Good, 30% Fair, 10% Poor
Self-reported Mental Health (Good/Fair/Poor)	45% Good, 40% Fair, 15% Poor	35% Good, 50% Fair, 15% Poor	55% Good, 30% Fair, 15% Poor
Chronic Health Conditions (Yes/No)	60% Yes, 40% No	65% Yes, 35% No	55% Yes, 45% No
Health Promotion Behaviors			
Physical Activity (Yes/No)	56.3% Yes, 43.7% No	60% Yes, 40% No	53% Yes, 47% No
Balanced Diet (Yes/No)	53.1% Yes, 46.9% No	50% Yes, 50% No	55% Yes, 45% No
Stress Management Techniques (Yes/No)	60% Yes, 40% No	65% Yes, 35% No	55% Yes, 45% No
Health Check-ups (Regular/Irregular)	68.8% Regular, 31.3% Irregular	70% Regular, 30% Irregular	68% Regular, 32% Irregular
Social Support (Strong/Weak)	78.1% Strong, 21.9% Weak	80% Strong, 20% Weak	75% Strong, 25% Weak
Psychosocial Factors			
Social Isolation (Yes/No)	34.4% Yes, 65.6% No	40% Yes, 60% No	30% Yes, 70% No
Caregiver Burnout (Yes/No)	28.1% Yes, 71.9% No	35% Yes, 65% No	22% Yes, 78% No

Health indicators and health promotion behaviors are crucial for understanding the well-being of caregivers and the impact that caregiving has on their physical and mental health. Health indicators typically include both self-reported and clinical measures of a caregiver's health status. These can involve physical health conditions such as chronic illnesses (e.g., hypertension, diabetes), fatigue, and sleep disturbances, as well as mental health issues like stress, anxiety, depression, and burnout, which are common among caregivers. Self-reported health assessments, along with objective data from electronic health records (EHR), help provide a comprehensive picture of a caregiver's health. These indicators are vital for identifying areas where caregivers may be at risk and require support or intervention to prevent negative health outcomes.

Health promotion behaviors refer to actions caregivers take to improve or maintain their health. These behaviors are often assessed using tools like the Health Promoting Lifestyle Profile (HPLP), which looks at key areas of well-being. Regular physical activity is one such behavior, helping caregivers manage the physical demands of caregiving and reduce stress. Nutrition also plays a critical role, as caregivers must prioritize their own diet to ensure they have the energy and stamina to care for others. Stress management is another key behavior, as caregiving can be emotionally taxing. Techniques such as relaxation exercises, mindfulness, or seeking social support help caregivers manage the stress that comes with caregiving responsibilities. Additionally, health responsibility behaviors—such as attending routine medical check-ups and managing existing health conditions—ensure that caregivers proactively care for their own health. Lastly, maintaining interpersonal relationships is essential, as strong social networks provide emotional support and reduce feelings of isolation, which are common among caregivers. By assessing both health indicators and health promotion behaviors, healthcare professionals can gain a better understanding of how caregiving affects caregivers' health and identify strategies to support them in maintaining their well-being.

Table 2 presents the caregiving measures for all participants, as well as for high-intensity and low-intensity caregivers. It provides insights into the caregiving workload, caregiver characteristics, and the impact of caregiving on various aspects of health and well-being.The hours of caregiving per week are significantly higher for high-intensity caregivers, with an average of 35.0 ± 12.4 hours, compared to 16.0 ± 6.8 hours for low-intensity caregivers. The overall average for all participants is 25.5 ± 10.0 hours. Similarly, the duration of caregiving is also higher for high-intensity caregivers (5.0 ± 2.5 years) compared to low-intensity caregivers (4.0 ± 2.0 years), with an overall average of 4.5 ± 2.1 years for all participants. Regarding the primary caregiver role, most participants (90.6%) identify as the primary caregiver, with 93% of high-intensity caregivers and 88% of low-intensity caregivers fulfilling this role. The caregiver's age shows an average of 68.0 ± 10.0 years for all participants, with high-intensity caregivers being older (70.5 ± 9.4 years) compared to low-intensity caregivers (65.5 ± 10.4 years). The gender distribution among caregivers shows that 64.3% of all participants are female, with 70% of high-intensity caregivers and 60% of low-intensity caregivers being female. In terms of marital status, the majority of caregivers are married, with 85.7% of all participants, 88% of high-intensity caregivers, and 83% of low-intensity caregivers being married. Most participants are retired (82.1%), with 20% of high-intensity caregivers and 15% of low-intensity caregivers still employed. In terms of caregiver burden, 28.1% of all participants report experiencing burden, with 35% of high-intensity caregivers and 22% of low-intensity caregivers reporting burden. Similarly, 34.4% of all participants report caregiving-related stress, with 40% of high-intensity caregivers and 30% of low-intensity caregivers reporting stress. Social support is generally strong, with 78.1% of all participants reporting strong support, 80% of high-intensity caregivers, and 75% of low-intensity caregivers. Physical activity is engaged in by 56.3% of all participants, with 60% of high-intensity caregivers and 53% of low-intensity caregivers participating in physical activity. The sleep quality data reveals that 50% of all participants report good sleep, with 40% reporting fair and 10% poor sleep. High-intensity caregivers report slightly lower sleep quality, with 40% rating their sleep as good, 50% as fair, and 10% as poor. In contrast, low-intensity caregivers report 60% good sleep, 30% fair, and 10% poor sleep. Regarding chronic health conditions, 60% of all participants report having at least one chronic condition, with 65% of high-intensity caregivers and 55% of low-intensity caregivers reporting chronic conditions.

Table 2. Care giving measures table

Caregiving Measure	All Participants (n=32)	High-Intensity Caregivers (n=16)	Low-Intensity Caregivers (n=16)
Hours of Caregiving per Week (Mean [SD])	25.5 ± 10.0	35.0 ± 12.4	16.0 ± 6.8
Duration of Caregiving (Mean [SD])	4.5 ± 2.1	5.0 ± 2.5	4.0 ± 2.0
Primary Caregiver (Yes/No)	90.6% Yes, 9.4% No	93% Yes, 7% No	88% Yes, 12% No
Caregiver's Age (Mean [SD])	68.0 ± 10.0	70.5 ± 9.4	65.5 ± 10.4
Gender (Male/Female)	35.7% Male, 64.3% Female	30% Male, 70% Female	40% Male, 60% Female
Marital Status (Married/Single)	85.7% Married, 14.3% Single	88% Married, 12% Single	83% Married, 17% Single
Employment Status (Employed/ Retired)	17.9% Employed, 82.1% Retired	20% Employed, 80% Retired	15% Employed, 85% Retired
Caregiver Burden (Yes/No)	28.1% Yes, 71.9% No	35% Yes, 65% No	22% Yes, 78% No
Caregiving-related Stress (Yes/ No)	34.4% Yes, 65.6% No	40% Yes, 60% No	30% Yes, 70% No
Social Support (Strong/Weak)	78.1% Strong, 21.9% Weak	80% Strong, 20% Weak	75% Strong, 25% Weak
Physical Activity (Yes/No)	56.3% Yes, 43.7% No	60% Yes, 40% No	53% Yes, 47% No
Sleep Quality (Good/Fair/Poor)	50% Good, 40% Fair, 10% Poor	40% Good, 50% Fair, 10% Poor	60% Good, 30% Fair, 10% Poor
Chronic Health Conditions (Yes/No)	60% Yes, 40% No	65% Yes, 35% No	55% Yes, 45% No

Table 3 presents a comparison of health indicators across all participants, high-intensity caregivers, and low-intensity caregivers, providing insight into various physical and mental health aspects. The data reveals differences between the two groups in terms of self-reported physical and mental health, chronic conditions, sleep quality, body mass index (BMI), and the presence of specific diseases such as diabetes and cardiovascular disease. In terms of self-reported physical health, 50% of all participants report their health as good, 40% as fair, and 10% as poor. For high-intensity caregivers, 40% report their health as good, 50% as fair, and 10% as poor, indicating a slightly lower physical health perception. In contrast, 60% of low-intensity caregivers rate their physical health as good, 30% as fair, and 10% as poor, suggesting that low-intensity caregivers perceive their health more positively than high-intensity caregivers. For self-reported mental health, 45% of all participants report their mental health as good, 40% as fair, and 15% as poor. High-intensity caregivers report a lower percentage of good mental health (35%) with 50% indicating fair and 15% poor mental health. Low-intensity caregivers report 55% as good, 30% as fair, and 15% as poor, reflecting better mental health compared to high-intensity caregivers. Regarding chronic health conditions, 60% of all participants report having chronic conditions, with 40% reporting none. High-intensity caregivers experience a higher rate of chronic conditions at 65%, while low-intensity caregivers report 55% chronic conditions, indicating that high-intensity caregivers may be more susceptible to chronic health issues. The sleep quality data shows that 50% of all participants rate their sleep as good, 40% as fair, and 10% as poor. High-intensity caregivers report 40% as good, 50% as fair, and 10% as poor, suggesting slightly poorer sleep quality compared to low-intensity caregivers, who report 60% as good, 30% as fair, and 10% as poor.

In terms of body mass index (BMI), all participants have an average BMI of 26.5 ± 5.2, with high-intensity caregivers having a slightly higher average of 27.0 ± 5.5 and low-intensity caregivers reporting a lower average of 26.0 ± 4.8. The chronic conditions data indicates that high-intensity caregivers experience an average of 1.7 ± 0.9 chronic conditions, slightly higher than the 1.5 ± 0.8 chronic conditions reported by all participants and the 1.3 ± 0.7 chronic conditions for low-intensity caregivers. For blood pressure, the average for all participants is 130/85 ± 10/5, with high-intensity caregivers having slightly higher blood pressure readings at 135/90 ± 10/5, and low-intensity caregivers reporting 125/80 ± 10/5, reflecting healthier blood pressure levels among this group. Regarding specific diseases, 25% of all participants report having diabetes, with high-intensity caregivers having a slightly higher rate at 30%, and low-intensity caregivers reporting 20%. In terms of cardiovascular disease, 18.8% of all participants are affected, with similar rates observed in both caregiver groups (20% for high-intensity caregivers and 17.5% for low-intensity caregivers).

Lastly, 21.9% of all participants report mental health diagnoses, with high-intensity caregivers reporting 25% and low-intensity caregivers 18.8%.

Table 3. Health indicators

Health Indicator	All Participants (n=32)	High-Intensity Caregivers (n=16)	Low-Intensity Caregivers (n=16)
Self-reported Physical Health	50% Good, 40% Fair, 10% Poor	40% Good, 50% Fair, 10% Poor	60% Good, 30% Fair, 10% Poor
Self-reported Mental Health	45% Good, 40% Fair, 15% Poor	35% Good, 50% Fair, 15% Poor	55% Good, 30% Fair, 15% Poor
Chronic Health Conditions	60% Yes, 40% No	65% Yes, 35% No	55% Yes, 45% No
Sleep Quality	50% Good, 40% Fair, 10% Poor	40% Good, 50% Fair, 10% Poor	60% Good, 30% Fair, 10% Poor
Body Mass Index (BMI)	26.5 ± 5.2	27.0 ± 5.5	26.0 ± 4.8
Chronic Conditions (Number of Conditions)	1.5 ± 0.8	1.7 ± 0.9	1.3 ± 0.7
Blood Pressure (Mean [SD])	130/85 ± 10/5	135/90 ± 10/5	125/80 ± 10/5
Diabetes (Yes/No)	25% Yes, 75% No	30% Yes, 70% No	20% Yes, 80% No
Cardiovascular Disease (Yes/No)	18.8% Yes, 81.2% No	20% Yes, 80% No	17.5% Yes, 82.5% No
Mental Health Diagnoses (Yes/No)	21.9% Yes, 78.1% No	25% Yes, 75% No	18.8% Yes, 81.2% No

Table 4 presents a comparison of caregiving activities across all participants, high-intensity caregivers, and low-intensity caregivers. The table highlights various types of caregiving tasks, with frequencies of activity reported as the average number of times caregivers engage in each task, measured on a scale. For Activities of Daily Living (ADL), all participants report an average of 4.3 ± 1.2 activities, with high-intensity caregivers engaging in 5.0 ± 1.1 activities and low-intensity caregivers engaging in 3.5 ± 1.0 activities. This suggests that high-intensity caregivers are significantly more involved in tasks related to basic daily activities compared to their low-intensity counterparts.In Instrumental Activities of Daily Living (IADL), high-intensity caregivers report 4.5 ± 0.9 activities, compared to 3.3 ± 1.2 for low-intensity caregivers and 3.9 ± 1.0 for all participants. This indicates that high-intensity caregivers also take on more complex daily tasks such as managing finances or meal preparation.For mobility assistance, high-intensity caregivers report 3.7 ± 0.9 activities, while low-intensity caregivers report fewer tasks at 2.3 ± 0.6. All participants have an average of 3.0 ± 0.8 activities in this category, showing that mobility support is a key aspect of caregiving, especially for those with higher caregiving intensity. In health system logistics, which includes tasks like coordinating medical appointments, high-intensity caregivers report 4.7 ± 1.1 activities, more than the 3.7 ± 0.9 reported by low-intensity caregivers, with all participants engaging in 4.2 ± 1.0 activities on average. This indicates that high-intensity caregivers are more involved in managing the healthcare needs of the patient. Health management tasks, including overseeing the patient's health and wellness, are also more frequent among high-intensity caregivers (4.4 ± 1.0) compared to low-intensity caregivers (3.2 ± 1.1), with an overall average of 3.8 ± 1.1 for all participants. This trend highlights the increased responsibility taken on by high-intensity caregivers for managing the patient's health. When it comes to monitoring medication and health status, high-intensity caregivers report 4.2 ± 0.8 activities, while low-intensity caregivers report 3.0 ± 1.0 activities. All participants engage in this task 3.6 ± 0.9 times on average, underscoring the importance of regular monitoring of the patient's health in caregiving. For providing emotional support, high-intensity caregivers report 4.3 ± 0.9 activities, whereas low-intensity caregivers engage in 3.1 ± 1.0 activities. Overall, all participants report an average of 3.7 ± 1.0 emotional support activities, suggesting that emotional support is a central component of caregiving but is more frequently required by high-intensity caregivers. Supervising and monitoring the patient, including ensuring their safety, is also more common among high-intensity caregivers (4.4 ± 1.0) compared to low-intensity caregivers (3.2 ± 1.2), with all participants averaging 3.8 ± 1.1 activities in this area. For tasks related to assisting with hygiene and grooming, high-intensity caregivers engage in 4.6 ± 0.9 activities, while low-intensity caregivers report 3.4 ± 1.1 activities, with all participants averaging 4.0 ± 1.0. This shows that high-intensity caregivers tend to be more involved in the personal care of patients. Finally, handling financial and legal tasks is the least frequent activity, with all participants engaging in 2.8 ± 1.2 activities on average. High-intensity caregivers report 3.4 ± 1.1 activities, while low-intensity caregivers report 2.2 ± 1.0. This suggests that financial and legal responsibilities are more often managed by those providing high-intensity care.

Table 4. Comparisons in frequencies of care giving activities by care giving intensity

Caregiving Activity	All Participants (n=32)	High-Intensity Caregivers (n=16)	Low-Intensity Caregivers (n=16)
Activities of Daily Living (ADL)	4.3 ± 1.2	5.0 ± 1.1	3.5 ± 1.0
Instrumental Activities of Daily Living (IADL)	3.9 ± 1.0	4.5 ± 0.9	3.3 ± 1.2
Mobility Assistance	3.0 ± 0.8	3.7 ± 0.9	2.3 ± 0.6
Health System Logistics	4.2 ± 1.0	4.7 ± 1.1	3.7 ± 0.9
Health Management	3.8 ± 1.1	4.4 ± 1.0	3.2 ± 1.1

continued on following page

Table 4. Continued

Caregiving Activity	All Participants (n=32)	High-Intensity Caregivers (n=16)	Low-Intensity Caregivers (n=16)
Monitoring Medication/Health Status	3.6 ± 0.9	4.2 ± 0.8	3.0 ± 1.0
Providing Emotional Support	3.7 ± 1.0	4.3 ± 0.9	3.1 ± 1.0
Supervising and Monitoring	3.8 ± 1.1	4.4 ± 1.0	3.2 ± 1.2
Assisting with Hygiene and Grooming	4.0 ± 1.0	4.6 ± 0.9	3.4 ± 1.1
Handling Financial/Legal Tasks	2.8 ± 1.2	3.4 ± 1.1	2.2 ± 1.0

Table 5 presents a comparison of physical health indicators and health behaviors among all participants, high-intensity caregivers, and low-intensity caregivers. The table highlights key health measures, providing insights into the health status and habits of caregivers based on their caregiving intensity. In terms of Body Mass Index (BMI), the average BMI for all participants is 26.5 ± 5.2, with high-intensity caregivers having a slightly higher average BMI (27.0 ± 5.5) compared to low-intensity caregivers (26.0 ± 4.8). This suggests a potential impact of caregiving intensity on physical health, although the differences are modest. Regarding chronic health conditions, 60% of all participants reported having chronic conditions, with high-intensity caregivers exhibiting a slightly higher rate of 65% compared to 55% in low-intensity caregivers. This could indicate a correlation between higher caregiving intensity and a higher prevalence of chronic health conditions. When looking at blood pressure, the average systolic and diastolic pressure for all participants is 130/85 ± 10/5. High-intensity caregivers have a slightly higher blood pressure (135/90 ± 10/5) compared to low-intensity caregivers (125/80 ± 10/5), which could reflect the increased stress associated with high-intensity caregiving responsibilities. For physical activity, about 56.3% of all participants engage in physical activity, with high-intensity caregivers having a 60% participation rate and low-intensity caregivers showing a slightly lower participation rate of 53%. This suggests that high-intensity caregivers might prioritize physical activity more than low-intensity caregivers. Sleep quality is categorized into good, fair, and poor. Overall, 50% of all participants report good sleep quality, 40% fair, and 10% poor. High-intensity caregivers show a tendency toward poorer sleep quality, with 40% reporting good sleep, 50% fair, and 10% poor. Conversely, low-intensity caregivers report 60% good sleep, 30% fair, and 10% poor, suggesting that less intense caregiving may be associated with better sleep quality. Diet adherence shows that 45% of all participants adhere to a good diet, 45% to a fair diet, and 10% to a poor diet. The distribution is fairly similar across caregiving intensity levels, though high-intensity caregivers have a slightly higher rate of 50% fair diet adherence compared to low-intensity caregivers at 40%. Regarding smoking status, 20% of all participants currently smoke, and high-intensity caregivers have a slightly higher percentage (25% current smokers) compared to low-intensity caregivers (15% current smokers). This suggests that high caregiving intensity may be linked with higher smoking rates, though the overall percentage remains low. For alcohol consumption, 40% of all participants report drinking alcohol, with 35% of high-intensity caregivers consuming alcohol compared to 45% of low-intensity caregivers. This indicates no significant difference between the two caregiving groups in alcohol use. In terms of stress levels, 30% of all participants report high stress, with high-intensity caregivers showing a slightly higher percentage of 35% reporting high stress compared to 25% of low-intensity caregivers. This highlights a potential link between high caregiving intensity and higher stress levels. Finally, sleep duration averages 7.5 ± 1.2 hours per night for all participants. High-intensity caregivers sleep an average of 7.2 ± 1.0 hours, while low-intensity caregivers sleep slightly more at 7.8 ± 1.3 hours, suggesting that more intense caregiving may lead to slightly less sleep.

Table 5. Comparisons in physical health indicators and health behaviors by care giving intensity

Health Indicator/Behavior	All Participants (n=32)	High-Intensity Caregivers (n=16)	Low-Intensity Caregivers (n=16)
Body Mass Index (BMI)	26.5 ± 5.2	27.0 ± 5.5	26.0 ± 4.8
Chronic Health Conditions	60% Yes, 40% No	65% Yes, 35% No	55% Yes, 45% No
Blood Pressure (Systolic/Diastolic)	130/85 ± 10/5	135/90 ± 10/5	125/80 ± 10/5
Physical Activity (Yes/No)	56.3% Yes, 43.7% No	60% Yes, 40% No	53% Yes, 47% No
Sleep Quality (Good/Fair/Poor)	50% Good, 40% Fair, 10% Poor	40% Good, 50% Fair, 10% Poor	60% Good, 30% Fair, 10% Poor
Diet Adherence (Good/Fair/Poor)	45% Good, 45% Fair, 10% Poor	40% Good, 50% Fair, 10% Poor	50% Good, 40% Fair, 10% Poor
Smoking Status (Current/Former/Never)	20% Current, 10% Former, 70% Never	25% Current, 10% Former, 65% Never	15% Current, 10% Former, 75% Never
Alcohol Consumption (Yes/No)	40% Yes, 60% No	35% Yes, 65% No	45% Yes, 55% No
Stress Levels (High/Moderate/Low)	30% High, 50% Moderate, 20% Low	35% High, 50% Moderate, 15% Low	25% High, 50% Moderate, 25% Low
Sleep Duration (Hours per Night)	7.5 ± 1.2	7.2 ± 1.0	7.8 ± 1.3

Table 6 presents a performance comparison of various models used for predicting caregiving activities associated with neuropsychological disorders. The table includes accuracy, precision, recall, and F1-score for each model, as well as their ability to handle temporal data, nonlinear relationships, and their interpretability. Among the models, Linear Regression and Logistic Regression show the lowest performance across all metrics, with accuracy values of 65% and 70%, respectively. These models also struggle with handling temporal data and nonlinear relationships, which are essential for caregiving activities. Their interpretability, however, remains high. Decision Trees perform moderately well, with an accuracy of 75%, and are better at handling nonlinear relationships compared to linear models. However, they still face limitations in terms of processing temporal data and generalizing to complex caregiving patterns. Random Forest, a more advanced ensemble method, shows a significant improvement, achieving an accuracy of 82%. It handles nonlinear relationships well but still struggles with temporal data, and its interpretability is low due to the complexity of the model. Support Vector Machines (SVM) and K-Nearest Neighbors (KNN) both demonstrate decent performance with accuracies of 80% and 73%, respectively. SVM excels in precision but struggles with temporal data. KNN performs modestly across all metrics and does not handle temporal data well, with moderate interpretability. Naive Bayes, with an accuracy of 71%, also struggles with temporal data and nonlinear relationships, but its high interpretability allows for straightforward understanding of the results. On the other hand, Neural Networks (MLP) show strong results with an accuracy of 85%, and are capable of handling both temporal data and nonlinear relationships effectively. However, like most complex models, they lack interpretability. Both Gradient Boosting Machines (GBM) and XGBoost achieve high performance with accuracy values of 87% and 88%, respectively, and are excellent at handling nonlinear relationships. However, they share a similar limitation in handling temporal data effectively and also have low interpretability. Finally, the Proposed CNN-LSTM model outperforms all other models, with the highest accuracy of 92%, precision of 90%, and recall of 89%. It excels in handling temporal data and nonlinear relationships, making it ideal for the dynamic nature of caregiving activities related to neuropsychological disorders. However, the CNN-LSTM model also faces challenges in interpretability due to its deep learning structure.

Table 6. Performance comparison for predicting caregiving activities associated with neuropsychological disorders

Model	Accuracy	Precision	Recall	F1-Score	Handling Temporal Data	Handling Nonlinear Relationships	Interpretability
Linear Regression(Duff et al.,2015)	65%	60%	55%	57%	Poor	Poor	High
Logistic Regression(Jiménez-Huete et al.,2014)	70%	65%	60%	62%	Poor	Poor	High
Decision Trees(Rostami et al.,2020)	75%	72%	68%	70%	Moderate	Good	Moderate
Random Forest(Kamarajan et al.,2020)	82%	80%	78%	79%	Moderate	Excellent	Low
Support Vector Machine (Bledsoe et al.,2020)	80%	85%	78%	81%	Poor	Good	Low
K-Nearest Neighbors(Rodrigues et al.,2015)	73%	71%	70%	70%	Poor	Moderate	Moderate
Naive Bayes(Bhagya Shree et al.,2018)	71%	68%	65%	66%	Poor	Poor	High
Convolution Neural Networks (Cheah et al.,2022)	85%	88%	84%	86%	Excellent	Excellent	Low
Gradient Boosting Machines(Chen et al.,2023)	87%	85%	83%	84%	Moderate	Excellent	Low
XGBoost(Yi et al.,2023)	88%	86%	85%	85%	Moderate	Excellent	Low
Proposed	92%	90%	89%	89%	Excellent	Excellent	Low

CONCLUSION

The comparison of physical health indicators and health behaviors between high- and low-intensity caregivers reveals significant differences in both caregiving activities and health outcomes. High-intensity caregivers are more frequently involved in caregiving tasks and report poorer physical health, including higher BMI, elevated blood pressure, and a higher incidence of chronic conditions. They also experience higher levels of stress and report lower sleep quality. In contrast, low-intensity caregivers tend to have better sleep quality, lower BMI, and lower stress levels. These findings suggest that the intensity of caregiving plays a crucial role in influencing caregivers' physical and mental well-being. The analytical prediction models, such as CNN-LSTM, were successfully used to predict caregivers' health status and the neuropsychological stage of patients, offering valuable insights into the impact of caregiving intensity on long-term health outcomes. Interventions aimed at reducing caregiving burdens, improving health management strategies, and providing emotional support are essential for mitigating the negative health impacts of caregiving. Future research should focus on identifying effective support systems and interventions to promote the health and well-being of caregivers, particularly those engaged in high-intensity caregiving.

REFERENCES

Al Yahyaei, A., Al Omari, O., Sharour, L. A., Cayaban, A. R., Shebani, Z., Al Hashmi, I., & Alhalaiqa, F. (2024). The Lived Experience of Parent Caregivers of Adolescents with Mental Illness: A Phenomenological Study. *International Journal of Community Based Nursing and Midwifery*, 12(1), 2. PMID: 38328010

Aljunaid, M. A., Alosaimi, R. M., Alazmi, E. A., Afandi, A. A., Musslem, M. T., Aljarameez, M. M., & Alzobaidi, H. H. (2024). Determinants of Depression in Caregivers of Geriatric Patients in Jeddah, Saudi Arabia: A Cross-Sectional Study. *Medicina*, 60(8), 1368. DOI: 10.3390/medicina60081368 PMID: 39202649

Bhagya Shree, S. R., & Sheshadri, H. S. (2018). Diagnosis of Alzheimer's disease using naive Bayesian classifier. *Neural Computing & Applications*, 29(1), 123–132. DOI: 10.1007/s00521-016-2416-3

Bledsoe, J. C., Xiao, C., Chaovalitwongse, A., Mehta, S., Grabowski, T. J., Semrud-Clikeman, M., Pliszka, S., & Breiger, D. (2020). Diagnostic classification of ADHD versus control: Support vector machine classification using brief neuropsychological assessment. *Journal of Attention Disorders*, 24(11), 1547–1556. DOI: 10.1177/1087054716649666 PMID: 27231214

Bookwala, J., Yee, J. L., & Schulz, R. (2000). Caregiving and detrimental mental and physical health outcomes. In *Physical illness and depression in older adults: A handbook of theory, research, and practice* (pp. 93–131). Springer US.

Cheah, W. T., Hwang, J. J., Hong, S. Y., Fu, L. C., Chang, Y. L., Chen, T. F., Chen, I.-A., & Chou, C. C. (2022). A digital screening system for Alzheimer disease based on a neuropsychological test and a convolutional neural network: System development and validation. *JMIR Medical Informatics*, 10(3), e31106. DOI: 10.2196/31106 PMID: 35262497

Chen, B., Xu, M., Yu, H., He, J., Li, Y., Song, D., & Fan, G. G. (2023). Detection of mild cognitive impairment in Parkinson's disease using gradient boosting decision tree models based on multilevel DTI indices. *Journal of Translational Medicine*, 21(1), 310. DOI: 10.1186/s12967-023-04158-8 PMID: 37158918

Duff, K., & Ramezani, A. (2015). Regression-based normative formulae for the repeatable battery for the assessment of neuropsychological status for older adults. *Archives of Clinical Neuropsychology*, 30(7), 600–604. DOI: 10.1093/arclin/acv052 PMID: 26289055

Felber, N. A., Lipworth, W., Tian, Y. J., Roulet Schwab, D., & Wangmo, T. (2024). Informing existing technology acceptance models: A qualitative study with older persons and caregivers. *European Journal of Ageing*, 21(1), 12. DOI: 10.1007/s10433-024-00801-5 PMID: 38551677

Hapsari, D. T. P., Nataliani, Y., Sembiring, I., & Wahyono, T. (2024, June). Smart Caregiving Support Cloud Integration Systems. In 2024 International Conference on Smart Computing, IoT and Machine Learning (SIML) (pp. 167-173). IEEE. DOI: 10.1109/SIML61815.2024.10578217

Jiménez-Huete, A., Riva, E., Toledano, R., Campo, P., Esteban, J., Barrio, A. D., & Franch, O. (2014). Differential diagnosis of degenerative dementias using basic neuropsychological tests: Multivariable logistic regression analysis of 301 patients. *American Journal of Alzheimer's Disease and Other Dementias*, 29(8), 723–731. DOI: 10.1177/1533317514534954 PMID: 24838533

Kalbe, E., Folkerts, A. K., Witt, K., Buhmann, C., & Liepelt-Scarfone, I.German Parkinson's Guidelines Group. (2024). German Society of Neurology guidelines for the diagnosis and treatment of cognitive impairment and affective disorders in people with Parkinson's disease: New spotlights on diagnostic procedures and non-pharmacological interventions. *Journal of Neurology*, 271(11), 1–28. DOI: 10.1007/s00415-024-12503-0 PMID: 39120709

Kamarajan, C., Ardekani, B. A., Pandey, A. K., Kinreich, S., Pandey, G., Chorlian, D. B., Meyers, J. L., Zhang, J., Bermudez, E., Stimus, A. T., & Porjesz, B. (2020). Random forest classification of alcohol use disorder using fMRI functional connectivity, neuropsychological functioning, and impulsivity measures. *Brain Sciences*, 10(2), 115. DOI: 10.3390/brainsci10020115 PMID: 32093319

Karunarathna, I., Kapila De Alvis, C., Rajapaksha, S., Warnakulasooriya, A., Aluthge, P., Perera, N., ... & Jayawardana, A. Effective Strategies for Alzheimer's Disease: Diagnosis, Treatment, and Caregiver Support.

Kelbling, E., Ferreira Prescott, D., Shearer, M., & Quinn, T. J. (2024). An assessment of the content and properties of extended and instrumental activities of daily living scales: A systematic review. *Disability and Rehabilitation*, 46(10), 1990–1999. DOI: 10.1080/09638288.2023.2224082 PMID: 37415395

Kelbling, E., Ferreira Prescott, D., Shearer, M., & Quinn, T. J. (2024). An assessment of the content and properties of extended and instrumental activities of daily living scales: A systematic review. *Disability and Rehabilitation*, 46(10), 1990–1999. DOI: 10.1080/09638288.2023.2224082 PMID: 37415395

Liu, Y. S., Lu, C. W., Chung, H. T., Wang, J. K., Su, W. J., & Chen, C. W. (2024). Health-promoting lifestyle and life satisfaction in full-time employed adults with congenital heart disease: Grit as a mediator. *European Journal of Cardiovascular Nursing*, 23(4), 348–357. DOI: 10.1093/eurjcn/zvad104 PMID: 37847800

Maristany, A. J., Sa, B. C., Murray, C., Subramaniam, A. B., & Oldak, S. E. (2024). Psychiatric manifestations of neurological diseases: A narrative review. *Cureus*, 16(7). Advance online publication. DOI: 10.7759/cureus.64152 PMID: 39119372

Oliver, T. L., Hetland, B., Schmaderer, M., Zolty, R., & Pozehl, B. (2024). A Feasibility Study of Qualitative Methods Using the Zarit Burden Interview in Heart Failure Caregivers. *Applied Nursing Research*, 79, 151826. DOI: 10.1016/j.apnr.2024.151826 PMID: 39256009

Patil, R. S., & Tupe, R. S. (2024). Communal interaction of glycation and gut microbes in diabetes mellitus, Alzheimer's disease, and Parkinson's disease pathogenesis. *Medicinal Research Reviews*, 44(1), 365–405. DOI: 10.1002/med.21987 PMID: 37589449

Riffin, C., Cassidy, J., Smith, J. M., Begler, E., Peereboom, D., Lum, H. D., & Wolff, J. L. (2024). Care Partner Perspectives on the Use of a Patient Portal Intervention to Promote Care Partner Identification in Dementia Care. [Rodrigues, Y. E., Manica, E., Zimmer, E. R., Neto, P. R., & Pascoal, T. A. Featuring Alzheimer Disease with Neuropsychological Tests and Proteomic Attributes using kNN-SMOTE Algorithm.]. *Journal of Applied Gerontology*, •••, 07334648241262649. PMID: 38901834

Rostami, M., Farashi, S., Khosrowabadi, R., & Pouretemad, H. (2020). Discrimination of ADHD subtypes using decision tree on behavioral, neuropsychological, and neural markers. *Basic and Clinical Neuroscience*, 11(3), 359. PMID: 32963728

Shaffer, K. M., Jacobs, J. M., Nipp, R. D., Carr, A., Jackson, V. A., Park, E. R., Pirl, W. F., El-Jawahri, A., Gallagher, E. R., Greer, J. A., & Temel, J. S. (2017). Mental and physical health correlates among family caregivers of patients with newly-diagnosed incurable cancer: A hierarchical linear regression analysis. *Supportive Care in Cancer*, 25(3), 965–971. DOI: 10.1007/s00520-016-3488-4 PMID: 27866337

Sun, W., Ashtarieh, B., & Zou, P. (2021). The safety challenges of therapeutic self-care and informal caregiving in home care: A qualitative descriptive study. *Geriatric Nursing*, 42(2), 491–501. DOI: 10.1016/j.gerinurse.2020.07.013 PMID: 32807555

Vos, E. E., De Bruin, S. R., van der Beek, A. J., & Proper, K. I. (2021). "It's like juggling, constantly trying to keep all balls in the air": A qualitative study of the support needs of working caregivers taking care of older adults. *International Journal of Environmental Research and Public Health*, 18(11), 5701. DOI: 10.3390/ijerph18115701 PMID: 34073386

Wang, L., Smriti, D., Yuan, H., & Huh-Yoo, J. (2024, May). Artificial Intelligence Systems for Supporting Informal Caregivers of People Living with Alzheimer's Disease or Related Dementias: A Systematic Review. In *Extended Abstracts of the CHI Conference on Human Factors in Computing Systems* (pp. 1-11). DOI: 10.1145/3613905.3650846

Watland, S., Solberg Nes, L., Hanson, E., Ekstedt, M., Stenberg, U., & Børøsund, E. (2023). The Caregiver Pathway, a Model for the Systematic and Individualized Follow-up of Family Caregivers at Intensive Care Units: Development Study. *JMIR Formative Research*, 7, e46299. DOI: 10.2196/46299 PMID: 37097744

Wolff, J. L., Cagle, J. G., Hanna, V., Dy, S. M., Echavarria, D., Giovannetti, E. R., Boyd, C. M., Saylor, M. A., Hussain, N., Reiff, J. S., Scerpella, D., Zhang, T., Sekhon, V. K., & Roth, D. L. (2024). Sharing health care wishes among older adults with cognitive impairment in primary care: Results from a randomized controlled trial. *Alzheimer's & Dementia*, alz.14210. DOI: 10.1002/alz.14210 PMID: 39189632

Wolff, J. L., Mulcahy, J., Huang, J., Roth, D. L., Covinsky, K., & Kasper, J. D. (2018). Family caregivers of older adults, 1999–2015: Trends in characteristics, circumstances, and role-related appraisal. *The Gerontologist*, 58(6), 1021–1032. DOI: 10.1093/geront/gnx093 PMID: 28637266

Yi, F., Yang, H., Chen, D., Qin, Y., Han, H., Cui, J., Bai, W., Ma, Y., Zhang, R., & Yu, H. (2023). XGBoost-SHAP-based interpretable diagnostic framework for alzheimer's disease. *BMC Medical Informatics and Decision Making*, 23(1), 137. DOI: 10.1186/s12911-023-02238-9 PMID: 37491248

Chapter 18
Developments, Hardships, and Prospective Directions in the Field of Neuroscience and Neurological Machine Learning for Behavioral Evaluation

Ridhima Sharma
https://orcid.org/0000-0002-7851-0292
Vivekananda Institute of Professional Studies-TC, India

Timcy Sachdeva
https://orcid.org/0000-0001-9978-9459
Vivekananda Institute of Professional Studies-TC, India

ABSTRACT

This study examines the current state of neuroscience, emphasizing the use of machine learning to improve behavioral assessment and its therapeutic applications. Progress in neuroscience has facilitated the comprehension of cognitive aging, neurological illnesses, and the essential function of cognition in detecting cognitive decline. The increasing potential of neurological machine learning likely overcomes the aforementioned deficiencies—consistent monitoring and early identification in mental health—through automation. This research will ultimately address AI-related concerns regarding the longitudinal monitoring of individuals with mental illness-

DOI: 10.4018/979-8-3693-9341-3.ch018

es. Neurocognitive testing may leverage machine learning to significantly advance the evaluation and early management of cognitive health, hence facilitating future research to enhance and broaden the capabilities of neurolearning and cognitive neuropsychology.

INTRODUCTION

Neuroscience is a multifaceted discipline that investigates the nervous system, including its structure, function, and development. Our comprehension of neurological disorders and brain functions has been substantially improved by recent developments. Nevertheless, the field is confronted with significant obstacles, particularly in the integration of machine learning (ML) techniques for behavioral evaluation and clinical trials. This paper investigates the current state of neuroscience and neurological machine learning, as well as the ongoing challenges and potential future directions. Neuroscience provides significant understanding of the brain processes that govern cognitive aging and how cognitive learning might promote healthy aging. Cognitive evaluation is crucial in aging neuroscience, since it allows researchers to understand the effects of aging on cognitive performance. With advancing age, individuals may encounter cognitive decline, leading to difficulties in memory, attention, and decision-making. Researchers can quantify alterations in cognitive function over time and uncover factors that may lead to cognitive decline using cognitive assessment. Conventional cognitive assessment tools include inherent limitations, including their failure to accommodate individual variations in cognitive ability and their restricted sensitivity to nuanced alterations in cognitive performance. The integration of machine learning techniques into neurocognitive testing, together with the development of automated and sustainable solutions for the speedy and accurate assessment of cognitive health, positions the emerging area of neurological learning to overcome existing limits. Conventional approaches depend on subjective interpretation, and there are difficulties in identifying nuanced alterations in cognitive function over time. Nonetheless, neurological machine learning methodologies have potential for improving cognitive evaluation. The application of data-driven approaches to detect cognitive impairment allows these models to provide objective and accurate assessments, leading to improved patient care, superior treatment outcomes, and individualized evaluations. Further study is necessary to explore the whole potential of neurological learning models in cognitive evaluation and to rectify their shortcomings. Conversely, neurolearning is a contemporary field that focuses on employing neuroscientific methods and instruments to improve cognitive function and learning. The integration of these two disciplines has the capacity to revolutionize our understanding and enhancement of human learning.

Cognitive neuropsychology is a multidisciplinary field that combines neurology and psychology to provide a practical understanding of the inherent abilities and characteristics of individuals. Patients may experience transformative consequences as a result of cerebral trauma. These may range from minor disruptions to routine activities to significant impairments in hepatic function. Cognitive neuropsychology is the study of the negative effects of brain injury on cognitive function. A cognitive function is the ability to effectively employ fundamental abilities, such as memory, conscious cognition, language, and perception (Ajith et al., 2024). Individuals, their families, and society incur substantial expenses as a consequence of mental illnesses or disorders. The evaluation of an individual's mental state is crucial for the diagnosis of mental diseases; however, it is a challenging process. The efficiency and precision of this investigation may be improved by incorporating modern technology, statistics, and analytics. According to the National Institute of Mental Health, approximately 20% of Americans are affected by mental illness.

Neuropsychology is predominantly concerned with three domains: cognitive, behavioral, and neurological. The behavioral level is determined by the score obtained during the assessment, which is the actual performance on a test. The cognitive level is indicative of the fundamental cognitive processes that are incorporated into the trial scores. The neurological bases and foundations of the aforementioned cognitive processes are elucidated at the brain level (Akhtar,2024). Neuropsychologists conducted a meticulous examination of the potential of computer-automated neuropsychological assessment in the 1980s. Additionally, they were placed in contrast to conventional methodologies, which frequently included assessments conducted with paper and pencil (Badrulhisham et al., 2024, Bhardwaj et al., 2024, Bom et al., 2024, Boudries et al., 2024). Diamond argues that it is impossible to suspend the creation of galaxies, instigate and cease hurricanes and ice eras, experimentally eradicate grizzly bears in specific national parks, or replicate the trajectory of dinosaur development. Other methods, such as observation, comparison, and natural experimentation, must be employed to acquire knowledge of these historical sciences. In the same vein, it is impossible to prevent the formation and progression of tumors, cure or postpone dementia, avert strokes, or rectify the repercussions of catastrophic neurological maladies. It is imperative to perform thorough analyses through experimentation, comparison, and observation. Based on the knowledge acquired from this research, neuropsychologists are capable of conducting animal experiments. In these investigations, neuropsychologists may also implement quasi-experimental methodologies (Akhtar, 2024, Calderone et al., 2024, Liu et al., 2024).

LITERATURE REVIEW

Artificial Intelligence is a field that seeks to emulate human talents and potential in automated systems. It can be an essential element of human learning, reasoning, adaptability, and introspection. In the domain of artificial intelligence (AI), neural networks and image processing are utilized to create a rigorously developed categorization model. This approach subsequently facilitates the extraction of patterns and distinctive qualities. The amalgamation of these two disciplines may be utilized across several areas, including precision agriculture, regenerative medicine, hematology, tumor detection, and microbiology. Artificial neural networks represent a substantial progression in the domain of artificial intelligence. This approach has been utilized to tackle complex global challenges across several machine learning sectors, including banking, agriculture, healthcare, and the automotive industry. Machine learning models may analyze research data with known outcomes by integrating auxiliary data from non-cognitive sources (e.g., biomarker data, blood glucose levels, and neuroimaging) and use therapy as clinical endpoints. These models allow doctors to assess the compatibility of a cognitive profile derived from one patient with that of another patient exhibiting similar, established health issues, after validation using fresh datasets (e.g., real-world examples) (Li et al., 2020, Palmisani et al., 2024). Machine learning may leverage big data as an extensive dataset to facilitate the evaluation of the current state and deliver more accurate forecasts. It can also facilitate the comparison of various datasets (Ngcukayitobi et al., 2024, Qu et al., 2024).

Support vector machines (SVMs) and convolutional neural networks (CNNs) have been thoroughly studied and utilized in image categorization owing to their remarkable specificity, sensitivity, and accuracy. Computerized analysis has become prevalent in neuropsychological assessment due to its ability to streamline diagnostic decision-making, test validity, and standardization (Rane et al., 2024). Visual analysis approaches extract shape-specific static information from offline drawing samples, whereas procedural analysis techniques depend on dynamic features obtained from online drawing responses. Both approaches need precise measurement of clinical abnormalities, which might be challenging to represent in a computable feature space. Researchers have explored many multidisciplinary strategies to tackle this difficulty and reconcile current research with traditional behaviors (Rane et al., 2024). Convolutional Neural Networks (CNNs) excel in image classification as they can extract distinguishing characteristics from different areas of the entire image without the need for localization or segmentation. The CNN model has enabled feature extraction and improved accuracy and performance by offering swift access to hidden layers. Compared to other algorithms, SVMs are notable for their remarkable efficiency and speed, along with their unique characteristics in feature extraction (Safitra et al., 2024).

Our understanding of cognitive-based brain-behavior linkages has been enhanced by recent research. However, the neuropsychological comprehension of emotion and empathy remains restricted (Badrulhisham et al., 2024, Dinov, 2024, Salles & Farisco, 2024]. Automated machine learning methodologies can be implemented to improve clinical decision-making and neuropsychological evaluation. Using an intelligent device or application, individuals can promptly acquire high-quality, graded data. The primary issues are addressed by the paradigm: The ability to systematically and perpetually monitor patients and their behaviors, while considering the significant amount of historical data (Sokołowska, 2024). Extended surveillance for several years is necessary for individuals who have been diagnosed with mental disorders. Neuropsychologists and clinicians encounter this logistical challenge. Additionally, the current methodologies and protocols do not provide the necessary conditions for more frequent analysis and critical appraisal, nor do they facilitate recurrent evaluations of this magnitude (Voigtlaender et al., 2024, Xu et al., 2024). By enabling the storage of clinical data that is rapidly evolving over an extended period and by accommodating specific thresholds and situations, an automated machine learning technique can address this constraint (Srivastava & Bag, 2024). The machine learning study of both individual and global mental states is facilitated by the extensive data generated. Reports suggest that individuals may frequently attempt suicide or relapse within a few days of consulting with a therapist. This demonstrates the rapid deterioration of patients' mental health. In order to ensure the effective and efficient surveillance of all patients with mental diseases, a substantial number of physicians is required. This process may be facilitated by the deployment and dissemination of automated machine learning. The emergence of this technology has the potential to considerably increase the frequency of examinations, facilitate the early detection of cases, and ensure a precise diagnosis.

This framework has the potential to serve as a model for the critical improvement of the integrity of mental health treatments. It can be used as a basis for providing each patient with the necessary assistance and attention (Akbar et al., 2024, Di Nunno et al., 2022). The technical feasibility of longitudinal monitoring, which involves the surveillance and transmission of patient data, has been enhanced by recent technological advancements. This data contains critical information regarding suicidal ideation and inclinations, activation levels, and effects (Gao et al., 2024, He et al., 2024). Machine learning has the potential to generate actionable alarms that will necessitate human intervention when combined with appropriate clinical research (Srivastava et al., 2024, Jawed et al., 2024).

Recent Advancements in Neuroscience Technological Innovations

The capacity to analyze brain activity and structure has been enhanced by the emergence of advanced imaging techniques, including MRI and machine learning algorithms. For instance, mild cognitive impairment (MCI) and Alzheimer's disease (AD) are being diagnosed using magnetic resonance imaging (MRI) measurements of hippocampal volume (Suttie et al., 2024). New laboratory models, such as brain-on-a-chip technologies, facilitate comprehension of intricate neurological conditions by simulating human brain environments (Tanaka & Vécsei, 2024, Akhtar, 2024]. AI has been increasingly incorporated into the various phases of drug discovery for central nervous system (CNS) disorders. Target identification, lead optimization, and drug toxicity prediction are all facilitated by machine learning algorithms (Ajith et al., 2024). The objective of this integration is to enhance the success rates of clinical trials and decrease the associated expenses. Research has underscored the influence of memory, neurodegeneration, consciousness, human-machine interaction, and creativity on cognitive processes. These regions are essential for comprehending the impact of external stimuli on mental health. Industry 5.0 encourages intelligent collaboration between humans and machines to achieve enhanced, adaptable, and sustainable production techniques, with a focus on the role of humans as the primary agents in production processes (Tanaka & Vécsei, 2024, Tanaka et al., 2024]. It includes the essential components of networked manufacturing and human-machine cooperation. Initially, human-machine collaboration requires a more collaborative relationship between humans and automata (Akbar et al., 2024). Secondly, networking is the term used to describe the interconnection of information, individuals, and equipment, which facilitates the development of a more secure, efficient, and intelligent networked production system (Tanaka et al., 2024). The implementation of sophisticated technologies is required to accomplish a digital, networked, intelligent, and automated production model that improves production efficiency and quality, as intelligent manufacturing is considered a critical component of Industry 5.0. Cybernetics provides a theoretical framework for the analysis of the design, control, and optimization strategies of intelligent industrial systems. Cybernetics may also be applied to humans, which are a multifaceted biosocial system (Vaidya et al., 2024). The inputs of our system are human activities and decisions, while the outputs and feedback from these behaviors are the results. The regulation and introspection of human activities, in conjunction with the perception and comprehension of the external world by humans, are determinants in the process of human functioning. Nevertheless, the evaluation of human dynamics and the establishment of correlations between cognitive processes and sophisticated engineering systems remain a significant challenge (van et al., 2024). In this context, ergonomics data can clarify the cognitive and affective states of the human brain during task execution, thereby enabling the development of user-centric products with specific functionalities (Voigtlaender et al., 2024, Boudries et al., 2024]. The proposal of multi-source data fusion in healthcare has been prompted by the advancement of artificial intelligence (AI) and big data technologies. Multimodal ergonomics data integration techniques offer numerous advantages in the context of improving system design and understanding the human body's condition.

DISCUSSION

Humanity is significantly burdened by cognitive neuropsychology and its range of maladies and disorders. In order to improve the accuracy and dependability of forecasting and identifying these diseases, automated algorithms have been developed. Big data, the Internet of Things, artificial intelligence, computer data, block chain, and machine learning were all proposed as viable solutions. The primary focus of this review was on deep learning and machine learning, with a particular emphasis on CNNs and SVM models. In terms of the optimal classification of data, the construction of stable linear- and non-linear hyperplanes, and the efficient management of chaotic data, SVM models are robust. In a variety of fields, such as neuroscience, neuromuscular disorder diagnosis, clinical practice, and neuropsychological disease prediction, Support Vector Machines (SVMs) have exhibited substantial potential, offering substantial advantages. Convolutional Neural Networks are predominantly used to process visual data, such as images. Additionally, CNN systems required fewer parameters than alternative networks. Particularly in the field of brain tumor segmentation, convolutional neural networks (CNNs) have demonstrated substantial efficacy in the areas of neuroimaging segregation, recognition, and classification. They have exhibited efficacy in the fields of disease forecasting, robotic neurosurgery, and radiation therapy. SVM and CNN are distinguished by a few limitations, including the inference of the function of each parameter, the generalization of the results, and a restricted pool of test subjects, despite their advantages. Additional research is being conducted to improve the predictive capabilities of SVMs and CNNs. However, it is undeniable that SVMs and CNNs are becoming more valuable for the detection and prediction of neuropsychological diseases. Support Vector Machine (SVM) models can generate optimal functions that distinguish between two distinct classes when trained with classified data. Support Vector Machines (SVMs) are distinguished from other classification in statistics methods, such as linear regression and discriminant function analysis, in that they construct their functions using only a portion of the data and sample cases that are challenging to group. These instances are subsequently recognized as support vectors. The primary objective of an SVM is to effectively reduce the span between the decision boundary and the support vectors. SVMs have been employed in numerous studies for recognizing neuromuscular diseases. These models conduct a comprehensive evaluation of accuracy by utilizing numerous matrices as input. This method has been demonstrated to be beneficial in the fields of neuroscience and clinical practice. Support Vector Machines (SVMs) are a valuable instrument for the analysis of extensive datasets, including neuroimaging data and behavioral observations. This method has been employed to estimate cognitive decline, identify biomarkers for neurological disorders, and classify various brain states. In research, variables that were either manually or automatically generated have been employed to identify stress using machine learning and deep learning algorithms. These implementations have demonstrated potential for the identification and management of cognitive impairments and mental health disorders. Convolutional Neural Networks are notably beneficial in the detection early of Alzheimer's disease, as they significantly aid in the processing of neuroimaging data. In recent years, they have been increasingly employed for precise image recognition and labeling, as they perform exceedingly well with photographs. In general, neural networks are more effective when combined with MRI scan data to effectively teach and enhance the classifier for tasks such as predicting Alzheimer's disease.

In domains including classification, segmentation, and image recognition, convolutional neural networks (CNNs) have demonstrated efficacy and efficiency. This system can be characterized as a feed-forward artificial neural network that acquires image features in the convolutional layer. Convolutional Neural Networks (CNNs) have demonstrated potential in the segmentation of brain lesions. The following factors should be taken into account when employing machine learning for neuropsychological detection and prediction:

- The training and evaluation of machine learning models in neuropsychological detection and prediction necessitate the availability and quality of large and diverse datasets. The acquisition of such datasets may be challenging and expensive, and it may also raise ethical and privacy concerns.
- Neuropsychological diseases are multifaceted and diverse, exhibiting varying manifestations across individuals and over time. Consequently, it is challenging to create machine learning models that are capable of accurately identifying and forecasting these ailments across a variety of populations and scenarios. Choosing the most suitable data pieces and representations to accurately depict the neurological and cognitive systems associated with neuropsychological disorders is a challenging task.
- Deep learning models can be difficult to comprehend and convey. Consequently, it is challenging to assess the model's predictive capabilities

and identify its constraints. Machine learning algorithms are frequently instructed on a single dataset, which may limit their capacity to generalize to new, unexplored data. This may reduce the model's value by restricting its application to new individuals or situations.

- Verification: The absence of ground truth data, the complexity of the disease, and the volatility of data can make it challenging to validate the outputs of machine learning models for neuropsychological diagnosis and prognosis. The acquisition and utilization of substantial quantities of sensitive personal data, particularly brain imaging data, for the purpose of machine learning research raises significant ethical and privacy concerns.

Comprehending systems that are characterized by inadequately understood physics and limited data is a significant challenge in the biological, biomedical, and behavioral sciences. Machine learning could be employed to investigate design spaces and identify correlations with a comprehensive collection of high-resolution data. Multiscale modeling could be employed to forecast system dynamics and establish causality with a validated and calibrated set of physical equations and material parameters. Ultimately, we can provide quantitative predictive insights into biological systems by combining machine learning and multiscale modeling.

A set of technologies that are specifically engineered for individual-level clinical predictions is provided by machine learning. Predictive models are conceptually located between genetic risk variations, which represent an individual's blueprint at one extreme, and clinical symptoms, which reflect an individual's behavioral manifestations at the other extreme. The potential to improve clinical management in mental care is present through the early diagnosis, illness classification, and selection of medication therapies, therapy modification, and individualized prognosis of diverse intermediate phenotypes (Qadri et al., 2024). Learning algorithms can be directly applied to individual patients to predict therapeutic outcomes that are intrinsically valid and immediately applicable, such as determining the appropriate dosage of medication. The inherent applicability of a variety of machine learning techniques for prospective clinical predictions at the individual level is influenced by a variety of factors, whereas the predominant statistical approaches are frequently more suitable for group-level research. The increasing costs of mental disorders are a global concern for our societies. Statistical analysis is the foundation of the feasibility of customized medicine in enhancing psychiatric treatment. "The group" has served as the primary operational entity for mental health researchers for an extended period of time. The individual patient is now a viable focus for study due to the improved collection of more specific and diversified information on mental patients. Rather than presuming the existence of illness categories and formally validating predetermined neurobiological hypotheses, a more appealing objective is to allow the facts to guide the inquiry. Certain statistical procedures that have been historically reliable may become less optimal as data complexity increases and research inquiries evolve. The rapid, economical, and practicable therapeutic application of experimentally validated single-patient predictions may be facilitated by the statistical characteristics of learning algorithms.

Obstacles in Neuroscience

The intricate nature of central nervous system (CNS) disorders presents significant challenges in the development of treatments. The high failure rates of clinical trials are ascribed to a limited comprehension of disease mechanisms and inadequate target selection (Ajith et al., 2024, Badrulhisham et al., 2024). For instance, despite the extensive research conducted, the pathophysiology of diseases such as Alzheimer's remains inadequately understood. The advancement of neuroscience is impeded by the insufficient exchange of data among researchers. The collaborative efforts that are essential for the advancement of knowledge in the field are restricted by the reluctance of many scientists to share their findings (Ajith et al., 2024). The democratization of data sharing may be facilitated by recent developments in computational methods; however, a cultural transformation within the research community is necessary. As neuroscience explores the intricacies of human brain functions through the application of innovative technologies, ethical concerns regarding the manipulation and study of human brain circuits have arisen. It is imperative to establish guidelines for this type of research in order to guarantee that ethical standards are upheld (Akhtar, 2024). Neurological machine learning algorithms have the potential to improve cognitive evaluation; yet, challenges remain in recognizing small differences in cognitive function over time, and conventional methods rely on subjective interpretation. These models provide objective and exact evaluations of cognitive impairment utilizing data-driven approaches, resulting in personalized assessments, improved treatment outcomes, and better patient care. Additional research is needed to overcome limitations and explore the full potential of neurological learning models in cognitive evaluation.

Future Directions

The integration of machine learning techniques can improve behavioral evaluations by offering a deeper understanding of cognitive processes through the analysis of large amounts of data. The future research should concentrate on the refinement of these algorithms to enhance their predictive capabilities with respect to behavioral outcomes (Gao et al., 2024, He et al., 2024. Bridging the divide between neuroscience and disciplines such as computer science and engineering could be a catalyst for interdisciplinary collaboration. The development of novel technologies that improve our comprehension of brain functions can be achieved through collaborative endeavors (Jawed et al., 2024). The implementation of a precision medicine approach that takes into account the individual variability in cognition and behavior has the potential to revolutionize the treatment of neurological disorders. This change is consistent with the growing popularity of neurodiversity and inclusiveness in healthcare (Akhtar et al., 2024). The implementation of longitudinal studies that monitor cognitive changes over time can offer valuable insights into the progression of neurodegenerative diseases. These investigations have the potential to identify early biomarkers for conditions such as Alzheimer's disease. (Akhtar et al., 2024, Li et al., 2020).

CONCLUSION

The discipline of neuroscience is currently at a critical juncture, marked by substantial challenges and significant advancements. Although technological advancements and the integration of AI present promising opportunities for advancement, it is imperative to address the intricacies of neurological disorders and cultivate collaborative research environments in order to achieve future success. The further investigation of these domains will not only improve our comprehension of the brain but also enhance therapeutic strategies for individuals affected by neurological conditions. In Neurodevelopmental diseases, like in healthcare overall, machine learning can help rectify persistent issues such as significant diagnostic inaccuracies, treatment errors, and resource misallocation. Machine learning will certainly assist in scientifically redefining the categories of neurodevelopmental disorders and other mental diseases, facilitating early identification and contributing to better tailored therapies. The emergence of machine learning presents an opportunity to enhance the standardization of practices and to promote the widespread use of open research through preregistration and data sharing or federated learning. Moreover, the domain must exhibit superior and consistent performance in actual clinical settings. Ultimately, significant philosophical, ethical, and socio-technical difficulties must be confronted.

REFERENCES

Ajith, M., Aycock, D. M., Tone, E. B., Liu, J., Misiura, M. B., Ellis, R., Plis, S. M., King, T. Z., Dotson, V. M., & Calhoun, V. (2024). A deep learning approach for mental health quality prediction using functional network connectivity and assessment data. *Brain Imaging and Behavior*, 18(3), 1–16. DOI: 10.1007/s11682-024-00857-y PMID: 38340285

Akbar, K., Passaro, A., Di Gioia, M., Martini, E., Dragone, M., Zullo, A., & Stasolla, F. (2024). Reviewing the Horizon: The Future of Extended Reality and Artificial Intelligence in Neurorehabilitation for Brain Injury Recovery. *Information (Basel)*, 15(8), 501. DOI: 10.3390/info15080501

Akhtar, Z. B. (2024). Exploring Biomedical Engineering (BME): Advances within Accelerated Computing and Regenerative Medicine for a Computational and Medical Science Perspective Exploration Analysis. *J Emerg Med OA, 2*(1), 01-23.

Badrulhisham, F., Pogatzki-Zahn, E., Segelcke, D., Spisak, T., & Vollert, J. (2024). Machine learning and artificial intelligence in neuroscience: A primer for researchers. *Brain, Behavior, and Immunity*, 115, 470–479. DOI: 10.1016/j.bbi.2023.11.005 PMID: 37972877

Bhardwaj, S., Thapa, S. B., & Gandhi, A. (2024). Advances in neuromarketing and improved understanding of consumer behaviour: Analysing tool possibilities and research trends. *Cogent Business & Management*, 11(1), 2376773. DOI: 10.1080/23311975.2024.2376773

Bom, H. S. H., Kim, J., Yun, M., & Kang, D. Y. (2024). Are the Nuclear Neuro-Imaging Biomarkers Reliable? *Nuclear Medicine and Molecular Imaging*, •••, 1–2. PMID: 38932761

Boudries, R., Williams, H., Paquereau—Gaboreau, S., Bashir, S., Hojjat Jodaylami, M., Chisanga, M., Trudeau, L.-É., & Masson, J.-F. (2024). Surface-Enhanced Raman Scattering Nanosensing and Imaging in Neuroscience. *ACS Nano*, 18(34), 22620–22647. DOI: 10.1021/acsnano.4c05200 PMID: 39088751

Calderone, A., Latella, D., Bonanno, M., Quartarone, A., Mojdehdehbaher, S., Celesti, A., & Calabrò, R. S. (2024). Towards Transforming Neurorehabilitation: The Impact of Artificial Intelligence on Diagnosis and Treatment of Neurological Disorders. *Biomedicines*, 12(10), 2415. DOI: 10.3390/biomedicines12102415 PMID: 39457727

Di Nunno, V., Fordellone, M., Minniti, G., Asioli, S., Conti, A., Mazzatenta, D., Balestrini, D., Chiodini, P., Agati, R., Tonon, C., Tosoni, A., Gatto, L., Bartolini, S., Lodi, R., & Franceschi, E. (2022). Machine learning in neuro-oncology: Toward novel development fields. *Journal of Neuro-Oncology*, 159(2), 333–346. DOI: 10.1007/s11060-022-04068-7 PMID: 35761160

Dinov, I. D. (2024). Neuroinformatics Applications of Data Science and Artificial Intelligence. *Neuroinformatics*, 22(4), 1–3. DOI: 10.1007/s12021-024-09692-4 PMID: 39316274

Gao, J., Heng, F., Yuan, Y., & Liu, Y. (2024). A novel machine learning method for multiaxial fatigue life prediction: Improved adaptive neuro-fuzzy inference system. *International Journal of Fatigue*, 178, 108007. DOI: 10.1016/j.ijfatigue.2023.108007

He, Q., Li, L., Li, D., Peng, T., Zhang, X., Cai, Y., Zhang, X., & Tang, R. (2024). From digital human modeling to human digital twin: Framework and perspectives in human factors. *Chinese Journal of Mechanical Engineering*, 37(1), 9. DOI: 10.1186/s10033-024-00998-7

Jawed, S., Faye, I., & Malik, A. S. (2024). Deep learning-based assessment model for Real-time identification of visual learners using Raw EEG. *IEEE Transactions on Neural Systems and Rehabilitation Engineering*, 32, 378–390. DOI: 10.1109/TNSRE.2024.3351694 PMID: 38194390

Li, X. T., & Huang, R. Y. (2020). Standardization of imaging methods for machine learning in neuro-oncology. *Neuro-Oncology Advances*, 2(Supplement_4), iv49–iv55. DOI: 10.1093/noajnl/vdaa054 PMID: 33521640

Liu, S., Wang, L., & Gao, R. X. (2024). Cognitive neuroscience and robotics: Advancements and future research directions. *Robotics and Computer-integrated Manufacturing*, 85, 102610. DOI: 10.1016/j.rcim.2023.102610

Ngcukayitobi, M., Tartibu, L. K., & Bannwart, F. (2024). Enhancing Thermo-Acoustic Waste Heat Recovery through Machine Learning: A Comparative Analysis of Artificial Neural Network–Particle Swarm Optimization, Adaptive Neuro Fuzzy Inference System, and Artificial Neural Network Models. *AI*, 5(1), 237–258. DOI: 10.3390/ai5010013

Palmisani, F., Segelcke, D., & Vollert, J. (2024). Navigating the light and shadow of scientific publishing faced with machine learning and generative AI. *European Journal of Pain (London, England)*, ejp.4736. DOI: 10.1002/ejp.4736 PMID: 39360710

Patil, D. (2024). The future of artificial intelligence in healthcare: Opportunities, challenges, and ethical considerations. *Challenges, and Ethical Considerations (November 08, 2024).*

Qadri, Y. A., Ahmad, K., & Kim, S. W. (2024). Artificial General Intelligence for the Detection of Neurodegenerative Disorders. *Sensors (Basel)*, 24(20), 6658. DOI: 10.3390/s24206658 PMID: 39460138

Qu, J., Cui, L., Guo, W., Bu, L., & Wang, Z. (2024). Development of a novel machine learning-based approach for brain function assessment and integrated software solution. *Advanced Engineering Informatics*, 60, 102461. DOI: 10.1016/j.aei.2024.102461

Rane, J., Mallick, S. K., Kaya, O., & Rane, N. L. (2024). Artificial intelligence, machine learning, and deep learning in cloud, edge, and quantum computing: A review of trends, challenges, and future directions. *Future Research Opportunities for Artificial Intelligence in Industry 4.0 and, 5*, 2-2.

Rane, J., Mallick, S. K., Kaya, O., & Rane, N. L. (2024). Scalable and adaptive deep learning algorithms for large-scale machine learning systems. *Future Research Opportunities for Artificial Intelligence in Industry 4.0 and, 5*, 2-40.

Rane, N. L., Mallick, S. K., Kaya, O., & Rane, J. (2024). Applications of machine learning in healthcare, finance, agriculture, retail, manufacturing, energy, and transportation: A review. *Applied Machine Learning and Deep Learning: Architectures and Techniques*, 112-131.

Safitra, M. F., Lubis, M., Kusumasari, T. F., & Putri, D. P. (2024). Advancements in Artificial Intelligence and Data Science: Models, Applications, and Challenges. *Procedia Computer Science*, 234, 381–388. DOI: 10.1016/j.procs.2024.03.018

Salles, A., & Farisco, M. (2024). Neuroethics and AI ethics: A proposal for collaboration. *BMC Neuroscience*, 25(1), 41. DOI: 10.1186/s12868-024-00888-7 PMID: 39210267

Sokołowska, B. (2024). Being in Virtual Reality and Its Influence on Brain Health—An Overview of Benefits, Limitations and Prospects. *Brain Sciences*, 14(1), 72. DOI: 10.3390/brainsci14010072 PMID: 38248287

Srivastava, G., & Bag, S. (2024). Modern-day marketing concepts based on face recognition and neuro-marketing: A review and future research directions. *Benchmarking*, 31(2), 410–438. DOI: 10.1108/BIJ-09-2022-0588

Srivastava, G., Wu, D., Liu, C., & Xu, J. (2024). Neuroscience and neurological machine learning for cognitive assessment: Advancements, challenges, and future directions. *Frontiers in Aging Neuroscience*, 16, 1406184. DOI: 10.3389/fnagi.2024.1406184 PMID: 38872631

Suttie, M., Kable, J., Mahnke, A. H., & Bandoli, G. (2024). Machine learning approaches to the identification of children affected by prenatal alcohol exposure: A narrative review. *Alcohol, Clinical & Experimental Research*, 48(4), 585–595. DOI: 10.1111/acer.15271 PMID: 38302824

Tanaka, M., Battaglia, S., Giménez-Llort, L., Chen, C., Hepsomali, P., Avenanti, A., & Vécsei, L. (2024). Innovation at the intersection: Emerging translational research in neurology and psychiatry. *Cells*, 13(10), 790. DOI: 10.3390/cells13100790 PMID: 38786014

Tanaka, M., Tuka, B., & Vécsei, L. (2024). Navigating the Neurobiology of Migraine: From pathways to potential therapies. *Cells*, 13(13), 1098. DOI: 10.3390/cells13131098 PMID: 38994951

Tanaka, M., & Vécsei, L. (2024). A Decade of Dedication: Pioneering Perspectives on Neurological Diseases and Mental Illnesses. *Biomedicines*, 12(5), 1083. DOI: 10.3390/biomedicines12051083 PMID: 38791045

Tanaka, M., & Vécsei, L. (2024). From lab to life: Exploring cutting-edge models for neurological and psychiatric disorders. *Biomedicines*, 12(3), 613. DOI: 10.3390/biomedicines12030613 PMID: 38540226

Vaidya, N., Marquand, A. F., Nees, F., Siehl, S., & Schumann, G. (2024). The impact of psychosocial adversity on brain and behaviour: An overview of existing knowledge and directions for future research. *Molecular Psychiatry*, 29(10), 1–23. DOI: 10.1038/s41380-024-02556-y PMID: 38658773

van der Meulen, M., & Wijnenga, M. M. (2024). Education and training in neurology: Developments and future challenges. *European Journal of Neurology*, 31(11), 16332. DOI: 10.1111/ene.16332 PMID: 38773718

Voigtlaender, S., Pawelczyk, J., Geiger, M., Vaios, E. J., Karschnia, P., Cudkowicz, M., Dietrich, J., Haraldsen, I. R. J. H., Feigin, V., Owolabi, M., White, T. L., Świeboda, P., Farahany, N., Natarajan, V., & Winter, S. F. (2024). Artificial intelligence in neurology: Opportunities, challenges, and policy implications. *Journal of Neurology*, 271(5), 2258–2273. DOI: 10.1007/s00415-024-12220-8 PMID: 38367046

Xu, A., Hou, Y., Niell, C., & Beyeler, M. (2024). Multimodal deep learning model unveils behavioral dynamics of V1 activity in freely moving mice. *Advances in Neural Information Processing Systems*, •••, 36. PMID: 39005944

Xu, K., & Kang, H. (2024). A review of machine learning approaches for Brain Positron Emission Tomography Data Analysis. *Nuclear Medicine and Molecular Imaging*, 58(4), 1–10. DOI: 10.1007/s13139-024-00845-6 PMID: 38932757

Compilation of References

Aazam, M., Zeadally, S., & Harras, K. A. (2018). Deploying fog computing in industrial internet of things and industry 4.0. *IEEE Transactions on Industrial Informatics*, 14(10), 4674–4682. DOI: 10.1109/TII.2018.2855198

Abadal, S., Galván, P., Mármol, A., Mammone, N., Ieracitano, C., Giudice, M. L., & Morabito, F. C. (2025). Graph neural networks for electroencephalogram analysis: Alzheimer's disease and epilepsy use cases. *Neural Networks*, 181, 106792. DOI: 10.1016/j.neunet.2024.106792 PMID: 39471577

Abd-Alrazaq, A. A., Alajlani, M., Alalwan, A. A., Bewick, B. M., Gardner, P., & Househ, M. (2019). An overview of the features of chatbots in mental health: A scoping review. *International Journal of Medical Informatics*, 132, 103978. DOI: 10.1016/j.ijmedinf.2019.103978 PMID: 31622850

Abdollahifard, S., Farrokhi, A., Mowla, A., & Liebeskind, D. S. (2024). Performance Metrics, Algorithms, and Applications of Artificial Intelligence in Vascular and Interventional Neurology: A Review of Basic Elements. *Neurologic Clinics*, 42(3), 633–650. DOI: 10.1016/j.ncl.2024.03.001 PMID: 38937033

Abi-Dargham, A., Moeller, S. J., Ali, F., DeLorenzo, C., Domschke, K., Horga, G., Jutla, A., Kotov, R., Paulus, M. P., Rubio, J. M., Sanacora, G., Veenstra-VanderWeele, J., & Krystal, J. H. (2023). Candidate Biomarkers in Psychiatric Disorders: State of the Field. *World Psychiatry; Official Journal of the World Psychiatric Association (WPA)*, 22(2), 236–262. DOI: 10.1002/wps.21078 PMID: 37159365

Aboukadri, S., Ouaddah, A., & Mezrioui, A. (2024). Machine learning in identity and access management systems: Survey and deep dive. *Computers & Security*, 139, 103729. DOI: 10.1016/j.cose.2024.103729

Abou-Zahra, S., Brewer, J., & Cooper, M. (2018). Artificial intelligence (AI) for web accessibility: Is conformance evaluation a way forward? In *Proceedings of the internet of accessible things* (pp. 1–4). DOI: 10.1145/3192714.3192834

AbuAlrob, M. A., & Mesraoua, B. (2024). Harnessing artificial intelligence for the diagnosis and treatment of neurological emergencies: A comprehensive review of recent advances and future directions. *Frontiers in Neurology*, 15, 1485799. DOI: 10.3389/fneur.2024.1485799 PMID: 39463792

Addae, S., Kim, J., Smith, A., Kang, M., & Rajana, P. (2024). Smart Solutions for Detecting, Predicting, Monitoring, and Managing Dementia in the Elderly: A Survey. *IEEE Access : Practical Innovations, Open Solutions*, 12, 100026–100056. DOI: 10.1109/ACCESS.2024.3421966

Agrawal, S., & Vagha, S. (2024). A Comprehensive Review of Artificial Intelligence in Prostate Cancer Care: State-of-the-Art Diagnostic Tools and Future Outlook. *Cureus*, 16(8). Advance online publication. DOI: 10.7759/cureus.66225 PMID: 39238711

Ahmed, B., & Khan, S. (2023). Cognitive rehabilitation strategies for traumatic brain injury survivors. *Review Journal of Neurological & Medical Sciences Review*, 1(02), 28–51. DOI: 10.1016/j.rjnmsr.2023.06.001

Ahuja, A., Agrawal, S., Acharya, S., Batra, N., & Daiya, V. (2024). Advancements in Wearable Digital Health Technology: A Review of Epilepsy Management. *Cureus*, 16(3), e57037. DOI: 10.7759/cureus.57037 PMID: 38681418

Aizenstein, H., Moore, R. C., Vahia, I., & Ciarleglio, A. (2023). Deep learning and geriatric mental health. *The American Journal of Geriatric Psychiatry*. PMID: 38142162

Ajith, M., Aycock, D. M., Tone, E. B., Liu, J., Misiura, M. B., Ellis, R., Plis, S. M., King, T. Z., Dotson, V. M., & Calhoun, V. (2024). A deep learning approach for mental health quality prediction using functional network connectivity and assessment data. *Brain Imaging and Behavior*, 18(3), 1–16. DOI: 10.1007/s11682-024-00857-y PMID: 38340285

Akbar, K., Passaro, A., Di Gioia, M., Martini, E., Dragone, M., Zullo, A., & Stasolla, F. (2024). Reviewing the Horizon: The Future of Extended Reality and Artificial Intelligence in Neurorehabilitation for Brain Injury Recovery. *Information (Basel)*, 15(8), 501. DOI: 10.3390/info15080501

Akhtar, Z. B. (2024). Exploring Biomedical Engineering (BME): Advances within Accelerated Computing and Regenerative Medicine for a Computational and Medical Science Perspective Exploration Analysis. *J Emerg Med OA, 2*(1), 01-23.

Akhtarkhavari, D. D. (2023). *Toward Private and Personalized Mental Healthcare with Fast and Efficient Machine Learning Methods* (Doctoral dissertation, La Sierra University).

Al Meslamani, A. Z., Jarab, A. S., & Ghattas, M. A. (2023). The role of machine learning in healthcare responses to pandemics: Maximizing benefits and filling gaps. *Journal of Medical Economics*, 26(1), 777–780. DOI: 10.1080/13696998.2023.2224018 PMID: 37293941

Al Yahyaei, A., Al Omari, O., Sharour, L. A., Cayaban, A. R., Shebani, Z., Al Hashmi, I., & Alhalaiqa, F. (2024). The Lived Experience of Parent Caregivers of Adolescents with Mental Illness: A Phenomenological Study. *International Journal of Community Based Nursing and Midwifery*, 12(1), 2. PMID: 38328010

Alhuwaydi, A. M. (2024). Exploring the Role of Artificial Intelligence in Mental Healthcare: Current Trends and Future Directions–A Narrative Review for a Comprehensive Insight. *Risk Management and Healthcare Policy*, 17, 1339–1348. DOI: 10.2147/RMHP.S461562 PMID: 38799612

Ali, M. T., Turetta, C., Pravadelli, G., & Demrozi, F. (2024). ICT-based solutions for Alzheimer's Disease Care: A systematic review. *IEEE Access : Practical Innovations, Open Solutions*, 12, 13944–13961. DOI: 10.1109/ACCESS.2024.3356348

Ali, N. H., Abdulmunem, M. E., & Ali, A. E. (2021). Learning evolution: A survey. *Iraqi Journal of Science*, •••, 4978–4987. DOI: 10.24996/ijs.2021.62.12.34

Aljunaid, M. A., Alosaimi, R. M., Alazmi, E. A., Afandi, A. A., Musslem, M. T., Aljarameez, M. M., & Alzobaidi, H. H. (2024). Determinants of Depression in Caregivers of Geriatric Patients in Jeddah, Saudi Arabia: A Cross-Sectional Study. *Medicina*, 60(8), 1368. DOI: 10.3390/medicina60081368 PMID: 39202649

Almazaydeh, l., Alsalameen, r., & Elleithy, k. (2022). Herbal leaf recognition using mask-region convolutional neural network (mask r-CNN). Journal of Theoretical and Applied Information Technology, 100(11).

Alnuaimi, A., & Albaldawi, T. (2024). An overview of machine learning classification techniques. *BIO Web of Conferences, 97*, 00133. https://doi.org/DOI: 10.1051/bioconf/20249700133

Alowais, S. A., Alghamdi, S. S., Alsuhebany, N., Alqahtani, T., Alshaya, A. I., Almohareb, S. N., Aldairem, A., Alrashed, M., Saleh, K. B., Badreldin, H. A., Yami, M. S. A., Harbi, S. A., & Albekairy, A. M. (2023). Revolutionizing healthcare: The role of artificial intelligence in clinical practice. *BMC Medical Education*, 23(1), 689. Advance online publication. DOI: 10.1186/s12909-023-04698-z PMID: 37740191

Alpaydin, E. (2020). *Introduction to Machine Learning*. MIT Press.

Altemimi, A., Lakhssassi, N., Baharlouei, A., Watson, D. G., & Lightfoot, D. A. (2017). Phytochemicals: Extraction, isolation, and identification of bioactive compounds from plant extracts. *Plants*, 6(4), 42. DOI: 10.3390/plants6040042 PMID: 28937585

Alzheimer's Association. (2023). 2023 Alzheimer's Disease Facts and Figures. *Alzheimer's & Dementia*, 19(1), 1–50. PMID: 36918389

Amuthalingeswaran, C., Sivakumar, M., Renuga, P., Alexpandi, S., Elamathi, J., & Hari, S. S. (2019, April). Identification of medicinal plants and their usage by using deep learning. In 2019 3rd International conference on trends in electronics and informatics (ICOEI) (pp. 886-890). IEEE.

Andreu-Perez, J., Emberson, L. L., Kiani, M., Wang, X., & Tiwari, P. (2021). Explainable Artificial Intelligence-Based Analysis for Interpreting Infant fnirs Data in Developmental Cognitive Neuroscience. *Communications Biology*, 4(1), 126. Advance online publication. DOI: 10.1038/s42003-021-02534-y PMID: 34526648

Annavarapu, R. N., Gavini, J., & Nair, S. (2019). Non-Invasive Imaging Modalities to Study Neurodegenerative Diseases of Aging Brain. *Journal of Chemical Neuroanatomy*, 97, 67–76. DOI: 10.1016/j.jchemneu.2018.02.006 PMID: 29474853

Ao, L., Bansal, R., Pruthi, N., & Khaskheli, M. B. (2023). Impact of social media influencers on customer engagement and purchase intention: A meta-analysis. *Sustainability (Basel)*, 15(3), 2744. DOI: 10.3390/su15032744

Arbabshirani, M. R.. (2017). Advanced machine learning in diagnostic neuroimaging. *NeuroImage*, 145, 215–228. DOI: 10.1016/j.neuroimage.2016.12.015

Arpaia, P., D'Errico, G., De Paolis, L. T., Moccaldi, N., & Nuccetelli, F. (2021). A Narrative review of Mindfulness-Based Interventions using Virtual Reality. *Mindfulness*, 13(3), 556–571. DOI: 10.1007/s12671-021-01783-6

Axelsson, M., Spitale, M., & Gunes, H. (2024). Robots as mental well-being coaches: Design and ethical recommendations. *ACM Transactions on Human-Robot Interaction*, 13(2), 1–55. DOI: 10.1145/3643457

Azadeh, A., Rouzbahmana, M., & Saberi, M. (2009). Utilization of an Artificial Intelligence approach for Assessment of Job satisfaction. *International Journal of Intelligent Information Technology Application*, 2(6).

Baba, A. (2024). Neural networks from biological to artificial and vice versa. *Bio Systems*, 235, 105110. DOI: 10.1016/j.biosystems.2023.105110 PMID: 38176518

Bacon, E. J., He, D., Wang, L., Li, H., Yao-Digba, P. D. Z., Monkam, P., & Qi, S. (2024). Neuroimage analysis using artificial intelligence approaches: A systematic review. *Medical & Biological Engineering & Computing*, 62(9), 1–29. DOI: 10.1007/s11517-024-03097-w PMID: 38664348

Badrulhisham, F., Pogatzki-Zahn, E., Segelcke, D., Spisak, T., & Vollert, J. (2024). Machine learning and artificial intelligence in neuroscience: A primer for researchers. *Brain, Behavior, and Immunity*, 115, 470–479. DOI: 10.1016/j.bbi.2023.11.005 PMID: 37972877

Bajwa, J., Munir, U., Nori, A., & Williams, B. (2021). Artificial intelligence in healthcare: Transforming the practice of medicine. *Future Healthcare Journal*, 8(2), e188–e194. DOI: 10.7861/fhj.2021-0095 PMID: 34286183

Bakariya, B., Singh, A., Singh, H., Raju, P., Rajpoot, R., & Mohbey, K. K. (2024). Facial emotion recognition and music recommendation system using CNN-based deep learning techniques. *Evolving Systems*, 15(2), 641–658. DOI: 10.1007/s12530-023-09506-z

Baker, E., Houghton, C., & Morris, J. (2019). Integrating cognitive assessments with AI: Benefits and challenges. *Frontiers in Aging Neuroscience*, 11, 329.

Bang, J., Spina, S., & Miller, B. L. (2015). Frontotemporal dementia. *Lancet*, 386(10004), 1672–1682. DOI: 10.1016/S0140-6736(15)00461-4 PMID: 26595641

Bansal, R., Gupta, A., Singh, R., & Nassa, V. K. (2021, July). Role and impact of digital technologies in E-learning amidst COVID-19 pandemic. In *2021 fourth international conference on computational intelligence and communication technologies (CCICT)* (pp. 194-202). IEEE. DOI: 10.1109/CCICT53244.2021.00046

Bansal, R., Pruthi, N., & Singh, R. (2022). Developing customer engagement through artificial intelligence tools: roles and challenges. In *Developing Relationships, Personalization, and Data Herald in Marketing 5.0* (pp. 130-145). IGI Global. DOI: 10.4018/978-1-6684-4496-2.ch008

Bansal, S. (2023). ANALYTIXLABS. *MACHINE LEARNING What is Classification Algorithm in Machine Learning? With Examples, 25 JANUARY 2023.[Online]. Available:https://www. analytixlabs. co. in/blog/classification-in-machine-learning.*

Bansal, R., Shukla, G., Gupta, A., Singh, A., & Pruthi, N. (2023). Optimizing Augmented Reality and Virtual Reality for Customer Engagement. In *Promoting Consumer Engagement Through Emotional Branding and Sensory Marketing* (pp. 24–35). IGI Global.

Bansal, R., Shukla, G., Gupta, A., Singh, A., & Pruthi, N. (2023). Optimizing augmented reality and virtual reality for customer engagement. In *Promoting consumer engagement through emotional branding and sensory marketing* (pp. 24–35). IGI Global., DOI: 10.4018/978-1-7998-7925-6.ch002

Barkley, R. A. (2015). *Attention-deficit hyperactivity disorder: A handbook for diagnosis and treatment* (4th ed.). Guilford Press.

Barocas, S., Hardt, M., & Narayanan, A. (2019). *Fairness and machine learning: Limitations and opportunities*. MIT Press.

Beardwell, J., & Claydon, T. (Eds.). (2007). *Human resource management: A contemporary approach*. Pearson Education.

Beck, A. (1967). Depression: clinical, experimental, and theoretical aspects. *Harper & Row google schola, 2*, 103-113.

Beck, A. T., Rush, A. J., Shaw, B. F., Emery, G., DeRubeis, R. J., & Hollon, S. D. (2024). *Cognitive therapy of depression*. Guilford Publications.

Beck, J. S. (2020). *Cognitive behavior therapy: Basics and beyond*. Guilford Publications.

Beck, J. S., & Fleming, S. (2021). A Brief History of Aaron T. Beck, MD, and Cognitive Behavior Therapy. *Clinical Psychology in Europe*, 3(2), e6701. DOI: 10.32872/cpe.6701 PMID: 36397957

Bengio, Y. (2019). The consciousness prior. *arXiv preprint arXiv:1709.08568*.

Bengio, Y., LeCun, Y., & Hinton, G. (2021). Deep learning for AI. *Nature Reviews. Physics*, 3(6), 447–456.

Bergstra, J., & Bengio, Y. (2012). Random Search for Hyper-Parameter Optimization. *Journal of Machine Learning Research*, 13, 281–305.

Bernal, J., Costa, A., Oliveira, J., Sanchez, I., & Hernandez, M. (2019). Deep Convolutional Neural Networks for Brain Image Analysis on Magnetic Resonance Imaging: A Review. *Artificial Intelligence in Medicine*, 97, 123–137. DOI: 10.1016/j.artmed.2018.08.008 PMID: 30195984

Berrezueta-Guzman, J., Pau, I., Martín-Ruiz, M.-L., & Máximo-Bocanegra, N. (2021). Assessment of a robotic assistant for supporting homework activities of children with ADHD. *IEEE Access : Practical Innovations, Open Solutions*, 9, 93450–93465. DOI: 10.1109/ACCESS.2021.3093233

Berrezueta-Guzman, S., Kandil, M., Martín-Ruiz, M.-L., Pau de la Cruz, I., & Krusche, S. (2024). Future of ADHD care: Evaluating the efficacy of ChatGPT in therapy enhancement. *Health Care*, 12(6), 683. DOI: 10.3390/healthcare12060683 PMID: 38540647

Bertacchini, F., Demarco, F., Scuro, C., Pantano, P., & Bilotta, E. (2023). A social robot connected with ChatGPT to improve cognitive functioning in ASD subjects. *Frontiers in Psychology*, 14, 1232177. DOI: 10.3389/fpsyg.2023.1232177 PMID: 37868599

Bhagya Shree, S. R., & Sheshadri, H. S. (2018). Diagnosis of Alzheimer's disease using naive Bayesian classifier. *Neural Computing & Applications*, 29(1), 123–132. DOI: 10.1007/s00521-016-2416-3

Bhardwaj, S., Thapa, S. B., & Gandhi, A. (2024). Advances in neuromarketing and improved understanding of consumer behaviour: Analysing tool possibilities and research trends. *Cogent Business & Management*, 11(1), 2376773. DOI: 10.1080/23311975.2024.2376773

Bhave, D. P., Teo, L. H., & Dalal, R. S. (2020). Privacy at work: A review and a research agenda for a contested terrain. *Journal of Management*, 46(1), 127–164. DOI: 10.1177/0149206319878254

Bhugra, D., Smith, A. J., Ventriglio, A., Rao, N., Ng, R., Javed, A., Chisolm, M. S., Malhi, G., Kar, A., Chumakov, E., & Liebrenz, M. (2024). World Psychiatric Association-Asian Journal of Psychiatry Commission on the Mental Health and Wellbeing of International Medical Graduates. *Asian Journal of Psychiatry*, 93, 103943. DOI: 10.1016/j.ajp.2024.103943 PMID: 38342035

Bini, S. A. (2018). Artificial intelligence, machine learning, deep learning, and cognitive computing: What do these terms mean and how will they impact health care? *The Journal of Arthroplasty*, 33(8), 2358–2361. DOI: 10.1016/j.arth.2018.02.067 PMID: 29656964

Birrenbach, T., Stuber, R., Müller, C. E., Sutter, P., Hautz, W. E., Exadaktylos, A. K., Müller, M., Wespi, R., & Sauter, T. C. (2024). Virtual reality simulation to enhance advanced trauma life support trainings – a randomized controlled trial. *BMC Medical Education*, 24(1), 666. Advance online publication. DOI: 10.1186/s12909-024-05645-2 PMID: 38886688

Bledsoe, J. C., Xiao, C., Chaovalitwongse, A., Mehta, S., Grabowski, T. J., Semrud-Clikeman, M., Pliszka, S., & Breiger, D. (2020). Diagnostic classification of ADHD versus control: Support vector machine classification using brief neuropsychological assessment. *Journal of Attention Disorders*, 24(11), 1547–1556. DOI: 10.1177/1087054716649666 PMID: 27231214

Boeldt, D., McMahon, E., McFaul, M., & Greenleaf, W. (2019). Using virtual reality exposure therapy to enhance treatment of anxiety disorders: Identifying areas of clinical adoption and potential obstacles. *Frontiers in Psychiatry*, 10, 773. Advance online publication. DOI: 10.3389/fpsyt.2019.00773 PMID: 31708821

Bohr, A., & Memarzadeh, K. (2020). The rise of artificial intelligence in healthcare applications. In *Artificial Intelligence in healthcare* (pp. 25–60). Academic Press., DOI: 10.1016/B978-0-12-818438-7.00002-2

Bom, H. S. H., Kim, J., Yun, M., & Kang, D. Y. (2024). Are the Nuclear Neuro-Imaging Biomarkers Reliable? *Nuclear Medicine and Molecular Imaging*, •••, 1–2. PMID: 38932761

Bookwala, J., Yee, J. L., & Schulz, R. (2000). Caregiving and detrimental mental and physical health outcomes. In *Physical illness and depression in older adults: A handbook of theory, research, and practice* (pp. 93–131). Springer US.

Bora, K. S., Sharma, A., & Singh, S. (2011). Evaluation of Antidepressant-like Activity of Glycyrrhiza glabra L. in Experimental Models of Depression. *Pharmacognosy Research*, 3(1), 21–25.

Botella, C., Fernández-Álvarez, J., Guillén, V., García-Palacios, A., & Baños, R. (2017). Recent Progress in Virtual Reality Exposure Therapy for Phobias: A Systematic Review. *Current Psychiatry Reports*, 19(7), 42. Advance online publication. DOI: 10.1007/s11920-017-0788-4 PMID: 28540594

Bottou, L. (2010). "Large-Scale Machine Learning with Stochastic Gradient Descent. "*Proceedings of the 19th International Conference on Machine Learning (ICML-10)*, 3-10.

Boudries, R., Williams, H., Paquereau—Gaboreau, S., Bashir, S., Hojjat Jodaylami, M., Chisanga, M., Trudeau, L.-É., & Masson, J.-F. (2024). Surface-Enhanced Raman Scattering Nanosensing and Imaging in Neuroscience. *ACS Nano*, 18(34), 22620–22647. DOI: 10.1021/acsnano.4c05200 PMID: 39088751

Brownlee, J. (2022). *Machine learning mastery*. Machine Learning Mastery.

Brown, M. R.. (2020). AI-based neuroimaging biomarkers for ADHD. *NeuroImage*, 204, 116223. DOI: 10.1016/j.neuroimage.2020.116223

Bui, J., Luauté, J., & Farnè, A. (2021). Enhancing upper limb rehabilitation of stroke patients with Virtual Reality: A mini review. *Frontiers in Virtual Reality*, 2, 595771. Advance online publication. DOI: 10.3389/frvir.2021.595771

Buolamwini, J., & Gebru, T. (2018). Gender Shades: Intersectional Accuracy Disparities in Commercial Gender Classification. *Proceedings of the 2018 Conference on Fairness, Accountability, and Transparency*, 77-91.

Burke, T. A., Ammerman, B. A., & Jacobucci, R. (2019). The use of machine learning in the study of suicidal and non-suicidal self-injurious thoughts and behaviors: A systematic review. *Journal of Affective Disorders*, 245, 869–884. DOI: 10.1016/j.jad.2018.11.073 PMID: 30699872

Cabibihan, J. J., Javed, H., Ang, M.Jr, & Aljunied, S. M. (2013). Why robots? A survey on the roles and benefits of social robots in the therapy of children with autism. *International Journal of Social Robotics*, 5(4), 593–618. DOI: 10.1007/s12369-013-0202-2

Cai, Y., Li, X., & Li, J. (2023). Emotion recognition using different sensors, emotion models, methods and datasets: A comprehensive review. *Sensors (Basel)*, 23(5), 2455. DOI: 10.3390/s23052455 PMID: 36904659

Calderone, A., Latella, D., Bonanno, M., Quartarone, A., Mojdehdehbaher, S., Celesti, A., & Calabrò, R. S. (2024). Towards transforming neurorehabilitation: The impact of artificial intelligence on diagnosis and treatment of neurological disorders. *Biomedicines*, 12(10), 2415. DOI: 10.3390/biomedicines12102415 PMID: 39457727

Cano, M., Velasco, C., & Bakos, S. (2023). Making Virtual Reality (VR) Accessible for People with Disabilities. In *Springer eBooks* (pp. 1–6). DOI: 10.1007/978-3-319-08234-9_523-1

Carl, E., Mason, J.E., Smits, J.A. and Asmundson, G.J., (2022). Exercise for mental health: Current perspectives, clinical practice implications, and future directions.

Carlson, C. G. (2023). Virtual and augmented simulations in mental health. *Current Psychiatry Reports*, 25(9), 365–371. DOI: 10.1007/s11920-023-01438-4 PMID: 37624512

Carrarini, C., Nardulli, C., Titti, L., Iodice, F., Miraglia, F., Vecchio, F., & Rossini, P. M. (2024). Neuropsychological and electrophysiological measurements for diagnosis and prediction of dementia: A review on machine learning approach. *Ageing Research Reviews*, 100, 102417. DOI: 10.1016/j.arr.2024.102417 PMID: 39002643

Cascella, M., Montomoli, J., Bellini, V., Vittori, A., Ianniello, D., & Cuocolo, R. (2023). Crossing the AI Chasm in Neurocritical Care. *Computers*, 12(4), 83. DOI: 10.3390/computers12040083

Cavaliere, L. P. L., Nath, K., Wisetsri, W., Villalba-Condori, K. O., Arias-Chavez, D., Setiawan, R., . . . Regin, R. (2021). *The impact of E-recruitment and artificial intelligence (AI) tools on HR effectiveness: the case of high schools* (Doctoral dissertation, Petra Christian University).

Celedonia, K. L., Karukivi, M., Valenti, M. W., Geldsetzer, P., & Wilson, M. L. (2024). Temporal Patterns of Suicidality Among Adolescents Receiving Behavioral and Mental Health Services in the Community: A Survival Analysis. *Community Mental Health Journal*, •••, 1–8.

Ceradini, M., Losanno, E., Micera, S., Bandini, A., & Orlandi, S. (2024). Immersive VR for upper-extremity rehabilitation in patients with neurological disorders: A scoping review. *Journal of Neuroengineering and Rehabilitation*, 21(1), 75. Advance online publication. DOI: 10.1186/s12984-024-01367-0 PMID: 38734690

Cerda, I. H., Therond, A., Moreau, S., Studer, K., Donjow, A. R., Crowther, J. E., Mazzolenis, M. E., Lang, M., Tolba, R., Gilligan, C., Ashina, S., Kaye, A. D., Yong, R. J., Schatman, M. E., & Robinson, C. L. (2024). Telehealth and virtual reality Technologies in Chronic Pain Management: A Narrative review. *Current Pain and Headache Reports*, 28(3), 83–94. DOI: 10.1007/s11916-023-01205-3 PMID: 38175490

Ceyhan, B., Bek, S., & Onal-Suzek, T. (2024). Smart Wristband Monitoring: A Caregiver-Oriented Mobile Application for Tracking Cognitive Decline in Mild Cognitive Impairment Patients. medRxiv, 2024.2005. 2031.24307874. DOI: 10.1101/2024.05.31.24307874

Chaddad, A., Wu, Y., Kateb, R., & Bouridane, A. (2023). Electroencephalography signal processing: A comprehensive review and analysis of methods and techniques. *Sensors (Basel)*, 23(14), 6434. DOI: 10.3390/s23146434 PMID: 37514728

Challa, V. N. S. K. (2022). AI-Driven Resource Allocation. *International Journal Of Advanced Research in Engineering and Technology, 13*(12).

Chamorro-Premuzic, T., Winsborough, D., Sherman, R., & Hogan, R. (2016). New talent signals: Shiny new objects or a brave new world? *Industrial and Organizational Psychology: Perspectives on Science and Practice*, 9(3), 621–640. DOI: 10.1017/iop.2016.6

Chan, S., et al. (2021). AI and sleep monitoring for ADHD management. *Journal of Medical Informatics.*

Chancellor, S., Baumer, E. P., & De Choudhury, M. (2019). Who is the" human" in human-centered machine learning: The case of predicting mental health from social media. *Proceedings of the ACM on Human-Computer Interaction, 3*(CSCW), 1-32. DOI: 10.1145/3359249

Chancellor, S., Birnbaum, M. L., Caine, E. D., Silenzio, V. M., & De Choudhury, M. (2019, January). A taxonomy of ethical tensions in inferring mental health states from social media. In *Proceedings of the conference on fairness, accountability, and transparency* (pp. 79-88). DOI: 10.1145/3287560.3287587

Chand, S., Kuckel, D., & Huecker, M. (2022). [*StatPearls*][*Internet*] [. *Treasure Island*] [*FL*][: *StatPearls Publishing.*]. *Cognitive Behaviour Therapy*, 2022(May), 29.

Chaplin, E., Karatzios, C., & Benaim, C. (2023). Clinical Applications of Virtual Reality in Musculoskeletal Rehabilitation: A scoping review. *Health Care*, 11(24), 3178. DOI: 10.3390/healthcare11243178 PMID: 38132067

Cheah, W. T., Hwang, J. J., Hong, S. Y., Fu, L. C., Chang, Y. L., Chen, T. F., Chen, I.-A., & Chou, C. C. (2022). A digital screening system for Alzheimer disease based on a neuropsychological test and a convolutional neural network: System development and validation. *JMIR Medical Informatics*, 10(3), e31106. DOI: 10.2196/31106 PMID: 35262497

Chen, B., Xu, M., Yu, H., He, J., Li, Y., Song, D., & Fan, G. G. (2023). Detection of mild cognitive impairment in Parkinson's disease using gradient boosting decision tree models based on multilevel DTI indices. *Journal of Translational Medicine*, 21(1), 310. DOI: 10.1186/s12967-023-04158-8 PMID: 37158918

Chen, I. Y., Pierson, E., Rose, S., Joshi, S., Ferryman, K., & Ghassemi, M. (2021). Ethical machine learning in healthcare. *Annual Review of Biomedical Data Science*, 4(1), 123–144. DOI: 10.1146/annurev-biodatasci-092820-114757 PMID: 34396058

Chen, S., Janies, D., Paul, R., & Thill, J. C. (2024). Leveraging advances in data-driven deep learning methods for hybrid epidemic modeling. *Epidemics*, 48, 100782. DOI: 10.1016/j.epidem.2024.100782 PMID: 38971085

Chen, X., Wang, S., Yang, X., Yu, C., Ni, F., Yang, J., Tian, Y., Ye, J., Liu, H., & Luo, R. (2023). Utilizing artificial intelligence-based eye tracking technology for screening ADHD symptoms in children. *Frontiers in Psychiatry*, 14, 1260031. DOI: 10.3389/fpsyt.2023.1260031 PMID: 38034916

Chen, X., Zhang, X., Xie, H., Tao, X., Wang, F., Xie, N., & Li, J. (2021). A Bibliometric and Visual Analysis of Artificial Intelligence Technologies-Enhanced Brain MRI Research. *Multimedia Tools and Applications*, 80(11), 17335–17363. DOI: 10.1007/s11042-020-09062-7

Chen, Z. (2023). Ethics and discrimination in artificial intelligence-enabled recruitment practices. *Humanities & Social Sciences Communications*, 10(1), 1–12. DOI: 10.1057/s41599-023-02079-x

Chen, Z. S., Galatzer-Levy, I. R., Bigio, B., Nasca, C., & Zhang, Y. (2022). Modern views of machine learning for precision psychiatry. *Patterns (New York, N.Y.)*, 3(11), 100602. Advance online publication. DOI: 10.1016/j.patter.2022.100602 PMID: 36419447

Cheong, P. H. (2020). Robots, religion and communication: Rethinking piety, practices and pedagogy in the era of artificial intelligence. In *Religion in the Age of Digitalization* (pp. 86–96). Routledge. DOI: 10.4324/9780367809225-9

Chopra, H., Annu, , Shin, D. K., Munjal, K., Priyanka, , Dhama, K., & Emran, T. B. (2023). Revolutionizing clinical trials: The role of AI in accelerating medical breakthroughs. *International Journal of Surgery*, 109(12), 4211–4220. DOI: 10.1097/JS9.0000000000000705 PMID: 38259001

Chudzik, A., Śledzianowski, A., & Przybyszewski, A. W. (2024). Machine learning and digital biomarkers can detect early stages of neurodegenerative diseases. *Sensors (Basel)*, 24(5), 1572. DOI: 10.3390/s24051572 PMID: 38475108

Cichy, R. M., & Kaiser, D. (2019). Deep neural networks as scientific models. *Trends in Cognitive Sciences*, 23(4), 305–317. DOI: 10.1016/j.tics.2019.01.009 PMID: 30795896

Clak, D. A., & Beck, A. T. (1999). *Scientific foundations of cognitive theory and therapy of depression*. John Wiley & Sons.

Clemmensen, L., Bouchard, S., Rasmussen, J., Holmberg, T. T., Nielsen, J. H., Jepsen, J. R. M., & Lichtenstein, M. B. (2020). STUDY PROTOCOL: EXPOSURE IN VIRTUAL REALITY FOR SOCIAL ANXIETY DISORDER - a randomized controlled superiority trial comparing cognitive behavioral therapy with virtual reality-based exposure to cognitive behavioral therapy with in vivo exposure. *BMC Psychiatry*, 20(1), 32. Advance online publication. DOI: 10.1186/s12888-020-2453-4 PMID: 32000725

Corsi, M. C. (2023). Electroencephalography and Magnetoencephalography. *Machine learning for brain disorders*, 285-312. DOI: 10.1007/978-1-0716-3195-9_9

Cosic, K., Kopilas, V., & Jovanovic, T. (2024). War, emotions, mental health, and artificial intelligence. *Frontiers in Psychology*, 15, 1394045. DOI: 10.3389/fpsyg.2024.1394045 PMID: 39156807

Cossich, V. R. A., Carlgren, D., Holash, R. J., & Katz, L. (2023). Technological breakthroughs in sport: Current practice and future potential of artificial intelligence, virtual reality, augmented reality, and modern data visualization in performance analysis. *Applied Sciences (Basel, Switzerland)*, 13(23), 12965. DOI: 10.3390/app132312965

Creed, C., Al-Kalbani, M., Theil, A., Sarcar, S., & Williams, I. (2023). Inclusive AR/VR: Accessibility barriers for immersive technologies. *Universal Access in the Information Society*. Advance online publication. DOI: 10.1007/s10209-023-00969-0

D'Hotman, D., & Loh, E. (2020). AI enabled suicide prediction tools: A qualitative narrative review. *BMJ Health & Care Informatics*, 27(3), e100175. Advance online publication. DOI: 10.1136/bmjhci-2020-100175 PMID: 33037037

Dash, A., & Agres, K. (2024). AI-based affective music generation systems: A review of methods and challenges. *ACM Computing Surveys*, 56(11), 1–34. DOI: 10.1145/3672554

Das, S., Mohapatra, S. K., & Mishra, S. K. (2021). An in silico approach to evaluate the potential of Withania somnifera bioactives for inhibiting SARS-CoV-2 viral proteins. *Informatics in Medicine Unlocked*, 24, 100579.

Davatzikos C., (2019), "Machine Learning in Neuroimaging: Progress and Challenges," neuroimage, vol. 197, pp. 654-665.

Davatzikos, C., Bhatt, P., & Formisano, E. (2019). Predicting cognitive decline using AI in neuroimaging. *Journal of Alzheimer's Disease*, 68(3), 1223–1234. DOI: 10.3233/JAD-181148

Davenport, T. H., & Ronanki, R. (2018). Artificial intelligence for the real world. *Harvard Business Review*, 96(1), 108–116.

Dave, R., Sargeant, K., Vanamala, M., & Seliya, N. (2022). Review on psychology research based on artificial intelligence methodologies. *Journal of Computer and Communications*, 10(5), 113–130. DOI: 10.4236/jcc.2022.105008

Daviglus, M. L., Bell, C. C., & Berrettini, W. (2011). The role of early diagnosis and intervention in Alzheimer's disease: Impact on quality of life. *American Journal of Preventive Medicine*, 41(4), S236–S243.

De Prisco, R., Guarino, A., Malandrino, D., & Zaccagnino, R. (2022). Induced emotion-based music recommendation through reinforcement learning. *Applied Sciences (Basel, Switzerland)*, 12(21), 11209. DOI: 10.3390/app122111209

de Souza, G. C., & Roveroni, A. J. (2023). INTELIGÊNCIA ARTIFICIAL (IA): O PAPEL CRUCIAL DA REGULAMENTAÇÃO. *Revista Ibero-Americana de Humanidades. Ciência & Educação (Bauru)*, 9(10), 1982–1993. DOI: 10.51891/rease.v9i10.11896

Dechsling, A., Orm, S., Kalandadze, T., Sütterlin, S., Øien, R. A., Shic, F., & Nordahl-Hansen, A. (2021). Virtual and Augmented Reality in Social Skills Interventions for Individuals with Autism Spectrum Disorder: A Scoping Review. *Journal of Autism and Developmental Disorders*, 52(11), 4692–4707. DOI: 10.1007/s10803-021-05338-5 PMID: 34783991

Dehaene, S., Lau, H., & Kouider, S. (2017). What is consciousness, and could machines have it? *Science*, 358(6362), 486–492. DOI: 10.1126/science.aan8871 PMID: 29074769

Delgado, S., Vignola, R. C. B., Sassi, R. J., Belan, P. A., & de Araújo, S. A. (2024). Symptom mapping and personalized care for depression, anxiety and stress: A data-driven AI approach. *Computers in Biology and Medicine*, 182, 109146. DOI: 10.1016/j.compbiomed.2024.109146 PMID: 39265480

Deloitte. (2017). The 2017 Deloitte state of cognitive survey. Accessed 10 July 2021. Web Link https://tinyurl.com/4kn2c35s

Deng, W., Hu, D., Xu, S., Liu, X., Zhao, J., Chen, Q., Liu, J., Zhang, Z., Jiang, W., Ma, L., Hong, X., Cheng, S., Liu, B., & Li, X. (2019). The efficacy of virtual reality exposure therapy for PTSD symptoms: A systematic review and meta-analysis. *Journal of Affective Disorders*, 257, 698–709. DOI: 10.1016/j.jad.2019.07.086 PMID: 31382122

Dennis, A. P., & Strafella, A. P. (2024). The role of AI and machine learning in the diagnosis of Parkinson's disease and atypical parkinsonisms. *Parkinsonism & Related Disorders*, 126, 106986. DOI: 10.1016/j.parkreldis.2024.106986 PMID: 38724317

DeRubeis, R. J. (2019). The history, current status, and possible future of precision mental health. *Behaviour Research and Therapy*, 123, 103506. DOI: 10.1016/j.brat.2019.103506 PMID: 31706160

Dhanka, S., & Maini, S. (2021, December). Random forest for heart disease detection: a classification approach. In *2021 IEEE 2nd International Conference On Electrical Power and Energy Systems (ICEPES)* (pp. 1-3). IEEE. DOI: 10.1109/ICEPES52894.2021.9699506

Dhiman, R. (2023). Machine learning techniques for electroencephalogram based brain-computer interface: A systematic literature review. *Measurement. Sensors*, 28, 100823. DOI: 10.1016/j.measen.2023.100823

Di Nunno, V., Fordellone, M., Minniti, G., Asioli, S., Conti, A., Mazzatenta, D., Balestrini, D., Chiodini, P., Agati, R., Tonon, C., Tosoni, A., Gatto, L., Bartolini, S., Lodi, R., & Franceschi, E. (2022). Machine learning in neuro-oncology: Toward novel development fields. *Journal of Neuro-Oncology*, 159(2), 333–346. DOI: 10.1007/s11060-022-04068-7 PMID: 35761160

Dignum, V. (2018). *Responsible AI: How to develop and use AI in a responsible way*. Springer.

Dinov, I. D. (2024). Neuroinformatics Applications of Data Science and Artificial Intelligence. *Neuroinformatics*, 22(4), 1–3. DOI: 10.1007/s12021-024-09692-4 PMID: 39316274

Dixit, S., Bohre, K., Singh, Y., Himeur, Y., Mansoor, W., Atalla, S., & Srinivasan, K. (2023). A Comprehensive review on AI-enabled models for Parkinson's disease diagnosis. *Electronics (Basel)*, 12(4), 783. DOI: 10.3390/electronics12040783

Doyle, A. E., Bearden, C. E., Gur, R. E., Ledbetter, D. H., Martin, C. L., McCoy, T. H.Jr, Pasaniuc, B., Perlis, R. H., Smoller, J. W., & Davis, L. K. (2024). Advancing Mental Health Research Through Strategic Integration of Transdiagnostic Dimensions and Genomics. *Biological Psychiatry*. Advance online publication. DOI: 10.1016/j.biopsych.2024.10.006 PMID: 39424167

Drigas, A., & Sideraki, A. (2024). Brain Neuroplasticity Leveraging Virtual Reality and Brain–Computer Interface Technologies. *Sensors (Basel)*, 24(17), 5725. DOI: 10.3390/s24175725 PMID: 39275636

Duff, K., & Ramezani, A. (2015). Regression-based normative formulae for the repeatable battery for the assessment of neuropsychological status for older adults. *Archives of Clinical Neuropsychology*, 30(7), 600–604. DOI: 10.1093/arclin/acv052 PMID: 26289055

Duffy, M. E., Twenge, J. M., & Joiner, T. E. (2019). Trends in mood and anxiety symptoms and suicide-related outcomes among US undergraduates, 2007–2018: Evidence from two national surveys. *The Journal of Adolescent Health*, 65(5), 590–598. DOI: 10.1016/j.jadohealth.2019.04.033 PMID: 31279724

Dzianok, P., & Kublik, E. (2024). PEARL-Neuro Database: EEG, fMRI, health and lifestyle data of middle-aged people at risk of dementia. *Scientific Data*, 11(1), 276. DOI: 10.1038/s41597-024-03106-5 PMID: 38453963

Ehrlich, K.. (2021). AI insights in workplace ADHD support. *Organizational Behavior and Human Decision Processes*.

Ehrlich, S.. (2021). Advances in AI for ADHD management. *Nature Reviews. Neurology*, 17(5), 276–287. DOI: 10.1038/s41582-021-00473-x

Emmelkamp, P. M. G., Meyerbröker, K., & Morina, N. (2020). Virtual reality therapy in social anxiety disorder. *Current Psychiatry Reports*, 22(7), 32. Advance online publication. DOI: 10.1007/s11920-020-01156-1 PMID: 32405657

Epelbaum, S., Chupin, M., & Lebihan, D. (2021). AI-enhanced neuroimaging: Algorithms and applications. *NeuroImage*, 224, 117430.

Ernala, S. K., Birnbaum, M. L., Candan, K. A., Rizvi, A. F., Sterling, W. A., Kane, J. M., & De Choudhury, M. (2019, May). Methodological gaps in predicting mental health states from social media: Triangulating diagnostic signals. In *Proceedings of the 2019 chi conference on human factors in computing systems* (pp. 1-16). DOI: 10.1145/3290605.3300364

Esteva, A., Robicquet, A., Ramsundar, B., Kuleshov, V., DePristo, M., Chou, K., Cui, C., Corrado, G. S., Thrun, S., & Dean, J. (2021). A guide to deep learning in healthcare. *Nature Medicine*, 25(1), 24–29. DOI: 10.1038/s41591-018-0316-z PMID: 30617335

Ezzati, A., & Lipton, R. B. (2020). Machine Learning Predictive Models Can Improve Efficacy of Clinical Trials for Alzheimer's Disease. *Journal of Alzheimer's Disease*, 74(1), 55–63. DOI: 10.3233/JAD-190822 PMID: 31985462

Fabrizio, C., Termine, A., Caltagirone, C., & Sancesario, G. (2021). Artificial Intelligence for Alzheimer's Disease: Promise or Challenge? *Diagnostics (Basel)*, 11(8), 1473. DOI: 10.3390/diagnostics11081473 PMID: 34441407

Fan, J., Han, F., & Liu, H. (2020). Challenges of big data analysis. *National Science Review*, 6(5), 712–721. DOI: 10.1093/nsr/nwx153 PMID: 25419469

Farahani, F. V., Fiok, K., Lahijanian, B., Rostami, M., & Zeinali, S. (2022). Explainable AI: A Review of Applications to Neuroimaging Data. *Frontiers in Neuroscience*, 16, 791229. Advance online publication. DOI: 10.3389/fnins.2022.906290 PMID: 36583102

Faraone, S. V., et al. (2021). Optimizing ADHD medication using AI. *Journal of Clinical Psychiatry, 82*(4), 21r13944. https://doi.org/DOI: 10.4088/JCP.20r13944

Faraone, S. V., Banaschewski, T., Coghill, D., Zheng, Y., Biederman, J., & Franke, B. (2021). The world federation of ADHD international consensus statement: 208 evidence-based conclusions about the disorder. *Neuroscience and Biobehavioral Reviews*, 128, 789–818. DOI: 10.1016/j.neubiorev.2021.01.022 PMID: 33549739

Farhud, D. D., & Zokaei, S. (2021). Ethical Issues of Artificial Intelligence in Medicine and Healthcare. *Iranian Journal of Public Health*, 50(11), i–v. DOI: 10.18502/ijph.v50i11.7600 PMID: 35223619

Felber, N. A., Lipworth, W., Tian, Y. J., Roulet Schwab, D., & Wangmo, T. (2024). Informing existing technology acceptance models: A qualitative study with older persons and caregivers. *European Journal of Ageing*, 21(1), 12. DOI: 10.1007/s10433-024-00801-5 PMID: 38551677

Felsenstein, O., Oren, N., & Tal, O. (2019), "Multi-Modal Neuroimaging Analysis and Visualization Tool (MMVT)," arxiv preprint arxiv:1910.13543.

Fiorente, N., Mojdehdehbaher, S., & Calabrò, R. S. (2024). Artificial Intelligence and Neurorehabilitation: Fact vs. Fiction. *Innovations in Clinical Neuroscience*, 21(1-3), 10. PMID: 38495602

Fırat, H., Asker, M. E., Bayındır, M. İ., & Hanbay, D. (2023). Hybrid 3D/2D complete inception module and convolutional neural network for hyperspectral remote sensing image classification. *Neural Processing Letters*, 55(2), 1087–1130. DOI: 10.1007/s11063-022-10929-z

Fitzpatrick, K. K., Darcy, A., & Vierhile, M. (2017). Delivering CBT via AI chatbots. *Journal of Medical Internet Research*, 19(5), e132. DOI: 10.2196/jmir.7277

Fitzpatrick, K. K., Darcy, A., & Vierhile, M. (2017). Delivering Cognitive Behavior Therapy to Young Adults With Symptoms of Depression and Anxiety Using a Fully Automated Conversational Agent (Woebot): A Randomized Controlled Trial. *JMIR Mental Health*, 4(2), e19. DOI: 10.2196/mental.7785 PMID: 28588005

Forcier, M. B., Gallois, H., Mullan, S., & Joly, Y. (2019). Integrating artificial intelligence into health care through data access: Can the GDPR act as a beacon for policymakers? *Journal of Law and the Biosciences*, 6(1), 317–335. DOI: 10.1093/jlb/lsz013 PMID: 31666972

Franklin, G., Stephens, R., Piracha, M., Tiosano, S., Lehouillier, F., Koppel, R., & Elkin, P. L. (2024). The Sociodemographic Biases in Machine Learning Algorithms: A Biomedical Informatics Perspective. *Life (Basel, Switzerland)*, 14(6), 652. DOI: 10.3390/life14060652 PMID: 38929638

Freeman, D., Haselton, P., & Lister, R. (2017). Virtual reality in psychological therapy. *Annual Review of Clinical Psychology*, 13, 209–245. DOI: 10.1146/annurev-clinpsy-032816-045901

Freitas, J. R. S., Velosa, V. H. S., Abreu, L. T. N., Jardim, R. L., Santos, J. V., Peres, B., & Campos, P. F. (2021). Virtual Reality Exposure Treatment in Phobias: A Systematic Review. *The Psychiatric Quarterly*, 92(4), 1685–1710. DOI: 10.1007/s11126-021-09935-6 PMID: 34173160

Frey, C. B., & Osborne, M. A. (2017). The future of employment: How susceptible are jobs to computerisation? *Technological Forecasting and Social Change*, 114, 254–280. DOI: 10.1016/j.techfore.2016.08.019

Friedman, L. G., Zhang, D., & Zhou, W. (2018). Prediction of Alzheimer's disease with machine learning. *Journal of Neuroscience Methods*, 305, 88–97.

Friston, K. J. (2021). The new science of complex systems and artificial intelligence. *Frontiers in Computational Neuroscience*, 15, 669928. DOI: 10.3389/fncom.2021.669928

Friston, K., Zeidman, P., & Litvak, V. (2020). Empirical Bayes for DCM: A group inversion scheme. *Frontiers in Systems Neuroscience*, 12, 76. DOI: 10.3389/fnsys.2020.00076 PMID: 26640432

Frosolini, A., Franz, L., Caragli, V., Genovese, E., de Filippis, C., & Marioni, G. (2024). Artificial Intelligence in Audiology: A Scoping Review of Current Applications and Future Directions. *Sensors (Basel)*, 24(22), 7126. DOI: 10.3390/s24227126 PMID: 39598904

Fulmer, R., Joerin, A., Gentile, B., Lakerink, L., & Rauws, M. (2018). Using psychological artificial intelligence (Tess) to relieve symptoms of depression and anxiety: Randomized controlled trial. *JMIR Mental Health*, 5(4), e9782. DOI: 10.2196/mental.9782 PMID: 30545815

Ganesh, S., Chithambaram, T., Krishnan, N. R., Vincent, D. R., Kaliappan, J., & Srinivasan, K. (2023). Exploring Huntington's Disease Diagnosis via Artificial Intelligence Models: A Comprehensive Review. *Diagnostics (Basel)*, 13(23), 3592. DOI: 10.3390/diagnostics13233592 PMID: 38066833

Ganguly, C., Nayak, S., & Gupta, A. K. (2022). *Mental health impact of COVID-19 and machine learning applications in combating mental disorders: a review.* Artificial Intelligence, Machine Learning, and Mental Health in Pandemics. DOI: 10.1016/B978-0-323-91196-2.00016-8

Gao, J., Heng, F., Yuan, Y., & Liu, Y. (2024). A novel machine learning method for multiaxial fatigue life prediction: Improved adaptive neuro-fuzzy inference system. *International Journal of Fatigue*, 178, 108007. DOI: 10.1016/j.ijfatigue.2023.108007

Gao, K., Xu, A., & Krulwich, T. A. (2018). Roles of Resveratrol in Improving the Antioxidant Deficiency of Chronic Fatigue Syndrome. *Nutrients*, 10(10), 1395. DOI: 10.3390/nu10101395 PMID: 30275418

Garg, A., Chaturvedi, V., Kaur, A. B., Varshney, V., & Parashar, A. (2022). Machine learning model for mapping of music mood and human emotion based on physiological signals. *Multimedia Tools and Applications*, 81(4), 5137–5177. DOI: 10.1007/s11042-021-11650-0

Garg, M. (2024). WellXplain: Wellness concept extraction and classification in Reddit posts for mental health analysis. *Knowledge-Based Systems*, 284, 111228. DOI: 10.1016/j.knosys.2023.111228

Gazzaniga, M. S., Ivry, R. B., & Mangun, G. R. (2020). *Cognitive neuroscience: The biology of the mind.* W.W. Norton & Company.

Gerke, S., Minssen, T., & Cohen, G. (2020). Ethical and legal challenges of artificial intelligence-driven healthcare. *Artificial Intelligence in Healthcare*, 295–336. DOI: 10.1016/B978-0-12-818438-7.00012-5

Ghahramani, Z. (2015). Probabilistic Machine Learning and Artificial Intelligence. *Nature*, 521(7553), 452–459. DOI: 10.1038/nature14541 PMID: 26017444

Ghazi, M. M., & Nielsen, M. (2022), "FAST-AID Brain: Fast and Accurate Segmentation Tool Using Artificial Intelligence Developed for Brain," arxiv preprint arxiv:2208.14360.

Ghedabna, L., Ghedabna, R., Imtiaz, Q., Faheem, M. A., Alkhayyat, A., & Hosen, M. S. (2024). Artificial Intelligence in Human Resource Management: Revolutionizing Recruitment, Performance, and Employee Development. *Nanotechnology Perceptions*, •••, 52–68.

Gheorghe-Moisii, M., & Gheorghe, C. G. (2024). *Ethical Considerations on the Use of AI Technology in ehealth Applications for Neurodegenerative Diseases*. Romanian Journal.

Giang, V. (2018). *The potential hidden bias in automated hiring systems*. Fast Company.

Gifford, R., & Nilsson, A. (2014). Personal and social factors that influence pro-environmental concern and behavior: A review. *International Journal of Psychology*, 49(3), 141–157. PMID: 24821503

Gill, A., & Mathur, A. (2024). Emotional Intelligence in the Age of AI: Enhancing Workforce Development for Human-Machine Collaboration. In Sustainable Innovation for Industry 6.0 (pp. 263-285). IGI Global.

Gjorevska, N. (2021).. *Workplace Spirituality and Well-Being among the Workforce in Social Businesses in Scotland* (Doctoral dissertation, Budapesti Corvinus Egyetem).

Gomes, N., Pato, M., Lourenço, A. R., & Datia, N. (2023). A Survey on Wearable Sensors for Mental Health Monitoring. *Sensors (Basel)*, 23(3), 1330. DOI: 10.3390/s23031330 PMID: 36772370

Gonçalves, R., Pedrozo, A. L., Coutinho, E. S. F., Figueira, I., & Ventura, P. (2012). Efficacy of Virtual Reality exposure therapy in the treatment of PTSD: A Systematic review. *PLoS One*, 7(12), e48469. DOI: 10.1371/journal.pone.0048469 PMID: 23300515

Gonzalez, C. S., Morin, P., & Hinton, S. (2020). Detecting early signs of cognitive impairment using wearable technology: A review. *Journal of Neuroengineering and Rehabilitation*, 17(1), 65. PMID: 32430036

Goodfellow, I., Bengio, Y., & Courville, A. (2016). *Deep learning*. MIT Press.

Gorriz Sáez, J. M., Álvarez Illán, I., Arco Martín, J. E., Castillo Barnes, D., Formoso, M. A., Gallego Molina, N. J., ... & Shoeibi, A. (2023). Computational approaches to Explainable Artificial Intelligence: Advances in theory, applications and trends. DOI: 10.1016/j.inffus.2023.101945

Goveas, J. S., Steinman, M. A., & Gonzales, M. (2021). Behavioral analysis using AI for diagnosing Frontotemporal Dementia. *Frontiers in Aging Neuroscience*, 13, 711–723.

Govindarajan, R., Vijayakumar, M., Pushpangadan, P., & Suresh, B. (2005). Antioxidant approach to disease management and the role of 'Rasayana' herbs of Ayurveda. *Journal of Ethnopharmacology*, 99(2), 165–178. DOI: 10.1016/j.jep.2005.02.035 PMID: 15894123

Graham, S., Depp, C., Lee, E. E., Nebeker, C., Tu, X., Kim, H. C., & Jeste, D. V. (2019). Artificial Intelligence for Mental Health and Mental Illnesses: An Overview. *Current Psychiatry Reports*, 21(11), 116. DOI: 10.1007/s11920-019-1094-0 PMID: 31701320

Greenberg, M. S., & Beck, A. T. (1989). Depression versus anxiety: A test of the content-specificity hypothesis. *Journal of Abnormal Psychology*, 98(1), 9–13. DOI: 10.1037/0021-843X.98.1.9 PMID: 2708648

Güçlü, U., & van Gerven, M. A. J. (2015). Deep neural networks reveal a gradient in the complexity of neural representations across the ventral stream. *The Journal of Neuroscience : The Official Journal of the Society for Neuroscience*, 35(27), 10005–10014. DOI: 10.1523/JNEUROSCI.5023-14.2015 PMID: 26157000

Haddadi, A.. (2020). Wearable AI for ADHD monitoring. *IEEE Transactions on Biomedical Engineering*, 67(12), 3441–3450. DOI: 10.1109/TBME.2020.3006708

Haddadi, H.. (2020). Wearable AI systems for hyperactivity monitoring. *IEEE Transactions on Neural Systems and Rehabilitation Engineering*.

Hadjipanayi, C., Banakou, D., & Michael-Grigoriou, D. (2023). Art as therapy in virtual reality: A scoping review. *Frontiers in Virtual Reality*, 4, 1065863. Advance online publication. DOI: 10.3389/frvir.2023.1065863

Hager, P., Jungmann, F., Holland, R., Bhagat, K., Hubrecht, I., Knauer, M., Vielhauer, J., Makowski, M., Braren, R., Kaissis, G., & Rueckert, D. (2024). Evaluation and mitigation of the limitations of large language models in clinical decision-making. *Nature Medicine*, 30(9), 2613–2622. DOI: 10.1038/s41591-024-03097-1 PMID: 38965432

Hahn, T., Nierenberg, A. A., & Whitfield-Gabrieli, S. (2017). Predictive analytics in mental health: Applications, guidelines, challenges and perspectives. *Molecular Psychiatry*, 22(1), 37–43. DOI: 10.1038/mp.2016.201 PMID: 27843153

Haimson, O. L., Ringland, K., Simpson, S., & Wolf, C. T. (2014). *Using depression analytics to reduce stigma via social media: BlueFriends. iConference 2014*. Social Media Expo.

Haleem, A., Javaid, M., Singh, R. P., & Suman, R. (2021). Telemedicine for healthcare: Capabilities, features, barriers, and applications. *Sensors International*, 2, 100117. DOI: 10.1016/j.sintl.2021.100117 PMID: 34806053

Hallowell, E. M., & Ratey, J. J. (2011). *Driven to distraction: Recognizing and coping with attention deficit disorder from childhood through adulthood*. Anchor.

Hamida, S. U., Chowdhury, M. J. M., Chakraborty, N. R., Biswas, K., & Sami, S. K. (2024). Exploring the Landscape of Explainable Artificial Intelligence (XAI): A Systematic Review of Techniques and Applications. *Big Data and Cognitive Computing*, 8(11), 149. DOI: 10.3390/bdcc8110149

Hamilton, R. H., & Sodeman, W. A. (2020). The questions we ask: Opportunities and challenges for using big data analytics to strategically manage human capital resources. *Business Horizons*, 63(1), 85–95. DOI: 10.1016/j.bushor.2019.10.001

Handa, P., Lavanya, , Goel, N., & Garg, N. (2024). Software advancements in automatic epilepsy diagnosis and seizure detection: 10-year review. *Artificial Intelligence Review*, 57(7), 181. DOI: 10.1007/s10462-024-10799-y

Hapsari, D. T. P., Nataliani, Y., Sembiring, I., & Wahyono, T. (2024, June). Smart Caregiving Support Cloud Integration Systems. In 2024 International Conference on Smart Computing, IoT and Machine Learning (SIML) (pp. 167-173). IEEE. DOI: 10.1109/SIML61815.2024.10578217

Haque, M. D. R., & Rubya, S. (2023). An Overview of Chatbot-Based Mobile Mental Health Apps: Insights From App Description and User Reviews. *JMIR mHealth and uHealth*, 11, e44838. DOI: 10.2196/44838 PMID: 37213181

Haraldsen, I. H., Hatlestad-Hall, C., Marra, C., Renvall, H., Maestú, F., Acosta-Hernández, J., Alfonsin, S., Andersson, V., Anand, A., Ayllón, V., Babic, A., Belhadi, A., Birck, C., Bruña, R., Caraglia, N., Carrarini, C., Christensen, E., Cicchetti, A., Daugbjerg, S., & Rossini, P. M. (2024). Intelligent digital tools for screening of brain connectivity and dementia risk estimation in people affected by mild cognitive impairment: The AI-Mind clinical study protocol. *Frontiers in Neurorobotics*, 17, 1289406. DOI: 10.3389/fnbot.2023.1289406 PMID: 38250599

Harrer, S., Shah, P., Antony, B., & Hu, J. (2019). Artificial intelligence for clinical trial design. *Trends in Pharmacological Sciences*, 40(8), 577–591. DOI: 10.1016/j.tips.2019.05.005 PMID: 31326235

Hasnain, S. (2020). Artificial neural networks (ANNs) in neuroscientific research: Revolutionizing mental health assessments and therapies. *Neuroscience Research Journal*, 28, 142–153.

Hassabis, D., Kumaran, D., Summerfield, C., & Botvinick, M. (2021). Neuroscience-inspired artificial intelligence. *Neuron*, 95(2), 245–258. DOI: 10.1016/j.neuron.2017.06.011 PMID: 28728020

Hassouneh, A., Mutawa, A. M., & Murugappan, M. (2020). Development of a real-time emotion recognition system using facial expressions and EEG based on machine learning and deep neural network methods. *Informatics in Medicine Unlocked*, 20, 100372. DOI: 10.1016/j.imu.2020.100372

He, H., Wu, D., Wang, Y., & Lu, B. (2020). EEG-based brain-computer interfaces for communication and rehabilitation: Advances and challenges. *Frontiers in Neuroscience*, 14, 814. DOI: 10.3389/fnins.2020.00814

Helm, J. M., Swiergosz, A. M., Haeberle, H. S., Karnuta, J. M., Schaffer, J. L., Krebs, V. E., Spitzer, A. I., & Ramkumar, P. N. (2020). Machine Learning and Artificial Intelligence: Definitions, Applications, and Future Directions. *Current Reviews in Musculoskeletal Medicine*, 13(1), 69–76. DOI: 10.1007/s12178-020-09600-8 PMID: 31983042

He, Q., Li, L., Li, D., Peng, T., Zhang, X., Cai, Y., Zhang, X., & Tang, R. (2024). From digital human modeling to human digital twin: Framework and perspectives in human factors. *Chinese Journal of Mechanical Engineering*, 37(1), 9. DOI: 10.1186/s10033-024-00998-7

Hernández-Capistran, J., Sánchez-Morales, L. N., Alor-Hernández, G., Bustos-López, M., & Sánchez-Cervantes, J. L. (2023). Machine and deep learning algorithms for ADHD detection: A review. In *Innovations in Machine and Deep Learning* (pp. 163–191). Case Studies and Applications. DOI: 10.1007/978-3-031-40688-1_8

Hochreiter, S., & Schmidhuber, J. (1997). Long Short-Term Memory. *Neural Computation*, 9(8), 1735–1780. DOI: 10.1162/neco.1997.9.8.1735 PMID: 9377276

Ho, D., Quake, S. R., McCabe, E. R. B., Chng, W. J., Chow, E. K., Ding, X., Gelb, B. D., Ginsburg, G. S., Hassenstab, J., Ho, C. M., Mobley, W. C., Nolan, G. P., Rosen, S. T., Tan, P., Yen, Y., & Zarrinpar, A. (2020). Enabling Technologies for Personalized and Precision Medicine. *Trends in Biotechnology*, 38(5), 497–518. DOI: 10.1016/j.tibtech.2019.12.021 PMID: 31980301

Holmes, J.. (2018). AI in adaptive learning systems for ADHD. *Computers in Human Behavior*, 92, 66–75. DOI: 10.1016/j.chb.2018.10.016

Houssein, E. H., Hammad, A., & Ali, A. A. (2022). Human emotion recognition from EEG-based brain–computer interface using machine learning: A comprehensive review. *Neural Computing & Applications*, 34(15), 12527–12557. DOI: 10.1007/s00521-022-07292-4

Howard, J., & Ruder, S. (2018)." Universal Language Model Fine-tuning for Text Classification. "*Proceedings of the 56th Annual Meeting of the Association for Computational Linguistics (ACL)*, 328-339.

Howard, M. C., & Gutworth, M. B. (2020). A meta-analysis of virtual reality training programs for social skill development. *Computers & Education*, 144, 103707. DOI: 10.1016/j.compedu.2019.103707

Hsu, C. Y., Yang, Y. H., & Wu, Y. T. (2019). Neuroimaging biomarkers for Lewy body dementia: A review of MRI and PET studies. *Journal of Neural Transmission (Vienna, Austria)*, 126(6), 765–777.

Huang, C., Wang, J., Wang, S. H., & Zhang, Y. D. (2022). Applicable Artificial Intelligence for Brain Disease: A Survey. *Neurocomputing*, 504, 223–239. DOI: 10.1016/j.neucom.2022.07.005

Huang, Y., Yang, B., Wong, T. W., Ng, S. S. M., & Hu, X. (2024). Personalized robots for long-term telerehabilitation after stroke: A perspective on technological readiness and clinical translation. *Frontiers in Rehabilitation Sciences*, 4, 1329927. Advance online publication. DOI: 10.3389/fresc.2023.1329927 PMID: 38259875

Huang, Z. Y., Chiang, C. C., Chen, J. H., Chen, Y. C., Chung, H. L., Cai, Y. P., & Hsu, H. C. (2023). A study on computer vision for facial emotion recognition. *Scientific Reports*, 13(1), 8425. DOI: 10.1038/s41598-023-35446-4 PMID: 37225755

Huang, Z., Dai, X., Zheng, J., Zhang, Z., & Wang, S. (2021). Machine learning for clinical diagnosis from electroencephalography (EEG) signals: A review. *IEEE Reviews in Biomedical Engineering*, 14, 131–151. DOI: 10.1109/RBME.2020.2985792

Hussain, S. S., Degang, X., Shah, P. M., Islam, S. U., Alam, M., Khan, I. A., Awwad, F. A., & Ismail, E. A. A. (2023). Classification of Parkinson's Disease in Patch-Based MRI of Substantia Nigra. *Diagnostics (Basel)*, 13(17), 2827. DOI: 10.3390/diagnostics13172827 PMID: 37685365

Ijichi, S., & Ijichi, N. (2007). Computerized lifelong mentoring support using robots for autistic individuals. *Medical Hypotheses*, 68(3), 493–498. DOI: 10.1016/j.mehy.2006.08.016 PMID: 17023117

Inamdar, M. A., Raghavendra, U., Gudigar, A., Chakole, Y., Hegde, A., Menon, G. R., Barua, P., Palmer, E. E., Cheong, K. H., Chan, W. Y., Ciaccio, E. J., & Acharya, U. R. (2021). A Review on Computer Aided Diagnosis of Acute Brain Stroke. *Sensors (Basel)*, 21(24), 8507. DOI: 10.3390/s21248507 PMID: 34960599

Inkster, B., Sarda, S., & Subramanian, V. (2018). An empathy-driven, conversational artificial intelligence agent (Wysa) for digital mental well-being: Real-world data evaluation mixed-methods study. *JMIR mHealth and uHealth*, 6(11), e12106. DOI: 10.2196/12106 PMID: 30470676

Insider, B. (2017). *Consumer goods giant Unilever has been hiring employees using brain games and artificial intelligence—And it'sa huge success*. Business Insider.

Islam, M. M., Hassan, S., Akter, S., Jibon, F. A., & Sahidullah, M. (2024). A comprehensive review of predictive analytics models for mental illness using machine learning algorithms. *Healthcare Analytics*, 100350, 100350. Advance online publication. DOI: 10.1016/j.health.2024.100350

Islam, Z. (2023). Optimizing Human Resource Operations through AI-Driven Advanced Computing Systems. *Journal of Advanced Computing Systems*, 3(12), 18–25.

Ismail, Y., & Voleti, V. K. (2024). A review on usage of artificial intelligence for early detection and management of Alzheimer's disease. *Journal of Pharma Insights and Research, 2*(5), 007–013. https://doi.org/DOI: 10.1016/j.jpir.2024.05.002

Jack, C. R., Bennett, D. A., Blennow, K., Carrillo, M. C., Feldman, H. H., & Frisoni, G. B. (2018). NIA-AA research framework: Toward a biological definition of Alzheimer's disease. *Alzheimer's & Dementia*, 14(4), 535–562. DOI: 10.1016/j.jalz.2018.02.018 PMID: 29653606

Jacobs, A. Z., & Wallach, H. (2021, March). Measurement and fairness. In *Proceedings of the 2021 ACM conference on fairness, accountability, and transparency* (pp. 375-385). DOI: 10.1145/3442188.3445901

Jain, N., & Gautam, V. (2016). Artificial Intelligence in Human Resource Management: An Emerging Role in 21st Century. *International Journal of Management*, 7(3), 1–7.

Jain, R., & Triadafilopoulos, T. (2020). AI and HR Analytics: Redefining Talent Management in the 21st Century. *Human Resource Management International Digest*, 28(2), 12–15.

Jangra, A., Dwivedi, V., Sharma, M., & Joshi, R. (2019). Centella asiatica attenuates neurobehavioral, neurochemical and neurohistological abnormalities in MPTP-induced parkinsonism in mice. *Metabolic Brain Disease*, 34(6), 1781–1794. PMID: 31478182

Javed, A. R., Saadia, A., Mughal, H., Gadekallu, T. R., Rizwan, M., Maddikunta, P. K. R., Mahmud, M., Liyanage, M., & Hussain, A. (2023). Artificial intelligence for cognitive health assessment: State-of-the-art, open challenges and future directions. *Cognitive Computation*, 15(6), 1767–1812. DOI: 10.1007/s12559-023-10153-4

Jawed, S., Faye, I., & Malik, A. S. (2024). Deep learning-based assessment model for Real-time identification of visual learners using Raw EEG. *IEEE Transactions on Neural Systems and Rehabilitation Engineering*, 32, 378–390. DOI: 10.1109/TNSRE.2024.3351694 PMID: 38194390

Jeong, S. (2022). *Designing and Deploying Robotic Companions to Improve Human Psychological Wellbeing* (Doctoral dissertation, Massachusetts Institute of Technology).

Jeong, S., Aymerich-Franch, L., Arias, K., Alghowinem, S., Lapedriza, A., Picard, R., Park, H. W., & Breazeal, C. (2023). Deploying a robotic positive psychology coach to improve college students' psychological well-being. *User Modeling and User-Adapted Interaction*, 33(2), 571–615. DOI: 10.1007/s11257-022-09337-8 PMID: 38737788

Jeyaraman, M., Balaji, S., Jeyaraman, N., & Yadav, S. (2023). Unraveling the Ethical Enigma: Artificial Intelligence in Healthcare. *Cureus*, 15(8), e43262. DOI: 10.7759/cureus.43262 PMID: 37692617

Jha, A., Peterson, J. C., & Griffiths, T. L. (2023). Extracting low-dimensional psychological representations from convolutional neural networks. *Cognitive Science*, 47(1), e13226. DOI: 10.1111/cogs.13226 PMID: 36617318

Jiang, M., Zhao, Q., Li, J., Wang, F., He, T., Cheng, X., . . . Fu, G. (2024). A Generic Review of Integrating Artificial Intelligence in Cognitive Behavioral Therapy. *arXiv preprint arXiv:2407.19422*.

Jiang, F.. (2020). Natural language processing for cognitive assessments. *AI in Medicine*, 102, 101762. DOI: 10.1016/j.artmed.2020.101762

Jiang, F., Jiang, Y., Zhi, H., Dong, Y., Li, H., Ma, S., Wang, Y., Dong, Q., Shen, H., & Wang, Y. (2020). Artificial intelligence in healthcare: Past, present, and future. *Stroke and Vascular Neurology*, 2(4), 230–243. DOI: 10.1136/svn-2017-000101 PMID: 29507784

Jiang, Y., Wang, X., & Zhang, D. (2021). Artificial intelligence in early diagnosis and monitoring of cognitive decline. *Journal of Neuroscience Methods*, 356, 108201.

Jilka, S., Odoi, C. M., van Bilsen, J., Morris, D., Erturk, S., Cummins, N., Cella, M., & Wykes, T. (2022). Identifying schizophrenia stigma on Twitter: A proof of principle model using service user supervised machine learning. *Schizophrenia*, 8(1), 1. DOI: 10.1038/s41537-021-00197-6 PMID: 35132080

Jiménez-Huete, A., Riva, E., Toledano, R., Campo, P., Esteban, J., Barrio, A. D., & Franch, O. (2014). Differential diagnosis of degenerative dementias using basic neuropsychological tests: Multivariable logistic regression analysis of 301 patients. *American Journal of Alzheimer's Disease and Other Dementias*, 29(8), 723–731. DOI: 10.1177/1533317514534954 PMID: 24838533

Jimenez-Mesa, C., Arco, J. E., Martinez-Murcia, F. J., Suckling, J., Ramirez, J., & Gorriz, J. M. (2023). Applications of machine learning and deep learning in SPECT and PET imaging: General overview, challenges, and future prospects. *Pharmacological Research*, 197, 106984. DOI: 10.1016/j.phrs.2023.106984 PMID: 37940064

Jingili, N., Oyelere, S. S., Nyström, M. B. T., & Anyshchenko, L. (2023). A systematic review on the efficacy of virtual reality and gamification interventions for managing anxiety and depression. *Frontiers in Digital Health*, 5, 1239435. Advance online publication. DOI: 10.3389/fdgth.2023.1239435 PMID: 38026832

Johnason, P. (2009). HRM in changing organizational contexts. In Collings, D. G., & Wood, G. (Eds.), *Human resource management: A critical approach* (pp. 19–37). Routledge.

Johnson-Glenberg, M. C. (2018). Immersive VR and education: Embodied design principles that include gesture and hand controls. *Frontiers in Robotics and AI*, 5, 81. Advance online publication. DOI: 10.3389/frobt.2018.00081 PMID: 33500960

Johnson, K. B., Wei, W. Q., Weeraratne, D., Frisse, M. E., Misulis, K., Rhee, K., Zhao, J., & Snowdon, J. L. (2021). Precision Medicine, AI, and the Future of Personalized Health Care. *Clinical and Translational Science*, 14(1), 86–93. DOI: 10.1111/cts.12884 PMID: 32961010

Johnston, M., O'Mahony, M., O'Brien, N., Connolly, M., Iohom, G., Kamal, M., Shehata, A., & Shorten, G. (2024). The feasibility and usability of mixed reality teaching in a hospital setting based on self-reported perceptions of medical students. *BMC Medical Education*, 24(1), 701. Advance online publication. DOI: 10.1186/s12909-024-05591-z PMID: 38937764

Jones, M. (2001) Rapid object detection using a boosted cascade of simple. In: *Proceedings of the IEEE Computer Society Conference on Computer Vision and Pattern Recognition*, HI, Kaua'i, USA, pp. 8–14.

Jurafsky, D., & Martin, J. H. (2020). *Speech and Language Processing* (3rd ed.). Pearson.

Jurafsky, D., & Martin, J. H. (2021). *Speech and language processing*. Pearson.

Kalani, M., & Anjankar, A. (2024). Revolutionizing Neurology: The Role of Artificial Intelligence in Advancing Diagnosis and Treatment. *Cureus*, 16(6), e61706. DOI: 10.7759/cureus.61706 PMID: 38975469

Kalbe, E., Folkerts, A. K., Witt, K., Buhmann, C., & Liepelt-Scarfone, I.German Parkinson's Guidelines Group. (2024). German Society of Neurology guidelines for the diagnosis and treatment of cognitive impairment and affective disorders in people with Parkinson's disease: New spotlights on diagnostic procedures and non-pharmacological interventions. *Journal ofNeurology*, 271(11), 1–28. DOI: 10.1007/s00415-024-12503-0 PMID: 39120709

Kamarajan, C., Ardekani, B. A., Pandey, A. K., Kinreich, S., Pandey, G., Chorlian, D. B., Meyers, J. L., Zhang, J., Bermudez, E., Stimus, A. T., & Porjesz, B. (2020). Random forest classification of alcohol use disorder using fMRI functional connectivity, neuropsychological functioning, and impulsivity measures. *Brain Sciences*, 10(2), 115. DOI: 10.3390/brainsci10020115 PMID: 32093319

Kamran, A., Dawood, J., & Hilal, S. B. (2015). Analysis of the recruitment and selection process. In *Proceedings of the Ninth International Conference on Management Science and Engineering Management* (pp. 1357-1375). Springer Berlin Heidelberg. DOI: 10.1007/978-3-662-47241-5_114

Karstoft, K. I., Eskelund, K., Gradus, J. L., Andersen, S. B., & Nissen, L. R. (2023). Early prediction of mental health problems following military deployment: Integrating pre-and post-deployment factors in neural network models. *Journal of Psychiatric Research*, 163, 109–117. DOI: 10.1016/j.jpsychires.2023.05.014 PMID: 37209616

Karunarathna, I., Kapila De Alvis, C., Rajapaksha, S., Warnakulasooriya, A., Aluthge, P., Perera, N., ... & Jayawardana, A. Effective Strategies for Alzheimer's Disease: Diagnosis, Treatment, and Caregiver Support.

Karyotaki, E., Efthimiou, O., Miguel, C., Bermpohl, F. M. G., Furukawa, T. A., Cuijpers, P., & Forsell, Y. (2021). Internet-Based Cognitive Behavioral Therapy for Depression: A Systematic Review and Individual Patient Data Network Meta-analysis. *JAMA Psychiatry*, 78(4), 361–371. DOI: 10.1001/jamapsychiatry.2020.4364 PMID: 33471111

Katiyar, K. (2022). AI-based predictive analytics for patients' psychological disorder. In *Predictive Analytics of Psychological Disorders in Healthcare: Data Analytics on Psychological Disorders* (pp. 37–53). Springer Nature Singapore. DOI: 10.1007/978-981-19-1724-0_3

Katwaroo, A. R., Adesh, V. S., Lowtan, A., & Umakanthan, S. (2023). The diagnostic, therapeutic, and ethical impact of artificial intelligence in modern medicine. *Postgraduate Medical Journal*. Advance online publication. DOI: 10.1093/postmj/qgad135 PMID: 38159301

Ke, L., Tong, S., Cheng, P., & Peng, K. (2024). Exploring the frontiers of LLMs in psychological applications: A comprehensive review. *arXiv preprint arXiv:2401.01519*.https://doi.org//arXiv.2401.01519DOI: 10.48550

Kelbling, E., Ferreira Prescott, D., Shearer, M., & Quinn, T. J. (2024). An assessment of the content and properties of extended and instrumental activities of daily living scales: A systematic review. *Disability and Rehabilitation*, 46(10), 1990–1999. DOI: 10.1080/09638288.2023.2224082 PMID: 37415395

Kessler, R. C., Adler, L., Barkley, R., Biederman, J., Conners, C. K., Demler, O., Faraone, S. V., Greenhill, L. L., Howes, M. J., Secnik, K., Spencer, T., Ustun, T. B., Walters, E. E., & Zaslavsky, A. M. (2006). The prevalence and correlates of adult ADHD in the United States: Results from the National Comorbidity Survey Replication. *The American Journal of Psychiatry*, 163(4), 716–723. DOI: 10.1176/ajp.2006.163.4.716 PMID: 16585449

Kessler, R. C., Berglund, P., Demler, O., Jin, R., Merikangas, K. R., & Walters, E. E. (2005). Lifetime Prevalence and Age-of-Onset Distributions of DSM-IV Disorders in the National Comorbidity Survey Replication. *Archives of General Psychiatry*, 62(6), 593–602. DOI: 10.1001/archpsyc.62.6.593 PMID: 15939837

Khalid, U. B., Naeem, M., Stasolla, F., Syed, M. H., Abbas, M., & Coronato, A. (2024). Impact of AI-powered solutions in rehabilitation process: Recent improvements and future trends. *International Journal of General Medicine*, 17, 943–969. DOI: 10.2147/IJGM.S453903 PMID: 38495919

Khare, S. K., March, S., Barua, P. D., Gadre, V. M., & Acharya, U. R. (2023). Application of data fusion for automated detection of children with developmental and mental disorders: A systematic review of the last decade. *Information Fusion*, 99, 101898. DOI: 10.1016/j.inffus.2023.101898

Khatib, O. (2016). Robotics and AI: Synergies and challenges. *AI Magazine*, 37(2), 1–7.

Khatiwada, P., Yang, B., Lin, J.-C., & Blobel, B. (2024). Patient-Generated Health Data (PGHD): Understanding, Requirements, Challenges, and Existing Techniques for Data Security and Privacy. *Journal of Personalized Medicine*, 14(3), 282. DOI: 10.3390/jpm14030282 PMID: 38541024

Kim, H., & Hong, T. (2024). Emotion-oriented recommender system for personalized control of indoor environmental quality. *Building and Environment*, 254, 111396. DOI: 10.1016/j.buildenv.2024.111396

Kim, J. H., Lee, S. M., & Kim, J. (2022). Neuroimaging Modalities in Alzheimer's Disease: Diagnosis and Clinical Features. *International Journal of Molecular Sciences*, 23(11), 6112. DOI: 10.3390/ijms23116079 PMID: 35682758

Kim, T., Hwang, Y., & Lee, J. (2020). Optimizing psychotherapy with machine learning: Personalized approaches for anxiety and depression. *Psychiatry Research*, 295, 113–122.

Klein, M.. (2019). Genetic insights into ADHD. *Nature Genetics*, 51(1), 7–8. DOI: 10.1038/s41588-018-0317-3 PMID: 30514911

Knapp, P., & Beck, A. T. (2008). Cognitive therapy: Foundations, conceptual models, applications and research. *The British Journal of Psychiatry*, 30, s54–s64. DOI: 10.1590/S1516-44462008000600002 PMID: 19039445

Koch, C., Massimini, M., Boly, M., & Tononi, G. (2016). Neural correlates of consciousness: Progress and problems. *Nature Reviews. Neuroscience*, 17(5), 307–321. DOI: 10.1038/nrn.2016.22 PMID: 27094080

Köchling, A., Riazy, S., Wehner, M. C., & Simbeck, K. (2021). Highly accurate, but still discriminatory: A fairness evaluation of algorithmic video analysis in the recruitment context. *Business & Information Systems Engineering*, 63(1), 39–54. DOI: 10.1007/s12599-020-00673-w

Kohavi, R. (1995). A Study of Cross-Validation and Bootstrap for Accuracy Estimation and Model Selection. *Proceedings of the 14th International Joint Conference on Artificial Intelligence (IJCAI)*, 1137-1145.

Kooij, J. J. S., Bijlenga, D., Salerno, L., Jaeschke, R., Bitter, I., Balázs, J., Thome, J., Dom, G., Kasper, S., Nunes Filipe, C., Stes, S., Mohr, P., Leppämäki, S., Casas, M., Bobes, J., Mccarthy, J. M., Richarte, V., Kjems Philipsen, A., Pehlivanidis, A., & Asherson, P. (2019). Updated European Consensus Statement on diagnosis and treatment of adult ADHD. *European Psychiatry*, 56(1), 14–24. DOI: 10.1016/j.eurpsy.2018.11.001 PMID: 30453134

Kraguljac, N. V., McDonald, W. M., Widge, A. S., Rodriguez, C. I., Tohen, M., & Nemeroff, C. B. (2021). Neuroimaging Biomarkers in Schizophrenia. *The American Journal of Psychiatry*, 178(6), 509–521. DOI: 10.1176/appi.ajp.2020.20030340 PMID: 33397140

Krichen, M. (2023). Convolutional neural networks: A survey. *Computers*, 12(8), 151. DOI: 10.3390/computers12080151

Krishnan, G., Singh, S., Pathania, M., Gosavi, S., Abhishek, S., Parchani, A., & Dhar, M. (2023). Artificial intelligence in clinical medicine: Catalyzing a sustainable global healthcare paradigm. *Frontiers in Artificial Intelligence*, 6, 1227091. DOI: 10.3389/frai.2023.1227091 PMID: 37705603

Kruzan, K. P., Fitzsimmons-Craft, E. E., Dobias, M., Schleider, J. L., & Pratap, A. (2022). Developing, deploying, and evaluating digital mental health interventions in spaces of online help-and information-seeking. *Procedia Computer Science*, 206, 6–22. DOI: 10.1016/j.procs.2022.09.081 PMID: 37063642

Kumar, A., Dhanka, S., Bansal, R., Sharma, A., Singh, J., Khan, A. A., & Maini, S. Agriculture in the Era of Industry 5.0. *Industry 5.0 and Emerging Technologies: Transformation Through Technology and Innovations*, 111.

Kumar, A., Nayyar, A., Sachan, R. K., & Jain, R. (Eds.). (2023). *AI-assisted special education for students with exceptional needs*. IGI Global., DOI: 10.4018/979-8-3693-0378-8

Kumar, A., Singh, J., & Khan, A. A. (2024). A comprehensive machine learning framework with particle swarm optimization for improved polycystic ovary syndrome (PCOS) diagnosis. *Engineering Research Express*, 6(3), 035233. DOI: 10.1088/2631-8695/ad76f9

Kumar, D., Bhat, Z. A., & Shah, M. Y. (2013). Neuroprotective Effect of Dry Fruits of Ficus carica L. in Mice. *Indian Journal of Pharmaceutical Sciences*, 75(4), 424–429.

Kumar, S., Asthana, R., Upadhyay, S., Upreti, N., & Akbar, M. (2020). Fake news detection using deep learning models: A novel approach. *Transactions on Emerging Telecommunications Technologies*, 31(2), e3767. DOI: 10.1002/ett.3767

Kumar, S., Keefe, B., & Feldman, H. (2021). Personalized cognitive training using AI: Applications and outcomes. *IEEE Transactions on Biomedical Engineering*, 68(1), 23–32. PMID: 34086560

Kumar, Y., Koul, A., Singla, R., & Ijaz, M. F. (2023). Artificial intelligence in disease diagnosis: A systematic literature review, synthesizing framework and future research agenda. *Journal of Ambient Intelligence and Humanized Computing*, 14(7), 8459–8486. DOI: 10.1007/s12652-021-03612-z PMID: 35039756

Ladakis, I., Filos, D., & Chouvarda, I. (2024). Virtual reality environments for stress reduction and management: A scoping review. *Virtual Reality (Waltham Cross)*, 28(1), 50. Advance online publication. DOI: 10.1007/s10055-024-00943-y

Lan, L., Sikov, J., Lejeune, J., Ji, C., Brown, H., Bullock, K., & Spencer, A. E. (2023). A Systematic Review of using Virtual and Augmented Reality for the Diagnosis and Treatment of Psychotic Disorders. *Current Treatment Options in Psychiatry*, 10(2), 87–107. DOI: 10.1007/s40501-023-00287-5 PMID: 37360960

Larkins, A., Knight, B., Keokhamphavanh, B., Taggart, K., Keatley, S., Insisiengmay, B., & Ash, A. (2024). Sensitivity and specificity of microscopic and molecular techniques for the diagnosis of taeniasis. *Acta Tropica*, 260, 107414. DOI: 10.1016/j.actatropica.2024.107414 PMID: 39362512

Lebedev, M. A., & Nicolelis, M. A. (2017). Brain-machine interfaces: From basic science to neuroprostheses and neurorehabilitation. *Physiological Reviews*, 97(2), 767–837. DOI: 10.1152/physrev.00027.2016 PMID: 28275048

LeCun, Y., Bengio, Y., & Hinton, G. (2020). Deep learning. *Nature*, 521(7553), 436–444. DOI: 10.1038/nature14539 PMID: 26017442

Lee, E. E., Torous, J., De Choudhury, M., Depp, C. A., Graham, S. A., Kim, H. C., Paulus, M. P., Krystal, J. H., & Jeste, D. V. (2021). Artificial intelligence for mental health care: Clinical applications, barriers, facilitators, and artificial wisdom. *Biological Psychiatry: Cognitive Neuroscience and Neuroimaging*, 6(9), 856–864. DOI: 10.1016/j.bpsc.2021.02.001 PMID: 33571718

Lee, L. Y., Vaghari, D., Burkhart, M. C., Tino, P., Montagnese, M., Li, Z., Zühlsdorff, K., Giorgio, J., Williams, G., Chong, E., Chen, C., Underwood, B. R., Rittman, T., & Kourtzi, Z. (2024). Robust and interpretable AI-guided marker for early dementia prediction in real-world clinical settings. *EClinicalMedicine*, 74, 74. DOI: 10.1016/j.eclinm.2024.102725

Lee, S. H., Lee, J. H., & Lee, Y. S. (2019). Multimodal deep learning for early detection of cognitive impairments. *Journal of Biomedical Informatics*, 94, 103–114.

Lee, S., Kim, H., Park, M. J., & Jeon, H. J. (2021). Current advances in wearable devices and their sensors in patients with depression. *Frontiers in Psychiatry*, 12, 672347. DOI: 10.3389/fpsyt.2021.672347 PMID: 34220580

Lee, Y., Mansur, R., & McIntyre, R. S. (2019). Machine learning and big data: Implications for disease modeling and therapeutic discovery in psychiatry. *Artificial Intelligence in Medicine*, 99, 101704. DOI: 10.1016/j.artmed.2019.101704 PMID: 31606109

Le, K. B. Q., & Cayrat, C. (2024). Howdy, Robo-Partner: Exploring artificial companionship and its stress-alleviating potential for service employees. *Journal of Service Management*. Advance online publication. DOI: 10.1108/JOSM-09-2023-0408

Leng, M., Liu, P., Zhang, P., Hu, M., Zhou, H., Li, G., Yin, H., & Chen, L. (2019). Pet robot intervention for people with dementia: A systematic review and meta-analysis of randomized controlled trials. *Psychiatry Research*, 271, 516–525. DOI: 10.1016/j.psychres.2018.12.032 PMID: 30553098

Li, J., He, Z., Cui, Y., Wang, C., Chen, C., Yu, C., Zhang, M., Liu, Y., & Ma, S. (2022). Towards ubiquitous personalized music recommendation with smart bracelets. *Proceedings of the ACM on Interactive, Mobile, Wearable and Ubiquitous Technologies*, 6(3), 1–34. DOI: 10.1145/3550333

Li, L., Pomeroy, J. E., Zhou, J., Qu, G., Zhang, X., & Yuan, J. (2021). AI-driven cognitive neuroscience: From brain imaging to neural signal analysis. *NeuroImage*, 236, 118–173. DOI: 10.1016/j.neuroimage.2021.118173

Lin S Y, Lin C P, Hsieh T J, Lin C F, Chen S H, Chao Y P, (2019), "Multiparametric Graph Theoretical Analysis Reveals Altered Structural and Functional Network Topology in Alzheimer's Disease," neuroimage: Clinical.

Lin, K. Y., Liu, Y., Li, L., & Dou, R. (2021). A review of explainable artificial intelligence. In *Advances in Production Management Systems. Artificial Intelligence for Sustainable and Resilient Production Systems: IFIP WG 5.7 International Conference, APMS 2021, Nantes, France,September 5–9, 2021,Proceedings, Part IV* (pp. 574-584). Springer International Publishing. DOI: 10.1007/978-3-030-85910-7_61

Lindner, P. (2020). Better, Virtually: The Past, Present, and Future of Virtual Reality Cognitive Behavior Therapy. *International Journal of Cognitive Therapy*, 14(1), 23–46. DOI: 10.1007/s41811-020-00090-7

Lindner, P., Hamilton, W., Miloff, A., & Carlbring, P. (2019). How to Treat Depression with Low-Intensity Virtual Reality Interventions: Perspectives on translating cognitive behavioral techniques into the virtual reality modality and how to make Anti-Depressive use of Virtual Reality–Unique Experiences. *Frontiers in Psychiatry*, 10, 792. Advance online publication. DOI: 10.3389/fpsyt.2019.00792 PMID: 31736809

Liu, Y., Li, Y., Zhao, Y., & Na, X. (2021, October). Image Classification and Recognition of Medicinal Plants Based on Convolutional Neural Network. In 2021 IEEE 21st International Conference on Communication Technology (ICCT) (pp. 1128–1133). IEEE. DOI: 10.1109/ICCT52962.2021.9658028

Liu, D., Cui, J., Pan, Z., Zhang, H., Cao, J., & Kong, W. (2024). Machine to brain: Facial expression recognition using brain machine generative adversarial networks. *Cognitive Neurodynamics*, 18(3), 863–875. DOI: 10.1007/s11571-023-09946-y PMID: 38826642

Liu, F., Shi, Y., & Liu, Y. (2017). Intelligence quotient and intelligence grade of artificial intelligence. *Annals of Data Science*, 4(2), 179–191. DOI: 10.1007/s40745-017-0109-0

Liu, S., Wang, L., & Gao, R. X. (2024). Cognitive neuroscience and robotics: Advancements and future research directions. *Robotics and Computer-integrated Manufacturing*, 85, 102610. DOI: 10.1016/j.rcim.2023.102610

Liu, X., Zhang, Y., & Wang, Z. (2018). Predicting depression with machine learning models based on behavioral data: A review. *Journal of Affective Disorders*, 243, 63–72.

Liu, Y. S., Lu, C. W., Chung, H. T., Wang, J. K., Su, W. J., & Chen, C. W. (2024). Health-promoting lifestyle and life satisfaction in full-time employed adults with congenital heart disease: Grit as a mediator. *European Journal of Cardiovascular Nursing*, 23(4), 348–357. DOI: 10.1093/eurjcn/zvad104 PMID: 37847800

Li, X. T., & Huang, R. Y. (2020). Standardization of imaging methods for machine learning in neuro-oncology. *Neuro-Oncology Advances*, 2(Supplement_4), iv49–iv55. DOI: 10.1093/noajnl/vdaa054 PMID: 33521640

Li, X., Hu, Y., Yang, X., Bi, X., Zhang, J., & Tao, P. (2024). The effectiveness of virtual reality training on social skills in education: A meta-analysis. *Education and Information Technologies*. Advance online publication. DOI: 10.1007/s10639-024-12941-3

Li, Y., Wang, M., Wang, L., Cao, Y., Liu, Y., Zhao, Y., & Zhang, L. (2024). Advances in the Application of AI Robots in Critical Care: Scoping Review. *Journal of Medical Internet Research*, 26, e54095. DOI: 10.2196/54095 PMID: 38801765

Loies, S. E. (2025). Combating Mental Health Stigma With Artificial Intelligence: Improving Societal Understanding. In *Supporting Psychological and Emotional Wellbeing Among Entrepreneurs* (pp. 75-92). IGI Global. Ganguly, C., Nayak, S., & Gupta, A. K. (2022). Mental health impact of COVID-19 and machine learning applications in combating mental disorders: a review. *Artificial Intelligence, Machine Learning, and Mental Health in Pandemics*, 1-51.

Lombardo, R., Walther, N., Young, S., Gorbatkin, C., Sletten, Z., Kang, C., Tran, O., & Couperus, K. (2022). Ready Medic One: A feasibility study of a Semi-Autonomous Virtual Reality Trauma Simulator. *Frontiers in Virtual Reality*, 2, 719656. Advance online publication. DOI: 10.3389/frvir.2021.719656

Luan, L., Lin, X., Dai, Y., Allen, L., & Hu, S. (2024). Transforming STEM education: Leveraging ChatGPT for enhanced learning in psychology and neuroscience. In *ChatGPT and Global Higher Education: Using Artificial Intelligence in Teaching and Learning* (p. 100). *IGI Global.*https://doi.org/DOI: 10.4018/978-1-7998-6987-6

Luan, H., Geczy, P., Lai, H., Gobert, J., Yang, S. J., Ogata, H., Baltes, J., Guerra, R., Li, P., & Tsai, C. C. (2020). Challenges and future directions of big data and artificial intelligence in education. *Frontiers in Psychology*, 11, 580820. DOI: 10.3389/fpsyg.2020.580820 PMID: 33192896

Luckin, R.. (2016). AI in education: A transformative force. *Journal of Educational Technology & Society*, 19(3), 1–9.

Lu, Z., Seo, J. H., Khandan, P., Maxa, T., Garcia-Pi, B., & Wells-Beede, E. (2024). The work behind an interdisciplinary team: Creating a postpartum hemorrhage virtual reality training platform. *Clinical Simulation in Nursing*, 94, 101595. DOI: 10.1016/j.ecns.2024.101595

Maftei, G. A., Martu, M. A., Ciurcanu, O. E., Busuioc, A., Luca, E. O., Onofrei, A., & Popa, C. (2024). The advent of artificial intelligence in oral pathology. *Romanian Journal of Medical and Dental Education*, 13(2). Advance online publication. DOI: 10.2478/rjmde-2024-0009

Mahadev Madgule, N. (2023). Vinayaka, Yeshwant M. Sonkhaskar, Dhiren Ramanbhai Patel, R. Karthikeyan, P. Selvakumar, (2023). Mechanical properties and microstructure of activated TIG welded similar joints of Inconel alloys by desirability approaches. *Materials Today: Proceedings*, 77, 528–533. DOI: 10.1016/j.matpr.2022.12.250

Mahmood, H., Nawar, F., Islam, S. M. S., & Iqbal, A. (2024), "neuroatlas: An Artificial Intelligence-Based Framework for Annotation, Segmentation and Registration of Large Scale Biomedical Imaging Data," *biorxiv*.

Makarius, E. E., Mukherjee, D., Fox, J. D., & Fox, A. K. (2020). Rising with the machines: A sociotechnical framework for bringing artificial intelligence into the organization. *Journal of Business Research*, 120, 262–273. DOI: 10.1016/j.jbusres.2020.07.045

Mak, J. N.. (2018). AI-integrated brain-computer interfaces. *Neurorehabilitation and Neural Repair*, 32(7), 602–612. DOI: 10.1177/1545968318787687

Maleki Varnosfaderani, S., & Forouzanfar, M. (2024). The role of AI in hospitals and clinics: Transforming healthcare in the 21st century. *Bioengineering (Basel, Switzerland)*, 11(4), 337. DOI: 10.3390/bioengineering11040337 PMID: 38671759

Manning, C. D., Raghavan, P., & Schütze, H. (2008). *Introduction to Information Retrieval*. MIT Press.

Mao, C. P., Wang, G., Cao, J., Meshberg, N., Huang, Y., Zhang, Y., & Liu, X. (2022). Functional Connectivity of the Thalamo-Sensorimotor Circuit in Chronic Low Back Pain: Resting-State Functional Magnetic Resonance Imaging and Diffusion Tensor Imaging. *Neuroscience*, 493, 1–12. DOI: 10.1016/j.neuroscience.2022.02.001 PMID: 35134490

Mao, T., Shi, Z., & Zhou, D. X. (2023). Approximating functions with multi-features by deep convolutional neural networks. *Analysis and Applications*, 21(1), 93–125. DOI: 10.1142/S0219530522400085

Ma, Q. G., & Wang, X. Y. (2006). Cognitive neuroscience, neuroeconomics, and neuromanagement. *Guanli Shijie*, 10, 139–149.

Maristany, A. J., Sa, B. C., Murray, C., Subramaniam, A. B., & Oldak, S. E. (2024). Psychiatric manifestations of neurological diseases: A narrative review. *Cureus*, 16(7). Advance online publication. DOI: 10.7759/cureus.64152 PMID: 39119372

Martinek, R., Ladrova, M., Sidikova, M., Jaros, R., Behbehani, K., Kahankova, R., & Kawala-Sterniuk, A. (2021). Advanced bioelectrical signal processing methods: Past, present, and future approach—Part III: Other biosignals. *Sensors (Basel)*, 21(18), 6064. DOI: 10.3390/s21186064 PMID: 34577270

Mathe, M., Padmaja, M., & Krishna, B. T. (2021). Intelligent approach for artifacts removal from EEG signal using heuristic-based convolutional neural network. *Biomedical Signal Processing and Control*, 70, 102935. DOI: 10.1016/j.bspc.2021.102935

Maturi, M. H., Satish, S., Gonaygunta, H., Meduri, K., Rajan, R., & Srinivasan, R. (2022). The Intersection of Artificial Intelligence and Neuroscience: Unlocking the Mysteries of the Brain. *International Journal (Toronto, Ont.)*.

Mazzolenis, M. V., Mourra, G. N., Moreau, S., Mazzolenis, M. E., Cerda, I. H., Vega, J., Khan, J. S., & Thérond, A. (2024). The role of virtual reality and Artificial intelligence in Cognitive Pain therapy: A Narrative review. *Current Pain and Headache Reports*, 28(9), 881–892. Advance online publication. DOI: 10.1007/s11916-024-01270-2 PMID: 38850490

McGowin, G., Sonnenfeld, N. A., & Fiore, S. M. (2024). Navigating Cognitive Demand in virtual Reality: Implications for education and training. *Proceedings of the Human Factors and Ergonomics Society Annual Meeting*. DOI: 10.1177/10711813241278286

McGraw, D., & Mandl, K. D. (2021). Privacy protections to encourage use of health-relevant digital data in a learning health system. *NPJ Digital Medicine*, 4(1), 2. DOI: 10.1038/s41746-020-00362-8 PMID: 33398052

McKeith, I. G., Boeve, B. F., Dickson, D. W., Halliday, G., Taylor, J.-P., Weintraub, D., Aarsland, D., Galvin, J., Attems, J., Ballard, C. G., Bayston, A., Beach, T. G., Blanc, F., Bohnen, N., Bonanni, L., Bras, J., Brundin, P., Burn, D., Chen-Plotkin, A., & Kosaka, K. (2017). Diagnosis and management of dementia with Lewy bodies: Fourth consensus report of the DLB consortium. *Neurology*, 89(1), 88–100. DOI: 10.1212/WNL.0000000000004058 PMID: 28592453

Medenica, V., Ivanovic, L., & Milosevic, N. (2024). Applicability of artificial intelligence in neuropsychological rehabilitation of patients with brain injury. *Applied Neuropsychology. Adult*, •••, 1–28. DOI: 10.1080/23279095.2024.2364229 PMID: 38912923

Mehrabi, N., Morstatter, F., Saxena, N., Lerman, K., & Galstyan, A. (2021). A survey on bias and fairness in machine learning. *ACM Computing Surveys*, 54(6), 1–35. DOI: 10.1145/3457607

Mehra, S., Raut, G., Purkayastha, R. D., Vishvakarma, S. K., & Biasizzo, A. (2023). An empirical evaluation of enhanced performance softmax function in deep learning. *IEEE Access : Practical Innovations, Open Solutions*, 11, 34912–34924. DOI: 10.1109/ACCESS.2023.3265327

Mehta, A., Niles, A. N., Vargas, J. H., Marafon, T., Couto, D. D., & Gross, J. J. (2021). Acceptability and effectiveness of artificial intelligence therapy for anxiety and depression (Youper): Longitudinal observational study. *Journal of Medical Internet Research*, 23(6), e26771. DOI: 10.2196/26771 PMID: 34155984

Mejia-Puig, L., & Chandrasekera, T. (2022). The virtual body in a design exercise: A conceptual framework for embodied cognition. *International Journal of Technology and Design Education*, 33(5), 1861–1882. DOI: 10.1007/s10798-022-09793-8

Mennella, C., Maniscalco, U., De Pietro, G., & Esposito, M. (2024). Ethical and regulatory challenges of AI technologies in healthcare: A narrative review. *Heliyon*, 10(4), e26297. DOI: 10.1016/j.heliyon.2024.e26297 PMID: 38384518

Merayo, N., Ayuso-Lanchares, A., & González-Sanguino, C. (2024). Machine learning and natural language processing to assess the emotional impact of influencers' mental health content on Instagram. *PeerJ. Computer Science*, 10, e2251. DOI: 10.7717/peerj-cs.2251 PMID: 39314721

Merk, T., Peterson, V., Köhler, R., Haufe, S., Richardson, R. M., & Neumann, W. J. (2022, May 1). Machine learning based brain signal decoding for intelligent adaptive deep brain stimulation. *Experimental Neurology*, 351, 113993. DOI: 10.1016/j.expneurol.2022.113993 PMID: 35104499

Miller, B. L., Cummings, J. L., & Benson, D. F. (2022). Advances in understanding and diagnosing cognitive impairments: The role of AI. *Journal of Neurology*, 269(1), 12–21. PMID: 34085094

Miller, J. P., Chen, C., & Lee, M. (2017). Analyzing changes in speech patterns for detecting mild cognitive impairment using NLP techniques. *Journal of Biomedical Informatics*, 70, 103–113.

Mirkin, S., & Albensi, B. C. (2023). Should artificial intelligence be used in conjunction with Neuroimaging in the diagnosis of Alzheimer's disease? *Frontiers in Aging Neuroscience*, 15, 1094233. DOI: 10.3389/fnagi.2023.1094233 PMID: 37187577

Mishra, S., Chouhan, V., & Garg, R. (2021). Deep learning for early detection of schizophrenia through brain scan analysis. *Journal of Neural Engineering*, 18(2), 134–146.

Mishro, P. K., Agrawal, S., & Panda, R. (2021). A Survey on State-of-the-Art Denoising Techniques for Brain Magnetic Resonance Images. *IEEE Reviews in Biomedical Engineering*. PMID: 33513109

Misselhorn, C. (2018). Artificial morality. Concepts, issues and challenges. *Society*, 55(2), 161–169. DOI: 10.1007/s12115-018-0229-y

Mitsea, E., Drigas, A., & Skianis, C. (2023). Digitally assisted mindfulness in training self-regulation skills for sustainable mental health: A systematic review. *Behavioral Sciences (Basel, Switzerland)*, 13(12), 1008. DOI: 10.3390/bs13121008 PMID: 38131865

Mittal, G., & Bansal, R. (2023). Driving force behind consumer brand engagement: the metaverse. In *Cultural marketing and metaverse for consumer engagement* (pp. 164–181). IGI Global. DOI: 10.4018/978-1-6684-8312-1.ch012

Mnih, V., Kavukcuoglu, K., Silver, D., Rusu, A. A., Veness, J., Bellemare, M. G., Graves, A., Riedmiller, M., Fidjeland, A. K., Ostrovski, G., Petersen, S., Beattie, C., Sadik, A., Antonoglou, I., King, H., Kumaran, D., Wierstra, D., Legg, S., & Hassabis, D. (2015). Human-level control through deep reinforcement learning. *Nature*, 518(7540), 529–533. DOI: 10.1038/nature14236 PMID: 25719670

Mohammadi, A. T., Ghanbarzadeh, E., Zamiri, R., Dana, M. K., Far, Y. K., Avarani, M. A. J. N., & Shamshiri, M. (2024). *Advancements in neuroscience: Modern tools and techniques fueling thrilling discoveries in the 21st century*. Nobel Sciences., DOI: 10.1016/j.nobel.2024.03.004

Morales, S., & Bowers, M. E. (2022). Time-frequency analysis methods and their application in developmental EEG data. *Developmental Cognitive Neuroscience*, 54, 101067. DOI: 10.1016/j.dcn.2022.101067 PMID: 35065418

Mukherjee, G., Tudu, B., & Chatterjee, A. (2021). A convolutional neural network-driven computer vision system for identifying species and maturity stage of medicinal leaves: Case studies with Neem, Tulsi, and Kalmegh leaves. *Soft Computing*, 25(22), 14119–14138. DOI: 10.1007/s00500-021-06139-9

Müller, VC. (2016) Fundamental Issues of Artificial Intelligence. Springer Nature. 12.

Muneer, A., & Fati, S. M. (2020). Efficient and automated herbs classification approach based on shape and texture features using deep learning. *IEEE Access : Practical Innovations, Open Solutions*, 8, 196747–196764. DOI: 10.1109/ACCESS.2020.3034033

Murad, A. (2000). *HR—A complete guide*. Book Press and Printers.

Murthy, Y. S., Chandra, B. S. R., Reddy, M. G., & Mahek, A. (2024). Building Trust in Digital Health Marketing Strategies for Successful Integration of Digital Twins. In *Exploring the Advancements and Future Directions of Digital Twins in Healthcare 6.0* (pp. 24–47). IGI Global. DOI: 10.4018/979-8-3693-5893-1.ch002

Murthy, Y. S., & Chandra, R. (2024). AI Chatbots as a Catalyst for Customer Loyalty Investigating Digital Experience Preferences Across Age Groups. In *Future of Customer Engagement Through Marketing Intelligence* (pp. 143–160). IGI Global. DOI: 10.4018/979-8-3693-2367-0.ch007

Nasir, A., Shah, M. H., & Tiwari, A. (2019). Using machine learning to predict PTSD treatment efficacy. *Psychiatry Research*, 279, 276–284.

Nazer, L. H., Zatarah, R., Waldrip, S., Ke, J. X. C., Moukheiber, M., Khanna, A. K., Hicklen, R. S., Moukheiber, L., Moukheiber, D., Ma, H., & Mathur, P. (2023). Bias in artificial intelligence algorithms and recommendations for mitigation. *PLOS Digital Health*, 2(6), e0000278. DOI: 10.1371/journal.pdig.0000278 PMID: 37347721

Neudorf, J., Ekstrand, C., Kress, S., & Borowsky, R. (2020). Connectivity Predicts Brain Functional Complexity: Diffusion Tensor Imaging Derived Centrality Accounts for Variance in Fractal Properties of Functional Magnetic Resonance. *Neuroscience*, 438, 1–8. DOI: 10.1016/j.neuroscience.2020.04.048

Ngcukayitobi, M., Tartibu, L. K., & Bannwart, F. (2024). Enhancing Thermo-Acoustic Waste Heat Recovery through Machine Learning: A Comparative Analysis of Artificial Neural Network–Particle Swarm Optimization, Adaptive Neuro Fuzzy Inference System, and Artificial Neural Network Models. *AI*, 5(1), 237–258. DOI: 10.3390/ai5010013

Ngoc, T. M., Li, M. S., Liu, S. H., Wu, C. F., Yen, J. H., & Su, Y. J. (2019). Neuroprotective effects of Alpinia oxyphylla extract against glutamate-induced oxidative stress and apoptosis in PC12 cells. *Nutrients*, 11(10), 2469. PMID: 31618902

Ngo, D., Nguyen, A., Dang, B., & Ngo, H. (2024). Facial expression recognition for examining emotional regulation in synchronous online collaborative learning. *International Journal of Artificial Intelligence in Education*, 34(3), 1–20. DOI: 10.1007/s40593-023-00378-7

Nielsen, A. N., Kjær, L., Møller, J. R., & Nielsen, J. A. (2020), "Machine Learning with Neuroimaging: Evaluating Its Applications in Psychiatry," neuroimage: Clinical, vol. 26.

Nielsen, T. L., Hsu, W. H., & Brubaker, R. (2020). Artificial intelligence in personalized medicine: Early diagnostic and therapeutic interventions. *Frontiers in Medicine*, 7, 152.

Nigro, S., Filardi, M., Tafuri, B., De Blasi, R., Ciccarelli, N., & Di Iorio, A. (2022). The Role of Graph Theory in Evaluating Brain Network Alterations in Frontotemporal Dementia. *Frontiers in Neuroscience*. PMID: 35837233

NISC. (2004). The Wealth of India: A Dictionary of Indian Raw Materials & Industrial Products. National Institute of Science Communication, Council of Scientific &. *Industrial Research*, ISBN-13, 9788172362089.

Nishad, N. (2019). Robotic process automation for recruitment process. 10, 608-611.

Noreen, R., Zafar, A., Waheed, T., Wasim, M., Ahad, A., Coelho, P. J., & Pires, I. M. (2023). Unraveling the inner world of PhD scholars with sentiment analysis for mental health prognosis. *Behaviour & Information Technology*, •••, 1–13. DOI: 10.1080/0144929X.2023.2289057

Nosrati, S., Sabzali, M., Heidari, A., Sarfi, T., & Sabbar, S. (2020). Chatbots, counselling, and discontents of the digital life. *Journal of Cyberspace Studies*, 4(2), 153–172. DOI: 10.34296/jcs.2020.4203

Nwoye, E. O., Muslehat, A. A., Umeh, C., Okodeh, S. O., & Woo, W. L. (2024). SchizoBot: Delivering Cognitive Behavioural Therapy for Augmented Management of Schizophrenia. *Digital Technologies Research and Applications*, 3(2), 24–40. DOI: 10.54963/dtra.v3i2.225

O'Brien, J. T., & Thomas, A. (2015). Vascular dementia. *Lancet*, 386(10004), 1698–1706. DOI: 10.1016/S0140-6736(15)00463-8 PMID: 26595643

Obradovich, N., Khalsa, S. S., Khan, W. U., Suh, J., Perlis, R. H., Ajilore, O., & Paulus, M. P. (2024). Opportunities and risks of large language models in psychiatry. *NPP-Digital Psychiatry and Neuroscience*, 2(1), 8. DOI: 10.1038/s44277-024-00010-z PMID: 39554888

Office for AI. (2019). Understanding artificial intelligence. Retrieved December 1, 2021.

Ogawa, S. (2024). Predicting Dropout From Cognitive Behavioral Therapy for Panic Disorder Using Machine Learning Algorithms. *Journal of Clinical Medicine Research*, 16(5), 251–255. DOI: 10.14740/jocmr5167 PMID: 38855785

Oh, S., Joung, Y.-S., Chung, T.-M., Lee, J., Seok, B. J., Kim, N., & Son, H. M. (2024). Diagnosis of ADHD using virtual reality and artificial intelligence: An exploratory study of clinical applications. *Frontiers in Psychiatry*, 15, 1383547. DOI: 10.3389/fpsyt.2024.1383547 PMID: 38887727

Oktavianus, A. J. E., Naibaho, L., & Rantung, D. A. (2023). Pemanfaatan Artificial Intelligence pada Pembelajaran dan Asesmen di Era Digitalisasi. *Jurnal Kridatama Sains Dan Teknologi*, 5(02), 473–486. DOI: 10.53863/kst.v5i02.975

Oliveira, A. L. S., Matos, L. N., Junior, M. C., & Delabrida, Z. N. C. (2021). An Initial Assessment of a Chatbot for Rumination-Focused Cognitive Behavioral Therapy (RFCBT) in College Students. Computational Science and Its Applications–ICCSA 2021: 21st International Conference, Cagliari, Italy, September 13–16, 2021, Proceedings, Part VI 21, Penninx, B. W., Benros, M. E., Klein, R. S., & Vinkers, C. H. (2022). How COVID-19 shaped mental health: from infection to pandemic effects. *Nature Medicine*, 28(10), 2027–2037.

Oliver, T. L., Hetland, B., Schmaderer, M., Zolty, R., & Pozehl, B. (2024). A Feasibility Study of Qualitative Methods Using the Zarit Burden Interview in Heart Failure Caregivers. *Applied Nursing Research*, 79, 151826. DOI: 10.1016/j.apnr.2024.151826 PMID: 39256009

Ore, O., & Sposato, M. (2022). Opportunities and risks of artificial intelligence in recruitment and selection. *The International Journal of Organizational Analysis*, 30(6), 1771–1782. DOI: 10.1108/IJOA-07-2020-2291

Paganoni, S., & Amato, A. (2013). Electrodiagnostic evaluation of myopathies. *Physical Medicine and Rehabilitation Clinics of North America*, 24(1), 193–207. DOI: 10.1016/j.pmr.2012.08.017 PMID: 23177039

Painoli, A. K., Bansal, R., Singh, R., & Kukreti, A. (2021). Impact of digital marketing on the buying behavior of youth with special reference to Uttarakhand state. In *Big data analytics for improved accuracy, efficiency, and decision making in digital marketing* (pp. 162–182). IGI Global. DOI: 10.4018/978-1-7998-7231-3.ch012

Pallavicini, F., & Bouchard, S. (2019). Editorial: Assessing the therapeutic uses and effectiveness of virtual reality, augmented reality and video games for emotion regulation and stress management. *Frontiers in Psychology*, 10, 2763. Advance online publication. DOI: 10.3389/fpsyg.2019.02763 PMID: 31920816

Palmisani, F., Segelcke, D., & Vollert, J. (2024). Navigating the light and shadow of scientific publishing faced with machine learning and generative AI. *European Journal of Pain (London, England)*, ejp.4736. DOI: 10.1002/ejp.4736 PMID: 39360710

Palombi, T., Galli, F., Giancamilli, F., D'Amico, M., Alivernini, F., Gallo, L., Neroni, P., Predazzi, M., De Pietro, G., Lucidi, F., Giordano, A., & Chirico, A. (2023). The role of sense of presence in expressing cognitive abilities in a virtual reality task: An initial validation study. *Scientific Reports*, 13(1), 13396. DOI: 10.1038/s41598-023-40510-0 PMID: 37591908

Palta, P., Kumar, A., & Palta, A. Leveraging Dielectric Properties, Remote Sensing, and Sensor Technology. *Industry 5.0 and Emerging Technologies: Transformation Through Technology and Innovations*, 89.

Palta, N. P., & Kumar, N. A. (2024). -Soil Dielectric Response to Chemical Fertilizers in Northern India's Key Agricultural Areas. *Physics and Chemistry of the Earth Parts A/B/C*, •••, 103806.

Palta, P., & Kumar, A. (2024). Effect of vermicompost additive on physical, chemical and dielectric properties of soil and its modeling. *The Journal of Microwave Power and Electromagnetic Energy*, 58(3), 186–206. DOI: 10.1080/08327823.2024.2378668

Palta, P., Kumar, A., & Kaur, P. (2024). Evaluation of the impact of wastewater irrigation on the soil's dielectric parameters. *Land Degradation & Development*, 35(7), 2643–2657. DOI: 10.1002/ldr.5088

Palta, P., Kumar, A., & Palta, A. (2024). Leveraging Dielectric Properties, Remote Sensing, and Sensor Technology in Agriculture: A Perspective on Industry and Emerging Technologies. *Industry 5.0 and Emerging Technologies: Transformation Through. Technology and Innovation*, •••, 89–109.

Palumbo, A. (2022). Microsoft HoloLens 2 in Medical and Healthcare Context: State of the art and Future Prospects. *Sensors (Basel)*, 22(20), 7709. DOI: 10.3390/s22207709 PMID: 36298059

Panayides, A. S., Amini, A., Filipovic, N. D., Konstantinidis, G., Lungren, M. P., & Mitsouras, D. (2020). AI in Medical Imaging Informatics: Current Challenges and Future Directions. *IEEE Journal of Biomedical and Health Informatics*, 24(7), 1931–1941. DOI: 10.1109/JBHI.2020.2991043 PMID: 32609615

Panda, M., Abraham, A., Gopi, B., & Ajith, R. (2024). *Computational Intelligence for Oncology and Neurological Disorders: Current Practices and Future Directions*. CRC Press. DOI: 10.1201/9781003450153

Panesar, K., & de Alba, M. B. (2023, December 1). Natural language processing-driven framework for the early detection of language and cognitive decline. *Language and Health.*, 1(2), 20–35. DOI: 10.1016/j.laheal.2023.09.002

Pang, B., & Lee, L. (2008). Opinion Mining and Sentiment Analysis. *Foundations and Trends in Information Retrieval*, 2(1–2), 1–135. DOI: 10.1561/1500000011

Parincu, A. M. T., Capatina, A., Varon, D. J., Bennet, P. F., & Recuerda, A. M. (2020). Neuromanagement: the scientific approach to contemporary management. In *Proceedings of the International Conference on Business Excellence* (Vol. 14, No. 1, pp. 1046-1056). DOI: 10.2478/picbe-2020-0099

Park, H. J. (2024). Patient perspectives on informed consent for medical AI: A web-based experiment. *Digital Health*, 10, 20552076241247938. DOI: 10.1177/20552076241247938 PMID: 38698829

Parsapoor, M., Koudys, J. W., & Ruocco, A. C. (2023). Suicide risk detection using artificial intelligence: The promise of creating a benchmark dataset for research on the detection of suicide risk. *Frontiers in Psychiatry*, 14, 1186569. DOI: 10.3389/fpsyt.2023.1186569 PMID: 37564247

Parsons, T., & Duffield, T. (2020). Paradigm shift toward digital neuropsychology and high-dimensional neuropsychological assessments. *Journal of Medical Internet Research*, 22(12), e23777. DOI: 10.2196/23777 PMID: 33325829

Parveen, A., Akhtar, M., Zainuddin, M., & Khan, N. A. (2018). Neuroprotective Effect of Ethanol Extract of Gentiana kurroo Royle on Aluminum Chloride-Induced Neurotoxicity in Rats. *BMC Complementary and Alternative Medicine*, 18(1), 1–10. PMID: 29295712

Patil, D. (2024). The future of artificial intelligence in healthcare: Opportunities, challenges, and ethical considerations. *Challenges, and Ethical Considerations (November 08, 2024)*.

Patil, R. S., & Tupe, R. S. (2024). Communal interaction of glycation and gut microbes in diabetes mellitus, Alzheimer's disease, and Parkinson's disease pathogenesis. *Medicinal Research Reviews*, 44(1), 365–405. DOI: 10.1002/med.21987 PMID: 37589449

Pavlopoulos, A., Rachiotis, T., & Maglogiannis, I. (2024). An overview of tools and technologies for anxiety and depression management using AI. *Applied Sciences (Basel, Switzerland)*, 14(19), 9068. DOI: 10.3390/app14199068

Pels, E. G., Aarnoutse, E. J., Ramsey, N. F., & Vansteensel, M. J. (2019). Brain-computer interfaces in the fully locked-in state and chronic stroke. *Progress in Brain Research*, 245, 317–335. DOI: 10.1016/bs.pbr.2018.12.011

Pereira, J., Li, W., & Chauhan, A. (2020). Real-time stress detection using machine learning and physiological data. *Psychophysiology*, 57(9), e13592. PMID: 32412112

Pereira, V., Hadjielias, E., Christofi, M., & Vrontis, D. (2023). A systematic literature review on the impact of artificial intelligence on workplace outcomes: A multi-process perspective. *Human Resource Management Review*, 33(1), 100857. DOI: 10.1016/j.hrmr.2021.100857

Perivolaris, A., Adams-McGavin, C., Madan, Y., Kishibe, T., Antoniou, T., Mamdani, M., & Jung, J. J. (2024). Quality of interaction between clinicians and artificial intelligence systems. A systematic review. *Future Healthcare Journal*, 100172(3), 100172. Advance online publication. DOI: 10.1016/j.fhj.2024.100172 PMID: 39281326

Petersen, R. C., Smith, G. E., Waring, S. C., Ivnik, R. J., Tangalos, E. G., & Kokmen, E. (1999). Mild cognitive impairment: Clinical characterization and outcome. *Archives of Neurology*, 56(3), 303–308. DOI: 10.1001/archneur.56.3.303 PMID: 10190820

Peth-Nui, T., Wattanathorn, J., Muchimapura, S., Tong-Un, T., Piyavhatkul, N., Rangseekajee, P., Ingkaninan, K., & Vittaya-areekul, S. (2011). Effects of 12-Week Bacopa monnieri Consumption on Attention, Cognitive Processing, Working Memory, and Functions of Both Cholinergic and Monoaminergic Systems in Healthy Elderly Volunteers. *Evidence-Based Complementary and Alternative Medicine*, 2012, 1–10. DOI: 10.1155/2012/606424 PMID: 23320031

Phelan, I., Furness, P. J., Matsangidou, M., Babiker, N. T., Fehily, O., Thompson, A., Carrion-Plaza, A., & Lindley, S. A. (2021). Designing effective virtual reality environments for pain management in burn-injured patients. *Virtual Reality (Waltham Cross)*, 27(1), 201–215. DOI: 10.1007/s10055-021-00552-z PMID: 36915632

Piñeros-Fernández, M. C. (2023). Artificial intelligence applications in the diagnosis of neuromuscular diseases: A narrative review. *Cureus*, 15(11). Advance online publication. DOI: 10.7759/cureus.48458 PMID: 37942130

Praba, R., Darshan, G., Roshanraj, T., & Prakash, B. (2021). Study on machine learning algorithms. *Int. J. Sci. Res. Comput. Sci. Eng. Inf. Technol*, 7, 67–72.

Prajapati, R., & Emerson, I. A. (2021). Global and Regional Connectivity Analysis of Resting-State Function MRI Brain Images Using Graph Theory in Parkinson's Disease. *The International Journal of Neuroscience*, 131(2), 105–115. DOI: 10.1080/00207454.2020.1733559 PMID: 32124666

Privitera, A. J., Ng, S. H. S., Kong, A. P. H., & Weekes, B. S. (2024). AI and aphasia in the digital age: A critical review. *Brain Sciences*, 14(4), 383. DOI: 10.3390/brainsci14040383 PMID: 38672032

Pruitt, J. M., Koski, S., & O'Leary, D. (2020). Adaptive cognitive assessments: A new approach to evaluating cognitive function. *Journal of Cognitive Neuroscience*, 32(4), 591–603.

Purtle, J., Nelson, K. L., Counts, N. Z., & Yudell, M. (2020). Population-Based Approaches to Mental Health: History, Strategies, and Evidence. *Annual Review of Public Health*, 41(1), 201–221. DOI: 10.1146/annurev-publhealth-040119-094247 PMID: 31905323

Putri, Y. A., Djamal, E. C., & Ilyas, R. (2021, March). Identification of medicinal plant leaves using convolutional neural network. [). IOP Publishing.]. *Journal of Physics: Conference Series*, 1845(1), 012026. DOI: 10.1088/1742-6596/1845/1/012026

Qadri, Y. A., Ahmad, K., & Kim, S. W. (2024). Artificial General Intelligence for the Detection of Neurodegenerative Disorders. *Sensors (Basel)*, 24(20), 6658. DOI: 10.3390/s24206658 PMID: 39460138

Quan, W., Liu, S., Cao, M., & Zhao, J. (2024). A Comprehensive Review of Virtual Reality Technology for Cognitive Rehabilitation in Patients with Neurological Conditions. *Applied Sciences (Basel, Switzerland)*, 14(14), 6285. DOI: 10.3390/app14146285

Qu, J., Cui, L., Guo, W., Bu, L., & Wang, Z. (2024). Development of a novel machine learning-based approach for brain function assessment and integrated software solution. *Advanced Engineering Informatics*, 60, 102461. DOI: 10.1016/j.aei.2024.102461

Raghavan, M., Barocas, S., Kleinberg, J., & Levy, K. (2020, January). Mitigating bias in algorithmic hiring: Evaluating claims and practices. In *Proceedings of the 2020 conference on fairness, accountability, and transparency* (pp. 469-481). DOI: 10.1145/3351095.3372828

Raghavendra, U., Acharya, U. R., & Adeli, H. (2020). Artificial intelligence techniques for automated diagnosis of neurological disorders. *European Neurology*, 82(1-3), 41–64. DOI: 10.1159/000504292 PMID: 31743905

Raghavendra, U., Acharya, U. R., & Adeli, H. (2020). Artificial Intelligence Techniques for Automated Diagnosis of Neurological Disorders. *European Neurology*. PMID: 31743905

Rahman, M. A., Brown, D. J., Mahmud, M., Harris, M., Shopland, N., Heym, N., Sumich, A., Turabee, Z. B., Standen, B., Downes, D., Xing, Y., Thomas, C., Haddick, S., Premkumar, P., Nastase, S., Burton, A., & Lewis, J. (2023). Enhancing biofeedback-driven self-guided virtual reality exposure therapy through arousal detection from multimodal data using machine learning. *Brain Informatics*, 10(1), 14. Advance online publication. DOI: 10.1186/s40708-023-00193-9 PMID: 37341863

Raikar, A. S., Andrew, J., Dessai, P. P., Prabhu, S. M., Jathar, S., Prabhu, A., Naik, M. B., & Raikar, G. V. S. (2024). Neuromorphic computing for modeling neurological and psychiatric disorders: Implications for drug development. *Artificial Intelligence Review*, 57(12), 318. DOI: 10.1007/s10462-024-10948-3

Rajaraman S., (2024), "Artificial Intelligence in Neuro Degenerative Diseases: Opportunities and Challenges," AI and Neuro-Degenerative Diseases: Insights.

Rajasankar, S., Manivasagam, T., Surendran, S., Ashokkumar, N., & Sankaralingam, P. (2017). Neuroprotective effect of Centella asiatica extract (CAE) on experimentally induced parkinsonism in aged Sprague-Dawley rats. *Journal of Toxicology*, 2017, 1–13.

Rajkomar, A., Dean, J., & Kohane, I. (2019). Machine learning in medicine. *The New England Journal of Medicine*, 380(14), 1347–1358. DOI: 10.1056/NEJMra1814259 PMID: 30943338

Rakhmatulin, I., Dao, M. S., Nassibi, A., & Mandic, D. (2024). Exploring convolutional neural network architectures for EEG feature extraction. *Sensors (Basel)*, 24(3), 877. DOI: 10.3390/s24030877 PMID: 38339594

Ram, A. (2022). Short Review on Machine Learning and its Application. *Special Education*, 1(43).

Ramakrishnan, T., Mohan Gift, M. D., Chitradevi, S., Jegan, R., & Subha Hency Jose, P. Nagaraja, Rajneesh Sharma H.N., Selvakumar P., Sintayehu Mekuria Hailegiorgis, (2022). "Study of Numerous Resins Used in Polymer Matrix Composite Materials", Advances in Materials Science and Engineering, vol. 2022, Article ID 1088926, 8 pages, 2022. DOI: 10.1155/2022/1088926

Ramón-Arbués, E., Gea-Caballero, V., Granada-López, J. M., Juárez-Vela, R., Pellicer-García, B., & Antón-Solanas, I. (2020). The prevalence of depression, anxiety and stress and their associated factors in college students. *International Journal of Environmental Research and Public Health*, 17(19), 7001. DOI: 10.3390/ijerph17197001 PMID: 32987932

Rane, J., Mallick, S. K., Kaya, O., & Rane, N. L. (2024). Artificial intelligence, machine learning, and deep learning in cloud, edge, and quantum computing: A review of trends, challenges, and future directions. *Future Research Opportunities for Artificial Intelligence in Industry 4.0 and, 5*, 2-2.

Rane, J., Mallick, S. K., Kaya, O., & Rane, N. L. (2024). Scalable and adaptive deep learning algorithms for large-scale machine learning systems. *Future Research Opportunities for Artificial Intelligence in Industry 4.0 and, 5*, 2-40.

Rane, N. L., Mallick, S. K., Kaya, O., & Rane, J. (2024). Applications of machine learning in healthcare, finance, agriculture, retail, manufacturing, energy, and transportation: A review. *Applied Machine Learning and Deep Learning: Architectures and Techniques*, 112-131.

Rani, K., Vishnoi, H., & Mishra, M. (2023). A mental health chatbot delivering cognitive behavior therapy and remote health monitoring using NLP and AI. 2023 International Conference on Disruptive Technologies (ICDT), Rastogi, V., Satija, S., Sharma, D. P. K., & Singh, S. (2020). Machine learning algorithms: Overview. *International Journal of Advanced Research in Engineering and Technology*, 11(9).

Rathee, P., Chaudhary, H., Rathee, S., Rathee, D., Kumar, V., Kohli, K.,... & Kumar, R. (2009). Mechanism of action of flavonoids as anti-inflammatory agents: A review. Inflammation & Allergy-Drug Targets (Formerly Current Drug Targets-Inflammation & Allergy), 8(3), 229-235.

Ravishankar, V. (2022). Designing an assistive technology for self-reflection for students suffering from ADHD at Malmö University (Dissertation). Retrieved from https://urn.kb.se/resolve?urn=urn:nbn:se:mau:diva-55292

Rebsamen, M., Bansal, V., Chatel-Goldman, J., Bevilacqua, F., & Jerbi, K. (2021). Deep learning for neuroimaging: Leveraging brain signal complexity for clinical insights. *Journal of Neuroscience Methods*, 348, 109001. DOI: 10.1016/j.jneumeth.2020.109001

Reilly, P. (2018). The impact of artificial intelligence on the HR function. *Which way now for HR and organisational changes*, 41-58.

Rezaei, M., Pironti, M., & Quaglia, R. (2024). AI in knowledge sharing, which ethical challenges are raised in decision-making processes for organisations? *Management Decision*. Advance online publication. DOI: 10.1108/MD-10-2023-2023

Riaz, H., & Ghanghas, S. (2024). Artificial Intelligence in Employee Performance Evaluation and Its Managerial Implication. *Journal of Informatics Education and Research*, 4(1).

Ribé-Viñes, J., Gutiérrez-Maldonado, J., Zabolipour, Z., & Ferrer-Garcia, M. (2023). Efficacy of virtual reality-based exposure therapy for the treatment of fear of flying: A systematic review. *Cognitive Behaviour Therapist*, 16, e19. Advance online publication. DOI: 10.1017/S1754470X23000119

Riffin, C., Cassidy, J., Smith, J. M., Begler, E., Peereboom, D., Lum, H. D., & Wolff, J. L. (2024). Care Partner Perspectives on the Use of a Patient Portal Intervention to Promote Care Partner Identification in Dementia Care. [Rodrigues, Y. E., Manica, E., Zimmer, E. R., Neto, P. R., & Pascoal, T. A. Featuring Alzheimer Disease with Neuropsychological Tests and Proteomic Attributes using kNN-SMOTE Algorithm.]. *Journal of Applied Gerontology*, •••, 07334648241262649. PMID: 38901834

Ritter, S. M., Damian, R. I., Simonton, D. K., van Baaren, R. B., Strick, M., Derks, J., & Dijksterhuis, A. (2020). Creativity: Cognitive, social, and neurocognitive perspectives. *Psychological Bulletin*, 146(7), 745–781. DOI: 10.1037/bul0000294

Riva, G., Wiederhold, B. K., Di Lernia, D., Chirico, A., Riva, E. F. M., Mantovani, F., Cipresso, P., & Gaggioli, A. (2019). Virtual reality meets artificial intelligence: The emergence of advanced digital therapeutics and digital biomarkers. *Annual Review of Cybertherapy and Telemedicine*, 17, 3–7. https://psycnet.apa.org/record/2020-34322-001

Rizea, A. (2022). Deep Learning-based Solution for Mental Health Issues. *DATABASE SYSTEMS*, 57.

Rizzo, A., Goodwin, G. J., De Vito, A. N., & Bell, J. D. (2021). Recent advances in virtual reality and psychology: Introduction to the special issue. *Translational Issues in Psychological Science*, 7(3), 213–217. DOI: 10.1037/tps0000316

Roark, B., Mitchell, M., & Hosom, J. P. (2011). Spoken language markers of dementia with Lewy bodies. *Proceedings of the IEEE International Conference on Acoustics, Speech and Signal Processing (ICASSP)*, 5956-5959.

Robinson, N. L., Ward, B., & Kavanagh, D. J. (2021, August). A robot-delivered program for low-intensity problem-solving therapy for students in higher education. In *2021 30th IEEE International Conference on Robot & Human Interactive Communication (RO-MAN)* (pp. 945-950). IEEE. DOI: 10.1109/RO-MAN50785.2021.9515532

Roggeveen, L. F., Hassouni, A. E., de Grooth, H. J., Girbes, A. R. J., Hoogendoorn, M., & Elbers, P. W. G.Dutch ICU Data Sharing Against COVID-19 Collaborators. (2024). Reinforcement learning for intensive care medicine: Actionable clinical insights from novel approaches to reward shaping and off-policy model evaluation. *Intensive Care Medicine Experimental*, 12(1), 32. DOI: 10.1186/s40635-024-00614-x PMID: 38526681

Rosenfeld, A., Benrimoh, D., Armstrong, C., Mirchi, N., Langlois-Therrien, T., Rollins, C., Tanguay-Sela, M., Mehltretter, J., Fratila, R., Israel, S., & Snook, E. (2021). Big Data analytics and artificial intelligence in mental healthcare. In *Applications of big data in healthcare* (pp. 137–171). Academic Press. DOI: 10.1016/B978-0-12-820203-6.00001-1

Ros, T., Enriquez-Geppert, S., Zotev, V., Young, K. D., Wood, G., Whitfield-Gabrieli, S., & Vuilleumier, P. (2020). More than a feeling: How neurofeedback training improves human cognitive abilities. *Trends in Cognitive Sciences*, 24(6), 506–519. DOI: 10.1016/j.tics.2020.03.006

Rostami, M., Farashi, S., Khosrowabadi, R., & Pouretemad, H. (2020). Discrimination of ADHD subtypes using decision tree on behavioral, neuropsychological, and neural markers. *Basic and Clinical Neuroscience*, 11(3), 359. PMID: 32963728

Rudroff, T. (2024). Artificial intelligence's transformative role in illuminating brain function in long COVID patients using PET/FDG. *Brain Sciences*, 14(1), 73. DOI: 10.3390/brainsci14010073 PMID: 38248288

Rumiantcev, M., & Khriyenko, O. (2020) Emotion based music recommendation system. In: *Proceedings of the Conference of Open Innovations Association FRUCT* (edited by Oy, F.).

Ruppert, D., (2004). The elements of statistical learning: data mining, inference, and prediction.

Rush, A. J., Beck, A. T., Kovacs, M., & Hollon, S. (1977). Comparative efficacy of cognitive therapy and pharmacotherapy in the treatment of depressed outpatients. *Cognitive Therapy and Research*, 1(1), 17–37. DOI: 10.1007/BF01173502

Russell, S., & Norvig, P. (2020). *Artificial intelligence: A modern approach*. Pearson.

Ryu, S., Kim, K. S., & Kim, K. H. (2018). Economic impact of early detection and intervention in dementia. *Health Economics Review*, 8, 8.

Saad, M., & Islam, S. M. R. (2019), "Brain Connectivity Network Analysis and Classifications from Diffusion Tensor Imaging," 2019 International Conference on. DOI: 10.1109/ICREST.2019.8644080

Saboo, S., Gupta, S., Nailwal, I., Gandhi, R., & Rana, S. (2021, October). Diagnosing Mental Health Patient WhileMaintaining Anonymity. In *2021 IEEE Mysore Sub Section International Conference (MysuruCon)* (pp. 244-248). IEEE. DOI: 10.1109/MysuruCon52639.2021.9641727

Sabour, S., Zhang, W., Xiao, X., Zhang, Y., Zheng, Y., Wen, J., Zhao, J., & Huang, M. (2023). A chatbot for mental health support: Exploring the impact of Emohaa on reducing mental distress in China. *Frontiers in Digital Health*, 5, 1133987. DOI: 10.3389/fdgth.2023.1133987 PMID: 37214342

Saboury, B., Morris, M., & Siegel, E. (2021). Future Directions in Artificial Intelligence. *Radiologia Clinica*. PMID: 34689876

Sachdeva, C., Gangwar, V. P., Grover, V., & Gochhait, S. (2024). Cognitive Dissonance in Banking Employees: Exploring Factors Amid the Artificial Intelligence Revolution. 2024 ASU International Conference in Emerging Technologies for Sustainability and Intelligent Systems (ICETSIS), Sachdeva, C., & Grover, V. (2024). Balancing Technology and Humanity: Perspectives on AI in Healthcare. In *Analyzing Explainable AI in Healthcare and the Pharmaceutical Industry* (pp. 1-12). IGI Global.

Sachdeva, C., Grover, V., & Gangwar, V. P. (2024). Business Science Dynamics: Unraveling Cognitive Dissonance for Innovation. *Unleashing the Power of Basic Science in Business*, 212-221.

Sachdeva, C., Grover, V., Kaur, P., & Gangwar, V. P. (2024). Regulatory Landscapes: Navigating Compliance in the Commercialization of Basic Science. In *Unleashing the Power of Basic Science in Business* (pp. 118-137). IGI Global.

Saeidnia, H. R., Fotami, S. G. H., Lund, B., & Ghiasi, N. (2024). Ethical Considerations in Artificial Intelligence Interventions for Mental Health and Well-Being: Ensuring Responsible Implementation and impact. *Social Sciences (Basel, Switzerland)*, 13(7), 381. DOI: 10.3390/socsci13070381

Safitra, M. F., Lubis, M., Kusumasari, T. F., & Putri, D. P. (2024). Advancements in Artificial Intelligence and Data Science: Models, Applications, and Challenges. *Procedia Computer Science*, 234, 381–388. DOI: 10.1016/j.procs.2024.03.018

Saha, S., Sadhukhan, P., & Sil, P. C. (2015). Mangiferin: A xanthonoid with multipotent anti-inflammatory potential. *BioFactors (Oxford, England)*, 41(3), 141–159. PMID: 27219011

Salazar, E., Chopra, A., & Pradhan, S. (2020). Machine learning for optimizing medication adherence in patients with mental health disorders. *The Journal of Clinical Psychiatry*, 81(5), e1–e7.

Salles, A., & Farisco, M. (2024). Neuroethics and AI ethics: A proposal for collaboration. *BMC Neuroscience*, 25(1), 41. DOI: 10.1186/s12868-024-00888-7 PMID: 39210267

Samuel, A. L. (1959). Machine learning. *Technology Review*, 62(1), 42–45.

Samy, R. P., & Gopalakrishnakone, P. (2010). Therapeutic potential of plants as anti-microbials for drug discovery. *Evidence-Based Complementary and Alternative Medicine*, 7(3), 283–294. DOI: 10.1093/ecam/nen036 PMID: 18955349

Sandhya, N., & Charanjeet, K. (2016). A review on machine learning techniques. *International Journal on Recent and Innovation Trends in Computing and Communication*, 4(3), 451–458.

Sarker, I. H. (2021). Machine learning: Algorithms, real-world applications and research directions. *SN Computer Science*, 2(3), 160. DOI: 10.1007/s42979-021-00592-x PMID: 33778771

Sarmento, R. M., & Vasconcelos, F F X. (2019). Automatic Neuroimage Processing and Analysis in Stroke—A Systematic Review. *IEEE Reviews in Biomedical Engineering*. PMID: 31449031

Sarter, L., Heider, J., Kirchner, L., Schenkel, S., Witthöft, M., Rief, W., & Kleinstäuber, M. (2021). Cognitive and emotional variables predicting treatment outcome of cognitive behavior therapies for patients with medically unexplained symptoms: A meta-analysis. *Journal of Psychosomatic Research*, 146, 110486. DOI: 10.1016/j.jpsychores.2021.110486 PMID: 33879330

Sarubbo, F., Ramis, M. R., Kienzer, C., Aparicio, S., Esteban, S., Miralles, A., & Moranta, D. (2015). Neuroprotective Effects of Flavonoids on Transient Cerebral Ischemia in Mice: Structural Requirements for Activity. *Pharmacological Research*, 100, 363–373.

Savekar, A., Tarai, S., & Singh, M. (2022). Linguistic markers in individuals with symptoms of depression in bi-multilingual context. In *Research Anthology on Bilingual and Multilingual Education* (pp. 1535–1559). IGI Global. DOI: 10.4018/978-1-6684-3690-5.ch077

Schirrmeister, R. T., Springenberg, J. T., Fiederer, L. D. J., Glasstetter, M., Eggensperger, K., Tangermann, M., Hutter, F., & Ball, T. (2017). Deep learning with convolutional neural networks for EEG decoding and visualization. *Human Brain Mapping*, 38(11), 5391–5420. DOI: 10.1002/hbm.23730 PMID: 28782865

Schulze, B. (2007). Stigma and mental health professionals: A review of the evidence on an intricate relationship. *International Review of Psychiatry (Abingdon, England)*, 19(2), 137–155. DOI: 10.1080/09540260701278929 PMID: 17464792

Scoglio, A. A., Reilly, E. D., Gorman, J. A., & Drebing, C. E. (2019). Use of social robots in mental health and well-being research: Systematic review. *Journal of Medical Internet Research*, 21(7), e13322. DOI: 10.2196/13322 PMID: 31342908

Scott, J., & Beck, A. T. (2008). Cognitive behavioural therapy. *This page intentionally left blank*, 636.

Scott, J., & Beck, A. T. (2008). Cognitive behavioural therapy. In Murray, R. M., Kendler, K. S., McGuffin, P., Wessely, S., & Castle, D. J. (Eds.), *Essential Psychiatry* (4th ed., pp. 636–651). Cambridge University Press., https://doi.org/DOI, DOI: 10.1017/CBO9780511544125.029

Sebastian, J., & Richards, D. (2017). Changing stigmatizing attitudes to mental health via education and contact with embodied conversational agents. *Computers in Human Behavior*, 73, 479–488. DOI: 10.1016/j.chb.2017.03.071

Seelye, A. M., Schmitter-Edgecombe, M., Das, B., & Cook, D. J. (2012). Application of cognitive rehabilitation theory to the development of smart prompting technologies. *IEEE Reviews in Biomedical Engineering*, 5, 29–44. DOI: 10.1109/RBME.2012.2196691 PMID: 23231987

Seh, A. H., Zarour, M., Alenezi, M., Sarkar, A. K., Agrawal, A., Kumar, R., & Khan, R. A. (2020). Healthcare Data Breaches: Insights and Implications. *Healthcare (Basel)*, 8(2), 133. DOI: 10.3390/healthcare8020133 PMID: 32414183

Selvakumar, P., Mariappan, P., Shunmugam, S., Paul, R., & Jabez, S. (2024). Removal of chemicals from effluent using photobioreactor technology to improve environmental and health impacts. *Zeitschrift für Physikalische Chemie*, 2024(7), 1295–1302. Advance online publication. DOI: 10.1515/zpch-2023-0450

Selvakumar, P., Palanisamy, S. K., Cinthaikinian, S., Palanisamy, V., Mariappan, R., & Selvakumar, P. K. (2024). Biosensors and its diverse applications in healthcare systems. *Zeitschrift für Physikalische Chemie*, 2024. Advance online publication. DOI: 10.1515/zpch-2023-0406

Senapati, B. R., Swain, S., & Khilar, P. M. (2024). The Role of Artificial Intelligence, Machine Learning, and Deep Learning to Combat the Socio-Economic Impact of the Global COVID-19 Pandemic. *Modeling and Optimization of Signals Using Machine Learning Techniques*, 173-207.

Shaffer, K. M., Jacobs, J. M., Nipp, R. D., Carr, A., Jackson, V. A., Park, E. R., Pirl, W. F., El-Jawahri, A., Gallagher, E. R., Greer, J. A., & Temel, J. S. (2017). Mental and physical health correlates among family caregivers of patients with newly-diagnosed incurable cancer: A hierarchical linear regression analysis. *Supportive Care in Cancer*, 25(3), 965–971. DOI: 10.1007/s00520-016-3488-4 PMID: 27866337

Shaheed, K., Mao, A., Qureshi, I., Kumar, M., Hussain, S., Ullah, I., & Zhang, X. (2022). DS-CNN: A pre-trained Xception model based on depth-wise separable convolutional neural network for finger vein recognition. *Expert Systems with Applications*, 191, 116288. DOI: 10.1016/j.eswa.2021.116288

Shajari, S., Kuruvinashetti, K., Komeili, A., & Sundararaj, U. (2023). The emergence of AI-based wearable sensors for digital health technology: A review. *Sensors (Basel)*, 23(23), 9498. DOI: 10.3390/s23239498 PMID: 38067871

Shamsutdinova, D., Das-Munshi, J., Ashworth, M., Roberts, A., & Stahl, D. (2023). Predicting type 2 diabetes prevalence for people with severe mental illness in a multiethnic East London population. *International Journal of Medical Informatics*, 172, 105019. DOI: 10.1016/j.ijmedinf.2023.105019 PMID: 36787689

Shang, S., Shi, Y., Zhang, Y., Liu, M., Zhang, H., Wang, P., & Zhuang, L. (2024). Artificial intelligence for brain disease diagnosis using electroencephalogram signals. *Journal of Zhejiang University. Science. B.*, 25(10), 914–940. DOI: 10.1631/jzus.B2400103 PMID: 39420525

Sharma, A., Dhanka, S., Bansal, R., Kumar, A., & Maini, S. Industry 5.0 with Sustainable Development. *Industry 5.0 and Emerging Technologies: Transformation Through Technology and Innovations*, 347.

Sharma, V. P., Gaded, A. S., Chaudhary, D., Kumar, S., & Sharma, S. (2021) Emotion-based music recommendation system. In: 9th International Conference on Reliability, Infocom Technologies and Optimization (Trends and Future Directions)(ICRITO), Vol. 2021. IEEE Publications, pp. 1–5. DOI: DOI: 10.1109/ICRITO51393.2021.9596276

Sharma, A., Dhanka, S., Kumar, A., & Maini, S. (2024). A comparative study of heterogeneous machine learning algorithms for arrhythmia classification using feature selection technique and multi-dimensional datasets. *Engineering Research Express*, 6(3), 035209. DOI: 10.1088/2631-8695/ad5d51

Sharma, A., Lin, I. W., Miner, A. S., Atkins, D. C., & Althoff, T. (2021, April). Towards facilitating empathic conversations in online mental health support: A reinforcement learning approach. In *Proceedings of the Web Conference 2021* (pp. 194-205). DOI: 10.1145/3442381.3450097

Sharma, S., Gupta, M., & Singh, A. (2022). Challenges in implementing machine learning in mental health care: A systematic review. *Journal of Mental Health (Abingdon, England)*, 31(1), 12–22.

Sharma, S., Mansoori, S., Goyal, M., Goyal, K., & Sharma, P. (2024). Educating healthcare professionals on AI in Alzheimer's disease. In *AI-Driven Alzheimer's Disease Detection and Prediction* (pp. 372–388). IGI Global., DOI: 10.4018/979-8-3693-3605-2.ch024

Shatte, A. B. R., Hutchinson, D. M., & Teague, S. J. (2019). AI in psychological assessments. *PLoS One*, 14(3), e0212935. DOI: 10.1371/journal.pone.0212935 PMID: 30840663

Shen, H., Wang, L., Liu, Y., & Hu, D. (2017). Discriminative analysis of resting-state functional connectivity patterns of schizophrenia using low-dimensional embedding of fMRI. *NeuroImage*, 124, 704–714. DOI: 10.1016/j.neuroimage.2015.06.034 PMID: 19931396

Shen, L., Liu, Y., & Zhang, D. (2021). Predictive modeling of biomarkers for cognitive impairment using AI. *Journal of Biomedical Informatics*, 114, 103664.

Shibata, K., Watanabe, T., Sasaki, Y., & Kawato, M. (2019). Neurofeedback training induces changes in white and gray matter. *The Journal of Neuroscience : The Official Journal of the Society for Neuroscience*, 39(25), 5342–5355. DOI: 10.1523/JNEUROSCI.1018-18.2019

Sibley, M. H., Bickman, L., Atkins, D., Tanana, M., Coxe, S., Ortiz, M., Martin, P., King, J., Monroy, J. M., Ponce, T., Cheng, J., Pace, B., Zhao, X., Chawla, V., & Page, T. F. (2024). Developing an implementation model for ADHD intervention in community clinics: Leveraging artificial intelligence and digital technology. *Cognitive and Behavioral Practice*, 31(4), 482–497. DOI: 10.1016/j.cbpra.2023.02.001

Sigcha, L., Borzì, L., Amato, F., Rechichi, I., Ramos-Romero, C., Cárdenas, A., Gascó, L., & Olmo, G. (2023). Deep learning and wearable sensors for the diagnosis and monitoring of Parkinson's disease: A systematic review. *Expert Systems with Applications*, 229, 120541. DOI: 10.1016/j.eswa.2023.120541

Sim, J. A., Huang, X., Horan, M. R., Baker, J. N., & Huang, I. C. (2024). Using natural language processing to analyze unstructured patient-reported outcomes data derived from electronic health records for cancer populations: A systematic review. *Expert Review of Pharmacoeconomics & Outcomes Research*, 24(4), 467–475. DOI: 10.1080/14737167.2024.2322664 PMID: 38383308

Simonite, T. (2021). What really happened when Google Ousted Timnit Gebru.

Singh, A. P., Saxena, R., Saxena, S., Sharma, P., & Kumar, V. (2024). *Mind Unveiled: Cutting-Edge Neuroscience and Precision Brain Mapping*. Asian Journal.

Singh, J., Pandey, B., Karna, S., Arora, A. S., & Kumar, A. (2024). Enhancing the thermographic diagnosis of maxillary sinusitis using deep learning approach. *Quantitative InfraredThermography Journal*, •••, 1–15. DOI: 10.1080/17686733.2024.2349976

Singh, N. M., Harrod, J. B., Subramanian, S., Robinson, M., Chang, K., Cetin-Karayumak, S., Dalca, A. V., Eickhoff, S., Fox, M., Franke, L., Golland, P., Haehn, D., Iglesias, J. E., O'Donnell, L. J., Ou, Y., Rathi, Y., Siddiqi, S. H., Sun, H., Westover, M. B., & Gollub, R. L. (2022). How Machine Learning is Powering Neuroimaging to Improve Brain Health. *Neuroinformatics*, 20(4), 943–964. DOI: 10.1007/s12021-022-09572-9 PMID: 35347570

Singh, S., Gambill, J. L., Attalla, M., Fatima, R., Gill, A. R., & Siddiqui, H. F. (2024). Evaluating the clinical validity and reliability of artificial intelligence-enabled diagnostic tools in neuropsychiatric disorders. *Cureus*, 16(10), e71651. DOI: 10.7759/cureus.71651 PMID: 39553014

Sitaram, R., Veit, R., Stevens, B., Caria, A., Gerloff, C., Birbaumer, N., & Hummel, F. (2017). Acquired self-regulation of insula cortex modulates emotion recognition and brain network connectivity in schizophrenia. *Human Brain Mapping*, 38(4), 2019–2035. DOI: 10.1002/hbm.23500

Sivarajan, I. B. (2017). Ayurvedic Drugs and Their Plant Sources. *CBS Publishers & Distributors Pvt Ltd, India.*, ISBN-13, 9788120408289.

Smith, E. E., & Kosslyn, S. M. (2021). *Cognitive psychology: Mind and brain*. Pearson.

Snoek, L., Miletić, S., & Scholte, H. S. (2021). How to control for confounds in decoding analyses of neuroimaging data. *NeuroImage*, 184, 741–744. DOI: 10.1016/j.neuroimage.2018.09.074 PMID: 30268846

Sokolova, M., & Lapalme, G. (2009). A Systematic Analysis of Performance Measures for Classification Tasks. *Information Processing & Management*, 45(4), 427–437. DOI: 10.1016/j.ipm.2009.03.002

Sokołowska, B. (2024). Being in Virtual Reality and Its Influence on Brain Health—An Overview of Benefits, Limitations and Prospects. *Brain Sciences*, 14(1), 72. DOI: 10.3390/brainsci14010072 PMID: 38248287

Soori, M., Arezoo, B., & Dastres, R. (2023). Artificial intelligence, machine learning and deep learning in advanced robotics, a review. *Cognitive Robotics*, 3, 54–70. DOI: 10.1016/j.cogr.2023.04.001

Sorger, J. M. (2024). How to Objectively Evaluate the Impact of Image-Guided Surgery Technologies. *European Journal of Nuclear Medicine and Molecular Imaging*, 51(10), 2869–2877. DOI: 10.1007/s00259-023-06504-w PMID: 37971499

Soula, M., Maslarova, A., Harvey, R. E., Valero, M., Brandner, S., Hamer, H., Fernández-Ruiz, A., & Buzsáki, G. (2023). Interictal epileptiform discharges affect memory in an Alzheimer's disease mouse model. *Proceedings of the National Academy of Sciences of the United States of America*, 120(34), e2302676120. DOI: 10.1073/pnas.2302676120 PMID: 37590406

Sowndhararajan, K., Deepa, P., Kim, M., Park, S. J., & Kim, S. (2018). Neuroprotective and cognitive enhancement potentials of baicalin: A review. *Brain Sciences*, 8(6), 104. DOI: 10.3390/brainsci8060104 PMID: 29891783

Spiegel, B. M., Liran, O., Clark, A., Samaan, J. S., Khalil, C., Chernoff, R., Reddy, K., & Mehra, M. (2024). Feasibility of combining spatial computing and AI for mental health support in anxiety and depression. *NPJ Digital Medicine*, 7(1), 22. DOI: 10.1038/s41746-024-01011-0 PMID: 38279034

Spitale, M., Axelsson, M., & Gunes, H. (2023, March). Robotic mental well-being coaches for the workplace: An in-the-wild study on form. In *Proceedings of the 2023 ACM/IEEE International Conference on Human-Robot Interaction* (pp. 301-310). DOI: 10.1145/3568162.3577003

Sreenivasulu, A., & Manimozhi, T. Satheesh kumar P., Selvakumar P. And Singh P.,(2022). "The Model of Smart Sensing Device For Sensitive Nanoclusters Modification in Sensing Properties," 2022 2nd International Conference on Advance Computing and Innovative Technologies in Engineering (ICACITE), Greater Noida, India, 2022, pp. 1043-1047, DOI: 10.1109/ICACITE53722.2022.9823846

Srinivasan, S., & Rajavel, N. (2025). Artificial intelligence approach to psychological wellbeing among the ageing population. In *AI Technologies and Advancements for Psychological Well-Being and Healthcare* (pp. 187–218). IGI Global., DOI: 10.4018/978-1-7998-9516-5

Srivastava, G., & Bag, S. (2024). Modern-day marketing concepts based on face recognition and neuro-marketing: A review and future research directions. *Benchmarking*, 31(2), 410–438. DOI: 10.1108/BIJ-09-2022-0588

Srivastava, G., Wu, D., Liu, C., & Xu, J. (2024). Neuroscience and neurological machine learning for cognitive assessment: Advancements, challenges, and future directions. *Frontiers in Aging Neuroscience*, 16, 1406184. DOI: 10.3389/fnagi.2024.1406184 PMID: 38872631

Srivatsa, S., Singh, A., & Singh, P. K. (2021, December). Combating Depression Through the Neural Analysis of Web Behavior. In *International Conference on Hybrid Intelligent Systems* (pp. 128-139). Cham: Springer International Publishing.

Steen, C. W., Söderström, K., Stensrud, B., Nylund, I. B., & Siqveland, J. (2024). The effectiveness of virtual reality training on knowledge, skills and attitudes of health care professionals and students in assessing and treating mental health disorders: A systematic review. *BMC Medical Education*, 24(1), 480. Advance online publication. DOI: 10.1186/s12909-024-05423-0 PMID: 38693509

Steerling, E., Siira, E., Nilsen, P., Svedberg, P., & Nygren, J. (2023). Implementing AI in healthcare-the relevance of trust: A scoping review. *Frontiers in Health Services*, 3, 1211150. DOI: 10.3389/frhs.2023.1211150 PMID: 37693234

Stober, S., Sternin, A., Owen, A. M., & Grahn, J. A. (2017). Deep feature learning for EEG recordings. *International Conference on Learning Representations (ICLR)*. https://arxiv.org/abs/1511.04306

Stone, D. L., Deadrick, D. L., Lukaszewski, K. M., & Johnson, R. (2015). The Influence of Technology on the Future of Human Resource Management. *Human Resource Management Review*, 25(2), 216–231. DOI: 10.1016/j.hrmr.2015.01.002

Stumpo, V., Salvetti, O., & Gori, R. (2022), "Machine Learning Algorithms in Neuroimaging: An Overview," Machine Learning in Neuroimaging, Springer.

Sugumaran, K. M. D., Pandiyarajan V., Y. B S, Selvakumar P. And M. S, (2024). "Analysis of Electromyography Signals for Control of Mechanical Prosthesis using Machine Learning Techniques," 2024 2nd International Conference on Intelligent Data Communication Technologies and Internet of Things (idciot), Bengaluru, India, 2024, pp. 1059-1067, DOI: 10.1109/IDCIoT59759.2024.10467707

Sui, J., Jiang, R., Bustillo, J., & Calhoun, V. (2020). Neuroimaging-Based Individualized Prediction of Cognition and Behavior for Mental Disorders and Health: Methods and Promises. *Biological Psychiatry*, 88(11), 818–828. DOI: 10.1016/j.biopsych.2020.02.016 PMID: 32336400

Suk, H. I., Lee, S. W., & Shen, D. (2017). Latent feature representation with stacked auto-encoder for AD/MCI diagnosis. *NeuroImage*, 101, 535–545.

Sun, W., Ashtarieh, B., & Zou, P. (2021). The safety challenges of therapeutic self-care and informal caregiving in home care: A qualitative descriptive study. *Geriatric Nursing*, 42(2), 491–501. DOI: 10.1016/j.gerinurse.2020.07.013 PMID: 32807555

Surianarayanan, C., Lawrence, J. J., Chelliah, P. R., Prakash, E., & Hewage, C. (2023). Convergence of Artificial Intelligence and Neuroscience Towards the Diagnosis of Neurological Disorders—A Scoping Review. *Sensors (Basel)*, 23(6), 3062. DOI: 10.3390/s23063062 PMID: 36991773

Su, S., Wang, Y., Jiang, W., Zhao, W., Gao, R., Wu, Y., & Li, K. (2022). Efficacy of artificial intelligence-assisted psychotherapy in patients with anxiety disorders: A prospective, national multicenter randomized controlled trial protocol. *Frontiers in Psychiatry*, 12, 799917. DOI: 10.3389/fpsyt.2021.799917 PMID: 35126211

Suttie, M., Kable, J., Mahnke, A. H., & Bandoli, G. (2024). Machine learning approaches to the identification of children affected by prenatal alcohol exposure: A narrative review. *Alcohol, Clinical & Experimental Research*, 48(4), 585–595. DOI: 10.1111/acer.15271 PMID: 38302824

Sutton, R. S., & Barto, A. G. (2018). *Reinforcement learning: An introduction*. MIT Press.

Sweet, L. B., Müller, C., Anand, M., & Zscheischler, J. (2023). Cross-validation strategy impacts the performance and interpretation of machine learning models. *Artificial Intelligence for the Earth Systems*, 2(4), e230026. DOI: 10.1175/AIES-D-23-0026.1

Takac, M., Collett, J., Conduit, R., & De Foe, A. (2021). A cognitive model for emotional regulation in virtual reality exposure. *Virtual Reality (Waltham Cross)*, 27(1), 159–172. DOI: 10.1007/s10055-021-00531-4

Tambe, P., Cappelli, P., & Yakubovich, V. (2019). Artificial intelligence in human resources management: Challenges and a path forward. *California Management Review*, 61(4), 15–42. DOI: 10.1177/0008125619867910

Tanaka, M., Battaglia, S., Giménez-Llort, L., Chen, C., Hepsomali, P., Avenanti, A., & Vécsei, L. (2024). Innovation at the intersection: Emerging translational research in neurology and psychiatry. *Cells*, 13(10), 790. DOI: 10.3390/cells13100790 PMID: 38786014

Tanaka, M., Tuka, B., & Vécsei, L. (2024). Navigating the Neurobiology of Migraine: From pathways to potential therapies. *Cells*, 13(13), 1098. DOI: 10.3390/cells13131098 PMID: 38994951

Tanaka, M., & Vécsei, L. (2024). A Decade of Dedication: Pioneering Perspectives on Neurological Diseases and Mental Illnesses. *Biomedicines*, 12(5), 1083. DOI: 10.3390/biomedicines12051083 PMID: 38791045

Tanaka, M., & Vécsei, L. (2024). From lab to life: Exploring cutting-edge models for neurological and psychiatric disorders. *Biomedicines*, 12(3), 613. DOI: 10.3390/biomedicines12030613 PMID: 38540226

Tan, Y. L., Chang, V. Y. X., Ang, W. H. D., Ang, W. W., & Lau, Y. (2024). Virtual reality exposure therapy for social anxiety disorders: A meta-analysis and meta-regression of randomized controlled trials. *Anxiety, Stress, and Coping*, •••, 1–20. DOI: 10.1080/10615806.2024.2392195 PMID: 39161295

Tariq, M. U. (2024). AI and the future of talent management: Transforming recruitment and retention with machine learning. In Christiansen, B., Aziz, M., & O'Keeffe, E. (Eds.), *Global practices on effective talent acquisition and retention* (pp. 1–16). IGI Global., DOI: 10.4018/979-8-3693-1938-3.ch001

Tariq, M. U. (2024). Application of blockchain and Internet of Things (IoT) in modern business. In Sinha, M., Bhandari, A., Priya, S., & Kabiraj, S. (Eds.), *Future of customer engagement through marketing intelligence* (pp. 66–94). IGI Global., DOI: 10.4018/979-8-3693-2367-0.ch004

Tariq, M. U. (2024). The role of AI ethics in cost and complexity reduction. In Tennin, K., Ray, S., & Sorg, J. (Eds.), *Cases on AI ethics in business* (pp. 59–78). IGI Global., DOI: 10.4018/979-8-3693-2643-5.ch004

Tariq, M. U. (2024). The role of AI in skilling, upskilling, and reskilling the workforce. In Doshi, R., Dadhich, M., Poddar, S., & Hiran, K. (Eds.), *Integrating generative AI in education to achieve sustainable development goals* (pp. 421–433). IGI Global., DOI: 10.4018/979-8-3693-2440-0.ch023

Tariq, M. U. (2025). The Belmont Report: Guiding Ethical Principles in Human Research. In Throne, R. (Ed.), *IRB, Human Research Protections, and Data Ethics for Researchers* (pp. 245–268). IGI Global Scientific Publishing., DOI: 10.4018/979-8-3693-3848-3.ch010

Tariq, M. U., & Sergio, R. P. (2025). Ethical Considerations and Social Impact of AI and Computational Intelligence in Society 5.0. In Pandey, R., Srivastava, N., Prasad, R., Prasad, J., & Garcia, M. (Eds.), *Open AI and Computational Intelligence for Society 5.0* (pp. 225–248). IGI Global Scientific Publishing., DOI: 10.4018/979-8-3693-4326-5.ch010

Thibault, R. T., Lifshitz, M., Jones, J. M., & Raz, A. (2018). Neurofeedback, self-regulation, and brain imaging: Clinical science and fad in the service of mental health. *Psychotherapy and Psychosomatics*, 87(4), 193–207. DOI: 10.1159/000371714 PMID: 29788029

Thomson K R, (2020), "Image-Guided Interventions: Expert Radiology Series," Tsoumakidou G, Saltiel S, Villard N, Duran R, Krokidis M, Brountzos E, (2021), "Image-Guided Marking Techniques in Interventional Radiology: A Review of Current Evidence," Journal of Interventional Radiology.

Timmons, A. C., Duong, J. B., Simo Fiallo, N., Lee, T., Vo, H. P. Q., Ahle, M. W., Comer, J. S., Brewer, L. C., Frazier, S. L., & Chaspari, T. (2023). A Call to Action on Assessing and Mitigating Bias in Artificial Intelligence Applications for Mental Health. *Perspectives on psychological science: a journal of the Association for Psychological Science, 18*(5), 1062–1096. DOI: 10.1177/17456916221134490

Toga, A. W., & Thompson, P. M. (2022). The role of neuroimaging in cognitive neuroscience. *Neuropsychopharmacology*, 27(2), 189–204. DOI: 10.1038/s41386-021-01235-5

Topol, E. J. (2019). *Deep medicine: How artificial intelligence can make healthcare human again*. Basic Books.

Topol, E. J. (2019). High-performance medicine: The convergence of human and artificial intelligence. *Nature Medicine*, 25(1), 44–56. DOI: 10.1038/s41591-018-0300-7 PMID: 30617339

Trigueiro, M. J., Lopes, J., Simões-Silva, V., De Melo, B. V., De Almeida, R. S., & Marques, A. (2024). Impact of VR-Based Cognitive training on working memory and inhibitory control in IDD young adults. *Health Care*, 12(17), 1705. DOI: 10.3390/healthcare12171705 PMID: 39273729

Tulay, E. E., Ozdemir, A., & Yilmaz, E. (2019). Multimodal Neuroimaging: Basic Concepts and Classification of Neuropsychiatric Diseases. *Clinical EEG and Neuroscience*, 50(3), 159–167. DOI: 10.1177/1550059418782093 PMID: 29925268

Turing, A. M. (1950). Computing machinery and intelligence. *Mind*, 59(236), 433–460. DOI: 10.1093/mind/LIX.236.433

Vaidya, N., Marquand, A. F., Nees, F., Siehl, S., & Schumann, G. (2024). The impact of psychosocial adversity on brain and behaviour: An overview of existing knowledge and directions for future research. *Molecular Psychiatry*, 29(10), 1–23. DOI: 10.1038/s41380-024-02556-y PMID: 38658773

Valtakari, N. V., Hessels, R. S., Niehorster, D. C., Viktorsson, C., Nyström, P., Falck-Ytter, T., Kemner, C., & Hooge, I. T. C. (2024). A field test of computer-vision-based gaze estimation in psychology. *Behavior Research Methods*, 56(3), 1900–1915. DOI: 10.3758/s13428-023-02125-1 PMID: 37101100

Van den Broek, E., Sergeeva, A., & Huysman, M. (2021). When the Machine Meets the Expert: An Ethnography of Developing AI for Hiring. *Management Information Systems Quarterly*, 45(3), 1557–1580. DOI: 10.25300/MISQ/2021/16559 van der Meulen, M., & Wijnenga, M. M. (2024). Education and training in neurology: Developments and future challenges. *European Journal of Neurology*, 31(11), 16332. DOI: 10.1111/ene.16332 PMID: 38773718

van Esch, P., & Black, J. S. (2019). Factors that influence new genera tion candidates to engage with and complete digital, AI-enabled recruiting. *Business Horizons*, 62(6), 729–739. DOI: 10.1016/j.bushor.2019.07.004

van Gerven, M. A., de Lange, F. P., & Heskes, T. (2020). Neural decoding with hierarchical generative models. *Trends in Cognitive Sciences*, 14(11), 616–624. DOI: 10.1016/j.tics.2020.10.004

Van Giffen, B., Herhausen, D., & Fahse, T. (2022). Overcoming the pitfalls and perils of algorithms: A classification of machine learning biases and mitigation methods. *Journal of Business Research*, 144, 93–106. DOI: 10.1016/j.jbusres.2022.01.076

Van Rijsbergen, C. J. (1979). *Information Retrieval* (2nd ed.). Butterworths.

Van Twillert, B., Bremer, M., & Faber, A. W. (2007). Computer-Generated Virtual Reality to control pain and anxiety in pediatric and adult burn patients during wound dressing changes. *Journal of Burn Care & Research; Official Publication of the American Burn Association*, 28(5), 694–702. DOI: 10.1097/BCR.0B013E318148C96F PMID: 17667488

Vaswani, A., Shankar, S., Parmar, N., Uszkoreit, J., Jones, L., Gomez, A.N., Kaiser, Ł., Kyllonen, J., & Polosukhin, I. (2017). Attention is All You Need. *Advances in Neural Information Processing Systems*, •••, 30.

Velana, M., Sobieraj, S., Digutsch, J., & Rinkenauer, G. (2022). The Advances of Immersive Virtual Reality Interventions for the Enhancement of Stress Management and Relaxation among Healthy Adults: A Systematic Review. *Applied Sciences (Basel, Switzerland)*, 12(14), 7309. DOI: 10.3390/app12147309

Verbeek, P., Wit, D., & Haan, J. (2020). Resource allocation and early detection of cognitive impairment: An AI-driven approach. *Health Care Management Review*, 45(3), 245–256. PMID: 30080714

Viderman, D., Tapinova, K., Dossov, M., Seitenov, S., & Abdildin, Y. G. (2023). Virtual reality for pain management: An umbrella review. *Frontiers in Medicine*, 10, 1203670. Advance online publication. DOI: 10.3389/fmed.2023.1203670 PMID: 37521355

Vidya S, Gupta K, Aly A, Wills A, Ifeachor E, Singh S, (2024), "Explainable AI for Autism Diagnosis: Identifying Critical Brain Regions Using fmri Data," arxiv preprint.

Vieira, S., Liang, X., Guiomar, R., & Mechelli, A. (2022). Can we predict who will benefit from cognitive-behavioural therapy? A systematic review and meta-analysis of machine learning studies. *Clinical Psychology Review*, 97, 102193. https://doi.org/https://doi.org/10.1016/j.cpr.2022.102193. DOI: 10.1016/j.cpr.2022.102193 PMID: 35995023

Vieira, S., Pinaya, W. H., & Mechelli, A. (2017). Using machine learning to predict psychiatric outcomes based on neuroimaging data: A systematic review. *NeuroImage*, 145, 267–282. DOI: 10.1016/j.neuroimage.2016.06.062

Vijayakumar, G., Rajkumar, M., Rajiv Chandar, N., Selvakumar, P., & Duraisamy, R. (2024). Muniyandi Rajkumar, Rajiv Chandar N, Selvakumar P and Ramesh Duraisamy, (2024). Environmentally friendly TDS removal from waste water by electrochemical ion exchange batch-type recirculation (EIR) technique. *Environmental Science. Water Research & Technology*, 10(4), 826–835. DOI: 10.1039/D3EW00793F

Vistorte, A. O. R., Deroncele-Acosta, A., Ayala, J. L. M., Barrasa, A., López-Granero, C., & Martí-González, M. (2024). Integrating artificial intelligence to assess emotions in learning environments: A systematic literature review. *Frontiers in Psychology*, 15, 1387089. DOI: 10.3389/fpsyg.2024.1387089 PMID: 38966729

Voigtlaender, S., Pawelczyk, J., Geiger, M., Vaios, E. J., Karschnia, P., Cudkowicz, M., Dietrich, J., Haraldsen, I. R. J. H., Feigin, V., Owolabi, M., White, T. L., Świeboda, P., Farahany, N., Natarajan, V., & Winter, S. F. (2024). Artificial intelligence in neurology: Opportunities, challenges, and policy implications. *Journal of Neurology*, 271(5), 2258–2273. DOI: 10.1007/s00415-024-12220-8 PMID: 38367046

Von Krogh, G. (2018). Artificial intelligence in organizations: New opportunities for phenomenon-based theorizing. *Academy of Management Discoveries*, 4(4), 404–409. DOI: 10.5465/amd.2018.0084

Vos, E. E., De Bruin, S. R., van der Beek, A. J., & Proper, K. I. (2021). "It's like juggling, constantly trying to keep all balls in the air": A qualitative study of the support needs of working caregivers taking care of older adults. *International Journal of Environmental Research and Public Health*, 18(11), 5701. DOI: 10.3390/ijerph18115701 PMID: 34073386

Wahlang, I., Singh, P., Singh, R., & Gupta, P. (2022). Brain Magnetic Resonance Imaging Classification Using Deep Learning Architectures with Gender and Age. *Sensors (Basel)*, 22(11), 4231. DOI: 10.3390/s22051766 PMID: 35270913

Walter, M., Tanovic, E., & Moller, H. E. (2019). Translational Machine Learning for Psychiatric Neuroimaging. *Progress in Neurobiology*, 175, 53–66. PMID: 30290208

Wang, C., Kong, J., & Qi, H. (2023). Areas of Research focus and trends in the research on the application of VR in rehabilitation medicine. *Health Care*, 11(14), 2056. DOI: 10.3390/healthcare11142056 PMID: 37510497

Wang, G., Wang, J., Feng, J., & Liu, Y. (2019). Application of machine learning in EEG signal processing. *IEEE Access : Practical Innovations, Open Solutions*, 7, 68733–68744. DOI: 10.1109/ACCESS.2019.2918456

Wang, L., Smriti, D., Yuan, H., & Huh-Yoo, J. (2024, May). Artificial Intelligence Systems for Supporting Informal Caregivers of People Living with Alzheimer's Disease or Related Dementias: A Systematic Review. In *Extended Abstracts of the CHI Conference on Human Factors in Computing Systems* (pp. 1-11). DOI: 10.1145/3613905.3650846

Wang, R.. (2021). Digital phenotyping and AI for ADHD. *Nature Digital Medicine*, 4(6), 322–333. DOI: 10.1038/s41746-021-00492-7

Watanabe, T., Sasaki, Y., Shibata, K., & Kawato, M. (2017). Advances in fMRI real-time neurofeedback. *Trends in Cognitive Sciences*, 21(12), 997–1010. DOI: 10.1016/j.tics.2017.09.010 PMID: 29031663

Watland, S., Solberg Nes, L., Hanson, E., Ekstedt, M., Stenberg, U., & Børøsund, E. (2023). The Caregiver Pathway, a Model for the Systematic and Individualized Follow-up of Family Caregivers at Intensive Care Units: Development Study. *JMIR Formative Research*, 7, e46299. DOI: 10.2196/46299 PMID: 37097744

Weaver, D. T., King, E. S., Maltas, J., & Scott, J. G. (2024). Reinforcement learning informs optimal treatment strategies to limit antibiotic resistance. *Proceedings of the National Academy of Sciences of the United States of America*, 121(16), e2303165121. DOI: 10.1073/pnas.2303165121 PMID: 38607932

Webb, C. A., Rosso, I. M., & Rauch, S. L. (2017). Internet-based cognitive-behavioral therapy for depression: Current progress and future directions. *Harvard Review of Psychiatry*, 25(3), 114–122. DOI: 10.1097/HRP.0000000000000139 PMID: 28475503

Wei, L. (2023). Artificial intelligence in language instruction: Impact on English learning achievement, L2 motivation, and self-regulated learning. *Frontiers in Psychology*, 14, 1261955. DOI: 10.3389/fpsyg.2023.1261955 PMID: 38023040

Weizenbaum, J. (1966). ELIZA—A Computer Program for studying Natural Language Communication between Man and Machine. *Communications of the ACM*, 9(1), 36–45. DOI: 10.1145/365153.365168

Wierenga, B. (2010). Marketing and artificial intelligence: Great opportunities, reluctant partners. In *Marketing intelligent systems using soft computing: Managerial and research applications* (pp. 1–8). Springer Berlin Heidelberg. DOI: 10.1007/978-3-642-15606-9_1

Williams, J. E., & Pykett, J. (2022). Mental health monitoring apps for depression and anxiety in children and young people: A scoping review and critical ecological analysis. *Social Science & Medicine*, 297, 114802. DOI: 10.1016/j.socscimed.2022.114802 PMID: 35192989

Williams, K. S. (2024). Evaluations of artificial intelligence and machine learning algorithms in neurodiagnostics. *Journal of Neurophysiology*, 131(5), 825–831. DOI: 10.1152/jn.00404.2023 PMID: 38533950

Williamson, S. M., & Prybutok, V. (2024). Balancing Privacy and Progress: A review of privacy challenges, systemic oversight, and patient perceptions in AI-Driven healthcare. *Applied Sciences (Basel, Switzerland)*, 14(2), 675. DOI: 10.3390/app14020675

Wimbarti, S., Kairupan, B. R., & Tallei, T. E. (2024). Critical review of self-diagnosis of mental health conditions using artificial intelligence. *International Journal of Mental Health Nursing*, 33(2), 344–358. DOI: 10.1111/inm.13303 PMID: 38345132

Wolff, J. L., Cagle, J. G., Hanna, V., Dy, S. M., Echavarria, D., Giovannetti, E. R., Boyd, C. M., Saylor, M. A., Hussain, N., Reiff, J. S., Scerpella, D., Zhang, T., Sekhon, V. K., & Roth, D. L. (2024). Sharing health care wishes among older adults with cognitive impairment in primary care: Results from a randomized controlled trial. *Alzheimer's & Dementia*, alz.14210. DOI: 10.1002/alz.14210 PMID: 39189632

Wolff, J. L., Mulcahy, J., Huang, J., Roth, D. L., Covinsky, K., & Kasper, J. D. (2018). Family caregivers of older adults, 1999–2015: Trends in characteristics, circumstances, and role-related appraisal. *The Gerontologist*, 58(6), 1021–1032. DOI: 10.1093/geront/gnx093 PMID: 28637266

Wolpaw, J. R., & Wolpaw, E. W. (Eds.). (2012). *Brain-computer interfaces: Principles and practice*. Oxford University Press. DOI: 10.1093/acprof:oso/9780195388855.001.0001

World Health Organization. (1999). *WHO monographs selected medicinal plants* (Vol. 2). World Health Organization.

Wu, J., Sun, Y., Zhang, G., Zhou, Z., & Ren, Z. (2021). Virtual Reality-Assisted Cognitive Behavioral Therapy for Anxiety Disorders: A Systematic Review and Meta-Analysis. *Frontiers in Psychiatry*, 12, 575094. Advance online publication. DOI: 10.3389/fpsyt.2021.575094 PMID: 34366904

Xie, B., Liu, H., Alghofaili, R., Zhang, Y., Jiang, Y., Lobo, F. D., Li, C., Li, W., Huang, H., Akdere, M., Mousas, C., & Yu, L. (2021). A review on virtual Reality skill training applications. *Frontiers in Virtual Reality*, 2, 645153. Advance online publication. DOI: 10.3389/frvir.2021.645153

Xu, A., Hou, Y., Niell, C., & Beyeler, M. (2024). Multimodal deep learning model unveils behavioral dynamics of V1 activity in freely moving mice. *Advances in Neural Information Processing Systems*, •••, 36. PMID: 39005944

Xu, C., Wang, Q., & Zhang, Y. (2020). Anxiety disorder prediction using machine learning and behavioral data: Insights from smartphone usage patterns. *Computers in Human Behavior*, 102, 113–121.

Xue, C., Li, A., Wu, R., Chai, J., Qiang, Y., Zhao, J., & Yang, Q. (2024). VRNPT: A neuropsychological test tool for diagnosing mild cognitive impairment using virtual reality and EEG signals. *International Journal of Human-Computer Interaction*, 40(20), 6268–6286. DOI: 10.1080/10447318.2023.2250605

Xu, K., & Kang, H. (2024). A review of machine learning approaches for Brain Positron Emission Tomography Data Analysis. *Nuclear Medicine and Molecular Imaging*, 58(4), 1–10. DOI: 10.1007/s13139-024-00845-6 PMID: 38932757

Xu, L., Sanders, L., Li, K., & Chow, J. C. (2021). Chatbot for health care and oncology applications using artificial intelligence and machine learning: Systematic review. *JMIR Cancer*, 7(4), e27850. DOI: 10.2196/27850 PMID: 34847056

Yadollahi, A., Shahraki, A. G., & Zaiane, O. R. (2017). Current state of text sentiment analysis from opinion to emotion mining. *ACM Computing Surveys*, 50(2), 1–33. DOI: 10.1145/3057270

Yamijala, S. M. S., Chodisetty, R. M., Chakravorty, C., & Sai, K. P. (2025). AI-Powered Learning Revolutionizing Smart Education With Personalized Learning Styles. In *Internet of Behavior-Based Computational Intelligence for Smart Education Systems* (pp. 191–212). IGI Global.

Yamijala, S. M., Chodisetty, R. C. M., & Chakravorty, C. (2025). Adapting HR Practices for a Transhumanist Future: An Empirical Study on Policy and Implementation. In *Enhancing the Modern Workforce Through Transhumanism* (pp. 117–146). IGI Global.

Yanamala, K. K. R. (2022). Integrating machine learning and human feedback for employee performance evaluation. *Journal of Advanced Computing Systems*, 2(1), 1–10. https://market.us/report/ai-in-hr-market/. DOI: 10.69987/JACS.2022.20101

Yang, S., & Kar, S. (2023). Application of artificial intelligence and machine learning in early detection of adverse drug reactions (ADRs) and drug-induced toxicity. *Artificial Intelligence Chemistry.*, 100011(2), 100011. Advance online publication. DOI: 10.1016/j.aichem.2023.100011

Yao, Y., & Cui, Z. (2020). An Automatic Epilepsy Detection Method Based on Improved Inductive Transfer Learning. *Computational and Mathematical Methods in Medicine*, 5046315, 1–13. Advance online publication. DOI: 10.1155/2020/5046315 PMID: 32831900

Yasmeen, K., Imran, H., Abbas, M. M., Bibi, A., Nadeem, S., Anwar, Z., & Noreen, H. R. (2024). Analyzing the Influence of AI in Predictive Analytics for Mental Health and Its Impact on Early Intervention, Anxiety Levels, And Treatment Adherence. *Social Science Review Archives*, 2(2), 232–243.

Yeh, J. F., Lin, K. M., Chang, C. C., & Wang, T. H. (2023). Expression recognition of multiple faces using a convolution neural network combining the haar cascade classifier. *Applied Sciences (Basel, Switzerland)*, 13(23), 12737. DOI: 10.3390/app132312737

Yeung, J. A., Wang, Y. Y., Kraljevic, Z., & Teo, J. T. (2023). Artificial intelligence (AI) for neurologists: Do digital neurones dream of electric sheep? *Practical Neurology*, 23(6), 476–488. DOI: 10.1136/pn-2023-003757 PMID: 37977806

Yi, F., Yang, H., Chen, D., Qin, Y., Han, H., Cui, J., Bai, W., Ma, Y., Zhang, R., & Yu, H. (2023). XGBoost-SHAP-based interpretable diagnostic framework for alzheimer's disease. *BMC Medical Informatics and Decision Making*, 23(1), 137. DOI: 10.1186/s12911-023-02238-9 PMID: 37491248

Yim, D., Khuntia, J., Parameswaran, V., & Meyers, A. (2024). Preliminary Evidence of the Use of Generative AI in Health Care Clinical Services: Systematic Narrative Review. *JMIR Medical Informatics*, 12, e52073. DOI: 10.2196/52073 PMID: 38506918

Ying, H., Pranolo, A., Nuryana, Z., & Syafitri, A. I. (2024, November 2). Emerging trends in the evolution of neuropsychology and artificial intelligence: A comprehensive analysis. *Telematics and Informatics Reports.*, 100171, 100171. Advance online publication. DOI: 10.1016/j.teler.2024.100171

Yoo, R. E., & Choi, S. H. (2024). Deep Learning-Based Image Enhancement Techniques for Fast MRI in Neuroimaging. *Magnetic Resonance in Medical Sciences*, 23(3), 341–351. DOI: 10.2463/mrms.rev.2023-0153 PMID: 38684425

Zafar, F., Alam, L. S., Rauf, S., & Usman, M. (2024). Advancing neuropsychology: Artificial intelligence models for detecting neurodegenerative diseases. *Brain Sciences*, 14(2), 199. DOI: 10.3390/brainsci14020199

Zafar, F., Fakhare Alam, L., Vivas, R. R., Wang, J., Whei, S. J., Mehmood, S., Sadeghzadegan, A., Lakkimsetti, M., & Nazir, Z. (2024). The Role of Artificial Intelligence in Identifying Depression and Anxiety: A Comprehensive Literature Review. *Cureus*, 16(3), e56472. DOI: 10.7759/cureus.56472 PMID: 38638735

Zahra, M. A., Al-Taher, A., Alquhaidan, M., Hussain, T., Ismail, I., Raya, I., & Kandeel, M. (2024). The synergy of artificial intelligence and personalized medicine for the enhanced diagnosis, treatment, and prevention of disease. *Drug Metabolism and Personalized Therapy*, 39(2), 47–58. DOI: 10.1515/dmpt-2024-0003 PMID: 38997240

Zhai, Y., Zhang, Y., Chu, Z., Geng, B., Almaawali, M., Fulmer, R., Lin, Y.-W. D., Xu, Z., Daniels, A. D., Liu, Y., Chen, Q., & Du, X. (2024). Machine learning predictive models to guide prevention and intervention allocation for anxiety and depressive disorders among college students. *Journal of Counseling and Development*, jcad.12543. DOI: 10.1002/jcad.12543

Zhang, T., Schoene, A. M., Ji, S., & Ananiadou, S. (2022). Natural language processing applied to mental illness detection. DOI: 10.1038/s41746-022-00589-7

Zhang, F., Hoffmann, N., Karayumak, S. C., & Rathi, Y. (2019), "Deep White Matter Analysis: Fast, Consistent Tractography Segmentation Across Populations and dmri Acquisitions," *Conference on Medical*. DOI: 10.1007/978-3-030-32248-9_67

Zhang, F., Karayumak, S. C., Hoffmann, N., & Rathi, Y. (2020). *Deep White Matter Analysis (deepwma): Fast and Consistent Tractography Segmentation*. Image Analysis.

Zhang, F., Wu, Y., Norton, I., Rathi, Y., Golby, A. J., & O'Donnell, L. J. (2019). Test-Retest Reproducibility of White Matter Parcellation Using Diffusion MRI Tractography Fiber Clustering. *Human Brain Mapping*, 40(10), 3041–3057. DOI: 10.1002/hbm.24579 PMID: 30875144

Zhang, H., Zhao, Y., Wang, Y., & Liao, W. (2020). Brain-computer interface for neural rehabilitation: Engineering and clinical perspectives. *Frontiers in Neurorobotics*, 14, 87. DOI: 10.3389/fnbot.2020.00087

Zhang, J., & Zhang, Z. M. (2023). Ethics and governance of trustworthy medical artificial intelligence. *BMC Medical Informatics and Decision Making*, 23(1), 7. DOI: 10.1186/s12911-023-02103-9 PMID: 36639799

Zhang, L., Wang, W., & Wang, X. (2020). AI in genetic research for cognitive impairments. *Nature Reviews. Genetics*, 21(6), 341–354.

Zhang, S., Chen, M., Yang, N., Lu, S., & Ni, S. (2021). Effectiveness of VR based mindfulness on psychological and physiological health: A systematic review. *Current Psychology (New Brunswick, N.J.)*, 42(6), 5033–5045. DOI: 10.1007/s12144-021-01777-6

Zhang, W., Xie, J., Zhang, Z., & Liu, X. (2024). Depression detection using digital traces on social media: A knowledge-aware deep learning approach. *Journal of Management Information Systems*, 41(2), 546–580. DOI: 10.1080/07421222.2024.2340822

Zhang, X., Fan, H., Guo, C., Li, Y., Han, X., Xu, Y., Wang, H., & Zhang, T. (2024). Establishment of a mild cognitive impairment risk model in middle-aged and older adults: A longitudinal study. *Neurological Sciences*, 45(9), 1–10. DOI: 10.1007/s10072-024-07536-2 PMID: 38642322

Zhang, X., Tan, Y., & Xu, H. (2020). Neural correlates of consciousness: Progress and challenges in artificial intelligence. *Frontiers in Psychology*, 11, 1953. DOI: 10.3389/fpsyg.2020.01953

Zhang, Y. D., Dong, Z., Wang, S. H., Yu, X., Yao, X., Zhou, Q., Hu, H., Li, M., Jiménez-Mesa, C., Ramirez, J., Martinez, F. J., & Gorriz, J. M. (2020). Advances in multimodal data fusion in neuroimaging: Overview, challenges, and novel orientation. *Information Fusion*, 64, 149–187. DOI: 10.1016/j.inffus.2020.07.006 PMID: 32834795

Zhang, Z., Zhang, S., Ni, D., Wei, Z., Yang, K., Jin, S., Huang, G., Liang, Z., Zhang, L., Li, L., Ding, H., Zhang, Z., & Wang, J. (2024). Multimodal sensing for depression risk detection: Integrating audio, Video, and Text Data [Video]. *Sensors (Basel)*, 24(12), 3714. DOI: 10.3390/s24123714 PMID: 38931497

Zhao, H., Wu, S., & Li, C. (2023). Exploring AI solutions for personalized neuropsychological rehabilitation in the elderly population. *Journal of Neural Engineering*, 20(4), 046029. DOI: 10.1088/1741-2552/ad618b PMID: 37336205

Zhao, X., Wang, L., Zhang, Y., Han, X., Deveci, M., & Parmar, M. (2024). A review of convolutional neural networks in computer vision. *Artificial Intelligence Review*, 57(4), 99. DOI: 10.1007/s10462-024-10721-6

Zhao, X., & Zhao, X. M. (2021). Deep Learning of Brain Magnetic Resonance Images: A Brief Review. *Methods (San Diego, Calif.)*, 187, 94–103. DOI: 10.1016/j.ymeth.2020.09.007 PMID: 32931932

Zheng, T., Feng, W., Yu, C., & Wu, Q. (2023). Feature extraction analysis method of pre-trained CNN model for SAR target recognition. *International Journal of Remote Sensing*, 44(7), 2294–2316. DOI: 10.1080/01431161.2023.2198654

Zhou, J., Cui, G., Hu, S., Zhang, Z., Yang, C., Liu, Z., ... & Sun, M. (2020). Graph neural networks: A review of methods and applications. *AI open, 1*, 57-81. DOI: 10.1016/j.aiopen.2021.01.001

Zhou, X., Liu, C., Fan, X., & Sun, J. (2020). Machine learning for brain disease neuroimaging. *IEEE Reviews in Biomedical Engineering*, 13, 7–19. DOI: 10.1109/RBME.2019.2932311

Zhu, G., Jiang, B., Tong, L., Xie, Y., & Zaharchuk, G. (2019). Applications of Deep Learning to Neuro-Imaging Techniques. *Frontiers in Neuroscience*. PMID: 31474928

Zuboff, S. (2019). *The age of surveillance capitalism: The fight for a human future at the new frontier of power*. PublicAffairs.

About the Contributors

Rohit Bansal is working as an adjunct faculty in Stanford Institute of Management & Technology, Australia as well as Professor in Department of Management Studies in Vaish College of Engineering, Rohtak, India. He is a perseverant, passionate academician cum seasoned professional. He obtained Ph.D. in Management from Maharshi Dayanand University, Rohtak. With a rich experience of 16 years, he has achieved growth through robust and proactive academic initiatives. Moreover, he is working as an Online Adjunct Faculty in Optics Teacher Training Institute, Liberia. He is also working as online Instructor on Udemy.com having launched six online courses with 15, 000 students enrolled till date. He has authored & edited 47 books with renowned national & international publishers including Springer Nature, IGI Global, Scrivener-Wiley Publishing, De Gruyter, Central West Publishing etc. In addition to, he has published 160 research papers and chapters in national and international journals of repute as well as edited books. His research work is published in leading publishers like Springer, MDPI, HIndawi, IGI Global, Cell Press, De Gruyter, Elseveir, Inderscience, Wiley etc. He has also presented papers in 60 conferences and seminars including IIM Indore, IIM Ranchi, IIM Jammu and IIM Kozhikode. His area of interest includes marketing management, organizational behavior, mental health and well-being, customer engagement, digital marketing, influencer marketing, emerging technologies, industry 5.0, sustainable development, e-learning . He is on Editorial Advisory Board as a member in 120 national and international peer reviewed journals. He is Managing Editor of International Journal of 360° Management Review. He has served as member of technical committee in many international conferences. Dr. Rohit has acted as session chair and speaker in many international conferences. He has been awarded many times for contribution to academics and research.

Tariq Maqableh is an experienced academic with over 6 years of experience in an Accounting and finance discipline as a lecturer and tutor at various universities including University of Western Sydney, Charles Sturt University, southern cross Institute, Canterbury Institute of Management and ECA with a proven track record. He has taught both undergraduate and postgraduate Accounting and Management courses like Financial Management, Foundation of Accounting, Foundation of Management, Mathematics and Statistics, Strategic Management, Project Integration and change management and concepts to both face-to-face and online students' cohorts. His teaching skills are his strength such as working in groups with the students which enable them to participate and have a better understanding of their subject, enabling the development of their soft skills which is his core research area.

Gunjan Shuklaa is currently working as a Principal in SICA College, Indore. She is an erudite academician with Ph.D. (Management), M.Phil., PG (GOLD MEDALIST) and with an 18 years of experience in academics, corporate sector and as an educational entrepreneur in developing results driven curriculum and delivering enthusiastic instruction to students. She is also working with MSME for teaching hospital administration and six sigma to professionals from industry. Moreover, she has published few books as well as research papers in peer-reviewed journals. With a rich blend of industry and academic experience, she is dedicated to fostering academic excellence and driving impactful research initiatives. She has participated as resource person in many national and international events.

Fazla Rabby is an accomplished academic and professional with a diverse background in education, management, and marketing. Holding a Ph.D. from the University of Southern Queensland, their education includes degrees and diplomas in management, leadership, and information systems from Central Queensland University and the University of Madras. As a Teaching Academic at Macquarie University and Lecturer at Canterbury Institute of Management, Dr. Rabby designs and delivers educational activities, assesses student progress, and contributes to curriculum development. Their role as Academic Director at Stanford Institute of Management and Technology highlights their leadership in stakeholder relationships, business strategies, and HR management. Previously, Dr. Rabby excelled in sales and marketing roles, including Director of Australian Sales and Marketing and Managing Director of Sales Solutions Australia.

Remya Lathabhavan is an Assistant Professor of Indian Institute of Management Bodh Gaya, India. She had completed her PhD from NIT Tiruchirappalli in OB and HRM. She is a B Tech holder in Computer Science and Engineering and MBA in HRM. Her research interests include Glass Ceiling, Human Resource Management, HR analytics, Data Analytics, Artificial Intelligence, Career Progression, mental health and psychology. She has authored more than 50 articles in peer reviewed journals.

***

Aashish A. Gadgil, Department of E&C, KLS Gogte Institute of Technology, Belagavi, Karnataka 590008, India.

Aashu Aggarwal is an Assistant Professor at the Vivekananda Institute of Professional Studies, affiliated to Guru Gobind Singh Indraprastha University, New Delhi. She has completed her Ph.D. in Management from Jamia Millia Islamia, New Delhi. She holds MBA from Jamia Millia Islamia and a B.Com (H) from the University of Delhi. She qualified NET, December 2013. She is a keen researcher and has many research papers presented and published in various conference proceedings and journals. Her areas of interest include Marketing, Entrepreneurship, Business, and General Management. She can be reached at aashuaggarwal30@gmail.com.

Parag Chatterjee received the B.E. degree in Computer Science & Engineering from the Karnatak University, Dharwad, India, in 1998 and received M.Tech. degree from IIEST Shibpur, Kolkata, India, in 2007. He has an academic experience of 20 years. Currently he is working as an Assistant Professor in the Department of CSE at Global Institute of Management and Technology, Krishnanagar, West Bengal, India. His current research interests include Data ware Housing, Data mining and Wireless sensor. He has 15 publication in national and international journals and 3 Patents.

Renuka Devi D currently serves as an Assistant Professor in the Department of Computer Science at Stella Maris College(Autonomous) in Chennai, India. With over 15 years of extensive teaching experience, she holds a Ph.D. from the University of Madras. Her academic expertise spans areas such as Data Mining, Machine Learning, Big Data, and Artificial Intelligence. She has authored a book titled "Research Practitioner's Handbook on Big Data Analytics," published by Apple Academic Press, CRC Press, USA, and has contributed articles to various publications, including IEEE, Springer, Scopus, and Web of Science. In addition, she holds patents in the fields of virtual network security and AI. She presented papers at international conferences, earning accolades such as the Best Paper Award and the Best Researcher Award. She is associated with various international societies. She is also an editorial member of the Journal of Advances in Management Sciences & Information Systems and has represented India as a panelist in the "Global Perspectives on Artificial Intelligence in Higher Education - A virtual roundtable on AI" in 2023 organized by Alamo Colleges District, San Antonio, USA.

Malathi G. is an accomplished academic faculty currently serving as an Assistant Professor of Biochemistry at Sri Akilandeswari Women's College in Tamil Nadu, India. With a passion for biochemistry and a commitment to education, she has significantly contributed to both the academic development of her students and the broader scientific community.

Sabeena Gnanaselvi is a dedicated academician with a strong background in computer science and engineering. She holds a Bachelor of Engineering and a Master of Engineering in Computer Science and Engineering, demonstrating her commitment to the field. Currently, she is actively contributing to the academic community as a faculty member at Sathyabama Institute of Science and Technology.

Rajnish Kumar Gupta completed his PhD in Behavioral Neuroscience in 2016 at Sapienza University of Rome, Italy. He is an assistant professor (senior scale) at Manipal University Jaipur. His research focuses on understanding normal brain functioning versus brain disorders to improve predictive accuracy and develop a non-invasive and non-pharmacological intervention. He has published several articles in national and international peer-reviewed journals and supervised over 15 MSc dissertations.

Lokesh Jasrai has a Ph.D. and is currently a professor in the Marketing Department at Lovely Professional University in Jalandhar, Punjab. His research mainly focuses on consumer behavior and marketing strategies. Dr. Jasrai studies various topics, such as predicting opinion leadership in the mobile telecom services sector based on demographics, analyzing e-loyalty among female apparel shoppers in India, creating customer segments for telecom services using the Motivated Consumer Innovativeness (MCI) Scale, and exploring consumer innovativeness for environmentally friendly durable goods through factorial designs. With his expertise in these areas, Dr. Jasrai provides important insights to both academia and industry.

Prabhjeet Kaur is a doctoral research scholar currently pursuing a Ph.D. in Marketing, focusing on Artificial Intelligence for Customer Relationship Management, at Lovely Professional University. Her research interests also include plate tectonic movements in geography, E-STEM, higher education, and Morse code. She has already published four chapters in Scopus-indexed books covering various aspects of her research interests. In the future, she aims to publish more research on multi-domain topics that benefit both industry and the general community.

Deepak Kumar is an accomplished pharmacology professional with an M. Pharma from I.T.S College of Pharmacy, Ghaziabad. With extensive research experience, he has published impactful studies on psoriasis, AI in pharmaceuticals, and cancer pharmacology. Currently an Assistant Professor, he is passionate about innovative pharmaceutical technologies and aspires to contribute to healthcare advancements and entrepreneurial ventures.

Puneet Kumar is an accomplished Associate Professor of Pharmaceutical Chemistry at Shri Gopichand College of Pharmacy, Baghpat, India. Affiliated with Dr. APJ Abdul Kalam Technical University, Lucknow, he completed his Bachelor's and Master's degrees in Pharmacy from IFTM University, Moradabad, in 2015 and 2017, respectively. With 7 years of dedicated teaching experience, Mr. Kumar has made significant contributions to the field, including securing an Indian patent and publishing one international book. Additionally, he has authored 8 research articles and 18 review articles, reflecting his expertise and commitment to advancing pharmaceutical sciences.

Swetha Margaret T A is an accomplished professional with a diverse background in academia, research, and industry, specializing in Cyber and Network Security, Cloud Computing, Computer Networks, IoT, IIoT, Big Data, and Artificial Intelligence. With 12 years of experience, she currently serves as an Assistant Professor in the Department of Computer Science at Stella Maris College, bringing seven years of dedicated teaching expertise. Dr. Margaret holds a Ph.D., earned during her three-year tenure as a full-time Doctoral Research Scholar at Quaid E Millath College, Chennai. Prior to her academic pursuits, she gained valuable industry experience with IBM and Citrix, focusing on IBM mainframe backend support, task management, and load creation. Her commitment to professional development is evident through various international certifications, including those from IBM, Big Data University, and Udemy, covering Cloud Computing, Data Science Methodology, and more. As the Chief Information Security Officer (CISO) at Stella Maris College since 2023, she has demonstrated leadership in securing information assets. Dr. Margaret's research contributions extend to over 20 publications in international journals, including Scopus, IEEE, and Springer. Her expertise has been recognized through accolades such as the "Best Researcher Award" from D K International Research Foundation and the 'Young Faculty in Science' Award during the Contemporary Academic Meet-CAM by Venus International Foundation, both in 2018-2019. Her commitment to innovation is evident through patents, including Innovation patent for "Un Nanban," an AI-based interactive web and voice application, and a Design patent for a "Smart Walking Stick" for visually impaired individuals in 2023. Represented India as a panellist in the "Global Perspectives on Artificial Intelligence in Higher Education - A virtual roundtable on AI" in 2023 organised by Alamo Colleges District, San Antonio, USA

Chodisetty Murthy is an Associate Professor in the Department of Management Studies at Vardhaman College of Engineering, Shamshabad, Hyderabad, Telangana, with over 16+ years of teaching experience. Dr Murthy former Associate Dean, Research & Development (SNIST). He Published 70+ Research papers in various Journals like Scopus, WoS, ABDC, UGC Care etc. He published 8 Book chapters. He Filed and Published 12 Patents. He completed 4 R&D Projects (3 Internal+1 Consultancy). He Attended nearly 280+ workshops across India. He organized 8 FDPs, 6 International Conferences in the field of Commerce & Management. He guided nearly 320+ students projects. He presented papers in 68 conferences. He was Editor in Sreenidhi Journal of Management. He acts as a Coordinator in NBA/ NAAC/AICTE/JNTU-H/Task Force/Other Inspections.

Yamijala Murthy is a versatile individual who dons many hats as a Facilitator, Researcher, Author and Mentor. He believes in Innovative teaching pedagogy and student centric learning. His sessions incorporate various practical assignments like taking part in fests, thereby leading to rich contribution by students to sessions. He possesses 11 years in Teaching and 1 year 11 months of rich Industrial Experience from Assam Bengal Carriers limited. He is pursuing Ph.D. from Andhra University in the area of Human Resources. He completed M.B.A (Marketing & HR) from GITAM Institute of Management, GITAM University, Vishakhapatnam. His primary research interests include Human Resources, Marketing and Statistics. He has attended various National and International Workshops, national and international conferences. He has published 58 articles to his credit which includes ABDC-B,C, Scopus, Web of Science, UGC and peer reviewed articles. He has published 6 books, 9 patents and acted as resource person to train individuals on various aspects related to art of research. A tally of 21 citations to the current date is the reflection of my research work to the field of business management.

N. Sasikaladevi received her Ph. D. Degree in Computer Science in 2013. She has published more than 42 papers in reputed International journals and conferences including publications in SCI-Indexed Journals. She is a reviewer of more than a dozen of reputed journals including IEEE transactions on Services Computing and IEEE Journal of Internet of Things. s. Her research focus includes the design of machine learning strategies to solve Discrete Logarithm Problem. She published several books and chapters in reputed publisher including Prentice Hall of India, Lambert Academic Publisher, IGI Global, Springer and Science Direct. She has received fund from Department of Science and Technology, Government of India to carry out projects in the domain of Services computing and Security System. She has received young scientist award and women scientist award from DST, India. She is also involved in the security enriched payment system design as a part of

Digital India Initiative. Her current research interests include information security, digital authentication, security of wireless sensor networks, computer vision, deep learning and security of vehicular ad-hoc networks.

P. Selvakumar is currently an Associate Professor in the Department of Science and Humanities at Nehru Institute of Technology, Coimbatore, Tamil Nadu, India. Since 2023, he has served as the Department IQAC Coordinator at the institute. Prior to joining Nehru Institute of Technology, he held positions as an Assistant Professor in the Department of Science and Humanities various engineering colleges in Coimbatore, Tamil Nadu, India, spanning from 2011 to 2023. Dr.P. Selvakumar's academic and research interests lie primarily in the field of phytochemistry. He has made significant contributions to his field, with an impressive record that includes 30 journal publications, 12 patents, and 20 conference papers. Additionally, he has organized 5 seminars and conferences, further demonstrating his commitment to academic and scientific exchange. Throughout his career, Dr. P.Selvakumar has been recognized for his dedication and excellence in teaching, having been honored with several awards, including the Best Teacher Awards. He holds a prominent position in the academic community, contributing actively to research.

Sushma Pal is an accomplished pharmaceutics professional with an M. Pharma from RGPV University. With extensive research experience, she has published impactful studies Articulation of mouth dissolving film, A review on COVID-19 disease. Currently an Assistant Professor, She is passionate about innovative pharmaceutical technologies and aspires to contribute to healthcare advancements and entrepreneurial ventures.

Channi Sachdeva is pursuing a PhD in Human Resource Management at Lovely Professional University, Phagwara, Punjab, India. She also serves as an Editor for the Emerald book HR 5.0 Integration: Unleashing the Potential of the Digital Twin Revolution. Her research interests encompass the AI revolution, technology readiness, cognitive dissonance, digital twins, virtual reality, and workplace happiness. She is currently working on enhancing the theory of cognitive dissonance. Channi has authored several articles on public issues for prominent newspapers, including The Tribune, Times of India, and Hindustan Times Ludhiana. Her work includes a bibliometric paper published in a journal, a research framework for which she has received a copyright certificate from the Government of India, and additional research papers published in IEEE (Scopus-indexed). Taylor & Francis, Emerald and other Scopus-indexed publishers have published her book chapters. Several of her book chapters and conference proceedings have been published (Scopus Indexed), and some publications are pending. In addition to her academic and research accomplishments, Channi is a successful businesswoman based in Ludhiana, Punjab, India. She has previously worked as an HR Generalist at DSB Edutech and has two years of teaching experience at a reputed management institution in India.

Timcy Sachdeva holds a doctorate degree in management, specializing in finance from Guru Gobind Singh Indraprastha University. With a teaching and research experience of 14 years, she has various publications in international journals viz., listed in Cabell's Directory, and Ulrich's Periodical, USA; Scopus indexed and ABDC listed journals. Dr. Sachdeva has participated in many national and international conferences including IIMs, IIT and MDI and has chaired sessions in them as well. She is a sought-after trainer for financial econometrics and modeling and has conducted many FDPs for faculty and research scholars across India. She has also authored book on Fundamentals of Financial Modeling using Excel. Dr. Timcy Sachdeva is currently working as an Assistant Professor in Vivekananda Institute of Professional Studies, affiliated to Guru Gobind Singh Indraprastha University.

Sharma Ruchika is working as an assistant professor at Vivekananda Institute of Professional Studies affiliated with Guru Gobind Singh Indraprastha University, Delhi. She has a Ph.D. from B.I.T Mesra, Ranchi, and a Gold Medallist in MBA. She has more than eleven years of experience in Academics. Her area of specialization is Human Resources and Marketing. She was conferred with the Best Teacher Award and has published articles in various international journals listed in ABDC and Scopus. She has also authored a book titled 'Services Marketing: Text and Cases' in 2019.

Sangam Singh earned his Bachelor's degree in Pharmacy in 2010 and his Master's degree in Pharmacy in 2013. With a decade of teaching experience, he has established himself as a dedicated educator and researcher. His scholarly contributions include 6 review and research articles published in reputable international journals. Currently, Sangam Singh is actively engaged in research focused on the potential of natural compounds in the treatment of skin cancer.

Ranjit Singha is a Doctorate Research Fellow at Christ (Deemed to be University) and holds a prestigious membership in the American Psychological Association (APA). With a strong background in Research and Development, he has significantly contributed to various fields such as Mindfulness, Addiction Psychology, Women Empowerment, UN Sustainable Development Goals, and Data Science. With over 15 years of experience in Administration, Teaching, and Research, both in Industry and Higher Education Institutions (HEI), Mr Ranjit has established himself as a seasoned professional. Mr Ranjit is dedicated to research and teaching endeavours, primarily focusing on mindfulness and compassion-based interventions. His work in these areas aims to promote well-being and foster positive change in individuals and communities.

Surjit Singha is an academician with a broad spectrum of interests, including UN Sustainable Development Goals, Organizational Climate, Workforce Diversity, Organizational Culture, HRM, Marketing, Finance, IB, Global Business, Business, AI, K12 & Higher Education, Gender and Cultural Studies. Currently a faculty member at Kristu Jayanti College, Dr. Surjit also serves as an editor, reviewer, and author for prominent global publications and journals, including being on the editorial review board of Information Resources Management Journal and contributing to various publications. With over 15 years of experience in Administration, Teaching, and Research, Dr. Surjit is dedicated to imparting knowledge and guiding students in their research pursuits. As a research mentor, Dr. Surjit has nurtured young minds and fostered academic growth. Dr. Surjit has an impressive track record of over 150+ publications (SCOPUS Indexed 74), including articles, book chapters, and textbooks, holds two US Copyrights, and has successfully completed and published two fully funded minor research projects from Kristu Jayanti College. PhD, M.Phil, MBA (Distinction) from Christ University, M.Com, BBM from KJC (Bangalore University), PGDHE (Higher Education) from IGNOU (Central University), UGC-NET Commerce, Examiner for IB.

Muhammad Usman Tariq has more than 16+ year's experience in industry and academia. He has authored more than 200+ research articles, 110+ case studies, 120+ book chapters and several books other than 4 patents. He is founder and CEO of The Case HQ, a unique repository for courses, narrative and video case studies. He has been working as a consultant and trainer for industries representing six sigma, quality, health and safety, environmental systems, project management, and information security standards. His work has encompassed sectors in aviation, manufacturing, food, hospitality, education, finance, research, software and transportation. He has diverse and significant experience working with accreditation agencies of ABET, ACBSP, AACSB, WASC, CAA, EFQM and NCEAC. Additionally, Dr. Tariq has operational experience in incubators, research labs, government research projects, private sector startups, program creation and management at various industrial and academic levels. He is Certified Higher Education Teacher from Harvard University, USA, Certified Online Educator from HMBSU, Certified Six Sigma Master Black Belt and has been awarded PFHEA, SFSEDA, SMIEEE, and CMBE.

Geetha Valavan received her B.E degree in Computer Science and Engineering from Regional Engineering College, Tiruchirappalli, India in 1996. She obtained

M.Tech. in computer science and Ph.D. from the National Institute of Technology, Tiruchirappalli. Her research was in the area of memory architecture - Web caching and its applications. She worked as Research Associate in National Institute of Technology from 2000 to 2006. She also worked as a faculty in the same institute from 2012 to 2014. She has worked on projects related to network security, web technology, computer architecture and digital design. Currently she is working with SASTRA University, Tanjore as a Senior Assistant Professor. Her research interests include Web caching, Digital design, Hardware cryptography, and High-performance computing.

Yashasvi Walia completed her postgraduation at National Forensic Sciences University, specializing in clinical psychology. Currently, she is pursuing a PhD in psychology, with 2 years of experience in hospital/clinical settings and education. She is dedicated to a holistic approach to mental health and education, aiming to contribute across various domains to enhance mental health outcomes.

Index

A

B

C

D

N

P

R

S

T

V

W

www.ingramcontent.com/pod-product-compliance
Lightning Source LLC
LaVergne TN
LVHW080353011026
849161LV00009B/2289